JOHN BAXTER, PRINTER, JAMES COURT, HEAD OF MOUND,
EDINBURGH

TITLE II

OF WRITINGS OF A PUBLIC AND OFFICIAL CHARACTER AND OF ANALOGOUS WRITINGS

---

§ 1051 Public and official written evidence comprehends all those documents which are prepared under the care of official persons, for the purpose of preserving evidence of matters in which the public are interested Some of these documents relate to the affairs of the nation, and are preserved in the national archives Others are immediately connected with private transactions, but are intrusted to official care, on account of the matters which they embody affecting the interest of third parties, or with a view to preserving them There are also documents which, relating to private affairs and prepared by private persons, are compiled systematically with the same kind of care as is observed in public offices, for example, the business books of banking and railway companies and of extensive mercantile houses The *quasi* official character of such writings, and their general trustworthiness, has given them a position in the law of evidence analogous to that occupied by official registers

---

CHAPTER I —ACTS OF PARLIAMENT

§ 1052 Acts of Parliament, the originals of which are preserved in the rolls of Parliament, are divided into classes, to which different rules of evidence apply

A treatise on the law of evidence in Scotland

William Gillespie Dickson, John Skelton

A TREATISE

ON

THE LAW OF EVIDENCE

IN SCOTLAND

BY

WILLIAM GILLESPIE DICKSON

ADVOCATE

PROCUREUR AND ADVOCATE GENERAL OF THE MAURITIUS

SECOND EDITION

EDITED BY

JOHN SKELTON, ADVOCATE.

IN TWO VOLUMES

VOL. II

EDINBURGH:

BELL & BRADFUTE, 12 BANK STREET.

WILLIAM MAXWELL, LONDON.

MDCCCLXIV

(1) Public Acts—that is, those which concern the Sovereign, the public generally, all persons or offices of any class within the country, and the like—are the general law of the realm, and are presumed to be known to every person. They are not matter of fact, and do not require to be given in evidence; but when any dispute arises as to their terms, these may be proved by copies bearing to be printed by the Queen's Printer, the theory being, that the judge only requires to have his memory refreshed upon them (*a*).

(2) Local and personal acts relate to the concerns of particular districts or corporations, joint-stock companies, and similar bodies. For many years it has been customary to insert in them a clause providing that they shall be deemed to be public acts, and be judicially noticed or received in evidence; and when there is such a provision they may be proved in the same way as public statutes (*b*). This is also the rule as to acts which merely provide that they shall be deemed and taken to be public acts (*c*). When they do not contain either of these clauses, they can only be proved by copies sworn to have been collated with the Parliament roll (*d*), unless they were passed after the commencement of the session of Parliament 14th Victoriae. Every act passed subsequently to that time must be deemed and taken notice of judicially as a public act, unless the contrary is expressly provided and declared by the act itself (*e*).[1]

(3) Private acts, when printed, are in the same position in these respects as local and personal acts; the distinction between those passed before and after 14th Victoriae applying also to them (*f*).

(*a*) 41 Geo III c 90 § 9—Bell's Pr, § 2208—Tait Ev, 201—2 Phill, 127, 8—Taylor, 1016, 7. (*b*) Bell's Pr, *supra*—Tait, 202—Phill, *supra*—Taylor, *supra*—Macf Pr, 185. (*c*) Woodward v Cotton, 1831, 1 Cr Me and Ro, 44—Beaumont v Mountain, 1834, 10 Bing 404—2 Phill, 128—Taylor, 1016 explaining Brett v Beales, 1829, 1 Mo and Mal 421—*Contra*, Bell's Pr *supra*.

(*d*) Authorities in preceding note. (*e*) 13 and 14 Vict c 21 § 7.

(*f*) 13 and 14 Vict, ib.

[1] In England the Courts without requiring proof judicially notice a variety of facts, such as "the existence and titles of the sovereign powers in the civilised world" "facts which may certainly be known from the invariable course of nature," and others of a like kind, Taylor on Evidence, 3d edition, p 3. They have noticed judicially that an affidavit sworn abroad was notarially sealed, Cole v Sherard, 11 Exch Rep 482—that the colony of Victoria is beyond seas, Cooke v Wilson, 2 Jur N S, 1094—that the University of Oxford is a national institution, the purposes of which are the advancement of learning and religion, The Oxford Poor-rate, 8 El and Bl 184—and that a place is east or west of Greenwich, Curtis v March, 4 Jur N S, 1112.

When unprinted, they may be proved by copies sworn to have been collated with the Parliament roll (*g*).

These rules are very loosely dealt with in practice in Scotland, printed copies of private acts being constantly received without opposition in cases where, according to strict law, they are inadmissible But, if the objection were raised, it would be dealt with according to the rules above stated (*h*)

§ 1053 Errors in the authorised printed copies of acts of Parliament may be proved by persons who have compared them with the Parliament roll (*i*)

§ 1054 Foreign statutes may be proved by sworn copies They must also be supported by the evidence of foreign lawyers, swearing that they are in force, and explaining (if necessary) any peculiarities in the phraseology (*k*).[2]

§ 1055 Public statutes are admissible in evidence of all the facts which they contain, because they are open to challenge at their several stages, and are prepared with great care, and also because every subject is held to be privy to the making of them (*l*)

(*g*) Bell's Pr, *supra*—Tait, *supra*—Phill, *supra*—Taylor *supra*

(*h*) Bell's Pr, § 2208, note The act 8 and 9 Vict, c 113, § 3, provides, that all copies of local and personal acts, if purporting to be printed by the Queen s printer may be admitted without proof that they were actually so printed But this act does not extend to Scotland, ib, § 5

(*i*) 2 Phill, 129—1 Starkie, 277—R *v* Jeffries, 1720, 1 Str, 446—Spring *v* Eve, 1676, 2 Mod, 240

(*k*) Taylor, 946 1017—See the sections on examining foreign lawyers *infra*

(*l*) Taylor Ev 1088—Roscoe's Nisi Pr (8th ed), 85 Thus the preamble of a public act, narrating the existence of certain outrages, was received to prove that fact R *v* Sutton, 1816 4 Mau and Sel, 532, and where several public acts recognised war with France, the Court of King's Bench said, they must judicially notice it, R *v* De Berenger, 1714, 3 Mau and Sel, 67—See R *v* Greene (next note)

[2] The English Evidence Amendment Act, 14 and 15 Vict, c 99, enacts, § 7, 'All proclamations, treaties and other acts of state of any foreign state or of any British colony, and all judgments, decrees, orders, and other proceedings of any Court of Justice, in any foreign state or in any British colony, and all affidavits, pleadings, and other legal documents, filed or deposited in any such Court," may be proved either by examined copies, or by copies to which the Seal of the State is attached, or in the case of proceedings before a Court by the Seal of the Court, or, in the event of the Court having no seal, by the signature of a judge In Abbot *v* Abbot 1860 (29 L J Mat Causes, 57), it was held that an extract certificate of a foreign marriage, being an extract from a register of marriages kept at Santiago in Chili, and signed by the curate-rector of the church where the marriage was solemnised, was admissible,—the signature of the curate being attested by a notary and other witnesses In this case Justice Keating cited Biddulph *v* Lord Camoys (unreported) where copies of French registers were admitted on its being proved by French lawyers that such registers were kept by official authority

But they may be contradicted as to matters which they do not enact (*m*) The statements in local and private acts, however, are not received in evidence against third parties This is the rule, notwithstanding a provision in an act that it shall be received as a public act, which is only intended for convenience in pleading and proof not to extend the effect of the act (*n*) Such acts, however, are admissible to prove reputation in questions of prescription, pedigree and the like (*o*) [3]

CHAPTER II —JOURNALS OF PARLIAMENT

§ 1056 The journals of the Houses of Parliament must be proved by examined copies (*a*), a late statute, which admits copies printed by her Majesty's printer, not extending to Scotland (*b*)

These journals only prove the proceedings of Parliament—not the truth of facts set forth in the resolutions (*c*)

A copy of the judgment of the House of Lords in an appeal case, certified by the proper officer is sufficient proof to guide the Court of Session in applying the judgment But if their Lordships are satisfied that the judgment as written out contains a clerical error,

(*m*) Thus, the mention of a place as a borough, and of its members as a corporation, in the schedule to a public act, although *prima facie* evidence may be contradicted, R v Greene, 1837 6 Ad and Ell, 548—See also per L Ellenborough in R v Sutton, *supra* (*n*) Brett v Beales, 1836 1 Mo and Mal 421—Ballard v Way, 1836, 1 Me and Wel, 520—Taylor v Parry, 1840, 1 Man and Gr, 604—2 Phill, 128—Taylor, 1088 (*o*) E Carnarvon v Villebois, 1844, 13 Me and Wel, 313—Wharton Peerage case 1845, 12 Cl and Finn, 295, 302—Starkie (4th ed) 278

(*a*) Bell's Pr, § 2210—Rose Ni Pr 85—R v Lord G Gordon, 1781 2 Doug, 593—R v L Melville, 1806, 29 State Tr 683—Jones v Randal, 1774 Cowp, 17

(*b*) 8 and 9 Vict, c 113, § 3, 5 (*c*) Bell's Pr, *supra*—But see R v Franklin, 1731, 17 St Tr, 635, where the journals of the House of Lords were admitted to prove the existence of differences between this country and France which they stated See also Rose Ni Pr, 86

[3] Recitals in private acts of Parliament of very recent date are not evidence of the facts stated in them such recitals being no longer submitted to the previous approval of the judges Lord St Leonards—'That used to be the practice, but it is not so now The evidence in support of private bills is not now submitted to and reported on by the judges and future recitals will not therefore be evidence,' Shrewsbury Peerage Case, 1857-1858 7 Clark's H of L Cases 13

they will give effect to it according to what they deem to be its proper tenor (*d*)

CHAPTER III.—*ROTULI SCOTIAE*

§ 1057 The ancient *Rotuli Scotiae*, which contain a number of state papers, chiefly relating to the political transactions between Scotland and England in the 14th, 15th, and 16th centuries are evidence in questions of peerage, propinquity, and the like Their contents may be proved by a sworn copy or excerpt, but as the originals are in existence a copy printed under the superintendence of Royal Commissioners not proved on oath is inadmissible (*e*)

CHAPTER IV.—GAZETTES

§ 1058 Gazettes being prepared officially and with care, for the purpose of announcing matters of state procedure and acts of the Crown, are admissible and full proof of such transactions (*a*) This is the case in regard to entries of proclamations of war and peace, for performance of quarantines, and the presentation of public addresses to the Crown (*b*). But gazettes are not received as evidence of individual or private rights although flowing from the Crown, *e g*, presentations to benefices, commissions in the Army, grants of land to subjects (*c*) On such matters the gazette contains merely an announcement that a certain grant has been made or dignity conferred, the party receiving a written title as the pro-

---

(*d*) Aberdeen Ry Co *v* Blaikies, 1851, 16 D, 570 (*e*) Crawford and Lindsay Peerage case, 1848, 2 Cl and Finn, 534, 547 (*a*) Bell's Pr, § 2209—Tait, 51—2 Phill, 108—Taylor, 1089 (*b*) King *v* Holt, 1793, 5 Durn and E, 443—Att-Gen *v* Theakson 1820, 8 Price, 89 In Omeron *v* Dowick, 1809, 2 Camp 42, the Court of King's Bench refused to listen to a plea that cutlasses were contraband, because the statute founded on only allowed the King to make them so by proclamation, and the gazette was not tendered to prove the proclamation (*c*) Authorities in note (*a*)—R *v* Gardner, 1810, 2 Camp, 513 Kirkman *v* Cockburn, 1803, 5 Esp, 233 Per Kenyon in R *v* Holt, *supra*

per evidence of his right whereas in public matters the proclamation is full, and the original is preserved in the national archives

§ 1059 Gazettes also contain publications on some matters of private interest, with which the Crown is not connected but which concern a number of individuals *e g* sequestrations cessios, and petitions under the disentailing act Such notices are only proof of publication, and, being secondary evidence of the fact published, they are inadmissible as evidence of it They may go to the jury in a question whether a certain party knew of the fact, but the mere publication does not necessarily prove knowledge, and, therefore, there must in general be evidence tending to show that the party read the paper, as, from a copy of it having been found in his custody, from his having attended a reading-room where it was taken in, and having been acquainted with other matters contained in it, and the like (*d*) Such proof is especially necessary as to matters which are published in the gazette without statutory authority, as, for example, dissolutions of partnership (*e*) Even as to matters of public interest, a gazette notice alone does not raise a presumption of knowledge to which the jury are obliged to give effect, and, therefore, in an action on a policy of marine insurance in England, where the underwriters pleaded that the policy was void because the voyage was to a port which the master knew was blockaded, the Court held that the jury were justified in negativing the issue of knowledge, although it appeared that the master had been in this country some time after the publication of the gazette in which the blockade was notified (*f*) Of course, wherever it is provided by statute that a gazette notice shall be held to prove knowledge, it must receive that effect (*g*)

CHAPTER V —RECORDS OF COURTS OF LAW

§ 1060 The interlocutors and decrees of courts, the verdicts of juries, and the different steps of procedure throughout a cause, are set forth in the record prepared by the clerk of court, and in most

(*d*) Bell's Pr § 2209—Taylor, 1092—Jenkins v Blizard 1816 1 Stark R, 420—Godfrey v M'Aulay, 1795, 1 Esp, 371—Graham v Hope 1793 1 Pea R 151, per L Kenyon (*e*) Taylor, *supra*—Bell's Pr *supra* (*f*) Harratt v Wise, 1820, 9 B and C, 712 (*g*) See *e g*, 6 Geo IV, c 16, § 83

instances signed by the judge. These records being made up by sworn and in general careful officers, and passing under the eyes both of the judge and of the parties to the cause, are entitled to high credibility.

1. To what extent they are Probative

§ 1061. As to the extent to which judicial records are probative, a distinction exists between matters which fall immediately within their object, and incidental or collateral matters.

The record, when duly authenticated, is competent and full proof on all matters of the first class which are set forth in it. Thus in civil causes the interlocutors and minutes of Court are the materials from which the extract decree is prepared as the warrant of legal executorials. And the record of a criminal court, proved by an official extract (of which hereafter), is full proof of the conviction or acquittal of the person accused, provided he be identified as the person to whom the conviction applies; as, where it is tendered to prove that he has tholed an assize, or that he has been convicted of a crime, when that either forms part of the charge against him in a subsequent trial, or is founded on as impairing his credibility as a witness (*a*).[4]

§ 1062. Judicial records are also *probatio probata* on all matters falling immediately within their province, except when they are challenged on grounds which, if true, infer that they contain a falsehood or flaw in some essential particular (*b*). Averments that the proceedings, when set forth on record as having been duly conducted, were irregular in some matter of form or technical detail, will not be entertained; for the probative quality of the record is supported by the presumption *omnia rite et solenniter acta*, and no real injustice is occasioned by giving effect to it. Thus the Court

(*a*) Burnett, 171—2 Hume, 316 (note 2)—2 Al., 50, 596—Tait, 43. Conviction of a crime inferring infamy disqualified a witness before the passing of the act 15 Vict., c. 27. (*b*) As to such exceptions, see *infra*, § 1065, *et seq.*

[4] A certificate or extract of a conviction for theft in an English court, proved to apply to the panel, has been admitted by the Court of Justiciary as instructing the aggravation of "previous conviction of theft", Jane M'Pherson or Dempster and Others, 1862, 4 Irv., 143. But see observations on Dempster by Lord Deas, in H. M. Adv. v. Davidson and Francis, 1863, 35 Sc. Jur., 270. A previous conviction must be sufficiently proved; it is not sufficient that the judge before whom the trial takes place is aware that the previous conviction applies to the panel, Morrison v. Munro, 1851, 1 Irv., 599.

of Justiciary refused to allow a prisoner to prove that five of the jurors in a trial before them had not been sworn, the objection having been stated the day after the verdict had been returned and the jury discharged, and when the Court were about to pronounce sentence (c).[5] And where, after a verdict of guilty had been returned, it was pleaded in arrest of judgment that the jury had been sworn in the absence of the presiding judge, the objection was repelled, with the observation that his Lordship had been only absent from the bench for a few minutes, that no objection had been stated at the time and that the record could not be redargued (d).[6] In like manner the Court repelled the objection to the record of an oral verdict, that it did not bear that the jury had chosen a chancellor or that the verdict had been delivered from his mouth (e). So, where the records of trials in inferior Courts bore that the judge had heard the "evidence adduced," and had "taken evidence" the Court of Justiciary, construing these words to mean that the witnesses had been examined on oath according to the usual practice, refused to allow a proof that they had not (f). And a similar decision was pronounced in regard to a record which merely set forth that the witnesses had been "examined," without also stating that they had been put on oath (g).

§ 1063. On the same principle, when an omission or mis-statement occurs in any essential part of the record, it will be fatal, and, except in the cases mentioned afterwards (h), the Court will not allow a proof that the proceedings were regular. This rule was applied to the record of a conviction in a police court, which bore that all the witnesses except one had been 'sworn and examined,'

(c) Hannah, 1809, 2 Hume, 316—Burnett, Apx. p. 70, S. C. (d) M'Ginnes v. Harvey, 1833, Bell's Notes, 239. (e) M'Kinlay, 1819, Sh. Just. Ca., 58. But see M'Leod, 1819, ib., 30, where the Justiciary Court *before answer* allowed a proof that one of the jury was erroneously designed, the objection having been pleaded in arrest of judgment. There can be little doubt, it is thought, that the objection would not ultimately have been sustained, as it struck only at the description, not at the identity, of the juror. (f) Cobb, 1836, 1 Swin., 354—Macqueen v. Robson, 1832 (not rep.) noted in 2 Al., 51. (g) Connor, 1826, and Gunn v. M'Gregor, 1829, 2 Al., 51, 597. (h) *Infra*, § 1074, 5.

[5] Reg. v. Mellor, 1858, 7 Cox's Crim. Cases, 455. See *infra*, § 1072, note [11].

[6] Proof that the magistrate, before whom a declaration was emitted, was absent during part of the time when it was being taken, has been admitted. H. M. Advocate v. Mahler, 2 Irv., 634. As to the effect of his absence on the admissibility of the declaration, see *infra*, § 1406.

and that he had been "examined" The Court of Justiciary holding this to mean that the witness had not been sworn, suspended the sentence *simpliciter* (*i*) And where it is customary in records of particular courts to set forth that the witnesses were examined on oath, it would seem that the omission of such a statement in an individual case will be fatal (*k*)

§ 1064 Nor may extrinsic evidence be admitted for the purpose of giving to the record a different meaning from its true construction For example, a recorded verdict must be construed as it stands, without the aid of extrinsic evidence, although it is ambiguous (*l*) Thus, also where a prisoner charged with murder and assault pleaded *res judicata*, and founded on an extract conviction which bore that she had been punished for "drunkenness, fighting, and returning from banishment," the Court, holding that these terms described a different offence, refused to allow parole proof to show that they related to the same affair as that for which she was indicted (*m*) The rules against admitting parole evidence to explain deeds (*n*) illustrate the same principle

§ 1065 An exception to the rule by which judicial records are conclusive proof, occurs in regard to objections which go not merely to the regularity of the proceedings, but to the essential justice of the case For such a wrong (which experience shows may exist) there must be a remedy, and, therefore, an objection of this nature may be established by extrinsic evidence in the same way as allegations of fraud or want of substantial consent may be proved to the effect of annulling private deeds Thus, where an entailed estate had been sold judicially as if for payment of the entailer's debts, and a subsequent heir challenged the proceedings on the ground that they were a fraudulent device for breaking the fetters of the entail by raising up fictitious debts and overstating the amount of such debts as really existed the House of Lords held

---

(*i*) Purves 1825 Cr Just Ca, 183, 2 Al, 50 But where the record in a justice of peace case did not state that the principal witness had been sworn, while stating that the others had the Court repelled the objection, as the deposition of that witness concluded in the usual terms, "All which is truth, as the deponent shall answer to God," and bore to be signed by the justice, as the witness could not write, Rankin v Alexander, 1836, 1 Swin, 44 Bell's Notes, 239, S C (*k*) Grant 1827, Syme, 114—Dykes, 1829 ib, 262—See also Nimmo v Stewart, 1832, 10 S 841 The admission that witnesses in a small debt case were not sworn is fatal to the decree although appearing on record to be regular Home v Henderson, 1825 4 S 30

(*l*) *Supra* § 18 *et seq* (*m*) Paterson 1823 2 Al, 617 (*n*) *Supra* § 191, *et seq* that the decree of sale did not form a bar to reduction (*o*). Thus, also where the common agent in a process of ranking and sale had purchased part of the bankrupt estate, and the decree in his favour bore that the sale had been legally and orderly proceeded in, and therefore adjudged the estate to him as his absolute property, in an action of reduction which the bankrupts raised of the decree and subsequent title, on the ground that the common agent could not legally purchase because his duty to obtain the highest price for the creditors and to protect their interest was incompatible with a sale to himself, the House of Lords (reversing the decision of the Court of Session) held the sale to be null. This is a strong case, because the decree had been pronounced *causa cognita*, upon a report by one of the judges to the whole Court, stating that he had satisfied himself by investigation as to the propriety and regularity of the proceeding (*p*).

§ 1066. The same principle is illustrated by a recent and important case. A person possessed of landed estate in Scotland, emigrated to America, where, shortly before his death, he married a woman by whom he had had a son and daughter. A nephew was served heir to him, on the footing that these children were bastards, whereupon an action of reduction of the service was raised at the instance of a factor *loco tutoris* who had been appointed by the Court of Session to the son, on the application of his next of kin. In this action of reduction decree of absolvitor was pronounced by the Court of Session in 1803, and affirmed by the House of Lords in 1808. In 1848 the son raised an action of reduction in the Court of Session, for the purpose of setting aside the service and the judgments in the previous action of reduction. In this action the son averred that the former proceedings had been adopted and carried through in pursuance of a fraudulent conspiracy to deprive him of his right of succession, entered into between the nephew and certain other persons in collusion with the factor *loco tutoris*, and that in pursuance of this device, certain facts which it was alleged, would have led to an opposite decision in the first action, had been fraudulently concealed. The Court of Session dismissed the action, on the ground that the summons was irrelevant, as no specification of facts inferring fraud was set forth in it. In the House

(*o*) Irvine v. E. Aberdeen, 1770, 2 Pat. Ap. Ca. 219, reversing.

(*p*) York Buildings Co. v. Mackenzie, 1795, 3 Pat. Ap. Ca. 378. The agent pleaded homologation and acquiescence, but the House of Lords held that the circumstances did not raise that bar to the action.

of Lords a question was raised as to the jurisdiction of the Court of Session to entertain an action of reduction of a decree of a superior tribunal, but no doubt was supposed to exist as to the competency of inquiring by some means into the question, whether the former proceedings had been carried through in furtherance of a fraudulent conspiracy. The House of Lords affirmed the judgment of the Court of Session but chiefly on a different ground (r).

§ 1067. The principle on which these decisions proceeded has also been followed in regard to recorded verdicts of juries when impugned on similar grounds. Thus the allegation that the jury in a civil case had cast lots for their verdict was held to be provable by evidence other than the jurors, who were held to be incompetent under the constitution of the tribunal (s).[7] In another case, where an unsuccessful party moved for a new trial on the ground that the jury had been tampered with and had misconducted themselves, the Court, before answer, allowed a proof of the allegations by witnesses other than the jurors (t). Again, where in a jury trial in a Sheriff-court for assessing the value of certain lands under a special statute the verdict had been sealed up before the jury, had been handed to the clerk of court, and by him delivered to the Sheriff, and where the next day several of the jurors gave in to the Sheriff a declaration stating that the verdict erroneously bore that the sum set forth in it had been found by a majority of the jury, the Court of Session held it to be fatal to the verdict that it had been returned to Court out of the presence of the judge, and without having been read over to the jury and approved of by them in open Court (u). Their Lordships, accordingly (holding it to be unnecessary to inquire into the other objection) ordered a new trial.[8]

§ 1068. In the following cases, also, the Court allowed investi-

---

(r) Sheddan v. Patrick, 1852, 14 D., 721; aff'd, 15th May 1854, 22 Sc. Jur., 420.

(s) Stewart v. Fraser, 1830, 5 Mur., 166; Adam on Jur. Tr., 176, 209, and ib., App. No. 14, S. C. (t) M'Whir v. Maxwell, 1836, 15 S. 299. The proof entirely failed. See also Black v. Croall, 1854, 16 D., 431. (u) Forbes v. Magistrates of Aberdeen, 11 Feb. 1809, F. C. The facts as to the irregularity on which the Court proceeded were not disputed.

---

[7] How far affidavits by jurymen, as to the circumstances under which a verdict was returned, are admissible, was considered in the late case of Dobbie v. Johnston and Russell, 23 D., 1139.—See *supra*, § 48, note [4].

[8] A motion for a new trial on the ground of the verdict having been returned and delivered to the clerk of court in absence of the judge, was refused,—no exception to his absence having been taken by the parties at the time. Brownlie v. Tennant & Co., 1855, 17 D., 422.

gation, where the records of inferior courts were impugned on the ground of error *in substantialibus*, or of irregularities which amounted to a denial of justice. Where an accused person imprisoned for examination applied to the Sheriff to be admitted to bail, and his petition was marked by the sheriff-clerk with the date 9th July, which was the date of the first deliverance on it, in an action of damages at his instance against the Sheriff for wrongous imprisonment under the act 1701, c. 6, it was held by the House of Lords to be competent for him to prove that the petition had actually been presented on the 2d of the month (x). In an action regarding the settlement of a schoolmaster, where a formal extract from the books of the presbytery bore that intimation of the proceedings of that court had been made to the heritors the Court of Session allowed a proof not only that the extract was disconform to the record, but also that the procedure set forth in the record had not taken place (y). Again where regulations which had been framed under the powers contained in a general police act, for the proceedings in summary trials before Sheriffs, required that if the accused applied for time to summon witnesses and was refused, the clerk of court should make a note of the application and refusal and where a party who had been convicted for theft in a trial falling under the regulations brought a suspension on the ground that no complaint had been served on him, that the judge had refused his application for time to summon witnesses and to employ an agent, or to prepare for his defence, and where no note to that effect had been made by the clerk the Court, before answer, allowed a proof of the allegations. Afterwards on considering the evidence, they found that it did not actually ' amount to proof of the specific allegation contained in the previous interlocutor, but found that it appeared that the suspender had not been aware that the case could be proceeded with without a summons and warning thereby to be prepared, and that he did express some surprise or complaint that the matter could be then disposed of and that the right to apply for time was not intimated to the suspender, to whom the new regulations were unknown, and hence that he was not enabled to put his application into any correct form, and, under the whole circumstances, as there appears to be some want of explanation although unintentional and accidental on the part of the magistrate in not making

(x) Andrew v. Murdoch 1814 2 Dow, 401 reversing, Buch Rep., 1

(y) Philp v. Heritors of Cruden, 1724, M. 12,389 13,122, S. C.

the purport of the new regulations fully known,' their Lordships suspended the sentence, but without expenses (z) [9]

§ 1069 In treating of this subject, Sir A Alison (a) distinguishes between cases where the objection is merely that the offer of proof was rejected, and those where it is also alleged that the judge refused to note the offer and rejection In the latter case he holds the objection to be provable, because it does not contradict the record, the allegation being that the judge refused to make up a record, whereas in the former case, the prisoner admits that he did not require the judge to note the rejection, and there is therefore nothing to shake the presumption that the record is full and accurate (b) But the decision which has just been cited, and (it is also thought) correct principle, exclude this distinction, which is founded, not on the character of the respective objections, but on the extent of acquaintance which accused persons, who are generally uneducated, may have with forms of process

§ 1070 The decision referred to is further important, as showing that an accidental error of the judge, if materially affecting the justice of the case, will be a sufficient ground for suspending the sentence, and this is just, because the injury to the accused does not depend on the motives which gave rise to the error

§ 1071 Contrasted with these cases, but not conflicting with them, is one in which the Court of Session held it to be incompetent for them to inquire whether the chancellor of the jury in a trial before a Circuit Court of Justiciary had controlled the other jurors, had prevented them from retiring for deliberation and had returned as unanimous a verdict of acquittal, which (it was alleged) had not been unanimous (c) The question occurred in an action of damages at the instance of a private party (who had been prosecutor in the Criminal Court) against the chancellor of the jury, and the sum-

(z) Blyth v M'Bain 1852 J Shaw R, 554 (a) 2 Al, 51, 2

(b) Sir A Alison founds his distinction on two unreported cases, Gillespie and Mills, 1831 and Russel, 1829, both noticed in 2 Al, 51, 2 (c) Mackintosh v Fraser, 1834, 12 S, 872

[9] The Court of Justiciary allowed proof that the sentence pronounced in a prosecution before a magistrate was not read over to the prisoner before being signed, the record being formal, Wilson v Hanning 1844, 2 Broun, 328 The proof failed, same parties, Arkley, 80 In Ord v M'Callum the Court of Justiciary allowed the complainer a proof of his averment, that for the purpose of excluding parties friendly to him the door of the police court was kept closed, 1855, 2 Irv 183, but in M'Lean v Macfarlane, 1863, 35 Sc Jur, 319, the Court refused an application for suspension, on the ground that it was not sufficiently averred by the suspender that delay had been asked and refused, although at the bar that averment was made, and proof offered

mons libelled malice Here it will be observed, the objection was, not that the jury had not consented to the verdict, or that they had left it to chance, but that they had consented to it under improper influence, whereas the allegation that it had not been unanimous was contradicted by the fact that they had allowed it to be recorded as such, after having been read out to them in open court There was also a conflict of jurisdictions involved in the objection, as the verdict had been returned in a Court of co-ordinate jurisdiction, and independent of that in which it was afterwards challenged A similar decision, in so far as the first point is concerned, occurred in regard to a criminal trial of two persons before the Sheriff and a jury The verdict finding both prisoners guilty was signed by the chancellor, returned to Court, read over by the clerk, and openly assented to, and was then duly recorded in common form Sentence was pronounced against one of the prisoners a few days afterwards but was delayed for several weeks in regard to the other In the interval she offered, in a suspension before the Court of Justiciary, to prove that the verdict had not been agreed to by a majority of the jury But the Court held the proof to be incompetent (*d*) Such an attempt *ex intervallo* to contradict by parole a verdict which had been assented to in open court, and recorded in the terms in which the jury had announced it, was manifestly inconsistent with the fundamental principles of judicial procedure — Again, where, after a unanimous verdict of guilty, but qualified by alleviating circumstances, had been returned in a prosecution before the Court of Justiciary for abduction and rape and where the day afterwards when the Court were about to pronounce sentence, a large majority of the jury tendered a declaration stating that they understood that the finding in mitigation would have exempted the prisoner from capital punishment, the Court "absolutely refused" to receive the declaration, and signified their disapproval of the step (*e*) It was an attempt to review a returned and recorded verdict on the ground that the jury had miscalculated its consequences, which did not fall within their province, and the Court justly considered that allowing such a procedure would hold out dangerous temptations to tampering with juries [10]

(*d*) Mill *v* Nicol, 1767, Maclau., 372

(*e*) Macgregor, 1752, ib 149

[10] In Dobie *v* Johnston and Russell, *supra*, the jury returned a verdict finding that the pursuer had been induced to purchase bank stock by the false representations of the defenders but that these representations were not fraudulent The foreman stated at the time that the jury intended the verdict to be for the pursuer, and affidavits by the foreman and nine of the jurymen in which they declared that unless they had intended

The Court proceed so strictly in such matters that they will not allow a recommendation to mercy to be added to a verdict of guilty, which has been recorded and assented to by the jury without such a qualification (*f*)

§ 1072 The most eminent Scotch writer on criminal law (*g*) considers it doubtful whether an inquiry could be allowed, where it is averred (without undue delay) that a mistake in a material word has by inadvertence occurred in a written verdict, as, for example, where "not" has been omitted or inserted before "guilty" The difficulty arises from the fact that the jury, by acquiescing in the verdict as read out in Court and recorded may be held to have abandoned their previous intention to pronounce a different finding, and that, whether they did so or not, is a matter on which they alone can speak On the other hand, the palpable injustice of excluding inquiry in such a case should overcome all mere technical difficulties The effect of such an error, however as Baron Hume observes, would not be to cast the proceedings, but, at the most, to make way for a new trial [11]

(*f*) Harvey 1830 Bell's Notes, 295 But the presiding judge observed in this case, that the Court might pay regard to the recommendation in determining the punishment (*g*) 2 Hume, 430

---

it to be for the pursuer they would not have returned it, were afterwards produced The Court held that the jury had no concern with the legal import of the facts found by their verdict, and strong observations on the statement in the affidavits that they had miscalculated its legal import, and would, had they not done so, have returned a different verdict, fell from several of the judges Lord Benholme observed — "What inference can be drawn from this declaration except that the jury, having an intention of giving the pursuer success, would have made an alteration upon their verdict in order to obtain that object? I mean an alteration upon their findings in point of fact—upon their finding as to fraud Until and unless such alteration were made, the verdict must remain inevitably a verdict for the defenders What then could the jury have done had they been sent back to revise their verdict so as to satisfy their own views of the justice of the case? I confess I can put no construction upon the declaration of the jury in regard to their contingent intentions, such as to make one regret that these intentions were defeated" 23 D, 1160

[11] At the trial of Aaron Mellor for murder, the name of Joseph Henry Thorne was called as one of the jury to try the cause A juror answered to the name, went into the box and was duly sworn, but next day it was discovered that William Thorncley, another on the list of assize, had, by mistake, answered to the name of Thorne Justice Wightman reserved the point for the consideration of the Court of Criminal Appeal, where it was held, by a majority of one, that the Court had no jurisdiction But the minority, consisting of six judges (among whom were Campbell, C-J and Cockburn, C-J) were of opinion that there had been a mis-trial, that the Court had jurisdiction, and that the proper course was to issue *venire de novo* The decision, therefore, cannot be regarded as one upon the general question, and, looking to the observations which fell from several of the judges who constituted the majority it is thought that the objection to the

§ 1073 The principle of allowing investigation into substantial objections to judicial records, is also applicable to the reports of commissioners appointed to take proofs Thus the Court allowed proof of the allegation that a justice of peace, acting as commissioner to take an oath on reference in a Sheriff-court case, had falsely and collusively signed a certificate that the party was not in a fit state of mind to undergo examination and that he had refused to take down the deposition which the party had really emitted (*h*) But in another case the Court refused to listen to the allegation that a commissioner appointed to take an oath on reference had refused either to allow certain questions to be put to the party or to record them. Here, however, the objection was not taken until after the commissioner's report had been for some time in process, and after the Lord Ordinary had decided the case on the merits against the party objecting (*i*) [12]

§ 1074 When the clerk of court in a civil case has, from inadvertence or mistake, written out the interlocutor in different terms from those which the Court directed or has omitted some portion of the judgment, the error may be corrected on application to the Court *de recenti* after the interlocutor has been signed (*k*)

(*h*) M'Laurin *v* Stewart, 1832, 10 S 333

(*i*) Anderson *v* Watson, 1833, 12 S, 273 The only note of what fell from the Court is in these terms — 'Bring your complaint against the commissioner We cannot listen to such a statement here, everything being *ex facie* regular' Notwithstanding this, it is thought probable that the Court were moved by the omission to state the objection *de recenti* of the procedure before the commissioner (*k*) Wishart *v* Hume, 1679, 2 B Sup, 250—Cathcart *v* Cathcart, 1830, 8 S, 497, affd, 5 W S, 315—Palmer *v* Stewart, 1832, 10 S, 252—Fletcher *v* Watson, 1825, 3 S, 439—Gray *v* Young, 1839 2 D, 128—Wright *v* Burns, 1832, 11 S, 180—Kerr *v* Bremner, 1835, 14 S 180—Ritchie *v* Ferguson, 1849, 12 D, 119 The technical, but important, word 'decerns' was allowed to be added to an interlocutor after an interval of more than two years, Lawrie *v* Donald, 1833, 11 S 246 Where two erasures in unimportant words

---

validity of the verdict, if stated before a competent tribunal, would have been sustained, Reg *v* Mellor, 1858, 7 Cox's Crim Cases 435 After the decision in H M Adv *v* Fraser, in which the Court of Justiciary held unanimously that, having once "tholed an assize," the panels could not be tried a second time for the same offence, it may be doubted how far the observations of Baron Hume, referred to in the text, can now be held to be a correct statement of the law It is thought that when a panel has once 'tholed an assize,' without a competent conviction being obtained, no second trial can in any case take place, H M Adv *v* Fraser, 1852, 1 Irv, 66

[12] Where the report of a commission was regular *ex facie* the Court allowed proof of the averment that the commissioner had been absent during part of the examinations, Jaffray *v* Murray, 1830, 8 S 667 See also M Kay *v* M'Lachlan, 1863, 1 Macph, 110, *infra* § 1401

The Court will also correct clerical errors which have occurred in recording the verdict of a jury in a civil case (*l*) and where the verdict is ambiguous, it may be corrected by the Court from the notes of the judge who presided at the trial (*m*) Nay more where the Court are satisfied that a clerical error has crept into a recorded judgment of the House of Lords, they will apply the judgment in the terms which they consider their Lordships of the Upper House intended (*n*) But the Court will not *ex intervallo* alter an interlocutor, except in a matter of mere form (*o*) And where the Court of Session corrected an error in their interlocutor after an appeal had been entered, the House of Lords were not satisfied as to the competency of the proceeding and the case was compromised on a suggestion from the woolsack (*p*) [13]

§ 1075 Clerical errors in the record may also be corrected in criminal cases (*r*) But more strictness will be observed in regard to these than as to errors occurring in civil proceedings

§ 1076 As the probative quality of judicial records depends on their being written at the time when the proceedings in the cause are fresh in the memory of the clerk of court and the parties, any considerable interval between the judgment or other procedure and

---

occurred in an interlocutor granting power to disentail, the Court, on application made at a short interval, pronounced the interlocutor of new, observing that the former interlocutor was sufficient, Caddell, 1853, 15 D, 282 The cases on this subject are collected in Shand's Pr, 346 (*l*) Kirk v Guthrie, 1817, 1 Mur, 279—Dalziel v D Queensberry's Exs, 1826, 4 Mur 18—Macf Pr, 239 (*m*) Marianski v Cairns, 1852 1 Macq, 212 noted *supra*, § 50 (*n*) Aberdeen Ry Co v Blaikies, 1854, 16 D, 470 (*o*) Martin v Crawford, 1685 2 B Sup, 69—Anderson v Watson, 1833, 12 S, 273 (noted *supra*, § 1073)—compared with Lawrie v Donald, *supra*

(*p*) Duguid v Mitchell, 1824, 3 S 96, 1 W S, 216, foot-note

(*r*) Burnett, 480—Henry v Young, 1846, Arkl, 105—Headrick 1773, Burnett, 476—2 Al Cr Law, 596

---

[13] *Supra* §§ 48, 49, and 50 In ordinary civil actions in the Sheriff-courts it is "competent to any Sheriff-substitute or Sheriff to correct any merely clerical error in his judgment at any time before the proceedings have been transmitted to the judge or court of review, not being later than seven days from the date of such judgment" 16 and 17 Vict, c 80, § 20 The Act of Sederunt 11th July 1828, § 63, allows the Lord Ordinary, of consent, to correct or alter any interlocutor before extract The Court, after final judgment is orally pronounced, will not except of consent alter the substance of an interlocutor, Cuthill v Burns, 1862, 24 D, 849—Hard v Anstruther, 1862, 1 Macph, 14 When a judgment of the House of Lords contains a remit to the Court of Session to carry out the judgment, it is the duty of the Court, 'instead of insisting that they are bound to give a purely literal meaning to the words of this House, and unable on such a construction to execute the order, to consider that there is imposed upon them the performance of the judicial act necessary to complete the procedure and to give effect to the judgment" *per* Lord Chancellor (Westbury) in Whitehead & Morton v Galbraith, 1861, 4 Macq, 283

the recording of it will be fatal. Accordingly, a decree was held to be ineffectual which bore to proceed on consent to decree under a judicial reference, but which consent had been written out from the recollection of the judges six months after its supposed date (s). And where a defender had given his oath on reference, and decree of absolvitor had been pronounced thereupon, but the clerk of court had omitted to minute either the oath or the decree, the Court would not allow the omission to be supplied *ex intervallo* from the oaths of the pursuer's counsel and of the judge and clerk (t).

§ 1077. The probativeness of judicial records is limited to matters which fall directly within their province, as the verdict and decree, interlocutory orders, findings and acts of the judge throughout the cause; and it does not extend to extrinsic or collateral matters. Thus a decreet by magistrates of a burgh, stating that the fines which it imposed had been applied to the use of the town, was held not to be probative *per se* of that fact, because it was not an *actus officii* wherein the town clerk's statement was to be credited (u). Thus also a decree enacting a person as cautioner *judicio sisti* is not effectual, unless it proceed on the cautioner's signed consent (x). And a confirmation as tutor, bearing that the party accepted the office, was held not to be probative against him of that fact, not being instructed by an acceptance under his hand (y).

§ 1078. It is partly on this principle that a statement on record, authenticated merely by the judge or clerk of court, is not probative of admissions by a party on the merits of the cause; for the record so authenticated is designed for minuting the proceedings of the judge and jury, not the pleas or admissions of the parties; and in practice all important admissions are authenticated by the parties or their procurators. Accordingly, a sentence or decree bearing to proceed on a confession or admission of the party, which is not signed by him or by his procurator in his name, is null both in civil (z) and criminal (a) causes. This rule applies also to church

(s) L. Buchanan v. Osborn, 1661, M., 12,528. (t) Brown v. Wilson, 1680, M., 12,267; 3 B. Sup. 373, S. C. (u) Stuart v. Mag. of Edinburgh, 1697, M., 12,536. (x) L. Lovat v. Sheriff of Nairn, 1628, M., 7661; 12,526.—Strowan v. Cameron, 1674, M., 7541; 12,533. (y) Kirkton v. L. Hunthill, 1665, M., 12,531.—Hamilton v. Porterfield, 1686, M., 12,534. (z) Cases in Mor., pp. 12,525 to 12,535.—Davidson v. Heddell, 1829, 8 S., 219.

(a) 9 Geo. IV., c. 29, § 14.—ib., c. 50, sch. A, 4.—Mackay v. Milne, 1679, M., 12,533.—See Burnett, 480. If the prisoner pleads guilty after the case has been sent to a jury, the verdict may proceed on the confession made in their presence, the confession being minuted and subscribed by the panel or his procurator. Until the act 9 Geo. IV.,

courts (*b*), although these are not strictly dealt with as to the forms of their procedure. In like manner a judicial ratification by a wife is not probative unless it is signed not only by the magistrate before whom it is emitted, but also by the party herself, or if she cannot write, by notaries subscribing for her in common form (*c*).

§ 1079. But while important judicial admissions must be subscribed by the party or his procurator, it is the practice for counsel to consent orally at the bar in matters occurring incidentally in the course of the process, as in consents to commissions for examining witnesses, to prorogations, and even to the repelling or sustaining of particular pleas. In such cases the interlocutor bears to proceed on consent, and it is effectual, unless the statement is challenged without delay (*d*). In jury trials, also, it is the practice for counsel to consent verbally to proof of certain facts being dispensed with, or to witnesses tendered being held to concur with others who have already been examined, and similar incidental matters. And this consent is marked by the judge in his notes. The trust placed in such admissions arises from the mutual confidence of the counsel on each side, rather than from definite rules of practice.

§ 1080. The rule which requires confessions in criminal cases to be signed by the prisoner was departed from in a complaint by the procurator-fiscal to the Magistrates of Glasgow against 640 dealers in wine and spirits for using false measures, where the record, which bore that "all severally acknowledged the matter therein charged," was not signed by any of them. In a suspension by one of them the Court of Justiciary held that "the record in a case of this nature afforded sufficient evidence without the signature of the party" (*e*). The Police Acts in several large towns dispense with the prisoner's subscription, and there is perhaps a similar power in inferior courts at common law in summary trials for minor offences (*f*). But in summary trials before the Sheriff without a jury, it is the practice for prisoners to sign their confessions, and

---

all pleas of guilty were made and subscribed in presence of the jury, who returned the verdict proceeding on the judicial confession, Justiciary Records.

(*b*) Kerr *v* Steedman, 1661, M, 12,528—Ross *v* Findlater, 1826, 4 S, 514. See Miller *v* Baird 1755, M, 12,539—Cuthbert 1842, 1 Broun, 311.

(*c*) Mitchelson *v* Mowbray 1635, M, 5960, 6073, 1 B Sup, 354 357, S C—Bell *v* Mow, 1636, M, 12,526—Swinton *v* Brown, 1668, M, 3412 8408 S C—Gordon *v* Maxwell, 1678, M, 12,533—1 Fraser Pers and Dom Rel, 431.

(*d*) Compare Brown *v* Henderson, 1693, M, 12,535—Fraser *v* Maitland 1821, 2 Sh Ap, 37—Miller *v* Edinburgh and Glasgow Railway Company, 1849, 11 D, 1012—and see Tait Ev, 15.

(*e*) Jardine *v* Simpson, 1823, Sh Just Ca, 91.

(*f*) See Tait Ev, 17, and Cockburn *v* Johnston, 1851, 1 Irvine, 492.

if they cannot write, the judge signs for them (*g*) The Court, in an old case, sustained a decree by a burgh court, not signed by the accused, which imposed a fine and bore to proceed on a complaint for "abusing the provost, adhered to and owned by the defender in face of the Court" (*h*) This decision may be defended on the ground that the party by his conduct before the Court (a narrative of which fell within the province of the record), repeated the offence and warranted the punishment which had been inflicted for it

II *How far the Verdict or Decree in one case is admissible in another case involving the same facts*

§ 1081 To prevent rights from being precarious and fluctuating, decrees *in foro* are conclusive of the interests of the parties and their successors, so as to exclude any subsequent action embracing the same conclusions and *media concludendi* (*i*) 14 But a subsequent suit relating to a different interest, or on different *media* is competent although it should be founded on the same facts, so that one who has been either convicted or acquitted in a criminal prosecution may be sued for damages at the instance of the injured party, be-

(*g*) 9 Geo IV c 29 sch G 3 (*h*) Prov of Forfar v Cuthbert, 1682, M, 12,533 (*i*) Stair, 4, 40 16—Ersk 4 3, 3—Tait Ev 406—Henderson v Malcolm 1814 2 Dow 287, 8—Graham v Maxwell 1814, ib, 314

14 It has been decided in England that a colonial verdict is not pleadable in bar in an action brought in England for the same cause, Bank of Australasia v Harding, 1850—9 Manning and Scott's C P C 661 In Houlditch v the Marquis of Donegal 8 Bligh N S, 301 it was held that a foreign judgment is not conclusive but is merely *prima facie* evidence The decree or judgment of a foreign court may be made the ground of a valid proceeding and with fruit and effect in each country But a question has been raised, Whether it is only *prima facie* evidence, a ground of action or conclusive, not to be traversed or rebutted, and not to be averred against? The leaning of my opinion is so strong that I can hardly call it the inclination of an opinion, and we know it is the general sense of lawyers in Westminster Hall that the judgment of a foreign court in courts of this country is only *prima facie* evidence—is liable to be averred against, and not conclusive It would seem a strange thing to hold that our courts were bound conclusively to give execution to the sentence of foreign courts, when for aught we know there is not any one of those things which are reckoned the elements or the corner stones of the due administration of justice present in the procedure of these foreign courts,' *per* Lord Chancellor Lyndhurst in Houlditch v Marquis of Donegal In Whitehead v Thomson 1861 23 D, 772, the Court of Session gave decree for a sum "conform to extract or exemplification" of a judgment obtained in the Court of Queen's Bench Lord Curriehill was of opinion that, before the Court could give decree as asked, they must be satisfied that the judgment would be *res judicata* in England, but this was doubted by Lord Deas, see *infra* § 1283

cause the one process is carried on *ad vindictam publicam*, while the object of the other is reparation of the patrimonial loss occasioned to a private individual (*j*). In the same way, the right of the Crown to prosecute is not impaired by a previous civil action at the instance of the injured party (*k*). Thus, also, one who had been acquitted in a criminal prosecution for attempting to bribe the solicitor of excise failed to recover the money in a subsequent action for payment, the Civil Court holding that it had been given for an illegal purpose (*l*).

§ 1082. But the rules regarding *res judicata* are not so pertinent to the subject of this treatise, as is the question whether the decree or verdict in one cause can be used as evidence *valeat quantum* in another laid upon the same facts. The authorities on this point are not uniform. On the one hand, where a person had been convicted of robbery and the injured party raised an action of reparation against him which was opposed by his creditors, the Court refused to hold the conviction as *res judicata*, but no question was raised, and no doubt seemed to be entertained, as to the competency of receiving it in evidence (*m*). So it has been held that a conviction before a court-martial for murder is sufficient evidence in a subsequent action of assythment (damages claimed by the deceased's relations), unless the defender's innocence is proved (*n*). And where a person had been acquitted on a trial for culpable homicide, caused by the fall of a tree which he had been cutting, it was observed in a subsequent civil action of damages by the deceased's relations against that person and his employer, that the acquittal was a circumstance in favour of the defenders (*o*). Such seems, also, to have been the opinion of Baron Hume, who observes that the testimonies given in the criminal case are lawful evidence in the civil case, so far as they go, without excluding new pleas or evidence for the defender "whereby to obviate the presumption against him, and invalidate, if he can, the previous conviction" (*p*). But, however

---

(*j*) 2 Hume, 71, 479—2 Al. Cr. Law, 64—Bell's Pr. § 2216—Ker v. Sun Fire Office, 1793, M., 14,078—Wilsons v. M'Knight, 1830, 8 S. 398—Hill v. Fletcher, 1847, 10 D., 7.

(*k*) Hume, ib.—Al. ib.—Bell, ib.—Tait, ib.—Miller v. Moffat, 11th March 1820, 2 Mur., 308, afterwards tried criminally as L. Advocate v. Moffat, 12th June 1820, 2 Hume, 260.

(*l*) Stein v. Bonar, 4th Dec. 1789, 2 Hume, 72.

(*m*) Bontein v. Buchanan's Crs., 1739, M., 11,013; Elch., "Proof," No. 5. The proof failed in the civil action.

(*n*) MacHargs v. Campbell, 1767, M., 12,541; Hailes, 192, S. C.

(*o*) Per Lords Just.-Clerk Boyle and Bannatyne in Linwood v. Hathorn, 14th May 1817, F. C., affirmed on merits 1 Sh. Ap., 20.

(*p*) 2 Hume, 180. See also ib. 72.

just this view may have been under the old practice, when the depositions in the criminal cause were entered at length on the record, and when the civil court proceeded on written proofs without the aid of a jury, it is inapplicable to modern procedure, where, from the witnesses being examined orally without such a record, the jury in the civil case cannot discover whether the former verdict was well or ill founded (*r*). Professor Bell seems to have overlooked this distinction, when he laid down that the verdict in a criminal case, although not conclusive in a subsequent civil case regarding the same matter, and *vice versa*, may serve as *prima facie* proof (*s*)

§ 1083 The strict view is more consistent with principle, as well as with modern practice In many cases the verdict in another case should be excluded on the ground of *res inter alios*, while in every case the jury ought to decide on the evidence adduced before them, without regard to the opinion which another judge or jury may have formed upon the same issue but perhaps erroneously, or from different evidence (*t*) The former verdict must either coincide with, or differ from, the view which the jury would take on the second trial independently of it In the one event, it would be useless in the other, it would produce misdecision, the risk of which can only be avoided by excluding the proof Accordingly, in an action of proving the tenor where the issue was whether a certain deed of settlement had been destroyed by the testator's directions the interlocutor pronounced by the Lord Ordinary in a previous action of reduction between the same parties and relating to the same matter, in which his Lordship found it proved by the oaths of havers that the deed had been destroyed after the testator's death, was held by Lord Cringletie to be inadmissible, because the jury "must judge for themselves on the evidence before them" (*u*) In like manner, in an action of damages for maltreatment when the

---

(*r*) See 2 Al, 66 (*s*) Bell's Pr § 2216 See also Macf Prac, 184

(*t*) A striking illustration of the independence of different juries judging on the same facts occurred in Stone v General Marine Insurance Company, 1851, 13 D, 1288, where there were separate actions and trials against two sets of underwriters upon the same ship The same evidence was adduced in each case, in the one the jury found for the pursuer, and in the other for the defender, yet the Court refused the pursuer's motion in the second case for a new trial, holding that the verdict in each case must stand unless palpably inconsistent with the evidence adduced before the jury therein See also Cleland v Cleland 1838, 1 D, 254 noted *supra* § 917 (*y*)

(*u*) Andersons v Jefrey 1826, 4 Mur 90 See also Dalziel v D Queensberry's Executors 1825 4 Mur, 13

pursuer was in a prison, in which the defenders were the governor and two turnkeys, where the defence was that the defenders had acted in accordance with the prison regulations, which the pursuer had violated, the Lord Chief Commissioner refused to admit an incidental decision of an inferior court as to what regulations were in force, and he observed,—"If the point had been incidentally decided even in a supreme court, I should have held it not to be binding and that I must here decide the point on the facts proved, and not by proof of the conclusion to which others have come" (x) In another trial (y) before the same learned judge, the sentence which had been pronounced in a criminal prosecution was produced, without objection for the pursuer in an action of damages at the instance of the injured party, but his Lordship observed that he would have doubted whether one who had been examined as a witness in a criminal prosecution could make such a use of the sentence His Lordship, accordingly, guarded against the case being drawn into a precedent lest parties should attempt to make evidence for themselves, by getting a conviction on their own testimony in a criminal prosecution This reason, however for doubting the admissibility of the sentence does not apply now, as parties are competent witnesses in this class of civil cases.

Sir A Alison also lays down, that while a civil action is competent in regard to acts which have been prosecuted criminally, and *vice versa*, "the verdict of the one court is no evidence in the other" (z) And this is supported by recent practice, as in several cases where actions of damages have followed criminal prosecutions for the same delict, the verdict in the criminal court seems not to have been tendered for the pursuer (a)

(x) Macfarlane v Young, 1824, 3 Mur, 412 His Lordship also observed,—"If this had been a suit in the Supreme Court instead of an inferior one and having for its direct object to ascertain which set of regulations were in force and had there been a final adjudication in that case, I must have held it to be binding" (y) Mackie v Wight, 1822, 3 Mur, 25 (z) 2 Al Cr Law, 67

(a) See Hill v Fletcher, 1847, 10 D. 7—Ronald v Robertson, Jan 1820 (not reported) noted in 2 Al, *supra* See also M'Arthur v Croall, 1852, 24 Sc Jur, 170, where, in an action of damages at the instance of a widow against the proprietor of a stage coach, on the ground that her husband's death had been caused by the negligence of the drivers of two coaches belonging to the defender the defender pleaded that he had taken proper precautions for the safety of passengers, by having skilful drivers, good horses, &c,—the pursuer tendered two criminal convictions against one of the drivers for careless driving several years before (but not any applicable to the occasion in issue) and the presiding judge held them to be admissible as anticipating the defender's proof but observed that they would not be of much avail to the pursuer, upon which they

§ 1084 In England the conviction in a criminal case is inadmissible in a civil suit, and *vice versa*, on the ground that it is *res inter alios* (*b*), and before parties were admissible as witnesses in civil causes it used to be rejected on the ground that the party had, by his own evidence, aided in bringing about the verdict (*c*)[15]

§ 1085 Yet a conviction proceeding on a plea of guilty will be received in a subsequent civil action, as proof of a deliberate admission of the acts charged, and, although not conclusive as if it had been an admission on record in the civil case, it will be an important item of evidence (*d*)

§ 1086 Of course where a new trial is granted the former verdict on the same issues cannot be used in evidence before the second jury, for it was set aside on the ground that it did not meet the justice of the case, in consequence of the erroneous admission or exclusion of evidence, from surprise, being against evidence, or the like (*e*) But where a new trial is granted on some of the issues, or where new issues on other points of the case are tried before a second jury, the verdict in the former trial may be referred to as settling all matters of fact which are not embraced by the new issues (*f*)

III *Authentication of Judicial Records*

§ 1087 The act 1686 c 3, ordains that "all interlocutors pronounced by the Lords of Council and Session, and all other judges within the kingdom, shall be signed by the President of the Court, or the judge pronouncer thereof", and it prohibits "the clerks upon their peril to extract any acts or decreets unless the interlocutors,

---

were withdrawn[16] (*b*) 2 Phill, 23—Taylor 1114—1 Starkie (4th ed), 363

(*c*) Smith *v* Rummens, 1807, 1 Camp, 9—Hathaway *v* Barrow, 1807, ib, 151

(*d*) 2 Phill, 25—Taylor 1115—See also Griersoun *v* L Zester, 1541, M, 14,021—Vicar of Kinghorn *v* L Scotfield, 1541, M, 14,022—Same parties, 1542, M, ib—Home *v* Scott, 1541, M, 14,023 In these cases the previous confession was held not to be available because the party at making it had protested that it should not prejudice him in subsequent proceedings (*e*) See O'Connor *v* Malone, 1839, M'Lean and Rob, 468, 485—Cleland *v* Cleland, 1838, 1 D, 254, *supra*, § 917 (*y*)

(*f*) Fife *v* L Fife's Tr, 1816, 1 Mur, 125, 6—Watson *v* Hamilton, 1824, 3 Mur, 486—See also Dalziel *v* D Queensberry's Ex, 1825, 4 Mur, 13

---

[15] In England, a conviction under statute is not admissible as a previous conviction in a prosecution at common law, R *v* Ferne, 4 Jur N S, 300

[16] R *v* Moore, 1 F and F, 73 where in a prosecution for forgery proof of previous acts of forgery was not admitted

which are the warrants thereof, be signed as said is,—declaring hereby, the extracts which shall be given out otherways to be void and null." The want of the judge's signature to an interlocutor of importance cannot be supplied by homologation, and may be pleaded after several steps of procedure have followed on it. Thus where an interlocutor by a Sheriff-substitute ordering a proof was unsubscribed, the objection was allowed to be taken for the first time in the Circuit Court, on appeal from the judgments of the Sheriff-substitute and principal successively, proceeding on a proof led on the unsigned interlocutor (*g*). But Lords Fullerton and Mackenzie considered that such an objection of nullity would only apply to the essential interlocutors in a cause. In a late case (*h*) the Lord Chancellor (St Leonards) observed, that the act 1686 'does not say that interlocutors shall be signed at the time, but simply that they shall be signed, and subsequent signature has always been deemed sufficient.'

§ 1088. In practice the original minutes of proceedings of presbyteries and other courts of the Established Church are not authenticated at the time, but are inspected half-yearly or at other intervals by a committee of the court, when one signature is then adhibited by the moderator, which is understood to extend to all the proceedings since the previous authentication (*i*). On account of this long continued practice, as interpreting the act 1686, c. 3, that statute has been found not to apply to the records of church courts, which will be sustained if authenticated according to the forms observed in the church (*k*).

(*g*) Smith *v.* M'Aulay, 1846, 9 D., 190. (*h*) Ferguson *v.* Skirving, *infra*.

(*i*) See Report by Principal Lee and Mr Bell (Procurator for the Church), in Ferguson *v.* Skirving, *infra*. (*k*) Ferguson *v.* Skirving, 1850, 12 D. 1145, affd. 1 Macq. 232. Here the deposition by a presbytery of a schoolmaster was sustained, although the original record of the sentence, consisting of eleven pages and on six separate sheets, was only signed by the moderator (preses) at the foot of the eighth and last pages, and on marginal notes on the eighth, ninth, tenth, and last pages, and by the moderator and clerk about the middle of the sixth page, the first five pages being altogether unauthenticated. The certified copy engrossed in the presbytery records was not signed at all by the moderator who presided during the deposition, but by him who presided when the minute was read over and approved of. The Court, after an inquiry and report as to the practice in authenticating ecclesiastical records, sustained the one so authenticated. See also Dickson *v.* Heir of Newlands, 1768, M., 7464, as noticed in this case.

CHAPTER VI —REGISTERS OF DEEDS AND OTHER PRIVATE WRITINGS

§ 1089 One of the most distinctive features of Scottish jurisprudence is its system of public registers for private writings Originating in the infancy of our common law, these records have been regulated and expanded into a system of great public utility They form an important branch of the law of evidence

The registers referred to are divided, according to their respective purposes, into—

(1) Registers for preservation—in which writings or copies of them are preserved in order to prevent the evils arising from loss or destruction,

(2) Registers for preservation and execution—in which documents are recorded as an indispensable preliminary towards their being enforced by diligence —and

(3) Registers for publication—in which writings or copies or abstracts of them are entered in order that their existence may be advertised to all the lieges whom they may concern

§ 1090 The second class, being the earliest in date, will be first noticed These registers are coeval with, and form part of, the records of our civil courts Originally the mode of enforcing deeds was by an action of registration, in which the granter of the deed was summoned before a competent court at the instance of the grantee, to show cause why the deed should not be registered in the court books, in order that diligence might pass upon it About the fourteenth century it became the practice for the parties to important deeds to appear before a judge, and in person acknowledge their subscriptions, whereupon a decree setting forth the confession was pronounced, and, with a copy of the deed, was recorded in the court books, an extract of the entry being the warrant for diligence (*a*) When personal attendance was inconvenient to a party, he authorised a procurator to confess judgment in his name The authority was contained in a written mandate, which at first was separate from the deed, and after having for some time been indorsed upon it at last came to form (as at present) one of its concluding

(*a*) Kames' Law Tracts (ed 1792) 77—1 Ross Lec 109—Act 1581 c 4 This proceeding was similar to that observed at a very early period in verbal contracts, where the parties appeared in Court and orally admitted the contract, which was thereupon recorded in the books of Court See Kames, *ut supra*, 72

clauses The mandate when contained in the deed, or indorsed upon it, was blank in the name of the mandatory, and was completed by the grantee filling in the name of an advocate, who then had authority to appear for the granter and consent to the deed being registered He did so by personal attendance in court, and latterly by a written consent (*b*) In course of time the attendance and consent were abolished as unnecessary (*c*), and every deed containing a clause consenting to registration came to be entered by the clerk of court in the court books on mere presentation to him for that purpose, without any formality or procedure in presence of the judge In this state the matter has stood till now Registration takes place of course, but the theory that it proceeds upon an order of the judge remains (*d*), and by a fiction of law the record and extract still narrate a decree of registration, interponed by the judge on the motion of a procurator for the granter of the deed, or for both parties if it is bilateral

Originally the principal deeds were returned to the parties But in course of time they came to be preserved *in publica custodia*, only an extract of the decree of registration, embodying an official copy of the deed, being given out (*e*) The principals can only be recovered under the order of a judge, as afterwards mentioned

"In this manner the several Courts of Law in Scotland came to hold registers and were made the custodiers of private deeds, without any special establishment, act of Parliament, or grant from the Crown, as is the case of all the other registers in the kingdom" (*f*)

§ 1091 The register in the books of Council and Session was originally kept by the clerks of session, like the other records of the Court (*g*) But after the records of deeds and of judicial procedure had been for some time practically separate, the former was placed under separate superintendence (*h*) The registers of inferior courts are still kept by the clerks of court

§ 1092 The advantage of allowing summary diligence to proceed on bills of exchange caused two acts (*i*) to be passed, by which instruments of protest, having copies of the relative bills

(*b*) Kames' Law Tracts, 78—1 Ross Lec, 111 (*c*) A S, 9th Dec 1670

(*d*) This theory is well illustrated by the case of Fleming *v* Newton, 1818 6 Bell's Ap Ca, 175, reversing, 8 D, 677, which related to protests of bills recorded in terms of the acts noticed *infra*, § 1092 (*e*) 1 Ross Lec, 108 (*f*) 1 Ross Lec 108 (*g*) See 1685 c 38 (*h*) 55 Geo III c 70 § 1

(*i*) 1681 c 20, 1696 c 36 The former applies to foreign, the latter to inland bill

prefixed, may be recorded within a limited time in the books of all competent judicatories for execution, like deeds bearing a clause of registration And this privilege was afterwards extended to protests on promissory-notes (*k*) The instrument is retained in the register as the ground of the decree and extract, which narrate a fictitious decree, but the bill or note, if produced is returned to the party, as it is often required for procedure elsewhere

§ 1093 Deeds which bear a consent to register *for preservation* (and not also for execution) are entered in the books of competent courts The principals are retained in order to give full effect to the granter's intention—only an extract being given out to the parties interested (*l*)

§ 1094 At common law registration even for preservation, could only proceed in virtue of a decree of registration *causa cognita*, or on consent of the parties to the deed This defect was remedied by the act 1698, c 4 On the preamble that "it will be of great ease and advantage to the lieges that probative writs be allowed to be registrate albeit they want a clause of registration," this statute enacts that it shall be lawful and leisume to registrate for conservation all charters granted by subjects, dispositions, bonds, contracts, tacks, reversions and all other probative writs in any public authentic register that is competent, albeit the said writs want a clause of registration, and the principal to be given back to the party

§ 1095 The extract of deeds so registered do not set forth a fictitious decree Nor is the principal deed preserved *in publica custodia* The registers, therefore, merely contain authentic copies of the deeds recorded in them

§ 1096 Formerly registration, either for preservation or for preservation and execution, used to be competent in the books of all inferior courts having civil jurisdiction, and of Commissary Courts But this practice having become inconvenient, it was restricted by the act 49 Geo III c 42 which on the preamble that "irregularities and inconveniences have arisen, or may arise, from the unnecessary multiplication of registers in Scotland," &c, prohibits (§ 1) clerks of royal burghs or burghs of regality or barony from receiving deeds or writings for the purpose of registration in their respective books either under the act 1698 c 4, or in virtue of a clause of registration And the same act also prohibits (§ 2)

(*k*) 12 Geo III, c 72 § 36 made perpetual by 23 Geo III c 18 § 55

(*l*) 1 Ross Lec 92 *et seq*—Kames' Law Tr 77 *et seq*

clerks of Commissary Courts from receiving writings for registration in virtue of the statute or clause of registration referred to, or of the acts authorising the registration of protests on bills and promissory-notes From those prohibitions, however, are excepted (§ 1) the right of clerks of royal burghs to record instruments of protest on bills and notes, and to record instruments of sasine and other writs relative to burgage property within their respective burghs and liberties thereof, under the act 1681, c 11, and any deeds and instruments relating exclusively to the property or possession of such subjects, or to which all the parties are burgesses or domiciled within the burgh at the date of presentment

§ 1097 The books and warrants of the records thus abolished were directed to be transmitted as follows —that kept by the Edinburgh Commissary Clerks to the Clerk Register, and those of the Inferior Commissary Courts, and of burghs of regality and barony, to the Sheriff-clerks of their respective counties (*m*)

§ 1098 On account of the interest of the lieges in certain writings, chiefly those which affect real estate, *publication in appropriate registers* has been made essential to their full legal effect This is the case as to letters of horning and relaxations, with their executions (*n*), inhibitions and interdictions (*o*) Deeds of entail (*p*), adjudications (of which an abbreviate is recorded) (*r*), instruments and summonses for interrupting prescription in real rights (*s*), and ' reversions regressions, bonds and writs for making reversions, or regresses, assignations thereto, and discharges of the same, renunciation of wadsets, and grants of redemption, and instruments of sasine (*t*),' and instruments of resignation *ad remanentiam* (*u*) [1] Recording the instrument of sasine now constitutes infeftment (*w*) And deeds required for creating or transmitting heritable securities may now be recorded in the appropriate register of sasines, so as to complete the creditor's real right (*x*).[2]

(*m*) 49 Geo III, c 42, §§ 4, 5, 6 (*n*) 1579 c 75—1600 c 13

(*o*) 1581, c 119 (1)—1600, c 13—Stair, 1 6, 10 and 4, 50 8—Ersk , 2, 11, 5—See 1597, c 268 , repealed by 20 Geo II, c 43, § 11 (*p*) 1685, c 22

(*r*) Regulations, 1695 art 24 (*s*) 1696, c 19 (*t*) 1617, c 16 (as to lands, not burgage)—1681, c 11 (as to burgage property) (*u*) 1669, c 3

(*w*) 8 and 9 Vict , c 35 (as to lands not burgage)—10 and 11 Vict c 49 (as to burgage property) (*x*) 8 and 9 Vict , c 31—10 and 11 Vict , c 50—extended to

---

[1] Instruments of sasine and of resignation *ad remanentiam* are not now required , 21 and 22 Vict , c 76 (Titles to Land Act)—See *infra*, § 1187

[2] The 20 and 21 Vict c 26, on the registration and assignation of long leases,

§ 1099 The records of Chancery in Scotland contain retours and decrees of services of heirs, copies of charters and precepts by the Crown and Prince of Scotland, patents, and some other writings

§ 1100 The retour (*y*) of a service is the verdict of an inquest under a brieve issued from Chancery for trying whether the claimant's ancestor died at the faith and peace of the Crown, whether the claimant is his heir, and, in cases of special service what is the valued rent of the land succeeded to, and some other matters The finding of the jury is returned or "retoured" to Chancery The ancient practice of that office was to record a memorandum of the "retours," and give back the principal But for a considerable time the principals have been retained and preserved under the charge of the Lord Clerk Register and Director of Chancery, the parties receiving only an extract

§ 1101 The earliest portion of the record of Chancery is not extant. It is supposed to have been destroyed about the year 1544, when the English army under Lord Hertford burnt the city of Edinburgh and the monastery and palace of Holyrood This is consistent with the fact that the series of original retours in Chancery commences only in 1547, although the record also embraces some older retours which, long after that date, had been found in private custody and deposited in the office From 1547 till a comparatively recent period, the series of retours is very imperfect the want of a proper place for preserving them having caused many to be lost and destroyed by damp, while some were carried away by Cromwell In 1807 the originals in preservation at that date were for the first time arranged by the indefatigable Mr Thomas Thomson

§ 1102 The practice of engrossing retours in books of record was begun in 1630, by the Director of Chancery getting all the retours then in existence booked It has been continued by engrossing all subsequent retours But the completeness and accuracy of this record cannot be implicitly relied on, as it exhibits throughout many instances of negligent transcription, which can only be de-

all classes of heritable securities by 17 and 18 Vict, c 62 Under these acts the old forms of completing the creditor's title are still competent (*y*) The term 'Retour' is also frequently applied to the extract registered retour

provides, by § 1, that long leases are to be registered in Register of Sasines, and by § 15 that certified extracts shall make faith as writs registered

tected by collation with the originals. Notwithstanding its defects and its unauthorised origin, this record is of considerable value and extracts from it have long been received in our Courts. The 5th volume, containing the retours from 1611 to 1614, has unfortunately been lost (*z*).

§ 1103. An act passed in 1821 directed the clerks to services of retourable brieves to transmit to Chancery for preservation, under the orders of the Lord Clerk Register, not only the verdicts of inquest, but also the original claims of service, minutes of the proceedings and depositions of the witnesses in services (*a*).

§ 1104. Recent legislation has substituted for the old brieve and retour a petition and decree of service before the Sheriff of the bounds or the Sheriff of Chancery. But the original proceedings and decrees in all services are transmitted to Chancery, and there preserved. They are entered by the Director of Chancery or his depute in the "Record of Services," under superintendence of the Lord Clerk Register, the parties receiving extracts certified from the Chancery Office, which are equivalent to extracts of retours. An index or abridgment of this register is directed to be prepared annually and to be printed and published in such manner as the Lord Clerk Register shall direct (*b*).

§ 1105. The retours and books of the Record of Chancery are important evidence in cases of pedigree. Under the former election law, extracts from them were the proper evidence of the valued rent of persons claiming right to vote (*c*).[3]

§ 1106. Charters from the Crown and the Prince of Scotland are entered in the Record of Chancery before being delivered. Formerly no record of the sealing of them was preserved, in consequence of which the register did not prove that a completed charter had been expede (*d*). This defect has been remedied as to all writs which may have passed the Great Seal since the year 1809, when the Director of Chancery was ordained before delivering the writ, to enter the sealing in the Register of the Great Seal—extracts of writs so recorded being made probative, except in improbations (*e*).

(*z*) The foregoing sketch is taken from Mr Thomson's preface to the Abridgment of Retours, published in 1811. See also Tait, 187.

(*a*) 1 and 2 Geo. IV, c. 38, § 12.

(*b*) 10 and 11 Vict., c. 47 (Service of Heirs Act), §§ 12, 13, 14.

(*c*) 16 Geo. II, c. 11, § 8. See the chapter on extracts from records of deeds, *infra*.

(*d*) Ersk., 4, 1, 22.

(*e*) 49 Geo. III, c. 42, §§ 15, 16. This is also the prac-

---

[3] For the present evidence of qualification see note on the Valuation Roll, *infra*, § 1161.

§ 1107 The Director of Chancery also keeps a "Record of Precepts," in which are recorded at length all precepts issued from Chancery after 1st October 1847 for infefting heirs in crown or principality lands (*f*) [4]

CHAPTER VII —REGISTRY OF SHIPS

§ 1108 Great Britain, like all other commercial countries, extends certain privileges to vessels belonging to her subjects (*a*) In connection with these privileges and in order to preserve a public record of the constitution and transmission of rights in British ships, registers are established at certain British possessions and at all ports and places throughout the kingdom, which may be fixed by the Commissioners of Customs for the purpose (*b*) The enactments regarding these registers are contained in several statutes, and have been consolidated and re-enacted by a statute passed in 1854 (*c*) [1] They will be noticed shortly in their bearing upon the law of evidence

---

tice under the Crown Charter Act, 10 and 11 Vict c 51, § 15 (*f*) 10 and 11 Vict c 51 § 20

(*a*) The original object of the Registry Acts was to advance the public policy of the State at a time when extensive monoplies of trade were enjoyed by British vessels, and the rules as to constituting and transmitting rights in ships were subsidiary to the national objects The exclusive right to trade has been almost entirely abolished by the acts 12 and 13 Vict c 29 and 17 and 18 Vict c 5 But the Queen in council may impose retaliatory restrictions on the voyages of the ships of any foreign country, so as to place them on the same footing in British ports as that on which British ships are placed in the ports of the foreign country, 16 and 17 Vict, c 107, §§ 324, 5, 6—17 and 18 Vict c 5, § 1 (*b*) 17 and 18 Vict, c 104 (Merchant Shipping Act) § 30

(*c*) The Registry Acts were consolidated by 4 Geo IV, c 41 The act 6 Geo IV c 110 came in its place, and was supplanted by the 3 and 4 Will IV c 55 The act 8 and 9 Vict, c 89, consolidated all previous acts on the subject It has been repealed by the act 17 and 18 Vict, c 120 (Merchant Shipping Repeal Act, 1854), which, with 17 and 18 Vict, c 104 ("Merchant Shipping Act, 1854"), now constitutes the law as to registration of ships

---

[4] The 157th section of the Bankruptcy Act 19 and 20 Vict, c 79, provides that a book entitled 'The Register of Sequestrations' shall be kept by the Accountant in Bankruptcy, in which he is to enter the particulars of any sequestration awarded by the Sheriff or by the Court of Session

[1] Amended by 25 and 26 Vict, c 63 (Merchant Shipping Acts Amendment Act, 1862

§ 1109 In this respect the general scope of the enactments as to registration of ships consists in preserving a double record of the rights in every ship or share of a ship, one of these records being preserved in the register of the port to which the ship belongs, the other, called the certificate of registry, being carried about in the ship throughout her voyages Each of these records is altered from time to time, as the rights of the parties interested in the ship are transmitted, lost, or otherwise changed

§ 1110 Every British ship except certain small craft engaged in the river and coasting trade of the United Kingdom, and in the fishing and coasting trade of our North American possessions, must be registered, and (with these exceptions) no ship, unless registered, can be recognised as a British ship, or can receive from the custom-house a clearance for enabling her to proceed to sea (*d*) When a foreign ship becomes the property of British owners at a foreign port, the master may obtain from the British consular officer there a provisional certificate, which possesses the same force as a regular certificate of registry, but only for six months, or till such earlier time as the ship arrives at a port where there is a British registrar (*e*)

§ 1111 With a view to registration, the property in every ship is held to be divided into sixty-four shares, but not more than thirty-two persons can at the same time be registered as owners of any ship (*f*),—except in the case of corporate bodies, who may be registered by their corporate names, and who are reckoned as individual owners (*g*),—and in the case of joint owners, who, to the number of five, may hold any share or number of shares, and who are also reckoned as one person (*h*). No one can be registered as owner of a fractional part of a share (*i*) nor can joint owners dispose in severalty of their interests in the share or shares which they hold (*k*) These rules however, do not affect the beneficial title of any number of persons, or any company represented by, or claiming through, any registered owner or joint owner (*l*) In case of the death of an owner, his representatives acquiring right to his share or shares are reckoned as one person (*m*), and there is a similar provision as to persons coming in right of a bankrupt or insolvent owner (*n*) No notice of any trust, express, implied or constructive, can be entered on the register, but each person appearing

(*d*) 17 and 18 Vict, c 104 (Merchant Shipping Act), § 19 (*e*) Same act, § 51 (*f*) Same act, § 37 (*g*) Ib (*h*) Ib (*i*) Ib (*k*) Ib (*l*) Ib (*m*) Same act, §§ 58, 60 (*n*) Same act, §§ 59, 60

there to be owner has power (subject to any rights appearing on the register to be vested in any other person) absolutely to dispose of the ship or share standing in his name, and to give effectual receipts for any money therefor paid or advanced by way of consideration (*o*)

§ 1112 The entry in the registry contains (1) the name of the ship, and of the port to which she belongs, (2) the details as to her tonnage, build and description, specified by the act, (3) the particulars as to the time and place of her building, and in case of a foreign ship a statement of her foreign name and (if she was condemned) of the time, place and court of condemnation, (4) the names and descriptions of her registered owner or owners, and, if there are more than one the proportions in which they are interested (*p*)

§ 1113 Upon the completion of the registry, the registrar is required to grant a "Certificate of Registry" in the statutory form, which embraces the particulars entered in the register, along with the name of the master of the ship (*q*)

§ 1114 On the death or bankruptcy of a registered owner the person or persons coming in his place may be registered, on producing evidence of their right in terms of the act (*r*), and there is a similar power as to shares transmitted by marriage (*s*)

§ 1115 Registration of an appropriate instrument in the form prescribed by the Merchant Shipping Act is also essential to the completion of the real right of a purchaser (*t*), or mortgagee (*u*), in any ship or share of a ship and the rights of competing mortgagees are determined by priority of registration, not by priority in date of their respective instruments (*x*) These rules, however, do not affect the personal right which a party, holding an obligation to transfer an interest in a ship or share, has to sue the registered owner to execute the writings necessary for having the right made real by registration (*y*).

There are also provisions for recording the conveyance, trans-

---

(*o*) 17 and 18 Vict, c 104 (Merchant Shipping Act), § 53 (*p*) Same act, § 42 (*q*) Same act, § 44 (*r*) Same act, §§ 58, 59 60

(*s*) Ib (*t*) Same act § 55 *et seq*—Under the corresponding rules of a previous statute (8 and 9 Vict, c 89, § 34) it was held, that where a coasting vessel under fifteen tons burden had been registered, the owner might transfer the right without a written instrument, and without an entry in the register, because the vessel was not one of those requiring to be registered by the act 8 and 9 Vict, c 88, §§ 13, 14, Benyon *v* Cresswell, 1848, 12 Ad and Ell N S, 899 (*u*) Same act, § 66 *et seq*

(*x*) Same act, § 69 (*y*) See Boyd's Ex *v* Martin's Ex, 1847, 9 D, 1234 This decision was pronounced in regard to the corresponding provisions of the act 3 and

mission, and extinction of mortgages (*z*) The certificate of registry does not, by statute, contain any evidence of them

§ 1116 It is also enacted that, if any change takes place in the registered ownership of a vessel, a memorandum of the change shall be indorsed on the certificate of registry If the change takes place when the ship is at her port of registry, the memorandum is indorsed by the registrar there, and if it occurs when the ship is absent from her port of registry the indorsation is made by the registrar of that port on the first return of the ship, or, if she previously arrives at any other port where there is a British registrar, such registrar on being advised by the registrar of the port of registry of the change having taken place, is required to indorse a like memorandum thereof on the certificate of registry (*a*)

Whenever the master of a ship is changed, a memorandum of the change must be indorsed on the certificate of registry If it is made in consequence of the sentence of a Naval Court, the indorsation must be made and subscribed by the presiding officer of such court, and if it takes place from any other cause, the indorsation must be made and subscribed by the registrar or (if there is no registrar) by the British consular officer of the place where the change is made The officers of customs at any port may refuse to admit any person to act as master, unless his name is indorsed on the certificate as the last appointed master (*b*)

§ 1117 It is enacted that every register and every certificate of registry of any British ship, purporting to be signed by the registrar or other proper officer shall be received in evidence as *prima facie* proof of all the matters contained or recited in such register when the register is produced, and of all the matters contained in or indorsed on such certificate of registry, and purporting to be authenticated by the signature of a registrar, when such certificate is produced (*c*) There is a similar provision as to certified copies of the register

§ 1118 As already seen, every person registered as owner is vested with the absolute right to dispose of the shares standing in his name (*d*) It follows that the shares thus appearing to be the property of any registered owner form on his bankruptcy part of the estate to which his creditors have right Accordingly in a case

4 Will IV, c 55, § 31

(*z*) 17 and 18 Vict c 104, §§ 68, 73, *et seq*

(*a*) Same act, § 45

(*b*) Same act, § 46

(*c*) Same act § 107

(*d*) Same act, § 43

arising on the corresponding provisions of a previous statute (*e*), (which were not so clear as to the right of the registered owner), where the vessels belonging to a shipping company, instead of being registered in the company's name, were entered in the names of the partners, as owners respectively of certain shares, and where, on the bankruptcy of one of the partners, the trustee on his estate claimed the shares standing in his name, and the other partners maintained that they were to be regarded as company property under the deed of copartnery, which provided that notwithstanding the registrations, each of the partners should be held as equally interested in each and all of the vessels, the Court sustained the claim of the trustee (*f*). In another case, arising on the same statute, where shares registered in the name of one partner of a company were averred to be company property by the trustee on the sequestrated estate of another partner, the Court held it incompetent to prove *prout de jure* that they were company property, and accordingly, they disregarded a proof which had been allowed before answer in the inferior court, and which seems to have supported the trustee's allegation (*g*). This decision, however, did not touch the question whether the latent right of the company (which was of the nature of a trust) could be proved by the writ or oath of the partner registered as owner. The Merchant Shipping Act of 1854 seems to save all such questions, both under the clause which provides that the register and certificate of registry shall be received merely as *prima facie* proof of the matters which they contain (*h*), and under the proviso that the rule which entitles no more than thirty-two individuals to be registered as owners at one time, "shall not affect the beneficial title of any number of persons or of any company represented by or claiming under or through any registered owner or joint owner" (*i*). Accordingly, it is thought that any latent right of the nature referred to may be proved by writ or oath of the registered owner if it resolves into an averment of trust in him (*k*). If, however, it involves fraud or collusion, it seems to be provable *prout de jure* (*l*).[2] It is also thought that such evidence

(*e*) 3 and 4 Will IV, c 55, § 32. (*f*) M'Arthur v. M'Brair and Johnston's Tr, 1844, 6 D, 1174. (*g*) Ord v Barton 1846, 8 D, 1011. From the way in which this case arose the whole question as to the right to the shares was not before the Court. See also, in support of the text, Yallop, 1808, 15 Vesey, 60.

(*h*) 17 and 18 Vict, c 104, § 107. (*i*) Same act, § 37.

(*k*) See *supra*, § 674, *et seq*. (*l*) See *supra*, § 578, *et seq*. Would parole be admitted to prove that the registered owner was a fictitious party and that the real owners were aliens, and therefore not entitled to hold shares? In Scott v Miller, 1828,

[2] A certificate of registry was held such *prima facie* evidence of the title of the holders

is admissible to prove that the name of a party appearing as owner has been entered in the register without his authority (*m*), or without the authority of another person, who is the true owner (*n*)

§ 1119 Registration is indispensable to the active title of owner; the Court not recognising as owners those who have failed to comply with the statutory requirements (*o*) But action by unregistered owners to recover from their agent sums received by him is competent, because an agent may not challenge his principal's title (*p*).

§ 1120. Registration is not essential to the passive title of ownership, an unregistered owner being liable for sums expended upon the ship on his order, or that of any one having his authority (*q*)

§ 1121 There was considerable difference of opinion as to the extent to which registration under the former acts created liability for repairs or furnishings to the ship In one case in this country where a person registered as owner, contended that he had only a right in security, he was held liable for furnishings ordered in London by the master, who he alleged was the true owner, and it was laid down as fixed law, that a registered owner is liable for such debts (*r*) More recently, where Cockburn's Trustees, of whom his son Isaac was one, were registered owners of certain ships, and where Isaac and another son acquired right to the ships under an

---

7 S, 56, 5 Mur, 236, 11 S, 21, S C, parole of such an averment was admitted This case, however, arose under an act which did not make the entry in the register *prima facie* proof of ownership (*m*) Under the former registry acts, the entry in the register was not *prima facie* proof of ownership, when the authority was disputed, see Fraser *v* Hopkins, 1809, 2 Taunt, 5—Smith *v* Fuge, 1813, 3 Camp, 456—Reusse *v* Meyers 1813, ib, 475—Tinkler *v* Walpole, 1811, 14 East, 226—Tead *v* Martin, 1814, 4 Camp, 90 (*n*) It will be a difficult question how far such proof can affect third parties (*o*) See this illustrated in regard to the former registration acts in Walker *v* Pollock, 1825, 3 S, 625—Tod, &c *v* Boag &c, 1825, 3 S, 622—See also *per curiam* in Scott *v* Miller, *supra* (*p*) So held under the former registry acts in Lumsden *v* Allen, 1823, 2 S, 585—Dixon *v* Hamond, 1819, 2 Barn and Ald, 310 See also Walker *v* Pollock, *supra* (*q*) So held under the former registry acts in Pearse *v* Turner, 1829 7 S 412—Ritchie *v* Lang, 1829, ib—Inglis *v* Lane, 1833, 12 S, 67 (*r*) Leslie *v* Curtis, 1836, 14 S, 994

---

that they obtained unconditional recal of arrestments used by creditors of the former owners, though it was pleaded by the arresters that the transference was fraudulent and collusive, Duffus and Lawson *v* Mackay, 1857, 19 D, 430, and in Schultze *v* Robinson and Niven, 1861, 21 D, 120, an unregistered bill of sale executed in Prussia, was held to transfer the property in a vessel, to the effect of defeating arrestments used by creditors of the former owner But see Bell *v* Gow, 1862, 1 Macph 183, where an arrestment was held effectual—although at the time the ship stood registered in name of the debtor's infant son, and not of the debtor himself,—the transfer in favour of the son having been subsequently reduced

arrangement with the trustees, but without being registered, on these brothers becoming bankrupt and the ships being sold under venditions in the names of the trustees, action was sustained against the trustees for furnishings which had been made on Isaac's order before the sale (s). This case was decided on the grounds that there was no proof of the trustees having ceased to be beneficially interested in the ships, and that, as the orders had been given by one who was likely to have acted for the trustees, the furnishings must be held to have been made on the credit of the trustees and not of that person individually The general question therefore, was not decided, and Lord Moncreiff observed that the decisions, both in this country and in England, at one time gave more force to the registry than the Courts had recently approved of.

§ 1122 In England it was at one time held that registered ownership created liability for repairs or furnishings (*t*) But the later decisions (none of which have been pronounced in regard to the act of 1854) settled that the question in each case was, On whose credit were the repairs or furnishings made? and that this the jury had to determine on the evidence before them, without being obliged to give effect to the registration unless they believed that the furnishings were made on the credit and actual or implied authority of the person registered as owner (*u*) These decisions proceed on the fair principle that a person contracting on the credit of certain parties should not have action against others on whose credit he did not reckon, and who did not derive profit from the contract The same principle seems to apply under the existing statute, with this difference, that as the register is now *prima facie* proof of ownership the registered owner might have to bear the burden of proving that the furnishings were not made on his authority or credit [3]

§ 1123 When any registered ship is so altered as not to corre-

(*s*) Hay v Cockburn's Tr, 1850, 12 D, 1298 (*t*) Westerdell v Dale, 1797, 7 Durf and East, 306—Rich v Coe 1777, 2 Cowp, 636—Abbot on Shipping (9th ed), 25 (*u*) Young v Brander, 1806 8 East, 10—M'Iver v Humble, 1812 16 ib, 169—Baker v Buckle, 1822, 7 Moore, 349—Jennings v Griffiths 1822, 1 Ry and Moo 42—Curling v Robertson, 1844, 8 Scott's New Ca 12—Abbot on Shipping (9th ed), 25 26

[3] It has been held in England that the register of a ship is not conclusive evidence of the liability of the person appearing thereon as owner for the acts of the master done within the scope of his general authority The owner of a ship, then at sea transferred it to the defendant by absolute bill of sale (the bill of sale being however, intended only as a collateral security for a loan) which was duly registered. The defendant was

spond with her description entered in the register, a corresponding alteration must be made on the entry in the register book, and either a new certificate of registry must be granted, or a memorandum of the alteration must be indorsed and subscribed on the old certificate. The alteration on the certificate is made by the registrar of the port where the ship is at the time of alteration, if there is such an officer there, and, if not, by the registrar of the first port having a registrar at which the ship arrives after the alteration. If the registrar who makes the alteration is not the registrar of the port of registry, he must report it to the latter officer, in order that a corresponding alteration may be made on the register book (*x*).

§ 1124. The registry of a ship may be transferred from one port to another on an application made in writing and subscribed by all the parties appearing on the register to be interested in her, whether as owners or mortgagees (*y*). In such cases the registrar of the new register enters the ship in his books, and grants a fresh certificate of registry (*z*).

§ 1125. If the certificate of registry of a ship has been mislaid, lost, or destroyed, a new certificate may be granted by the registrar of the port of registry. A provisional certificate may be granted by the registrar of another port at which the vessel is at the time or which she first reaches thereafter, in those cases specified by the act where access cannot readily be had to the registrar of the port of registry (*a*).[4]

(*x*) 17 and 18 Vict., c. 104, § 84. (*y*) Same act, § 89.
(*z*) Same act, § 90. (*a*) Same act, § 48.

held not to have incurred liability for contracts entered into by the master while abroad, and before the return of the vessel. "It has been admitted that, in the case of a mortgagee of a vessel who takes merely the security of the ship, not intending to incur liability as owner, a mere entry by him into possession does not render him liable for the contracts of the master, made after the execution of the mortgage and before entry, because that alone does not prove an intention on the part of the mortgagee to adopt the master as his agent", *per* Jervis C.-J.—Meyers *v.* Willis, 1855, 25 L. J. C. P., 43; affirmed 1856, 2 Jur. N. S., 788. Each case must, therefore, depend on the particular circumstances which determine whether the relation of principal and agent existed between the master and the person sought to be made liable.

[4] *By the 56th section of the 25 and 26 Vict., c. 63, it is provided, that in any proceeding against a ship owner in respect of loss of life, the master's list or the duplicate list of passengers shall, in the absence of proof to the contrary, be sufficient proof that the persons, in respect of whose death such proceeding is instituted, were passengers on board such ship at the time of their deaths. The 54th section limits the liability of ship-owners in the cases specified in the section.*

CHAPTER VIII.—REGISTERS OF BIRTHS, DEATHS AND MARRIAGES

I. *Before the Registration Act of* 1854.

§ 1126. For a long period there have been in most of the parishes throughout Scotland, registers intended for recording the births, deaths and marriages, in their respective localities. These *Parish Registers* were introduced in the year 1551 by a provincial council of the clergy held in Edinburgh. They were originally confined to births and marriages, or rather to baptisms and proclamations of marriage; but in the year 1574 an act of the General Assembly enjoined the readers at every kirk to preserve a catalogue of the names of the persons deceased within their parishes. The keeping of a register of "baptisms, marriages, and defuncts," was again enjoined in 1616 in the instructions which the Lord Commissioner produced to the Assembly of that year; whereupon the reverend court passed an act ordaining *inter alia*, "that every minister have a perfyte and formall register, quherin he sall have registrat the particular of the baptisme of every infant within his paroch, and quho wer witnesses thereto; the tyme of the marriages of all persons within the same, and the special tyme of the buriall of every ane deceisand within thair parochin," to be presented at their next synod assembly, under pain of suspension. In the same year, (on 10th December 1616), the Scottish Privy Council passed an enactment in similar terms, and further requiring the entries in the register to be authenticated by the subscription of the minister or reader and two of the kirk-session, in the case of marriages and births; and two persons present at the burial, in the case of deaths. This act also ordained that the register should be "repute and haldin as famous and authentic," and that the extracts thereof, subscribed by the minister or reader, as well as the original record, should "mak faith in all and qtsomeuer judgmentis within this kingdome." The "Directory for Public Worship," which was approved of by act of Assembly and act of Parliament in 1645, required a register to be kept of both the proclamation and celebration of marriages; and about this time it appears that a register of baptisms also was kept in most parishes. An act of Assembly, passed in 1746, recommended and appointed kirk-sessions to have a register, in which they should record the names of all persons dying and interred within their bounds, and the times of their deaths The subject was again brought under the notice of the General Assembly in 1810, and in 1816 that reverend body recommended "that the several presbyteries should take the steps necessary to secure the keeping of three separate registers in every parish, in one of which the names of all children and of their parents should be recorded, with the dates of their births, whether their parents belong to the Church or are Dissenters, in another, the names of all persons married, with the dates of their marriages, whether legally solemnized or not, with the specialties of any particular cases that may occur, and in the third, the names of all persons who have died, with the particular dates of their deaths, whether they have been buried in the parish burying ground or elsewhere" This recommendation, however, seems not to have been followed by a uniform improvement in the system of registration throughout the country, although it produced reform in several instances

§ 1127. These repeated regulations (none of which, it will be observed flowed directly from the Legislature) did not secure anything like a complete system of registration The imperfection arose from a complication of causes.

In the case of births, the registers, except in a very few parishes, contain entries only of baptisms No record therefore appears of the birth of infants who died before being baptised, or of adult persons to whom that ordinance has not been administered while most registers are also entirely blank as to children baptised by the dissenting clergy In many cases, where baptisms are entered, the name of one or other of the parents is omitted, and this is still more frequently the case as to the important item of the mother's maiden name In general, the sex of the child is indicated by the name under which it was baptised, but this test does not appear either in regard to names which are enjoyed by both sexes, or where the first name of the child is properly a surname Sometimes, also, a christian name, usually enjoyed by one sex, is conferred on a child of the other, especially in cases of posthumous birth Equally deficient are the parish registers in regard to the ages of the children', and on this head they can only be regarded as showing birth at a date, which was probably not less than a fortnight, or more than a year, before baptism

§ 1128 In like manner, the registers of marriages are blank in regard to such as were not celebrated *in facie ecclesiae* after regular proclamation of banns In most instances they do not record the fact that the marriage took place, but only that intention to marry was proclaimed Consequently, where the marriage was not completed in consequence of death, change of purpose or forbidding of the banns the register in most instances contains the same entry as if the marriage had been celebrated

§ 1129 Not more complete are the registers of deaths They only record the decease of persons who were interred in the parish burying ground, and not even of all these, for in general no entry appears unless the parish "mortcloths" was used and it became the custom in many places to use private mortcloths In some instances also landed proprietors and their families were interred in mausoleums on their estates, while many dissenting bodies have burial grounds attached to their places of worship The greatly increased use of cemeteries belonging to joint-stock companies, has still more extensively impaired the value of the registers of deaths The effect of these causes has been, that in very many instances the parish registers contain entries of only a fractional part of the deaths in the district Some parishes, including the extensive city parish of Edinburgh have no register either of deaths or of burials

Where entries of burials occur they do not in general afford better evidence of the sex of the deceased than do the registers of baptisms while they are lamentably deficient as to the age of the individual and as to the date and cause of death

§ 1130 To these causes of the incompleteness of the parish registers must be added the apathy of the people, who, especially among the poorer classes, were often deterred by having to pay a fee for an entry, although it might in many cases, have proved their propinquity to wealthy relations This apathy was increased by the unwise provisions of the act 23 Geo III, c 67, which imposed a duty on all entries made in the registers That statute was repealed eleven years after its enactment, but its bad effects remained for a much longer period

The want of a proper system for securing accuracy in the entries combined with the frequent carelessness and incompetency of the session-clerks, has still farther impaired the value of the registers The entries in them were sometimes made from memory or loose jottings, at considerable intervals after the proper dates, and there are examples of entries interpolated at the distance even of years The custom of the keepers of many records, to allow unrestricted access to them without check or supervision, afforded opportunities for fabricating and obliterating or altering entries (a)

(a) In a recent succession case, where the stake was about £100,000, one of the

while the want of proper arrangements for preserving the different books has caused the loss of many volumes and the obliteration of many entries in those which are in existence.

§ 1131. The foregoing sketch, which is abridged from a useful and interesting little work by Mr George Seton, Advocate (*b*), will have shewn that the parochial registers throughout Scotland are (with a few honourable exceptions) very far from being complete or accurate. The circumstance that a certain birth, death, or marriage, is not entered in the proper record raises no presumption against its existence; while the trustworthiness of every entry depends on the regularity with which the particular register has been kept, which ought therefore to be investigated in each case, both by scrutinising the register books and by examining the keeper of them.

§ 1132. The recent Registration Act provides that the system of parish registers which has thus been described shall cease and determine from and after 31st December 1854, in so far as regards births, deaths, and marriages taking place after that day; but that it shall be competent for any person, on or before 31st December 1855, to record in these registers any birth, death, or marriage which shall have taken place on or before 31st December 1854 (*c*). The existing parochial registers, minutes, and relative documents,

---

claimants founded on a parish register containing an entry of a baptism as in 1735. But this was evidently an interpolation, as it did not occur at its proper date, and was written in ink of a different colour and with letters of a different form from the other entries about the same time; while the marginal summation of entries had been altered, although not so as to suit the page in its altered state. The keeper of this register deponed that he had not kept it locked up, that he had been in the practice of allowing it to be inspected by any person of apparent respectability without himself being present, and that he had also been accustomed to enter births, deaths, and marriages out of their proper order, and at considerable intervals from the dates of the events; Morgan *v.* Morris, 1853, 16 D., 82, noted in Seton on Scottish Parish Records, p. 62. In another succession case, which was very anxiously litigated, the session-clerk of Dunnottar deponed, as to a certain volume, that he was not aware of its containing any authentication by the keeper, and that there was not in any part of it a title stating what it really was. The session-clerk of Kintore deponed that the register of that parish, about the year 1720 (the period in question), was almost illegible, and that in one of the entries material to the case several words appeared to have been retraced; Willox *v.* Farrell, 1846, noted in Seton, ib. 58, and reported on other points in 8 D., 1226; 9 D., 766.

(*b*) "Sketch of the History and Imperfect Condition of the Parochial Records of Births, Deaths, and Marriages, in Scotland." Edinburgh: Constable & Co., 1854. This work has been carefully compiled from Parliamentary Returns, the Statistical Account of Scotland, and other trustworthy sources of information. Shortly after its publication Mr Seton was appointed Secretary to the Registrar General under the Registration Act of 1854.

(*c*) 17 and 18 Vict., c. 80, § 1.

in so far as regards such of them as have been made and entered prior to 1st January 1820, are to be transmitted to the Registrar-General for preservation in the General Registry Office in Edinburgh, and in so far as regards those from the year 1820 inclusive to January 1855, they are to be delivered over to the person to be appointed registrar in each parish under the new statute (*d*) The officer last mentioned shall, if required by the Registrar-General, make, or cause to be made inventories and indexes of these papers, mentioning any blanks or deficiencies which may occur in them The registers and relative documents and indexes from the year 1820 to the 1st January 1855 are, at the end of thirty years from the date last mentioned, to be transmitted to the Registrar-General for preservation as aforesaid (*e*)

Where a parish register contains entries of births, deaths, and marriages mixed up with sessional or other matters, the Sheriff may direct either that copies of the former shall be made and delivered to the registrar, the existing register remaining in the custody in which it formerly was, or that copies of the entries relating to the sessional or other matters shall be made and delivered to the persons interested therein, the record itself being delivered to the registrar of the parish (*f*)

§ 1133. Parish registers are competent, and, if regularly kept, are good evidence of the facts of birth, death, and marriage set forth in them (*g*) They may also be received in questions as to the age of the persons to whom the entries refer, when that is set forth (*h*) But on such matters they are seldom of much value The entry of a baptism is an adminicle of evidence in a question whether the individual was minor at some interval less than twenty-one years after its date, but it is far from being sufficient proof of that fact, as the person may have been baptised when one or more years of age (*i*)

§ 1134 It is competent to prove that a register has been kept irregularly (*k*), and the Court will probably direct the jury to pay little regard to registers in which irregularities are considerable Inquiries may also be made as to the authority or information on which the session-clerk or his predecessors used to make the en-

(*d*) 17 and 18 Vict, c 80, § 18 (*e*) Ib (*f*) Ib, § 19

(*g*) Bell's Pr, 2212—Tait Ev, 51 (*h*) Cuming *v* Cuming, 1628, M, 12,630—Watson *v* Glass, 1837, 15 S, 753 (*i*) Wilson *v* Aitken, 1626, M, 12,700—Thomson *v* Stevenson, 1667 M 12,701 (*k*) Watson *v* Glass, *supra*—Miller *v* Fraser, 1826, 4 Mur, 122—Willox *v* Farell, *supra*, § 1130, note—Morgan *v* Morris ib—Tait, 52

tries (*l*), whether they correspond with those in a duplicate copy (*m*), and on any other matters pertinent to the credibility of the register. Entries which have been made a considerable time after their proper dates ought to be received with great caution, and if they were interpolated after the cause of action arose, they ought to receive little or no credit. In one case, in 1854 between two parishes as to the birth settlement of a pauper, the register of one of the parishes contained an entry of his birth as in the year 1778, but it had been made in the handwriting of a session-clerk who had not been appointed till twenty-one years afterwards, and the pauper stated that his birth had been recorded about the year 1811. The Court held that the register was admissible, and that, being corroborated by the belief of the pauper, it was sufficient to prove the parish of his birth. But their Lordships doubted whether it would have been admissible in a question of propinquity (*n*). It was held in England that an entry in the register book of the baptism of a child as the legitimate son of a certain person was not admissible in a question as to the child's legitimacy, the entry having been made by a minister who was not in the cure, and had no connection with the parish when the child was baptised, but who made the entry at an interval of a year and a half from information received by him from the parish clerk (*o*). In the same case a private memorandum made by the parish clerk, who had been present at the baptism, was excluded.

§ 1135. In some cases the register has been prepared from a day-book in which the entries were made in draft. When this is the fact, the fair copy is held in England to form the register (*p*). But any discrepancy between it and the original may be proved by exhibition of the latter (*q*).

The admissibility of extracts from these registers is noticed afterwards.

II. *Registers introduced by the Registration Act of* 1854.

§ 1136. The registers of births, deaths, and marriages through-

(*l*) Miller *v* Fraser, *supra*. (*m*) Morris *v* Morgan, 1853, noted in Seton on Parish Registers, 62. (*n*) Hay *v* Murdoch, 1854, 16 D., 364. In cases of settlement, slight evidence suffices to shift the burden of proof. (*o*) Warren *v* Bray, 8 Barn. and Cres., 813. (*p*) May *v* May, 1737, 2 Strange, 1073. But see Mathers *v* Lawrie, 1849, 12 D., 433. (*q*) See Sturrock *v* Greig, 1849, 12 D., 166—Ferguson *v* Skirving, 1850, 12 D., 1145, affd., 1 Macq., 232—Morris *v* Morgan, 1853, noted in Seton on Par. Reg. 62—See *contra*, May *v* May, *supra*.

out Scotland, have been put on a satisfactory footing by a recent statute, which came into operation from and after 31st December 1854 (s) This statute makes anxious regulations for securing the trustworthiness of each entry the regular supervision and examination of all the registers, and their preservation in safe places, where access cannot be obtained to them for improper purposes It also contains provisions calculated for making registration compulsory, and thereby securing completeness as well as accuracy in this class of public records

§ 1137 In order to attain these purposes, the whole registers in the country are placed under the supervision of a "Registrar-General" for Scotland with a Secretary and staff of clerks and other assistants (t) The record in each parish is intrusted to an officer called the "Registrar," and the Sheriff of the bounds has power to divide parishes, as well as to unite parishes or portions of parishes into one district, each such district being held as a separate parish for the purposes of the act (u) The registrar in every parish is entitled, with the approval of certain persons, to appoint an assistant to act in case of his illness or unavoidable absence, or of his ceasing to hold office, and until the appointment of another registrar, and the entries made by the assistant, and the duties performed by him, have the same force and effect as those of the registrar (x) The Sheriff of each county has the control and superintendence of the registrars of the parishes within his jurisdiction, and where a parish is partly situated in more counties than one, it is for the purposes of the act held to be within the county where the parish church is situated (y)

§ 1138 The former parish registers, or authenticated copies of the entries in them, require to be transmitted to the Registrar-General or registrar of each parish, as already mentioned (z), and authenticated copies of the registers kept at private burial grounds or cemeteries before 31st December 1854 are directed to be prepared and delivered to the registrar of the parish (a).

§ 1139 The act also provides that all the register books and relative documents shall be kept in locked iron boxes or fire-proof-places, to which there shall be two keys, and no more, one of them

(s) 17 and 18 Vict, c 80 A useful analysis of the Registration Act has been published, from the pen of Mr George Seton, Advocate, Secretary to the Registrar-General

(t) Same act, §§ 2, 3, 4 (u) Same act, § 14 (x) Same act, §§ 10, 76 (y) Same act § 21 (z) *Supra*, § 1132 (a) Same act § 20

being kept by the registrar and the other by the Sheriff of the bounds (*b*)

§ 1140 Uniformity in the registers and their due authentication, is secured by requiring the entries to be made according to certain statutory forms—which may be altered by the Registrar-General, with consent of the Queen in council (*c*)—and to be attested as afterwards mentioned, the Registrar-General being ordained to furnish to the local registrars books, certificates, notices and forms, in sufficient numbers (*d*)

§ 1141 To obviate the evils arising from loss or obliteration, as well as to afford security against vitiation of the local registers, the statute requires each register to be kept in duplicate, both duplicates being paged continuously alike, and each page being authenticated by the initials of the Sheriff before the books are delivered to the registrars The contents of each page of both duplicates are to be the same A careful comparison and revisal is to be made annually by the Sheriff, and a signed docquet appended to each duplicate, mentioning the fact of the examination, and any marginal additions or alterations appearing on either duplicate. One of the duplicates is to be retained by the registrar, and the other to be transmitted by the Sheriff to the Registrar-General on or before 31st August in each year, the Sheriff reporting at the same time any circumstance relating to the registers to which he thinks the attention of the Registrar-General should be called (*e*)

§ 1142 The *Register of Births* contains, in separate columns, (1) the number of the entry in the book (2) the name of the child, if any is given, (3) its sex, (4) the year, day of month, and hour of birth, (5) the place of birth, and whether it happened in lodgings, (6) the name, rank, profession or occupation of the father, with his age and birth-place, (7) when and where he was married, and his issue, living and deceased, (8) the mother's name, maiden name, age, and birth-place, and how many children she has had, (9) the signature of the father or mother, or other informant, with their residence, if out of the house in which the birth occurred, and (10) the date and place of registration, with the signature of the registrar (*f*)

§ 1143 In order to have these particulars properly completed, the statute requires the parents or parent, or (in case of their death or inability) the person in charge of the child, and the occupier of

(*b*) 17 and 18 Vict c 80, § 22 (*c*) Same act, § 71

(*d*) Same act, § 23 (*e*) Same act § 58 (*f*) Same act, sch (A) every house in which to his or her knowledge any birth takes place, and the nurse present at the birth, and in the case of an illegitimate child the mother, or in case of her death, illness or inability the person in charge of the child, or the occupier of the house, or the nurse present at the birth, to attend personally upon the registrar of the parish or district, within twenty-one days after the birth, and give information to the best of their knowledge on the particulars referred to, and sign the register in presence of the registrar Any other person having knowledge of the facts may also be called on by the registrar personally, or by written requisition, to attend and give information thereupon (*g*), and the registrar may require the child to be produced, in case of doubt existing as to its sex or birth (*h*) Any person finding a new-born child exposed, whether it is alive or dead, is required to give notice to the registrar, or to the inspector of the poor, or constable of the district who must thereupon give notice to the procurator-fiscal (*i*).

§ 1144 In the case of a child of a Scottish parent being born at sea on board of a British vessel, the commanding officer is required to minute in his log-book, or otherwise, the particulars above mentioned, so far as known, and on arriving in a British port, or by any earlier opportunity to send a certified copy of the minute to the office of the Registrar-General, by whom the same shall be filed, and a copy of it entered in the "Marine Register," and another copy transmitted to the registrar of the place where the parents are supposed to be domiciled, if that is known, the latter officer entering the particulars in his register, and noticing the transmission in the manner prescribed by the Registrar-General (*j*)

§ 1145 When the parish of birth is different from that in which the parents are domiciled, the registrar of the former parish is required to transmit a copy of the entry to the registrar of the parish of domicile, who shall transcribe the same, and mark on the margin of the entry the name of the parish of birth (*k*)

§ 1146 To prevent the concoction of entries at an interval after the birth, it is provided that registration cannot take place after the expiry of three months from birth, except under authority of the Sheriff, proceeding upon a written declaration of the parents or parent, or guardians of the child, and in such cases the Sheriff shall sign the entry in the register, and (except in cases of children born

(*g*) 17 and 18 Vict c 80 § 27 (*h*) Same act, § 28
(*i*) Same act, § 29 (*j*) Same act, § 30 (*k*) Same act § 26

at sea), no register shall, unless the entry is signed by the Sheriff, be admitted to prove the birth of a child, wherein it shall appear that more than three months intervened between the birth and registration (l)

But the name given to a child, either in baptism or by its parents, if they do not recognise infant baptism, may be added to the register within six months, or, with the Sheriff's authority beyond six months after birth, on production of certain evidence (m) And the minister officiating at a baptism, unless a certificate of registration of the birth is produced to him is required to intimate the baptism, and any information he may have as to the birth and parentage to the registrar of the parent's domicile (n)

§ 1147 In cases of illegitimate children, the registrar may not enter the name of any person as father except at the joint request of the mother and the person acknowledging the paternity, and who, along with the mother, must sign the register When the paternity has been found by the decree of a competent court, the clerk of court, within ten days, is required to transmit notice thereof to the registrar, by whom a corresponding entry is made A similar procedure takes place when a child registered as illegitimate is found by decree of court to be legitimate (o) Again, in the case of children registered as illegitimate being legitimated *per subsequens matrimonium*, the registrar shall, on the production of an extract of the registration of the marriage, note on the margin of the register, opposite the entry of the birth of the child the legitimation and the date of the marriage, but unless the paternity was acknowledged or found by decree, as above mentioned, the entry of legitimation can only be made on an order of the Sheriff, on joint application of the parents, and after intimation and hearing of parties (if any) having interest, who may oppose the application (p)

§ 1148 The *Register of Deaths* contains, in separate columns, (1) the number of the entry, (2) the name rank, and profession or occupation of the deceased (3) the sex, (4) the age, (5) the birthplace and how long resident in the district where the death occurred, (6) parents' names, and rank, profession, or occupation, and whether they are alive or dead, (7) whether the deceased was married, and, if so, to whom, (8) the number names, and ages of his or her children, and the dates of decease of such as have died, (9) the hour and day of the month and year when the death occurred,

(l) 17 and 18 Vict, c 80 § 31 (m) Same act, §§ 32, 33
(n) Same act, § 34 (o) Same act, § 35 (p) Same act, § 36

(10) the place of death (11) the cause of death, the particulars as to the duration of the deathbed illness, and the date of the last visit of a medical attendant, as certified by him, (12) the burial-place as certified by an undertaker (13) the signature of the informant and (14) the date and place of registration and the registrar's signature (r)

§ 1149 In order to have these particulars filled up, the statute requires the nearest relatives who were present at the death of any person, and the occupier of the house, or, if the occupier be the person who has died, his nearest relatives and the inmates of the house, to attend personally upon the registrar within eight days after the death, and give the requisite information, and in presence of the registrar sign the entry In the event of failure, they and any other person having knowledge of the death may be required to attend within fourteen days after the death, for the purpose of making up and signing the register (s) There are also regulations for completing the register where death did not take place within a house (t), and in cases where any precognition touching the death of any person shall be held, the procurator-fiscal is required to intimate the result to the registrar by whom a corresponding entry shall be made in the register (u) The medical person who attended the deceased during his last illness is required, within fourteen days after the death, to transmit to the registrar a certificate in the statutory form, for completing the particulars contained in the 4th, 9th, 10th, and 11th columns of the register (x), and the undertaker or other person having charge of the burial must transmit the statutory certificate as to the interment, for completing the entry in the 12th column (y) The person in charge of the place of interment (unless a certificate of registration of death is produced to him before interment by the person having charge of the funeral) is required to give notice of the interment to the registrar within three days thereof (z)

§ 1150 In the case of any Scottish subjects of Her Majesty dying at sea on board of a British vessel, the commanding officer is required to enter the particulars, so far as known to him, in his logbook or otherwise and on arriving in any port in the United Kingdom or by any earlier opportunity, to transmit a certified copy of the entry to the Registrar-General, by whom a copy thereof, veri-

(r) 17 and 18 Vict, c 80, § 36, sch B. (s) Same act, § 38 (t) Same act, § 39 (u) Same act, § 40 (x) Same act, § 41, sch G (y) Same act, § 42, sch H (z) Same act § 44

fied by his signature, shall be entered in the "Marine Register," and another copy be transmitted to the registrar of the deceased's domicile (if known), by whom the same shall be registered accordingly In the case of shipwreck, any of the officers who may have escaped, or, if they all perished, any person who may have escaped, is required, to the best of his ability, to comply with these provisions (*a*)

§ 1151 In case of the persons bound to give information not attending at the registrar's office, their attendance may be enforced, under order of the Sheriff, on application by the registrar (*b*)

§ 1152 The *Register of Marriages* contains a copy, under the hand of the registrar, of the particulars inserted in the schedule afterwards noticed, which contains, in separate columns, (1) the number of the entry, (2) the date, place, and form of marriage, (3) the signatures of the husband and wife, (4) their residences at the time, (5) their usual residences, (6) their ages; (7) their ranks or professions, and relationship if they are related, (8) whether a widower or a widow, and whether entering into a second or third marriage, (9) their children (if any), living or dead, by former marriages, (10) their birth places, and when and where registered, (11) the names of their parents; (12) the rank, profession, or occupation, of their parents, (13) the signatures of the officiating clergyman, and the witnesses, where the marriage is regular, or (14), if it is irregular, the date of the extract sentence of conviction, or decree of declarator of marriage, and in what court pronounced, (15) the date and place of registration, with the registrar's signature (*c*)

§ 1153 In all cases of regular marriages, a schedule containing columns for these particulars is required to be given out with the certificate of proclamation of banns and to be filled up with the particulars contained in the 2d, 13th, and intervening columns, in presence of the persons solemnizing the marriage, and to be signed by the spouses, by the witnesses, male or female, who are present (not being fewer than two), and by the minister or other person officiating It is then delivered to the parties contracting the marriage, who are required, within three days, to deliver or transmit it to the registrar of the district where the marriage is solemnized. That officer enters the particulars in the duplicates of the register, and the original schedules are transmitted by the Sheriff to the Re-

---

(*a*) 17 and 18 Vict, c 80, § 43 (*b*) Same act, § 45
(*c*) Same act, sch C

gistrar-General for preservation (*d*). Persons intending to marry may require the registrar to attend with the register-book at the solemnization of the marriage on payment of a certain fee additional to those exigible in other cases (*e*).

§ 1154. When persons are convicted before a justice of the peace or a magistrate of having celebrated an irregular marriage (*f*), either of them may, and they are severally required, to enter the same in the register of the parish where the conviction takes place. And it is competent to either party to a marriage, which is established by decree of declarator of any competent court to record the same in the register of the domicile of the parties or of their usual residence. The production of an extract of the conviction, or decree of declarator, is a sufficient warrant for such registration (*g*). The magistrate or clerk of court in which such conviction takes place and the clerk of the court in which such decree is pronounced, are required to give information thereof in the statutory form, to the registrar respectively of the parish in which the conviction takes place or of the parish of the domicile or usual residence of the parties (*h*).

§ 1155. In case any of the parties whose signatures are required by the act are unable to write, they may sign by a cross or other mark in presence of the registrar or Sheriff, or of two witnesses, who must adhibit their designations to their subscriptions, and such mark is as effectual as a proper signature (*i*).

§ 1156. When any additions or alterations competent under the act are made on any register, the registrar shall make a minute in duplicate of such alterations, and deliver one of the duplicates to the Sheriff, with the relative documents, and the Sheriff shall, if necessary, inquire into the accuracy of the facts therein set forth, and, if they are erroneous, correct the minute. The duplicate minutes are then examined and authenticated by the Sheriff, one is retained by the registrar, and the other is transmitted to the Registrar-General, and such minutes are to be deemed and taken as part of the registers, and to be given effect to on or opposite to the relative entries in the duplicate registers previously transmitted (*k*).

§ 1157. If the duplicate register in the custody of any registrar

---

(*d*) 17 and 18 Vict, c 80, § 46. (*e*) Same act, § 47.

(*f*) In some districts the parties to an irregular marriage appear before a magistrate or justice of peace under a pretended criminal complaint, and confess the marriage, whereupon they are fined, and a record of the procedure is preserved.

(*g*) 17 and 18 Vict, c 80, § 48. (*h*) Same act, § 49, sch K.

(*i*) Same act, § 72, sch B. (*k*) Same act, § 54.

shall be lost destroyed, or mutilated, or shall have become illegible in whole or part, he shall forthwith communicate the fact to the Registrar-General, who shall require the said register to be transmitted to him, and shall thereupon apply by petition to the Court of Session, in the terms set forth in the statute, to have the register restored, and the Court, on being satisfied on the matter, and after such intimation as they may think proper, shall order such register to be corrected or completed at the sight of the Registrar-General, and to be authenticated by him, whereupon it shall become of the same force and validity as the original duplicate (*l*) The act also provides machinery for having errors in any register corrected under authority of the Sheriff after examinations on oath, the particulars regarding every such correction being also entered in a separate book, called the "Register of Corrected Errors" and a copy of the entry being transmitted to the Registrar-General, if the duplicate has been previously sent to him The Register of Corrected Errors is also to be transmitted to the Registrar-General annually, along with the duplicate of the register (*m*) But any errors committed in the form or substance of any entry may be corrected according to the truth of the case before the entry is signed Correction by deletion must be made by drawing a line through the erroneous words or figures (but so as to leave them legible), and must be authenticated by the registrar affixing his signature thereto (*n*)

§ 1158 The statute provides for the genuineness and truth of the registers and relative documents, by introducing punishments by transportation or imprisonment in the case of persons wilfully destroying, obliterating, or otherwise injuring entries in the register and relative documents, or falsely making or counterfeiting any part of them, or knowingly causing to be inserted any false statement, or wilfully giving any false certificate or extract touching any birth, death, or marriage (*o*) [1]

§ 1159 In order to facilitate the searching of the registers,

(*l*) 17 and 18 Vict, c 80, § 55

(*m*) Same act, § 63

(*n*) Same act, § 64

(*o*) Same act, § 62

[1] In the first prosecution which occurred under the act the panel was dismissed from the bar, the public prosecutor declining to move for sentence, H M Adv *v* David Greig, 2 Irv, 357, but in H M Adv *v* Askew, 2 Irv, 491, the panel for a contravention of the act, by making a false entry in the register of births was sentenced to twelve months imprisonment The indictment ought to set forth the entry alleged to be false and fictitious, ib, 493, *per* Lord Justice Clerk (Hope)

tabular alphabetical indexes are directed to be made by every registrar, and to be accessible at all reasonable hours to parties who may search the same, on payment of certain fees (*p*)

§ 1160 Extracts of entries in these registers authenticated as afterwards mentioned (*r*), are admissible in evidence in all parts of Her Majesty's dominions (*s*)

After the foregoing statement as to the care with which the registers require to be prepared and preserved it need hardly be added that they will be records of very high trustworthiness But neither by the Registration Act, nor according to legal principle, are they *probatio probata* of the facts which they record The registers of births and deaths, being merely an authenticated statement by the persons who furnish the information to the registrar, will not exclude contradictory evidence on the matters set forth, while the register of marriages may be impugned, not only on such grounds as forgery, collusion, force, or pupillarity, but also on the ground of any errors which may be detected by comparing it with the original returns preserved in the General Registry Office [2]

CHAPTER IX — OTHER OFFICIAL REGISTERS

Besides the important registers which have thus been explained, the law of Scotland admits a number of minor records of a public or official character

§ 1161 The books of a burgh are admissible to prove facts of which they are the proper record Thus they have been held to be

(*p*) 17 and 18 Vict c 80, § 56

(*r*) See chapters on Extracts, *infra* § 1219 *et seq*

(*s*) 17 and 18 Vict c 80 § 58

[2] Further provision for registration of births deaths &c is made by the 18 Vict, c 29, and by the Registration of Births &c (Scotland) Act, 1860, 23 and 24 Vict c 85 By section 2 of the latter act, it is provided that a book, to be called "the Register of Neglected Entries,' shall be kept in the General Register Office in which it shall be competent for any person to require the registrar to enter any birth, death, or marriage, which has taken place in Scotland between the 31st December 1800 and the 1st January 1855, on a warrant by the Sheriff (granted on a petition, and after proof) to that effect being produced Section 2 provides for the correction of errors in registers kept prior to 1st January 1855

not only admissible, but necessary, to prove the *res gestæ* at the election of magistrates (*a*), and whether certain persons were members of council (*b*) And the appointment of the burgh officers may be proved by minutes entered in the burgh books (*c*) In one case parole was held to be inadmissible, when tendered in contradiction of the minute prepared by the clerk to an incorporation of a royal burgh, the object being to prove that the clerk had erroneously entered certain votes (*d*) As, however, the objection had been taken at the time, but had not been insisted in before the meeting broke up, the question as to the admissibility of parole did not arise purely, and the observations made on the Bench show that their Lordships avoided deciding whether they would have interfered if the party had insisted at the time that the alleged error should be corrected

§ 1162 Cess books are official registers, which the collector is bound to produce or exhibit, as the Court may direct in actions between private persons, and entries in them were admissible in questions as to qualifications to vote before the Reform Act (*e*) [1]

(*a*) Gardner *v* Reekie 1828, 4 Mur , 138 (*b*) Black *v* Campbell, 1819 5 Dow, 23 (*c*) Hunter *v* Hill, 1833, 11 S 989 (*d*) Ogilvy *v* Mag of Edinburgh, 6th Feb 1810 F C (*e*) Mackintosh *v* Mackintosh, 1829, 8 S , 181

---

[1] By the 17 and 18 Vict , c 91, § 1, the Commissioners of Supply are directed annually to cause to be made up a Valuation Roll showing the yearly rent or value for the time of the whole lands and heritages within the counties and burghs of Scotland The roll is to be authenticated in counties by the signature of the convener or other person authorised by the Commissioners, in burghs by the signature of the provost, or other person authorised by the magistrates Section 30 provides that no valuation of lands or heritages shall be rendered void or be affected by reason of any mistake or variance in the names of such lands or heritages, or in the christian or surname or designation of any proprietor or tenant or occupier thereof, nor be challengeable by reason of any informality in the proceedings for making up the roll Section 34 enacts that, in all questions relating to the franchise before any Registration or Appeal Court, the entry in the roll shall be conclusive proof that the gross yearly value or rent of the lands and heritages specified are correctly stated in the roll The 19 and 20 Vict , c 58, § 17 (Burgh Voters), while making the roll *prima facie* evidence in all proceedings under the act provides that it shall be competent to prove that the specified lands or heritages are, or have been, of a greater or less annual value than the value stated in the roll The Annual Register of Voters, made up as authorised by the act, is declared by § 14 to be conclusive evidence, at every future election of a Member of Parliament for the burgh or burghs, that the persons therein named "continue to have the qualifications which are annexed to their names" The 24 and 25 Vict , c 83 contains similar provisions for the registration of voters in counties In Leith *v* Leith 1862, 24 D 1059, it was held, in a question between the heir of entail and the younger children, as to the amount of their provisions, that the valuation roll did not afford conclusive proof of the value of the home farm, which was not let, and the Court remitted to a land valuator to report

§ 1163 Books kept at Government offices, as the War Office (*f*), the office of the Board of Inland Revenue (*g*), and Board of Customs (*h*), are admissible to prove facts within their proper purposes (*i*)

§ 1164 The log-book of a man-of-war is admissible to prove a storm, or the separation of merchant vessels from their convoy, and similar facts of which it is the official record (*k*) But the log of a private vessel, although it may be used to refresh the memory of witnesses, has been held not to be admissible as an official record, because it is merely the statement of the master and mate, who are private persons (*l*) Yet it may be used as an admission made by parties representing the owners, and it has been ruled that the latter are not entitled to impugn the statements which it contains when these are to their prejudice (*m*)

§ 1165 The official books of a prison are sufficient proof of the time of each prisoner's entry and discharge (*n*), but it was held in England that the cause of commitment not being an essential part of the register, must be proved by other evidence (*o*) Parole has been received of the fact that a prisoner had undergone his sentence, the point occurring in an objection to his competency as a witness (*p*) It has been held in England that a book containing a record of the marriages celebrated at the Fleet Prison is inadmissible being a private unauthorised register (*r*)

§ 1166 The books of the Bank of England are admissible as an official register to prove transfers of stock and other matters falling within their sphere (*s*)

§ 1167. The register kept at Stationers' Hall [2] is *prima facie*

(*f*) See Kay *v* Roger, 1836, 10 S, 831 (*g*) See Dunbar *v* Harvie, 1820, 2 Bligh 351 (*h*) Tomlins *v* Attorney-General, 1813, 1 Dow 404

(*i*) The privilege of public boards to refuse access to their documents is noticed, § 1845, *et seq* (*k*) Watson *v* King, 1815 4 Camp, 275—D'Israeli *v* Jowett, 1795, 1 Esp, 427 (*l*) Wright *v* Liddell 1829, 5 Mur, 36—Innes *v* Glass, 1827, 4 ib, 164—Cairns *v* Kippen 1828, 1 Bell's Com, 612, note 5, correcting Carleton *v* Strong, 1816, 1 Mur 27 (*m*) Campbell *v* Fryson, 1841, 4 D, 342, per L Pres Boyle This ruling may be questioned as a general doctrine of law (*n*) R *v* Aickes, 1785 1 Lea C C, 391—Salte *v* Thomas 1824, 3 Bos and Pull, 188 (*o*) Salte *v* Thomas *supra* (*p*) Aitchison *v* Patrick, 1836, 15 S, 360 (*r*) Read *v* Passer, 1794 1 Esp 213 There is some conflict in the previous cases (*s*) Marsh *v* Colnett, 1798, 2 Esp, 665—Breton *v* Cope, 1791, Pea Ca, 30—2 Phill 115—Taylor, 1158 As to the books of private banking companies see *infra* § 1179

---

[2] The copyright in photographs is secured by 25 and 26 Vict, c 86 and in the

proof of the copyrights which are entered in it (*t*) And the registers of shareholders of joint-stock companies have similar effect as to the shares held by the several partners (*u*) [3] The minute-book kept by order of the directors of a public joint-stock company, if signed by the chairmen of the meetings respectively is evidence of the orders, proceedings, and meetings of the company, directors and committees of directors, without the signature of the chairman, or the fact of his having been such, requiring to be proved (*x*)

§ 1168 The minute-book kept by the trustee and commissioners in a sequestration is the proper evidence of the procedure recorded in it, and in this way it may prove that a sequestration subsisted at a certain date (*y*) Parole has been held inadmissible to prove the fact of sequestration and of a claim having been made by a creditor on the estate, where no reason appeared for withholding the proper record of these facts (*z*) But under the rule which requires the best evidence, the minute-book has been held inadmissible to prove the terms of documents of which it only contained copies (*a*) Under the former Sequestration Act the statutory

(*t*) 5 and 6 Vict, c 45 § 11—7 and 8 Vict c 12, § 8 As to how patents are proved see 15 and 16 Vict c 83, § 33 (*u*) 8 and 9 Vict, c 17 (Companies' Consolidation Act) §§ 10, 12 (*x*) Same act § 101 The signature is essential, Whitehaven &c, Ry Co *v* Macfadyen, 1849, 11 D, 846 But where a meeting of committee had been adjourned, subscription of the minute of the adjourned meeting was held to authenticate the whole, Great Northern Ry Co *v* Inglis, 1851, 13 D 1315, aff'd, 1 Macq, 112 (*y*) Smith *v* Mackay, 1835, 13 S 323—Hunter *v* Carson, 1822, 3 Mur 232 (*z*) Smith *v* Kemp, 1828, 4 Mur, 401

(*a*) Thus the minute-book containing copy of the act of Court sequestrating the

pharmacopœia by 25 and 26 Vict, c 91 The 5 and 6 Vict, c 45, § 11, makes registration at Stationers' Hall *prima facie* evidence of proprietorship of copyright in printed works, and it has been held that the title of an assignee, possessing such *prima facie* evidence, was sufficiently instructed without production of a formal instrument of assignment attested by two witnesses, Jeffreys *v* Kyle 1856 18 D, 907

[3] It was decided, in Caledonian Railway Co *v* Lockhart, 1855, 17 D 917, that while the register of a railway company is, under the Companies Clauses Act (8 and 9 Vict, c 17, §§ 10, 12) *prima facie* evidence that those named in it are shareholders, if it has been kept in the way prescribed by the statute, yet that its accuracy may be impeached by counter-evidence and that a very slender deviation from the statutory forms will render it inadmissible The Court held that the failure to enter the paid up subscriptions in the register was not merely a slender deviation, but 'a systematic departure from the directions of the statute," and they refused to receive a register in which these, in many cases, had not been entered The same view had been previously adopted by the House of Lords, Bain *v* Whitehaven Railway Co 1850 7 Bell's App Ca 95 But see Henderson *v* the Royal British Bank 1857 7 Ell and Black 356

duplicate of the minute-book was equally admissible with the principal (*b*)[4]

§ 1169. The minutes of meetings of a *Senatus Academicus* have been held not only to be admissible, but to be necessary evidence of their proceedings, so as to exclude parole of them (*c*) And a similar ruling has been given as to parole of the proceedings of road trustees (*d*) But these cases seem to go too far Minutes of an hospital (although not signed) were once admitted by the Lord Chief Commissioner (*e*)

§ 1170 The admissibility of the minute-books thus noticed in so far as depending on common law, arises from the bodies whose acts are recorded having a recognised legal *status* and of the records of their proceedings being usually intrusted to qualified officials, under some supervision or securities for accuracy But the law does not recognise as evidence minutes of meetings of private bodies, *e g*, dissenting congregations (*f*), creditors meeting extrajudicially (*g*), or a deceased person's relations sealing up his repositories (*h*) So it has been held in England that the register of burials in the ground attached to a Wesleyan chapel is not admissible not being a public register (*i*) Nor is the report made to Government by one of the Government Inspectors of Schools admissible as an official register to prove the qualifications of a teacher (*k*) The minutes of an *ex parte* riding of marches is inadmis-

---

estates of A B, which was dated 17th April 1827, was held not to be admissible to prove that the sequestration was granted on that day the proper evidence being an extract of the act of sequestration or of the deliverance of the Court, Smith *v* Mackay, 1835 13 S, 323 In one case, the minute-book was held inadmissible as evidence of the bankrupt s discharge where that was founded on by the trustee, Mansfield *v* Maxwell, 1835 13 S, 721, per L Pres Hope This ruling may be questioned

(*b*) Hunter *v* Carson *supra*—Smith *v* Mackay *supra*—Stevenson *v* Macpherson 1827 4 Mur, 275—*supra*, § 135 (*c*) Hamilton *v* Hope, 1827, 4 Mur, 239 per L Ch Commissioner (*d*) M'Ghie *v* M'Kirdy, 1850, 12 D, 442 See also Wilson *v* Jameson 1827, 4 Mur, 366 (*e*) Oswald *v* Lawrie, 1828, 5 Mur, 8 (*f*) Arneil *v* Robertson, 1843, 5 D, 400—Mathers *v* Laurie 1849 12 D, 433 See also Auchinutie *v* Ferguson, 1817 1 Mur, 208 per Lord Chief Commissioner, as to the books of the "Gilt Box Society of Kirkaldy"

(*g*) Mackenzie *v* Mackartney, 1831, 5 W S, 513 The contrary decision of Lea *v* Landale, 1828, 6 S, 350, is thought to be erroneous See also *contra*, Wright s Tr *v* Hamilton s Tr, 1834, 12 S, 692, 13 S, 380, S C (*h*) Kers *v* Penman 1830 5 Mur, 115 (*i*) Whittuck *v* Waters, 1830, 4 Car and Pa 375 See also Read *v* Passer, 1794 1 Esp 213 noted *supra*, § 1165 (*k*) Sturrock *v* Greig 1849 12 D, 166

---

[4] The bankrupt s statutory oath is the best evidence of the statements made by him at his examination, Elmslie *v* Gabriel 1862, 1 Macph 209

sible as evidence for the heritor for whom it was made, because it is in effect a statement by the party in his own favour (*l*) Yet a minute of a meeting seems to be admissible where it has been signed by the parties (although without the solemnities required by the act 1581), for the purpose of preserving a record of their proceedings (*m*) And in an action raised against a company of manufacturers by their servant for wages, entries in the minute-book of the company were received for the pursuer, although some of them had not been signed (*n*)

§ 1171 These authorities show that the doctrine of Professor Bell, that minutes of a public meeting are probative of what took place, cannot be received without considerable qualification (*o*). The proper mode of proving meetings of bodies not recognised by law is by the oath of the person who prepared the minute, and who may use it to refresh his memory, but the oath of any other person who was present is equally admissible

§ 1172 A distinction must also be taken as to the purposes for which the minute-books of a public body can be used Thus while they are the proper proof of all matters occurring at the meetings, in so far as the different members of the body are concerned, and in favour of any person having a legal interest in the proceedings, they seem not to be admissible against third parties on matters in which the body acts as an individual, *e g*, in regard to the constitution of obligations in its favour, or the discharge of obligations granted by it (*p*)

§ 1173 It seems not to be settled whether subscription by the proper officer is essential at common law to the admissibility of minutes of public bodies (*r*) It is thought not to be indispensable that they be signed by the person who presided at the meeting to which the minutes apply, provided they are subscribed by the preses of that at which they were read over and approved of (*s*) And

(*l*) Hunter v Dodds, 1832, 10 S 833

(*m*) Hill v Lindsay, 1847, 10 D 78 But such a writing would not be admissible as a deed of obligation, discharge, or the like

(*n*) Ivison v Edinburgh Silk Company 1846, 9 D, 1039

(*o*) Bell's Pr § 2222

(*p*) See Inglis v Cunningham, 1826, 4 Mur, 77—Mansfield v Maxwell, 1835 13 S, 721, *supra*, § 1168—Mackenzie v Town of Elgin, 1693 1 B Sup 54—King v Mag of Elgin, 1711, M, 12,537—Tait Ev, 52—Taylor, 1161—2 Phill 122, 1 ib, 307 (2)—Marriage v Lawrence, 1819, 3 Barn and Ald, 142

(*r*) See Forbes v Morrison, 1851 14 D, 134—Ivison v Edinburgh Silk Co, 1846, 9 D, 1039, *supra* (*n*)—Oswald v Lawrie, 1828, 5 Mur, 8, *supra* (*e*)—Great Northern Railway Co v Inglis, 1850, 13 D, 1315, affd 1 Macq 112—King v Mag of Elgin, 1711 M 12,537 As to cases under the Companies Consol Act, see *supra* § 1167

(*s*) See Ferguson v Skirving 1850 12 D, 1145, affd, 1 Macq 232—Northern Railway Co v Inglis *supra* when minutes are taken down in scroll, the fair copy extended by the clerk and signed by the preses after the dissolution of the meeting is admissible (*t*) [5]

CHAPTER X —HISTORIES, TOMBSTONES, ETC

§ 1174 In matters of ancient date—*e g* questions of pedigree, precedence, the creation and extinction of peerages—chronicles and books of history compiled at the time are received, as the testimony of those acquainted with the facts either personally or from credible information, and because they were not prepared with reference to the case in issue (*a*) Of course, the weight due to such evidence depends on the historian's character for accuracy and impartiality, and on the extent to which he is supported or contradicted by contemporary writers (*b*) Modern compilations, however (*e g*, peerage books), seem to be inadmissible, because the older records or histories from which they have been made up ought to be produced (*c*) But in a question of pedigree, peerage books were received to prove that persons whose names were found only in them had died childless (*d*)

(*t*) See Lea *v* Landale, 1828, 6 S, 353, per Lord Balgray (*a*) Stair 4 42, 16—Ersk 4 2, 7—Tait, 53—Crawford and Lindsay Peerage Case, 1848, 2 Cl and Fin (new ser), 534—Swinton's Rep of case of *soi-disant* Earl of Stirling p 173, and Bell's Notes, 283, S C See also Gardner *v* Beekie, 1828, 4 Mur, 439 where an old printed list of burgesses was received (*b*) Stair, *supra*—Tait *supra*

(*c*) 2 Phill 123—Taylor, 1161—Crawford and Lindsay case, *supra* In this case, also a printed copy of the *Rotuli Scotiæ* was rejected, the original being in existence *supra* § 1057 See Tait, 53 (*d*) Crawford and Lindsay case *supra*

---

[5] It was held in Johnson *v* Scott, 1860, 22 D, 393, that the minutes of a provisional railway meeting are not the writ of any person present who does not sign them See observations by Lord Justice-Clerk (Inglis), *supra*, § 118 note [9] In an action of divorce, on the ground of adultery, brought against a husband by his wife, it was held that the minutes of certain meetings of kirk-session and presbytery, at which the defender was not present, were not competent or admissible as evidence against him generally, but that there was evidence of a letter having been written by the defender as to the baptism of a child, and of the loss of the letter, sufficient to warrant the introduction of secondary evidence of the contents of the letter, and that the minutes of a meeting of kirk session containing a copy of the letter were admissible Minutes containing a statement made by a party who had since died were also held admissible as hearsay of a witness deceased A *v* B 1858 20 D 407

§ 1175 In England, books of general history are received to prove events relating to the kingdom at large, as the death of a sovereign, or the time when he assumed a certain title (e) because they are as good evidence as could be expected on such matters, and errors in them can easily be detected But they have been held inadmissible as evidence of private matters e g, the custom of a town, or whether a certain abbey was of an inferior order (f) And a history of a district or county is not admitted in England, when tendered as evidence of boundaries, and the like, because the writer may have had an interest or bias on the matter, which is in a measure private (g) These rules would probably be applied here (h) The House of Lords, in Warren Hasting's trial, allowed Cantemir's history of the Ottoman empire to be read to prove a universal custom of the Mahomedan religion (i) The testimony of persons speaking from personal knowledge is the proper proof on such matters

§ 1176 Not only histories, but even memorials of a private character, are admissible on ancient matters, as, for example, entries made in family bibles regarding the birth or death of members of the household, old plans, inscriptions on tombstones, and the like (k) And where the matter is so remote that better evidence cannot be expected, any light which can be thrown upon it by deeds between third parties will be admitted (l) The ingenuity which has sometimes been displayed in fabricating evidence of the class referred to in this paragraph makes it necessary to use great circumspection in dealing with it [1]

(e) Bull N P, 248—2 Phill, 123—Taylor, 1164 (f) Bull *supra*—Phill *supra*—Taylor *supra*—1 Greenl, 617 (g) Evans v Getting, 1834—6 Car and Pay, 586—Taylor, *supra* (h) Tait Ev, 52 (i) Warren Hasting's case (not reported on this point), as noted in 2 Phill, 123, and per L Ellenborough in 30 State Tr 492 (k) Tait, 53 In Humphrey's (*soi disant* Earl of Stirling) case, almost all these kinds of proof were admitted, and all were proved to be forgeries Among them was a pretended copy of the inscription on a tombstone, with certificates of its being genuine, Swinton's Report, p 173, *et seq* In Willox v Farrell, Autumn 1816, a tombstone with a certain inscription was produced in Court In Bullen v Michel, 1816, 4 Dow, 320, an old chartulary of an abbey was admitted in England in a question as to the right to tithes (l) Stair, 3, 5, 35—Ersk, 3, 8, 66—Tait Ev, 53—Lady Ivy's case, 10 State Tr, 555, noted *supra*, § 929

---

[1] In Hope v Fulcher, 1858, 1 Ell and Ell, 3, the Court of Queen's Bench held that a map on which a public road was marked, and which had been used by deceased stewards on the manor through which the road ran for more than thirty years, was not admissible as evidence of the public right of way claimed In Darby v Ousely, 1856, 1 Hurl and Nor Exch Rep, 1, the following points were laid down —(1) Counsel at

§ 1177 An almanack is not evidence, but it may be looked at by the Court or jury as a memorandum, *e g*, to show what day of the month was Good Friday, whether a certain day of the month was a Sunday, and the like (*m*) It does not require to be produced in process in order to be so used (*n*)

§ 1178 Books of science (*e g*, works on medical jurisprudence) are not admissible, the matters which they contain requiring to be proved by the oral evidence of scientific witnesses (*o*) But passages in treatises regarding the subject of examination may be made evidence by the witnesses deponing that they coincide with the views which the author there expresses (*p*) [2]

(*m*) Goodwin, 1837 1 Swin 431, Bell's Notes, 283 S C—Taylor, 22

(*n*) Goodwin, *supra*

(*o*) M'Kay *v* Davidson, 1828, 6 S, 367 (affd on merits, 3 W S, 210)—M'Gavin, 1846, Arkley, 67 See also Donaldson, 1836, Bell's Notes, 283

(*p*) See as to examining scientific witnesses, *infra*, § 1994

a trial may refer to matters of general history provided the license be exercised with prudence but cannot refer to particular books of history or read particular passages from them to prove any fact relevant to the case (2) Works of standard authority in literature may, provided the privilege be not abused, be referred to at a trial in order to show the general course of composition explain the sense in which words are used and matters of a like nature but cannot be resorted to to prove facts relevant to the cause (3) Medical books cannot be cited by counsel, but a medical man may be asked in cross-examination whether he has read a particular medical book (4) It is not competent, in order to show the doctrine of the Church of Rome relative to the mode of dealing with heretics to read from the canons and decrees of that church the bulls of popes, or works published by members of it, or the oath taken by its bishops, nor to read from history the excommunications of sovereigns by the popes, although reference may be made to the general fact that there have been such excommunications In a case before the Committee for Privileges, the following documents were admitted —a copy of a plate of the arms of the Knights of the Garter, now existing in the Chapel Royal at Windsor, the plate itself not being removeable except by authority of the Queen and no such plate having been removed since first put up in the reign of Henry V, declarations of deceased members of families, a visitation taken by deputation from Clarence King-of-Arms, a record of a royal warrant of precedence from the Herald's Office, &c An old ' Collection of Monumental Inscriptions" in country churches was tendered to show what had been the inscription on a partly defaced tombstone, but, on the counsel for the opposing parties objecting that in the Leigh case Dugdale's History was refused, the reception of the volume was not pressed W T married M D, in whose uncle's will occurred the expression ' All this I give to my nephew W T" The will, along with an entry from the Act Book of Doctor's Commons granting administration to "W T, nephew minor and universal legatee," of the uncle, was received as proof (no certificate of marriage having been recovered) that a marriage had taken place between W T and M D The Shrewsbury Peerage Case, 7 Clark, H of L Cases, 1 See also Report of the Claim to the Dukedom of Montrose by Lord Lindsay, 1855

[2] In H M Adv *v* John Thomson, 1857 2 Irv, 747, the Lord Justice-Clerk (Hope) observed that "to read to a jury the opinions of living men, who might have changed their opinions, was improper"

CHAPTER XI.—MERCANTILE BOOKS AND OTHER ACCOUNT BOOKS

§ 1179 Mercantile books are akin to official registers in this respect, that they are usually made up with care for the purpose of preserving a true record of the transactions set forth in them, and in many cases they are intrusted to accurate book-keepers under supervision and comparison similar to those observed in official registers. Accordingly, when appearing to be regular, they are admissible not only (as afterwards noticed) against the person or company whose transactions they record, but also in his favour, although in general a party may not found on writings which have been prepared by himself or under his directions. In cases not tried by jury, a merchant suing for payment of his account is allowed to produce his business books with a view to establishing a *semiplena probatio*, and being thereby entitled to emit his oath in supplement (*a*). And in jury trials entries in them may form part of the evidence in his favour (*b*).

§ 1180 The only books admissible under this rule are those kept in the ordinary course of trade or business (*c*), which, although chiefly applying to books of merchants and shopkeepers, include those kept by bankers (*d*), law-agents (*e*), and the like. So the Court have admitted books kept at a toll-bar, and made up each evening from jottings noted at the time of the number and weights of the carts which passed through (*f*). But a tenant's books have

---

(*a*) Ersk 4, 2, 4—1 Bell's Com., 331—Tait Ev., 274—Wood *v* Kello, 1672, M., 12,728—Cuming *v* Marshalls, 1752, M., 10,095—Maxwell *v* Reid, 1685, M., 12,625—Balfour *v* Sharp, 1833, 11 S., 784. See also Dunbar *v* Harvie, 1820, 2 Bligh, 351—Ivory *v* Gourlay, 1816, 4 Dow, 467—Hutton *v* Buckmaster, 1853, 15 D., 574.

(*b*) Edinburgh, Leith, and Hull Shipping Co *v* Ogilvie, 1819, 2 Mur., 139—Forbes *v* Hudson, 1822, 3 Mur., 46—Macqueen *v* M'Intosh, 1827, 4 Mur., 193—Dickson *v* Ponton, 1824, 3 Mur., 440—Macf. Pr., 175. See also Grant *v* Johnston, 1845, 7 D., 390—Stuart *v* Mitchell, 1833, 11 S., 1004; *contra*, Britton *v* Lang, 1820, 2 Mur., 367.

(*c*) Ersk., 4, 2, 4—Macf. Pr., 176.

(*d*) British Linen Co *v* Thomson, 1853, 15 D., 314—Grant *v* Johnston, 1845, 7 D., 390. In Cuming *v* Marshalls, 1752, M., 10,095, which was an action by a merchant for payment of an account containing an entry, "To bank notes sent per post £100," his books were admitted in his favour, there being evidence that he had been in use (like a private banker) to send bank notes to his correspondents, and in particular to the defender. See also Furness *v* Cope, 1828, 2 Mo. and Pa., 197.

(*e*) Macqueen *v* M'Intosh, 1827, 4 Mur., 193. They were admitted without objection in an action by the agent for the expenses of law proceedings, the Lord Chief Commissioner remarking that he had not been accustomed to see such evidence admitted. See also Macqueen *v* Colvin, 1827, 4 Mur., 193.

(*f*) Balfour *v* Sharp, 1833, 11 S., 784.

been held not to be evidence against his landlord of the quantity of manure laid on the farm (*g*) or of the sum expended by the tenant on repairs (*h*). And the private books of one partner were held not to be admissible against the representatives of his copartner (who was not proved to have seen them), to instruct payments alleged to have been made by the former to the latter (*i*). The books in these cases were considered not to have the trustworthy character of those which are made up in the ordinary course of business. Yet where a question as to the intromissions of a person (*e.g.*, an executor) arises at an interval of several years, the Court will pay regard to entries appearing to have been made *in bona fide* at the time in books which do not come within the category of mercantile or business books (*k*). And if such books are adduced to prove the receipt of money, they will also be admitted to show that it was paid away again (*l*). A factor's or steward's books will probably be admitted to prove payments made on behalf of his constituent (*m*).

§ 1181. Mercantile and business books will only be received if they appear to have been regularly kept, and if they are free from interpolations and marks of concoction; for if a party were allowed to found on books which are open to the suspicion of having been fabricated, a very wide door would be opened to fraud (*n*). The admissibility of books, when regularly kept, is limited to such mat-

---

(*g*) Paterson *v.* Blair, 1819, 2 Mur., 179.

(*h*) Laing *v.* Hay, 1829, 1 De. and And., 23.

(*i*) Smith *v.* Logan, 1826, 5 S., 32; affd. 4 W. S., 47. There were no company books.

(*k*) Fisher *v.* Fisher, 1850, 13 D., 245, per L. Just.-Clerk.

(*l*) Campbell *v.* M'Cartney, 1848, 14 D., 1086—M'Kay *v.* Ure, 1847, 10 D., 89. See *infra*, § 1182.

(*m*) The view in the text is supported by Ersk., 4, 2, 14, and Tait Ev., 275, where it appears that the factor's oath in supplement is admissible.

(*n*) Ersk., 4, 2, 4—Tait Ev., 274—Ivory *v.* Gourlay, 1816, 4 Dow, 467. This was an action by Gourlay's assignee against a bankrupt estate for payment of four parcels of flax, furnished by Gourlay to the bankrupt. The first item was instructed by an account with a note indorsed in the bankrupt's handwriting, and was regularly entered in Gourlay's books. The second had been entered in his day-book to the debit of another person connected with the bankrupt, but had been carried to the bankrupt's debit in the ledger, a marking to that effect in a different handwriting appearing on the margin of the day-book. The third parcel was entered in the day-book at the bottom of a page, out of its order in date, and seemingly interpolated. The fourth was regularly entered, and latterly it was not disputed. The pursuer founded on his books to prove resting-owing of all the items, and to prove continuousness of the account as eliding prescription of the first item. On this and other evidence the Court of Session gave decree for the whole, but the House of Lords reversed the judgment, and remitted the case, with a finding that there was sufficient evidence of the first item (unless it was prescribed), but not of the second and third items.

ters as fall directly within their province, and of which they are the ordinary and proper record Accordingly, in an action founded on alleged guarantee for the price of goods, where goods had been previously furnished on the defender's credit and paid for by him, and where the books of the pursuer contained an entry that the furnishings for which payment was demanded had been made to the same person and on the same order, the Court held that the books, with the oath in supplement of the pursuer's salesman, was "not a lawful course of evidence" to establish the averment of guarantee (*o*)

§ 1182 Nor are mercantile books full proof in favour of the merchant, being his own writings, made up *ex parte* (*p*) This principle was applied in a narrow case where a bank account, containing entries to the debit and credit of the same person, was entered in separate books (a "deposit journal" and a "ledger"), and the bank failed in consequence to prove their advances, although it was admitted that if the entries had been in a continuous account, the customer could not have founded on the one side of it without giving effect to the other (*r*)

§ 1183 Partly on the principles above illustrated, but chiefly on account of their being written admissions, a party's books may be used in evidence against him, notwithstanding the general principle that undelivered documents are like unuttered thoughts and not admissible in evidence The competency is not limited to the business books of a party Thus private books holograph either of a merchant (*s*), or of one who is not in trade (*t*) are admissible to prove payments made to him, goods received by him, and similar facts And business books in the handwriting of a party's bookkeeper are admissible for the same purpose, the party being presumed to have authorised or been privy to their contents (*u*) Entries in a pass-book kept by the creditor in certain debts, and made either by her or by her daughter under her directions, were held to prove payments to account, which, being indefinite, were attributed

(*o*) Buchanan *v* Scott, 1816, noted in Hume D 422 (*p*) Hatton v Buckmaster, 1853, 15 D 574 (*r*) British Linen Co *v* Thomson, 1853, 15 D, 314, see *supra*, § 1180 (*s*) Purveyance *v* Cunningham, 1677, M, 12,623 The books proved both the receipt of the principal sum and the payment of several years' interest (*t*) Wardlaw *v* Gray, 1662, M, 12,620—Lowrie *v* Drummond, 1675, M, 12,622 To understand this report see the case between the same parties in 1675 2 B Sup (Stair's Decisions), 181—Burnett, 1662, 2 B Sup, 296—Currie *v* Halyburton, 1688, M, 12,625 (*u*) Knox *v* Martin, 1850, 12 D, 719 This rule is observed in daily practice

to interest on a bond, although in her oath of calumny she deponed that they were made to account of bills (x) So the triennial or sexennial prescription may be overcome by entries of payments of interest &c in the debtor's books written by himself or by his book-keeper (y) and in questions of onerosity of bills, the books of the holders are often important evidence against themselves (z) A party's books are also admissible against him to prove a course of dealing, when that is relevant to the issue (a) [1]

§ 1184 The books and balance sheet of a company are conclusive in questions between the partners or their respective executors as to the share which each partner drew (b) And on the ground that all the partners are presumed to be aware of entries made by the company's book-keeper, these were admitted in a question whether a private debt of one partner had been paid from the company's funds, or with money furnished by a third party (c)

§ 1185 A detached account charge and discharge was once held to prove repayment of money advances, having been holograph of the creditor and found in his repositories after his death (d) But the more just view seems to be against admitting such accounts, unless docqueted or signed, because they are often made in anticipation of transactions which may have never been completed (e)

The rules as to the effect of the books of an agent against his principal, a cedent against his assignee and the like, are noticed elsewhere (f) as are also the rules as to the authentication of docqueted accounts (g) [2]

(x) Couper v Young, 1849, 12 D 190 (y) Black v Shand's Crs, 1823, 2 S 118 See also Berry's Reps v Wight, 1822, 1 S, 433 (z) See *supra*, §§ 342, 362 (a) Blair v Russell, 1828, 6 S, 836—Calder v Calder, 1825, 4 S, 331 (b) Blair v Russell, *supra* (c) Kenney v Walker, 1836, 14 S, 803 (d) Millar v Bonar, 1708, M, 12,626 (e) Nasmyth v Bower 1665 M, 12,621 (f) See the chapter on Admissions *infra*, § 1434, *et seq* (g) *Supra*, § 788, *et seq*

---

[1] In an action of resting-owing, where the defence was non-liability, a proof was allowed, and partial excerpts from the pursuer's books produced It was held incompetent to tender these excerpts with a view to prove payment, no such plea having been stated, and no excerpts or productions made with reference to such a defence, Goodwin v Maclean, 1857 19 D, 878

[2] It was held by the Second Division that an entry in a bank pass-book, duly initialed by the officers of the bank, being a writ *in re mercatoria*, is a probative writ as against the bank, and cannot be challenged *ope exceptionis*, but only by reduction But the House of Lords, reversing the decision of the Court of Session, held that such an entry was merely *prima facie* evidence against the bank, and was challengeable *ope ex-*

CHAPTER XII.—OF NOTARIAL INSTRUMENTS

§ 1186 A notarial instrument is the narrative under the hand of a notary, detailing procedure which has been transacted by or before him in his official capacity It is not made on oath, but is within the general oath *de fideli administratione*, which the notary takes when he enters on his office A notarial instrument is the only competent mode of proving those facts of which it is the recognised record, whereas upon other matters it is usually inadmissible, because, being beyond the powers intrusted by law to the notary, it is non-official

§ 1187 Thus on the one hand, an instrument of sasine is indispensable to the proof of infeftment by symbolical delivery (*a*), while under the modern system infeftment is constituted by expeding and recording an instrument in the statutory form (*b*) [1] A no-

(*a*) Stair 4, 42, 9—Ersk 2, 3, 34

(*b*) 8 and 9 Vict, c 35 § 1—10 and 11 Vict, c 49, § 5

---

ceptionis, Rhind *v* Commercial Bank, 1857, 19 D, 519 Lord Cowan considered that these entries in pass books were in every respect equivalent to deposit-receipts —"I think it clear that, in the absence of written evidence, or of an offer to prove the entry a mistake by the oath of the pursuer, the pass-book must be taken *hoc statu*, and until reduced, as good evidence of the debt,' reversed, House of Lords, 10th February 1860 3 Macq, 643 In Fraser *v* Bruce it was held that an entry in a depositor's pass book with a savings bank, of a payment made to a third party, who affixed his signature to an entry, is competent evidence of the receipt of the money by the third party, 1857, 20 D, 115 Many recent cases as to the admissibility of entries in the books of deceased persons against their interest will be found in the English reports, Dickett *v* Corser, 21 Beav, 52—Webster *v* Webster 1 F and F, 401—Bright *v* Legerton, 7 Jur N S, 559—Rawlins *v* Rickards, 28 Beav, 370

[1] It may be convenient to note briefly the alterations, in so far as they bear upon the forms of deeds noticed in this and other chapters, effected by the Titles to Land Act 21 and 22 Vict, c 76 The main feature of the act is the recording a conveyance of lands in the Register of Sasines in place of an instrument of sasine following upon the conveyance An instrument of sasine is therefore (§ 1) no longer necessary Where it is not desired to record the whole of the conveyance, the act (§ 2) authorises a notarial instrument to be expede in favour of the party to whom the conveyance is granted, in which such parts of the conveyance as relate to the lands in which a real right is desired to be obtained are set forth "The object of the notarial instrument is simply to furnish a certified excerpt from the conveyance" Section 4 dispenses with instruments of resignation *ad remanentiam*, and provides that, in place thereof, the warrant of resignation be recorded in the Register of Sasines, or a notarial instrument be expede and recorded as in the case of an ordinary conveyance When an instrument of resignation *ad remanentiam* is used, it may be recorded (§ 19) at any time during the life of

tarial instrument is the only competent proof of resignations *ad remanentiam* (c), and at one time it was required to resignations *in favorem* but, after having fallen into desuetude (d), it was abolished by statute with regard to the latter class of *actus legitimi* (e) An instrument by a notary is necessary to prove intimation of an assignation or translation (f), unless when the intimation is acknowledged by a writing under the debtor's hand (g) By statute a notarial instrument is indispensable to a disentail (h), and to completing the title of the creditor's lien, and in some cases that of his singular successor under the Heritable Securities Acts (i) The protest of a bill or promissory-note, and all other protests, can only be proved by notarial instruments (k) [2] A writ of this nature was also required for proving requisition and consignation of the sum borrowed under the obsolete security of wadset (l)

§ 1188 On the other hand, wherever law does not require the interference of a notary, his acts are unauthorised, and his instruments are inadmissible Thus an instrument of protest upon the fact was rejected as evidence of wrongous imprisonment in an ac-

---

(c) Stair, 2, 2, 2—Ersk 2, 7, 19, 20 (d) Renton *v* Anstruther, 1848, 11 D 37 (e) 8 and 9 Vict c 35, § 9 (f) Stair, 4, 42, 9—Ersk 3, 5, 3—2 Bell's Com, 17 (g) Ersk 3, 5, 4—Bell's Com, *supra*—Bell's Pr, § 1465—*Supra*, § 766 There are also equivalents to intimation, which do not require the intervention of a notary, *e g*, the assignee's raising action against the debtor, and the debtor's paying him interest, see Bell's Com, *supra*

(h) 11 and 12 Vict, c 36, §§ 3, 12 (i) 8 and 9 Vict, c 31, §§ 1, 4, 5, extended to all heritable securities by 17 and 18 Vict, c 62 (k) 1 Bell's Com 413—Bell's Pr, § 339—Thomson on Bills, 443 (l) Ersk 2, 8, 19, 25

---

the party in whose favour it is expede An instrument of sasine being no longer necessary, the precept of sasine is by section 5, dispensed with By sections 6, 7, 8, and 9, writs of confirmation and resignation (written on the conveyance itself) are substituted for charters of confirmation and resignation Other sections of the act provide for the simplifying and shortening of the forms by which a party conveys lands to which he has only a personal right Section 33 extends the provisions of 6 and 7 Will IV, c 33 (by which instruments of sasine are declared free from challenge on the ground of erasures), to recorded notarial instruments None of the provisions of the act are compulsory (§ 20), so that all the forms for the constitution, transmission, and completion of land rights in use before the passing of the act may still be employed See Analysis of the Titles to Land Act by Mr George Ross, Advocate, and Menzies' Lectures on Conveyancing, 3d edition, 1863 Similar changes as to the forms applicable to burgage tenure are effected by a later statute 23 and 24 Vict, c 143

2 A notarial protest is not now necessary to prove the presentment and dishonour of a bill or promissory-note, in order to preserve recourse against the drawer or indorser That may be proved *prout de jure* to the effect of preserving such recourse, 19 and 20 Vict c 60, § 13

tion of damages (*m*), and as evidence of the state of a vessel in an action on a policy of insurance (*n*), and as evidence of the insufficient state of a mill in an action for abstracted multures (*o*) In these cases the instrument was held probative of the fact that a protest had been taken, that being a proceeding in presence of a notary,—but inadmissible to prove the state of matters on which the party thought fit to protest, the proper evidence of these being by witnesses examined on oath This is a more correct mode of dealing with such evidence than that which was sometimes adopted when the Court used to sit both as judge and jury, and when it was not unusual to admit notarial instruments as evidence on matters on which they were non-official provided they were adminiculated by evidence on oath (*p*). But even at that time the Court more than once refused to admit notarial instruments as evidence of such facts (*r*) In like manner a notarial instrument is inadmissible as evidence of such intimations or citations as are by law intrusted to messengers-at-arms (*s*).

§ 1189 On the same principle, while a notarial instrument is probative of the facts which are intrinsic to its purpose as an official narrative (*t*), it is not admissible to prove such as are extrinsic (*u*) So an instrument of intimation of an assignation is not admissible to prove the existence either of the assignation or of the right assigned (*x*) Nor is an instrument of sasine presumptive evidence of the existence of its warrant (*y*), except in ancient matters, or when prescriptive possession has followed on it (*z*) Owing to the sasine in favour of an heir entering by hasp and staple not proceeding on a precept, the instrument thereupon is probative both of the fact of the entry and of the heir s propinquity (*a*)

It is also thought that a notarial instrument will be admissible on extrinsic matters, where, from the notary and witnesses having died, secondary evidence may be received

---

(*m*) Hosie *v* Baird, 1828, 4 Mur, 417 (*n*) Thomson *v* Bisset, 1823, 3 Mur, 297 (*o*) Clark's Tr *v* Hill, 1827, 4 Mur, 205

(*p*) Lawrie *v* Gibson, 1671, M, 12,501—Glass *v* Stuart, 1715, M, 12,507—Stair, 4, 42, 9—Ersk, 1, 2, 6 (*r*) Anstruther *v* Thomson, 1611, M, 12,499—Lawrie *v* Miller, 1629, M, ib—See also Malvenius *v* Hepburn, 1686, M, 583

(*s*) Haswell *v* Mag of Jedburgh, 1714, M, 12 270 (*t*) Stair, 4, 42, 9—Ersk, 2, 3, 34, and 4, 2, 5—Bell's Pr, § 2220, 1—Tait Ev, 4—Balfour *v* Lyle, 1832, 10 S, 853 (*u*) Ersk, 1, 2, 5—Bell s Pr, *supra* (*x*) Ersk, *supra*

(*y*) Stair, 2, 3, 19—Ersk, *supra*—Bell s Pr, *supra*—D Roxburghe *v* Kerr, 1822 1 Sh Ap Ca, 157—Ker *v* Ker 1583, M, 12,509 -Norval *v* Hunter, 1661, M, 12,517—Mitchell *v* Cowie, 1672, M, 12,520 (*z*) Stair, *supra*—1591 c 218

(*a*) Stair, 2 3, 19—Ersk, 2, 3 38—Cases in M, 12,513 *et seq*

§ 1190. A notarial instrument is only admissible to prove facts palpable to the senses, not to prove matters of opinion (*b*).

§ 1191. The admissibility of notarial instruments arises from their being executed by persons duly qualified.[3] But in order to prevent fraud, and to protect instruments *ex facie* probative, it is enough if the persons whose signatures they bear were habit and repute notaries at the time (*c*). Acts by a notary for his own behoof in matters in which he is personally interested are invalid (*d*), but it is doubtful whether he may not act against his interest, *e.g.* by giving sasine upon a precept granted by himself (*e*).[4] The validity of an instrument, however, will not be impaired by an interest which has emerged after its date (*f*). It is 'irregular and unsuitable' in the managing partner of a bank to act as notary in the affairs of the bank, but a mere stock-holder seems not to be disqualified (*g*). In instruments which require a procurator the same person cannot act as such and notarially (*h*). A notary may act in matters in which his relations are concerned (*i*), although it would seem that he cannot officiate in favour of his wife (*k*).

(*b*) Miller *v.* L. Cullernie, 1541, M., 12,498. (*c*) Cunningham *v.* Sempil, 1573, M. 3091—Seton *v.* Cant, 1598, M., 12,448—L. Huntly *v.* L. Forbes, 1619, M. 12,449—Spence *v.* Reid, 1610, M., 3092—Douglas *v.* Chieslie, 1615, M., ib.—Stair, 4, 42, 9—See *infra*, § 1215. (*d*) Leith Bank *v.* Walkers, 1836, 14 S., 332—Russell *v.* Kirk, 1827, 6 S., 133—Office of a notary, 36—Duff Feud., 14, 117—See also L. Gormock *v.* the Lady, 1583, 16,874. See *infra*, § 1215. (*e*) See More's Notes, 401—Duff Feud., 117—Cheap *v.* Philp, 1667, Dal. Dec., 34—Howieson *v.* Gibson, 1629, M. 615, 16,879—Sim *v.* Clark, 1831, 10 S., 85—Russell *v.* Kirk, *supra*.

(*f*) Mackenzie *v.* Smith, 1830, 9 S., 52. (*g*) Ferries *v.* Smith, 9th June 1813, F. C. (*h*) Scott *v.* L. Drumlanrig, 1628, M., 846—Mack. Inst., 3, 5, 3.

(*i*) Reid *v.* Grindlay, 1830, 9 S., 31—Duff Feud., 14, 117. (*k*) See Tait, 1848, 10 D., 1365.

---

[3] The act 18th Vict., c. 25, enacts (§ 1), that when any person called as a witness in any court of civil judicature in Scotland, or requiring or desiring to make an affidavit or deposition, shall refuse or be unwilling from alleged conscientious motives to be sworn, it shall be lawful for the judge or other presiding officer, to allow him to make a solemn affirmation or declaration. In the case of Andrew Marshall, petitioner, 1862, 24 D., 376, it was held that the act did not apply to the case of a notary-public, and that the oath *de fideli* which a notary is required to take on his admission, could not be dispensed with.

[4] A trust-disposition and settlement of heritage and moveables, executed for the granter by two notaries, was reduced as not validly authenticated, because one of the notaries (who was a law-agent, and there being a declaration in the deed that the trustees might employ and pay one of their number as law-agent) was nominated a trustee under the deed. Ferrie *v.* Ferrie's Trustees, 1863, 1 Macph. 291. See *supra*, § 676, note 7.

By a revenue statute (*l*) it is made incompetent for notaries to act, unless they have complied with certain requisites as to admission, and taken out stamped certificates There seems to be no decision in which an instrument was cut down on this ground (*m*)

§ 1192 In general, a notary's powers extend over all Scotland. But the town-clerk of a royal burgh has an exclusive privilege to act in instruments in burgage holdings (*n*) [5] Until recently, sasines in crown lands, on such precepts as passed to heirs upon retours, could only be expede by the sheriff-clerk of the county, or his depute (*o*), the latter of whom officiated in his principal's sasines (*p*) This privilege has been abolished (*r*)

§ 1193 Every "consul-general or consul appointed by Her Majesty at any foreign port and place" has the same powers there as has a notary in the United Kingdom (*s*)

§ 1194 Acts and instruments under the hand of a foreign notary seem to be effectual in this country the office being of a European character (*t*) But in an *ex parte* proceeding, where an instrument of disentail had been executed before a French notary, the Court recommended that the notary's subscription should be attested by the Maire or in some other way in order to show that the person subscribing held the notarial office (*u*) [6]

§ 1195 *As to the authentication of notarial instruments*—At first the notary attested his instruments by his seal, and afterwards by his initials in a *cypher*—called also a *monogram, paraph,* or *rack*—which latterly became a fanciful signature surrounded by a motto (*x*) The motto is still required in the more important instruments (*y*), except those noted below (*z*) Notaries now sign

(*l*) 39 and 40 Geo III, c 72, § 7 (*m*) See Tait Ev, 7

(*n*) 1567 c 27—Ersk, 2, 3, 41—Dawson *v* Mag of Glasgow, 1827, 6 S, 19—M'Gilchrist *v* Rowan 1667, 1 B Sup, 535 The clerk of a burgh of regality has not this privilege, and cannot acquire it by prescription, Mag of Edinburgh *v* Howart, 2d February 1814, F C The Court of Session authorise the sheriff-clerk to act in instruments on burgage rights in favour of the town clerk, Duff, 1823 2 S, 117, or of the town clerk's wife, Tait 1848, 10 D 1365 (*o*) 1540 c 77—1606, c 15—Ersk, 2, 3 37 See also 1555, c 34 (*p*) Duff Feud, 117

(*r*) 8 and 9 Vict, c 35, § 6 (*s*) 6 Geo IV, c 87, § 20—Cunningham, 1850 12 D, 743 (*t*) Story's Confl, § 632 (*a*)—Story on Bills, 277—Cunningham, *supra* (*u*) Cunningham *supra* (*x*) 2 Ross, 189

(*y*) Tait Ev, 26—See H M Advocate *v* Urquhart, 1755, Cr and St, 586

(*z*) The motto is not required to instruments of disentail, 11 and 12 Vict, c 36, sch, or to instruments in favour of the creditor's heir, under the Heritable Secu-

5 This privilege, except in certain cases, is abolished, 23 and 24 Vict c 143 § 21

6 In Cole *v* Sherard, 1855, 11 Exch Rep, 482 the Court of Exchequer received an

their names to all their instruments (*a*) and must sign each leaf of instruments of sasine written bookways on more than one sheet (*b*) In all instruments each page should be subscribed by the notary And he ought to add the letters N P to his signature

§ 1196 Each leaf of instruments of sasine in the old style, written bookways, and consisting of more than one sheet, must also be signed by the witnesses to the ceremony (*c*), who must be above pupillarity (*d*), and must not be fewer than two (*e*) Their subscriptions are indispensable to instruments of sasine written in the old form of rolls, and to instruments of resignation *ad remanentiam*, and of intimation of assignations, translations or retrocessions to bonds, contracts, or other writs (*f*) The witnesses need only sign the last page of instruments of sasine in the new style, of whatever length, since they attest the notary's subscription, and not (as formerly) the act of symbolical delivery (*g*) They must sign the last page of instruments of disentail (*h*) and of instruments in favour of the creditor's lien under the Heritable Securities Act of 1845 (*i*) It is the common practice for instruments of protest of bills not to be signed by the witnesses (*k*) But the probative value of all instruments is increased by their subscriptions (*l*)

§ 1197 The witnesses must be designed in instruments of sasine in the old form, and instruments of resignation *ad remanentiam*, and of intimation of assignations and retrocessions (*m*)

---

rities' Act, 8 and 9 Vict, c 31, sch 3 It is adhibited in the statutory schedule for instruments of sasine in the new form in burgage property 10 and 11 Vict, c 49, sch D, but omitted in the forms for other instruments of sasine in the new form in 8 and 9 Vict, c 35, sch B—10 and 11 Vict, c 47, sch C—10 and 11 Vict c 48, sch L

(*a*) The act 1540, c 76, requiring the signature to be the same as that in a book kept by the Sheriff (if it was ever in observance) has long been in desuetude, Ersk, 4, 2, 6

(*b*) 1686, c 17—Carnegie *v* Scott 1696 M 8858—See *supra*, § 658

(*c*) 1686 c 17—2 Ross 192—Duff *v* L Buchan, 1725, Rob Ap, 525—*contra* former decisions in M 16,954, 6

(*d*) See *supra*, § 689

(*e*) Ersk 3, 2, 15—2 Ross Lec, 190—1584, c 1

(*f*) 1681, c 5

(*g*) See Duff on Recent Stat 7—The act as to sasines in burgage property (10 and 11 Vict, c 49, sch D) requires only the last page to be signed by the witnesses

(*h*) 11 and 12 Vict c 36, sch

(*i*) 8 and 9 Vict, c 31, sch 1

(*k*) Thomson on Bills, 119—Tait Ev, 22

(*l*) This is recommended in Stair, 2, 3 19 (*ad finem*)—Ib, 4, 42 9 (*ad finem*)—Tait Ev, 21

(*m*) 1681 c 5 In Morton *v* Hunters, 1828, 7 S 172, affd, 4 W S, 879, an erasure in the christian name of a witness in the body of an instrument of sasine was overlooked This was before the act 6 and 7 Will IV, c 33 noticed *infra*, § 1208

---

affidavit sworn abroad and notarially sealed An instrument of protest on a bill, formed according to the law of the foreign country where the protest was taken, is a good warrant for summary diligence in this country on the bill Elder *v* Young, 1851, 17 D, 56

Their designations are also necessary in instruments of sasine in the modern form (*n*), and in all other instruments which conclude with an ordinary testing clause (*o*)

§ 1198 Instruments of sasine and resignation *ex propriis manibus*, being in effect deeds of conveyance, must be signed not only by the notary and witnesses, but also by the granter (*p*) The witnesses to such deeds, however, do not require to subscribe or to be designed with special reference to the subscription of the granter, their signatures and designations being held to apply to it as well as to the subscription of the notary (*r*) The subscription of the granter of a sasine or resignation *propriis manibus* is not necessary, when the instrument is adminiculated by a writing under his hand (*s*) Instruments of resignation and sasine in burgage property in favour of disponees will not be sustained, unless they are either signed by the party from whom they bear to flow, or are adminiculated by a writing signed by him (*t*) A reversion in burgage property by instrument under the hand of the town-clerk, without the party's subscription, was sustained in an old case on account of the practice (*u*)

An instrument of disentail must be signed not only by the notary, but also by the disentailer, before witnesses in common form (*x*)

§ 1199 Until recently, notaries required to append to all important instruments (*e g*, of sasine and resignation) a holograph (*y*) attestation or "docquet" Its essentials are nowhere authoritatively defined (*z*) Among them seems to be a statement that the notary

(*n*) 8 and 9 Vict, c 35, sch A—10 and 11 Vict, c 47, sch C—10 and 11 Vict, c 49, sch D (*o*) 8 and 9 Vict, c 31 sch No 3—10 and 11 Vict, c 48, sch L

(*p*) 1555, c 38—Ersk, 2, 3, 38—Ib, 2, 7, 20—2 Ross Lec, 195

(*r*) Kibbles *v* Ross, 1804, M 14,314, 1 Ross Ca, 19 See also Anderson *v* Anderson, 1828, 6 S, 163 Nor is it necessary to design the writer of such instruments, Kibbles *v* Ross, *supra*—Ivory's Ersk, 281, note 51

(*s*) Stair, 2 3, 19—Ersk, *supra*—2 Ross Lec, *supra* As to what is a sufficient written adminicle, see Gray *v* Finlayson, 1615, M, 12,509—Murray *v* Shaw, 1618, M, 12,510—Lady Mountquhannie *v* St Andrews, 1632, M 12,516—Buchan *v* Taits, 1669, M, 12,519—Young *v* Thomson, 1672, M, 12,520—Mackenzie *v* Monro, 1731, M, 12,524 Sasine by a man *intuitu matrimonii* has been sustained without any written adminicle, where the provision was reasonable, Stair, 2 3, 19—Compare Clapperton *v* Hume, 1628, M, 12,512—Kell *v* Morrison, M, 12,508—Hamilton *v* Hamilton, 1639, M, 12,516—Wallace *v* Kennal, 1669 M, 12,315

(*t*) Stair, 2 3, 19—Ersk, 2, 3, 38 (*u*) Galloway *v* Burgh of Dumbarton, 1551, M, 3104 (*x*) 11 and 12 Vict c 36 § 32, sch (*y*) According to uniform practice the docquet should be holograph, see 1 Juridical Styles, 70, note †

(*z*) For the form of the docquet, see Office of a Notary, 27, 28—Ersk, Apps, 1—2 Ross Lec, 187 Bad grammar does not destroy the docquet, M'Intosh *v* Inglis 1825,

was present (*a*), and that he saw, knew, and heard (or words to that effect) the procedure which he records (*b*) The docquet to an instrument of sasine in the old form must mention the number of pages of which the instrument consists, if it is written bookwise on more than one sheet (*c*) The notary's name ought to be both stated at length in the beginning of the docquet (*d*), and subscribed to it But the subscription has been dispensed with, where the name was set out in the notary's handwriting in the body of the docquet (*e*) Any alterations by way of deletion, superinduction, or the like in the instrument should be mentioned in the docquet (*f*)

A shorter docquet is used in less important instruments, and was once sustained in the case of a sasine (*g*)

§ 1200 The docquet is no longer necessary to instruments of resignation *ad remanentiam* (*h*), and an ordinary testing clause has come in its place in instruments of sasine in the new form (*i*) Instruments of disentail (*k*), and instruments in favour of the creditor's heir under the Heritable Securities Act of 1845 (*l*) also, conclude by a testing clause

§ 1201 As to the *contents of notarial instruments*, reference

---

4 S 190 and a docquet has been sustained in which there were three omissions and three other clerical errors, none of them being *in substantialibus*, M'Ghie *v* Leishman, 1827, 5 S, 758 (*a*) M'Intosh *v* Inglis, *supra* It is usual, but not necessary, to state that the notary was asked and required to officiate, Duff Feud, 118 See Craig, 2, 7, 8 (*b*) Primrose *v* Dury, 1612, M, 14,326 (*c*) 1686, c 17 —A S, 17th January 1756—Kirkham *v* Campbell, 1822, 1 S, 423 Immaterial errors on this point have been overlooked, as in Morrison *v* Ramsay, 1826, 5 S, 150—M'Ghie *v* Leishman, *supra*—Dickson *v* Cunningham, 1829, 7 S, 503, affd, 5 W S 657

(*d*) As to whether this is requisite see Maxwell *v* E Nithsdale's Tenants, 1680, M, 16,837, questioned in M'Intosh *v* Inglis, *supra* (*e*) Gordon *v* Murray, 1765 M, 16,818—Cullen *v* Thomsons, 1731, M, 16,842, *supra*, § 758 (*f*) 2 Ross, 189—Anderson *v* Thomson, 1828, 6 S 463—Howden *v* Ferrier, 13 S, 1097 As to erasures in instruments of sasine and resignation, see 6 and 7 Will IV, c 33, *infra*, § 1208 (*g*) Maxwell *v* E Nithsdale's Tenants, *supra* (*h*) 8 and 9 Vict c 35, § 8 Instruments of resignation *in favorem* are abolished, same act, § 9

(*i*) 8 and 9 Vict c 35 sch B—10 and 11 Vict, c 47 sch C—10 and 11 Vict, c 48 sch L—10 and 11 Vict, c 49, sch D The statutory form in the first noted act (for sasine in lands not burgage) contains no blank for the number of pages, but bears merely that the instrument is on 'this and the preceding pages' It is thought that this, although evidently an omission will protect sasines under the act in which the number of pages is not mentioned Mr Duff (on Recent Stat, p 7) entertains a different opinion

(*k*) 11 and 12 Vict c 36, sch (*l*) 8 and 9 Vict, c 31 sch 3

must be made to books of forms, a summary of the general rules on the subject being sufficient for the purpose of this treatise

The only safe rule to observe in practice regarding all instruments is, that they ought to narrate fully and accurately the procedure which they are designed to record

§ 1202 An *instrument of sasine* in the old form is the narrative of an act of infeftment in land and its accessories, by delivery of appropriate symbols of possession in presence of a notary It commences with an invocation of the Deity ('In the name of God, Amen') as a solemn adjuration to the truth of the narrative (*m*) It then sets forth the date of the formal act, by the day of the month and the year, both of the Christian era and of the Sovereign's reign (*n*) It requires to coincide with the precept or warrant to infeft (*o*), as well as to narrate the formal act by the appropriate symbol (*p*), although slight inaccuracies on these points have been overlooked, especially where the sasine had been followed by possession (*r*) If the sasine is in favour of the heir or singular successor of the party whose name appears in the precept, the con-

---

(*m*) This is necessary, Office of a Notary, 49

(*n*) Office of a Notary, 49—Duff Feud, 104 An instrument is null if its date is not mentioned in one or other of these modes, but it is an open question whether it must bear both the year of the Sovereign's reign and of the Christian era, Macfarlan, 1853, 15 D, 708 It seems that omitting the day of the month is not fatal if there is no doubt, from the date given, that the recording took place within sixty days from the sasine, Dickson *v* Goodall, 1820, Hume D, 925, note A discrepancy between the years of the era and the reign has been held fatal Mag of Brechin *v* Arbuthnot, 1810, 3 D 216 An instrument of sasine fell (before the act 6 and 7 Will IV, c 33) in consequence of the year of the Christian era being written on erasure, Hoggan *v* Rankin, 1835, 13 S, 461, affd 1 Rob 173 as did also an instrument of sasine bearing date 4th October 1820, in the 58th year of the reign of Geo IV, Lindsay *v* Giles, 1844, 6 D, 771

(*o*) Hoggan *v* Rankin, 1 Rob Ap, 173, per L Brougham (questioning Gordon *v* L Fife, 1827, 5 S, 550)—Guthries *v* L Guthrie, 1667 3 B Sup, 140—Murray *v* Murray, 1708, 4 B Sup 701—Wallace *v* Dalrymple, 1742 M, 6919 A precept to infeft in the granter's lands, described by a general name, covers sasine in every particular part of them, Graham's Tr *v* Hislop 1753, M, 6921—Mackenzie *v* Buchanan, 1743, M 14,323—Hill *v* D Montrose, 1833, 11 S 958 See Belshes *v* Stewart, 21st January 1815, F C And an infeftment in an annuity, proceeding on an assignation to that effect of a warrant to infeft in the full fee, has been sustained, Bonthrone *v* Bonthrone's Tr, 1805, Hume D, 238

(*p*) Davidson *v* M'Leod 1827, 6 S, 8—Ker *v* Scot's Crs, 1702, M, 14,310—Stirling, 1724, M ib—Mag of Brechin *v* Arbuthnot, 1810, 3 D, 216

(*r*) Inaccuracies in mentioning sasine by delivering the appropriate symbol were overlooked in E Wigton *v* E Cassilis, 1630, M, 14,320—L Lamerton *v* Home, 1682, M 14 309 14 321—Gordon *v* Brodie 5 B Sup 587—Pringle *v* Murray 1725 M 14 312—Urquhart *v* Officers of State, 1752, M 9014, 16,903—5 B Sup 257 S C

necting title must be deduced (s) The name of the party infeft must be stated and sasine is incompetent in favour of the heirs or representatives of a person (t) or in favour of a company firm (u) The description of the lands must be in accordance with the terms of the precept (x), but errors on this head have been held not to be fatal, *si constat de subjecto* (y)

In noticing the cases where the Court had sustained instruments which did not fully and accurately set forth the infeftment, Lord President Hope observed, "I think that we have gone too far in sanctioning blunders I cannot understand how it can be maintained, that because we have passed over one blunder, we must sanction every other blunder, or how it is possible to argue from one blunder to another" (z)

§ 1203. An instrument of sasine in the new form is a statement by a notary that there was presented to him by or on behalf of the grantee, the deed (or an extract of it), or an extract of the decree of service, or of adjudication or sale, containing the warrant to infeft, in virtue of which the instrument bears that the notary "hereby gives sasine" to the grantee, according to the nature of his right (a) This instrument, therefore is not (like the former one) a narrative of a symbolical act of giving sasine, but expeding and recording the instrument constitute the infeftment (b) The instrument does not contain an invocation of the Deity, or mention the presence of a bailie or attorney for the respective parties It states the place where it was expede which does not require to be any part of the subject in which the sasine is given It concludes with a testing clause in the same terms as that appended to

affd, Cr and St, 586—Maxwell v L Portrack, 1628, M, 14,318—Kennedy v Graham 1629, M, 14 319—L Smeaton v Dunfermline Vassals, 1631, M, 14,320—Somervil v Somervil, 1631, M, ib—M Clydesdale v Menzies' Crs, 1729, M, 14,312 Inaccuracies in other parts of the narrative were overlooked where the fact of infeftment was substantially set forth, Douglas v Chalmers 5 B Sup, 587—Hilton v Lady Cheynes 1676, M 14 331—Livingston v L Napier 1762, 5 B Sup, 587—Morton v Hunters & Co, 1838, 7 S, 172, affd, 4 W S, 379—M'Glue v Leishman, 1827, 5 S, 758—Henderson v Dalrymple 1776, 5 B Sup, 586—Kirkham v Campbell, 1822, 1 S, 423—M'Gillivray v Campbell, 1824, 3 S, 378—Gordon v Brodie, 1773 5 B Sup, 587

(s) 1693, c 35 But see Proctor v Carnegy, 1796, M 8871

(t) Blackwood v E Sutherland, 1740, M, 14 327—Melville v Swinton's Crs, 1794, M, ib

(u) Morrison v Miller, 1818, Hume D, 720

(x) See *supra* (o)

(y) L Clackmanan v L Allardice, 1630, 1 B Sup 314, 323—Farie v Drummond, 1830, 8 S, 550—Hill v D Montrose, 1833, 11 S, 958

(z) Davidson v M'Leod, 1827, 6 S, 8

(a) 8 and 9 Vict c 35, sch B—10 and 11 Vict c 47, sch C—10 and 11 Vict, c 48 sch I—10 and 11 Vict c 49 sch D

(b) 8 and 9 Vict c 35, § 1—10 and 11 Vict c 49 §§ 5 6

deeds (c), but it does not contain a date, the precedency of competing sasines being regulated entirely by their order in registration

§ 1204 An *instrument of resignation* is a notarial narrative of the symbolical act of resignation by a vassal into the hands of his superior Instruments of resignation *in favorem*, after having been generally discontinued in practice (d), were abolished from and after 1st October 1845 (e) But instruments of resignation *ad remanentiam* subsist [7] They ought to refer accurately to their warrants (f), and ought to detail fully and correctly the *res gestæ* They must specify the proper symbol, namely staff and baton (g), and must deduce the title, when they are made in favour of the heir or singular successor of the party whose name appears in the procuratory (h) The ceremony may be performed anywhere (i) The docquet is now unnecessary, the instrument being authenticated by the notary's subscription and motto, with the subscriptions of the witnesses (k)

§ 1205 There are statutory forms for *instruments of disentail* (l), and instruments *in favour of the creditor's heir* under the Heritable Securities Act of 1845 (m)

§ 1206 An *instrument of protest* of a bill must have a copy of the bill prefixed (n) It should state where the protest was taken, but this is not necessary if the instrument bears that the bill was duly protested (o) Where the protest was at the instance of one party, the instrument may be extended in favour of another who has subsequently acquired right to the bill (p) Under the stamp laws it has been held that each instrument can include only one bill (r)

There are no settled rules or styles for other instruments of pro-

---

(c) See the schedules to the acts above noted (a), and see *supra*, § 703, *et seq*

(d) Renton v Anstruther, 1848, 11 D, 37

(e) 8 and 9 Vict, c 35, § 9

(f) M'Millan v Campbell, 1831, 9 S, 551

(g) A S, 11th Feb 1708—Ersk, 2, 7 17—Carnegy v Cruikshank's Crs, 1729, M, 14,316—E Aberdeen, 1742, M, ib, but see Young v Calderwood, 1708, M, 3105

(h) 1693, c 35

(i) Ersk, 2, 7, 18—Office of a Notary, 106

(k) 8 and 9 Vict, c 35, § 8—Duff Recent Stat, 60

(l) 11 and 12 Vict c 36, sch

(m) 8 and 9 Vict, c 31, sch No 3

(n) See Thomson on Bills, 449, where the requisites of these instruments are stated

(o) Commercial Bank v Hanna 24th Feb 1818, F C

(p) Mackie v Hilliard, 1822, 1 S 499—Allan v Galli, 1829, 7 S, 706 See also Swanston v Archibald, 1837, 16 S, 308

(r) Barbour v Newall, 1822, 1 S, 257, and 1823, 2 S, 328—Napier v Carson, 1824, 2 S, 622

---

[7] See *supra*, § 1187, note [1]

test or instruments of intimation of assignations, all of which, however, come under the general rule, already mentioned, that the *res gestæ* should be narrated fully and accurately

§ 1207 The tenor and contents of notarial instruments, except those introduced by the recent statutes regarding infeftment, heritable securities, services, and disentails (*s*), have been regulated by the practice of conveyancers under occasional directions from the Court of Session Errors in form have sometimes crept in, and have not been brought before the Court until after they had become common throughout the country To avoid the evils which would have arisen from holding such errors to be fatal the Court have repeatedly overlooked them when not *in essentialibus* (*t*). But in several cases they have intimated that they would exact the proper formalities in future (*u*) The neglect of an Act of Sederunt passed for the purpose of reforming an erroneous practice as to the symbol used in resignations was visited with nullity (*x*)

§ 1208 At common law notarial instruments, if vitiated *in substantialibus* are null (*y*), for the reasons mentioned in treating of vitiations in private deeds (*z*) The consequences of this rule in regard to instruments of sasine and resignation led to the passing of a statute (*a*), which, proceeding on the narrative of the acts regarding public registers, and of various questions having arisen as to the validity of recorded instruments of sasine and resignation *ad remanentiam* containing erasures, whereby a want of confidence in the security of land rights had been produced, enacted that no challenge of such instruments should thereafter receive effect on the ground that any part of them had been written on erasure unless it were averred and proved that such erasure had been made for the purpose of fraud or that the record was not conformable to the instrument as presented for registration The act applies retro-

---

(*s*) *Supra* §§ 1203, 4, 5 (*t*) Galloway *v* Dumbarton, 1554, M, 3104—Edmiston, 1623, M, 3105—Kibbles *v* Ross, 1804 M 14,314, note—Skelly *v* Duff, 1774, 5 B S, 589—Ersk, 2, 7 17 (See analogous cases regarding messengers' executions, *infra*) (*u*) Young *v* Calderwood, *supra*—Skelly *v* Duff, *supra*—A S 11th Feb 1708—Ersk, *supra* (*x*) E Aberdeen *v* Duncan, 1742, M 14 316 (*y*) Innes *v* E Fife, 1827, 5 S 559, affd, 2 W S, 637—M'Millan *v* Campbell, 1831, 9 S 551—Hoggan *v* Ranken 1835 13 S, 461, affd, 1 Rob Ap, 173—Howden *v* Ferrier 1835, 13 S, 1097 It was held not to be fatal to an instrument of sasine in the old style, that the name of one of the witnesses was on erasure in the body of it, Morton *v* Hunters 1828, 7 S 172, affd, 4 W S, 379

(*z*) *Supra*, § 871 (*a*) 6 and 7 Will IV, c 33

spectively to all instruments of resignation and sasine except those which had been reduced before 12th May 1835 Instruments of sasine and resignation *propriis manibus*, being in effect deeds of divestiture, are excepted from the operation of the act [8]

It will be observed that the statute only protects instruments containing words on erasure, and not those in which interlineations or marginal additions occur Such alterations must, therefore, be mentioned in the docquet or testing clause (as the case may be), in order to be effectual as parts of the instrument (*b*) The act is limited to instruments of sasine and resignation *ad remanentiam*

§ 1209 Instruments of sasine in the old form (*c*), and instruments of resignation (*d*) require to be recorded—and, therefore, to be executed—within sixty days of their dates, which are the dates of the ceremonies respectively set forth in them There is no fixed period within which other instruments must be extended; and accordingly, they are admissible, although they were not written out till several years after their dates (*e*) It is also competent to extend a new and amended instrument in room of one which is defective (*f*) But if a title has been made up on an irregular instrument, it will not be validated by extending another instrument correctly narrating the same ceremonial act (*g*) [9]

§ 1210 Before the establishment of public registers for instruments of sasine and registration, each notary used to record duplicates of his instruments in a private register or "protocol book", and these records were so important that an act was passed requiring

(*b*) *Supra*, §§ 884, 1199 (*c*) 1617, c 16 (*d*) 1669, c 3 This is also the rule as to instruments of resignation and sasine in lands held burgage, 1681, c 11 (*e*) In Alexander *v* Scott, 1827, 6 S 150, an instrument of protest of a bill extended at an interval of 15 years was sustained See also Brown & Co *v* Dunbar, 1807, M, "Bill of Exchange," Appx, No 21—Hop Pringle *v* Home, 1623, M, 2215—L Wigton *v* E Cassilis 1630, M, 2216 (*f*) Barbour *v* Newall, 1823, 2 S, 328—Balfour *v* Lyle, 1832, 10 S, 853—Scott Moncrieff, 1830, 8 S, 116—Alexander *v* Scott 1827, 6 S, 150—Kibbles *v* Stevenson, 1830, 9 S, 233, affd, 5 W S, 553—Fulton *v* Macalister, 1831, 9 S, 412 Formerly a notary was held to be *functus officio* by extending a defective instrument, Jaffray *v* L Wamphray, 1677, M, 3630, 8310, S C—Maxwell *v* L Innerwick, 1628, M, 12,265 Under the Sasine Act, an instrument made and recorded of new takes effect from the date of recording, 8 and 9 Vict, c 35, § 4 (*g*) See M'Intosh *v* Inglis, 1825, 4 S, 190

[8] *Supra*, § 1187 note [1], 21 and 22 Vict, c 76, § 33
[9] *Supra*, § 1187, note [1], 21 and 22 Vict c 76, §§ 19 31

them to be delivered after the notary's death to the Clerk-Register for preservation (*h*). An instrument made up from the protocol book, and signed by the notary and witnesses, is probative as the original instrument (*i*), and if these persons have died, the entry in the protocol may be made available by an action of transumpt (*k*). The entry of a sasine in a protocol book was sustained in an action of transumpt although it was not in the notary's handwriting and not signed by him, because it was among genuine entries, and there was no ground to doubt its credibility, and because the party offered to prove by the witnesses that sasine was given (*l*). An instrument of sasine made up from the notary's protocol may, on a petition to the Court, be marked with the date of registration of the original instrument (*m*). Since the establishment of the registers of sasines, &c., the use of protocol books has been almost entirely discontinued.

A lost instrument of sasine may also (like any other writing) be supplied by an action of proving the tenor (*n*).

§ 1211. A notarial instrument, if regular *ex facie*, and narrating facts of which such a record is required by law, is probative of its tenor (*o*), and cannot in general be contradicted except by means of an action of reduction (*p*). Vitiations and patent informalities however, may be pleaded by exception. And this seems also to be the rule where an instrument is alleged to be disconform to its warrant, and the latter document is produced (*r*). So the objection, that the notary has a disqualifying interest may be pleaded by exception if it appears on the face of the instrument, *e.g.*, in the case of a notary protesting a bill to which he is a party (*s*).

§ 1212. In weighing the evidence in improbation of notarial

(*h*) 1587, c. 45. (*i*) Stair, 2, 3, 25—Ersk. 2, 3, 43.

(*k*) Stair, *supra*—Ersk., *supra*—Striviling v. Menteith, 1566, M., 12,447.

(*l*) Brown v. Nisbet, 1630, 1 B. Sup., 311. With this case compare D. Monmouth v. Scott, 1667, M., 12,266. (*m*) Ramsay, 1678, M., 13,553—L. Lindores v. Foulis, 1706, 4 B. Sup. 648. (*n*) See the chapter on actions of Proving the Tenor, *infra* § 1287, *et seq.* (*o*) See *supra*, § 1187 *et seq.* (*p*) Telfer v. Barrow, 1814, 7 D., 170—L. Crawford v. Ogilvie, 1583, M., 2708—Thomson on Bills, 449—Tait Ev., 4—Baron Hume notes a case (Campbell v. Campbell, 1810, Hume D., 723) where the Court refused to entertain the objection (to be proved by witnesses) to an instrument of sasine that the ceremony had not taken place on the lands, but on a contiguous tenement. The question arose twelve years after the date of the sasine.

(*r*) See Watts v. Barbour, 1828, 6 S., 1048—L. Kirkconnell v. L. Barnbarroch, 1628, M., 3682—Lamb v. Blackburn, 1628, M., 3683. (*s*) Russell v. Kirk, 1837, 6 S., 133.

instruments, the same principles apply as in improbations of private writings (*t*) The written attestation by the notary and witnesses cannot be cut down upon their merely deponing *non memini* (*u*), while their oaths admitting their subscriptions, but denying that the facts set forth took place, are to be received with suspicion (*x*) It is presumed that dead witnesses would have deponed affirmatively (*y*)

Several cases analogous to those in this chapter have occurred in regard to messengers' executions (*z*)

CHAPTER XIII —OF OFFICIAL WRITINGS BY MESSENGERS-AT-ARMS AND OTHER OFFICERS OF THE LAW

§ 1213 The citation of parties and witnesses called to appear in courts of law, the intimation of various steps of legal procedure and the execution of legal diligence are intrusted to official persons, whose formal written narratives are the proper, and in general, the only competent proof of the officers' proceedings These writings are of two classes, **1***st*, the citation or schedule, by which the officer intimates the service to the party on whom it is made, and, 2*d*, the execution, which is returned by the officer to the Court or to his employer, and which is an authenticated narrative of the official act Before noticing these writings separately, a few matters common to them both will be adverted to

§ 1214 All writs or letters running in the name of the Sovereign may be executed by messengers-at-arms, and in civil matters by them only (*a*) Criminal letters and indictments, and warrants from the Court of Justiciary, may be served by messengers-at-arms, by macers of the court, or by sheriff-officers of the county in which they are executed (*b*). Services and intimations in the Court of Session are usually made by messengers-at-arms But the Court

---

(*t*) See *supra*, § 909, *et seq*

(*u*) *Supra*, § 910—Berry *v* Balfour, 1822, 2 Mur, 116

(*x*) *Supra*, § 911

(*y*) *Supra* § 915—Wood *v* Cramond, 1562, M, 12,650—L Newbottle *v* Simpson, 1591, M, 12 651

(*z*) *Infra*, § 1226, *et seq*

(*a*) Darling's Office of a Messenger, 3, *et seq* —Acts 1672, c 6, and 1693, c 12

(*b*) 11 and 12 Vict, c 79, § 6—2 Hume, 242—2 Al, 327

sometimes direct warrants for the apprehension of delinquents to be executed by its own macers and in such cases these officers only are competent. The macers of the Court of Session also execute captions for the return of processes which have been borrowed (c). Services and intimations in other courts are intrusted to their respective officers. By statute, warrants by a Sheriff against parties charged with crimes committed within his jurisdiction, and warrants against parties as *in meditatione fugæ*, may be executed in another county without being indorsed by the Sheriff or sheriff-clerk of that county provided they are executed by a messenger-at-arms, or by an officer of the court from which they are issued (d). Witnesses in criminal proceedings and prosecutions for pecuniary penalties before any courts or magistrates in Scotland, although residing beyond their respective jurisdictions, may be cited by a messenger-at-arms, by an officer of the court or magistrate who grants the warrant, or by an officer of the place where the person cited may be at the time (e).

The Court of Session once authorised a sheriff-officer to cite witnesses and havers in Shetland in a case before them, the nearest messenger having been distant 300 miles from the place of service (f).[1]

A notary is not qualified to act as a messenger-at-arms or officer of court, and therefore, a notarial instrument is not admissible in place of an execution (g).

§ 1215. The faith placed in citations and executions thus depends on their being under the hand of the proper officers. They

(c) Bell's Law Dic., voce Macer—Shand's Prac., 119. (d) 1 and 2 Vict., c. 118, § 25. (e) 11 Geo. IV. and 1 Will. IV., c. 37, § 8.
(f) Mitchell, 1764, M., 7355. The application was not opposed.
(g) Haswell v. Mag. of Jedburgh, 1714, M., 12,270.

[1] The Court have refused to grant warrant to sheriff-officers to execute a decree of the Court of Session against a party at Kirkwall, in Orkney, although it was stated that there was no messenger-at-arms in the county of Orkney,—the nearest messenger residing at Thurso, in the county of Caithness. The Lord President (M'Neill) observed,—"I do not think there is such a case of necessity as will warrant us in granting the prayer of this petition, unless we are prepared to do so in every similar case." Miller's Trustees, petitioners, 1856, 19 D., 130. In a previous case, however, the Second Division granted warrant to have a summons served in Orkney by a sheriff-officer. As such warrant can only be granted in virtue of the *nobile officium* of the Court, it is necessary that it should be signed in the Inner House, James Cooper and Others, petitioners, 1854, 16 D., 1104. See also Kennedy, June 10, 1862, 24 D., 1131, and James Hoseason, petitioner, June 9, 1863 (not yet reported), where the application was made direct to the Inner House.

will, however, be sustained, if the persons whose signatures they bear were habit and repute qualified (*h*) Baron Hume doubts whether this applies to executions of criminal libels (*i*) A messenger, like a notary, cannot act in matters where he is personally interested (*k*) Relationship to the parties seems not to disqualify (*l*)

§ 1216 Two witnesses used to be required in citations and executions, but one is now sufficient in all of them, whether in civil or criminal processes (*m*), and in all diligences except poindings, where two witnesses are still required (*n*) Witnesses are not now required to citations of parties, witnesses, or havers under the Small Debt Acts (*o*), services and citations under the Sequestration Act (*p*), and citations of jurors or witnesses in civil or criminal cases (*r*)

§ 1217 All executions, and citations or schedules may be either written or printed, or partly both (*s*)

I *Of the Officer's Citation or Schedule*

§ 1218 The citation or schedule—the writ by which the officer certifies the fact of service to the person upon whom it is made—varies in its form and requisites according to the nature of the service

The citation on a summons in the Court of Session must be sub-

---

(*h*) Stuart *v* Hay, 1676, M, 3092—Lermont *v* Lermont's Heirs, 1699, M, 3096—See Ogilvie, 1681, 3 B Sup, 410—Tait Ev, 7—*Supra*, § 1191 An execution by a messenger who had been deprived of office, and his deprivation advertised in the public prints, was held ineffectual in Hunter *v* Montgomery, 1732, M, 3097, and in Somerville *v* Jarviswood, 1608, M, 3091, the Court seem to have considered that publication at the market-cross of the head burgh where the officer dwelt would exclude the plea of habit and repute qualified The "Regulations for Messengers-at-Arms," which were approved of, and confirmed by the Court of Session, by A S, 10th March 1772, prescribe (§ 10) the mode of publishing deprivation and suspension of these officers at the market-cross and church doors, and by advertisement in the newspapers, but they do not declare that all executions under the hand of persons so published shall be null

(*i*) 2 Hume, 212 (*k*) Dalgliesh *v* Scott 1822, 1 S, 506—*Supra*, § 1191

(*l*) *Supra*, § ib (*m*) 9 Geo IV, c 29, § 6—7 Will IV and 1 Vict, c 41, § 21—1 and 2 Vict, c 114, § 32 (explained and re-enacted on this point by 9 and 10 Vict, c 67)—13 and 14 Vict, c 36, sch B—16 and 17 Vict, c 80, sch F, J

(*n*) 1 and 2 Vict, c 114, § 32—9 and 10 Vict, c 67—7 Will IV, and 1 Vict, c 41, § 20 (*o*) 6 Geo IV, c 48, sch—7 Will IV, and 1 Vict, c 41, § 3

(*p*) 2 and 3 Vict, c 41, § 138 (*r*) 11 Geo IV, c 37, § 7—16 and 17 Vict, c 80 sch G (*s*) 9 Geo IV, c 29, § 8—1 and 2 Vict, c 114, § 32, explained by 9 and 10 Vict, c 67—2 and 3 Vict c 41, § 138

scribed by the messenger (*t*) It does not require to be signed by the witness who was present at the service (*u*) In compliance with an act passed in 1693, the witnesses should be named and designed in "all copies of summonses charges, inhibitions arrestments, or other letters left with the parties cited (*x*) But the observance of this provision is not indispensable, as its sanction is not nullity of the citation, but deprivation of the messenger (*y*) In the form given in the Act of Sederunt of 8th July 1831 for citations on summonses before the Court of Session the witnesses are named and designed the effect of which in the opinion of a writer on practice (*z*), is that the omission will now probably be held a nullity This however, may be doubted because the act does not contain any express regulation on the point, and its relative provisions (§ 1) were not intended for increasing the solemnities of the citation, but to prescribe the form for citations applicable to the altered style of wills of summonses

§ 1219 The citation ought to describe the warrant on which it proceeds and to name and design the parties But these are not statutory requisites and errors in them will be overlooked if enough remains for the purpose of identification (*a*) The date on which the writ is served must be specified in words, not merely in figures (*b*), and of course the day to which the citation is given ought to appear with equal distinctness It used to be mentioned by specifying the day of the month, but in order to correspond with the altered style of wills of summonses, the citation is now

---

(*t*) 1592, c 141—Shand's Pr 249 The service copy of the summons (if in the Court of Session) does not require to be signed by the messenger, Izatt *v* Kennedy, 1840 2 D, 476 (*u*) Beattie *v* Lee, 1823, 2 S 224—Connel *v* Faulie, 1824, 2 S, 664—Shand Pr, 249 The act 1686, c 4, in requiring the subscriptions of witnesses to "citations," uses that word in place of "executions, Shand, ib—Cases in note (*y*), *infra* (*x*) 1693, c 12 (*y*) Holmes *v* Reid 1829, 7 S 535—Thomson *v* Gavin, 1830, 8 S, 921, overruling Stewart *v* Brown 1824 3 S, 56

(*z*) Shand's Pr 249 (*a*) Munn *v* Hood, 1845, 7 D 1009—M'Lellan *v* Graham, 30th June 1841, F C See also Brodie *v* Thomson 1836, 14 S, 983 A citation which omitted the name of the real raiser of a multiplepoinding was sustained in Miller *v* Ure, 1838, 16 S, 1204 (*b*) 1693, c 12 In Holmes *v* Reid, 1829 7 S 535 and Thomson *v* Gavin 1830, 8 S 921 *supra*, the omission of one requisite prescribed by this act was held not to infer nullity, because the sanction of the act is merely deprivation of the messenger The same rule of construction seems to apply to the omission to state the date at length But the citation would not (it is thought) be sustained unless the date were set forth either at length or in figures The form in A S, 8th July 1831, sch, evidently means that the date should be filled up in words But the act itself does not ordain this

given to the last day of the induciæ, counting from the date of service (*c*).

§ 1220. Citations in the Sheriff-court must be signed by the officer (*d*), but do not require the signature of the witness (*e*). The name of the pursuer's procurator should be marked upon them. The Act of Sederunt, however, which directs this to be done does not declare that its omission shall infer nullity (*f*). The citation must be conform to its warrant (*g*). In the service of libels in the Sheriff-court the citation is accompanied by a copy of the libel each page of which must be signed by the officer (*h*). "Edicts for choosing curators, summonses for curators giving up inventories, multiplepoindings, transferences, transumpts, wakenings, and cognitions, may be executed by delivering a copy of citation before one witness, containing the names and designations of the pursuer and defender, and bearing the extent and special grounds of the pursuer's claim, without any copy of the summons (*i*). There is a statutory form for such notices to remove as proceed on a probative lease or extract lease, or on a letter of obligation to remove under the hand of the tenant in the terms prescribed by the late Sheriff Courts Act (*k*).

§ 1221. There are also statutory forms for citations of defenders and witnesses under the Sheriff Small Debt Act (*l*), and of defenders in summary removings before the Sheriff (*m*). The act which regulates procedure in small debt cases before justices of the peace refers (*n*) to a schedule as containing a form of citation. But the schedule has been omitted.

With regard to all cases in which styles for citations are prescribed by statute, the only safe or proper rule is to follow the forms implicitly. The Court deal strictly with deviations from them (*o*).

§ 1222. The form of citations or notices of compearance on criminal libels is prescribed by statute (*p*), and must be accurately

---

(*c*) A. S., 8th July 1831, sch. (*d*) A. S., 10th July 1839, §§ 13, 139. (*e*) Calder *v.* Calder, 1825, 4 S., 331. (*f*) A. S., ib. § 19. The omission is thought not to be fatal, see Buchanan *v.* Yuills, 1832, 10 S., 235, 555—M'Glashan (Barclay's ed.) 182. (*g*) A. S. 10th July 1839, § 20. (*h*) A. S., ib., §§ 13, 139—M'Glashan's Prac., § 182. (*i*) A. S., ib., § 14. (*k*) 16 and 17 Vict. c. 80, §§ 30, 31, sch. I. This act makes the lease or extract, or a letter of obligation signed by the tenant, and either holograph or attested by one witness, without the authority of a judge being interponed thereto, a sufficient warrant to a sheriff officer to serve notice of removal. (*l*) 7 Will. IV, and 1 Vict. c. 41, sch. A. (*m*) 1 and 2 Vict. c. 119, sch. A. (*n*) 6 Geo. IV. c. 48, § 3. (*o*) See Beattie *v.* M'Lellan, 1844, 6 D. 1088. (*p*) 9 Geo. IV. c. 29, § 6, sch. A. This form does not re

observed (*r*) It is appended to the service copy of the libel (*s*). Slight inaccuracies in naming or designing the prisoner will not be fatal, *si constat de persona* (*t*) The days of service and compearance must be the same in the notice and execution (*u*) The notice must also correspond with the libel, but where the notice was to compear on the 1st of May, and the indictment called the panel to a Circuit Court to be held in April, but which was continued for some days in May the citation was sustained (*w*)[2] The officer executing, and the witness—both of whom must be the same in the notice and execution (*x*)—must sign the notice (*y*) The service copy of the libel does not require to be signed by either of them (*z*) The want of the officer's designation, along with other irregularities, has been held fatal (*a*), but the objection that the word "witness" was written over "messenger," so as partly to delete and obscure it has been repelled (*b*)

§ 1223 A person cited to attend Court as a witness in a summary case cannot be tried or dealt with as an accused party (*c*).

§ 1224 Jurymen and witnesses, unless summoned by a written citation cannot be proceeded against on failure to attend Formerly a citation was required to make it competent for witnesses or jurymen to appear, and they were deemed to be ultroneous if they attended without having been duly summoned (*d*) But witnesses in every case are now admissible without being cited (*f*), and a citation is not necessary to entitle jurymen to appear in criminal prosecutions (*g*)

§ 1225 Citations of witnesses and havers in the Sheriff-court must be in the statutory form (*h*), which is a good style to follow

---

quire to be observed in cases before Justices of the Peace, M'Cartney *v* Guthrie 1838 2 Swin, 23, Bell's Notes, 223, S C (*r*) Chalmers, 1836, 1 Swin 268, Bell's Notes, 222, S C—Lacy, 1837, 1 Swin 493—2 Al, 321 (*s*) 9 Geo IV, c 29, § 8 But see Gibb and Others, 1828 Bell's Notes, 223, Shaw Just Ca, 201, S C—Fraser, 1835, Bell's Notes, ib—M'Callum 1836, ib—1 Swin 207, S C

(*t*) Arthur and Others, 1829, Bell's Notes, 224—M'Callum, 1836, ib

(*u*) Aughterlony, 1716—2 Hume, 261—2 Al, 340, 1 (*w*) M'Farlane, 1843, 1 Broun, 550—M'Neill, 1844 2 Broun, 149 (*x*) 2 Al, 341, citing Ferguson 1825, and Ronald, 1818, both unreported (*y*) 9 Geo IV, c 29, sch A

(*z*) Same act, § 6—Watson, 1831 Sh Just Ca, 218 (*a*) Rodgers, 1830, Bell's Notes 223 (*b*) M'Callum, 1836 1 Swin, 207 (*c*) Ritchie *v* Palmer 1818, 1 Shaw 112—Welsh *v* Macpherson, 1870, ib 345

(*d*) Ful Le 369 (*f*) 15 Vict, c 27 § 1—9 Geo IV c 29 § 10—1 and 2 Vict, c 119 § 21—7 Will IV and 1 Vict, c 41 § 12 (*g*) 9 Geo IV c 29 § 10 (*h*) 16 and 17 Vict c 80, sch G

---

[2] See also H M Adv *v* M'Kay and Broadley 1861 4 Irv 97

in other cases. There is also a prescribed form for citations in Sheriff Small Debt cases (*i*). In cases not regulated by statute the rule to be observed is, that the person should be named and designed, and should be distinctly informed as to the day, place, and purpose of his compearance.[3]

II. *Of Executions by Messengers and other Officers.*

§ 1226. An execution is the return or report under the hand of a messenger-at-arms or other officer setting forth the *res gestæ* of a service. Upon all matters intrusted to such official care the execution (if formal) is not only admissible, but probative (*k*). In general also it is the only competent proof of the officer's proceeding (*l*). It was held, however, when writing was not a common accomplishment, that the citation of a tenant to his landlord's baron court (*m*), and the service within burgh of a warning of removal by chalking the door (*n*), might be proved by parole. Execution is dispensed with by statute in several cases of minor importance. The service of summonses or complaints under the Justice of Peace Small Debt Act may be proved either by an execution, or by the officer deponing in court that he duly cited the party (*o*). And the citation of witnesses, as well as the executing of the diligences of poinding and imprisonment, under the same statute, may be proved by the officer either verbally or by a written return, as the justices may require (*p*). Citations of parties, witnesses,

(*i*) 7 Will. IV. and 1 Vict. c. 41, sch. A. (*k*) Ersk., 4, 2, 5—Tait Ev., 5—Shand's Pr., 250, 256. (*l*) Tait Ev., 6—Shand's Pr., *supra*—Haswell *v.* Mag. of Jedburgh, 1714, M., 12,270—M'Kean *v.* ———, 1691, M., 3781. (*m*) Hay *v.* Gight, 1634, M., 3782. (*n*) Hart *v.* his Tenants, 1634, M., 3783—See also Dickson *v.* Anderson, 1626, M., 3108. (*o*) 6 Geo. IV., c. 48, § 3. (*p*) Same act, §§ 4, 13.

[3] The act 17 and 18 Vict., c. 34, §§ 1, 2, enacts, that if, in any action depending before the Court of Session in Scotland, it shall appear to the Court before which such action is pending or, if such Court is not sitting, to any Judge of the Court, that it is proper to compel the personal attendance at a trial of a witness who may not be within the jurisdiction of the Court, it shall be lawful for such Court or Judge to order that a warrant of citation shall issue in special form, which shall be as valid and effectual as if issued within the jurisdiction of the Court. It has been held that under the act a Lord Ordinary may issue such warrant of citation during the sitting of the Court as well as during vacation,—the Lord Ordinary, as representative of the Court, exercising the jurisdiction of the Court, Smith *v.* Hall, 1856, 18 D., 1002. A citation, issued the day before a complaint for breach of the peace was presented, and for which the Sheriff had given no warrant, was held bad, Stevenson *v.* Watson, 1857, 2 Irv., 592. The day of compearance must be correctly set forth in the citation, Waddel *v.* Romanes, 1857, 2 Irv., 611.

and havers under the Sheriff Small Debt Act may be proved either by the officer's oath or by his written execution (r) In criminal trials the prosecutor does not require to produce a written execution of the libel, except when he moves for sentence of fugitation or forfeiture of the bail-bond (s) The oath of an officer citing jurors and witnesses is sufficient evidence in support of the citation both in civil and criminal cases (t) And in trials by jury in civil causes the oath of 'some credible person' is sufficient to prove that a juryman failing to appear was duly cited (u) Services or intimations which do not require to be made by a messenger may be proved by a regular execution, by a notarial instrument, or by such a signed attestation as will satisfy the judge upon the fact (x) But where a messenger or officer of Court is required for any service or intimation, the *res gestæ* cannot be proved by a notarial instrument (y)

§ 1227 An execution like a notarial instrument (z), is only admissible on matters which are intrinsic to its purpose as a narrative of the service (a) Accordingly, in actions against a magistrate and sheriff for failure to apprehend a person denounced as rebel, the Court disregarded the messenger's executions bearing respectively that he had pointed out the rebel to the defender, and that the rebel was in the defender's company at the time of the service these facts being extraneous to the narrative of the service (b)

§ 1228. Executions of letters in the Sovereign's name, and of charges, used to be authenticated by a stamp bearing the officer's initials or some other thing universally known to be their signet, cut upon it (c) This mode of authentication was abolished by an act passed in 1686, which ordained that executions should be signed by the officer and witnesses under pain of nullity (d) It is pro-

---

(r) 7 Will IV and 1 Vict, c 41, § 3 (s) 9 Geo IV, c 29, § 7 But if the execution is produced, objections to it cannot be obviated by the officer's oath, Smith, 1836, 1 Swin 27—Soutar, 1828, Sh Just Ca, 209 (t) 11 Geo IV, and 1 Will IV c 37, § 7 (u) 55 Geo III c 42, § 22 (x) M'Millan v Campbell, 1832, 10 S, 220 (y) Haswell v Mag of Jedburgh, 1714, M 12,270

(z) *Supra*, § 1189 (a) Ersk, 4, 2, 5—Tait Ev, 5, 6

(b) Halyburton v Prov of Jedburgh, 1626, M, 11 694, 12 494, S C—Home v L Renton 1631, M, 12 496—See also Smith v Williamson, 1642, M, 12,497

(c) 1540 c 71—Ersk 3 2, 17 (d) 1686, c 4 (The word "citations" is used in this act in place of executions) The sanction of this act was enforced in Mon v Dons, 1711, M, 16,893—Orrok v Peter, 1769, 5 B Sup, 435—Baillie v Doig 1790, M 11 286—Henderson v Thomson, 1828, 7 S 51—Allan v Miller, 1848, 10 D, 1060 In an old case (which would probably not be followed now) an execution of a removing

vided by another act that none but subscribing witnesses shall be probative in executions of 'inhibitions, of interdictions, hornings or arrestments, and that no execution whatsoever to be given hereafter shall be sufficient to infer interruption of prescription in real rights, unless the same be done before witnesses present at the doing thereof subscribing' (e) The subscription of the witness—one being now sufficient in all cases except executions of poindings (f)—is required under the Court of Session Act to executions of summonses, notes of advocation and suspension, and notes of suspension and liberation, or suspension and interdict (g), and under the Sheriff Courts Act to executions of summonses and petitions, and to certificates of notice to remove (h) Executions of criminal libels must also bear this authentication (i) The executions which do not require witnesses have been mentioned already (k)

§ 1229 The witnesses attest the truth of the narrative (l), and do not require to see the messenger sign the execution (m) Of course they must be present when the citation or service takes place (n) In cases where their subscription is required they cannot sign merely by initials (o) When an execution contains more pages than one, it ought to be signed by the messenger and witnesses on each page (p) If, however, it consists only of one sheet, then subscription to the last page will suffice (r), and, if it consists of several sheets the omission to sign some of the pages seems not to be fatal, provided each separate sheet is authenticated, and there is no ground for suspecting interpolation (s)

§ 1230 At one time it was the practice for messengers to return their executions signed blank, the party or his agent filling up the narrative of the service This gross and dangerous irregularity was overlooked on account of the common practice (t) But the Court passed an Act of Sederunt declaring that all executions which should thereafter be signed blank would be held null, and that the executor would be deprived of office, and he and the wit-

signed by a baron-officer with his initials was sustained because persons who could sign their names could not always be got to undertake such an office, Irvine 1739, M, 16,810 (e) 1681, c 5 (f) *Supra*, § 1216 (g) 13 and 14 Vict c 36, sch B (h) 16 and 17 Vict, c 80, schs F and I—1 and 2 Vict, c 119, § 23—A S, 10th July 1839, § 15 (i) 9 Geo IV, c 29, sch B

(k) *Supra* § 1216 (l) A S, 28th June 1701 (m) Ersk, 3, 2, 17—L Gray v Hope, 1710, M, 16,892 (n) 1681, c 5—Campbells v M'Neill, 1799 M 11 120 (o) Meck v Dunlop, 1707, M, 16 806 (p) A S 28th June 1704—Fat Lv, 8—Shand's Pr, 256 (r) See *supra*, § 659—Shand's Pr, *supra* (s) Peter v Ross, 1793 M 16,937—*Supra* § 659—Shand's Pr *supra*

(t) Abernethy v Ogilvy, 1700, M 3781—Sinclair v Sinclair, 1701 M 3785

nesses would be held infamous (*u*). The question was once raised, but not decided, whether this act applies to executions in the Sheriff-court, or only to those returned by messengers-at-arms (*w*). There can be no doubt that any execution signed blank by the officer and witnesses, and filled up by the party, would now be held null (*x*).[4]

§ 1231. Under the Court of Session Act the statutory form for executions of summonses, executions of intimations of notes of suspension, suspension and interdict, suspension and liberation, and of advocation, requires the witness before whom the writ was served to be named and designed (*y*). This is also the case as to executions of summonses and petitions (*z*), and certificates of notice to remove proceeding on a probative lease or tested letter from the tenant under the recent Sheriff Courts Act (*a*). Designing the witness (one being now sufficient) is essential to executions of inhibitions, interdictions, hornings and arrestments, and executions for interrupting prescription in real rights (*b*), and in executions of charges under the Diligence Act (*c*). Under the statutory form for executions of criminal libels it is not necessary for the witness to be named or designed (*d*).

§ 1232. Executions of summonses and petitions used to be on papers separate from the writs to which they applied, and several regulations were made for securing in each execution a description of the writ to which it referred (*e*). A late statute requires that every execution "of a summons, and every execution of intimation of a note of suspension, or of suspension and interdict, or of suspension and liberation," in the Court of Session "shall be written at the end of the summons itself, or at the end of the usual certified copy of the note of suspension, or of suspension and interdict, or of suspension and liberation, or of advocation, and, where necessary, on

---

(*u*) A. S., 28th June 1704. This act was enforced against the messenger and witnesses in Wilson and Philips, 12th July 1740, A. S. (folio ed.)—See also Wright, 19th July 1788, ib.

(*w*) Falconers *v.* Smith, 1777, 5 B. Sup. 435.

(*x*) See *supra*, § 672.

(*y*) 13 and 14 Vict. c. 36, § 20, sch. B. This used not to be required, Ersk. 3, 2, 17—Napier *v.* L. Elphinstone, 1736, M. 16,899.

(*z*) 16 and 17 Vict. c. 80, § 9, sch. F.

(*a*) Same act, § 31, sch. K.

(*b*) 1681, c. 5—See L. Gray *v.* Hope, 1710, M. 3760, 16,892.

(*c*) 1 and 2 Vict. c. 114, sch. No. 2.

(*d*) 9 Geo. IV. c. 29, sch. B. See Walker, 1839, Bell's Notes, 223.

(*e*) 1672, c. 6—A. S., 8th July 1831, sch. 5—Stair, 4, 38, 13—Tait Ev. 9. The rules applicable to the former practice are stated in Shand's Pr. 251 *et seq.*

[4] *Infra*, § 1248, note [10].

continuous sheets, but not on a separate paper" (*f*) The execution must be as nearly as may be in the form prescribed by the statute, which narrates in short terms that the summons or other writ was executed or intimated by the messenger (who must be named) against or to the defenders or respondents by name (but without their designations), and states whether the service was personal or otherwise (*g*)[5] Executions of summonses and petitions under the Sheriff Courts Act are in the same form (*h*), and must be written at the end of the summons or petition, and on continuous sheets if necessary, but not on separate papers (*i*)

§ 1233 In executions of charge under the Diligence Act, the names and designations of the debtor and creditor must be given, whether the execution is appended to the warrant or not (*k*),[6] and the date and nature of the extract-decree or writ on which the charge proceeds must also be stated (*l*) Other executions, if separate from their warrants must so describe them as to identify them (*m*) and although slight errors in the description will be overlooked (*n*), errors which substantially affect the identification will be fatal (*o*)

§ 1234 Executions of criminal libels are separate from the writs to which they apply (*p*) In terms of the statutory form, they must describe the principal libel by mentioning correctly the crime which it charges (*r*), and the number of pages of which it consists (*s*), and if there are more libels than one against the party, each of the executions must specify the libel to which it is

(*f*) 13 and 14 Vict, c 36 § 20 (*g*) Same act, sch B (*h*) 16 and 17 Vict c 80 sch F (*i*) Same act § 9 (*k*) 1 and 2 Vict, c 114 sch 2—A S, 24th Jan 1839 altering A S, 24th Dec 1838, § 2 (*l*) 1 and 2 Vict, c 114 sch 2 (*m*) Mentioning the date of the warrant is not indispensable, Forbes *v* Watson, 1711, M, 3753—Blackwood *v* Milne's Crs 1752, M, 3396

(*n*) M'Lellan *v* Graham 30th June 1841, F C See also Mitchell *v* Hepburn 1830, 8 S, 319—Glen *v* Black, 1841 4 D, 36 (*o*) Watts *v* Barbour, 1828, 6 S, 1048—Burleigh *v* Fearn, 1848, 10 D, 1517—May *v* Malcolm, 1825, 4 S, 76

(*p*) 9 Geo IV, c 29, sch B (*r*) Ib—Meldrum, 1826, Syme, 17 Sh Just Ca, 176, S C—Wright, 1827 Syme, 136—Grant, 1827, ib, 245—Wright *v* Moffat, 1827, Sh Just Ca, 178 The execution does not require to mention the aggravations to the crime charged, Innes, 1826, 2 Hume, 262—Smith 1836, Bell's Notes 227, 1 Swin 27, S C Compare with the cases in this note Moffat or M'Coull, 1820, 2 Hume, 260 note (*s*) 9 Geo IV *supra*—Wright *v* Dick, 1832 2 Al, 310—Robson, 1821, 2 Hume, 262 note

5 *Infra*, § 1243 note 9

6 Under the Small Debt Act the creditor need not be named, Crombie *v* M'Ewan 1861, 23 D 333

applicable (*t*) The execution on a criminal libel must correspond with the citation or notice of compearance in all important particulars, *e.g.* the officer and witness (*u*), and the days of service and compearance (*x*)

§ 1235 Every execution must be conform to its warrant (*y*) It has been held however, that a warrant to serve a summons edictally entitles the messenger to cite the defender personally (*z*), although it was decided otherwise in regard to the execution of an inhibition (*a*)

§ 1236 With regard to the mode in which the different executions must detail the *res gestæ* of the service or citation, reference must be made to books of form It is sufficient for the purpose of this treatise to observe, that the narrative should be full and accurate (*z**), and that a mere general statement that the writ was duly served, or the party lawfully cited, is not sufficient (*a**) As to the decisions upon this head it may be remarked that the leaning of the Court for a considerable time has been to discourage critical objections to the execution of summonses, although considerable strictness is still observed in executions of diligences, and in cases where there are competing creditors The Court are also more rigorous in requiring a narrative of statutory formalities prescribed in different cases, than in regard to those originating in the common law (*b*)

§ 1237 The foregoing rules as to the requisites of executions only apply when the officer has executed his warrant, and not when he has been unable to do so "An execution must mean something done in executing a writ, and unless this writ be executed, there is no execution This is an excuse for not having executed the writ, the writ being still in full force" (*c*) The point arose in an action for reducing a warrant to open doors and lock-fast places,

(*t*) See M'Gregor, 1753, 2 Hume, 261—M'Kinlay, 1819, Sh. Just. Ca., 49

(*u*) 2 Al. 341, citing Ferguson, 1821, and Ronald, 1818, both unreported

(*x*) 2 Hume, 261—2 Al., 340-1

(*y*) Cases in M., 3681, 3694, 3799—Craig *v* Brock, 1841, 4 D. 54

(*z*) Kirkonnell *v* L. Barnbaroch, 1628, M., 3682, 1 B. Sup., 149, S. C.—Cochrane *v* Urquhart, 1705, M. 3686, 4 B. Sup., 611, S. C.—Shand's Pr. 236

(*a*) Erskine *v* Erskine, 1627, M. 3681—Lamb *v* Blackburn, 1628, M., 3683

(*z**) 1540, c. 75—Stair, 3, 3, 2, *et seq.*—Ersk., 2, 5, 55—Tait Ev. 16—Shand's Pr., 252

(*a**) Sanders *v* Jardine, 1681, M., 3791—Cunningham *v* M'Leod, 1682, M., 3792—Scott *v* Grieve, 1694, 4 B. Sup. 231—A *v* B. 1734, Elch. 'Execution,' No. 1—Gillies *v* Murray, 1771, M. 3795—But see M'Intosh *v* M'Kenzie, 1675, M. 3788

(*b*) See Ersk., 2, 5, 55—Shand, 253 *et seq.*

(*c*) Per L. Campbell in Scott *v* Letham, 1846, 5 Bell's Ap. Ca. 126, affirming 6 D., 1221 which had been obtained upon a return under the hand of the officer (not signed by witnesses), stating that he had been unable to execute a poinding, not having got access to the premises on account of lock-fast places

§ 1238 Irregularities in executions, when not in essential particulars have sometimes been overlooked on account of the *communis error* (*d*) But in several cases the Court, while sustaining executions on the first occasion on which such irregularities were brought before them, intimated that they would exact the proper requisites in future cases (*e*) When the irregularity occurred in the narrative of the *res gestæ*, proof that the proper forms of service had been observed was required in several cases before the executions were sustained (*f*)

§ 1239 Executions, like instruments, may be extended *ex intervallo* of the service or citation which they set forth (*g*) And the messenger may return an amended execution in place of one which, from some error would have been inadequate At one time it was held only competent to do so, where the new execution was not inconsistent with the one which had been previously returned (*h*) But of late the Court have repeatedly admitted amended executions which were inconsistent with those returned previously (*i*). And the new execution seems to be admissible, although the erroneous one has been produced in process, provided judgment has not been pronounced finding that it is insufficient (*k*)

(*d*) Gordon *v* Forbes, 1681, M , 3768—Trotter *v* Lundie, 1681, M , 7049 , 12,268—Yeaman *v* Trotter, 1698, M , 3768—Abernethy *v* Ogilvy, 1700, M , 3784—Sinclair *v* Sinclair, 1704, M 3785—Orrok *v* Peter, 1769, 5 B Sup 435—Drummond *v* Kerr, 1824, 3 S , 311—Beattie *v* Park, 1830, 8 S , 784—Compared with Crawford *v* Wood, 1624, M , 3108

(*e*) Gordon *v* Forbes, *supra*—Abernethy *v* Ogilvy, *supra*—A S , 28th June 1704 See also Falconers *v* Smith, 1777, 5 B Sup , 435

(*f*) Drysdale *v* Sornberg, 1621, M , 3765—Somerville *v* ——, 1626, M , 3766—Scott *v* Scott, 1637, M , 12 266—Trotter *v* Lundie 1581, M , 7049 , 12 268 This would not be required if the messenger or witness had died , Somerville *v* ——, *supra*

(*g*) Jack *v* Pearson 1821, 2 S 691—Henderson *v* Richardson, 1848, 10 D , 1035—Cameron *v* M'Ewan, 1830, 8 S , 410—Cases in two following notes

(*h*) Stair, 4, 38 17—A *v* B, 1748, M , 8345—Hog *v* Maclellan, 1797, M , 8316—Shand's Pr 259

(*i*) May *v* Malcolm, 1825 4 S , 76—Cullen's Tr *v* Watson, 1825, ib , 133—Henderson *v* Richardson 1848, 10 D , 1035

(*k*) Beg *v* Rig, 1744, M , 8345—Stewart *v* M'Ra, 1831, 9 S , 261—Creightons *v* Dennis, 1832, 11 S , 30—Henderson *v* Richardson, 1848, 10 D , 1035—Shand's Pr , 259 In Allan *v* Miller, 1848, 10 D , 1060, where a Lord Ordinary had passed, in absence, a note of suspension and liberation, the execution of which was not signed by the witness, the Court refused to receive an amended execution because the note had been passed without legal proof of service Formerly an amended execution was not received

There is some doubt whether an amended execution is admissible in competition of creditors (*l*)

§ 1240 Objections to executions of summonses and petitions, being preliminary defences, must be pleaded and disposed of *in initio litis* (*m*)[7] Under the former practice of the Court of Session they required to be pleaded before lodging defences on the merits, and this is still the rule in actions of reduction, in which the preliminary defences are pleaded separately In other actions, where the dilatory and peremptory defences are pleaded in the same paper, any objection to the execution must, in general, be insisted in before the parties have joined issue on the merits (*n*) But in an action of multiplepoinding, where the arrestee, after having pleaded that he did not owe the arrested sum, raised an objection to the execution of the arrestment, the Court sustained the plea, being of opinion that the due service of the arrestment was essential to the creation of the *nexus*, and that the execution of such a diligence was in an entirely different situation from that of a summons (*o*) Formerly falsehood in the execution could only be pleaded as a peremptory defence, and failure in that plea cut off the defender from his defences on the merits, the object of the rule having been to prevent defenders from raising such objections for the mere purpose of delay (*p*) The modern practice, of requiring all the defences to be stated at once, secures this object with equal effect and more justice Nor is there any modern instance in which the defence of falsehood in the execution has been required to be pleaded peremptorily, even in actions where dilatory defences are admitted before pleading to the merits

---

it the first had been produced in process, Butter, 1769, noted in Shand 259—Haddington Election, 1741 Elch, "Burgh Royal," No 14

(*l*) See Henderson *v* Richardson, *supra*—Opinions in May *v* Malcolm, *supra*—Hog *v* Maclellan, 1797, M 8346—Cullen's Tr *v* Watson 1824 4 S, 133—Shand's Pr 260 (*m*) Jamieson *v* Hay, 1674 M, 12,053—Wick Election 1773 5 B Sup, 457—Lamond *v* Reid, 1821, 1 S 232—Rankine *v* Corson, 1825, 4 S 127—Hamilton *v* Murray 1830, 9 S, 143—Atherton *v* Moffat, 1843, 1 Brown, 524—Shand's Pr, 258—*Contra*, M Lauchlans *v* M Dougal 1744, M, 6783 See Allan *v* Miller, 1848, 10 D, 1060, *supra* (*n*) Stat on act 1693, c 20, Appx § 6 (4)

(*o*) Stewart *v* Brown 1824 3 S, 56 The objection was to the schedule of arrestment, and to the execution in setting forth that the arrestment had been duly laid on With this case compare Zinzean *v* Kinloch 1667, M, 2721 (*p*) Wick Election 1773 5 B Sup, 457—Hamilton *v* Hunter, 1743, M, 6772—Bankt 1, 10, 217—Ibid, 4 25 3—Shand's Pr, 318

---

7 Hamilton *v* Monkland Iron and Steel Co 1863 1 Macph, 676

§ 1241 Where the objection that the execution of a summons is awanting is not taken until after a considerable interval (as where the action had fallen asleep before defences were lodged) the Court will presume that *omnia rite et solenniter actum*, and that a regular execution was either lodged in Court or was in the pursuer's hands for production, if necessary (*r*) But it was held that merely calling a summons did not, after a short interval, infer that an execution had been lodged with the clerk of Court along with it as there was no general practice to lodge the execution at that stage (*s*)

§ 1242 A party may be barred by personal exception from objecting to an execution as where he has agreed to hold the summons as executed (*t*), or where he has by writing acknowledged receipt of the service copy (*u*) [8]

§ 1243 An execution which is regular *ex facie* is probative of the facts which it sets forth, and, in general it cannot be challenged by exception (*x*). And if the execution narrates the service or citation in proper form, the objection that the schedule or the service copy of the libel was irregular cannot in general be pleaded without an action of reduction (*y*) On the other hand, any patent

(*r*) Walker v E Eglinton's Tutors, 1827, 5 S 240 (*s*) Cameron v M'Ewan, 1830 8 S, 410, 412, note—Per L Just-Clerk in Henderson v Richardson, 1848, 10 D, 1035, 8 (*t*) Shand's Pr, 261—Wilson v Pattie, 1826, 4 S, 623

(*u*) Fraser v Barnetson, 1826, 4 S 773 A party was held not to be barred from objecting to the service of the notice of an appeal to the Circuit Court of Justiciary, in consequence of having verbally admitted that he received the notice, M'Millan v Campbell, 1832, 10 S, 220 (*x*) Ersk, 4, 2, 5—Tait Ev, 4—Shand's Prac, 257—Logan v Carlile, 1583, M, 2712—Commendator of Kilwinning v L Blair, 1590, M ib—L Wintoun, 1621, M, 2713—E Galloway v Gordon, 1629, M, 2714—Montgomery v Montgomery, 1662, M, 2715—Ruthven v E Callender 1680, M, 12,502—Dun v Craig, 1824, 2 S 797 (*y*) Shand's Prac, 257—M'Donald v M'Leod, 1726, M, 3765—Calder v Calder, 1825, 4 S, 331—Ramsay v Pettigrew, 1828, 7 S, 193—Morrison v Forbes, 1826, 4 S, 668—Alison v Alison, 1829, 7 S 335—M'Queen v Clyne's Trs, 1834 12 S, 610—*Contra*, M'Laren v Finlay, 1835 14 S 143—Dunlop

[8] A company carried on business in the counties of Edinburgh and Haddington The company was dissolved, but one of the partners continued to carry on business in the county of Haddington under the same company name without giving notice of the dissolution of the partnership An action brought in the Sheriff court of Haddington, was served on the company at the place of business in that county The defender pleaded that the citation was inept, and that the Sheriff had no jurisdiction, as the firm was a fictitious one, and he was the sole partner, and domiciled in Edinburgh The Court held that he was barred from stating such a plea *personali exceptione*, whatever might have been its effect in a question with creditors or under his bankruptcy. Young v Livingstone 1860 22 D 9[illegible]

objection to an execution may be pleaded by exception, and this seems to be the case where it is apparent from the execution itself that the messenger had an interest which disqualified him from acting (z) Reduction seems also to be unnecessary where the objection is that the execution is not conform to its warrant (a) [9]

v Nicolson, 1827, 5 S, 915 ("a special case", per L President (Hope) in M'Queen v Cl. nes Trs, *supra*) In Fraser v Fraser 1825 3 S 590, where the execution of a charge differed from the service copy, the Court turned the charge into a libel See also Clarkson v Bell 1831 10 S, 17—Connel v Faulie 1824 2 S, 664

(z) Dalgliesh v Scott, 1822 1 S, 506 But the objection that the subscriber is not a messenger requires to be pleaded by reduction, Ersk 4 2 6—Mackenzie v Smith, 1829, 2 De and And 132 (a) L Kirkonnel v L Barnbarroch, 1628, M, 3682—Lamb v Blackburn, 1828 M, 3683

[9] In Stewart v Macdonald, 1860 22 D 1514, it was held by a majority of the whole Court that the provisions of the 20th section of the statute 13 and 14 Vict, c 36, as to the execution of summonses, and the direction contained in the relative schedule, "state whether personally or otherwise," made no alteration in the formalities appropriate to the various modes of executing summonses in use before the passing of the act The execution appended to the summons bore that it had been executed against 'Donald Macdonald, the defender, personally," but did not set forth that a copy had been delivered The majority were of opinion that, anterior to the statute, it had been settled, from time immemorial, that a messenger's execution, whether of a summons or other judicial writ required, in order to be valid, to set forth not merely the fact of service, but the mode in which the service took place It was considered necessary that the messenger should specify the solemnities actually used by him, for a reason which approves itself to sound policy—to wit that thereby the Court might be enabled to determine whether good service had been made Such specification was all the more necessary in consequence of the faith given to messengers executions until set aside by formal improbation Their claim to such faith lay in the particularity of detail, and it would not have been reasonably accorded to a mere general statement that everything had been lawfully gone about If the detail disclosed a defect the execution was liable to be set aside *ope exceptionis* If ostensibly all was right, the party complaining was not without his remedy, but he could make it effectual by a formal process of improbation In such a process it was essential to fairness of litigation that the execution should specify details in order that, if false, it might be redargued, by specific proof, to the contrary' They held, therefore, that the principle of specification, being a vital one in the law of Scotland could not be extinguished by a parenthesis in a schedule, and that the execution was bad The statute did not abrogate or affect the solemnities to be used, nor did it abrogate the most valuable part of the execution, which afforded the information which was indispensable to enable the Court to see whether the execution had been made so as to be unchallengeable *ope exceptionis*, it only shortened those parts of the forms of execution which, under the old law, were unnecessarily tedious, and adapted them to the change which the statute introduced, viz, the writing of the execution on the summons itself The minority held that, under the statute, it was enough to state that the summons had been executed personally, or otherwise, as the case might be, 'which implied that the messenger had adopted the formalities appropriate to the kind of execution mentioned by him, but left the execution open to challenge on the ground of falsehood as for-

§ 1244 In competitions of creditors, objections which cannot usually be pleaded except by reduction may be pleaded by way of exception (*b*)

§ 1245 When the ground of challenge of an execution infers fraud or falsehood in the messenger or witnesses, reduction-improbation seems to be necessary (*c*), whereas such blunders or irregularities as do not infer falsehood may be pleaded by simple reduction (*d*)

§ 1246 In inferior courts, where actions of reduction are incompetent, objections to executions of summonses or petitions may be pleaded by way of exception if they are of a patent character If not, they may, in the Sheriff-court, be pleaded by articles improbatory and approbatory, on which a record is made up as in actions of reduction-improbation (*e*) It is a preliminary to this procedure that the party challenging the execution shall consign a sum not exceeding £5 or under 10s, to be forfeited to the other party in case of the objection being repelled (*f*)

§ 1247. Executions of criminal libels may be challenged by exception on any relevant ground, there being no procedure in any criminal court corresponding to actions of reduction, or articles improbatory and approbatory (*g*) If the prisoner is absent, the ob-

---

(*b*) More's Notes, 378—Shand's Prac, 258, 597—Stewart *v* Brown, 1824, 3 S, 56—Holmes *v* Reid 1829, 7 S, 535, per L Mackenzie (*c*) M'Vittie *v* Barbour, 1838, 16 S, 1184—Balfour *v* Robertson 1839, 1 D 458—Shand's Prac, 258

(*d*) M'Lellan *v* Graham, 30th June 1841, F C—Shand, *supra* (*e*) A S, 10th July 1839 § 91 A recent writer on the practice of Sheriff-courts considers that this proceeding is only competent where the execution is fabricated, and that latent objections to genuine executions in the Sheriff-court cannot be pleaded except by reduction in the Court of Session, M'Glashan (Barclay's ed), 189 This view is supported by Macdonald *v* Sinclair 1843 5 D, 1253, notes to Lord Ordinary's interlocutor It is understood that the practice in Sheriff-courts upon the point is not uniform

(*f*) A S, 10th July 1831, § 91 (*g*) 2 Hume, 247—2 Al, 341, and Proudfoot, April 1823, there cited

---

merly, if he had not actually done so" The opinion of the majority, however, appears to be consistent with sound principle, for, were it true that the statute rendered specification unnecessary, one or other of two important alterations in practice would seem to follow—either (1) that the cases in which an execution could be challenged *ope exceptionis* on the plea that the solemnities had not in point of fact, been observed (a plea which could not previously have been stated *ope exceptionis* in face of the statement in the execution), would be indefinitely increased, or (2) that challenge of an execution *ope exceptionis* would be altogether excluded seeing that no patent objection could be stated to an execution which did not specify the formalities—thus leaving the defender in every such case only the cumbrous remedy of reduction

jection may be stated by his counsel, in order to prevent him from being fugitated (h) But the cautioner in his bail-bond may not plead the objection, unless the prosecutor moves for forfeiture of the bond (i)

§ 1248 The messenger and subscribing witnesses are admissible to prove that an execution under their hands is false, but their evidence ought to be weighed scrupulously (k) It seems not to be indispensable for the party challenging to examine these persons Indeed, his case may be that they concocted a false return, and are in a conspiracy against him (l) [10]

(h) Grant, 1827 Syme, 245—Anderson, 1834, Bell's Notes, 229—Lacy, 1837 1 Swin, 493—Ross, 1837, ib, note (i) Smith, 1836, 1 Swin, 301—Laird, 1838, 2 Swin, 178 (k) Aitchison v Patrick 1836 15 S, 360—Kay v Rodger, 1832, 10 S, 831—See *supra*, § 908, *et seq* (l) Kay v Rodger ib —*Supra* § 931, *et seq*

---

[10] Several cases on the subjects treated of in this chapter have been lately decided In service of note of suspension and interdict under 1 and 2 Vict c 86, § 6, a copy of the interlocutor ordering service must be served with note, Anderson v Drysdale, 1862, 1 Macph, 46 The citation need not be written on service copy of summons This was held in a case where the citation was attached to the summons by wafers, and the messenger's name was written across the junction between the two documents, Hamilton v Monkland Iron and Steel Co, 1863, 1 Macph, 676 A sheriff-officer who falsely adhibits the name of another person as a witness to a citation commits forgery, but if he gets a person to sign as a witness a blank sheet of paper, and thereafter writes an execution of citation above the signature, he may be indicted for a *crimen falsi*, but not for forgery, H M Adv v Fraser, 3 Irv, 467

TITLE III

OF EXTRACTS FROM OFFICIAL RECORDS, AND OF OFFICIAL COPIES OF DOCUMENTS.

§ 1249 In order to prevent the originals of public records from being lost or injured, as well to secure ready access to them by all the lieges, they usually remain in the custody of their respective keepers, and their terms may in most cases be proved by extracts or office copies Authenticated copies of documents may also be obtained by judicial procedure in cases where one party is entitled to the custody of writings in which others are interested, and where an original document has been lost or destroyed, it may be supplied by means of a decree of proving the tenor, extracted in common form

The admissibility of all these extracts and copies arises from their having the same characteristic—namely, being prepared under official care, and authenticated by the proper officer Their admissibility is an exception, for obviously good reasons, from the rule which rejects copies and excerpts on the ground that they are secondary evidence

CHAPTER I —EXTRACTS AND EXCERPTS FROM JUDICIAL RECORDS

§ 1250 The original processes, with the interlocutors and decrees in the courts in this country are preserved in the archives of the respective courts Their terms may be proved by extracts or excerpts duly certified by the proper officer, which are admissible without their being proved to be correct, and without the signature of the officer authenticating them requiring to be proved (*a*) This rule is in daily observance in criminal courts, where extracts by the respective clerks of court are received as full proof of previous convictions, *res judicata* and the like, without any evidence beyond what is required for identifying the prisoner as the person to whom they refer In civil cases, also, the extract-decree is the warrant for diligence by which the judgment may be enforced, and in proceedings relating to heritable property, *e g*, services, adjudications, and reductions and declarators regarding that kind of property, the extract-decree often forms an important link in a progress of titles

§ 1251 In most of the civil courts in Scotland the extract-decrees used to set forth the whole proceedings in the cause, a practice which occasioned many technical objections, as well as much useless expense and delay (*b*) The evil, although pointed out by Lord Stair (*c*), continued till the act 50 Geo III introduced the system of short extracts, which contain only the decerniture referring by date or description to the documents (if any) on which the action is laid (*d*) Under the powers conferred by a subsequent statute, the Court of Session framed similar styles for extracts of decrees in Sheriff-courts (*e*) In criminal cases the extracts have been confined within proper limits They set forth merely the prisoner's name and designation, the crime charged, the verdict (or if the case was not decided by jury, the finding of the magistrate or sheriff) and the sentence or absolvitor

§ 1252 By an Act of Sederunt, passed in 1829, it was ordained that extracts of decrees in the Court of Session, and other civil courts in Scotland, should bear 'a docquet in the handwriting of the officer by whom the extract is signed, stating by whom it is

---

(*a*) See *infra* § 1257 (*b*) See L Dirleton *v* L Eastnisbet, 1623 M, 12,180 —Pitcairn, 1671, M, 12,181—Lawrie *v* Gibson, 1671, M 12,532 (*c*) Stair, 4, 46, 27 (*d*) 50 Geo III, c 112, sch A and B The directions in this statute were not strictly observed until the office of extractor in the Court of Session was placed upon its present footing by 1 and 2 Vict, c 118 § 18 The short forms introduced by 50 Geo III, may be used for decrees obtained before the act, A S, 26th Feb 1831

(*e*) 6 Geo IV, c 23, § 2—A S, 27th Jan 1830, sch C A similar power was conferred on the Judge-Admiral for abridging extracts in the Admiralty Court by 1 and 2 Geo IV c 39, § 7, and a committee of Sheriffs were empowered to prepare forms for abridging extracts in Commissary Courts by 4 Geo IV, c 97, §§ 2, 17 These are no longer separate courts 11 Geo IV, and 1 Will IV, c 69, §§ 21 29 *et seq* written, by whom it has been collated, and at what date it was completed by the signature of the extractor, and in all cases where such docquet has not been duly made, the extracts shall be held as improbative' (*f*) A subsequent act of Parliament provided, that in all extracts (including extracts of fictitious decrees on registered deeds and on instruments of protest on bills) there should be inserted a warrant for execution of the decree, in terms of the schedule appended to the act (*g*), which also provided that the extracts should be "subscribed and prepared in other respects, as extracts are at present subscribed and prepared" (*h*) Another statute (*i*), passed on the same day, conferred full powers on the Court of Session for regulating their own forms of procedure, and the extractor of decrees in that Court was placed under the superintendence and direction of the junior Principal Clerk of Session, acting under the directions of the Court (*k*) Their Lordships considered that the forms introduced by the first of these acts superseded the provisions of the Act of Sederunt of 1829 in regard to extracts of all their decrees, and not merely of such as could be followed by diligence, and accordingly, their Lordships enacted that, instead of affixing a docquet, the extractor should specify, in writing on the last page of the extract the date on which the same was completed by his subscription (*l*) The Act of Sederunt of 1829, however, has not been expressly repealed as to extracts of decrees in inferior courts, in which a warrant for execution is not inserted in terms of the Diligence Act (*m*) But in the forms for extracts in the Sheriff-court prescribed by the Act of Sederunt of 27th January 1830, the docquet required by the Act of Sederunt of 1829 is omitted, and the extract concludes with a docquet in this form, 'Extracted by me, sheriff-clerk (or sheriff-clerk depute) of the county of '

§ 1253 Extract of decrees of the Court of Session must bear at the commencement the date of the decree (*n*), and at the termination the date on which the extract is signed (*o*) They ought also to specify the place where they are subscribed, but the want of this requisite was held not to vitiate an extract which commenced

(*f*) A S, 6th March 1829 This act was held not to apply to decrees for expenses in the Bill Chamber, Ross *v* Webster, 1837, 15 S, 1238 (*g*) 1 and 2 Vict c 114, §§ 1, 9, sch 1, 6 (*h*) Same act, §§ 1 9 (*i*) 1 and 2 Vict, c 118, §§ 18, 33 (*k*) 1 and 2 Vict, c 118, § 18 (*l*) A S, 24th Dec 1838 (as to form of extracts), § 6 (*m*) See M'Glashan (Barclay's ed), 359, 360

(*n*) Where a decree, dated 8th July, bore to be signed upon the 11th of that month the Court held that the extract was correct in setting forth the latter as the date of the decree, Cleland *v* Clark, *infra* (*o*) 1 and 2 Vict, c 114, sch No 1

in the usual terms, "At Edinburgh," and concluded, "Extracted upon this and the preceding page by me, principal extractor in the Court of Session, (signed) J Parker, November 4, 1848," the Court considering that, as it was held known that the extractor's office was in Edinburgh, the regulation had been practically observed (*p*) It has been held not indispensable that extracts of decrees in the Sheriff-court should specify the date and place of the extractor's subscription (*r*)

§ 1254 Every extract ought to specify the number of pages of which it consists (*s*) And this is thought to be indispensable, whenever the extract is written on more than one sheet (*t*) If there are deletions or marginal additions, they ought to be enumerated at the end of the extract in the same way as in the testing clause of a deed (*u*) And the extractor's signature must be adhibited, not only at the end of the extract, but at least once on each sheet, where there are more than one (*x*) Each page ought to be authenticated in this way (*y*) In a prosecution for breach of the peace, and intrusion at a communion service in a parish church an extract of a finding by the kirk-session suspending the prisoner from church privileges was rejected, because it was written on five pages and signed only on the last page (*z*)

§ 1255 Extracts are appropriate to final decrees, and to interlocutory judgments on which interim execution may pass Extracts of commissions and diligences also used to be required, as the warrants for citing witnesses and havers But by a recent act, a copy, certified by the clerk or assistant-clerk, of any interlocutor in the Court of Session granting a commission and diligence, or either of them, has the same effect as an extract under the former practice (*a*), and a copy, so certified, of the interlocutor fixing a trial is a sufficient warrant to any messenger-at-arms to cite witnesses and havers to the trial for either party (*b*) In the Sheriff-courts a copy of an interlocutor fixing a diet of proof, or of the portion of such interlocutor which relates to that matter, if certified by the sheriff-clerk is a sufficient warrant to cite witnesses and havers (*c*)

The Sequestration Act ordains that a copy of the act and warrant in favour of the trustee or interim factor certified by one of the

(*p*) Cleland *v* Clark, 1849, 11 D, 602 (*r*) Wilson *v* Wilson, 1848, 11 D 160 (*s*) Tait Ev, 191 (*t*) See *supra*, § 704 (*u*) *Supra*, § 724
(*x*) Fraser 1839, 2 Swin, 436—*Supra* § 659 (*y*) Tait Ev *supra*
(*z*) Fraser *supra* (*a*) 13 and 14 Vict c 36, § 25 (*b*) Same act § 43 (*c*) 16 and 17 Vict, c 80 § 11 The interlocutor may be enforced in another county, the certified copy being indorsed by the sheriff-clerk there, ib

clerks in the Bill-Chamber, and authenticated by the seal of the Court of Session, shall be received in all courts and places in Her Majesty's dominions, as evidence of the factor's title to sue for and recover debts due to the bankrupt (*d*).[1]

Copies of all or any parts of any proceedings in the Court of Session, if certified by a principal or assistant clerk of session, are admissible in evidence (*e*). And copies similarly certified of the printed papers given in to the Court of Session, and of any interlocutors or minutes in any cause in that Court, are admissible as evidence in appeals in the House of Lords, in the same manner as extracts of the whole proceedings used to be received (*f*).

Any person interested in proceedings in any Sheriff-court "may

---

(*d*) 2 and 3 Vict., c. 41, § 49. (*e*) 50 Geo. III, c. 112, § 14—1 and 2 Geo. IV, c. 38, § 24—Anderson, 1827, 5 S., 543—Monro, 1828, 7 S., 52—Meiklehem, 1839, 2 D., 165. (*f*) 50 Geo. III, c. 112, § 11—1 and 2 Geo. IV, *supra*.

---

[1] By section 83 of the 19th and 20th Vict., c. 89, it is enacted that a copy of the act and warrant in favour of the trustee, "purporting to be certified by the sheriff-clerk, and to be authenticated by one of the Judges of the Court of Session, shall be received in all courts and places within England, Ireland, and Her Majesty's other dominions as *prima facie* evidence of the title of the trustee, without proof of the authenticity of the signature or of the official character of the persons signing, and shall entitle the trustee to recover any property belonging, or debt due, to the bankrupt, and to maintain actions in the same way as the bankrupt might have done if his estate had not been sequestrated." Section 174 provides that "all deliverances under this act, purporting to be signed by the Lord Ordinary, or by any of the Judges of the Court of Session, or by the Sheriff, as well as all extracts or copies thereof, or from the books of the Court of Session or the Sheriff-court, purporting to be signed or certified by any clerk of court, or extracts from, or copies of, registers purporting to be made by the keeper thereof or extractor, shall be judicially noticed by all Courts and Judges in England, Ireland, and Her Majesty's other dominions, and shall be received as *prima facie* evidence, without the necessity of proving their authenticity or correctness, or the signatures appended, or the official character of the persons signing, and shall be sufficient warrants for all diligence and execution by law competent." The English "Bankruptcy Act, 1861," 24 and 25 Vict., c. 134, § 218, makes it lawful for the assignee, trustee, or other representatives of the creditors of any person who has been duly adjudged or declared bankrupt or insolvent in India, or any English possession or colony, and who is resident in or possessed of property in Scotland, to apply for and obtain an adjudication of bankruptcy, sequestration, or insolvency, in the proper Court in Scotland, and that on such application, it shall not be necessary to give proof of any act of bankruptcy or petitioning creditor's debt, or to produce any other evidence than a duly certified copy under the seal of the court of the order of adjudication by which such person was found or adjudged bankrupt or insolvent. The Confirmation of Executors Act, 21 and 22 Vict., c. 56, which (by § 12) gives effect in England to confirmation in Scotland, provides (§ 9) that the interlocutor of the Commissary, finding that the deceased died domiciled in Scotland, shall be conclusive evidence of that fact, but (§ 17) shall be evidence, and have effect for the purposes of this act only.

demand a full extract, or an authenticated copy by the clerk, of all or any part of the proceedings" (*g*)

Whenever letters of tutory or curatory are issued by the Director of Chancery, a certified copy of them, transmitted to one of the principal clerks of the Court of Session in terms of the Pupils Protection Act of 1839, is held to establish a summary process in regard to the estate to which such letters relate before the division of the Court to which the clerk belongs, to the same effect as if the tutor or curator to whom such letters are issued had been appointed judicial factor by the Court on a petition in ordinary form (*h*)

§ 1256 The probative character of extracts and excerpts from judicial records (as of all other official writings) depends on their being prepared in the proper form, under official responsibility and care (*i*) Accordingly as it is not the province of the judge to authenticate extracts of his own decrees, an extract of a decree by a commissary judge signed by him in absence of the clerk of court, was held to be null (*j*) And copies of proceedings before a magistrate, being certified by him, were held to be inadmissible (*k*) Copies of decrees or sentences, if not made by the extractor or clerk of court, are inadmissible, even where evidence on oath as to their accuracy is tendered (*l*) A certificate by one of the keepers of the records, that in a record of old extent made up in 1613 certain lands were marked as of a certain valuation, was held not sufficient to instruct the retour, the proper evidence being a formal extract (*m*) [2]

On the same principle extracts of the proceedings of courts of dissenting churches are inadmissible, because law does not recognise the official character either of the courts or of their clerks (*n*)

§ 1257 The extract, if regular *ex facie*, is admissible, without proof either that it is accurate or that it bears the signature of

(*g*) A S, 27th Jan 1830 § 4 (*h*) 12 and 13 Vict, c 51, § 28 The act does not specify under whose hand the certificate must be (*i*) See *supra* §§ 1134, 1164, 5 (*j*) M'Douall *v* Prior of Ardchattan, 1623 M 12,180

(*k*) Carmichael *v* Melville 1825 Sh Just Ca, 137 (*l*) Burnett, 483 Clark *v* Thomson 1816, 1 Mur 163—Carmichael *v* Melville, *supra*

(*m*) Gordon *v* ——— 1767 (affd on appeal), M, 8592—See *infra*, § 1267

(*n*) Mathers *v* Laurie, 1849, 12 D, 433

[2] The evidence of a short hand writer as to what took place in Court on the occasion of an issue being directed by the Court of Chancery was refused by Baron Bramwell, Green *v* Alston 1857, 1 F and F 12

the proper officer, these facts being presumed (*n*) And an extract bearing to be signed by a depute-clerk of court is probative, without proof of the deputation (*o*) Such an officer is the proper person to extract decrees in which his principal is interested (*p*)

§ 1258. But an extract may be challenged on specific grounds which impugn its accuracy or regularity as a copy of the record Thus it is fatal to an extract, and any diligence following on it, that it is disconform to its warrant (*r*), or that the decree is set forth as of a wrong date (*s*) Under the former practice, however, when the interlocutors in civil courts were written on separate papers, or on the different steps of process extracts challenged after an interval of several years from their relative decrees, on the ground that they contained findings or other matter for which there was not a subsisting warrant under the hand of the judge, were repeatedly sustained, because the interlocutors in question might have fallen aside (*t*) This rule is not applicable to the modern system of engrossing the interlocutors and decrees of Court in one paper, which is preserved in the office of the clerk of court

§ 1259 It is also competent to inquire whether an extract has been issued prematurely (*u*) But the Court will presume that such an irregularity has not occurred (*x*), and will probably not entertain the objection, if a number of years have elapsed since the date of the decree (*y*)

(*n*) Stair 4 42, 10—Ersk, 4, 2, 6—Burnett 482—Tait Ev, 189—2 Al 596

(*o*) Ockland *v* Clark, 1849 11 D 602—Hanna *v* Neilson, 1849, ib, 941—Macdonall *v* Prior of Ardchattan, *supra* In the first of these cases it was held that a certificate of registration bearing the signature of a person in the office of the register of hornings who, the party was entitled to assume, held a proper deputation, was valid, although he had not a written appointment (*p*) Williamson *v* Threipland, 1682, M 12,548 (*r*) Stair, 4 1, 45—Ib, 4, 42 10—Ersk, 4, 2, 6—Burnett, 483—Adjudgers of Fairhill *v* Cunningham, 1736, M, 12 185—Swan *v* Allan 1829, 7 S, 775—Dingwall *v* Gardiner, 1825, 4 S 216 A trifling error in this respect was disregarded in Adamson *v* Porteous, 1833, 12 S, 124 The rule in the text was applied to an extract from the records of a presbytery, Philip *v* Heritors of Cruden, 1724, M, 12 539 (*s*) Belshes *v* Elphingston 1737 Elch, "Writ," No 5

(*t*) Alexander *v* Oswald, 1810, 3 D, 40—Wischeart *v* Hume, 1679 2 B Sup, 250—Hume *v* Renton, 1679, ib, 252—Ersk, 4, 2, 6 The Court used to sustain extracts without production of their warrants, when twenty years had elapsed since the decrees, Brown's Synop title "Grounds and Warrants"—Mor, ib (*u*) Grindlay *v* Saunders, 1829, 7 S, 193 and 8 ib 612—M'Lachlan *v* Campbell, 1846, 8 D, 571—Badger *v* L Blantyre, 1811, 17 Sc Jur, 63—*Contra* Maxwell *v* Maxwell, 1675 M 12,322 (*x*) Grindlay *v* Saunders, *supra*—Badger *v* L Blantyre, *supra*

(*y*) Martin *v* Crawfurd, 1685, 2 B Sup 69

§ 1260. When extracts of decrees in the Court of Session are disconform to their warrants, they may be recalled by the Court (*z*) or corrected under their direction (*a*), and a Lord Ordinary may by an order upon the extractor direct an extract of a decree pronounced by himself to be corrected *de recenti* (*b*) Lord Stair (*c*) considers an action of reduction to be necessary in order to allow the Court to correct an extract of one of their own decrees, when it is challenged *ex intervallo* But in one case, an error in an extract was corrected *ex parte* on a petition, although the decree had been dated two years before, and the extract had been issued immediately thereafter (*d*) Where an extract of an inferior court was challenged shortly after its date on the ground that it had been issued prematurely, the Court held that the fact might be investigated in a suspension without a reduction of the extract requiring to be raised (*e*)

§ 1261. Notwithstanding the rule that only formal extracts are admissible, an irregular extract of a conviction was received as evidence for the officers of police, when defending an action of damages for having wrongfully apprehended and detained the pursuer as an accused person, because the document might have justly influenced the defenders in their treatment of the pursuer, and it was relevant to prove their defence of probable cause (*f*)

§ 1262 When judicial proceedings are required not merely as evidence, but for the purpose of review in a higher court, the original record must be transmitted, because it becomes part of the record in the process of review (*g*) An exception occurs in appeals to the House of Lords in which, as already mentioned, certified copies of the proceedings in the Court of Session are admitted (*h*)

CHAPTER II —EXTRACTS FROM REGISTERS OF PRIVATE WRITINGS

§ 1263 Extracts of deeds recorded in the books of a court con-

---

(*z*) Stair, 4 1, 45—M Vicar *v* M'Callum 1765, 5 B Sup, 426—Kirk-session of Borrowstounness, 1764, ib, 425—E Kinnoul *v* Hunter, 1804 M, 12 191, Hume D, 14 S C (*a*) Brown petitioner 1840 2 D 1467 (*b*) Miller *v* Lindsay, 1850, 12 D 964 (*c*) Stair, 4 1 45 (*d*) Brown, petitioner *supra*

(*e*) Grindlay *v* Saunders 1829 7 S 493 (*f*) Nimmo *v* Stewart, 1832 10 S, 844 (*g*) This is done on warrant from the court of review which, in certain cases is signed by the clerk (*h*) See *supra*, § 1255

respond to extracts of decrees, the registration taking place under a fictitious decree, of which an extract is issued, as in the case of decrees *causa cognita* (*a*) These extracts are admissible in evidence, and are probative of the terms of the original deeds (*b*), except when the latter are challenged as false by reduction-improbation (*c*) The Lord Chief-Commissioner once held that an extract was inadmissible, because the original was in court (*d*) But there does not seem to be any sufficient ground for this distinction, which would probably not have occurred to the learned judge if he had been familiar with the practice of the Scotch courts on the subject

§ 1264 At common law the probative quality seems to attach only to extracts of deeds, the originals of which are retained in the record, because where the original is returned to the party he ought to produce it, under the rule which requires the best evidence (*e*) By statute, however extracts are admissible from several registers in which the original writings are not preserved Extracts from the register of probative writs "make entire faith in all cases, in the same manner as if the said writs had been registered by virtue of a clause of registration, except in the case of improbation" (*f*) Extracts from the register of inhibitions and interdictions are probative, unless the party against whom they are used offer to improve them "by way of action or exception" (*g*) Extracts from the register of reversions regressions, instruments of sasine, &c, "make faith in all cases, except where the writs so registered are offered to be improven" (*h*) There is not a similar provision in the act requiring instruments of resignation *ad remanentiam* to be recorded But as the act ordains the registration to be made "in the same manner and way, and at the same rates as renunciations, sasines, or reversions" (*i*), it may be fairly inferred that extracts from the register would be admitted (*k*)[1] The register of summonses and in-

(*a*) See *supra*, § 1090, *et seq* (*b*) Ersk 4 1, 53—Bell's Pr § 2217—Bell's Law Dic, *voce* Evidence (Sections on Acts of Court), &c—Tait Ev 192—Alisons, 1829, 7 S, 552 (*c*) Ersk, *supra*—Bell's Dic, *supra*—Tait, *supra* As to production of an extract in order to prevent decree of certification in actions of reduction-improbation see *infra*, § 1274, *et seq* (*d*) Stothart *v* Johnston's Trs, 1821, 2 Mur 539

(*e*) Tait Ev, 192 (*f*) 1698, c 4 (*g*) 1581, c 119 (1) The extract is probative in a reduction *ex capite inhibitionis*, unless improbation is proponed

(*h*) 1617, c 16 There is a similar provision as to extracts of the same writs when recorded in burgh registers, 1681, c 11 Extracts of a sasine and its warrant (an heritable bond of corroboration) were held a sufficient title in an action of poinding the ground, unless improbation were alleged, Wallace *v* E Dundonald, 1693, M, 12,518, 1 B Sup, 12, S C (*i*) 1669, c 3 (*k*) Tait Ev, 193

[1] 21 and 22 Vict, c 76, § 19 22 and 23 Vict, c 113, § 13

struments of interruption of prescription in real rights stands in a similar position, the registration requiring to "be made in the same manner, and with the same formalities in all points, as are ordained by former acts in the case of registration of sasines and inhibitions, but without providing that extracts from the register should be received in evidence" (*l*)

§ 1265 Where letters of horning and their executions have been recorded "the copy thereof authentically extracted forth of the Sheriff-books, subscribed by the said Sheriff and clerk, shall be esteemed as authentic, and shall have effect and force in whatsoever judgment they happen to be produced" (*m*), there being no exception as to improbations The same act directs relaxations from denunciation and their executions to be registered, but does not provide for extracts of them being probative Under this act, an extract of registered letters of horning and caption has been held to exclude the sexennial prescription (*n*) But where letters of horning, containing also a warrant to arrest, had been recorded, an extract was held not to be a sufficient warrant for arrestment, and accordingly, an arrestment used upon it was not sustained in competition with the subsequent diligence of another creditor, although the principal letters had been lost (*o*) The reason probably was, that as the statute does not authorise registration of the warrant to arrest, an extract from the register could not be effectual in place of the original warrant remaining in the party's hands

§ 1266 The effect of extracts from the records of Chancery depends on the natures of the respective documents recorded Since the year 1809, the sealing of charters and other writs passing the Great Seal has been entered in the Register of the Great Seal, and extracts of writs so registered have been made probative, except in improbations (*p*) But previous to that time, charters from the Crown and Prince were registered before being sealed, and, therefore, extracts of them were not probative, as they did not prove that the principal deeds had been completed (*r*) Extracts

(*l*) 1696, c 19—Tait Ev, 194 (*m*) 1579, c 75—Stair, 3, 3, 23—Baillie *v* Dunbar, 1686 M, 6703 (*n*) Walker *v* Easton, 1831 9 S, 759

(*o*) Duff *v* Boyd 1629 M, 12,547—Stair, 3, 1, 36 (*p*) 49 Geo III c 42, §§ 15, 16 See *supra*, § 1106 Under the Crown Charters Act 10 and 11 Vict, c 51, §§ 15 16, charters from the Crown and Prince are sealed before being recorded

(*r*) Ersk, 4, 1, 22—Nisbet *v* Hope 1790 M, 8855—L Alva *v* Stirlingshire Freeholders 1790 M 8856—*Nicolson v* Chancellor 15th May 1819, F C So condescending on the date of registration of such charters was held not to satisfy the production in an action of simple reduction, King *v* Strathern 1633 M 6690

from the "Record of Precepts" for infefting heirs in crown and principality lands, if certified by the Director of Chancery, or his depute or substitute, "make entire faith in all cases, except in case of improbation" (*s*)

§ 1267 According to Lord Stair, retours of services are decreets of the Chancery (*t*) In another place his Lordship terms them decreets of the judge to whom the brieves from Chancery were issued (*u*) In either view, a retour entered in the record of Chancery corresponds to the decree of a court recorded in the court books Accordingly, an extract of a recorded retour (*vera copia retornatus in cancellaria remanen*) is admissible, and probative of the terms of the service (*x*) This is the case as to retours dated prior to the middle of the seventeenth century, although the originals may not be extant, the records up to that time having been much dilapidated, and a large portion of them carried off by Cromwell (*y*). If the original of an extract retour has been preserved in the record, the extract will, of course be corrected in regard to any discrepancies which may be discovered by comparison (*z*) And if the document in the record is not entitled to faith in judgment, the extract also will be inadmissible because a copy cannot have a greater probative value than its original (*a*)

(*s*) 10 and 11 Vict c 51, § 20

(*t*) The Chancery of Scotland was, to some extent, framed on the model of the English Court of Chancery, Stair, 4, 1, 2, and was originally presided over by the Chancellor of Scotland, Bell's Law Dic, *voce* "Chancellor" From the Chancery issued brieves or summonses, of which some (*e g*, brieves for service of heirs) were directed to inferior judges, and others (*e g*, brieves of tutory and of idiotcy) were carried out in Chancery In the former cases the decrees of the inferior judge when retoured to Chancery, were decrees of Chancery, while the latter were completed by decrees and precepts in which "the King himself decerneth and commandeth immediately without a subordinate judge", Stair, 4, 3, 8 9 See also M'Intosh v M'Intosh, 1698, M, 14,431

(*u*) Stair, 4, 47, 37—ibid, 3, 5 41

(*x*) Ersk, 3, 8, 61—Bell's Pr, § 1831 As to cases of improbation, see *infra*, § 1278

(*y*) Stewart v Maxwell, 1752, M, 8591—Mackie v Maxwell, 1761, M, 8589—Stewart v Dalrymple, 1761 M, 8579—Colquhoun v Dumbartonshire Freeholders, 1715, M, 8572—M'Intosh v M'Intosh, 1698, M, 14,431 (argument)—*Contra*, Kerr v Scot, 1628 M, 13,498, where, in an action of simple reduction, the Court required the defender to produce the original of an old retour, in order to prevent decree of certification See Tait Ev, 194—Wright on Elections, 171—*Supra*, § 1101

(*z*) See *supra*, 1102

(*a*) In Cathcart v Gordon, 9th March 1813, F C an extract from the record of Chancery, setting forth a retour as in 1578, was held not to be evidence of the old extent of the lands, because the original in the record was not a retour, or an authenticated copy of a retour but a scrap of paper having the tenor of a retour written upon it In Campbell v Murray, 1831, 9 S, 861, a document bearing to be a *vera copia* of a retour, dated in 1519, was held not to be sufficient evidence of the old extent the entry in the record having been taken from a fragment of an old book not authenticated in

§ 1268 At one time the old extent in questions of right to freehold could be proved by any evidence which was satisfactory to the Court (b) But on the preamble that difficulties had arisen from this practice it was enacted that no person should be entitled to vote or be enrolled as an elector, in respect of the old extent of his lands, unless such old extent were proved by a retour of the lands dated before 16th December 1681, and that no division of the old extent made after that date or to be made after the passing of the act, should be sustained as sufficient evidence of the old extent (c)

A certificate by the keeper of one of the records, that in a record of old extent certain lands were valued at a sum specified, was found not to be sufficient to instruct a retour, not being an extract duly authenticated (d)

§ 1269 Extracts of decrees of service under the modern practice, if authenticated by the Director of Chancery, or his depute, have the same effect as extracts of retours, and the decrees so recorded and extracted cannot be challenged, except by reduction in the Court of Session (e)

§ 1270 The Patent Law Amendment Act of 1852 provides that extracts of letters of patent recorded in Chancery in terms of the act "shall be received in evidence in all courts in Scotland to the like effect as the letters-patent themselves" (f)

Under the same act, copies of entries in the "Register of Proprietors" of patents kept in the English Court of Chancery if certified under the seal appointed by the Lord Chancellor to be used in the office, "shall be received in evidence in all courts and in all proceedings, and shall be *prima facie* proof of the assignment of such letters-patent or share or interest therein, or of the license or proprietorship, as therein expressed" (g)

---

any way, bearing to be minutes of procedure in a Sheriff-court, without any preliminary process to test its authenticity But see Fraser s Tr v Fraser, 11th July 1800, F C, where a copy of one of several retours in an old Sheriff-court book was held to prove an old extent in a process of cognition and sale (b) Wight on Elections 166

(c) 16 Geo II, c 11, § 8 As to contradicting retours by extrinsic evidence, see Gibson v Adinston, 13th June 1818 F C, compared with Montgomerie v Ainslie, 16th Nov 1816, F C See also Bell on Elections 163, *et seq* —Wight on Elections, 166 *et seq* (d) Gordon v —— 1767, M, 8592 (e) 10 and 11 Vict c 47 § 13 (f) 15 and 16 Vict, c 83, § 18 Before the passing of this act the Court of Session expressed a decided opinion that the specification recorded in Chancery might be proved by an extract certified by the Director of Chancery or his depute, Morton v Lord Clerk Register &c, 1831, 10 S, 162 (g) 15 and 16 Vict, c 83 § 35—*Supra*, § 558

The act also provides that copies or extracts of documents deposited in the office of the Commissioners of Patents, if certified under the seal of the office, shall be "taken notice of and received in evidence without farther proof or production of the originals (*h*)

§ 1271 There is some conflict of authority as to the admissibility of extracts from the registers of births, deaths, and marriages, under the former system In an action of reduction on the ground of minority and lesion, where the pursuer tendered a testimonial bearing the time of his baptism, signed by the keeper of the parish register, the Court "found it could not prove, on the ground (among others) that the register was "not of that authority that the extract thereof alone ought to make faith *per se*" (*i*) But in a later case of the same nature, where an extract was received as an adminicle of evidence, but not as full proof of minority, the Court seem to have regarded it as probative of the terms of the entry in the register (*k*) And more recently, where an extract from a register of deaths was rejected, because not lodged in proper time, Lords Pitmilly and Gillies observed that it would have been evidence, if timeously produced (*l*) Mr Erskine seems to have considered extracts from parish registers to be admissible (*m*), and this view is supported by the opinions of Mr Tait (*n*) and the author of the Law Dictionary (*o*), and by a provision in the late Registration Act that "all extracts and certificates from such registers, shall be and remain of the same legal force and effect in all respects as if this act had not been passed" (*p*) Mr Burnett (*r*) and Sir Archibald Alison (*s*), however, consider that extracts from parish registers are inadmissible and that the entries can only be proved by the originals or by sworn copies Although the preponderance of authority is thus decidedly in favour of admitting extracts, it is always desirable to have the original registers in court, in order that the jury may see whether they have been regularly kept (*t*)

§ 1272 The Registration Act of 1854 provides that "every extract of any entry in the register books, to be kept under the provi-

(*h*) 15 and 16 Vict, c 83, § 2 (*i*) Wilson *v* Aitken, 1626, M, 12,700 (*k*) Thomson *v* Stevenson, 1667, M, 12,701 (*l*) Auchinutie *v* Ferguson, 1817, 1 Mur, 211, 2 (*m*) Ersk, 1, 7, 36 (*n*) Tait Ev, 201 (*o*) Bell's Law Dic, *voce* Evidence (Public Instruments), &c (*p*) 17 and 18 Vict, c 80, § 1 (*r*) Burnett Cr Law, 485 (*s*) 2 Al, 599, 600 This seems also to be Professor Bell's opinion, Pr, § 2212 3 (*t*) See *supra*, §§ 1131, 3 4 A party who tenders merely an extract when the fact recorded is important to his case will justly lay himself open to the suspicion that production of the original register would have shown that it was not kept with accuracy and regularity

sions of this act, duly authenticated and signed by the Registrar-General, if such extract shall be from the registers kept at the General Registry Office, and by the (local) registrar if from any parochial or district register, shall be admissible as evidence in all parts of Her Majesty's dominions, without any other or farther proof of such entry" (*u*)

§ 1273 Copies purporting to be certified under the hand of the registrar or other person having charge of any register of ships in terms of the Merchant Shipping Act of 1854 are *prima facie* proof of all matters contained or recited in such register when the copy is produced (*w*) Declarations made in pursuance of the act may be proved in the same way (*x*) Examined copies are on the same footing as extracts (*y*) [1]

§ 1274 Some farther remarks require to be made as to the competency of extracts to satisfy the production in actions of reduction-improbation The proper object of this action is to cut down a deed which is false or fabricated It proceeds on the presumption that if the defender, after repeated orders of Court, fails to produce the deed in question the deed is forged And accordingly, in the event of such failure the pursuer is entitled to decree of reduction, or, as it is termed, of certification *contra non producta* (*z*) The action is sometimes raised for the purpose of forcing deeds into Court for reduction, fabrication being alleged *pro forma*, along with the grounds of challenge on which the party really means to insist.

It is manifest that merely registering a document cannot preclude and ought not to be allowed to impede, inquiry as to its genuineness Accordingly, at a time when the originals of deeds recorded in the books of Council and Session were returned to the party, it was held that an extract could not satisfy the production in an improbation (*a*) In like manner, as the originals are not re-

(*u*) 17 and 18 Vict, c 80 § 58 (*w*) 17 and 18 Vict, c 104, § 107, *supra*, § 1117 (*x*) Ibid (*y*) Ibid (*z*) Ersk, 4, 1, 2

(*a*) Farquhar *v* Lyon 1681, M, 6692 The opposite case of Ballandalloch *v* Dalvey, 1678 M, 6700, was decided on its special circumstances

[1] By the 20 and 21 Vict, c 26 (Registration and Assignation of Long Leases), it is provided (§ 15) that leases, &c, duly presented for registration in pursuance of the act, shall be registered in the register book, and thereafter delivered to the parties with certificates of due registration thereon, which shall be probative of such registration, and extracts of all such writs, registered in pursuance of the act, shall make faith in all cases in like manner as the writs registered, except where the writs so registered are offered to be improven

tained in the respective registers, improbations are excepted from the cases in which it is competent to use extracts from the registers of probative writs (*b*) of reversions, sasines, &c (*c*) and of inhibitions and interdictions (*d*) And this seems also to be intended by the terms of the acts which required registration of instruments of resignation *ad remanentiam* (*e*), and summonses and instruments for interrupting prescription in real rights (*f*) But the act as to registering hornings directs that extracts shall be received as authentic in whatever judgment they happen to be produced, without excepting improbations (*g*) And in an action of improbation raised against the donator to an escheat an extract from that record was held to prevent certification *contra non producta* (*h*) Lord Stair, however, lays down that producing extracts from the register of hornings will not bar certification, as the principals are not kept in the register (*i*)

§ 1275 With regard to deeds of which the principals are retained in the register, the general rule is, that, if they are recorded in the books of Council and Session extracts will bar certification in actions of improbation, because the originals are *in manibus curiae* (*k*) In general it is even enough for the defender, without producing an extract, to condescend on the date of registration in order that the pursuer may procure the original deed or an extract (*l*). But if the defender recorded the deed after the action of improbation was instituted, he must produce it, because he is not entitled to prejudice the rights of the pursuer after litigiosity has commenced (*m*) And he will also require to produce the original

---

(*b*) 1698, c 4—Paterson *v* Houston, 1837, 16 S, 225—*Supra*, § 1264

(*c*) 1617, c 16—1681 c 11—Stair, 4, 20, 21—Wallace *v* E Dundonald 1693 M 12,548, 4 B Sup, 42, S C—*Supra*, ib (*d*) 1581, c 119—Stair ib—*Supra* ib—Williamson *v* Threepland, 1682 M, 12,548—Monro *v* Gordon, 1681 M, 6700—L Borthwick *v* L Gallashiels, 1635, 1 B Sup, 90 But an extract of an inhibition was received where the register of warrants for the year had been lost Gordon *v* Forbes, 1679, M, 6700 And in two cases extracts of inhibitions, with the principal executions, were received, no special reason for doing so being mentioned in the reports Erskine *v* Renton, 1632, M, 6689—Dundas *v* Symington, there cited (*e*) 1669, c 3—*Supra* § 1264 (*f*) 1696, c 19—*Supra*, ib (*g*) 1579 c 75—*Supra*, § 1265 (*h*) Baillie *v* Dunbar 1686 M, 6703 (*i*) Stair, 4, 20, 21

(*k*) Stair, 4, 20, 21—Ersk, 4, 1, 22—Shand s Pr, 633—Tait Ev, 196

(*l*) Stair, *supra*—Ersk, *supra*—Shand, *supra*—Ly Kirkness, 1676 (2d case), 3 B Sup, 110—Strachan *v* Lindsay s Crs, 1706, M, 5172, 6711—Colvil *v* Haly, 1687, 2 B Sup, 100—Little *v* L Nithsdale, 1665, M, 5191, 6692—Saline's Children *v* Callender, 1681, M, 6675 (*m*) Ker *v* Scott 1628 M, 6689 It is otherwise in cases of simple reduction, A B, 1627, M, 13 197

deed, if, after the usual orders, he has failed to produce an extract, or to condescend on the date of registration (*n*)

Where the ground of challenge insisted on is forgery, the original deed must be in court before the action can proceed (*o*) But the Court will probably require the pursuer and not the defender, in the first instance to bear the burden of getting it from the register, if the latter produces an extract from the Books of Council and Session, or condescends on the date of registration (*p*)

§ 1276 If a deed proved to have been recorded in the books of Council and Session cannot be found after a diligent search, an extract of it will not in general bar certification in a reduction-improbation (*r*) But if the deed is only one of a number recorded about the same period, which have been lost during some public commotion, or in consequence of some accident to the register, or the like, an extract of it will satisfy the production (*s*) Where the loss of the original cannot be accounted for in this way, an action of proving the tenor of it may be raised, in which the absence of the original from the register, without there being ground to suspect fraud, will probably be held a sufficient *casus amissionis* and the extract will be a good adminicle to prove the tenor If this were not competent, the party interested in a deed might suffer irreparable loss on account of accident or the carelessness of a public officer, on whose care he was entitled to rely, but over whose acts he had no control

§ 1277 Certification in actions of improbation is not barred by producing an extract from the register of an inferior court (*t*) But in a special case an extract of a bond recorded in the books of a Sheriff-court was held sufficient, the original, with other writings of the period, having been lost many years before, and the debtor under the deed having by his conduct recognised its validity (*u*)

§ 1278 Lord Stair considers that the defender in an improbation

---

(*n*) Ersk 4 1 22—Tait Ev 167—Morro *v* Gordon, 1681 M 6700—Morrison *v* E Leven, 1713 M 6712—Law *v* Hume, 1683, 2 B Sup 44 (*o*) Ersk *supra*

(*p*) Shand's Pr, 633 (*r*) Stair, 4, 20, 21—Ersk, *supra*—Wilson *v* L Saltue, 1704 M, 6706—Tait, *supra* But see A B, 1682, M, 6703

(*s*) Ersk, *supra*—Tait *supra*—Baine *v* Balfour, 1668 M, 6693—Gordon *v* Forbes, 1679, M, 6700—Blackwood *v* Purves, 1666 M 5167, 6693—Thoirs *v* L Tolquhoun, *infra*—E Nithsdale *v* Westraw, 1628, M, 6689 (*t*) Stair, 4, 20, 21—Ersk 4, 1, 22—Dunmore *v* Lutfoot, 1675 M 6699—Strachan *v* Edzele's Crs, 1667 M 6711 So held as to writs recorded in Sheriff court books, which it was said had been lost in times of political commotion, Baine *v* Balfour, *supra*—Hay *v* Jameson 1671 M, ib

(*u*) Thoirs *v* L Tolquhoun, 1675 M 6694

is not bound to produce the originals of writings recorded in Chancery, but only to condescend on their dates, in order to enable the pursuer to institute a search for them, and that on their not being recovered decree of certification will be pronounced (*x*) But the Court held that this was not sufficient where charters and retours recorded in Chancery were challenged by reduction-improbation (*y*), or even by simple reduction (*z*) Certification, however was refused where the original retours were dated before the year 1544, when the registers were burnt by the English (*a*) As already mentioned, extracts of decrees of service have the same effect as extracts of retours (*b*).

Extracts of charters from the Crown or Prince of Scotland, recorded in terms of the act 49 Geo III, will not satisfy the production in improbations (*c*), and this is also the rule as to extracts of precepts from the Crown or Prince for infefting heirs (*d*)

§ 1279 The Court refused in an action of reduction-improbation to require production of a principal codicil, which had been recorded in Doctors' Commons, and followed by letters of administration which were in process (*e*) This is necessary for the protection of parties interested in deeds recorded in a foreign register over which the courts of this country have no control

---

CHAPTER III —CERTIFIED AND EXAMINED COPIES OF WRITINGS IN OFFICIAL RECORDS OR CUSTODY

§ 1280 Besides extracts from public registers, examined copies of writings in official custody are in some cases admissible on account of the inconvenience and risks which would arise if originals had to be produced in all cases where they might be used in evidence On this ground copies of documents attested by the Accountant of the Court of Session of records and papers relating to factories, tutories, and curatories retained in the Accountant's office,

(*x*) Stair, 4, 20, 21 (*y*) King *v* E Strathern, 1633 M 6690—Little *v* E Nithsdale, 1665, M, 5194, 6692 (*z*) Ker *v* Scot, 1628, M 13,498

(*a*) E Nithsdale *v* Westraw, 1628, M, 6689 (*b*) 10 and 11 Vict, c 47 § 13 (*c*) 49 Geo III, c 42, § 6 As to charters passed before this act see *supra*, § 1267 (*d*) 10 and 11 Vict, c 51, § 20 (*e*) Ross *v* Ross, 1782, M, 4600

have by statute the same authority as the originals (*a*) Copies, certified under the hand of the Collector or Comptroller of Stamps in Edinburgh of the statutory accounts or returns of the names and designations of the company firms, principal officers, and partners of banking companies in Scotland, must be received in evidence as "proof of the appointment and authority of the officer named in such account or return, and also of the fact that all persons named therein as members of such society or copartnership were members thereof at the date of such account or return" (*b*) [1] Copies of entries in the registry of copyrights, certified under the hand of the officer appointed by the Stationers Company under the Copyright Amendment Act, and impressed with the stamp of the company, are "*prima facie* proof of the proprietorship or assignment of copyright or license as therein expressed, but subject to be rebutted by other evidence, and in the case of dramatic or musical pieces shall be *prima facie* proof of the right of representation, or performance, subject to be rebutted as aforesaid" (*c*) [2] In like manner a certificate from the register of shareholders of a joint-stock company, if bearing the company's seal, is "*prima facie* evidence of the title of such shareholder, his executors, administrators, successors, or assigns, to the share therein specified" (*d*)

§ 1281 In these cases the certified copy is admissible without its genuineness or accuracy being proved at the trial But where there is not any statutory provision to that effect, examined copies of documents must be proved on oath by a person who has compared them with the originals Accordingly extracts of entries in the books of Excise, certified by the secretary of the Board, but not proved in this way, were held not to be evidence (*e*) And certified extracts from the books of the War Office with proof of the handwriting and signature of the clerks in the office were rejected, because not proved to be true copies (*f*)

§ 1282 Moreover the admissibility of copies proved to be correct is limited to registers of a public character (*g*), as books of pub-

(*a*) 12 and 13 Vict, c 51, § 36 (*b*) 7 Geo IV, c 67 § 4
(*c*) 5 and 6 Vict, c 45, § 11—7 and 8 Vict c 12 § 8 (*d*) 8 and 9 Vict, c 17 (Companies Clauses Consolidation Act, 1845) § 12 (*e*) Dunbar *v* Harvie, 1820, 2 Bligh, 351, reversing decision of Court of Session, which is not reported
(*f*) Kay *v* Rodger, 1832 10 S, 831. (*g*) Bell's Pr, § 2213—Burnett, 484

[1] By the Companies Act 25 and 26 Vict c 89, the register of members kept in terms of the act is made (§ 37) *prima facie* evidence of any matters directed or authorised to be inserted therein

[2] Extended to copyright of works of art 25 and 26 Vict c 68, § 5

he government offices (*h*), parochial registers (*i*), and registers of ships (*k*) Books of private corporations, road trustees, trading companies, and the like, unless coming within the Banking Companies Act, or the Companies Consolidation Act (*l*), cannot be proved by sworn copies prepared *ex parte* (*m*), the proper course being to have copies or excerpts taken from them at the sight of a commissioner of court, if great inconvenience would be occasioned by requiring the originals to be produced, or if these contain entries which the party or haver is entitled to withhold Unless in such exceptional cases, copies, whether taken before a commissioner of court or proved at the trial, are excluded under the rule which requires the best evidence (*n*) [3] It is unfortunately not the practice in criminal courts to grant commissions for taking excerpts, and therefore in criminal trials the originals of all documents must be produced, unless they are among those already described, whose terms may be proved by extracts or sworn copies (*o*) [4]

(*h*) Dunbar *v* Harvie, *supra*—Kay *v* Rodger, *supra*—Tomkins *v* Att -General 1813, 1 Dow, 104—*Contra*, Paris *v* Smith, 1823, 3 Mur , 337 (*i*) Burnett, 484—2 Al , 600 As to extracts by the keepers of these registers, see *supra*, § 1271 Entries in registers, under the act of 1854, should be proved by extracts, see *supra*, § 1272 (*k*) 17 and 18 Vict c 104, § 107—See *supra*, § 1117

(*l*) *Supra*, § 1280 (*m*) Bell s Pr 2213—*Supra*, § 134

(*n*) *Supra*, § 140 (*o*) Burnett, 484—2 Al , 600

---

[3] Beattie *v* Mackay and Paterson, 1863, 1 Macph , 279, *infra*, § 1364

[4] The 14th section of the English Law of Evidence Amendment Act (14 and 15 Vict c 99) provides, that whenever any book or other document is of such a public nature as to be admissible in evidence on its mere production from the proper custody, an examined or certified copy or extract shall be admissible in evidence, provided it be proved to be an examined copy or extract, or provided it purport to be signed and certified as a true copy or extract by the officer to whose custody the original is intrusted It has been held that if a certified copy of any public document is rejected as such for not containing the requisites of one, it may be received as an examined copy, if proved to have been duly examined, Reed *v* Lamb, 1860, 6 H and L Exch Rep, 75 The following have been held to be public books in the sense of the statute, of which examined or certified copies are admissible —The Register of Voters at a Parliamentary Election, Reed *v* Lamb, *supra*,—a "duplicate original" from the archives of the East India Company of a Register of Marriages celebrated in India, kept by authority of the Company, Ratcliff *v* Ratcliff and Anderson, 1859, 5 Jur N S, 714,—the original By-Laws of a Railway Company, framed under the Railway Clauses Consolidation Act, Motteram *v* the Eastern Counties Railway Company, 1859, 7 Scott s N C B Rep, 58 —Parish Registers, Porter, *in re*, 1856, 2 Jur , N S , 349 where extracts from a parish register, purporting to be signed by the curate were admitted in evidence without verification of the signature of the curate, or of his being the proper custodier of the register —Registers under the 6 and 7 Will IV, c 85, R *v* Mainwaring, 1856, 7 Cox's Crim Cases, 192,—Book of Queen s Bench, Grindel *v* Brendon, 1859, 5 Jur N S,

CHAPTER IV —INTERNATIONAL LAW REGARDING EXTRACTS AND EXAMINED COPIES

§ 1283 Extracts or (as they are frequently termed) exemplifications of decrees in foreign courts, like deeds concerning moveables executed in foreign countries (*a*), are admissible in evidence here, if they are prepared and authenticated according to the law of the country whence they proceed, but they will be rejected if they are not formal according to that law (*b*) This rule is illustrated by a case where a pursuer in the Court of Session, founding on a judgment on the question in issue, which he had obtained against the defender in a colonial court, produced an exemplification of it, bearing to be attested by the proper officer, and to be sealed by the Chief Justice of the colony, and where the Court, proceeding on the opinion of English counsel that the document was not formal, refused to sustain it *in hoc statu*, but allowed proof of its authenticity (*c*) So, where in order to prove the objection of infamy against a witness for the Crown in the Court of Justiciary, there was produced a copy of a conviction in Ireland, bearing to be signed by the proper officer but not impressed with the seal of the Irish Court, the document was rejected as sealing was considered to be necessary for its admissibility according to the law of Ireland (*d*)

§ 1284 An exemplification of a foreign judgment, however, although regular, and authenticated according to the forms of the court from which it proceeds, is, in general, not probative in another country, for a party founding on such a writing in a court which is not familiar with the rules regarding it, ought to prove its authenticity Accordingly it has been held in several English cases that a document bearing to be a decree of a foreign or colonial court, and impressed with the seal of court, is not admissible with-

(*a*) *Supra*, § 1026 *et seq* (*b*) 2 Hume, 255—Burnett, 483—Tait Ev, 191—2 Alison, 599—Sinclair *v* Fraser 1771 2 Pat Ap Ca, 253, reversing M 4542, noted *infra* (*f*) In most foreign countries exemplifications of decrees are attested by the signature of the proper officer, and impressed with the seal of court

(*c*) Robertson *v* Gordon 15th Nov 1814, F C (*d*) W Dean, 1729, 2 Hume 355 The prisoner did not offer proof that the copy was formal according to the practice of the Irish Court, but tendered witnesses to prove that the person convicted had stood on the pillory in terms of the sentence The Court justly considered that such evidence could not prove the terms of the sentence

1420,—and the Registry under the Bill of Sales Act (17 and 18 Vict, c 36) Sutton *v* Bath, 1858 1 F and F, 152

out proof that it is genuine (e)[1] So a certificate of probate, bearing to be signed by "D S Bacon, Judge of Probate," and impressed

(e) Henry v Adey, 1802, 3 East 221—Buchanan v Rucker, 1810, 1 Camp, 63, 9 East, 192, S C—Clark v Mullick, 3 Moore P C R 252, 280—Story's Confl, § 643—Taylor Ev, 1032

[1] A guardian appointed by the Court of Chancery presented a petition to the Court of Session for the custody of his pupil, the Marquis of Bute (who had been surreptitiously removed to Scotland), in order to carry out a scheme of education approved by the Court of Chancery and which involved the pupil's residence in England The Court held that the production in process of official copies of the appointment and scheme of education, and of an order for the custody of the pupil's person—the copies being full of erasures and interlineations—could not be regarded as sufficient evidence of the orders of a foreign court, Stuart v Moore, 22 D, 1504 The case was appealed and the orders pronounced by the Court of Session for the custody and education of the pupil were recalled Lord Chelmsford, referring to the point above stated, observed, 'I agree with my noble and learned friend opposite (Lord Cranworth), that, if the circumstances had been reversed, if the Scotch Court had assumed the guardianship of the infant, and the infant had been improperly removed from its jurisdiction and the guardian had come to this country to reclaim possession of his infant ward the English Courts would have facilitated the guardian in his object, and I think that they would not have examined with a very nice and critical eye the proof of the orders which had emanated from the Scotch authority, or, if there had been any imperfection in the proof, they would have facilitated the Court in obtaining the necessary means of establishing their authority", 23 D 912, 4 Macq, 72 Mr Macpherson, in commenting upon these observations, remarks that not only was the view adopted by the Scotch Court in consonance with the practice in previous cases, but that the practice of the English Courts has not been less 'nice and critical" 'Such being the undoubted state of the law of Scotland, is the law of England more liberal? In 1814, Lord Ellenborough spoke thus, 'By the *comitas gentium* the courts of different countries will recognise and enforce the judgments of each other, but these judgments are to be authenticated under the seals of the courts by which they are pronounced or distinct evidence should be given that the Court had no seal, and verified its judgments by the signature of the Chief Justice'—(Alves v Bunbury, 4 Camp, 28) Before Lord Brougham's Act (8 and 9 Vict, c 113), the order in Chancery which this foreign court is asked to recognise would not have been recognised at the other end of Westminster Hall—or why was that act passed? and Scotland is by a special clause, excepted from its operation There is reason to suspect that the Common Law Courts of England will not even yet recognise an order pronounced by a judge at chambers, if it have only an impressed stamp upon it—(Taylor on Evidence, § 11) A motion was made on a copy of such an order, bearing the stamp usual on such documents, the Court refused to notice judicially the impressed stamp, although it was contended that it was practically the seal of court, the Court held it to be merely the mark of the judge's clerk—(Barrett Navigation Co v Shower, 8 Dowl, 173) Yet the Court of Session is rebuked for not acknowledging the Chancery order above described which, although it may be, for aught we know precisely in the form usually adopted in the Court of Chancery, to the eye of a Scottish lawyer, with its erasures and deletions, would certainly appear a vitiated document"—The Appellate Jurisdiction of the House of Lords in Scotch Causes, by Norman Macpherson, Advocate, 1861

In an action in the Court of Session, for judgment conform to 'extract or exemplification" of a judgment obtained in the Court of Queen's Bench against the de-with the "seal of Probate Court Monroe," was held in the Court of Session not to be sufficient to entitle the alleged executor to be sisted as pursuer in room of the deceased, the Lord Justice-Clerk observing "It is an established rule that a document of this nature from a foreign court must be certified as genuine For this purpose if a notary-public cannot be procured, the signature of a British consul, or of the mayor of the town would be sufficient. But we have here no evidence that Mr Bacon is what he states himself to be" (*f*) In like manner the Lord Chief Commissioner

(*f*) Disbrow v Mackintosh, 1852 15 D, 128 In the case of Sinclair v Fraser, 1771, 2 Pat Ap Ca 253 (reversing M, 4542), where it was held that a decree for payment pronounced by the Supreme Court of Jamaica should be received as *prima facie* proof of the same debt, when sued for in the Court of Session, the decree was certified by the clerk of the foreign court, his subscription was certified by the Secretary of the Island, who was a notary-public and whose subscription was confirmed by that of the Governor and by the Great Seal of Jamaica The decree was held in the House of Lords to be sufficiently proved (see M, 4543) In the Court of Justiciary a certificate of a conviction by an English Assize Court was admitted for the Crown on proof by the inspector and sub-inspector of police at Newcastle "that it was the ordinary form of conviction, that it was authentic, that it applied to the prisoner, and that the witnesses had been brought forward in English courts to prove such convictions", Macrae 1839 Bell's Notes, 281 [2]

fender it was maintained that the exemplification, without proof led in support of it, is not evidence of anything' On this plea Lord Deas said "I have no doubt whatever that the exemplification is good and sufficient evidence for this Court to receive, so long as it is not impugned as being false and forged It bears to be attested by one of the Masters of the Court of Queen's Bench, as a true copy of the original judgment roll in the custody of the Masters The seal of the Court of Queen's Bench is attached to it and then you have a notarial instrument prefixed, in which the notary certifies that it is an office copy, and agrees in all respects with the original judgment roll, and that the signature at the foot thereof is the genuine subscription of Mr Hodgson, one of the Masters of Court Now I take it that such an exemplification, with its authenticity so attested, is evidence which would be received all over the world, at all events, I have no doubt that it is receivable in this Court as full legal evidence of that judgment, and that we must deal with it accordingly" It was, accordingly held that the foreign decree was sufficiently authenticated, and the Court further refused to allow the defender a proof that no notice of the proceedings in the English court had been given to him, and that the decree was really a decree in absence, which, according to the law of England could be opened up, holding that his averments as to the circumstances under which the decree had been obtained and the effect it would receive in England were not sufficiently precise But Lord Cuninghill was in favour of a proof being allowed—' Before we can give decree conform, without further evidence in support of the claim we must be satisfied that the judgment is such that it would be held as *res judicata* in England", Whitehead v Thomson, 23 D, 772—Frisell v Thomson, 1862, 22 D 1176 See, as to the effect of a foreign judgment in England *supra*, § 1081, and as to the admissibility of copies of foreign judgments &c, 14 and 15 Vict, c 99, § 7

[2] H M Adv v Dempster, 1862, 4 Irv, 143—H M Adv v Davidson and Francis 1863, 35 Sc Jur, 270

once held that an English probate is not admissible in this country, without some person being adduced to prove its correctness, and the genuineness of the signatures and seal (*g*) For a considerable time, however, it has been the practice to admit probates and letters of administration from English and Irish courts (although foreign courts in questions of Scotch law) without their authenticity being proved (*h*) This is an exception to the ordinary rule, on the ground that the Scotch courts and legal profession are familiar with these writings, and that their accuracy and genuineness can easily be investigated if any doubt arises regarding them [3]

In America another exception to the rule is recognised in the case of foreign Courts of Admiralty, the seals of which, appended to their decrees, are judicially noticed without proof of authenticity, on the ground that Courts of Admiralty are courts of the law of nations (*i*)

The Court of Session once ordained an extract of a decree pronounced by them to be written on parchment and sealed with the seal of Court, as it required to be used in Ireland, where (the party alleged) the judges would not receive it if unsealed (*j*)

§ 1285 With regard to deeds recorded in foreign registers in which the original documents are preserved, the practice of the courts of this country is to receive an extract or copy certified by the keeper of the record, or other official person appointed to authenticate such writings Thus, where a person had obtained letters of administration in England upon a will and codicils, which were deposited in Doctors' Commons, the Court of Session, in an action of reduction-improbation of one of the codicils, held that the defender was not obliged to produce the original document, and, consequently, that the production might be satisfied by the letters of administration (*k*). Thus also, an extract of a contract from the books of a foreign notary has been admitted where, according to the *lex loci contractus*, the original deed was preserved in the re-

(*g*) Fowler *v* Paul, 1820 2 Mur 433 (*h*) Wardlaw *v* Maxwell, 1715, M, 4500—Clark *v* Brebner 1759, M, 4471—Stewart *v* M'Donald, 1826, 5 S 29—Marchioness of Hastings *v* Marq Hastings' Exrs 1852, 14 D, 189—Disbrow *v* Mackintosh, *supra* per Lord Just -Clerk (Hope) See also Ross *v* Ross, *infra*, (*k*)

(*i*) Story's Confl, § 643—1 Greenleaf's Ev, § 514—Yeaton *v* Fry, 1808, 5 Cranch Ca in Supr Court, U S, 335—Thomson *v* Stewart, 1820, 3 Day's Connecticut Rep 171 (*j*) Murray, 29th March 1683, 1 Fount, 230 (*k*) Ross *v* Ross, 1782, M, 4600

[3] Since the change effected by 21 and 22 Vict c, 56, § 14 (by which probates and letters of administration granted by the English and Irish Courts operate as confirmation in Scotland), the reasons in favour of the exception are of course stronger

gister kept by that officer and only certified copies of it were issued (*l*) Again, in the trial of Humphreys for forging documents to establish his title to the Earldom of Stirling, an examined copy from the French "Register of the Secretary of State" or "Collection of Registers of the King's Household" was tendered by the prosecutor to prove the appointment of a certain person to the office of Geographer Royal The prisoner's counsel objected that there was no proof that the law of France either recognised the register as evidence or admitted the document produced as a copy of it Upon this the prosecutor proved, by a French lawyer, that the register was the only record for writings of the kind, and that the extract was regularly authenticated by the keeper, and would "have all possible authenticity in France" The witness farther deponed that he had thrice collated the certified copy with the register The prisoner's counsel thereupon withdrew his objection, but the presiding judge (Lord Meadowbank *secundus*) observed, 'We should have doubted the prisoner's argument at any rate I say this for the benefit of the profession' (*m*). With much deference to the learned judge, it is conceived that a person tendering an extract from a foreign register, except in the case of English or Irish letters of administration (*n*) must prove the document to be a formal office copy according to the rules of the register from which it is taken. Failing this proof of its accuracy will be required, whereupon it will be admitted as an examined and sworn copy (*o*) This view is supported by the cases already cited as to proving extracts of foreign decrees (*p*) and by a decision in which an extract of a will from the books of a notary in Paris having been founded on to instruct the claim to a legacy of certain jewels, was held not to be probative "unless it were further astructed and adminiculated" (*r*)

§ 1286 The admissibility in foreign countries of extracts of deeds preserved in the registers of this country, must be determined by the rules of evidence in the court in which such extracts are tendered This sometimes occasions difficulty because, as afterwards mentioned (*s*), the Court of Session is exceedingly unwilling

(*l*) Lamington *v* Kincaid, 1627, M, 4443—Davidson *v* Town of Edinburgh, 1682, M, 4444 This point is stated as doubtful in Story's Confl, § 630 See *infra*, (*r*)

(*m*) Humphreys' Trial (1839) reported by Swinton, 123

(*n*) *Supra*, § 1284 (*o*) See *supra*, § 1281 (*p*) *Supra*, § 1284

(*r*) Ly Boghall *v* Duchess Lauderdale, 1688, 3 B Sup, 669 In support of the text see also *supra*, § 1038 *et seq* (*s*) See the chapter on recovering documents from Public Registers *infra*, § 1366, *et seq*

to allow deeds to be removed from registers in Scotland for production as evidence abroad Their Lordships considered that an extract of letters of patent recorded in Chancery would be admitted in support of a petition to Parliament by the patentee for extension of the term of the patent, and they accordingly refused to grant warrant for having the original letters delivered up (*t*). They took the same view in a case where a party craved warrant to have an original deed recovered from the books of Council and Session for production at a jury trial in York (*u*) In like manner, extracts of deeds recorded in the registers of this country are received as originals in Doctors' Commons (*x*) On the other hand an extract of a will recorded in the books of Council and Session, was held not to be admissible in a peerage case before the Committee of Privileges, the proof not showing that the original could not be recovered, but, on the contrary, that it could be produced in the hands of an officer of the Court of Session (*y*) In some cases, also, the Court of Session have allowed the originals of recorded deeds to be exhibited in this way, on being satisfied that extracts would not be admitted in the court where the terms of the deed were in issue (*z*).[4]

(*t*) Morton *v* L Clerk Register, 1831, 10 S, 162 (*u*) Bartwhistle *v* L Clerk Register 1825, 3 S, 602 (*x*) Wharton Peerage Case, 1845, 12 Cl and Fin 303 (*y*) Wharton Peerage Case *supra* (*z*) Malcolm, 25th May 1847 19 Sc Jur, 483—Annandale 1828, 6 S, 657 See the chapter on recovering documents from public registers, *infra*, § 1366, *et seq*

[4] The Court has given effect to a distinction between deeds recorded in registers under their authority, and documents forming part of the record of the Court of Session in an extracted process In the case of the former they have granted warrant to the keeper of the register, or to the party founding upon them to exhibit them before the foreign court, but they have commonly declined to allow the latter to be taken beyond their jurisdiction, Adamson petitioner, 1852, 14 D, 1045—Power, petitioner, 1859 21 D 782—Sheddon, petitioner, decided 1860 reported 24 D 1446—Dunlop *v* Deputy Clerk Register, 1861 24 D, 107—Bayley petitioner 1862, 24 D 1021 In Dunlop *v* Deputy-Clerk Register the Lord Justice-Clerk (Inglis) observed that it was quite decided "that the Court will not, on any conditions, allow a part of the proper records of the Court to be carried out of the jurisdiction of the Court" It has not, however, been expressly settled that, if the foreign court will not receive copies or extracts of the records, the original papers will not be sent, but it was observed in the case of Power that, "even supposing no evidence to be admitted by this English court short of the process itself, I am not prepared to say that the Court would grant such an application as this An extracted process is public property, and is the record of judicial proceedings which may affect the rights and status of Scotsmen yet unborn", *per* Lord Justice-Clerk (Inglis) Where the deed is delivered for exhibition to the petitioner, he will be required to find caution with sufficient security to return it within a short specified period; and, in the case of Dunlop, the Court required an extract of the deed duly authenticated to be

CHAPTER V.—OF THE ACTION OF PROVING THE TENOR OF WRITINGS WHICH HAVE BEEN LOST OR DESTROYED.

§ 1287. A writing which has been lost, or wholly or partially destroyed, may be supplied by means of an action of proving the tenor. In this process the Court has to be satisfied that the writing in question originally existed as a valid writ in the terms libelled on, and that its disappearance or mutilation was not occasioned by its having been retired or cancelled. On these facts being substantiated, the Court pronounce decree of proving the tenor; and an extract of the decree, like an extract of a recorded deed, is probative of the terms of the original document (*a*).

Considerable care and delicacy are evidently required in this proceeding; for while, on the one hand, it is proper and highly useful for the purpose of supplying lost evidence of subsisting rights, it may, on the other hand, be misused for the purpose of setting up forged or invalid documents, or of reviving obligations which have been extinguished. On account of its importance and

(*a*) Ersk., 4, 1, 59—Tait Ev. 212.

lodged in the register prior to its removal. At one time the Court inclined to send the deed for exhibition in the custody of the keeper or deputy-keeper of the records, and in the most recent case (Bayley, *supra*) this course was followed by the First Division. In Dunlop *v.* Deputy-Clerk Register the deed was delivered to the petitioner (he being the sole beneficiary under it, and caution being found by him for its return within six months), but the Court seemed principally moved by what had occurred in the case of Shedden. In that case the deputy-keeper was authorised to exhibit the documents in Court, but not to part with them, and to bring them back after the trial; but the English court held that it had right to the documents when once tendered in evidence, and refused to allow the deputy-keeper to return them, according to his instructions. The Lord Justice-Clerk (Inglis), referring to the case of Shedden, intimated that, in view of what had happened in that case, it was unlikely that the Court would for the future send one of its officers with the documents,—"We had some conversation with our brethren on the effect of that proceeding, and I think we all came to be of opinion that to send an officer of the court to any foreign court or to England, with a document with instructions not to part with it, when it was out of his power to resist the power of the court there if ordered by it to leave the document, was to place him in a very awkward and unsatisfactory position, and, therefore, I believe that none of your Lordships will be inclined again to send an officer with such instructions", 24 D. 108. The Court has stated its unwillingness to take public registers out of the hands of their proper custodiers, and has declined to enforce the Act of Sederunt (as to the lodging of documents for jury trial) with regard to parochial registers, Cochrane *v.* Ferrier, 1859, 21 D., 749.

delicacy it is only competent in the Court of Session (*b*), except in cases of lost valuations or subvaluations of teinds the tenor of which may be proved either in the Court of Session, or before the judges of that Court sitting as the Court of Teinds (*c*)

I *When an Action of Proving the Tenor is competent*

§ 1288. The most common purpose of this action is for proving the tenor of private deeds which have been lost, or accidentally or fraudulently destroyed. By statute (*d*) the tenor of "letters of horning, executions, and indorsations thereof not extant and produced judicially," cannot be "proven by witnesses" This, however, does not exclude proof of the tenor of such documents by written adminicles (*e*) Nor does the statute apply to actions for proving the tenor of other executions (*f*) or of judicial acts and decrees (*g*)

(*b*) Ersk, 4, 1, 58—Shand's Pr, 828—Balnagown *v* Mackenzie, 1663, M, 15,790—Smart *v* Ewing 1673, 3 B Sup 149

(*c*) The act 1707, c 9 (or c 10) made it competent for the Court of Session as Commissioners of Teinds, to cognosce and determine (*inter alia*) such causes and things as had previously been referred to commissioners for planting of kirks and valuation of teinds "and through the loss of the registers of that court, which were burnt in the late fire," and "to make up the tenor" of decrees of valuation In Alexander *v* Oswald, 1840, 3 D, 40 the Teind Court, taking a liberal construction of this act, held that they had jurisdiction in an action of proving the tenor of the report of a subvaluation of teinds where the *casus omissionis* was libelled alternatively as lost in the great fire or by shipwreck The objection to the jurisdiction applied both to the proving of the tenor of a subvaluation, and to a case not limited to loss by the great fire From the opinions expressed by their Lordships, after an inquiry into the practice, it would seem that any action of proving the tenor of a valuation of teinds may be brought in the Teind Court There is no doubt of the jurisdiction of the Court of Session in these cases, see 6 Geo IV, c 120, § 54—Alexander *v* Oswald, *supra*—Cases in note (*g*), *infra*

(*d*) 1579, c 94 (*e*) Ersk, 4, 1, 58 (*f*) Ersk *supra*—Boyd *v* Malloch, 1677 M 15,798—A B, 1755, 5 B Sup 837

(*g*) Actions have been sustained to prove the tenor of decrees of comprising, Binnie *v* Montgomery, 1675, M, 15,796—Peppermill *v* Room, 1684, M, 15,803—Miln *v* Lauderdale, 1687, M, 15,805 decrees of adjudication, L Airth *v* Blackwood, 1707, M, 15,813, of declarator of irritancy *ob non solutum canonem*, D Argyle *v* M'Lean, 1781, M, 15,828, decrees of valuation of teinds, L Lynedoch *v* Liston, 1811, 3 D, 1078—Shaw Stewart *v* Macfarlane, 1835, 13 S, 765—Alexander *v* Oswald, 1840, 3 D, 40, the verdict of an assize finding a person's estates forfeited for treason, L Cranstone *v* Turnbull, 1681, M, 15,801, and pleadings which formed parts of a closed record, Clyne *v* Johnstone, 1832, 11 S, 131 In Duncan *v* Arnott, 1827, 5 S, 810, where a party raised an action for proving the tenor of certain interlocutors, which had been pronounced in a cause where the decree had not been extracted, the Court sustained the objection that the pursuer could not proceed without also proving the tenor of the summons, and their Lordships accordingly sisted process till a supplementary action should be raised

§ 1289 The action is competent to prove the tenor of a holograph writing, but considerable difficulty is usually felt in establishing the authenticity of such documents (*h*) [2]

§ 1290 The action may be used for the purpose of restoring a clause which had been obliterated from a deed (*i*), and where the party's subscription had been torn off (*k*), or the document had been torn in pieces (*l*)

II *When an Action of Proving the Tenor is necessary*

§ 1291 When a party interested in a deed which has been lost or destroyed wishes to prove its tenor, in anticipation of requiring to operate upon it, he must, of course, raise an action for that purpose But when the terms of a writing are involved in a process already depending, a party interested is sometimes entitled to prove them incidentally without an action of proving the tenor Whether this will be allowed in any individual case, depends on the nature of the writing, and the object for which it is founded on (*m*)

On this subject "it was laid down as a general rule that if a writ is one upon which a permanent right is to be set up, or on which execution is to follow, such writ cannot be supplied without a proving of the tenor But if the writ be only such as imports the extinction or restriction of a debt, it may be supplied by adminicles, without a proving of the tenor Accordingly where the question was concerning a contract said to have been entered into between Hay of Aberlady and Maxwell of Friarcase, for restricting to securities certain rights *ex facie* irredeemable in the person of Aberlady, to certain parts of the estate of Friarcase the Lords found that it was competent to Glenriddle, the pursuer, to found upon the documents produced to instruct the restriction of the rights in Aberlady's person by the contract, without a formal proving of the tenor of that contract, and found the documents produced sufficient for that purpose" (*n*) Lord Brougham took substantially the same

(*h*) Robertson *v* Hyndman, 1833, 11 S, 775—Lillies *v* Lillie 1832, 11 S, 160—Trotter *v* Home, 1707, M, 15,811—Compared with Fraser *v* Davies, 1784, M, 15,830

(*i*) Ronald, 1830, 8 S, 1008—Graham *v* Graham 1847, 10 D, 45—Hume *v* Hume, 1712 M, 14,967, 15,819

(*k*) M'Donald *v* M'Glue, 1713, 5 B Sup, 98—Graham *v* Graham, *supra*

(*l*) Dow *v* Dow, 1848, 10 D, 1465

(*m*) See Tait Ev 212—Shand's Prac 842

(*n*) Maxwell *v* Maxwell, 1742, M 15,820 Elch Notes, 'Tenor, No 4 S C

[2] Cousin *v* Gemmil 1862 24 D 758

view in an action by the trustees of a bankrupt banking company against an alleged partner, who, without an action of proving the tenor, founded on secondary evidence of a lost assignation by him of his share in the concern His Lordship observed—' The inclination of my mind is, that the question rests entirely on the validity of the assignation that it need not be proved by an action of proving the tenor, as it was set up by way of exception, and not by way of the foundation of the original suit I agree that an action of proving the tenor is not necessary where a deed is only founded upon as in this case, and where, without any such deed, the same matter might be shown otherwise Yet where there is the necessity of showing in the first instance the existence of the deed, as the very fundamental principle upon which the party can alone proceed, the admission of secondary evidence" (except by means of a proving of the tenor) "is not competent" (o)

§ 1292 In accordance with these views a formal action of proving the tenor was held to be necessary in the following cases Where a party claiming to represent a creditor of a certain person raised an action of reduction of a decree of preference, which had been obtained by a co-creditor, the Court sustained the objection that the pursuer did not produce a title to connect himself with the original creditor, and they would not allow him to repeat *incidenter* a proving of the tenor of such connecting title "because the pursuer, before he convened the defender in his reduction, ought to have made up a sufficient title for prosecuting his intended action, and he cannot be allowed an incident for making up his title" (p) And this decision was followed in an action of maills and duties, where part of the pursuer's title (an extract of an heritable bond) was torn and mutilated in many places, so as to be illegible (r). Where a party claiming right to certain heritable subjects raised an action of reduction of the title of a person who had for a long time been in possession as proprietor, and where part of the defender's titles was a disposition and sasine which he alleged had been lost, the Court sisted process till he should raise an action for proving their tenor (s) Again, in an action of declarator of nullity of a will, which had been found in the deceased's repositories torn in

---

(o) Drummond v Thomson's Tr 1834 7 W S 564, affirming, 12 S, 620 The Lord Ordinary (Corehouse) had considered the action unnecessary, "the deed being founded upon in defence only, and for various other reasons" See also Synod of Merse v Scott, 1753, M, 15,823, *infra*, § 1293 (a) (p) Inglis v Hay 1709, M, 13,293 See also Geikie v Hutchison, 1848, 10 D, 351 (r) Dunbar v E Morton, 1711, M, 13,297 (s) Merry v Dun, 1833, 11 S, 36

two pieces, where both parties lodged issues on the question of the genuineness of the deed and its cancellation, the Court, *proprio motu*, sisted process till a proving of the tenor should be brought (*t*) In an action by the trustee on a sequestrated estate, for reducing a disposition granted by the bankrupt to his brothers and sisters, and proceeding on the narrative that it was in implement of a deed by their father to them, which the bankrupt had destroyed, the Court, after examining havers to prove the original existence of the deed, required the defenders to prove its tenor in an action, in order to show that its provisions had not been exceeded by those in the deed under challenge (*u*) Thus also, when any of the proceedings or interlocutors in the record in a cause have gone amissing, the Court will in general not allow their tenor to be proved incidentally except of consent (*x*) Formerly it seems to have been the practice to allow an incidental proof, where writs had been produced in process and after having been seen had been lost during the dependence (*y*) [2]

(*t*) Dow *v* Dow, 1848 10 D, 1465 The defender gave up the case soon afterwards

(*u*) Boyd *v* Anderson, 1821, 1 S 144, and 2 S, 363

(*x*) Hamilton *v* Durie's Tr, 1826 5 S 77—Clyne *v* Johnstone, 1832, 11 S, 131—Compared with Watson *v* Scott, 1839, 1 D, 518—Crs of Stenhouse 1769 (not rep), noted in Shand's Pr 843

(*y*) Allan *v* Ker, 1680, 3 B Sup, 368—Home *v* Home, 1680, M, 14,999

---

[2] In 1846 the Crown raised an action of declarator against James Sinclair of Forss, to have it found that he had no right to the fishings of the lands of Howburnhead and others It was answered for Sinclair that his title to the fishings was contained in a disposition and assignation, dated 30th November 1700, in favour of one of his predecessors and authors, but which disposition and assignation had been lost The process was sisted to allow Sinclair to bring an action for proving the tenor of the lost deed, which was brought The adminicles of evidence as to the existence and tenor of the deed alleged to have been lost consisted of an instrument of sasine thereon, excerpts from various contracts of wadset and dispositions of rights of reversion The instrument of sasine narrated the dispositive clause of the lost writ which was set forth as including "fishings It also narrated the infeftment of the disponee in "fishings," and "fishings were mentioned in the several contracts of wadset and dispositions of rights of reversion No specific *casus omissionis* was set forth, but it was proved by the evidence of the pursuer and his agents that they never saw the disposition, that they did not know how or when it was lost, and that the deed was not to their knowledge destroyed It was admitted that the pursuer and his authors had been in possession of the fishings for time immemorial On the case being advised the Lord President (M'Neill) said,—"The only question before the Court in this action is, as to the proving of the tenor of the writ alleged to be lost I have no doubt that the deed of 1700 did exist, and, looking to the nature of that deed, I think a sufficient *casus omissionis* has been established The same strictness is not necessary in regard to a deed of this description as is required in some other deeds But this is a matter which has of late

§ 1293 On the other hand, an action of proving the tenor was dispensed with in the following cases Where a party raised a summary process for having a neighbouring proprietor interdicted from opening up a road, and the respondent pleaded that he had a servitude of way under the complainer's original disposition, but that the complainer had destroyed that deed, and got a new deed in place of it with the clause omitted, the Court received an incidental proof of the destruction and tenor of the deed (*z*). Again, where the heritors of a parish were sued at the instance of the synod and presbytery of the bounds for the purpose of having the vacant cure supplied by a minister with an adequate stipend the Court held that an action was not necessary in order to enable the heritors to prove the tenor of a lost decree of suppression and annexation pronounced by the Commissioners for Plantation of Kirks (*a*) In an action of ranking and sale, one of the claimants was allowed to prove incidentally the tenor of two sheets of a disposition, which through carelessness had been torn from the portion of the deed containing the narrative (*b*) And in an action of count and reckoning between two brothers, one of them was allowed to prove incidentally the tenor of a lost bond granted by his father, which he had paid, and to which he produced an assignation in favour of himself (*c*) [3]

(*z*) Ross *v* Fisher, 1833, 11 S 467 The complainer, when examined as a haver, admitted that he had destroyed the first deed (*a*) Synod of Merse *v* Scott 1753 M, 15,823 (*b*) Hume *v* Hume, 1712, M, 14,967 (doubted by More, Notes, 385) (*c*) Home *v* Home, 1680, M, 14 999

years been looked to with great strictness by this Court I remember a case in which we refused to allow the tenor of a lost writ to be proved, and the writ itself was produced in a few weeks, having been placed inadvertently within another deed It is necessary to look strictly at the matter but the degree of stringency depends on circumstances The next point is as to the tenor of the deed This, I think, has been sufficiently made out Mere production of a sasine on a deed is not enough to prove the tenor of that deed, but, in this case, the sasine narrates the dispositive clause of the disposition at a time when there is no reason to suspect fraud on the part of the notary" The tenor of the deed was therefore held proven, Sinclair *v* the Lord Advocate, 7th Jan 1863 (not reported)

[3] In the case of the Advocate-General *v* Sinclair in the Court of Exchequer the plaintiff, on behalf of the Crown, claimed from the defendant certain arrears of tack-duty, and interest thereon from the terms of payment, due on a tack from the Crown of the bishops' teinds The tack was not produced, but secondary evidence of its terms was adduced, it was not proved that it had been lost or destroyed, and the defendants contended that, in these circumstances, an action of proving of the tenor should have been brought Lord Neaves, however, directed the jury 'that in this case, and in this Court in which the law administered is, in a certain degree, assimilated to the law of another

§ 1294 In an action of declarator of trust where the pursuer alleged that the defender had fraudulently obtained access to the back-bond and had destroyed it, proof of the fact was received without an action of proving the tenor (*d*) And where a party raised an action of exhibition of a deed containing a legacy in his favour, and the defender deponed that he had burnt the deed by the directions of the testator, but such directions were not proved otherwise, the Court granted decree for payment of the legacy without requiring the legatee to raise action of proving the tenor (*e*) These cases seem to have proceeded on the principle—which was also applied in a case arising upon an obligatory writing (*f*)—that where it is shown that the party prejudiced by a deed has destroyed it, he will not be allowed to insist that its tenor shall not be proved without an independent action

It was once held that an action of proving the tenor of a bond of annuity in favour of the granter's wife was not necessary where a disposition of liferent in nearly the same terms was extant, and sasine had followed on the bond (*g*)

§ 1295 The Court will dispense with an action of proving the tenor, where the parties consent to the terms of the missing deed being proved incidentally, and that course can be adopted without the process getting out of shape (*h*) And in an action of improbation of a lost bond, an incidental proving of the tenor of it was received, in order that the improbation might not be delayed (*i*)

§ 1296 Where the missing document is only to be used as part

(*d*) Kennoway *v* Ainslie, 1752, Elch, 'Trust,' 16 See also Fraser's Tr *v* Fraser, 1800, Mor, "Member of Parliament," Appx 5 (*e*) Fisher *v* Smith, 1771, M, 9366 (*f*) Seton *v* Paterson, 1766, 5 B Sup, 924 (*g*) M'Donald *v* M'Kinnon 1765, 5 B Sup, 904 (*h*) Compare M Bute *v* Cooper, 1827, 5 S, 831 (affirmed on merits 1 W S, 335)—Crs of Stenhouse, 22d December 1769 (not rep), cited in Shand's Prac 843—Watson *v* Scott, 1839, 1 D, 518—Dow *v* Dow 1848 10 D, 1465 (*i*) Mein *v* Dunse 1701 M 2742

country secondary evidence may be received And if evidence has been led that satisfies your minds that such a tack existed in the terms set forth, you are entitled to hold such evidence sufficient to supply its place," Advocate-General *v* Sinclair, 1855, 17 D 290 In a jury trial at Dumfries secondary evidence of a document of the nature of a decree-arbitral, which was alleged to give the defenders right to the ground in dispute, was rejected by Lord Neaves On advising a bill of exceptions, the Lord President (M'Neill) thought the question one of difficulty, and was not prepared to decide that a document, which was to have the effect of transferring property could be proved at all, except in an action of proving of the tenor Lord Deas and Ardmillan were of opinion that the evidence which had been disallowed should have been admitted Maxwell *v* Reid, June 17, 1863 (not yet reported)

of the evidence in a case, and not as the written constitution of a right or obligation, proof both as to the cause of its absence and as to its terms will be admitted incidentally (*j*) A strong illustration of this rule occurred in an action for setting aside an election of magistrates, on the ground of an illegal compact among the electors as to the mode in which they should vote, where it appeared that several of them had signed a deed for that purpose, and that some of the subscribers had destroyed the document with the view of suppressing proof of its terms The Jury Court, having entertained doubts as to whether a proving of the tenor was necessary, retransmitted the case to the Court of Session in order to have that point determined, whereupon the latter Court held that the tenor of the deed might be proved incidentally (*k*)

§ 1297 In one case the Court on a summary petition remitted to the Depute-Clerk Register to take proper steps for restoring parts of a deed of settlement, which had become much mutilated, and in many places nearly illegible, from lying in a damp repository (*l*) This case may be questioned, as there does not seem to have been any special reason for dispensing with an action of proving the tenor in common form It is said that incidental provings of the tenor are admitted in cases of competition (*m*)

III *Of the Summons of Proving the Tenor*

§ 1298 The summons of proving the tenor must set forth the terms of the missing deed, the supposed cause of its loss or mutilation (called the *casus amissionis*), and the evidence by which the pursuer proposes to prove its tenor (*n*)

The first of these items must be libelled distinctly and correctly, and all conditions and stipulations which the deed contained must be set forth, otherwise a deed in essentially different terms from that which was lost might be substituted for it (*o*) The summons must also bear that the deed was legally executed as a completed writ (*p*) But, as afterwards mentioned, it is not indispensable to

---

(*j*) See *supra*, § 143 It is the everyday practice to admit in evidence copies of correspondence, intimations, and other writings, on proof that the originals are lost or withheld (*k*) Hutchinson *v* Tod, 17th May 1823, F C, 2 S, 318, 2 Sh Ap Ca, 386, S C (*l*) Jeffreys, 1827, 5 S, 331—See also Hume, 1712, M, 11,967 (*m*) Shand's Pr, 842 See § 1293 (*b*) (*n*) Ersk, 4, 1, 56—Shand's Pr, 830—Tait Ev, 205, 7 (*o*) Ersk, *supra*—Shand, *supra*—Tait, 207—Begbie *v* Fell, 1822, 1 S, 391 (*p*) Tait Ev 207 Accordingly, where a summons of proving the tenor of a crown charter only libelled on the tenor of the signet precept for

set forth the date or the names of the writer and instrumentary witnesses (*q*) In one case, where an action was raised for proving the tenor of an unextracted decree, the Court held that the tenor of the relative summons must also be libelled and proved, and they accordingly allowed a supplementary action to be raised for the purpose (*r*)

As to libelling the *casus amissionis*, the rule is that where a special cause of loss must be proved, it must also be libelled on, whereas a general averment of loss from some accidental or unknown cause will suffice, where no specific cause of disappearance requires to be substantiated What deeds fall under these two classes will be noticed immediately (*s*)

In libelling upon the evidence by which the tenor is meant to be proved, any written adminicles which the pursuer proposes to found upon must be specified (*t*), and therefore where a summons of proving the tenor of a marriage-contract set forth that the pursuer was in possession of a copy of the deed, and of ' various other adminicles to be produced in the process to follow hereon," the Court refused to sustain the adminicles as libelled on, but allowed the pursuer to amend the summons by enumerating the documents (*u*)

When no individual is known who can have an interest to oppose the action, it may be brought against the lieges generally (*x*)

IV *Of the* casus amissionis

§ 1299 With regard to libelling and proving the *casus amissionis*, there is a marked distinction between two classes of writings [4]

---

such a deed, the Court dismissed the action, because a precept of that nature is an inchoate writing, and might never have been followed up by an executed charter, E Stirling *v* L Advocate, 1833, 11 S, 506 (*q*) See *infra*, § 1312, 3

(*r*) Duncan *v* Arnott, 1827, 5 S, 840 (*s*) *Infra*, § 1299

(*t*) Shand's Pr, 830 (*u*) Jenkinson *v* Campbell, 1850, 12 D, 854

(*x*) Mitchell *v* the Lieges, 1852, 14 D, 932

---

[4] The distinction is clearly expressed in the opinion returned by the Lord President (M'Neill), Lords Curriehill and Ardmillan, in the recent case of Winchester *v* Smith ' The *casus amissionis* (which as we understand the phrase, means not only that the writing has been actually destroyed or lost, but that its destruction or loss took place in such a manner as implied no extinction of the right of which it was the evident) requires to be supported by much stronger evidence in some cases than in others For example if the writing be a disposition of land of which the tenor is satisfactorily esta-

On the one hand where a deed embodies an obligation or right which is usually extinguished by giving up the document without a separate discharge, a party who attempts to prove the tenor of the deed on the ground that, although amissing, it has not been extinguished, must aver and prove some special *casus amissionis*, sufficient to overcome the presumption that the document was retired or cancelled on the right being discharged (*y*) This rule holds strongly in regard to bills; on account of the constant practice to discharge these writings by merely redelivering them Accordingly, summonses of proving the tenor of bills have been dismissed which did not libel on a special *casus amissionis* (*z*) And where it was averred that the bill had been sent by the pursuer to his agent along with the papers in a certain process, although it did not form one of the productions, and was not marked in the inventory—that the agent for the defender (who was the acceptor of the bill) had borrowed the process with the document—which had not been seen afterwards, notwithstanding the strictest search—the Court considering that proving the tenor of a bill was a "matter of great delicacy, and should not be permitted except on strong grounds," dismissed the action *in hoc statu* (*a*) In like manner, in an action for proving the tenor of a personal bond (*b*), it was held not to be enough to state that the pursuer (who was a lady) had intrusted

(*y*) Stair, 4, 32 3—Ersk 4, 1, 54—More's Notes, 386—Tait Ev 204—Shand's Pr, 832 (*z*) Campbell *v* York Building Co Crs, 1780, M, 15 828—Carson *v* M'Micken, 14th May 1811, F C (*a*) M'Farlane *v* M'Nee, 1826, 4 S, 509

(*b*) As to heritable bonds see *infra*, § 1303, 4

blished, and which was followed by infeftment and long and uninterrupted possession, and the instrument of sasine on which is produced, a comparatively slight proof of the *casus amissionis* may be sufficient But if it be such a writing as is usually cancelled or destroyed when it has served its purpose—as, for example, a bill of exchange or promissory-note, or a personal bond—and if it has been destroyed or has been found in the hands or the repositories of the granter actually cancelled, the presumption is, that the right, of which it had been originally the evident, no longer subsists, and very clear evidence is requisite to overcome the presumption The same is the case where the right, of which the cancelled or destroyed writing, if it were effectual, would be the evident, is a revocable one, because such cancellation or destruction is itself an effectual mode of executing a power of revocation, and when such a writing has actually been destroyed, or has been found cancelled in the hands or in the repositories of the granter after his death, the presumption is, that such destruction or cancellation took place in the exercise of his power of revocation, and that presumption can be obviated only by very clear evidence to the contrary In order, therefore, to judge of the sufficiency of the evidence of the *casus amissionis* of a writing in an action of proving the tenor, the nature of the writing must be carefully attended to," Winchester *v* Smith 1863, 1 Macph 685

her papers to a certain person, "and that the deed must have been lost or fallen aside in his keeping" (*c*) And in an action to prove the tenor of two bonds, where the *casus amissionis* averred was that they had been given in to a Sheriff-court record for registration the Court required that cause of loss to be admimiculated, because at the date in question, the originals of deeds so registered used to be returned (*d*) But it was held a sufficient *casus amissionis* of a lost bond that, twenty years before, it had been produced to the Commissioners of Chancery in England and had miscarried (*e*) And in another case the Court sustained the averment that a bond had been lost in the hands of the keeper of a public register, at a time when the same accident happened to other bonds (*f*) In like manner, where part of the signatures to a bond recorded in a Sheriff-court register had been torn away, the Court presumed that it had been complete when given in for registration, as it was not probable that the keepers of the register would have recorded a cancelled deed (*g*) In an old case the Court allowed the tenor of a bond to be proved, where the *casus amissionis* averred was that the creditor's wife had recklessly and foolishly burnt it at a candle, when no one else was present, although the averment could not be proved in consequence of the wife being inadmissible as a witness (*h*) This decision may be questioned

It was held to be a relevant averment of the *casus amissionis* of a back-bond (which may be discharged without writing) that ten years before the defender had privately obtained possession of the document, and had "destroyed or away put it," or that it had fallen aside and been lost, the peculiarity of the case being that (according to the averment) the deed, while still undischarged, was traced into the hands of the party who was interested in destroying it (*i*) It has been held necessary to prove a special *casus amissionis* of an indenture between a master and apprentice (*j*)

§ 1300 The rule that a special *casus amissionis* is necessary in regard to deeds which are usually discharged by redelivery, does not prevent a proving of the tenor in cases where there is proof or

---

(*c*) Begbie *v* Fell 1822, 1 S 391 See also Hammermen of Glasgow *v* Crawford, 1628, M, 2247 (*d*) A *v* B 1682 M 15,802 (*e*) E Southesk *v* D Hamilton, 1682, M, 15 801 "There was great presumption of the not payment"

(*f*) E Lauderdale *v* Mackay, 1770, 2 Pat Ap Ca, 234 (*g*) M'Dowall *v* M'Ghie, 1713, 5 B Sup, 98 The deed had been followed by a bond of corroboration

(*h*) Walker *v* Ronald, 1670 2 B Sup, 476 (*i*) Millar *v* Millar 1832 10 S 362 See also § 1305 (*n*) (*j*) Scotland *v* Robertson 1801 M "Tenor" Appx No 1

strong probability that the deed was not given up or cancelled, but where the party who founds on it cannot condescend on the occasion of its loss. In one case as to a personal bond of old date granted by an entailer and his son and heir, where it was averred that the original creditor and his heirs had employed different agents, through whose hands their papers had passed at various times, and that in the course of these changes the bond had fallen aside or been lost, the defence that the pursuer did not aver a sufficient *casus amissionis* was repelled, on the ground that the deed had been repeatedly operated upon, had been followed by payments of annuity, and had been founded on in a process of multiplepoinding many years before, in which it had been admitted by the debtor although it had not been produced (*k*). In another case, a similar averment as to the *casus amissionis* of a written cautionary obligation was sustained, where there was reason to believe, from the evidence, that the obligation had not been discharged (*l*). It was here considered that the question in each case is, whether the circumstances show that the missing document was discharged; the rule as to requiring a special *casus amissionis* being subsidiary to the more general rule that, if there are sufficient grounds for believing that the deed was never retired or cancelled, its tenor as a subsisting writ may be established (*m*).

§ 1301. There is a peculiar delicacy in regard to the *casus amissionis* of testamentary writings. The intentions of many testators so frequently fluctuate upon changes in their own circumstances or companionship, upon some accidental estrangement, or some act of real or fancied unkindness in the persons they at one time favoured,—and their changes of purpose are so often carried out with studied secrecy,—that the bare fact that a testamentary writing existed some time before the testator's death does not raise a presumption that he retained the intentions which he there expressed. Accordingly, the party who tries to rear up such a writing by an action of proving the tenor must aver and prove a *casus amissionis* incompatible with the supposition that the testator intentionally cancelled it (*n*). Thus it was held not enough to state that a will had never been cancelled or altered by the testator in any shape,

(*k*) Mackenzie v. L. Dundas, 1835, 11 S., 144. (*l*) Forbes' Trs. v. Welsh, 1827, 5 S., 497. (*m*) See also Mein v. Dunse, 1701, M., 2712—E. Southesk v. D. Hamilton, *supra* (*e*)—and cases *infra*, § 1305. (*n*) See this principle illustrated in Dow v. Dow, 1848, 10 D., 1465—Forrester v. Forrester, 1836, 16 S., 1064 (noted fully in Tait Ev., 206).

and had been placed in his repositories but had been abstracted therefrom or at least had disappeared (*o*) And where, in an action of proving the tenor of two testamentary writings, it was averred that the testatrix had become insane, and continued so till her death, that the deeds had been seen in her possession after her derangement began, but were not found in her repositories after her death, although the envelope which had inclosed them was found there, the Court, before answer as to whether the averments disclosed a sufficient *casus amissionis*, allowed a proof On afterwards considering the evidence, they held that it had failed to establish any one of the three points which were necessary in such a case, namely, (1) that the testatrix was insane, (2) that she was so the last time the deeds were seen in her possession and (3) that she continued insane till her death (*p*) The proof of the *casus amissionis* of a will was more successful, where it was shown that the next of kin of the testator had violently taken possession of it and destroyed it (*r*) and where it was proved that an executrix had burnt a letter directing her to pay certain legacies (*s*) In a case which occurred a few years ago four persons in a respectable rank of life were tried in the Justiciary Court, and were punished on their own confession, on a charge of destroying a will of a person to whom they were next of kin (*t*) The tenor of the deed was afterwards proved [5]

§ 1302 Mr Tait (*u*) notices the case (which can easily be supposed) of a person having become aware of an accidental or fraudulent destruction of his will and not having repeated its bequests in a new deed, when he had time and opportunity to do so The most probable explanation of such a case is that the testator resolved either to allow his succession to be intestate, or to execute a new will in terms different from the previous one, while, if he intended to execute a similar deed, the case will generally come under the category *quod voluit et potuit non fecit* But there may be circumstances (*e g*, the absence or delay of the testator's law-agent the testator's bad health or engrossment in business) which if com-

(*o*) Ker *v* Ker 1830, 9 S, 204 (*p*) Lang *v* Bruce, 1838 1 D 59

(*r*) Boyter *v* Rintoul, 1832 5 De and And, 215, affd, 6 W S, 394 In Reid *v* Duff, 1843, 5 D 656 a case of this nature broke down in consequence of the pursuer's agent having precognosced the witnesses in presence of each other

(*s*) Lillies *v* Smith, 1832, 11 S 160 (*t*) Rattrays, 1848, Arkley, 406

(*u*) Tait Ev 205

[5] Russell's Trustees *v* Russell 1862 24 D 1141

bined with clear proof of intention to execute another will in similar terms, may prevent the rights of the parties favoured by the previous will from being defeated

§ 1303 Contrasted with the cases noticed in the preceding section are those of "deeds which are intended to remain constantly with the grantee or which require contrary deeds of renunciation to extinguish them, as dispositions, seisines, wadsets, &c, or where the debtor who makes payment does not commonly choose to rely for their extinction on the bare cancelling of them, as assignations," &c In actions of proving the tenor of such deeds "a more general *casus amissionis* is sufficient, insomuch that most lawyers are of opinion that it is sufficient to libel that the deed was lost anyhow even *casu fortuitu*" (x)

§ 1304 Thus a special *casus amissionis* was dispensed with or only a *talis qualis* proof of one was required in proving the tenor of a disposition followed by sasine and possession (y), and of a precept of *clare constat* (z) And it was held enough, as to a disposition which had been followed by resignation and sasine and by possession, to allege that it had been lost in passing through the hands of successive law-agents for the disponee (a), or when his agent changed his chambers which he had done twice after the deed had been placed in his hands (b) The same principle has been applied in actions for proving the tenor of a deed of entail (c)—a marriage-contract (d)—an assignation of a debt (e)—an agreement between the lessor and tenant of a coal field, bearing that no rent should be paid the first year, and other stipulations (f)—an heritable bond followed by sasine (g)—and an heritable bond of annuity (without sasine) by a husband in favour of his wife (h) So it was held not necessary to prove a special *casus amissionis* of a decree of declara-

---

(x) Ersk, 4, 1, 54 The same rule is stated in Stair, 4, 32, 4—See also More's Notes, 386—Tait Ev, 206—Shand's Pr, 833 (y) Merry v Masson, 1834, 12 S, 761—Ker v Kay, 1830, 8 S, 1008—M'Leod v M'Lean, 1835, 13 S, 581

(z) Limond, 1829, 8 S, 116 (a) D Roxburghe's Tr v Young, 1835, 13 S, 176 (b) Walker v Brock, 1852, 14 D, 362 (c) Gordon v Gray, 1749, 5 B Sup, 776, reported as A B in M, 15,823 There was a "pretty strong presumption" that the defender had taken the deed out of a charter-chest in which it was proved to have been placed With this case compare M Annandale v L Hope, 1738, Cr and St, 198, *infra*, § 1305 (n) (d) Mann v Mann, 1736, Elch, "Tenor" 3

(e) Main v Niddrie, 1663, M, 15,789—Watson v Erskine, 1847, 19 Sc Jur, 523

(f) Robertson v Hyndman, 1833, 11 S, 775 (g) Chancellor v Gray, 1735, Elch, "Tenor" 2 (h) Moffat v Moffat, 31st January 1809 F C Compare with this case Sinclair v Sinclair's Crs, 1734, Elch, "Tenor, No 1

tor of irritancy *ob non solutum canonem*, pronounced at a time when the records were not regularly kept (*i*)

§ 1305 But the rule which dispenses with a special *casus amissionis* in regard to such writings does not apply to a case where it is probable, from the circumstances, that the document was discharged or cancelled by the granter or was altered by a subsequent deed (*k*) Accordingly, where a widow claimed under a bond of annuity which had been granted by her husband in consideration of her executing a certain disposition, and where in an action for proving the tenor of the disposition, it appeared that, although executed during her husband's life, it had not been ratified by her judicially and that it had been found in her own hands cancelled, the Court of Session presumed that it had been cancelled by herself, and the House of Lords affirmed the judgment (*l*) Thus, also, where a husband and wife had entered into a marriage-contract, under which she had only right to an annuity much less than her legal rights in her husband's estate, which had greatly increased after their marriage and where, in an action raised by the husband's heir for proving the tenor of the marriage-contract ' the evidence adduced was such as to corroborate the presumption arising from the non-appearance, that the husband had purposed to undo it," the Court refused decree of proving the tenor, and their judgment was affirmed on appeal (*m*) Again, where the institute under an entail had altered the order of succession, and his disponee (who alleged that the deed of entail exempted the institute from its prohibitions) raised an action to prove its tenor, the House of Lords, reversing the decision of the Court of Session held that a special *casus amissionis* was necessary, because the deed had been traced into the hands of the institute's mother who was interested in freeing him from its fetters (*n*) In another case the Court of Session assoilzied in a proving of the tenor of a decree of apprising, the *casus amissionis* on the evidence being general and weak, compared with strong grounds for presuming that the apprising had been retired (*o*) In like manner, where an action of reduction of an entail on the ground of forgery had been raised and on the

(*i*) D Argyll *v* M'Lean 1781, M , 15,828

(*k*) This is the counter-part of the rule stated *supra*, § 1300 The principle is the same in both cases, namely, that the necessity for proving a special *casus amissionis* depends on the circumstances of each case, and that the nature of the deed only raises such a presumption regarding the cause of its loss or mutilation, as may be overcome by contrary probabilities arising from the circumstances

(*l*) Houston *v* Schaw 1726, Rob Ap Ca , 561

(*m*) Donald *v* Kircaldy, 1787, M 15,831

(*n*) M Annandale *v* Hope 1733, Cr and St 108

(*o*) Miln *v* L Lauderdale, 1687, M 15,805

deed being lodged in process, in order to satisfy the production, it was found that the portion which should have borne the witnesses' names and a great part of the testing clause had been torn off, the Court held that a general allegation that it had been accidentally torn in pulling the deed out of a bundle of papers was not sufficient (*p*). Thus, also, in an action of proving the tenor of a lease for 1000 years at a nominal rent, the Court refused decree, on account of the evasive and contradictory statements which the pursuer had made in three declarations emitted by him in a criminal investigation, and when examined as a haver in an action of reduction-improbation of the lease, combined with an improbable story, not supported by any evidence that he had missed the deed out of his pocket on recovering from a drinking bout (*r*).

§ 1306. Difficult questions sometimes arise where the *casus amissionis* alleged is that the deed was destroyed by a depositary in compliance with the granter's directions (*s*). The result of such cases depends on whether the alleged directions are proved. But it seems that the alleged destruction is a sufficient *casus amissionis* to warrant decree of proving the tenor, in order to restore matters to the state in which they were before the depositary destroyed the document, and that the granter's directions require to be established in a subsequent action of reduction (*t*).[6]

V. *Of the mode of Proving the Tenor.*

§ 1307. The pursuer has next to prove that the document in question was a valid deed or other writ in the terms libelled on. And this is required, although the defender does not appear to oppose decree (*u*). The evidence may be *prout de jure* (*x*), except in cases of "letters of horning, executions, and indorsations thereof, not extant and produced judicially," the tenor of which cannot be proved by witnesses (*y*).

(*p*) Graham v. Graham, 1847, 10 D., 45. See a case somewhat similar, Nasmyth v. Hare, 1821, 1 Sh. Ap. Ca., 65, noted *supra*, § 714. (*r*) Paterson v. Houston, 1837, 16 S., 225. (*s*) See these cases noticed *supra*, § 967.

(*t*) Falconer v. Stephen, 1848, 11 D., 220, 1338.—See *infra*, § 1319.

(*u*) Shand's Pr., 839.—M'Larty v. Borland, 1832, 5 D. and And., 95.—Fisher v. Nicolson, 1831, 1 ib., 379. (*x*) Ersk., 4, 1, 55.—Tait Ev., 208.

(*y*) 1579, c. 94.—*Supra*, § 1288.

[6] See observations on Falconer v. Stephen by the Lord Justice-Clerk (Inglis), and Lord Neaves in Winchester v. Smith, 1863, 1 Macph., 697, 700, *infra* § 1318 note 8.

As to what amount of evidence will suffice to prove the tenor of different writings it is impossible to lay down any precise rules, because every case depends on its own circumstances, and on a complex view of the nature of the deed, the *casus amissionis* and the adminicles or other evidence of the tenor. A few general observations, however, may be made on the subject.

§ 1308. When the written adminicles are probative writings under the hand of the granter of the lost deed or any of his successors in the subject, they are held to be sufficient proof of the tenor, without being corroborated by witnesses (z). And writs reciting the deed, although not under the hand of any of these parties, will suffice, if the writing is of an old date (a), or if it is merely a step in a progress of writings, and not a deed constituting a right or obligation (b), or if the parties interested to exclude the decree do not oppose (c). In one case, where there was a "pretty strong presumption" that the defender had abstracted a deed of entail the tenor of it was held to be proved by the retour of a general service as heir of entail mentioning the maker of the entail and the series of heirs but none of the provisions or limitations, the terms of which were established by scrolls and copies (d). When the missing deed is alleged to be the constitution of a right or obligation, and the adminicles are not under the hand of the defender or his predecessor, proof of some kind to show that the deed was acted upon, or was recognised as valid, will usually be required, otherwise there would be nothing to indicate that it was effectual (e). But if the *casus amissionis* is clearly established, and if there is no ground for questioning the original validity of the deed, proof that it was recognised or acted upon may be dispensed with (f). And still more will this be competent, where the *casus amissionis* was the wrongful act of the party prejudiced by the deed, and against whom or his heirs the action of proving is instituted,—because *omnia presumuntur contra spoliatorem*, and his act is strong circumstantial evidence that the deed was effectual (g).

(z) Stair, 4, 32, 10—Ersk., 4, 1, 56—Tait, *supra*—Mackay *v.* E. Lauderdale, 1766, affirmed, 21st March 1770 (not rep.), noted in Ivory's Ersk., 954, †—Gordon *v.* Gray, 1749, 5 B. Sup., 776. (a) See Kinnear *v.* Kellie, 1685, M., 15,804—Lesmore *v.* M. Huntly, 1682, M., 15,802—A. B. 1755, 5 B. Sup., 837. (b) Inglis *v.* Lord A. Hay, 1712, M., 15,819. (c) M'Leod *v.* M'Lean, 1835, 13 S., 581—Fleming *v.* M'Intosh, 1835, ib., 1002. (d) Gordon *v.* Gray, *supra*. (e) Graham *v.* Graham, 1847, 10 D., 15—Brodie *v.* Douglas, 1672, M. 15,703—Corsar *v.* Durie, noted in Harner *v.* Hartly, 1667, M. 15,792—Fumartoun *v.* Lutefoot, 1675, M. 1755.

(f) Walker *v.* Brock, 1852, 14 D., 362—Per Lord Elchies in Gordon *v.* Gray, 1749, 5 B. Sup. 776. See also Stair, 4, 32, 7—Ersk., 4, 1, 55. (g) See Gordon *v.*

§ 1309 When the written evidence is not full proof of the tenor it may be supplemented by parole, which ought, if possible, to include the oaths of the instrumentary witnesses (*h*) In favourable cases the scroll of the deed, with the oaths of the writer and witnesses to prove its identity and the execution of the principal deed, will suffice (*i*) The proof may also include writings which merely refer to the lost deed, improbative writs, and even scrolls of deeds referring to it as a finished writ, such writings, however, being excluded where, from their having been prepared after the destruction or loss, there is reason to suspect that they may have been made up in order to be used as evidence in the case (*k*) Nor does such indirect and make-shift written evidence obviate the necessity for proof of the validity of the missing deed by the oaths of the instrumentary witnesses, or by evidence that it was recognised as effectual by the parties bound by it (*l*) Considerable weight will be attached to evidence of admissions of the granter that he executed the deed, or that it was obligatory (*m*) Such evidence, or evidence that the party recognised its validity, is peculiarly requisite in proving the tenor of holograph writings, because evidence of the handwriting is lost, and there are seldom witnesses who can swear to having seen the party write the deed (*n*)

§ 1310 In the older cases the Court seem to have held written adminicles to be indispensable, except in very special circumstances (*o*), from "deference to the cardinal maxim of our law, that where writing is *de solennitate* necessary, the want of it can never be supplied by parole" (*p*) They, however, admitted witnesses without writing, where the *casus amissionis* was clearly proved (*q*), especially where it was the improper destruction or mutilation of

---

Gray, *supra*—Boyter *v* Rintoul, 1832, 5 De and And, 215, affd, 6 W S, 394—Ronald, 1830, 8 S, 1008 (*h*) Stair, 4, 32, 8—Ersk, 4, 1, 56—Tait Ev, 210—Graham *v* Graham, 1847, 10 D, 49, per Lord Jeffrey (*i*) Ronald 1830, 8 S, 1008—Anderson *v* Boyd, 1827, 5 S, 927 (*k*) Ersk, 4, 1, 55—Gordon *v* Gray, 1749 5 B Sup, 776 (*l*) Ersk, 4, 1, 56 (*m*) Forbes' Tr *v* Walsh 1827, 5 S, 497—Baillie *v* Pitillock, 1680, M 15,800—Ronald *v* Sang, 1852, 14 D 357 (*n*) Compare Robertson *v* Hyndman, 1833, 11 S, 775—Trotter *v* Home, 1707, M, 15,811—Fraser *v* Davies, 1784, M, 15,830—Lillies *v* Lillie, 1832, 11 S 160

(*o*) Stair, 4, 32, 5—Ersk 4, 1, 55—Douglas *v* Graham, 1619, 1 B Sup, 439—Countess Kincardine *v* Broomhall, 1684, M, 15,803—Cranstoun *v* Swinton, 1674, M, 16,791—Harroway *v* Hartley 1667, M, 15,791 (*p*) Per L Jeffrey in Graham *v* Graham, 1847, 10 D, 45—Ersk, 4, 1, 55 (*q*) Stair, 4, 32, 7—Ersk, *supra*—Graham *v* Graham, *supra*—Dickson *v* Veitch, 1541, M, 15,783—E March *v* Montgomery 1743, M 15 820 But see Douglas *v* Graham, 1619, 1 B Sup 439

the deed by persons prejudiced by it (r) Written adminicles will also be dispensed with where it is not likely that the lost document if genuine would have been referred to in other writings, for otherwise the benefit of the action would often be lost to persons in right of such documents (s)[7] This applies to "acquittances and writs of that nature" (t), to back-bonds of relief (u) and even to personal bonds, which are frequently neither registered nor referred to in subsequent writings (x) In such cases the *casus amissionis* usually requires to be proved, and the depositions as to the tenor must be specific and consistent (y)

§ 1311 It is not necessary that the witnesses should depone to the precise words of the deed, provided they prove that it was substantially in the terms libelled on, and that it bore the necessary subscriptions, without appearance of vitiation or forgery (z) The Court will even dispense with specific proof of clauses which are matters of style, in deeds like the one libelled on (a) whereas they will require clear proof of unusual or improbable stipulations (b)

§ 1312 It has sometimes been considered that the testing clause, with the witnesses' subscriptions, must be specially libelled on and proved (c) But the House of Lords reversed a decision (d) in which the Court of Session held this to be necessary in proving the tenor of a bond Since that time the Court have overlooked the defect when they were satisfied that the deed was genuine (e),

(r) Lillies *v* Lillie, 1832 11 S, 160—Boyter *v* Rintoul, 1832, 5 De and And, 215, affd, 6 W S, 394—Cunninghame *v* Greenlees, 1674 M 15,794—Nimmo *v* Sinclair 1771 M, 15,825 See also Gordon *v* Gray 1749, 5 B Sup, 776

(s) Ersk, 4, 1, 55—Tait, 210

(t) Ogilvy *v* Napier, 1612, M, 15,786

(u) L Frendraught *v* L Banff 1636, M, 15,788 But see the report of this case in 1 B Sup 218

(x) Ersk, 4 1 55—Per L Elchies in Gordon *v* Gray *supra*

(y) Ersk, *supra*—Gordon *v* Gray, *supra*

(z) Stair, 4, 32, 9—Ersk 4 1, 56—Tait Ev, 207

(a) Stair, 4, 32, 8, 9 In Boyter *v* Rintoul *supra* a will which had been improperly destroyed by the next of kin was held to have contained a clause dispensing with delivery, although that was not specially proved See also Kay *v* Gordon, 1767 5 B Sup, 935—Nimmo *v* Sinclair, 1771, M, 15 825

(b) See Stair, 4, 32, 5—M Annandale *v* Hope, 1733, Cr and St, 108

(c) Elphinston *v* Salton, 1611 M, 15,785—Campbell *v* M'Alister, 1757, Elch, "Tenor" 6—Ersk, 4, 1, 57

(d) Blackwood *v* Hamilton, 1713, Rob Ap Ca, 211, reversing, M, 15,819

(e) Mackenzie *v* L Dundas, 1835, 14

7 Winton & Co *v* Thomson & Co, 1862, 24 D, 1094 Lord Justice-Clerk (Inglis) —'I am not sure but that in such a case —an agreement by creditors to accept a composition—"adminicles might be dispensed with altogether if one were satisfied that they were not to be expected"

as they had previously done in two cases where the lost deeds were old and of undoubted authenticity (*f*) These decisions justly proceed on the presumption *omne rite et solenniter actum* If the testing clause and witnesses required to be proved in all cases, the use of this action would be confined within too narrow limits, for the party seeking to set up a genuine deed would often fail in proving this part of it, especially where a considerable interval had elapsed since its date (*g*) The absence of proof of the testing clause, however, may be important where there is reason for doubting whether the deed was genuine and duly authenticated, and, if the action is raised to prove the tenor of a testing clause which has been torn off, the Court will require strong proof that the deed was probative, or at least, that the mutilation was accidental (*h*) Where part of the debtor's subscription to a bond recorded in the books of a Sheriff-court had been torn away, the Court of Session presumed that the deed had been complete when given in for registration as it was not likely that the keeper of the register would have received and recorded a mutilated deed (*i*)

Where there was proof of the *casus amissionis* of a disposition, which was alleged to have been executed notarially, and which had been followed by possession for many years, the Court granted decree of proving the tenor of it, although the pursuer did not specify the names of the notaries, or of any of the witnesses (*k*).

§ 1313 It is not essential to prove either the date or place of subscription, these not being statutory requisites to a deed (*l*) But the want of the date may be important in cases of competition (*m*)

§ 1314 Nor does the pursuer require to prove that the deed was stamped, because it will be presumed *omne rite et solenniter actum*, and that the party did not commit a fraud on the revenue But slight evidence that the deed was unstamped, will throw the burden of proof on the pursuer (*n*)

§ 1315 A witness who could neither read nor write was once held inadmissible to prove the tenor of a lost deed (*o*) There are many facts, however, which might be well established by such evi-

---

S, 144—Merry *v* Dunn, 1835, ib, 36—Ronald *v* Sing, 1852, 11 D, 357—Ersk, 4, 1, 57—Tait Ev, 208—Shand's Pr, 831, noting Mitchie *v* Duncan, 3d Feb 1810 (not rep)

(*f*) Calderwood *v* Courtie, 1681, M, 15,800—Trotter *v* Home, 1707, M, 15,811—See also Peppermill *v* Room, 1684, M, 15,803 (*g*) Ersk, *supra*

(*h*) Graham *v* Graham, 1817, 10 D, 45 (*i*) M'Dowall *v* M'Ghie, 1713, 5 B Sup, 98 (*k*) Merry *v* Dun, 1835, 11 S, 36 (*l*) See *supra*, § 711 (*m*) See Ballender *v* Law, 1686, M, 15,804—Shand's Pr 832

(*n*) See *supra* § 1005 (*o*) Bruce *v* Bruce, 1616, M, 15,786

dence, *e g*, admissions by the granter, and the *res gestæ* of the subscription

§ 1316. On account of the delicacy of the investigation, it used to be the practice for the Inner House to examine witnesses in actions of proving the tenor (*p*), and commissions to take the proof were refused except in special cases (*r*) or were granted to one or more of the judges (*s*) An ordinary commissioner was sometimes appointed to examine infirm witnesses or such as resided beyond the jurisdiction of the Court (*t*) The modern practice has been for the Lord Ordinary in the cause to take the proof (*u*) But commissions to others than the judges have in several cases been granted without a special reason being assigned (*x*) the Court, however, being more particular in selecting their commissioner in actions of proving the tenor than in less difficult cases (*y*)

VI *Effect of the Decree and Extract-decree*

§ 1317 A decree of proving the tenor revives the missing deed to the same effect as if it had continued in existence (*z*) And an extract of the decree is probative, like an extract of a recorded deed (*a*)

§ 1318 The object of the action being thus to overcome the loss of a writing and not to determine its effect or validity, a decree of proving the tenor is not *res judicata* in a challenge of the deed on the head of forgery (*b*), or impetration, or collusion (*c*)

(*p*) Ersk, 4, 1, 58—Tait Ev, 211—Shand's Pr, 840 (*r*) Authorities in preceding note—Ferrier *v* Berry, 1823, 2 S, 305 (*s*) Ersk, *supra*—Gordon, 1752, M 15,823 (*t*) Ersk, *supra*—Scott, 1787, Hailes, 1015—Cases of Comb *v* M'Millan 1773, E Aberdeen *v* Forbes, 1775, and Pringle *v* St Clair, 1771 (not reported), noted in Shand's Pr, 840 (*u*) Shand's Pr, 840—Falconer *v* Stephen, 1849, 11 D, 1338 (*x*) Anderson *v* M'Connochie, 1843, 5 D, 494—Cases of Pringle *v* Mack, 1821, and Small *v* Smith, 1826 (not reported), noted in Beveridge's Forms of Process, 413, and Shand, *supra* (*y*) In M'Comb *v* M'Millan, Pringle *v* Mack, and Small *v* Smith, *supra*, the commission was taken to the sheriff of the county, whereas in Ferrier *v* Berry, *supra*, a commission to that officer was refused because a special reason for it was not assigned In Anderson *v* M'Connochie, *supra* a commission to two justices of the peace was refused, while in Boyter *v* Rintoul, 1832, (5 De and And, 215, aff'd, 6 W S 394), noted on this point in Shand's Pr, 840, the proof was taken by an advocate (*z*) Ersk 4, 1, 59—Tait's Ev 212—Shand's Pr, 842 (*a*) Ersk, *supra*—Tait, *supra*—Shand *supra*

(*b*) Stair, 4, 32, 11—Ersk, *supra*—Nory *v* Meikle, 1672, 1 B Sup, 657—Tait, *supra*—Shand *supra* (*c*) Inglis *v* Hay, 1712, M, 2744—Baillies *v* Johnston, 1730, M, 15,833 Still less will it be a good defence to the proving that the deed was executed by a minor without consent of his curators See Carse *v* Kennedy, 1714 M, 13,247 because such objections are not competent defences to an action of proving Again, where the defender in an action on a deed as revived by a decree of proving the tenor alleges that the right has been extinguished, a distinction seems to exist as to the competency of this plea If it is averred that the non-existence of the deed arose from its having been retired or cancelled on the right being extinguished, then such discharge was a competent defence to the action of proving, as it negatived the allegation of a proper *casus amissionis* (*d*). Accordingly, if that defence was pleaded and repelled in the action of proving, the decree is *res judicata* on the point Nay more, if such a defence is for the first time pleaded in an action to enforce the deed as restored, the Court may hesitate to entertain it, because it was "competent and omitted" as a defence to the action of proving On the other hand, if the supposed discharge and the *casus amissionis* are independent, then, as the discharge was not a good defence in the action of proving the tenor, it may be pleaded in defence to an action on the deed, as restored by the decree of proving (*e*) [2]

(*d*) See Miln *v* Duchess of Lauderdale, 1687, M , 15,805 See *supra*, § 1300

(*e*) Inglis *v* Hay, 1712, M , 2744 See also Hamilton *v* Hamilton, 1713, M , 15,819

[2] In the recent case of Winchester *v* Smith some important observations on the scope and effect of the action of proving of the tenor fell from the bench The circumstances out of which the case arose were these —A mutual disposition and settlement was executed by spouses in favour of the survivor It contained a clause providing for the distribution of the means and estates upon the death of "the longest liver," and a reserved power to revoke "at any time during our joint lives" On the death of the husband, William Smith, the deed was produced with the wife's signature and those of the instrumentary witnesses cancelled The action was brought by one of the beneficiaries under the settlement for the purpose of setting up the deed Some of the judges were disposed to doubt whether, in the circumstances, Grace Winchester, the pursuer, had a good title to sue The deed provided that, upon the death of the longest liver of the spouses, one-half of the whole means and estates was to be divided equally, share and share alike, among the surviving children of Robert Smith, "and one-fourth to Grace Winchester and the heirs of her body" It was argued that the declaration and provision [not being a conveyance of anything in favour of the parties named, but only a *mortis causa* destination of any succession which might actually be left by the survivor of the spouses, and seeing that the pursuer would have no *jus quæsitum* under it, unless she happened to survive the widow, her mother, who during her life might exhaust the whole means and estate] did not confer any right upon the pursuer which could enable her to maintain the action The opinion of the majority, however, seemed to be, that any party who on the face of a deed has a *prima facie* interest in it, is *in titulo* to prove the tenor of it, and that the pursuer here had a *prima facie* interest The *casus amissionis*, which the pursuer alleged and attempted to instruct, was,

§ 1319. When it is alleged that a deed was destroyed by a depositary in conformity with the granter's directions, decree of prov-

that Mrs Smith, during the life of her husband, but without his knowledge, and in a fit of passion at one of the beneficiaries had deleted her own name and the names of the instrumentary witnesses. Mrs Smith was examined as a witness, and deponed that she had destroyed the deed in the circumstances described, but that she had immediately repented of what she had done, and had, after the death of her husband, of new subscribed her own name, and inserted those of the instrumentary witnesses. Her evidence, however, was quite unsupported, and the majority of the Court held that the evidence of one witness having a material interest in the validity of the deed, was not sufficient to overcome the presumption that it had been duly cancelled during the lifetime of the husband. But Lords Cowan and Deas were of opinion that the real evidence of facts and circumstances was confirmatory of the widow's testimony, and showed that a mutual deed which was not revocable by one of the granters alone had been cancelled or mutilated without the knowledge of the husband. They held, therefore, that the *casus amissionis* had been established, and that the pursuer was entitled to succeed in her action. But they were willing that the terms of the interlocutor should be similar to those adopted in Falconer's case (11 D., 220 and 1338), which were: "In respect of the peculiar circumstances of the present case, find the terms of the writing or codicil proven, and decern, under reservation of all questions as to the effect of said writing or codicil." Lord Neaves thought that such a reservation was incompetent, "but, if such a reservation is necessary or proper, we had better not allow the proving of the tenor at all. The very object of this action is to undo the cancellation, and a decree in it, by its very nature, repones all parties against that act as if it had never taken place. The deed cannot, I conceive, be reared up by a proving of the tenor, without being reared up to its full effect." And the Lord Justice-Clerk (Inglis) observed, that while under ordinary circumstances he would think such a reservation very unmeaning, "because there is necessarily such a reservation implied in all decrees of proving of the tenor," he thought it objectionable here because the only question on which the pursuer desired a decision was that which it was proposed to reserve. But the opinion of the Lord Justice-Clerk principally proceeded on the view, that an action of proving of the tenor was inapplicable to the circumstances of the case, and that to decide the questions raised under the summons would be to decide questions which ought never to be decided under such a summons, and dangerously to extend the scope and effect of the action of proving of the tenor. The pursuer did not merely ask the Court to declare that a valid deed was of a certain tenor, but she asked the Court to set up an ineffectual will cancelled and obliterated in vital parts. "Whether the cancellation, in the circumstances under which the will was found, is to have the effect in law of destroying the will, or whether the will can be restored as a legal instrument against the effect of the cancellation, is a question wholly unsuited for a process like this." In the case of Falconer, the deed was destroyed after the death of the granter, and the Court, after finding and decerning that the deed was of a certain tenor, reserved the question, Whether in law the mandate which authorised the cancellation operated *ipso facto* as a revocation, and was effectual although the deed was not actually destroyed until after the death of the mandant? Although in Winchester, the deed was mutilated during the lifetime of the granters, the sufficiency of the mutilation to affect the rights of the beneficiaries appears to be a question very similar to that which was reserved in the case of Falconer. In both cases the deeds were cancelled, the one during the lifetime, the other after the death, of the granter, and the true question in either case appears substantially the same. Did the cancellation, mutilation, or destruction of the deed by the person who cancelled

ing the tenor will be pronounced in order that matters may be restored to the state in which they were before the *casus amissionis*, the parties prejudiced by the deed being entitled to show in another process that it ought not to be enforced (*f*)

§ 1320 An extract-decree of proving will prevent certification *contra non producta* in an action of reduction-improbation (*g*), but without prejudice to any investigations as to the genuineness of the original deed Such an improbation, however, is not likely to be successful, if the tenor has been proved by the writer and instrumentary witnesses, or even by other witnesses deponing that they saw a deed of the tenor libelled duly signed and attested, without any appearance of vitiation or forgery (*h*), or if the tenor has been proved by adminicles under the hand of the party who propones the improbation Lord Stair seems to hold that if the defender compeared in the action of proving, and if the tenor was proved by the instrumentary witnesses, the decree of proving will be equivalent to a decree of declarator of verity of the writ, and the defender will be excluded from afterwards insisting in an improbation (*i*)

(*f*) Falconer *v* Stephen 1849 11 D 1338 See also Forbes *v* Lady Culloden 1712, M, 13 286 (*g*) Stair, 4, 32, 11—Ersk 4, 1, 59—Stewart's Answ *voce* "Tenor," p 306—Tait Ev 212—Shand's Pr 636 and Tait's MS there cited—Mein *v* Dunse, 1701 M, 2742—Anderson *v* Lowes, 1675, M 15 796—Bogle *v* Anderson 1683 M 5192—Waddell *v* Waddell 1707, M, 12 593 See also Hill *v* Cuthbertson, 1692, 4 B Sup, 11—Brown *v* Craw, 1698, M, 15 806 4 B Sup, 401, S C

(*h*) Stair, 4 32, 11—Ersk 4 1, 59 (*i*) Stair, 4 32, 10

---

or destroyed it extinguish the right of which it was the evident? Had he authority to cancel or destroy it, and was the authority competently exercised? If the defender's argument in Falconer, that the mandate to destroy operated *ipso facto* as a revocation, was well founded, then the deed was not a valid instrument any more than the mutual deed in Winchester, a condition being attached to it which made it as inoperative as if it had been destroyed by the granter during his life, and on the other hand, if the mutual deed in Winchester was not revocable by the sole act of one of the spouses then although lost or mutilated before the death of either of the granters, it became, it would appear, when restored and set up after the death of either of them, a complete and operative deed It is not very obvious at first sight why parties seeking to restore a deed in such circumstances should be compelled to have recourse to a remedy other than the remedy which an action of proving of the tenor provides, and there is difficulty in drawing a distinction between the cases in which the validity of the lost or mutilated deed may be competently established in a proving of the tenor, and those in which its validity must be otherwise established In every such action indeed the Court is forced to consider, as the first question in the inquiry, whether the circumstances under which the deed was lost did or did not import the extinction of the right of which it was the evident, and it is only when satisfied that they did not, a sufficient *casus* being otherwise instructed that decree will be given, Winchester *v* Smith, 1863, 1 Macph, 685—Falconer *v* Stephen, 1849, 11 D, 1338

§ 1321 It may be added that there is sometimes considerable difficulty in extricating mutual actions of reduction-improbation and proving of the tenor If the improbation is first instituted, and the defender alleges that the deed has been lost, the Court will sist process, in order that he may raise a proving of the tenor And this is a just course, because if a party prejudiced by a lost deed could exclude a proving of its tenor by raising an improbation of it, and obtaining decree of certification *contra non producta*, the result would not depend on the real merits and justice of the case, but on the mere priority of institution of the actions, and such a course would leave room for fraud Yet where the defender in an action of improbation, instead of producing the deed called for, offers to set it up by proving its tenor there may be reason to suspect that the alleged loss is a device for having the deed sustained without some nullity or informality being exposed, or without its falsity being discovered by comparison with genuine writings of the party (*k*) In such cases the Court endeavour to discriminate between improbations which are *bona fide* challenges on the head of forgery, and those of which the object is to embarrass the party in right of a genuine deed in his attempt to prove its tenor Every case of this kind must depend on its own special circumstances If the fair inference from these is that the deed was lost accidentally, or was destroyed without the connivance of the party who founds on it, the Court will give decree of proving its tenor, leaving the other party afterwards to establish his averments of falsehood (*l*), whereas, if the circumstances throw suspicion upon the original validity of the deed, and if a special *casus amissionis* is not established, decree of proving the tenor will be refused (*m*), and the action of improbation will terminate by decree of certification *contra non producta*

§ 1322 Where an action was raised to prove the tenor of a deed which had been deposited with a third person for conditional delivery to the grantee the Court, while they decerned in the action directed that only one extract of the decree should be issued, to be placed in the hands of the depositary on the same terms as the original deed (*n*)

(*k*) See this difficulty noticed in Dirleton and Stewart, *voce* 'Tenor," and in Brown v Craw, 1699, M 15,806 4 B Sup, 401, S C (*l*) See Ker v Kay 1830, 8 S, 1008—F Lauderdale 1770, 2 Pat Ap Ca 284—Waddell v Waddell, 1707, M, 12 593—Anderson v Lowes, 1675, M 15 996 (*m*) See Fumarton v Lutefoot, 1675, M 1755—Paterson v Houston 1837, 16 S, 225—Graham v Graham, 1847 10 D, 45 (*n*) Ferrier v Berry 1824 3 S 226

§ 1323 Where the creditor in a bond had succeeded in proving the tenor against one co-obligant, the Court would not receive the decree as proving the *casus amissionis* and adminicles in an action by him against the other debtor, but required the creditor to lead his whole proof of new (*o*)

CHAPTER VI —OF ACTIONS OF TRANSUMPT

§ 1324 Where a person has an interest in a deed to the custody of which another has right, he may get an authenticated copy or "transumpt" of it prepared by means of an action of transumpt (*a*) This action was also used for the purpose of having a lost notarial instrument made up from the notary's protocol after his death (*b*) It is competent either before the Judge Ordinary or the Court of Session, and is chiefly useful where the deed cannot be recorded in a public register (*c*) The same action may comprehend a number of deeds, and may be laid either on an obligation under the hand of the defender to grant transumpts, or on the pursuer's interest in the subject of the deed (*d*), *e g*, where it forms part of the titles to his property The summons calls on the party having the custody of the deed to produce it for transumption The granter and grantee or their representatives, must either concur in the action, or be called as defenders All others claiming interest may be cited edictally (*e*)

§ 1325 The writings are produced in Court and correct duplicates, called "transumpts" of them, are made out, and are collated and signed by the clerk of court (*f*) The pursuer thereupon obtains decree declaring that the transumpts shall bear as full faith as extracts from the record of the court

---

(*o*) Broomhall *v* E Lauderdale, 1665 M, 14,028

(*a*) The substance of this section is taken from Ersk, 4, 1 53 and Tait Ev, 202 See also Stevenson *v* Pitcairn 1711, M, 2156

(*b*) Stair, 2, 3, 25—Ersk 2, 3, 43—Stirveling *v* Monteith, 1566, M 12,147 See also Irving *v* Corson 1681 M, 12 522—*Supra*, § 1210

(*c*) In Stevenson *v* Pitcairn *supra*, where two persons were interested in certain bonds, the Court ordered them to be recorded, each party taking out an extract at his own expense

(*d*) In the latter case the pursuer must bear the expense, Ersk, 4, 1, 53

(*e*) Ersk, 4, 1, 53

(*f*) Ersk, *supra* The style of the summons given in 3 Jurid Styles makes the transumpts be authenticated by the Clerk-Register when the action is in the Court of Session

Transumpts obtained by this means are probative in ordinary cases But they will not be received if the deeds are challenged on the ground of falsehood (*g*) A transumpt taken in the Court of Session—not one taken in an inferior court—would probably satisfy the production in reductions on other grounds (*h*)

§ 1326 As already mentioned, it is competent to have lost, destroyed, or mutilated registers of births, deaths, and marriages under the recent Registration Act transumed on a summary petition to the Court of Session (*i*)

§ 1327. Notarial copies of documents are excluded, under the rule which requires the best evidence (*k*) But they will be received if the original documents have been lost or destroyed (*l*), and they are evidence in any case where the parties consent to their admission Copies prepared and authenticated by foreign notaries of deeds which are retained by them, and of which only such copies are given out to the parties, seem to be admissible (*m*)

(*g*) Ersk., *supra* § 55, noted *supra*, § 1157

(*h*) See *supra* § 1275

(*i*) 17 and 18 Vict., c 80,

(*k*) See *supra*, § 134

(*l*) See *supra*, § 144

(*m*) See *supra*, § 128

TITLE IV.

OF THE RULES AS TO PRODUCING WRITINGS, AND RECOVERING THEM BY DILIGENCE

§ 1328 The rules as to the admissibility and effect of the different kinds of written evidence having thus been detailed, we proceed to consider how writings are produced in evidence, and recovered from persons who refuse access to them The rules on these matters vary according as a document is in the hands of the person who founds on it,—of his opponent,—or of a stranger to the suit

I *Of Writings in the hands of the party who founds on them*

When a writing is in the hands of the party who founds upon it, he may make it available in evidence by merely producing it and (if it is not probative) proving its authenticity. In cases in the Court of Session the production must in general be made at an early stage of the cause, in order that the party who has documents in his hands may not have an unfair advantage over his opponent It is necessary that, "along with the summons and with the defence, the parties shall respectively produce the deeds or writings on which they respectively found, so far as the same are in their custody or within their power" (*a*)

§ 1329 For the same reason, the parties are required with their

(*a*) 6 Geo IV, c 120 § 3 Under this regulation if a party founds on a document in his own hands, but does not produce it from not intending to use it in evidence, the other party can insist for production, West Middlesex Assur Co v Clough 1840, 2 D 1053

revised pleadings to produce any additional documents therein founded on, and which are in their hands (*b*) Documents in their hands which they mean to use in evidence, but on which they do not found in their pleadings, may be produced any time before the record is closed (*c*) But "after the record is made up and closed, it shall no longer be competent for the party in any case to produce any writing which was in his possession or within his power at the time of completing the record, unless he shall instruct it is *noviter veniens ad notitiam*, but it shall be competent to the parties" to "produce such writings previously in their power, as may be rendered necessary by the production of papers made by the other party after the record is closed" (*d*) It is the practice in the interlocutor closing the record to reserve right to the parties to make their productions within a short time, usually eight or ten days

§ 1330 In cases tried by jury in the Court of Session, the production of writings is regulated by the Act of Sederunt, 16th February 1841 which applies, although the writings are in the hands of the party who founds on them (*e*) It provides that "all writings which are meant to be put in evidence at the trial of a cause must be lodged eight days before the trial, with the clerks of the Register House, and notice shall be at the same time given to the agent for the opposite party of the writings being lodged, and no writings but those lodged as aforesaid shall be admitted, except by consent, as evidence at the trial But, nevertheless, it shall be competent to the Court to permit writings to be given in evidence at the trial on its being established to the satisfaction of the Court that they could not be lodged eight days before the trial, nor before the period at which they are actually produced or exhibited to the opposite party, and that notice to the opposite party had been given of the particular writing or writings proposed in such case to be produced" (*f*) [1]

(*b*) 6 Geo IV, c 120, § 8—A S 11th July 1828, § 55 (*c*) A S, 11th July 1828, § 54 55 (*d*) A S, 11th July 1828, § 55 This provision was enforced in Brodie *v* Brodie, 1827, 5 S, 900, and in the cases noted *infra* (*e*)

(*e*) Cameron *v* Cameron's Tr, 1850, 13 D, 412 (*f*) A S 16th Feb 1841 § 19

1 In Maclean *v* Maclean's Trustees, the pursuer moved for a warrant on the Lord Clerk Register or his deputes to transmit certain deeds, which had been recorded, to the clerk of the process, in order that the rule established by the Act of Sederunt, 16th February 1841, § 19, requiring all documents to be used at the trial to be lodged with the clerk eight days before the trial, might be complied with The Depute-Clerk Re-

§ 1331 These provisions apply to cases tried of consent of parties by the Lord Ordinary without a jury (*g*), or by arbiters sitting as a jury (*h*), under the late Court of Session Act

§ 1332 In applying the Act of Sederunt of 1828, the Court presume that documents are "within the power" of a party if they are in the hands of his law-agent or his servant (*i*) But he may overcome this presumption by showing that he applied unsuccessfully for the documents with a view to production before the record was closed (*j*) [2]

(*g*) 13 and 14 Vict c 36, § 46 (*h*) Same Act § 50

(*i*) Wright *v* Bell, 1836, 15 S 242—Hamilton *v* Cuthill 1828 7 S, 21—Peter *v* Mitchell, 1826, 5 S 193—But see Gordon *v* Trotter, 1831 10 S, 47

(*j*) Peter *v* Mitchell, *supra*—See also Kerr *v* D Roxburghe, 1822, 3 Mur 131

---

gister appeared, and objected to give up the deeds maintaining that he was bound to do no more than attend and produce the deeds at the trial The Court refused the motion, holding that the provision of the Act of Sederunt would be satisfied by the production of extracts of the deeds; Maclean *v* Maclean's Trustees 1861, 23 D, 1262

[2] Some uncertainty and difference of opinion has prevailed as to the application of section 55 of the Act of Sederunt, 11th July 1828 In Irvine *v* Irvine, 1857, 19 D, 284 a letter addressed to the defender in an action, and admittedly all along in his possession was allowed to be produced in the course of the defender's proof, after the record had been closed it being alleged to be necessary in order to meet a point made for the first time in the course of the pursuer's proof The Lord Ordinary (Handyside) held that the act applied only to writings and documents founded on by the parties in the record, or on which they meant to found and use in support of their respective averments on record, and that the letter in question—the use of which arose only in the course of the proof as a piece of evidence to clear up dates spoken to by witnesses—could have neither value nor relevancy as affecting the statements on record The Court adhered to the Lord Ordinary's interlocutor In Anderson *v* Gill the commissary refused to allow the claimant to produce after the record was closed a letter which had been all along in his possession, and the Court of Session and the House of Lords affirmed the judgment It was argued, in the House of Lords, that the Act of Sederunt did not apply to the Commissary Court, but it was held that the act regulated procedure in that court, and that from the position the objectors took up from the first, the claimant ought to have known the importance of the document and produced it, Anderson *v* Gill, 1858, 20 D, 1326, affirmed, April 16, 1858 3 Macq, 180 In Borthwick *v* Lord Advocate, where minutes of debate were laid before the whole judges two questions were chiefly argued —(1) Were the documents in the possession or within the power of the party at the time of completing the record? (2) Were the documents founded on in the record? The Court were of opinion that to bring a writing within the provisions of the act it required to have been within the power of the party, and to have been founded upon in the record But while they were of opinion that the act required the concurrence of these two conditions, considerable difference of opinion existed as to the application of the act to the documents in question The question arose in a suspension The suspender alleged that a decree and charge thereon obtained at the instance of the Lord Advocate on Her Majesty's behalf, proceeding upon an affidavit

§ 1333 Documents which a party attempts to produce after the record is closed, on the ground that they are *noviter venientes ad*

---

of danger by Donald Horne, W S alleging himself to be "interim receiver of Crown rents," was null and void in respect that the affidavit of danger on which the decree was obtained was not made by a revenue officer The respondent, the Lord Advocate for Her Majesty, averred that Horne had been duly appointed receiver of Crown rents and feu and other duties, but the record was closed without any document being produced instructing his appointment A proof of the fact that Horne held the appointment was allowed before answer, and certain documents instructing his appointment were then produced These documents were of two classes —*1st*, Letters written by the Commissioners of Woods and Forests to Horne It was argued that these documents could not be received, seeing that Horne was the law-agent of the respondent and the documents had, therefore been within the respondent's power and could have been produced by him at the time of completing the record *2d*, Documents in the possession of the Commissioners themselves, who were in fact, the parties against whom the action was brought On this branch of the case the majority were of opinion that in a dispute as to the fact of an appointment given to a Crown-officer at a certain previous period of time, the Crown could not be held to have in its possession or within its power the writings delivered to that officer, and that consequently, as regarded the letters in Horne's possession, the act did not apply, and they held, further that the principal and proper documents instructing the appointment being those in Horne's possession, the others could only be regarded as accessory to, and as explaining the principals, and as such, and tending to make the evidence complete, might be received Lord Curriehill thought that the letters in the possession of the Commissioners were within the power of the party while Lords Benholme and Kinloch held that the whole of the documents must be considered documents which, if the act applied, should have been produced On the other branch of the case the majority were of opinion that the documents were not documents "founded upon" in the record in the sense of the act "They are adminicles of evidence required to obviate an objection raised by the suspender to the regularity and efficacy of proceedings preliminary to the application on which the decree *ex facie* regular was obtained The statute required that the affidavit itself should be founded on and produced but documents which have only come to be required to obviate extrinsic objections raised to the character of the party who made the affidavit, or of the magistrate before whom it was made, or to the powers of the parties from whom the assumed appointment as an officer of the revenue, was derived, are, I think, in a different position from the affidavit itself They are not founded on, and did not require to be founded on as part of the respondent's case", *per* Lord President M Neill But the Lord Justice-Clerk and Lord Benholme were clearly of opinion that the documents were documents "founded on" in the sense of the act It was the intention of the Judicature Act to bring parties, when making up a record, as nearly as possible to an agreement on matters of fact, and this object was best served by requiring the parties to produce, along with their original or revised papers, any writs described or referred to in the record,—these writs being within the power and in the possession of the parties using them Lord Kinloch, in an elaborate opinion, held that the Act of Sederunt applied only to the case where judgment was given upon the closed record, and was not applicable when a proof *prout de jure* was allowed In the latter case parties were at liberty to produce any documents relevant to the case and the analogy of the Act of Sederunt 16th February 1841 (relative to trial by jury) was strongly insisted in "To allow the production if the proof at large is led before a jury and refuse it, if in the same case the same evidence on the

notitiam, will be rejected, unless their existence would have been unknown to one exercising a proper amount of observation, or unless a careful search had been made for them without success (*k*)

§ 1334 Production of documents within the power of a party has sometimes been allowed after the record was closed, where the Court considered that the case could not be properly decided without them (*l*) But this seems to be an evasion of the Act of Sederunt of 1828 (*m*)

II *Writings in which a party has a right, but of which another person has possession*

§ 1335 When a party requires production of a document which is in the hands either of his opponent, or of a stranger, a distinction must be taken between cases where he has a direct right or interest in the document and cases where he calls for production *in modum probationis* of a document which belongs entirely to another

Where a party has a direct right or interest in a document, he is entitled to insist on production of it at any time, without reference to the dependence of any question between himself and the person in whose hands it may happen to be Nor does he require to show that its contents are relevant to any matter in issue be-

(*k*) The writings were held not to be *noviter venientes ad notitiam* in L Fife *v* Pirie, 1852 14 D, 331—Wright *v* Bell, 1836, 15 S 242—Ross *v* M'Leay 1834 12 S, 631—Graham *v* Graham, 1821, 1 S, 35, affd, 1 W S, 353 See also Dundas *v* Aitken 9th March 1810 F C—Mag of Dumbarton *v* Campbell, 18th November 1813 F C, affd, 5 Dow, 266 With these cases compare Wilkie *v* Jackson, 1834 12 S 520—Threipland *v* Rutherford, 1848 10 D 506, where the writings were received

(*l*) Turnbull *v* Forsyth 1832 10 S, 228—Cubbison *v* Hyslop 1837, 16 S, 112—See also Hamilton *v* Cuthill, 1828, 7 S 21 (reported as A B), 6 S, 571 where the Court took the same view of their powers under the Act of Sederunt of 12th Nov 1825, § 15 which was in similar terms to that of 11th July 1828 above quoted

(*m*) See per Lords Cringletie and Meadowbank in Ross *v* M'Leay, 1834, 12 S, 632—Per L Medwyn in Wright *v* Bell, 1836, 15 S, 243—Per L Just-Clerk (Boyle) in Turnbull *v* Forsyth, *supra*

same issue is led before a commissioner, appears to me to involve an anomaly with which I should be sorry to think that our forms of process were chargeable", Borthwick *v* Lord Advocate, 1861, 24 D, 130 In a still later case, the Court held that a book, entitled "Visitors Book" of Doune Castle (referred to in the record) which, though in the actual possession of the party or of a friend of the party calling for its production, was still legally within the power of another party, as its proper custodier, might be produced after the record was closed Longworth *v* Yelverton, 1862, 24 D,

tween them (*n*) Thus, where the beneficiaries under a certain trust raised action against the trustees for the purpose of having the defenders ordained to pay a certain annuity to one of the pursuers, and to carry out the trust, and where the trustees pleaded, *inter alia*, that the trust-deed was under challenge in the Grand Courts of Jamaica (where the greater part of the trust property lay) and that the whole trust-estate might be swept away in that action, and where the pursuers, alleging that the proceedings in Jamaica had terminated two years before, moved for a diligence during the preparation of the record to recover all correspondence, deeds, and writings between the trustees, or their agents or factor, and the attorney whom they had employed in Jamaica, the Court granted the motion, mainly on the ground that the beneficiaries had the substantial interest in the negotiations which the trustees had carried on for their behoof (*o*). Thus, also, in an old case where Hepburn, as a creditor of Barclay who was bankrupt, raised action against Barclay's mother for exhibition of all bonds and writs belonging to her son, in order that he (Hepburn) might consider what execution he might seek thereon, the Court sustained the action in the general terms libelled, holding that the pursuer had a probable and excusable ignorance regarding his debtor's writs (*p*) In like manner, an apparent heir may call for a general exhibition of his ancestor's writs, in order that he may deliberate whether he will take up the succession (*q*)

§ 1336 Again, a party who has a joint interest in a document along with the person in whose hands it is, may insist for exhibition of it although there may not be any cause depending in which it would be required as evidence This right is the foundation of actions of transumpt at the instance of an heir-portioner or other joint proprietor (*s*) In like manner, in a process of augmentation at the instance of the ministers of Edinburgh against the magistrates, the Court ordained the defenders to produce "all charters and grants from the Crown, or from private persons, towards the sustenance or maintenance of the pursuers" (*t*) So, superiors are entitled to call on their vassals to exhibit deeds which they or any former superiors may have granted in relation to the feus (*u*) In

(*n*) Tait Ev, 175 As to mode of forcing exhibition, see *infra*, § 1346

(*o*) Provan v Telfer's Trustees, 1830, 8 S, 797, more fully reported in 3 De and And 49

(*p*) Hepburn v Barclay, 1637, M, 3964

(*q*) Stair 4, 33, 2—Ersk, 4, 1, 52—Tait Ev, 175

(*s*) See *supra* § 1321

(*t*) Ministers of Edinburgh v the Magistrates, 1763 M, 3969

(*u*) Ersk, 2, 5, 3—Rose v Grant, 1781, M, 3971

such cases, of course, the party must show that he has an interest in the document And, therefore, where one pursued for exhibition of a marriage-contract to which he was not a party the Court required him to condescend on the special clauses which he conceived were in his favour, because he could not get the deed exhibited unless he could show he had an interest under it (*w*) So in an action of accounting between the representatives of two brothers, who, the pursuers alleged, had been partners, the pursuers having called for production of a book kept by the defenders' ancestor, on the ground that it contained entries regarding the company affairs, the Court ordained it to be exhibited to one of their own number, in order that, if it should be found to contain accounts as between partners and factors, it should be produced to the pursuers even *ad fundandum litem*, and if not, that it should be returned to the defenders without being shown to the pursuers (*x*) A member of a corporation, or a joint-stock company, is entitled to exhibition of the books of the corporation or company, under such restrictions as may be necessary to prevent the production from prejudicing the general body (*y*)[3] In an action of count and reckoning by one partner's widow against his co-partner, the defender was ordained to produce the company books although he pleaded that he required them in order to carry on his business and was only bound to exhibit them in his shop (*z*)

(*w*) Crawford *v* L Lamington, 1626, M, 3960—Tait Ev, 176 (*x*) Paton *v* Paton, 1668, M, 3963—See also M'Clure *v* Jaffray 1827 5 S, 229

(*y*) Tait Ev, 176—See *infra*, § 1344 (*n*) (*z*) Stewart *v* M'Gregor, 1823, 2 S 461

[3] In an action by a railway company against a shareholder for payment of calls, access was allowed the shareholder, at the sight of a commissioner, and without anyone representing the company being present, as far as regarded his own shares, to the books of the company,—the company contending that a shareholder had no right to have access to the books except for the purpose of seeing the entries which regarded himself The books were produced in process eight days before the trial, Great North of Scotland Railway Company *v* Cadell 1856, 18 D 790 In Tulloch *v* Davidson, 1858, 20 D, 1319, a shareholder was allowed full access to all books and documents of a banking company, and diligence was granted for recovery of such documents, instructing, or tending to instruct, his averments, as he might point out In Dobbie *v* Johnston 1860, 22 D, 1113, a diligence was granted for recovery of the whole books of the Edinburgh and Glasgow Bank, that excerpts might be made tending to instruct the pursuer's averments It was held that entries made by the officials, and in the books of another company, with which the Edinburgh and Glasgow Bank had amalgamated, fell under the diligence Access to books for the purpose of getting excerpts does not entitle a party to make notes and carry them away as his private property, National Exchange Co *v* Drew & Dick, 1857 19 D 689

III *Writings which belong to, and are in the hands of an opposite party*

§ 1337 Even where one cannot establish any right in a document which is in the hands of another person, he may, in most cases obtain production of it *in modum probationis* in an action to which he is a party This rule is a branch of the system by which courts secure investigation into the facts of causes depending before them It is analogous to the rule, that a party may compel the attendance of witnesses on his behalf (*a*) It has, in one respect, a more general application, since persons whose testimony is inadmissible may be forced to deliver up documents in their hands. And this was the case as to parties to a cause before the recent statute (*b*) was passed which rendered them competent as witnesses in most civil proceedings

§ 1338 The primary and proper object of this rule is thus to enable parties to prove averments on which they have joined issue in a closed record, in the same manner as the right to require the attendance of witnesses arises at that stage And as a party cannot obtain a judicial precognition of his opponent or third persons, with a view to framing his averments so it is held that a diligence cannot, in general be obtained during the preparation of the record for recovering writings to which the party cannot qualify a right (*c*) This rule is also defended on the ground that granting diligences before the record is closed may tend to encumber it, and to create delay in its preparation (*d*) In some cases, however, it is essential to justice that access to documents should be obtained at an earlier stage otherwise a party might have to make his averments in the dark and at random whereby his pleadings might be inaccurate or incomplete, to his serious prejudice Nay more, eminent judges have thought that it would tend to elucidate the truth, as well as to make records more precise and consistent with the facts to be proved if the parties were in general allowed to recover documents before being tied down to the facts and pleas in a closed record The justice of this course is more especially manifest where, from one party having important documents in his hands, the other is

(*a*) Tait Ev 176, 7 (*b*) 16 Vict, c 20 (*c*) Mackintosh *v* M'Queen 1828, 6 S 784—Lumsdaine *v* Balfour 1828, 7 S, 7—National Exchange Co *v* Glasgow and Kilmarnock Ry Co 1849, 12 D, 249—Forbes *v* Ure, 1854, 16 D, 640—Tait's Ev 176—Shand's Pr, 378—Cases in following notes

(*d*) Per Lord Fullerton in M'Conochie *v* Paul 1841 3 D 1261, and in M'Ilquham *v* Caledonian Ry Co 1850 13 D, 402

not on equal footing with him in preparing his record Whether the strict or the more liberal rule will be applied depends on the circumstances of each case, and no general principle can be extracted from the decisions on the point (*e*), on which, indeed, considerable difference of opinion exists on the bench (*f*)[4] At the

(*e*) The diligence was granted during the preparation of the record in Davidson *v* Lyall 1824, 3 S, 8—Fullerton *v* Town of Dumbarton, 1833, 11 S 361—Henderson *v* Lumsden, 1838, 16 S 898—M'Conochie *v* Paul, 1841, 3 D 1261—Moreton *v* Lockhart 1849, 22 Sc Jur 81, with which cases compare those, *supra* (*c*), where the diligence was refused In M'Ilquham *v* Caledonian Railway Co *supra*, the Court held that no general rule could be laid down on the point

(*f*) Compare the opinion of Lord Jeffrey in Miller *v* Edinburgh and Glasgow Railway Co 1849, 11 D 1012, in favour of granting diligences at an early stage of the case with the more strict view entertained by Lord Fullerton in M'Conochie *v* Paul, *supra*, and M'Ilquham *v* Caledonian Railway Co, 1850 13 D 403 In the latter case Lord Cuninghame observed, "In the law commission there was a good deal of discussion on this point and we did not exactly know what to make of it," and the First Division of the Court seem to have considered that it lay with the Lord Ordinary to determine whether a diligence should be granted and that the Inner House ought not lightly to interfere with his discretion But it would seem that the Second Division do not take this view, see Forbes *v* Ure, 1854, 16 D, 640—National Exchange Co *v* Glasgow, Kilmarnock, &c Railway Co 1849, 12 D, 249, which cases indicate that their Lordships of that Division take a strict view as to granting diligences during the preparation of the record

[4] It does not appear that any precise rule has been adopted by either Division as to the circumstances in which diligence for the recovery of documents will be granted before the record is closed But since Forbes *v* Ure *supra*, opinions have been expressed by several of the Judges of the First Division which seem to indicate that they are inclined to concur in the view expressed in that case by the Lord Justice Clerk (Hope) In Greig *v* Crosbie, 1855 18 D, 193 which was an action at the instance of a trustee on a sequestrated estate for reduction of an alleged preference, and which concluded alternatively against a bank and against the bank-agent in his official and also in his individual capacity, the pursuer moved, in the course of making up the record, for diligence for the recovery of all documents relating to the transaction, and he alleged that, unless it was granted he would have difficulty in stating on record in which capacity the defender had acted The Lord President (M'Neill) held that the object of the diligence was not to enable the pursuer to make his statement more specific, but to ascertain what his grounds of action really were, and that such a use of diligence was not permissible Lord Curriehill in concurring with the Lord President, said that a mistake seemed to prevail in the Outer House as to the practice sanctioned by the Divisions "It is there thought that you have come to be of opinion that this is the proper stage for making recovery of documents required *in modum probationis* If such doctrine has prevailed, it is not one which your Lordship has ever sanctioned In every case you exercise your discretion, and the Lord Ordinary must exercise his discretion, and if the party knows the case which he is to make, but only requires information to enable him to make his record in the specific form which the statute requires, the diligence may be granted, but if he is seeking, at that stage documents necessary

same time it may be said generally, that if a party can satisfy the Court that he will be ultimately entitled to production of certain documents, and that the withholding of them during the preparation of the record is likely to defeat the justice of the case, an order for their production will be granted before the record is closed, whereas their pertinency to the question in issue is not of itself a sufficient reason for granting access to them during the preparation of the record, because if they are only required *in modum probationis*, they can be recovered after the case has been prepared for probation

§ 1339 Farther the right of a party to call for documents in the hands of another does not entitle him to a sweeping or "fishing" diligence for examining all his opponent's titles and other writings *per aversionem*, thereby becoming acquainted with private matters with which he has no concern, and searching for evidence in support of averments made at hap-hazard (*g*) In this sense the maxim applies, *nemo tenetur edere instrumenta contra se* (*h*) Accordingly a party applying for a diligence must lodge a condescendence or "specification" of the writings he calls for, and unless those specified are relevant to the cause, he will not be allowed to recover them (*i*) Thus, where the purchaser under a written con-

(*g*) Ersk, 1, 1, 52—Tait Ev, 176—Shand's Pr, p 277 (*h*) Ersk, *supra*

(*i*) Ersk, *supra*—Tait, *supra*—Shand, *supra* In Foggo *v* Hill, 1839, 1 D, 1238, after an issue had been adjusted the pursuer obtained a diligence on a specification, which besides several articles of rather too general a character, embraced "generally

in modum probationis, you will refuse it, and reserve the demand till the proper time for proof arises" Lords Ivory and Deas, however, declined to lay down any general rule, holding that the question whether a diligence should be granted or refused was purely a question of circumstances and discretion In an action of count and reckoning, which was brought on the allegation that the defender had been conducting a business for behoof of the pursuer for a number of years, the defender stated that, after some years, he had agreed to purchase the business, and had since carried it on for himself, but he produced no agreement Before the record was closed the Lord Ordinary granted diligence to recover the whole business books, both before and after the alleged sale In the Inner House it was observed, that if a written agreement had been produced by the defender, that would have given him a *prima facie* case to stand upon as having carried on the business for himself, and on his undertaking to produce the agreement, the Court refused the motion for a diligence to recover the books, Curror *v* Dickson, 1857, 19 D, 991 While it cannot be said therefore that any general rule has been adopted, it would appear that the Court is indisposed, on an open record, to grant diligence for the recovery of writings which are not absolutely necessary to the preparation of the record, and which can be obtained more conveniently when a proof is taken,—those documents only being deemed necessary which either party requires in order to frame his record in the articulate form required by the statute

tract of sale alleged that it had been agreed to under a latent condition, and where he sought to recover all minutes memoranda, correspondence and writings tending to instruct the alleged limitation, the Court, after allowing him an opportunity to specify any document which he could aver existed in support of his allegations, on his failure to do so, refused the diligence, being satisfied that the party did not know of any such writing, and was really endeavouring to get a fishing diligence, in the hope that he might discover traces of evidence in support of averments made at random (*k*) Thus, also, in an action of reduction-improbation, where the defender produced a title to exclude, founded on charter and sasine with prescriptive possession, the Court found that he was not obliged to depone under a general diligence obtained by the pursuer to prove interruptions of the prescription, but that the pursuer must specify the writings called for, and their Lordships afterwards refused to compel the defender to produce an inventory of his titles on the pursuer calling for production of it (*l*) In like manner, in a process by a minister against the magistrates of a royal burgh and the other heritors of his parish to have them ordained to provide a manse, where the defenders pleaded that the whole parish was burgal, and referred to the ancient charter of erection of the burgh by King William the Lion and where the pursuer craved access to the burgh records in order that he might discover whether there were any other crown charters restricting or explaining the one founded on or any other writings in the possession of the town explanatory of those charters, and also craved inspection of all inventories which might relate to such papers, the Court refused the application (*m*)

§ 1340 Where a person claiming to be an heir of line and provision had expede a general service, and, while he was in the course of obtaining charter and sasine, his right was challenged by two competitors, who had raised reductions of his service and taken out

---

all documents tending to instruct the averments and denials of the pursuer in the case, and the affirmative of the issues therein" But in Morton *v* Scott, 1844, 6 D, 1105, this was stated to be a special case, and on the Court expressing a doubt as to the competency of such a general article, it was withdrawn A condescendence, both of the writings called for and of the purpose for which they were to be produced, was required in Kennedy *v* Hope, 1830, 8 S, 1029 But the common practice is to state the latter orally at the bar

(*k*) Pattinson *v* Robinson, 1844, 6 D, 911 (*l*) Scott *v* L Napier, 1735, M, 358, 3965—Elch, "Witness," No 3, S C, affd, Cr and St, 411—See also Smith *v* E Airley, 11th March 1815 (not rep), noted in Tait's Ev, 178, 9, *infra*, § 1341 (*n*)

(*m*) Auld *v* Mag of Ayr, 7th Feb 1818 (not rep), noted in Tait's Ev, 179

competing brieves, the Court refused to allow these parties to inspect indiscriminately the contents of the ancestor's charter-chest (*n*). And the like was again found (*o*). But an opposite, and (it is thought) a more just, decision was pronounced a few years afterwards, where, after a person had been served heir and had taken possession of the ancestor's charter-chest, a competing heir, who had raised a reduction of the service, was allowed to have inspection of the charter-chest and all the family papers, the Court considering that the case was like a competition of brieves, in which neither party had a preferable right to the family papers, and that "the case was very different from the case where the right to the lands was attacked, not the possessor's title as heir" (*p*). In another case of the same kind a diligence was granted to a party during the preparation of the record, to recover writs tending to instruct the pedigree on which he founded, reserving to the commissioner to judge whether the entire documents should be exhibited, or only excerpts taken from them, in the event of their also relating to other matters (*r*). The object of the qualification was to prevent the diligence from being turned into a fishing diligence, by which documents applicable to an entirely different case from the one in issue might have been discovered.

§ 1341. The Court will probably allow a somewhat general diligence in cases of fraud, where the allegations are specific, because, if they are true, it is probable that considerable secrecy will have been observed in regard to such writings as bear on them, and therefore the pursuer should not be limited to the recovery of writings which he can specify. Accordingly, in an action for recovery of property which had been stolen from the pursuers, the defenders being the alleged accomplices of one who had been hanged for the theft, and one of them being his widow, where the pursuers craved diligence to recover all letters between certain dates, at the interval of a year from each other, addressed to the principal thief by his own name or certain assumed names, and where the defenders maintained that the dates and names of the persons by whom the letters were written must be given, the Court repelled the objection in the special circumstances of the case, holding that as the allega-

(*n*) D. Hamilton *v.* Douglas, 1761, M., 3966 (affd. on appeal, see note to 5 B. Sup., 912). The right of the parties to call for production of individual writings was admitted. (*o*) Ross *v.* Ross, 1762, noted in M. 3969. (*p*) Cairncross *v.* Heatley, 1765, 5 B. Sup. 912. (*r*) Fraser *v.* L. Lovat, 19th December 1840, F. C.

tions of theft were specific it was absurd to require a more precise condescendence (*s*)

Nor will the Court insist for a precise specification, by date or otherwise where the party calling for documents under a general description qualifies an interest in them, and is not trusting to such grounds of action or defence as may turn up under a fishing diligence (*t*) On the other hand, if the party's object is to hunt for flaws in his opponent's titles, where he has not condescended on any existing in individual writings, he will not be allowed access to the deeds, merely because he can describe them by their dates or other identifying marks (*u*)

§ 1342 As to what writings may be recovered from an opponent there is no definable rule every case depending on the nature of the writings called for, and the purpose for which production of them is required It may be observed, however, that private plans of an opponent's estate may not, whereas judicial plans may, be called for (*x*) [5] Defences prepared but not lodged (*y*), and letters written but not dispatched (*z*), may not be recovered, because they are private like the party's unuttered thoughts So (as afterwards fully illustrated) communications between parties on the same side of a case and relating to the conduct of it (*a*), and communications

(*s*) National Bank *v* Heath, 1832, 10 S 694 See also M'Cowan *v* Wright, 1852, 15 D, 229 (*t*) See this illustrated in the cases of Ministers of Edinburgh *v* Mag of Edinburgh, 1763, M, 3969—Rose *v* Grant 1781, M, 3971—Hepburn *v* Barclay, 1637, M, 3961, all noted *supra*, § 1336—See also Campbell *v* Campbell 1823, 2 S 139

(*u*) Thus in Smith *v* E Airley, 11th March 1815 (not rep), noted in Tait's Ev, 178, 9, where one of the heritors in a division of commonty produced a prescriptive title commencing eighty years before, the Court would not grant to competing parties a diligence to recover the heritor's prior titles, although these (twenty in number) were specified distinctly by date and otherwise, the object of the production being to discover whether there was any limitation of the party's right The Court also refused to ordain the heritor to produce certified copies of such parts of the writings as might throw light on the point at issue

(*x*) Ferrier *v* Young, 1827, 5 S, 332 (*y*) Gavin *v* Montgomery, 1830, 9 S, 213 (*z*) Livingstone *v* Murrays, 1831, 9 S, 757 (*a*) Rose *v* Medical Invalid Insur Co, 1847, 10 D, 156

[5] In a declarator of right of way or footpath the Court allowed the pursuers access to the defender's titles to the effect of getting extracts, at the sight of a commissioner, of such portions as related to the footpath, although there was no averment on record that the titles referred to it, and also to correspondence and specifications relative to the erection of a march wall between two estates across the footpath, but they refused access to the titles of an adjoining estate, from which the footpath claimed was separated by a stream, Riggs *v* Drummond, 1861 23 D, 1251

between parties and their legal advisers (*b*), are in general privileged.

§ 1343. When it cannot be ascertained without inspection of a writing, whether a party is entitled to production of it, the Court usually appoint it to be exhibited to the commissioner who conducts the examination, in order that he may determine how far it is private, and if necessary, may make a special report on the point, in order to obtain the advice of the Court (*d*). In matters of great delicacy the Court sometimes require the haver to state to the commissioner the nature of the document, and his objection to producing it, and if these are satisfactory to that officer, production of the document, even to him, will not be required (*e*). A remit for the same purpose is sometimes made to the clerk of court, or to one of the judges. This subject is resumed in a subsequent section (*f*).[6]

IV. *Of Production of Writings in the hands of Third Parties.*

§ 1344. Writings which a party to a suit requires *in modum probationis* may be recovered from third parties, whose property or in whose possession they are (*g*); and if access to them is necessary for enabling the party to prepare his record production may be obtained for that purpose (*h*). A specification of the writings called for is required (*i*); and the havers (who, not being parties to the cause, cannot oppose granting the diligence) may decline to produce the writings on any reasonable ground, *e.g.*, that they are

(*b*) See chapter on privileged communications, *infra*.

(*d*) See Campbell *v.* Campbell, 1823, 2 S. 189—Jarvis *v.* Anderson, 1841, 3 D., 990—Clark *v.* Mitchell, 1825, 4 S., 102—Fraser *v.* L. Lovat, 19th Dec. 1840, F. C. (*supra*, § 1340)—Paton *v.* Paton, 1668, M., 3963. See Houldsworth *v.* Walker, 1819, 2 Mur., 85, where the Court would not order a party (a large mercantile company) to produce their books at a trial, but of consent allowed them to be examined by the clerk of court. In Fullerton *v.* Town of Dumbarton, 1833, 11 S., 361, the Court allowed a party inspection at the sight of a commissioner of town council records, which he asked diligence to recover. See also Fraser *v.* Dunbar, 1835, 13 S., 950, where the Court allowed an inspection at sight of the Sheriff.

(*e*) See Graham *v.* Sprott, 1847, 9 D., 545, *infra* (*n*)—Fisher *v.* Bontine, 1827, 6 S., 330—Scott *v.* L. Napier, 1735, M., 358, 3965, and Cr. and St., 441, S. C.

(*f*) See *infra*, § 1362. (*g*) Shand's Pr.—Tait Ev. 179. (*h*) See *supra*, § 1338—Graham *v.* Sprott, 1847, 9 D., 545. (*i*) Tait Ev., *supra*—Shand's Pr., *supra*.

[6] Buchanan *v.* Cullen, 1863, 1 Macph. 258—Same case, 1863, 1 Macph. 818.

private papers (*k*), or are manifestly irrelevant to the issue (*l*) Thus in an action by an heir of entail against his father, who during his son's minority had possessed and managed and sold part of the estate, to constitute certain claims, estimated at £40,000, arising out of his father's intromissions with the estate where the law-agent of one of the purchasers (who was not called as a defender) when cited by the pursuer as a haver, was required to produce his client's title-deeds to the subjects sold, and other documents connected therewith, the Court (on an appeal from the finding of the commissioner) held that the agent was not bound to produce the writings called for, or even to exhibit them to the commissioner Their Lordships held the agent to be in the same situation as his client, who could not be required to produce his own title-deeds in a question between third parties, whereby flaws in them might be discovered so as to found an action against himself, for if the pursuer had any objection to the titles, it was considered that he ought to raise an action of reduction or exhibition of them, where the question as to his right to production would arise in proper form (*m*) Thus also in an action of damages for failure to deliver shares of railway stock sold by the defender to the pursuer where the defender obtained a diligence to recover all documents tending to show the price of the company's stock at certain dates (reserving to the havers all their objections to the production), and where the secretary of the company when examined as a haver declined to exhibit their books to the commissioner on the ground that they contained private transactions of the company, the Court ordained him to make such exhibition in order that the commissioner might judge whether the books should be produced or not, reserving to the haver to state to the commissioner any special ground on which exhibition even to that officer ought to be limited (*n*) The Court

(*k*) In an action of divorce for adultery, the alleged paramour having been called on to produce all letters which passed between him and the defender, all letters by or to him in any way connected with or relating to the defender, and all writings or papers relating directly or indirectly to the matter in issue declined to produce them, and appealed to the Court against the decision of the Sheriff-Commissary repelling his objection The pursuer having stated that he did not insist for production of any documents under the haver's hand, and that he was willing that the commissioner should inspect the other writings called for, and should determine whether they ought to be produced, the Court repelled the haver's objection, and ordained him to exhibit the writings called for to the commissioner, to be dealt with in the manner proposed, Don *v* Don, 1848, 10 D, 1046

(*l*) Tait Ev, 180—Fraser *v* Long, 1823, 2 S, 491

(*m*) Fisher *v* Bontine, 1827, 6 S, 330—See also Scott *v* L Napier, 1637 M 358 Elch Witness 9 No 7

(*n*) Graham *v* Sprott 1847, 9 D 545

considered that the company were entitled to the same protection as private individuals against such an exhibition as would be hurtful to their affairs, but that the objection stated by the secretary was too broad and indiscriminate.

As already noticed, where documents belonging to a third person contain entries which bear upon the case in issue, but are mixed up with others of a private character, the proper course is to have the former excepted at the sight of a commissioner of Court (o)

§ 1345 In general the question whether the writings called for are admissible in evidence will not be discussed on a motion for a diligence But if they are manifestly inadmissible, the diligence will be refused (p), and it will not be granted in order that the party may use the documents in cross-examining his opponent's witnesses (r) [7]

(o) *Supra*, § 140
(p) See Fraser v Lang 1823 2 S, 491
(r) M'Loskey v Glasgow Marine Ins Co, 1843, 5 D 1013

[7] In an action for reduction of a settlement on the ground of facility and circumvention, the Court refused a diligence, at the instance of the defenders to recover letters, or copies of letters, relative to the state of mind of the testator, passing between parties who had been called as defenders but who had not appeared and who might be adduced as witnesses at the trial The Lord Justice-Clerk (Inglis) after consultation stated the view which had been taken by the whole Judges As the letters could not be given in evidence the object of recovering them must be to use them in taking the precognition or in conducting the examination or cross examination of the writers at the trial As to the recovering them as aids in taking precognitions that was quite out of the question In the other view, it appeared to the Court that the proper use of a diligence was to recover writings of the nature of evidence, and capable of being used as evidence in the cause—'not that we ever determine beforehand whether the writings to be recovered will be admissible as evidence, but we must be satisfied that the writings are of such a kind as may be used in evidence' Here the writings were not of that kind The use which would be made of them would be to put them into the hands of a witness and make him read them, with a view to refresh his memory, or to furnish counsel with information to enable him to put questions in cross-examination to cut down the evidence in chief, and in either view such is a competent use of writings if the party happen to have them But we are all of opinion that it is not the proper office of a diligence to put a party in possession of writings of that kind to be used for such a purpose ' Such letters were not properly documentary evidence if any words in the documents were material, they could only get into the case and go before the jury as part of the deposition of the witness not being documentary evidence they did not require to be put in eight days before the trial, and the party who wished to use them might cite the person who had them, and so get them and use them at the trial, Livingston v Dinwoodie, 1860, 22 D, 1333 In Huxton v Edinburgh and Glasgow Railway Co, 1863 35 Sc Jur 596, where a widow claimed damages and *solatium* from the company for the death of her husband who had been killed in a railway collision, the defenders moved the Court for a diligence to recover from law-agents correspondence and other documents tending to show that at and for some time prior to, the death of her husband

V Of the means by which a party may compel production of Writings in the hands of another

§ 1346 In our older practice a person who claimed a document as his own recovered it by means of an action of exhibition and delivery, mere production of a writ being obtained by an action of exhibition (*s*)

The first of these proceedings is still in use It is an independent action, founded on the pursuer's right of sole property in the document or on his right to the custody of it, where he has a joint interest in its subject (*t*) Accordingly, where one who had been served heir under a charter conveying lands and a peerage, but whose right had not been recognised by the Crown, brought against the party having right to the lands an action of exhibition and delivery of all titles relating to the peerage, the House of Lords (reversing the judgment of the Court of Session) held that the action could not be maintained, because the pursuer was unable to instruct that right of property in the documents which was necessary to support his action (*u*)

§ 1347 A summary petition to the Sheriff is a more convenient procedure for recovering writings from wrongous possessors, and it is equally competent (*x*), unless the right to the possession involves a question of heritable title But it ought not to be used for obtaining production of documents in a depending process, the proper course being to apply for a diligence in the cause in common form (*y*)

§ 1348 An action of simple exhibition is competent as an independent process for the purpose of enforcing the pursuer's right to have a document exhibited to him, *e g* where an heir, deliberat-

(*s*) Stair, 1, 7, 11—Ib, 4, 33 1 to 5—Ersk, 4, 1, 52 (*t*) Stair, ib—Ersk, ib—Tait, 175 (*u*) Ly Crawford *v* Campbell, 1826, 2 W S, 410, reversing, 2 S, 737 Lord Gifford (who proposed the judgment) carefully avoided deciding that the pursuer was not entitled to a simple action of exhibition of the deeds in question

(*x*) M'Kirdy *v* M'Lachlan, 1840, 2 D, 949—Haig *v* Buchanan, 1823, 2 S, 412—*Per curiam* in Peter *v* Mitchell, 1826, 5 S, 193 (*y*) M'Lure *v* Jaffray, 1827, 5 S, 229

the pursuer had had in contemplation the bringing an action to have the marriage declared a nullity The application was supported on the ground that if this were so, she was not entitled to damage for injury to feelings, and was opposed by the pursuers on the ground of the irrelevancy of the matters sought to be proved and the confidentiality of the documents sought to be recovered The Court unanimously refused the application See also Elmslie *v* Alexander 1862, 1 Macph 209

ing whether he will take up the succession requires exhibition of documents inferring debt against his ancestor—where a superior calls on his vassal to exhibit titles flowing from himself or previous superiors—and where a party wishes to see the titles to his estate, when they embrace other properties also, and are in the hands of a person entitled to the custody of them (z)

§ 1349 There is also an accessory action of exhibition for getting writings produced *in modum probationis* in a depending process (a) But in modern practice it has given place to the incident diligence against havers (b) And where writings are in the hands of the opposite party, they may be recovered either by a diligence or by an order to produce them under certification (c) An action of exhibition, however, might still be useful where there is reason to fear that the haver, when not a party to the cause, will deny possession of the document, because, under an incident diligence, he can only be forced to produce if he admits the possession, whereas, in an action of exhibition, that fact may be proved by witnesses (d)

§ 1350 In cases of urgency the Court, on a summary application, will take measures for preserving documents where there is ground to suspect that they may be destroyed or made away with, before production of them can be obtained in a process in which they will be required as evidence Thus where a party had failed in an action of proving the tenor of certain deeds alleged to instruct his title to a peerage and where the Officers of State, who had raised an action of reduction-improbation of his service, and the grounds and warrants thereof, as false and fabricated, petitioned the Court to prohibit the clerk lending up certain documents which

---

(z) Stair, 1, 7, 14—Ib 4 33 2—Ersk, 2, 5 3—Ib, 4, 1 52—Tait Ev, 175—See examples of this action in Crauford v L Lamington, 1626, M 3960—Hepburn v Barclay 1637 M 3964—Paton v Paton 1668, M, 3968—Rose v Grant 1781, M, 3971—Clerk v Mitchell 1825 4 S, 102 See also Ly Crawford v Campbell *supra* (u)—per L Alloway in Fisher v Bontine, 1827 6 S 330

(a) Stair, 4, 33, 3—Ersk 4, 1 52

(b) Ersk *supra*—Tait Ev, 176—Shand's Pr, 368, 9 In criminal cases either the prosecutor or the prisoner may on petition obtain a commission and diligence to recover writings, Muckarsie, 1834, Bell's Notes 278—Cameron, 1832, ib 285 In practice, however, the prosecutor obtains access to documents under a warrant from the Sheriff to cite witnesses and open shut and lockfast places

(c) Ersk, *supra*—Tait Ev 177—Shand's Pr, 368

(d) Stair 1 7 14—Ib, 4, 33, 3 In the first of these passages Lord Stair lays down that although witnesses are admissible to prove the custody of the document they cannot be received to prove that it was fraudulently put away, because fraud being a matter concerning the mind and purpose, can only be proved by writ or oath of party In modern practice witnesses are admissible to prove fraud see *supra* § 628

had been produced in the action of proving, and which included the documents sought to be reduced and certain writings required as evidence in the action of reduction, the Court granted the application, by directing the clerk to the process to keep the custody of the documents, and not to lend them to either party without authority from their Lordships (*e*) [8]

§ 1351 Until recently, havers in the Court of Session used to be cited on letters of diligence, which were signed by the extractor and passed the signet (*f*) When a haver duly cited did not appear, the Court granted letters of second diligence, which were signed and signeted in the same way, and on which the haver might be apprehended and brought before the commissioner (*g*) If there was ground to suspect that the haver would not attend, or if there was reason for urgency, letters of first and second diligence were granted at once (*h*) In practice, they were given out together without cause shown, in order that, if necessary, the party might enforce attendance (*i*) A certified copy of the interlocutor granting the commission and diligence has now the same effect as the extract under the former practice (*k*) A certified copy of the

---

(*e*) Officers of State *v* E Stirling, 1833 11 S, 625 In Orrok *v* Gordon, 1847 10 D, 35, where the trustees of a deceased person had taken possession both of her papers and of some documents belonging to her niece, which were beside them, and which the trustees refused to deliver up on the ground that they instructed fraud and circumvention by her in regard to certain testamentary writings which the deceased had executed in her favour, and of which they had instituted an action of reduction the Court held that the trustees had no right to withhold the papers, and, as a sweeping diligence to recover them all would not have been granted they appointed them to be delivered up, but in order to prevent tampering with them before they would be produced in the reduction, directed that they should be inventoried In Barclay *v* Gifford, 1843, 5 D, 1136, where a person applied to the Court to interdict certain parties from parting with or destroying a letter not addressed to him, but containing (as he alleged) injurious statements regarding him, the Court refused his application because he did not set forth a proper right or interest in the document and had neither raised, nor stated that he intended to raise, an action in which it would be required as evidence But this decision is not of much weight, as the Inner House by a majority of two judges to one, altered the Lord Ordinary's interlocutor

(*f*) Shand's Pr, 371—Beveridge's Forms of Process, 604 (*g*) Shand, *supra* —Beveridge, 606—Tait's Ev, 182—Fraser *v* Nicholl, 1840, 2 D 1254

(*h*) Shand's Pr, 372—Beveridge, 607 (*i*) Macf Pr, 112

(*k*) 13 and 14 Vict, c 36, § 25 There is a similar regulation as to cases in the Sheriff-court, by 16 and 17 Vict, c 80, § 11

---

[8] The Court of Queen's Bench have held that, until a case has been brought into Court, they have no power over documents and that they cannot pronounce any order in reference to them, Burton and Saddlers Co, 1861 *in re*, 31 L J Q B, 62

interlocutor fixing a trial is a warrant to messengers-at-arms to cite havers to the trial (*l*) In other respects the mode of forcing havers to attend and produce remains as formerly [9]

§ 1352 The proceedings for recovery of writings may be directed against a *minor pubes* (*m*) But writings may not be recovered from a pupil, because he has not a legal person, and is incapable either of intromission or of judging whether he ought to produce (*n*) The proper parties to call are his tutors, if he has any There is a difference of opinion as to whether a *tutor ad litem* can be appointed for the purpose to a pupil who has no tutors (*o*) It is thought that a pupil may be examined as to where the documents are and as to their supposed removal or destruction (*p*)

(*l*) 13 and 14 Vict c 36, § 43 But if the haver does not attend letters of second diligence must be obtained In practice, letters of first and second diligence are taken out as formerly (*m*) E Mar *v* his Vassals, 1628, M 8918—Tait Ev, 182—Shand's Pr, 374—See Maitland *v* Cashogill, 1623, M, 8917 (*n*) Aitken *v* Hewat, 1528, M 8907—Shand's Pr, 374—2 Fraser Pers and Dom Rel, 69

(*o*) See Fraser *supra*—questioned in Shand, *supra* (as corrected in *errata*) If an action of exhibition is raised against a pupil without tutors, a tutor *ad litem* may be appointed although the competency of doing so in an incident diligence may be doubted

(*p*) See *infra*, § 1357

---

9 In the National Exchange Co *v* Drew and Dick, 1858, 20 D, 837, affirmed, April 20, 1860, 32 Sc Jur, 482 a diligence was granted at the instance of the defenders for the recovery of writs Having failed to recover under the diligence certain documents which they said were essential to their defence, and had been traced into the possession of the pursuers they moved the Court for letters of second diligence against one of the havers who had been examined under the diligence, and who had deponed that the documents were not in his possession They argued that as the documents had been traced into the haver's possession since the raising of the action and as he must either have improperly lent them away or must be improperly withholding them, second diligence, though more usually applied for to compel the attendance of a haver or witness, might competently be granted But the Court were of opinion that letters of second diligence were not the appropriate remedy "The style of such letters is familiar in practice, and the object of them is to apprehend and bring up for examination a haver who disobeys the ordinary citation I never heard before that under such letters a haver could be at once imprisoned in respect of his answers being unsatisfactory, or amounting to a withholding or fraudulent putting away of the writs called for That is a wrong for which, if it can be instructed, the remedy is quite different," *per* Lord Deas Lord Curriehill, however while holding that no foundation for the motion had been laid, was of opinion that letters of second diligence operating practically as a caption, might, in certain circumstances be a competent remedy It has been held that, although interlocutors disposing of the competency of an action and approving of issues are appealed to the House of Lords, the Court is not precluded from granting diligence for recovery of documents to prepare the case for trial Forbes *v* Campbell 1857 20 D 287 The Lord Ordinary, after adjustment of issues in the Outer House can grant diligence for the recovery of writings, Hornel *v* Gordon 1862 24 D 551

§ 1353 A peer must attend and depone if cited under a diligence against havers (r), and it seems that his compliance may be forced by imprisonment (s)

§ 1354 At one time there were no means of forcing havers who resided beyond Scotland to attend or depone before a commissioner of Court (t) This defect has been in a great measure remedied by a statute, which enables a party who has obtained a commission for the examination of havers from any court of law in Scotland to compel their attendance in any part of the United Kingdom within which the diligence may require to be executed (u) A certified copy of an interlocutor by a Sheriff, fixing a diet of proof, is a sufficient warrant for the citation of havers residing beyond the sheriffdom, provided it be indorsed by the sheriff-clerk of the county where the haver resides (x)

§ 1355 A diligence cannot be obtained from any court in Scotland for production of part of the records of a foreign court (under which term are included the courts in England and Ireland), or for production of writings in a foreign register (y) The Court of Session, however, has granted a recommendation to the proper authorities to allow access to writings in Chancery (z)

§ 1356 In submissions where parties require documents in the hands of their opponents, production may be secured by an order from the arbiter under certification And production of documents in the hands of third persons may be obtained on petition to the Court of Session, or Sheriff of the bounds, to interpone authority to a commission granted by the arbiter to examine havers (a) A commission of this kind, with authority of the Court of Session interponed thereto has been enforced in England under the act 6 and 7 Vict, c 82 (b) [10]

(r) D Montrose v M'Cauley 1711, M, 10 029—Fraser v Nicholl, 1840, 2 D, 1254

(s) Burnett Cr Law, 451 This subject is fully noticed in the chapter on compelling witnesses to attend, *infra*, § 1887 *et seq*

(t) Izatt, 13th June 1809, F C—Glyn v Johnston & Co, 1834, 13 S, 126

(u) 6 and 7 Vict c 82, § 5 See Appendix, and chapter on compelling witnesses to attend, *infra*, § 1887, *et seq*

(x) 16 and 17 Vict, c 80, § 11

(y) Jeffrey v M'Gregor, 1826, 5 S, 48—Richardson v Forbes' Tr, 1850, 22 Sc Jur, 431—Ross v Ross, 1782 M 4600

(z) Richardson v Forbes' Tr, *supra*

(a) Ker v Scott, 1670 M, 634—Stevenson v Young, 1696, M, ib—Harvey v Gibson, 1826, 4 S, 809—Blaikies Brothers v Aberdeen Railway Co, 1851, 13 D, 1307—See also Houldsworth v Walker, 1819, 2 Mur, 85 If the haver without good cause refuses to produce the documents warrant to imprison him may be obtained on a second petition

(b) Blaikies Brothers v Aberdeen Railway Co, *supra*

---

[10] As to the rules to be observed in the recovery and retention by the public prose-

VI. *Of the Procedure in examining Havers.*

§ 1357. The preliminary procedure in examining havers is the same as in proofs on commission. The haver attends before the commissioner, and after being sworn he is asked whether he can produce all or any of the writings in the specification. At one time havers could only be compelled to depone generally that they had not the writs at the time of examination, or since citation, and had not put them away at any time. But the Court passed an Act of Sederunt (*c*), which, on the preamble of the inconvenience of such depositions, ordained havers "to answer to all special pertinent interrogators in relation to their having of the writs or putting the same away, or as to their knowledge and suspicion by whom the same were taken away, or where they presently are, that the pursuer may thereby make discovery and recover the same," declaring that they will not be decerned against as havers, "unless it be found that they had had the writs since the citation, or fraudulently put them away at any time."

§ 1358. A haver cannot escape from producing a writing which is within the specification, by deponing generally that it will not support the party's pleas, because he is not entitled to judge of that matter, and admitting such depositions would give occasion to prevarication (*d*). Persons may be examined in order to prove that a document existed at a certain date (*e*), or with a view to adducing secondary proof of its terms (*f*), or to establish the *casus amissionis* in an action of proving the tenor (*g*).[11] And although a diligence

---

(*c*) A. S., 22d February 1688. (*d*) Ly. Campbell *v.* E. Crawford, 1783, M., 3973—Tait Ev., 182. (*e*) Boyd *v.* Anderson, 1821, 1 S., 144.

(*f*) Ewing *v.* Crichton, 1827, 4 Mur., 181—Scott *v.* Millar, 1830, 5 Mur., 242—Home *v.* Hardy, 1842, 4 D., 1184—*Contra*, Clark *v.* Spence, 1824, 3 Mur., 454.

(*g*) Boyd *v.* Anderson, 1823, 2 S., 363—Livingstone *v.* Murray, 1830, 9 S., 161—Falconer *v.* Stephen, 1849, 11 D., 1338.

---

cutor of documents in criminal cases, see observations by the Lord Justice Clerk (Hope) in H. M. Adv. *v.* Madeleine Smith, 2 Irv., 675.

[11] The pursuer in an action of declarator of marriage tendered herself as a haver for the purpose of proving the loss or destruction of certain documents, with a view to proving their contents by parole. The Lord Ordinary (Ardmillan) found that the proposed examination was without precedent or authority, and inadmissible, and the Inner House adhered. "The testimony of the pursuer as a witness is inadmissible. Then her examination merely as a haver on her own requisition is quite unnecessary. If she were a haver or holder of documents, of which she desired production, a diligence against herself was not required, for production of the document was within her power

cannot be put in force except by the party who obtained it, yet a haver who has been examined for that party is subject to cross-examination, and if he has produced documents or excerpts, he may be required to produce others which are cross to them, in order that the production may not be one-sided or partial (*h*)

§ 1359 The examination ought to be confined to matters which are relevant to the existence and recovery of the document, any examination as to the merits of the cause being irregular (*i*) It was partly on this ground that, in an action of proving the tenor of a codicil, after one of the defenders when examined for the pursuer as a haver had deponed that he destroyed the document, a co-defender was not allowed to ask him whether in doing so he had acted by the granter's directions (*k*) [12] It follows from this rule that the deposition of a haver cannot be used as that of a witness on the merits of the cause (*l*) It has even been rejected where the deponent had died before the trial (*m*)

(*h*) Dunlop's Tr v L Belhaven 1852 14 D, 825—Thorburn v Hoby 1853, 15 ib, 767 (*i*) Kerr v D Roxburghe, 1822, 3 Mur 133—Campbell v Davidson, 1827, 4 Mur, 178—Dye v Reid, 1831 9 S 342 (where the Court ordered the objectionable passages in the deposition to be deleted)—Tait Ev, 181 (*k*) Falconer v Stephen, 1849, 11 D, 1338, per Lord Wood (Ordinary) See *supra*, § 1306

(*l*) Cases noted *supra* (*i*)—Scott v M Gavin, 1821, 2 Mur, 494

(*m*) Campbell v Davidson 1827, 4 Mur, 178 per Lord Chief-Commissioner There is room for doubt on this point

---

But she was really not a haver It is explained, on the part of the pursuer, that the object of this proposed examination was not to recover or produce documents, but to enable her to depone in regard to the loss or destruction of documents of which she says that she was once in possession, and which she avers to have been lost, or to have been destroyed by the defender The defender was called as a haver for the pursuer, and fully examined In so far as he may have admitted the loss or destruction of any documents, it was open to the pursuer to tender secondary evidence of their contents But he has, on examination by the pursuer as a haver, sworn that he did not destroy the documents referred to, and the attempt to prove such a fact by the deposition of the pursuer herself, in a cause where she cannot be a witness, is contrary to the rules of evidence and the practice of the Court,' Longworth v Yelverton 1862, 24 D 696 Until a party has exhausted his powers under a diligence to recover principals he is not entitled to know the contents of documents of which the haver only holds copies, Mann v Smith, 1861, 23 D 683

[12] A haver, in the course of his deposition under a diligence to recover certain states and materials used in preparation thereof and copies in all instances where the principals could not be obtained, deponed that he had destroyed a state The Court held that it was incompetent to put the questions,—Did you destroy the state under instructions from any one? and, Do you know who prepared the destroyed state?—being questions intended to test the veracity of the haver, and not competently arising under such an examination, but they allowed him to be asked, When he destroyed the state? Where he destroyed it? and Why he destroyed it? Cullen v Thomson and Kerr, 1863 1 Macph 284

§ 1360 Where the haver produces the writings called for, the report of the commissioner states so specifying the documents, which are marked by the haver, commissioner and clerk to the commissioner, as relative thereto If they are numerous, they may be mentioned as enumerated and described in an inventory, signed by these persons, the individual documents being marked with their initials (*n*). The commissioner ought to report specially upon any matters which he considers ought to be brought under the notice of the Court, and the Court sometimes direct him to make a special report regarding documents exhibited to him (*o*)

VII *Of admitting and proving Documents at the Trial*

§ 1361 As the admissibility of a document depends in most cases on the purpose for which it is tendered, the recovery of writings under a diligence does not exclude any objection to their being received in evidence at the trial (*p*), or by the Court when the case is not tried by jury (*r*) But the Court sometimes decide upon the admissibility, when the diligence is granted (*s*) In such cases it will be proper to repeat the objection at the trial if there is any intention to bring the judgment of the Court under review, or if the circumstances under which the document is tendered present the question in a new shape (*t*) When a party means to object to a document being admitted, he ought to do so when it is first produced at the trial, and it is too late to object after the document has been examined upon and when it is formally tendered in evidence upon the case of the party who founds on it being closed (*u*) Yet if it is tendered for a purpose which is not covered by the previous examination, the opposite party is not barred from objecting to its admission for such additional purpose

§ 1362 It has been said that 'where documents alleged to be confidential are called for to be used at a jury trial, the practice in the Court of Session is the same as in England, viz, that the documents having been sealed up, the judge who is to try the case opens the packet, and, according to his opinion, treats them as confidential or not, that his decision may be brought by bill of exceptions

---

(*n*) Tait Ev 182 See the forms given in the Appendix (*o*) Fraser *v* Sandeman, 1836, 14 S, 377 (*p*) Simpson *v* Macfarlane, 1822, 3 Mur, 194—Paul *v* Commercial Insur Co, 1831, 9 S, 842—Brash *v* Steel, 1845, 7 D, 539—M'Cowan *v* Wright, 1853, 15 D, 229 494 (*r*) Hannay's Tr *v* E Galloway, 1828, 6 S 689—Noble *v* Scott, 1843 5 D 727 (*s*) See Brash *v* Steel *supra*
(*t*) See M'Cowan *v* Wright *supra* (*u*) Robertson *v* Thom, 1848, 11 D 353

before the Court, who, if the judge held the documents to be confidential open the packet in like manner, and decide according to their opinion, and so, if the matter be taken to the House of Lords" (*x*). But this practice occasions delay at the trial, while there is an obvious propriety in withholding from the presiding judge documents which are kept from the jury (*y*). Accordingly, where the objection of confidentiality was taken before the trial the Court ordered the documents to be transmitted to one of their number, whom they requested to examine them with a view to production of such as were not privileged, and to excerpts being taken from any which were only partially protected (*z*). In other cases this duty has been intrusted to the Lord Ordinary, when the cause was depending before him (*a*), to the principal Clerk of Court (*b*), and to the Commissioner who executed the diligence (*c*).[13]

§ 1363. Some documents, if formal, are probative—that is, they are admissible in evidence without their authenticity being proved. Of this nature are deeds bearing the statutory solemnities (*d*), deeds containing a statement that they are holograph (*e*), bills (*f*), notarial instruments (*g*), and messengers' executions (*h*), extracts from public records in Scotland (*i*), and some others. The rules as to such documents have been already considered.

§ 1364. Documents which do not fall under this class will only be received on being admitted or proved to be what they are alleged to be (*k*). This, for example, is required as to the private books of

(*x*) Per L. Meadowbank in Watt *v.* Mitchell, 1839, 1 D., 698.
(*y*) Per L. Justice-Clerk in M'Cowan *v.* Wright, 1853, 15 D., 236.
(*z*) M'Cowan *v.* Wright, *supra*. (*a*) Aitkenhead *v.* Black, 1838, 16 S., 1183. (*b*) M'Lean *v.* Reid, 1835, 14 S., 102. (*c*) Campbell *v.* Campbell, 1823, 2 S., 139—Jarvis *v.* Anderson, 1841, 3 D., 990. (*d*) *Supra*, § 636, *et seq.* (*e*) *Supra*, § 754. (*f*) *Supra*, § 793. (*g*) *Supra*, § 1186, *et seq.* (*h*) *Supra*, §§ 1226–7, 1243. (*i*) *Supra*, § 1250, *et seq.* As to extracts from foreign records see *supra*, § 1281, *et seq.* (*k*) Mack. Pr., 173—E. Fife *v.* E. Fife's Tr., 1816, 1 Mur., 105.

13 In Hay *v.* Edinburgh and Glasgow Bank, the defender objected to produce certain documents on the plea of confidentiality. The Court, having held that the plea of confidentiality was not limited to documents of a date subsequent to the raising of the action, remitted to Lord Cowan to ascertain whether the documents in question were of a confidential nature. Lord Cowan having reported that they were, the Court ordered the documents to be sealed up and redelivered to the owner. Hay *v.* Edinburgh and Glasgow Bank, 1858, 20 D., 701.

a person (*l*), a ship's articles (*m*), a log-book (*n*), correspondence (*o*), and writings (except bills and promissory-notes), privileged as in *in re mercatoria* (*p*) In general, the witness who proves a document must speak from his own knowledge, and therefore, where a book of accounts was tendered as the book of one named Law (who was not a party to the case), and where the party who tendered it offered to adduce Watt, from whom it had been recovered under a diligence, and who, it was said, would prove that he got it from Law as Law's book (Law, when examined as a haver, having deponed that it was in the hands of Watt) the Court held the proof to be incompetent And they afterwards refused to admit Law to prove the book, because he had been in court throughout the trial (*r*) But where a witness produced a bulker's book, the objection that the person who wrote it was not called to prove it was repelled, because the witness deponed that he held it to be an office-book, and had regulated his conduct by it (*s*) In England, entries in a banker's books, which are open to all the clerks, may be proved by any of them, as well as by the actual writer (*t*) But in this country there is not yet a fixed rule on the point (*u*) The rules as to proving excerpts taken before a commissioner are noticed above (*w*) [14]

§ 1365 It is a common practice for parties in order to save the necessity for proving documents, to lodge before the trial written notes of admissions of their authenticity (*x*) But it is often necessary to have documents proved, in order that the mode in which they were prepared may be brought before the jury

(*l*) Stuart *v* Mitchell, 1833, 11 S, 1004—Anderson *v* Wishart, 1818, 1 Mur 435
(*m*) Carleton *v* Strong, 1816, 1 Mur, 27 (*n*) Same case, ib, 32
(*o*) E Fife *v* E Fife's Tr, *supra* (*p*) *Supra*, § 784
(*r*) Stuart *v* Mitchell, *supra* (*s*) Edinburgh, Leith and Hull Shipping Company, 1819, 2 Mur, 138 (*t*) Furness *v* Cope, 1828, 2 Mo and Pa, 197
(*u*) See this subject noticed *supra*, § 80, *et seq* (*w*) §§ 141, 142
(*x*) Macf Pr, 86

[14] In a trial before a jury at the instance of an inspector of poor, the pursuer proposed to give in evidence excerpts from the minute-book of the board, which had been recovered under a diligence, in the course of which the books had been exhibited in presence of the defender's agent, but the excepts were not certified by the commissioner to be correct None of the principal minute-books had been lodged eight days before the trial, but some of them were produced at the trial, others were not On an admission that the excerpts from the books produced were correctly made, they were admitted as evidence The excerpts from the books not produced were refused, Beattie *v* Mackay and Paterson, 1863 1 Macph 279

VIII *Of getting up Documents from Public Registers*

§ 1366 The Court of Session, as the supreme civil court in Scotland, has power to ordain the keepers of the public registers to deliver up documents in their official custody (*y*) And ' when any deeds, or steps or warrants of extracted processes deposited with the Lord Clerk-Register are required in processes depending before the permanent Lords Ordinary, it shall not be necessary to apply to the Inner House for a warrant for the transmission of such documents, but the Lords Ordinary before whom the causes depend may grant such warrant when the productions appear to them to be necessary for the ends of justice, provided always that the motion is intimated to the opposite party, and also to the said Lord Clerk-Register, or his deputy, two days before the motion, and that no relevant objection is stated thereto And the said warrant shall be certified by the clerk, and delivered to the Lord Register or his deputy at receiving up the documents " (*z*) In jury causes, " when it is deemed necessary by either of the parties that the original of any registered instrument or any recorded process, or any process depending, or that may have depended in any other court, should be lodged in process, it shall be competent for the party to apply to the Lord Ordinary in the cause before the issues are signed, and thereafter to the Court," ' for a warrant to authorise and direct the Lord Clerk-Register and his deputes, or the keeper of any other register in whose custody the instrument or process is preserved, or the clerk of any court before which such process is depending, or may have depended, to deliver up the same to the clerks " appointed to act in the business of trial by jury, " at the office in the Register House, in order to be produced at the trial, upon delivery of the warrant, and a proper receipt and obligation, for redelivery after the trial, and provided such application has been intimated to the agent of the opposite party, and also to the Lord Clerk-Register or his deputes two days before such application is made, it shall be competent to the Lord Ordinary or the Court, if they shall see cause, to grant such warrant, in such terms, and under such conditions and qualifications as may be deemed necessary (*a*) If the

---

(*y*) See cases *infra* § 1369, *et seq* (*z*) A S, 24th Dec 1838 (Enrolment of New Causes, &c), § 15 Mansfield *v* Stewart, 1840 2 D, 1235 At common law a Lord Ordinary has not power to ordain the Lord Clerk Register to transmit documents in his custody Simpson 1829, 7 S 471 (*a* A S 16th Feb 1841 § 20

case has been set down for trial, and the motion is made during vacation, it shall be heard by the judge who is to preside at the trial, if in Edinburgh, or by a judge who is to be on the circuit if it is to be on circuit, and in case of their absence respectively, by the Lord Ordinary on the Bills it being shown to the satisfaction of the judge before whom the motion is made that it could not have been made during the session (*b*) [15]

§ 1367 Any writ given in by a person for registration in the books of Council and Session may without judicial authority be got up by him, or by any one employed by him within six months after the in-giving, provided it has not been booked (*c*)

§ 1368 In cases which do not fall within the provision just noticed it is for the Court, in the exercise of its discretion, to determine whether writings should be taken out of the public registers for any purpose, and if so, to prescribe proper means for securing their preservation and return The following cases illustrate the views of the Court on the subject

§ 1369 The Court have refused to grant warrant to transmit an extracted process from the records of their own Court, with a view to its production in evidence in a cause depending before them (*d*), or depending in a Sheriff-court (*e*), because an extract of the decree, or certified excerpts of part of the process, are sufficient for the purpose (*f*) In an action of simple reduction of a deed on the ground of error in the testing clause the Court refused to order the original to be put into process, but appointed one of the keepers of the record to attend with it, when it should be required *in modum probationis* (*g*) And in a reduction on the ground of facility and circumvention, the Court refused an application by the defender to have two deeds, which had been entered in the books of Council and Session, delivered up in order to be shewn to witnesses in Arbroath, but granted warrant for delivery of them to the clerk of process in

(*b*) A S, 16th Feb 1841, § 21 (*c*) 1685, c 38 See a striking illustration of the effect of this provision in M'Leod *v* Cuninghame 1841, 3 D, 1288, affd, 5 Bell's Ap Ca, 210, noted *supra*, § 727 There is not any corresponding power to get up deeds from inferior court records see Brown *v* Rankine, 11th March 1809, F C, and Barclay *v* Brown, 1811 Hume D, 923, noted *supra*, ib, § ib (*d*) Anderson, 1827, 5 S, 543—Monro, 1828, 7 S, 52 (*e*) Meikleham, 1839, 2 D, 165

(*f*) See *supra* § 1255 (*g*) Gaywood, 1828 6 S, 363 The alleged vitiation was at the fold, and would have been increased if the deed had been produced in process See also Alison, 1829, 7 S, 552

[15] MacLean *v* M'Lean's Trustees 1861 23 D, 1262, *supra*, § 1330, note [1]—Cochrane *v* Ferrier, 1859, 21 D 749

order that he might take them to the place and exhibit them to the witnesses or otherwise as might be necessary (*h*)

In an election case before the Reform Act where the complainer moved the Court for a warrant on the town clerk of Dunfermline to produce the burgh court-books in process, or at least in the hands of the clerk to the process, the motion was refused, on the ground that the books were a record which was by law kept at Dunfermline, and that parties who wished to examine them were entitled and bound to inspect them there (*i*)

§ 1370 It is not a sufficient reason for allowing a deed to be taken out of the register in order to be produced in a foreign Court, that its terms require to be proved in an action depending there, because most foreign Courts admit an extract from a public record (*k*) But where the Court of Session have been satisfied that the foreign Court would not allow the terms of the deed to be proved, except by the deed itself, they have granted warrant to have the original placed in the hands of an officer of Court to be exhibited by him (*l*), while in other cases they have allowed it to be delivered to the party, on his finding security to return it to the record within a limited time (*m*) In an old case the creditor in a bond got it up

(*h*) Mansfield *v* Stewart, 1840, 2 D, 1235 (*i*) Campbell *v* Black, 6th July 1813, F C (*k*) Bartwistle *v* L Clerk Register, 1825, 3 S, 602—Morton *v* L Clerk-Register, 1831, 10 S, 162—Wharton Peerage Case, 1815, 12 Cl and Fin, 303—See these cases noted *supra* § 1286

(*l*) In Malcolm, 1847, 19 Sc Jur 483, the Court allowed a deed to be taken out of the records of Council and Session, and placed in the hands of an assistant clerk of court, to be by him exhibited at a trial in England And in Annandale, 1828, 6 S, 657 they intrusted a deed in the same way to a depute clerk of court who had been subpœnaed to attend the trial In both of these cases warrant to deliver up the deed to a private party was refused See also Wharton Peerage Case, 1815, 12 Cl and Fin, 295, *supra*, § 1286

(*m*) In Cunningham, 1821, 1 S, 98 the creditor in a bond recorded in the books of Council and Session wishing to enforce it against the debtor in Jamaica, where an extract is not admissible, was allowed to get it up on finding caution to return it in a year, an authenticated copy being deposited in the record in place of it In Bloxam *v* E Rosslyn, 1825, 3 S, 126, a party who had raised an action of damages for infringement of a patent in England, obtained warrant on the Director of Chancery to deliver up the original specification of the patent on granting bond to return it within three months He produced an opinion of English counsel, stating that it was necessary for the case that the original should be produced (But compare this case with Morton *v* L Clerk-Register, 1831, 10 S, 162 noted *supra* § 1286) In Duncan *v* L Clerk-Register, 1812, 1 D, 1517, where the trustees under a trust deed of settlement which had been recorded in the books of Council and Session, applied for delivery of the deed, in order to enable them to administer property in the East Indies and where they stated that the Indian courts had refused to allow them to administer on their producing an extract, the Court granted the application, on the parties finding security to return the from the books of Council and Session for production in Dantzic in an action against the debtor, apparently without having been required to find security to return it (*n*) [15]

§ 1371 The Court granted a petition by the Lord Advocate for warrant to have a deed which was recorded in the books of Council and Session delivered up on the Crown agent's receipt, for the purpose of investigation, one of the persons whose name was affixed to the deed, having lodged information that it was a forgery (*o*) Where a patentee applied to have the royal warrant for letters of patent, which was recorded in Chancery, delivered up, that it might be transmitted to the Home Secretary for the purpose of having a misnomer corrected, the Court granted the application (*p*) And they granted warrant to have a deed, which had not been properly stamped, delivered up to the agent of a party founding on it, in order to get the proper stamp affixed, security being found to return it within a limited time (*r*)

§ 1372 The Crown Charters Act provides that when the last charter, or retour, or decree of service in favour of a party applying for a crown-charter cannot be lodged with the presenter of signatures it shall be competent to that officer, or to the person applying for the charter, to "refer to the copy thereof engrossed in the register of the great seal, or in the register of retours or decrees of service and to procure exhibition thereof as evidence of the terms of such last charter, or retour, or decree of service," and the Lord Clerk-Register is authorised and required to make regulations for such exhibition being obtained upon the joint application of the vassal and of the presenter of signatures (*s*)

---

deed within six months an extract of it, duly authenticated, being lodged in the register in its stead (*n*) Finlayson *v* Finlayson, 1627, M, 13 541

(*o*) King's Advocate, 1831, 9 S, 387 (*p*) Whitehead, 1836, 14 S, 450

(*r*) Laidlaw, 21st January 1840, F C—Adamson, 1852, 14 D, 1045

(*s*) 10 and 11 Vict c 51, § 5

---

[15] See cases in note [4] § 1286 *supra*

BOOK SECOND.

OF STATEMENTS AND OATHS OF THE PARTIES TO THE CAUSE, AND PERSONS REPRESENTING THEM

---

§ 1373 Evidence may be furnished by the parties to a cause in several ways—viz, 1st, by a writing under their hands, prepared as the record of a transaction, 2d by a statement (written or verbal) made without the sanction of an oath, 3d, by a statement on oath as a party under the common law, and 4th, by a statement on oath as a witness under the Law of Evidence Amendment Act The first of these kinds of evidence has been considered under the title "Private Writings" The last will be noticed in treating of "Testimony" The following chapters will embrace the second and third kinds of evidence, with their expansion under the rule *qui facit per alium facit per se*

§ 1374 Evidence furnished by the parties, or those for whom they are responsible, usually occupies a high place in regard to the knowledge which the individual has of the facts to which he speaks But as to its probable truthfulness, there is a marked contrast between that which is favourable, and that which is unfavourable, to the party This contrast is seen in the admissibility, as well as in the credibility, of the evidence in question

TITLE I.

OF STATEMENTS MADE (NOT ON OATH) BY A PARTY IN FAVOUR OF HIMSELF

§ 1375 It is a leading rule in the law of evidence that a party may not adduce in his own favour statements made by himself. And this is just, for even an honest litigant is rarely found to speak or write impartially on the subject of his suit, while false evidence would frequently be concocted if a party could have his own account of the matter in issue laid before the jury Besides, when such statements come (as they often do) through third persons to whom they have been made, they are subject to all the objections which render hearsay evidence inadmissible (*a*)

§ 1376 This rule is observed in every-day practice The following cases, in which there are some peculiarities, illustrates its application Although the statements of every partner of a company are evidence against the company in questions with third persons, yet in an accounting between the representatives of two deceased partners regarding the company affairs, it was held that entries in the private books of one partner are not evidence in favour of his representatives, where it is not proved that the other partner was privy to them (*b*) In an action of damages for breach of contract, the defenders, who were a body of road trustees, were not allowed to use their own minute-book to prove an arrangement between them and a third party, which was a fact relevant to their defence (*c*) Where Sir George Mackenzie sued the Town of Elgin for arrears of his salary as their advocate, entries in the town-books were admitted to prove the granting of the salary, but were held

(*a*) See *supra*, § 83, *et seq*

(*b*) Smith *v* Mitchell 1830, 5 S, 32, affd, 4 W S, 47

(*c*) Inglis *v* Cunninghame, 1826, 4 Mur, 77

not probative of yearly payments thereof by their treasurer, "seeing their books prove against them but not for them" (*d*). Where the trustee on the sequestrated estate of a company called upon one of the creditors to communicate a payment he had received in Jamaica on the allegation that it had been paid out of funds belonging to the company, the trustee was not allowed, with the view of proving that fact, to found on correspondence between him and his attorney in Jamaica (*e*) Where the trustee in a similar sequestration tendered one of the partners as a witness, Lord President Hope would not allow him to use the statutory Sederunt Book, in order to show that the partner had been discharged, and had therefore not an interest to render him inadmissible (*f*) This ruling, however, may be questioned as the discharge was a fact to the prejudice of the creditors, although in the particular case it was tendered as evidence for them and it would have been admissible as proof of the discharge in any proceedings at the instance of the creditors against the bankrupt

In a question of boundaries, minutes of an *ex parte* riding of marches were held inadmissible as evidence for the heritor at whose instance the riding took place, because they were in effect statements by him in his own favour (*g*)

The exception from this rule in the case of business books has been already noticed (*h*)

§ 1377 But a party may prove that he made a certain statement when that fact is relevant to his case, independently of the question whether the statement is true, because the fact which is thus laid before the jury does not come through the tainted channel of the party's own narrative, but admits of independent evidence like any other fact in the cause Upon this principle—which is analogous to that already noticed in treating of hearsay (*i*)—a party may prove that he made a certain complaint, or sent a certain notice (*k*), or took a protest (*l*), and the like, where such facts are relevant So, where the state of mind of a party or his feelings towards another, are in issue, his statements may be evidence for

(*d*) Mackenzie *v* Town of Elgin, 1693, 4 B Sup, 51—See *supra*, § 1172

(*e*) Young, Ross, Richardson, & Co *v* Muir, 1821, 2 Sh Ap Ca, 25, reversing, 22d January 1819 (not reported) (*f*) Mansfield *v* Maxwell, 1835, 13 S, 721 The rubric bears that the book was held not to be sufficient *per se* But the report itself is not so qualified (*g*) Hunter *v* Dodds, 1832, 10 S, 833 See also Rosenberg, 1812 Bell's Notes, 285 (*h*) *Supra*, § 1179, *et seq*

(*i*) See *supra*, § 86, and cases there cited (*k*) Gordon *v* Smith 18[illegible], 4 Mur, 88—Kerr *v* Penman 1830, 5 Mur, 144 (*l*) Cases noted *supra* [illegible]

him or persons in his right, because they are the natural indications of his thoughts and feelings (*m*). Accordingly where a number of obligatory documents granted by a person to his son-in-law, and bearing to be for value received were challenged by the granter's representatives, on the ground of having been extorted by intimidation, fraud and circumvention from him when in old age and facile, the summons also embracing a count and reckoning at the instance of the representatives against the son-in-law; and where the pursuers tendered certain account-books which had been kept by the deceased, and asked witnesses whether he had made certain statements as to payments by himself, and which were inconsistent with the apparent acknowledgments in the documents in issue, objections to the admission of both kinds of evidence were repelled in the Court of Session; and the judgment was affirmed on appeal. Lord Truro, in proposing the affirmance, pointed out with much clearness the distinction between using such evidence in an issue of resting-owing, and in a question as to the state of mind and memory, the imbecility or insanity of a person. As, therefore, the evidence was admissible for the latter purpose, the exception to its admissibility was ill founded; while from no exceptions having been taken to the judge's charge it was to be presumed that he directed the jury to what part of the issue the evidence in question ought to be applied (*n*).

This case shows that, when the utterance of a certain statement may be proved as a circumstance in the cause but not as evidence of the facts stated, the proper course is to admit the statement and to direct the jury to give effect to it only for its legitimate purpose, the party against whom the evidence is used excepting to the judge's charge if it tends to mislead the jury upon the point.

§ 1378. In like manner, a prisoner may show, as an exculpatory circumstance, that his statements regarding the matter libelled

---

(*m*) Cases noted *supra*, § 88, *et seq*.

(*n*) Cairns *v.* Marianski, 1850, 12 D., 919, 1286; affd., 1 Macq., 212. Lord Truro observed,—"I must ask by what test do you always try whether a man is of sane or weak mind? Shut out his declarations and his conduct, and what test will remain by which you are to try the state of his mind? If the issue had been whether Fairservice (the deceased) was indebted to Marianski (the defender) what Mr Fairservice had said or done about this, not in the presence of Marianski or to his knowledge, might be subject to objection. But when the question is imbecility of mind, or insanity, there is in truth no other evidence pertinent to that issue but the man's declarations and conduct, his sayings and doings." In this case (12 D., 1290) Lord Moncreiff mentioned a similar decision, Graham *v.* Macalpine, and observed that "innumerable cases of the same kind have occurred."

have been consistent (*o*), although none of them can be admitted as independent evidence of the facts which they set forth

§ 1379 Again a party may found upon his own letter or statement, when it has been recognised or admitted by the individual to whom it was addressed (*p*), and where the recognition of it is admissible, the point before the jury in such a case being the conduct of the person addressed, which cannot be proved without admitting the statement Upon the same principle a party may prove a statement made by himself in the presence of his antagonist, the relevant inquiry there being the conduct of the latter party on the occasion (*r*) And it is the constant practice in criminal courts to adduce this kind of evidence, in order to show the manner in which the prisoner conducted himself when he was charged with the offence, or when facts relating to it were mentioned in his presence (*s*)

A person has been allowed to found upon his letters to his opponent, in order to show that he made without contradiction the statements which they contain (*t*)

§ 1380 Farther, where a party has led evidence of statements made by his antagonist, the latter may prove other statements which he made on the occasion, in order that the jury may not receive a partial impression from selected passages in the conversation (*u*) And a party proving a conversation may commence with examining upon his own statement, when that is necessary to the proper understanding of expressions on which he is entitled to found (*x*) But a party will not be allowed to use this rule as a pretext for proving such statements made by him as are extrinsic to the subject of conversation

In like manner, when a party puts in letters written by his op-

---

(*o*) 2 Al, 555—Forrest, 1837, 1 Swin 404—Bell's Notes, 285

(*p*) Doe d Brune *v* Rawlings, 1806, 7 East, 279—Burgess *v* Burgess, 1817, 2 Hag Con Rep, 235—1 Phill Ev, 405 Where letters by the agent of one party had been referred to on both sides in the Court of Session, they were received as evidence in the House of Lords, Hall *v* Brown, 1814, 2 Dow, 376 (*r*) Hay *v* Boyd, 1822, 3 Mur, 13 (*s*) On this subject see *supra*, § 271, *et seq*

(*t*) Hamilton *v* Hope, 1827, 4 Mur, 238, compared with Hatton *v* Peddie, 1830 5 Mur, 158 (*u*) Chaplain *v* Baillie, 1821, 2 Mur, 159—Reid *v* Stoddart, 1820, ib, 241 See Paterson *v* Shaw, 1830, 5 Mur, 271, where, in an action of damages for slander, a witness for the pursuer having in his examination in chief been asked as to certain statements made by the defender, and having, in cross-examination for the defender, said he asked the defender what authority he had for making the statements, the defender was allowed to ask what answer he gave

(*x*) See Mills *v* Albion Ins Co, 1826, 4 Mur, 112

ponent, he may accompany them by those in his own hand, to which they are answers, or which are answers to them, and the other party may produce any additional letters under his hand during the correspondence on the same matter, which may tend to make the production complete (*y*)[1] So where one reads to the jury part of his opponent's pleadings, the latter may require him to read the whole of the statement on the same branch of the case (*z*) And if a party gives in evidence part of a letter or other document under the hand of his opponent, the latter may insist on his reading the remainder of it, if that seems to be necessary for the proper understanding of the part founded on (*a*) On the same principle, a party may produce writings under his own hand, where writings which are produced refer to them either expressly or by implication as *partes ejusdem negotii* (*b*)

§ 1381 Whenever statements by a party form part of the *res gestæ* of acts which are in evidence they may be proved by him, as tending to explain the acts with which they are connected[2] This doctrine has been so fully considered in treating of hearsay (*c*), that it will suffice for the present purpose to quote a few cases illustrating its application to proof by a party of his own statements Where a pursuer proved that he delivered a certain memorial to a witness, he was also allowed to prove the instructions which he

(*y*) Wight *v* Liddell, 1829, 5 Mur, 40—Stevenson *v* Kyle, 1849, 11 D 1086—See also Dunlop's Tr *v* L Belhaven, 1852, 14 D, 825—Thorburn *v* Hoby, 1853, 15 D, 767 (*z*) Jamieson *v* Main, 1830, 5 Mur 118 (*a*) Cameron *v* Camerons, 1820, 2 Mur, 233 (*b*) See this subject considered *supra*, § 180, *et seq* (*c*) *Supra*, § 92, *et seq*

[1] Longworth *v* Yelverton, 1862, 24 D, 696—Smith *v* Pickett, 1861, 7 Jur, N S, 610

[2] In an action of declarator of marriage, it was held that evidence of statements made by the pursuer to lodging-house keepers and others, in the absence of the defender was inadmissible, unless where the statements formed part of the *res gestæ* In the first place hearsay was not admissible, and, in the second, the pursuer was not a competent witness "Her testimony in her own cause, given on oath, cannot be received, and these statements by herself, which she proposes to prove through the testimony of others, were not on oath and cannot be received as evidence where the testimony on oath is excluded Where, however, any particular statements of the pursuer are so connected with acts and facts given in evidence that the dissociation of the statements from the acts and facts to which they relate would frustrate the ends of justice, and impede the discovery of truth, then that dissociation is prevented, the statements are treated as *partes rei gestæ*, and, on that ground, are viewed as within the exception to the rule, and are admitted accordingly", Longworth *v* Yelverton, 1862, 24 D, 696 In H M Adv *v* Stewart, 1855, 2 Irv, 179, evidence of expressions of malice by the panel as matter arising *de recenti* and forming part of the *res gestæ* was admitted

gave on the occasion (*d*). In an action of declarator of marriage, where the pursuer proved that she got from her agent certain letters addressed by the defender to her, and that the defender accompanied her on the occasion, and waited outside of the agent's house till she returned, she was allowed to ask the agent on what ground, or for what purpose, she requested him to give up the documents (*e*). In an action of damages for assault the pursuer may prove that he called for assistance at the time (*f*).

A narrow question on this head occurred in an action of separation and aliment. The pursuer proved that a quarrel had taken place between her and the defender, and a witness adduced by her deponed that she afterwards found the pursuer in her bedroom in a state of great distress, sobbing convulsively, and that she heard her make an exclamation, not addressed to any one, but just as if she had given way to her feelings. The pursuer's counsel then asked the witness what the exclamation was, whereupon the commissioner before whom the proof was led, after ascertaining from the witness that the exclamation involved a statement as to the cause of the pursuer's distress, sustained an objection to the question, and the Lord Ordinary (Ivory) affirmed his decision. The Inner House, however, by a majority of two judges to one, altered the Lord Ordinary's interlocutor, and held that the witness might be asked what the pursuer said on the occasion, provided it was confined to an explanation, and was not a detailed statement as to the cause of her distress. The majority of the Court (Lords President Boyle and Jeffrey) considered that the exclamation was part of the *res gestæ* of the scene in the bedroom upon which the witness was examined. But Lord Mackenzie and the Lord Ordinary considered that it did not enter into the *res gestæ* of any matter between the pursuer and the defender, but merely formed part of her own behaviour in her bedroom, after her husband had left her (*g*). The decision can have little value as a precedent. It seems to conflict with a ruling by the Lord Chief-Commissioner in an action of damages for judicial slander, where a witness for the pursuer having been asked whether that party expressed any distress, or appeared agitated, the learned judge held that it was competent to prove the agitation, but not the words uttered (*h*).

(*d*) Hamilton *v* Hope, 1827, 4 Mur., 241. (*e*) Craigie *v* Hoggan, 1837, 15 S., 379, affd on merits Macl. and Rob., 942. (*f*) Hall *v* Otto, 1818, 1 Mur., 444. (*g*) A B *v* C D, 1848, 11 D., 289. (*h*) Robertson *v* Barclay, 1828, 4 Mur., 530.

§ 1382 It seems to be still an open question whether statements which a party, injured by acts of violence of another, made *de recenti* of them, are admissible in an issue regarding it in a civil action at his instance against his assailant The admissibility of such statements in criminal cases is fully recognised (*i*), for, besides being in themselves part of the real evidence, they are useful as testing the truthfulness of the statement emitted by the injured party as a witness, while the absence of any direct interest on his part in the issue makes it not likely that his statements *de recenti* were uttered for the purpose of being afterwards proved in such a prosecution But the leaning of the decisions has hitherto been against admitting in a civil cause such statements as evidence for the injured party, because they may have been uttered with the view of being afterwards used in his own favour, and because (at the dates of the decisions) the party was not admissible as a witness The latter reason does not now apply, except in a few cases where party witnesses are still inadmissible (*k*), while in every case where a party is examined as a witness, a statement made by him on any other specified occasion may be proved by the other party under the Law of Evidence Amendment Act of 1852 (*l*) In this state of matters it is likely that the Court will seldom, if ever, exclude proof of statements made by a party *de recenti* regarding an outrage for which he seeks reparation At all events, the cases (*m*) in which the Court rejected evidence of this kind, before the recent changes on the law of evidence, cannot be regarded as fixing a rule applicable to our present practice

§ 1383 In an action of damages for assault the pursuer was not allowed to prove the statements which he made to his medical attendant a day or two after the attack, as to suffering pain from bruises (*n*) Such evidence appears to be admissible in England (*o*)

§ 1384 It does not seem necessary to discuss at length a question which till recently, was of some importance, namely how far written statements by a person may be admitted in favour of his

(*i*) See *supra* § 95 (*k*) 16 Vict, c 20 (*l*) 15 Vict, c 27, § 3

(*m*) Evidence of statements made *de recenti* by the pursuer of an action of damages for assault with intent to ravish, was rejected in Maclean *v* Miller, 1832, 5 De and And, 270, and Hill *v* Fletcher, 1847, 10 D 7 (the latter case, however, being somewhat special, see *supra*, § 99) In an action of separation and aliment on the ground of bad treatment, where the pursuer proved that two hours after a quarrel between her and the defender she left home and walked some distance to a neighbouring house she was not allowed to prove the story she then told the lady of the house regarding the quarrel, A B *v* C D, 1848, 11 D 289

(*n*) Hall *v* Otto, 1828, 1 Mur 444

(*o*) See *supra* § 90

successors, when the question in issue relates to matters of ancient date. In such cases the statement will be received as secondary evidence of a deceased witness. Even before the passing of the "Law of Evidence Amendment Act" such evidence seems to have been admissible (*p*), along with hearsay, histories, entries in family bibles, clauses in deeds between third parties, and other make-shift evidence, as being the best that cases of the kind usually admitted of. In England the statements are only admitted if, at the time of making them, they were against the interest of the persons by whom they were emitted (*r*).

§ 1385. In an action of damages for malicious prosecution it is competent, in England, for the defender, in support of his defence of probable cause, to prove the evidence which he gave on the trial of the prosecution in issue, "for otherwise one that would be robbed, &c., would be under an intolerable mischief, for if he prosecuted for such robbery, &c., and the party should at any rate be acquitted, the prosecutor would be liable to an action for a malicious prosecution, without a possibility of making a good defence, though the cause of prosecution were ever so pregnant" (*s*). No authority on this point has been found in Scotland.

(*p*) See Westenra *v* M'Neill, 1826, 4 S., 603. (*r*) Taylor Ev., 438, and cases there cited. (*s*) Johnson *v* Browning, 6 Mod., 216, per Holt—Jackson *v* Bull, 2 Moo. and Rob., 176—Bull. N. P., 14—Taylor, 882—1 Greenleaf, 497.

TITLE II.

OF STATEMENTS MADE (NOT ON OATH) BY A PARTY AGAINST HIS INTEREST

CHAPTER I.—ADMISSIONS AND CONFESSIONS ON RECORD

§ 1386. Both at common law and under the Judicature Act, the admission by a party on record in a civil cause is almost always both competent and conclusive proof on any fact in issue (*a*). It is conclusive even upon facts which are provable only by the party's writ or oath, *e.g.*, the constitution and resting-owing of debts due under prescribed bills and accounts (*b*),[1] and the constitution of trusts under deeds *ex facie* absolute (*c*). But where writing is es-

---

(*a*) Stair, 4, 45, 5—Ersk., 4, 2, 33—6 Geo. IV., c. 120, §§ 13, 14, 15—Per L. Truro in Scottish Marine Ins. Co. *v.* Turner, 1853, 1 Macq., 340—Grubb *v.* Mackenzie, 1818, 2 Mur., 3—Hay *v.* Boyd, 1822, 3 Mur., 20—Mackenzie *v.* M'Kay, 1825, 4 S. 614—Mackay *v.* M'Leods, 1827, 4 Mur. 280—Gibson *v.* Marr, 1822, 3 Mur. 265—Elliot *v.* Northumberland Glass Co., 1824, 3 S. 67. (*b*) See *supra*, §§ 407, 8, 9.

(*c*) See *supra*, § 584.

---

[1] The observations made by the Lord Justice-Clerk (Hope) and by Lord Rutherfurd, when commenting in Cullen *v.* Smeal upon the cases where judicial admissions had been given effect to in questions of prescription, rather seem to imply that the question, whether a judicial admission can be held to be proof *scripto*, within the meaning of the statutes, is still open. "Whether such admissions are the writ of party, or whether, if the defender requires it, the matter must not be put to his oath, are points which it is unnecessary in this case to consider."—*per* Lord Justice-Clerk (Hope) in Cullen *v.* Smeal, 1853, 15 D. 868. In a previous case, Lord Jeffrey remarked that he entertained great doubt about the effect of these admissions. "In the Outer House I took them as superseding the necessity of an oath, by holding them to be properly *scripta* of the party. But for that I should not have gone the length I did. On consideration, I think it is not a sound view. It is not the *scriptum* the statutes require, unless there was an express procuration to make and sign the statement. We have gone on grounds of convenience rather than otherwise—for that is at the bottom of it—that where a party

sential to the constitution of a right or obligation, an admission on record that the parties entered into a verbal agreement on the matter will not bind the party admitting, because he was entitled to resile so long as writing did not intervene Yet if *locus pœnitentiæ* has been barred by *rei interventus*, the terms of the obligation may be proved by an admission on record (*d*)

Where any proceeding requires to be proved by the written evidence of an official person, an admission on record that it took place does not exclude the objection that the only legal proof of it is awanting or defective (*e*)

§ 1387 Equally effectual with admissions in a closed record are other formal judicial admissions, as, for example, those prefixed to the issue (*f*), or made in a joint case for the opinion of foreign lawyers (*g*), or in a minute prepared to obviate the necessity of proof (*h*) It has been justly held in England that admissions made by minute previous to a first trial of the cause, but not expressly limited to it, are conclusive in a new trial on the same issue because they are made with reference to the trial at which the cause is decided, not to an abortive one (*i*).

§ 1388 Lord Stair (*k*) and Mr Erskine (*l*) considered that admissions contained in argumentative papers were equally conclusive But in modern practice it would seem that such admissions, although competent against the party, do not exclude him from proof to contradict them as having been made in error (*m*)

(*d*) See *supra* § 845 (*e*) Campbells v M'Neill, 1799, M, 11 120—See *supra* §§ 1187 1226 (*f*) Macf Pr, 71 As to interlocutor copied in bill of advocation see § 139 (*g*) R Bank *v* Broughton 1830, 8 S 424—Van Wort *v* Wooley 1823 1 Ry and Moo 4—and Edmunds *v* Newman 1823, note thereto

(*h*) 6 Geo IV c 120 § 33—M'Whir *v* Oswald, 1833, 11 S, 552—Young *v* Wright, 1807, 1 Camp, 139—Lluck's Tr *v* Duff 1824, 3 S 343 The A S 16th February 1841, § 22 provides "that when parties (in civil jury causes) are disposed to make admissions in regard to matters of fact or to admit the authenticity of writings a note of the admissions is to be made in writing signed by the party's counsel or agent, and lodged in process, and certified by the clerk, and all admissions so made may be used and read in evidence at the trial if otherwise competent" (*i*) Elton *v* Larkins, 1832, 5 Car and Pa 385, 1 Mo and Rob, 196 S C—Doe *v* Bird, 1835 7 Car and Pa, 6—Langley *v* E Oxford, 1836 1 Mee and Wel, 508—Van Wort *v* Wooley, *supra* —Edmunds *v* Newman *supra* (*k*) Stair, 4, 45, 5 6 (*l*) Ersk 4, 2, 33

(*m*) Macf Pr, 211—Tait Ev, 41—Ewing *v* Crichton 1827, 4 Mur, 1833, per Lord

he made a statement, his oath can only be in conformity with it, and it is therefore unnecessary to be at the expense of an oath" But Lord Mackenzie thought that, under the new forms of pleading, the party could not recall an admission and doubted whether if he swore the contrary his oath could be received, Dunley *v* Kirkwood, 1845, 7 D 595

§ 1389 When a party makes in his record an explicit averment of a fact within the knowledge of the other party, and the latter does not deny it on record, he is held to admit it, and further evidence on the point is unnecessary (*n*) And if it is a *factum proprium* the party will not escape from this consequence by pleading "not admitted" (*o*) But if the averment is only provable by writ or oath of party (as for example, a prescribed account), the party against whom it is made is not bound to confess or deny it, and his non-denial will therefore not be held as equivalent to an admission obviating the necessity for proof by writ or oath (*p*)

§ 1390 It is only those admissions to which a party commits himself in a closed record, or by a formal judicial admission of the nature above described (*r*), which are conclusive against him Admissions made in defences, but retracted in the answers to the pursuer's condescendence, were held not to be conclusive (*s*), although the circumstance that they had been made and retracted might be used against the party (*t*), and might be material if not satisfactorily explained So where certain statements had been made on record in an inferior court but departed from in a new record made up in the Court of Session, it was held competent to use the first record for the purpose of showing that the party had there given a different account of the matter in question (*u*) Where a defender in an action for arrears of rent in an inferior court admitted that he was tenant, but denied that arrears were due, and decree was pronounced against him, he was not allowed in a suspension of a charge given upon the decree to retract the admission (which he

---

Chief Commissioner The same learned judge refused to admit an answer to a petition in Watson *v* Hamilton, 1821 3 Mur, 132, and in Ballentine *v* Ross 1821 2 Mur, 534, his Lordship held a representation to be inadmissible, unless it were proved that the party had seen it before it was given into Court These rulings are thought to be too strict

(*n*) A S 1st February 1715, § 7 (repeated in temporary A S, 7th February 1810)—A S 11th July 1828, § 105—Dunns *v* Livingstone, 1828, 7 S, 218—Kay *v* Hazeel's Tr, 1830, 2 De and And, 227—Drysdale *v* Wood, 1832 10 S, 198—Laidlaw *v* Smith, 1841, 2 Rob Ap 490—Fraser *v* Mackay 1833 11 S, 391

(*o*) A S 1st February 1715, § 6—Stephen *v* Pirie, 1832 10 S, 279—Ellis *v* Fraser, 1840, 3 D, 271, *per curiam*

(*p*) Dick *v* Aiton, 1738, M, 12,041—Duncan *v* Forbes, 1829 7 S, 821—Alcock *v* Fasson, 1842, 5 D, 356—Darnley *v* Kirkwood, 1845 7 D, 595

(*r*) *Supra*, § 1387

(*s*) Bathgate *v* Macadam, 1840, 2 D, 811—Low *v* Taylor, 1843, 5 D, 1261 (Here a statement in the defences was held to be retracted by having been merely dropped out of the papers on which the record was closed) With these cases compare Elliot *v* Scott, 1800, Hume D, 33—Hunter *v* Broadwood 1854 16 D 441—and Anderson *v* Pott, 1829, 7 S, 499

(*t*) Bathgate *v* Macadam *supra*—Stewart *v* Mitchell, 1833 11 S 1004

(*u*) Stewart *v* Mitchell *supra*

said had been a mistake of his agent), and to plead that he merely managed the farm for his mother (x)

Where certain articles had been expunged by order of the Court from answers to a condescendence the pursuer was allowed to read them to the jury, although the defender pleaded that they were in the same position as if the paper containing them had been withdrawn (y)

§ 1391 The value of admissions manifestly arises from their being supposed to be made by a party against his own interest But in certain consistorial causes both parties are sometimes desirous to have decree pronounced in terms of the libel, whereas it is the policy of the law to watch with much jealousy against collusion in this class of actions Accordingly, it has been enacted (z) that "no decree or judgment in favour of the pursuer shall be pronounced in any of the consistorial cases herein-before enumerated, whether appearance shall or shall not be made for the defendant, until the grounds of action shall be substantiated by sufficient evidence" The actions to which this provision refers are declarators of marriage and of nullity of marriage, declarators of legitimacy and of bastardy, actions of divorce, and of separation *a mensa et thoro* (y*) The Court of Session, following the practice of the commissaries, require the pursuer to lead proof also in actions of adherence, although the statute does not make that necessary (z*) [2]

§ 1392 The meaning of the enactment thus quoted was recently before the Court in an action of separation (a), in which Lord Mackenzie observed, with the concurrence of the other judges

(x) M'Lean v L Macdonald's Commissioners, 1822 1 S, 333

(y) Leven v Young & Co, 1818, 1 Mur, 377, per L Chief-Commissioner

(z) 11 Geo IV and 1 Will IV, c 69, § 36 The older law was very loose on this subject, see Ferguson's rep in Divorce Cases, Appx, 54 to 58—Syme v M'Inroy, 1763, 5 B Sup, 433 (y*) Same act, § 33 (z*) Black v Anderson, 1842, 4 D 615—1 Fraser Pers and Dom Rel, 713—Lothian Con Law, 98—Shand's Pr, 436 (a) Muirhead v Muirhead, 1846 8 D, 786 In Macfarlane v Macfarlane, 1847, 9 D, 500 it was held that decree of separation cannot be pronounced of consent of parties, a proof which had been led being withdrawn of consent, because the Court ought neither to sanction a separation, the propriety of which it has not considered, nor to raise a *bona gratia* into a judicial separation With these cases compare Sinton v Irvine, 1833, 11 S, 402 In England the defender's admission although proved to the satisfaction of the Court to be free from suspicion of collusion, is not sufficient alone to found a divorce *a mensa et thoro*, Burgess v Burgess 1817, 2 Hag Con Rep, 227, per Sir W Scott—Mortimer v Mortimer, 1820 ib, 315, *per eund*

[2] In proceedings under the Conjugal Rights Act for an order of protection proof of desertion is required 24 and 25 Vict cap 86 § 1

of the First Division, "I read the words 'sufficient evidence' as meaning sufficient evidence independent of the admissions of party I think the act meant entirely to exclude admissions, and require extrinsic evidence In an action of divorce admissions would not do, and the words of the act are the same as to actions of separation The law does not sanction *bona gratia* separations *a mensa et thoro* Parties may make them, but the law does not sanction them, and they may be recalled at pleasure Can we, then, allow parties to convert a *bona gratia* separation into a judicial one, by admitting judgment?" While, however this is true, common sense dictates that the proof does not require to be so full, where the defender admits the averments, as where he strenuously denies them, for in the one case the Court has only to guard against being defrauded into pronouncing a collusive decree, while in the other it has to determine whether an important change of status is to be forced upon an unwilling and resisting defender (*b*) The amount of evidence necessary, in addition to the defender's admission on record, must also depend upon the nature of the cause Some of the actions included in the statutory provision are in a high degree above the risk of collusion as for example a declarator of bastardy, which the defender is likely to resist most strenuously, and a declarator of marriage (*c*), which is almost always useless where the parties are agreed (*d*) Nor is independent evidence to the same extent necessary in actions of separation and aliment, where collusion is unlikely (*e*), as in actions of divorce and nullity of marriage, where collusion ought to be jealously guarded against.

§ 1393 The prisoner's verbal confession in open court in answer to the judge's question, whether he is guilty or not guilty, is conclusive evidence in all criminal cases (*f*) At one time the confession was made before the jury, who returned a verdict proceeding upon it (*g*) But this was abolished by statute (*h*) The practice in the Justiciary Court is to repeat the question after a short interval, and the confession is entered on record and signed by the

---

(*b*) See Mortimer *v* Mortimer, 2 Hag Con Rep, 310—Bishop on Mar and Div, §§ 307, 312 (*c*) See Stewart *v* Lindsay, 1818, Hume D 380

(*d*) Probably the only cases where collusion would require to be guarded against in declarators of marriage, are where the interests of third parties claiming to be the wife and legitimate children of the defender are involved (*e*) *Per curiam* in Sinton *v* Irvine, *supra* But see 1 Fraser Pers and Dom Rel 711 (*f*) 9 Geo IV c 29, § 14 This is seen in every-day practice It is also the rule in trials for treason, Foster, 241—3 Trea Tr, 173—1 Al Cr Law, 619 (*g*) Justiciary Records

(*h*) 9 Geo IV, c 29, § 14

prisoner (or if he cannot write, by his counsel) and by the judge whereupon the judge pronounces sentence. This (as already noticed) is also the practice in other criminal proceedings, except in police cases, where confessions are not signed by, or on behalf of, the prisoner (*i*) A confession in a declaration emitted by the prisoner before a magistrate cannot be used as a confession on record because the declaration is not made as an answer to the libel in open court (*j*)

It has been shown in a former chapter that admissions and confessions (except in a few cases) cannot be proved by a minute on record prepared by the clerk of court, but not signed by the party (*k*)

CHAPTER II —JUDICIAL EXAMINATIONS

§ 1394 The rule which, before the passing of the Law of Evidence Amendment Act, excluded party witnesses was modified in some cases by allowing a party to have his opponent examined *in causa* The object of this proceeding was to prevent one of the parties from defeating justice, by concealing facts of which there was not likely to be evidence from the ordinary sources of information (*a*) The procedure is still competent, although its importance has greatly diminished since the admission of parties as witnesses [1] Still, however, it is useful where this class of witnesses are ex-

(*i*) See *supra* § 1080 (*j*) Logan *v* M'Adam, 1853, 1 Irv , 329—See also Clark *v* Stevenson, 1853, 1 Irv , 309 (*k*) See *supra*, § 1077, *et seq*

(*a*) See per L Just -Cl (Hope) in A B *v* C D, 1843, 6 D , 346 *infra*, § 1398

[1] The competency of taking judicial examinations, under the present Evidence Law, has been recently considered more particularly in regard to the judicial examination of the parties in actions of filiation It has been doubted whether, seeing that the parties can now be examined as witnesses in the cause, judicial examinations have not been rendered unnecessary, or should be allowed Lord Cowan thought that it was objectionable to take from them judicial declarations, at all events at the outset of the cause, Scott *v* Chalmers, 1856 19 D , 119 But in a later case the Lord President (M'Neill) observed, that the old system was not abolished, and might still be resorted to, M'Kellar *v* Scott 1862, 24 D 199 When a party is appointed to attend for examination, it should distinctly appear on the interlocutor whether he is called as a witness or for judicial examination In the case last mentioned it was doubted in what capacity the party had been cited, and observations as to the effect of his failure to appear as a witness fell from the bench See *infra*, § 1101 note [3] and § 1523

cluded, and in other cases, where it can be obtained (as it sometimes may) before the record is closed (*b*)

The examination, which is not upon oath, is taken down in writing, and is signed by the party

§ 1395 When this proceeding was introduced, and during the development of the rules regarding it, the examination of one party at the instance of the other, unless on a reference to his oath, was regarded as an exceptional and very delicate course It was held not to be matter of right in the party moving for it but of discretion in the judge (*c*), and could only be granted on special cause shown (*d*)

§ 1396 Under the just rule that no one ought to be forced or entrapped into criminating himself, a judicial examination is incompetent, not only in criminal prosecutions, but also in civil cases where the matter in issue might be prosecuted criminally (*e*) Yet in an action to recover property of which the pursuer had been robbed where the defender having been examined as a *socius criminis* in a criminal prosecution for the offence, was protected from its penal consequences, he was forced to undergo a judicial examination upon the facts (*f*) Nor is it a ground for refusing to allow this proceeding, that the allegations impugn the party's moral character (*g*), as in actions of filiation (*h*), or declarators of marriage by promise and subsequent *copula* (*i*) Even where the case is laid on fraud, the examination will be allowed, unless the fraud is such as to render the party liable to a criminal prosecution (*k*) The defender in an action of divorce for adultery cannot be forced to undergo an examination, as adultery is still a point of dittay (*l*) So, before the usury laws were abolished (*m*), a party could not be examined on usurious transactions (*n*) The decisions are contra-

---

(*b*) See *infra* § 1399 (*c*) Shand's Pr, 403—A S 10th July 1839, § 66

(*d*) Shand, *supra*—A B, 1843, 6 D, 342—Barrie *v* Tait, 1843, ib 102.

(*e*) Brown *v* Millar, 1828, 6 S, 561—See Gordon *v* Campbell, 22d December 1809, F C—Cases *infra*, in notes (*l*) (*n*) (*f*) Jantzen *v* Easton 3d Feb 1814, F C (*g*) Jantzen *v* Easton, ib (*h*) Patrick *v* Godwin, 1845, 8 D, 138—Kilpatrick *v* Donaldson, 1843, 5 D, 1104 The examination has been frequently allowed in this class of cases (*i*) A B *v* C D, 1843, 6 D, 342—Harvie *v* Inglis, 1837, 15 S, 964—Mackenzie *v* Stewart, 1848 10 D, 611 See also Reid *v* Lang, 1823, 1 Sh Ap Ca, 440 444—and Jolly *v* M'Gregor, 1828 3 W S, 99

(*k*) Goodfellow *v* Madden, 1785, M, 1483—Boyle *v* Yule, 1778, M, 4899—Shand's Pr, 403 (*l*) See Nicolson *v* Nicolson, 1770, M, 16,770—Marshall *v* Anderson, 1798, M, 16 787—Don *v* Don, 1848, 10 D, 1046—Lothian Con Law 251 But see *contra*, Jenner *v* Crofts, 1840, 2 D, 342—1 Fraser Pers and Dom Rel, 700—Shand's Pr 404 (*m*) By 17 and 18 Vict, c 90 (*n*) Nisbet *v* Cullen, 1st Feb 1811 F C

dictory as to the competency of examining the respondent in a complaint for breach of interdict (*o*)

The ground on which the examination is refused in civil matters inferring criminality is not its own incompetency, but the privilege of the party to refuse submitting to it It will therefore be granted if he consents (*p*) or does not oppose it (*q*) In proper criminal prosecutions it is altogether incompetent [2]

When an examination is resisted in such cases it will be refused; and the Court will not grant an order for examination, leaving the party to refuse to answer questions which infer criminality (*r*)

§ 1397 A judicial examination should never be allowed as to a matter provable only by writ or oath as, for example, a loan of money above £100 Scots (*s*), or a prescribed bill or account (*t*), because an admission in such an examination would not prove the fact in issue, and the party ought not to be subjected to it with a view to a subsequent reference to his oath On this principle, also examination of the holder of a bill of exchange will not in general be allowed in order to prove non-onerosity (*u*) But if the facts, as admitted on record, or proved by the holder's writ, leave room to

---

(*o*) Duncan 1853, 1 Irv, 208—*Contra*, Mackay, ib, 288—See also Beattie *v* Rodger, 1835, 14 S 6 (*p*) See Livingston *v* Murrays 1831, 3 De and And 627

(*q*) Thus the defender, in actions of divorce for adultery, may be examined if he does not object See 1 Fraser Pers and Dom Rel 700 See also Humphreys' (*soi-disant* Earl of Stirling) case, 1839, separate report by Swinton, Appx, p 37

(*r*) Nisbet *v* Cullen *supra*—Brown *v* Miller, *supra*—Gordon *v* Campbell, *supra*

(*s*) Tarbet *v* Bennet, 1803, Hume D, 500—M'Master *v* Brown, 1829, 7 S, 337

(*t*) Alcock *v* Easson, 1842, 5 D, 356 per L Just-Clerk (Hope)—Hamilton *v* Hamilton, 1824, 3 S, 283 (*u*) Goodfellow *v* Madden 1785, M 1483—Campbell

---

[2] In an action in the Sheriff-court founded on an alleged breach of interdict, where the forms appropriate to criminal process were adopted, the accused having appeared in terms of the warrant of citation, underwent a judicial examination The case having been appealed, Lord Wood held, on circuit, that it was not competent, under a prosecution so followed out, to subject him to a judicial examination and that there was a radical error in the proceedings which no supposed acquiescence on his part could bar him from objecting to, Duncan *v* Ramsay, 1853, 1 Irv, 208 In another case, where the petition and complaint were in the usual form of summary applications in civil matters, and a record was made up in terms of the act of sederunt applicable to civil cases, Lord Ivory held, on circuit, that a judicial examination after the petition had been served was in no way inconsistent with the form of process, and was clearly competent But his Lordship added that judicial examinations were often too precipitately taken in the inferior courts, and that they were discountenanced in the Court of Session Mackay *v* Ross, 1853 2 Irv 288

suspect collusion or fraud, an examination will be allowed (*x*) And in a case provable only by writ or oath a judicial examination has been granted in order to expiscate the terms and conditions of a latent trust the existence of which was proved by writings under the hand of the trustee (*y*)

In one case where a party had been examined, without objection, on allegations of a verbal cautionary obligation followed by *rei interventus*, the Court while disapproving of the proceeding, dealt with the examination as if it had been on oath on reference (*z*)

§ 1398 Where the examination is not excluded on any of the grounds thus noticed "the result of the decisions seems to be, that the Court, where they have solid grounds for suspicion of undue concealment of material facts within the knowledge of the parties have ordered one or both of the parties to be subjected to a judicial examination" (*a*) This is more especially the case where from the question in issue being of a private or secret character, the proof from other sources is likely to be meagre, as, for example, in actions of filiation (*b*), and actions of declarator of marriage or promise and subsequent *copula* (*c*), and in questions relating to transactions between parties in a confidential relation as copartners, or the like (*d*) Yet where an action is laid upon the fraudulent retention by the defender of property belonging to the pursuer the defender is not bound to submit to an examination as to how he had acquired his own means (*e*)

The successful candidate for the trusteeship in a sequestration

---

v Hill 1826 5 S 54—Dunlop *v* Reid, 1827, ib 796—Malcolm *v* Ballenden 1835, 13 S, 1021—Lyon *v* Butter, 1841 4 D 178—Little *v* Smith 1845, 8 D, 265, see also Beveridge *v* Henderson 1841 4 D 87 per L Jus-Clerk (Hope)—Scott *v* Dunn 1837, 15 S, 921—*Supra* §§ 336 348 352 (*x*) Campbell *v* Turner 1822 1 S, 292 (as noticed by Lord Glenlee in Campbell *v* Hill *supra*)—Cairncross *v* Mitchell, 1823, 2 S 774—Smith *v* Stark 1831, 10 S, 150—Fell *v* Lyon, 1830, 8 S, 513—Robertson *v* Annan, 1825 4 S 40—M'Lean *v* Morrison, 1834, 12 S 613—Compared with cases in preceding note See also *supra*, § 361 (*y*) Muir *v* Gemmel 1805 Hume D 342 (by a bare majority)—See *supra*, § 171 (*z*) Porteous *v* M'Beath 1812 Hume D, 98—See *supra*, § 601 (*a*) Per L Just-Clerk (Hope) in A B *v* C D 1843 6 D 316 (*b*) *Supra* § 1395 (*c*) *Supra*, ib

(*d*) M'Gavin *v* Stewart 1830 4 W S, 184—Wilson *v* Beveridge, 1831, 9 S, 485 10 S, 110—See also Couper *v* Young, 1849 12 D, 190 193—Nisbet *v* M'Clelland 1837, 15 S 439 (*e*) Gordon *v* Campbell 22d Dec 1809 F C (On this case see *per curiam* in Jantzen *v* Laston, 3d Feb 1814 F C)—M'Candlish *v* Forbes 1825, 4 S, 58 It will not be supposed from these cases that the jury must shut their eyes to the fact of possession of wealth of which the party refuses to give any explanation See *supra*, § 290

will not be required to submit to examination at the instance of an unsuccessful competitor, on an allegation that he aided one of the creditors in attempts to acquire an improper preference, at least ' there must be something very strong to warrant that course" (*f*)

§ 1399 The examination may be allowed at various stages of the cause, according to the nature of the question in issue In a case already noticed, where one who had given evidence as a *socius criminis* in a trial for robbery was afterwards required to submit to judicial examination in a civil action against him for restitution of the property abstracted, the examination was taken at the commencement of the suit, and before the pursuer had condescended on the facts which he offered to prove (*g*) The Court were moved by the great suspicion attaching to the defender, and by the risk of his escaping with his booty if the examination had been refused till after the pursuer had made his averments specific The summons, also, was laid on a letter from the defender, which fixed on him part of the sum sued for, and therefore required explanation This however, is an exceptional case The examination has frequently been allowed after the parties had prepared their record, but before it had been closed, and, therefore, when any alterations suggested by the declaration could still be made (*h*) It is more easily obtained after the record has been closed, and when the parties are proceeding to probation (*i*) In one case, where the defender in an action on a bill bearing to have been granted by his deceased father, pleaded that it was either a forgery or had been obtained without value, the Court refused his motion to have the pursuer examined before the record was closed (*k*). The indiscriminate examination of the defender, especially if a married man, in actions of filiation, even after the record had been closed, has been disapproved of, and it has been considered an improper proceeding, unless from the defender's statements on record, or from evidence adduced in the case, there were grounds for suspicion against him (*l*) In this class of cases it was held incompetent to examine the pursuer judicially after she had emitted her oath in supplement (*m*), and in other cases it has been considered irregular

(*f*) Couper *v* Leslie, 1847, 9 D, 909 (*g*) Jantzen *v* Easton, *supra*

(*h*) Mackenzie *v* Stewart, 1848, 10 D, 611—A S 10th July 1839, § 66—Shand's Pr 404, 6 (*i*) See Harvie *v* Inglis, 1837, 15 S, 964 (*k*) Barrie *v* Tait 1843 6 D, 102 (*l*) *Per curiam* in Kirkpatrick *v* Donaldson, 1843 5 D, 1101, and Patrick *v* Goodwin, 1845, 8 D, 138 (*m*) Jameson *v* Barclay, 11th Jan 1820, F C

to take an examination after the whole proof has been closed (*n*). It ought never to be taken after a decision on the proof has been pronounced, because at that stage the losing party can only have recourse, on matters of fact, to his adversary's oath on reference (*o*) Yet if a party at a late stage of the cause moves to have documents admitted as *noviter repert a*, the Court may examine him on the circumstances on which he founds (*p*)

§ 1400. It is only competent under this procedure to examine a party to the cause, not a third person, although closely connected with one of the parties (*r*). Nor will the examination of one party be received in favour of another with whom his case is identified, because the essential quality of a judicial examination is, that it be against the party's own interest (*s*)

§ 1401 A party who has been ordained to appear and submit to examination, and who, without good cause, has failed to do so, may be held as confessed and the case in so far as it depends on admissions which it might be supposed he would make, may be decided against him (*t*) [3] But it is otherwise as to cases where the

(*n*) Young *v* Watt, 1747, M, 6775—Livingstone *v* Menzies, 1832, 5 De and And 7 (*o*) Campbell *v* Hill, 1826, 5 S, 54 See also Spen *v* Dunlop, 1825, 4 S, 92 (*p*) Officers of State *v* Alexander (*soi-disant* Earl of Stirling) 1839 1 D, 1188 (*r*) Stewart *v* Russell, 11th July 1815, F C—M'Master *v* Brown 1829, 7 S, 337—Lyon *v* Butter, 1841, 4 D, 178, per Lord Mackenzie—Couper *v* Leslie 1847, 9 D 909, per L Jus-Clerk (Hope) But see Mitchell *v* Hepburn, 1830, 8 S, 319, 2 De and And, 175, S C (*s*) Lindsay *v* Chapman 1826, 4 S, 490 See also Scott *v* Erskine, 1829, 1 De and And, 225 (*t*) A B *v* C D, 1844 6 D, 932

[3] In an action of filiation and aliment the defender was appointed "to appear personally for examination, but repeatedly failed to do so, alleging afterwards as a reason that he was at the time in hiding from his creditors He was held as confessed —the Lord President (M'Neill) observing, 'Before the recent Evidence Act this was one of the cases in which *semiplena* proof, with the pursuer's oath in supplement, was allowed In such actions, also, the judicial examination of the party was often resorted to, and it was a common result of the party not appearing to be judicially examined, that he was held as confessed on the pursuer's allegations as to intercourse Then the woman's oath in supplement was taken The Evidence Act changed the law considerably, by allowing the parties to be examined as witnesses But the old method is not abolished, and it is still quite competent to order the judicial examination of the party, to hold him as confessed if he fails to appear, and thereupon, with the oath in supplement of the pursuer, to hold the paternity as proved" Lord Curriehill remarked, that if the appointment upon the defender had been an appointment to appear as a witness, a new and important question would have been raised, namely, whether a party failing to appear as a witness could be held as confessed, but Lord Deas, assuming that his failure to appear as a witness might not be enough to warrant the Court in holding him confessed upon the whole cause thought that at least it would have amounted to an ad-

Court are bound to proceed upon full proof, in order to prevent collusion, as, for example, in actions of divorce In such cases the party's non-attendance will have little or no effect on the result (*u*)

§ 1402 The examination may be taken either by the Court or on commission (*x*), and the report of it may be laid before the jury (*y*) Where the examination of a party was required when the case was in the Inner House, it was taken in Court and minuted by the clerk of court (*z*) It seems to be competent to examine a party judicially before the jury (*a*)

§ 1403 Admissions made in a judicial examination, although evidence of a highly trustworthy character, have not the conclusive effect of admissions on record They will not prevent the party from proving that he spoke from erroneous information, or from misrecollection Nor do they seem to be full proof, sufficient to warrant a decision without farther inquiry into the facts (*b*)

§ 1404 By the Sequestration Act of 1839 it is provided, that the Sheriff may at any time, on the application of the trustee order an examination of the bankrupt's wife and family, clerks, servants, factors, law-agents and others, who can give information relative to his estate, either by declaration or on oath as to the Sheriff shall seem fit, and issue his warrant requiring such persons to appear, and if they refuse or neglect to appear when duly summoned the Sheriff may issue another warrant to apprehend the person so failing to appear" (*c*)[4] If any of the persons referred

(*u*) See Crofts *v* Crofts, 1840 2 D, 312 (*x*) Shand's Pr, 647—Carrick *v* Martin, 14th Nov 1818, F C, affd 1 Sh Ap Ca, 257 (*y*) Miller *v* Moffat, 1820, 2 Mur, 317 (*z*) Officers of State *v* Alexander (*soi-disant* Earl of Stirling), 1839 1 D, 1188 (*a*) M'Gavin *v* Stewart, 1830, 4 W S 184 (see this case farther in 9 S, 17, 5 W S, 807) See also Crawcour *v* St George Steam Packet Co, 1842, 5 D, 10 (*b*) Wilson *v* Beveridge, 1830, 10 S 110

(*c*) 2 and 3 Vict, c 41, § 68

mission on his part of the particular averment made by the pursuer, and so completed the proof, M'Kellar *v* Scott, 1862, 24 D 499

[4] 19 and 20 Vict c 79, §§ 90, 91 The examinations of the bankrupt, and of the other persons specified in the act, being for the purpose of obtaining information, are not subject to the strict rules of evidence, Sawers *v* Balgarnie, 1858, 21 D 153—M'Kay *v* M'Lachlan 1 Macph, 140 "A bankrupt is bound to answer all relevant questions without requiring attention to such rules The examination of a bankrupt in his sequestration is not the leading of evidence, but an investigation for the purpose of informing the trustee and the creditors"—*per* Lord Justice-Clerk (Inglis) in M'Kay *v* M'Lachlan In Sawers *v* Balgarnie, the wife of the bankrupt refused during her examination, to answer certain questions, on the ground that she became aware of the fact to which the questions referred by communications made to her by her husband

to refuse, without good reason, to answer any lawful questions, or to sign the minute of the examination, the Sheriff may order the person so refusing to be imprisoned until compliance (*d*) It was held that a person subject to examination under these provisions, was not entitled to refuse to be re-examined at an interval of three years, although it was not averred that any discoveries had been made since his first examination (*e*) The statute does not apply to examination of a creditor with regard to his claim, and therefore an application for such an examination will be determined under the common law rules above noticed (*f*) [5]

CHAPTER III —PRISONERS' DECLARATIONS *

§ 1405 It is the practice in Scotland, whenever a person is charged with a criminal offence (except in petty cases), to take him before a magistrate, in order to obtain his account of the matter By this means innocent persons sometimes succeed in explaining circumstances which seem to throw suspicion upon them, but far more frequently declarations support the case of the Crown by containing express or implied admissions of guilt, or at least of circumstances prejudicial to the prisoner

§ 1406 The declaration must be emitted before a magis-

(*d*) 2 and 3 Vict, c 14, §§ 69, 70 (*e*) Clark v Cuthbertson 1848, 10 D 1471

(*f*) Redpath v Forth Marine Ins Co, 1844 6 D 1438—Pollock v King 1844, 7 D 172 This was the rule under the corresponding provisions of the former Bankrupt Act, 2 Bell's Com, 394 399—Nisbet v M'Lelland, 1837 15 S 439—M'Leay v Lehose, 1792 Bell's Octavo Ca, 75

* This subject is fully treated in 2 Hume, 324—Burnett Cr Law, 488—2 Al Cr Law, 557—Bell's Notes 239

---

during the subsistence of the marriage and that her answer might be used in following up a criminal charge against him But the Court held that she was bound to answer, because (1) the common law rules of evidence did not apply to the examination, (2) the examination was a collateral inquiry and not a case in which the husband was directly interested, (3) the rule as to the confidentiality of communications between husband and wife was not a rule of the common law, but was introduced by the statute 16 and 17 Vict, c 20 § 3 and that rule was intended to apply to matters of evidence only, and not to those investigations in bankruptcy which were controlled by statute, and at which the wife had been a competent witness before the Evidence Act was passed

[5] A B v Binny 1858 20 D, 1858—Sawers v Balgarnie 1868 21 D, 153

trate (a) And as the presence of such an official is intended for protecting the prisoner against an improper mode of examination, as well as for securing a correct narrative of his statements a declaration which has not been emitted before a magistrate, but has merely been adhered to in his presence, is inadmissible (b) Yet it is not fatal to a declaration that the magistrate was occasionally absent during its emission, if substantially it was taken in his presence, and was read over and adhered to by the prisoner before him (c) And accordingly, where the magistrate had fallen asleep at intervals during the emission of certain long and tedious declarations, the longest sleep at any one time having been a quarter of an hour and the whole time so spent having been half an hour the Court by a majority held the declarations to be admissible, Lords Justice-Clerk and Medwyn adverting particularly to the circumstance that the magistrate had been awake when the declarations were read over and explained to the prisoners (d) [1]

§ 1407 The declaration must be emitted while the prisoner is in his sound and sober senses (e), and that fact must be either admitted or proved at the trial (f) It is, therefore, a good objection that he was drunk, or labouring under hysteria or insanity, at the time and proof of such an objection will be admitted (g) [2]

(a) 2 Hume 328, 9, notes—Burnett, 492—2 Al 560 It is not necessary that the magistrate have jurisdiction to try the offence with which the prisoner is charged Burnett, ib (b) Davidson, 1829 Sh Cr 207—2 Hume, 327—2 Al, 561, citing Woodness and Smith 19th July 1819 not reported (c) 2 Al, 561

(d) Mackay and others 1831, Bell's Notes, 242 (e) 2 Hume 328—2 Al, 557—Elder 1827, Sh Just Ca, 178, Syme, 118, S C (f) Hume supra—Al supra—See infra, § 1425 (g) Elder, supra—Connacher, 1823 noted in Hume supra

[1] The declaration will not be admitted if the magistrate has been absent during a material part of the examination Where a magistrate although occasionally absent, had judicially admonished the prisoners and had himself read the declarations over, the declarations were admitted, H M Adv v Mahler and Berrenhard 1857, 2 Irv, 634 Where a magistrate was absent from the room where the declaration was being taken, during the substantial portion of the declaration, although he was in an adjoining room where it was possible to hear the statement made in the other room, the declaration was rejected, H M Adv v M Millan, 1858, 3 Irv, 213 It is incompetent for the sheriff-clerk to act as sheriff substitute—the two offices being incompatible,—and a declaration taken before a sheriff clerk, who held a deputation as sheriff-substitute, was rejected H M Adv v Stewart 1857 2 Irv, 614—Ross v Mitchell, 1847, 10 D 153

[2] In H M Adv v Milne, 1863, 35 Sc Jur 170, the panel was charged with murder,—the defence being that at the time when the offence was committed he was under the influence of insane delusions The Court allowed a declaration emitted by him shortly after his apprehension and when he was in a state of considerable excitement

§ 1408 It is indispensable that the declaration shall have been emitted by the prisoner "freely and voluntarily," and that this be proved or admitted at the trial (h) Accordingly, if it has been emitted under promises or threats from a person conducting the examination, whether the magistrate or procurator-fiscal, or even from a superintendent of police (i), it will not be admitted Even if a person in either of these situations made statements to the prisoner, which, while coming short of either a promise or a threat, may yet have induced him to emit a declaration which he would not otherwise have made, the declaration will be cast This was strikingly illustrated in a case where a prisoner had emitted declarations before two different magistrates The magistrate who took the first, deponed—"I think I told him that he was at liberty to say what he thought proper, but my opinion was that the more candid he was in his declarations the better it would be for himself I said he was at full liberty to say what he thought proper It would be taken down as he said it, but my opinion was he should be candid and tell the truth I said, if I were in the same situation I would be candid and speak explicitly" The Court, after hearing parties, intimated their opinion that the declaration could not be received The second declaration referred to the one so rejected, and stated, that after it had been read over to the prisoner he adhered to it, and declared in continuation The magistrate who took the second declaration did not recollect having given the prisoner more than the usual caution, that he was not bound to answer. Upon this the Court were of opinion that the second magistrate had not said anything to undo the impression which might have been made on the prisoner's mind by the recommendation and advice of the first magistrate, and that, as both declarations had thus been made under the same impression, both were inadmissible (k) On the converse of this case, the effect of inducements or recommendations which might cause a declaration to be cast,

(h) 2 Hume, 331, note—Burnett, 491—2 Al 561—See *infra*, § 1425

(i) M'Laren and others, 1828 2 Al, 564

(k) Wilson's case, 1820, 2 Trea Tr 45 170, noted in 2 Hume, 331 2

to be read, reserving power to direct the jury whether they should receive it in evidence or not In his charge the Lord Justice Clerk (Inglis) directed the jury to consider the declaration only as bearing upon the question of the prisoner's insanity, and for no other purpose The declaration thus appears to have been admitted, not as a declaration emitted in the ordinary way, forming part of the case for the Crown and used as such, but as an adminicle of evidence, which the jury might look at, tending to instruct the state of mind of the panel at a time shortly after the commission of the offence may be removed by subsequent explanations from the same person or from *one* in a higher situation, and accordingly inducements which have been held out by a subordinate official will probably not be fatal, if the magistrate told the prisoner to disregard them, whereas it may be doubtful whether the effect of inducements held out by one magistrate would be removed by a contrary statement from a functionary of no higher authority (*l*) [3]

§ 1409 Promises or inducements proceeding from such inferior officials as police constables or turnkeys, although they may impair the weight of a declaration with the jury will probably not cause it to be excluded, because the public prosecutor is not bound by the spontaneous interference of such persons, and their statements will seldom produce much effect on the mind of the prisoner (*m*) [4] Still less will promises proceeding from private persons, even those which come from the person injured by the crime, be fatal to the declaration (*n*) although they may affect its credibility No case seems to have occurred upon the effect of threats by private persons It is easy to conceive cases where these might be so serious, and the execution of them so much within the power of an individual, that the declaration emitted under their influence would be the result of concussion, instead of being made "freely and voluntarily" In such cases the only fair and humane course is to exclude the declaration

§ 1410 The magistrate ought to caution the prisoner before commencing his declaration, that it will probably be used against him at his trial, and that he is entitled to decline answering all or any questions which may be put to him. This caution, however, is not indispensable, and therefore it does not require to be either set forth in the declaration, or proved at the trial (*o*) [5]

§ 1411. Declarations are almost always emitted in answer to

(*l*) See per L President Hope in Wilson's case, *supra*, 2 Trea Tr, 186

(*m*) Ferguson, 1819, 2 Hume, 327, note—2 Al, 562—*Contra*, Dalling, 1832, Bell's Notes, 241

(*n*) Honeyman and Smith, 1815, 2 Al, 563—Ferguson, *supra* But see M'Kay *v* M'Neil, 1817, ib, 563

(*o*) 2 Hume, 330—2 Al, 564

[3] Information given to a superintendent of police by a prisoner, under a promise of safety, was held inadmissible as evidence against the prisoner, and a declaration subsequently emitted by him before a magistrate was rejected, on the ground that the magistrate had not given the prisoner more than the usual caution and had not disabused his mind of the impression produced by the promise, H M Adv *v* Mahler and Berrenhard, 1858, 2 Irv, 631

[4] H M Adv *v* Mahler and Berrenhard, *supra*

[5] H M Adv *v* Dempster, 1862, 4 Irv, 15[illegible]

questions put by the procurator-fiscal in presence of the magistrate, in order to direct the prisoner's attention to the matters on which his statement is required It would manifestly be an abuse of this practice to importune or press the prisoner by a searching examination, and a declaration obtained by such unfair means would be rejected [6]

§ 1412 A declaration cannot be emitted on oath, because it is most unfair and oppressive to place an accused person in the dilemma of either confessing his guilt or perjuring himself (*p*) Nay more, if a person has been precognosced on oath as a witness (a proceeding which has sometimes to be resorted to), his subsequent declaration emitted without an oath is inadmissible against him, because if facts tending to criminate him have been extorted

(*p*) Burnett, 491—2 Al 567 It was declared in the "Claim of Right" at the Revolution, "that the forcing the lieges to depone against themselves in capital crimes, however the punishment be restricted, is contrary to law" And the same just principle has been extended to all criminal cases It is even doubtful whether a person who has been precognosced on oath, can afterwards be indicted for the offence on which he was examined, 2 Al 568 [7]

---

[6] The objections that were stated in a recent case to the admissibility of declarations were of various kinds but substantially resolved into allegations of unfairness and oppression It was objected, that they could not be regarded as the voluntary statements of the prisoner, having been extorted from her by a minute and searching examination, and that it was oppressive to subject a prisoner to an examination lasting, without intermission, for more than four hours These objections were repelled But the point chiefly pressed was that the husband of the panel had been examined by the sheriff and procurator-fiscal before she emitted her first declaration, and at a time when they had no reason to suspect that he was in any way connected with the crime, with the view of using his declaration as a precognition by which to examine the panel It was proved that at the time when the offence (murder) was committed, the husband was not in the neighbourhood, but Lord Deas was of opinion, on the evidence that at the time when his declaration was taken the officials were ignorant of that fact The declarations were admitted, but looking to the policy of the law which refuses in criminal cases to permit either spouse to be made, either directly or indirectly a witness for or against the other it is thought that such examinations should be undertaken with extreme caution, and only, perhaps, when a strong suspicion of guilt attaches to both husband and wife The temptation to a prosecutor to avail himself of this mode of obtaining evidence against a prisoner must often be strong, and care should be taken to prevent him from resorting to it except in rare and peculiar cases In the case alluded to the procurator-fiscal stated that he had heard, before the husband was examined, that he had been away on the day when the crime was committed, and that, though not then satisfied he had no reason to doubt that such was the case It would probably be advisable, in similar circumstances, to refrain from putting any questions that might tend to implicate, or to furnish materials against, the wife, until it has been ascertained where the husband was when the offence was committed H M Adv *v* M Lachlan, 1862, 4 Irv , 220

[7] On this see *infra*, § 1694

when he was sworn and when he may have believed himself constrained to answer, a repetition of them may have been elicited in his declaration to his serious prejudice (r) Nor can a statement made by a prisoner on precognition (not on oath) as a witness be used as his declaration even where he admits explicitly that it was made freely or voluntarily, or where it was referred to as true in a subsequent declaration, because it is an essential characteristic of every declaration that it be emitted by the declarant as an accused person, when his attention is directed to his own protection (s) Accordingly, if a person who has been precognosced as a witness is afterwards charged with the crime, his declaration must be taken of new without reference to his precognition which he is entitled to have destroyed before commencing his statement as an accused person (t) It was held not fatal to a declaration in a case of murder that a day before it was emitted the prisoner was required to touch the dead body, and on denying all knowledge of it, was told "We are all in the presence of God" (v)

§ 1413 The fair principle which forbids all attempts at entrapping an accused person into committing himself, requires, moreover, that when one emits a second or third declaration those which he has previously made shall be read over to him before he commences his new statement (u), or at least before it is concluded (x), in order that his mind may be refreshed upon his former story, and that he may have an opportunity of supplementing or correcting it Accordingly, where four declarations had been taken from a prisoner and he proved that the fourth had been emitted without the three others having been read over to him on his desiring it the Court held that only the three could be used against him, but that he might call for the fourth if he should be so advised (y) And the same rule applies, where the omission to read over the prior declaration arose from omission on the part of the magistrate, and not from his refusal of a request by the prisoner (z) In one case

(r) Burnett, *supra*—2 Al, 567 (s) Burnett *supra*—2 Al, 568, citing Renton v Fullerton, 13th July 1826, not rep (t) 2 Al *supra*

(u) Adam v Anderson, 1835, Bell's Notes, 212 (w) 2 Hume 330—2 Al, 570 (x) In Grant, 1827, 1 Swin, 501, Bell's Notes, 213 it was held not to be a good objection to a second declaration, that it bore at the end that the first one had been *then* read over (y) Stewart, 1817, noted in 2 Hume, 330 and 2 Al, 571

(z) 2 Hume 331—2 Al, 571—Observed per Lord Pitmilly in M'Kechnie, 1817, noted in Hume and Al, ib—and by Lords Justice-Clerk Boyle and Pitmilly in Barnett 1818, noted in Al, ib In M'Kechnie and Campbell, 1828, also there noted, where three declarations were tendered the second was rejected, because when it was emitted the first was not read over where a first declaration had been transmitted from a distant part of Scotland to Edinburgh, for the consideration of Crown counsel and where the prisoner at his own request emitted a second declaration it was received, notwithstanding the objection that only a copy of the first declaration had been read over to him (*a*) Where the second declaration related to a new charge incidentally throwing light on that on which the first declaration had been emitted it was received although it had been made without the first one having been read over (*b*)

§ 1414 It is not necessary, however, that each subsequent declaration should bear that all those previously emitted were read to the prisoner, because *omnia presumuntur rite et solenniter acta* (*c*). If the later declarations state that such was the fact, they will be admitted as probative of it, the prisoner being allowed to disprove the statement (*d*) And, even if they are silent on the point, the prosecutor will not be required to prove that the prior declarations had been read over (*e*)

§ 1415 As it would be unfair to allow the prosecutor to select from a number of declarations such as are prejudicial to the prisoner, and to withhold the others, it is settled law that when any one declaration is laid before the jury, all the others must (if the prisoner wishes) be produced also (*f*) It has even been held that where three formal declarations had been followed by a fourth, duly emitted and read over to the prisoner, but not signed either by him or by the magistrate, the three could not be read unless the prosecutor also produced the fourth, although it wanted the solemnities requisite for making it evidence for the Crown (*g*) And where the second of the only two declarations emitted by a prisoner was libelled on by a wrong date, and consequently could not be produced as evidence for the Crown the Court held that the prisoner might call for production of it if he should be so advised but repelled his objection that the first declaration could not be produced in consequence of the mistake (*h*) And similar decisions were pronounced where the last of three declarations was inaccurately libelled on (*i*),

---

(*a*) Earl, 1823 2 Al 572 (*b*) Goodwin, 1837 1 Swin, 431—Barnett, 1818, 2 Al, 571 (*c*) 2 Hume, 331—2 Al, 571—Duncan and Hippisley 1821, Sh Just Ca 45 (*d*) 2 Al 571 (*e*) Duncan and Hippisley, 1821 Sh Just Ca, 45 (*f*) Whyte, 1814, 2 Hume, 326, note—2 Al, 572

(*g*) Loch, 1837 1 Swin 494, Bell's Notes 240 S C This decision is just, because the prisoner was entitled to rely on the fourth declaration being produced and the authentication of it was not intrusted to his care (*h*) Stanfield 1817 2 Hume, 327 (*i*) Gilchrist 1835, Bell's Notes, 240 and where a first declaration had been taken before one who was not a magistrate (*j*) In such cases the prisoner cannot plead that he is prejudiced by the Crown endeavouring to prove only a part of his statement, because the Crown is willing to lay the whole of it before the jury and the non-production of a part arises from the prisoner urging an objection in point of form

§ 1416 The existence of a prior declaration, not produced, may appear from its being mentioned in those tendered, or in the warrant of commitment (*k*). It would also seem that the prisoner may prove the fact by parole (*l*), although the Crown cannot by that means prove the contents of the absent document in order to show that it merely contained a refusal to answer (*m*)

§ 1417 When the prisoner declines answering certain questions (as he is entitled to do), the question and refusal are set forth in the declaration And it is competent for the prosecutor to lay before the jury a document bearing that the prisoner refused to make any statement beyond his name and age (*n*), or refused to answer any questions, or remained silent (*o*), the document in such cases being signed by the magistrate in presence of the prisoner, and by the witnesses A general declinature ought never to weigh with the jury, because it does not raise any inference tending to inculpate the prisoner Yet a refusal to answer individual questions may be material, especially where, from their being latently connected with the charge, the prisoner's unwillingness to speak upon them shows that he is aware of their importance (*p*)

§ 1418 It is essential to the admission of a declaration that it be read over to the prisoner, in order that he may observe whether his statement has been correctly taken down, and that he may have any additions or corrections made upon it (*r*) But the reading over does not require to be either set forth in the document (although that is customary and proper), or proved at the trial (*s*) If however, the prisoner seriously denies it, the prosecutor must prove that the proper course was followed (*t*) The prisoner may prove by the magistrate and witnesses present that the reading over was omitted (*u*)

§ 1419 In like manner, if the prisoner does not understand

(*j*) Wylie, 1817, 2 Hume, 329 (*k*) As in Carruthers, 1831 2 Al 572
(*l*) Whyte, 1814, 2 Hume, 326, note (*m*) Whyte, *supra* See *infra* § 1426 (*n*) Scott 1827, Syme, 278 (*o*) Bell, 1816, Arkley 1 — Thomson, 1814 2 Broun, 286 (*p*) See *supra*, § 275 (*r*) 2 Hume, 330—Burnett, 490—2 Al, 569 (*s*) Hume, *supra*—Al, *supra*
(*t*) Hume, *supra*—Al, *supra* (*u*) Purnell, *supra*—Al *supra*

the English language, his declaration must be translated by a sworn interpreter from the language in which it is emitted and, after being taken down in English, it must be interpreted and explained to the prisoner in his own tongue (*x*) The narrative and proof of this proceeding are subject to the same rules as when the declaration is emitted in English (*y*)

§ 1420 The same course will be adopted where the prisoner is deaf and dumb, but can communicate by signs Or the questions may be put to a deaf and dumb prisoner in writing his answers being written down on a slate or separate paper, and copied into the declaration, which must of course, be read over by him before being signed In a case where this was done the objection that the original answers (which, with the questions had been written on a slate) ought to have been produced, was repelled (*z*)

§ 1421 The declaration, on being read over and approved of by the prisoner, must be signed by him (if he can write), and by the magistrate (*a*) If he cannot write, it must be signed by the magistrate in his presence, the docquet bearing that he stated his inability to sign for himself (*b*) And if he refuses to sign, the magistrate will do so in his presence and the docquet will state the refusal (*c*) Such a declaration may be evidence against a prisoner, and all the stronger in consequence of the refusal (*d*), but the prosecutor will probably be required to prove that it is a true narrative of the prisoner's statements as he may have refused to sign in consequence of the narrative being inaccurate.

Each page ought to be subscribed by the magistrate and prisoner, if he will do so (*e*) But it is improbable that a declaration will be excluded on account of the omission to sign a few pages, provided each sheet is authenticated (*f*).[7]

§ 1422 The declaration must also be signed (but only on the

(*x*) 2 Al 569 See Campbell, 1837, Bell's Notes, 243 (*y*) Mackay and Others, 1831, Bell's Notes, 242—2 Al, 570 (*z*) Smith, 1841, 2 Swin, 547, Bell's Notes, 242 S. C. (*a*) A declaration, which was libelled on as only emitted (not also subscribed) by the prisoner, was rejected, Gordon 1846 Arkley, 106

(*b*) Burnett 490—2 Al, 566 In Plenderleith or Dewar it was considered to be an important defect that the magistrate did not sign in presence of the prisoner, 1841, Bell's Notes, 241 (*c*) Burnett *supra*—Al, *supra* (*d*) Burnett, *supra*

(*e*) 2 Al 566 (*f*) See *supra*, § 659

---

7 The objection to a prisoner's declaration, that it was not signed by him was repelled, seeing that it was written on the same sheet of paper with another declaration, formally taken and signed next day, and which bore that the previous examination had been adjourned at the desire of the prisoner, H M Adv *v* Wilson 1857 2 Irv, 626

last page), by two witnesses, who attest not merely the genuineness of the subscriptions of the magistrate and prisoner, but also the assent of the prisoner to the statement (g) The witnesses must therefore be present when the declaration is emitted or at least, when it is read over and assented to by the prisoner If he withholds his assent, the same form of authentication will be observed, but the declaration will not be received unless the witnesses heard it emitted

Where the declaration is emitted in a foreign language, it is held essential that the witnesses should understand the language, because they must know what is taking place (h)

§ 1423. The declaration usually concludes with a docquet mentioning the names and designations of the magistrate and witnesses, and the number of pages [8] But it does not require the solemnities of the act 1681, c 5, and therefore the name of the writer of it does not require to be stated (i) nor does the omission of the names or designations of the magistrate and witnesses seem to be fatal (k) A declaration extending to six pages was admitted, although the docquet bore that it was written on this and the six preceding pages (l)

§ 1424 Any alterations by way of deletion, or writing above erasure should be mentioned in the docquet And such alterations in substantial parts may be fatal if not so noticed Yet where the deletion did not affect the sense, and the words were still legible, the document was received, although the alteration was not mentioned (m) And where an erasure occurred on the margin of a declaration, and the prosecutor consented to the prisoner reading what words he chose at the place, the declaration was admitted, but the Court disapproved of the practice (n)

§ 1425 A declaration, when tendered in evidence must be

(g) Burnett, 490—2 Al, 565, 569 (h) In Robertson, 1770, and Cameron 1805, Burnett, 492, a declaration signed by two witnesses was rejected because it had been emitted in Gaelic, and only one of the witnesses who had acted as interpreter, understood that language And the same rule was again applied in Mackenzie, 1839, 2 Swin, 345, Bell's Notes, 241 (i) 2 Hume, 330—Watt, 1801, Burnett, 492—2 Al, 665 (k) Al, *supra* (l) Fulton, 1841, 2 Swin, 564, Bell's Notes, 241 (m) Swan, 1837, Appx, Syme, 11 (n) Todd, 1825, Bell's Notes, 242 In Cain and Quin, 1838, ib, the objection that an erasure occurred in the name of the place, was repelled It was very slight, affecting only a letter or two, and the existence of it at all was doubtful

[8] It is not fatal to the validity of a prisoner's declaration that a witness has not appended the word "witness" to his signature, H M Adv v Wilson, *supra*

identified as that made by the prisoner at the bar, and must be proved to have been emitted by him freely and voluntarily, when he was in his sound and sober senses[9] This must be done by two witnesses (o), who ought to be the magistrate and one of the attesting witnesses (p) The magistrate, however, is not an indispensable witness (r) The Court have disapproved of adducing clerks in the procurator-fiscal's office a superintendent of police, and other persons engaged in the prosecution, to prove the declaration (s).

Each declaration ought to be proved independently And therefore it was once held that, where the only proof of a first declaration was the witnesses to the second deponing that the first was read over to the prisoner in their presence, whereon he declared he had freely and voluntarily emitted it, when in his sound and sober senses, the Court considered the proof to be inadequate, and the declaration was withdrawn (t)[10] Yet it has been held several times that when the first declaration is mentioned in the second, as having been freely and voluntarily emitted by the prisoner and is docqueted as the declaration so referred to, it does not require to be separately proved, but is regarded as a part of the second, the witnesses to the latter proving if required the reading over and admission (u)

In practice, except in capital cases, proof of the declarations is usually dispensed with by the prisoner's counsel admitting them

---

(o) 2 Hume, 327—Burnett, 491—2 Al 558 (p) 2 Hume, 329
(r) Howden, 1850 Shaw, 351 (s) M'Gavin, 1846, Arkley, 70—Vallance, 1846, ib, 181 (t) M'Gavin *supra* (u) Wylie, 1817, 2 Hume, 329—Kelly, 1837, Bell's Notes 240—Reid, 1835, ib 241—See *supra*, § 180, *et seq*

---

[9] It is not essential that a declaration should bear that the charge was explained to the panel, and that he was duly cautioned, H M Adv v Dempster, 1862, 4 Irv, 143 It is competent to prove by parole evidence that a panel was in his sound and sober senses when he emitted a declaration, although the fact is not stated in the docquet annexed to the declaration The docquet is no part of the declaration 'It is nothing more than a marking made at the time by the magistrate and witnesses in order to recall to their recollection what actually passed at the time and it corresponds to the labels upon articles produced in evidence which are used for the same purpose" *per* Lord Justice-Clerk (Inglis) in H M Adv v Hay, 1858, 3 Irv, 181 It is not necessary that witnesses to a declaration should also identify each article referred to in the declaration, H M Adv v Smith, 1854, 1 Irv, 378

[10] See H M Adv v Wynne, 1857, 2 Irv 720, and H M Adv v Hossack, 1858, 3 Irv 1 In each case the ground of judgment was, that the reference to the first declaration, contained in the second, proved neither that the panel was duly warned nor that he was in his sound and sober senses when the first declaration was emitted

§ 1426 The written declaration, if extant, is the only competent evidence of what the prisoner said in presence of the magistrate (*x*) But if it has been lost or destroyed without negligence on the part of the prosecutor or persons for whom he is responsible its terms may be proved by a copy or by parole, under the rule which admits secondary evidence of lost writings (*y*)

§ 1427 Baron Hume lays down that "if a written declaration is *ex facie* unexceptionable, and has been duly confirmed in ordinary course by the testimony of creditable witnesses to the manner and circumstances of the emission, and has not been impeached or discredited generally by evidence on the other part of anything improper in the manner of conducting the inquiry, the paper seems then to be conclusive of its own contents as fairly and correctly taken down, and it shall not be liable to challenge in the way of parole evidence, touching particular phrases or passages as not expressing what the prisoner meant to say To admit this sort of scrutiny would be to set up the doubtful testimony of witnesses, and given too, at a distance of time, and respecting matters where memory is so little to be trusted, against the regular written evidence made up by the magistrate on the spot in the course by law appointed and with every reasonable precaution to ensure correctness" (*z*) But notwithstanding this general rule, it is thought that if a prisoner specifically avers and offers to prove that a written declaration tendered as his, contains statements of importance essentially different from those which he emitted, he ought to be allowed to prove his averment by parole, otherwise there would be no security against false narratives of procedure before a magistrate being, either from carelessness or designedly, used against a prisoner The competency of such proof is supported by the rules as to impugning recorded decrees and verdicts (*a*), reports of commissioners appointed to take proofs (*b*), notarial instruments (*c*) and messengers' executions (*d*), all of which may be challenged on the ground of being false records of the proceedings which they pretend to narrate (*e*) So where, after the Sheriff before whom certain declarations had been emitted, had proved them in the usual way, the

(*x*) 2 Hume, 332—Burnett, 493—2 Al, 576—White 1844, 2 Hume, 326 note (*supra*, § 1416)—Little v Smith, 1847, 9 D, 737 (*infra* § 1437)—See also Rewson and Tranters, 1722, 16 State Tr, 31—*Supra* § 110, *et seq* (*y*) 2 Al, ib—*Supra* § 113, *et seq* (*z*) 2 Hume, 332—2 Al, 576 (*a*) *Supra* § 1065 *et seq* (*b*) *Supra* § 1073 (*c*) *Supra*, § 1211 2 (*d*) *Supra* § 1213 *et seq*

(*e*) See also § 1072, as to proving that a material error has occurred in entering a prisoner's plea on record

prisoner's counsel proposed to ask him "whether there had been any dispute as to the manner in which parts of the declarations were emitted, and whether the panel had declared in the terms contained therein," and where the prosecutor objected to the question as highly irregular and unprecedented, the Court allowed it to be put under certain modifications (*e*) In another case, where the declaration emitted by a man charged with having murdered his wife, contained the word "scuffle" one of the witnesses who proved the declaration deponed that that was not the word which had been used by the prisoner, but some other expression, which denoted merely a verbal altercation (*f*) Thus, also in a trial for theft, the prisoner's counsel was allowed to put to one of the witnesses to the declaration some question (which has not been preserved) to which the answer was that the declaration contained a true account of the *res gestæ*, the natural inference being that the question was put in order to obtain an opposite answer (*g*)

Where a declaration bore date at the commencement 10th March 1847, and in the docquet 10th March 1848, the prosecutor was allowed to prove that the first date was a clerical error, as the libel stated it to be (*h*)

§ 1428 The declaration is not taken with the view of being used as evidence for the prisoner Nor can he lay it before the jury unless the Crown consents (*i*) If regular it may in all cases be used against the prisoner who emitted it But it cannot be used against a *correus*, for it is not emitted on oath, and nothing is more frequent than culprits attempting to shift the guilt from themselves to the shoulders of their fellow-prisoners (*k*) This rule, however, was held not to preclude the prosecutor from exercising his right to lead proof, including the declaration, against a prisoner who pleaded guilty, and whose *correus* objected that the declaration might injure him in his trial at the same time and for the same offence, on a plea of not guilty (*l*) The presiding judge usually

(*e*) M'Taggart and Others 1798 Burnett, 493 The report does not state what the modifications were (*f*) M'Naught, 1774, Burnett, 493, note It does not appear whether the Crown objected to the question The answer was entered on record along with the rest of the witness testimony (*g*) Cathie, 1833, Bell's Notes, 243 It is not mentioned whether the question was objected to by the prosecutor

(*h*) Robertson 1850 J Shaw 447 (*i*) M'Queen and Robson 1832 (not reported) noted in 2 Al, 577—Kennedy 1842 1 Broun 497, Bell's Notes 285, S C But the prosecutor cannot produce one of several declarations, and withhold the others See *supra* § 1415 (*k*) 2 Hume, 327—2 Al, 576—M'Callum and Corner, 1853, 1 Irv 259 (*l*) Peter and Smith 1840 Bell's Notes, 238 240 S C, 2 Swin 192 directs the jury not to give any effect to one prisoner's declaration as evidence against another [11]

§ 1429 It is a nicer question whether, if a prisoner in his declaration confesses his own guilt and absolves his *correus*, the latter can refer to the declaration as evidence in his favour. No doubt he will not be allowed to do so, unless the prosecutor produces the declaration (*m*) If however, the admissions in a declaration on which the prosecutor founds are inconsistent with the guilt of the declarant's *correus*, it seems anomalous to receive them against the one panel, but to disregard them entirely as evidence for the other for they ought only to receive effect, on the supposition that they are true, and if they are there seems to be no just ground for refusing to the *correus* the benefit of them The confession, also, gives a truthful character to the exculpatory statements, which will usually be prejudicial rather than favourable to the party who makes them On the other hand it is not unlikely that a prisoner, finding his own case desperate, may try to clear his associate, while the general rule against admitting statements not made on oath is against receiving the declaration of one prisoner in favour of another Mr Burnett's opinion is in favour of admitting it for such a purpose (*n*), and in one case where two persons were charged with the murder of a revenue officer, but one of them had died before the trial his declaration was, with the prosecutor's consent, read to the jury on behalf of the other, though the circumstances regarding it were not favourable to its truthfulness (*o*) In a subsequent case, however, where a prisoner confessed that she alone committed the crime charged (theft), and the other prisoner was proceeding to prove the declaration (which had been only libelled on, not produced, by the Crown), the Court interposed, holding that the declaration of a prisoner could not be founded on at all, if not pro-

(*m*) See *supra*, § 1428. Burnett, 495 (*n*) Burnett, 494 (*o*) Reid, 1781

[11] A panel having pleaded guilty was examined as a witness for several other panels who were charged with the commission of the same offence During the cross-examination of this witness, the Advocate-Depute frequently referred to her declaration, which contained statements tending to inculpate the other prisoners It having been objected that this was virtually putting her declaration in evidence against them, which was incompetent, Lord Ardmillan held, that while the declaration of one panel could not be referred to nor used in evidence against another, it was competent to test the truth of the witness' testimony on oath, by referring to different statements made in her declaration, H M Adv v Wilson 1860, 3 Irv, 623

duced by the Crown, and that what one prisoner said there, could not be evidence for or against another prisoner" (*p*)

§ 1430 A declaration before a magistrate, although important, is in no case conclusive, evidence against the prisoner who emitted it (*r*) Nor can a confession contained in it be treated as a plea of guilty on record, for it is taken from the prisoner before he is brought to trial or called to plead to the libel (*s*) [12] If the only evidence against a prisoner besides his declaration confessing the crime, is proof of the *corpus delicti*, the Court will direct the jury to acquit, on account of the evidence not being sufficient in point of law (*t*) And the same course has been followed where some slight suspicion attached to the prisoner from other evidence, as, for example, in a case of theft where a confession in the declaration was corroborated by proof that a boy about the size of the prisoner ran off from the scene of the offence (*u*), and where, besides the declaration and proof of the *corpus delicti*, it appeared that the prisoner, when sought for in order to be apprehended, had been found concealed in a small closet, and had endeavoured to keep the door fast against the officer (*x*) On the other hand prisoners are every day convicted upon confessions in their declarations, corroborated by circumstances which throw considerable suspicion upon them, but which would not of themselves prove the prosecutor's case And this is just, for a false confession in a declaration is very rare and unlikely, indeed, not many degrees less so than a false plea of guilty

§ 1431 The declaration often contains denials, and improbable explanations of circumstances throwing suspicion on the prisoner Juries have learnt to attach to such declarations little weight as indicating guilt, for the wish to escape from the trouble and vexation of a prosecution, or to help the real offender, by putting the officers of justice on a false scent, and many other motives may produce falsehood in persons of the class usually placed at our criminal bars It is only when a circumstance has not an obvious connection with the charge, and when, therefore, a person unac-

(*p*) M'Queen and Robson, 1832 (not reported), noted in 2 Al 577

(*r*) 2 Hume, 324—Burnett, 488—2 Al 578—Ramsay, 1798 noted in Burnett and Hume, ib (*s*) Logan v M'Adam, 1853, 1 Irv 329 (*t*) Hunter and Others, 1838, Bell's Notes, 239 (*u*) Douglas, 1834, Bell's Notes 240

(*x*) Duff v Falconer 1841 Bell's Notes, 239

12 Clark v Stevenson, 1853, 1 Irv, 309—Logan v M'Adam 1853 1 Irv 329—Bone v Bird 1855 2 Irv 279—Gordon v Millar 1856 2 Irv 284

quainted with its latent pertinency is likely to make a candid statement regarding it, that a falsehood on the point ought to weigh against the prisoner. Yet even in such a case his knowledge of its bearing may have been derived from the real criminal, or from expressions dropped by the officers, while its very want of obvious relevancy may awaken his suspicions and induce a denial. Besides, a person may have private reasons, entirely unconnected with the subject of the charge, for disguising the truth regarding matters embraced in his declaration (*y*).

§ 1432. It sometimes happens that a declaration from being probable in itself, and coinciding with the other evidence, assists the case of the prisoner, its general appearance of truthfulness leading the jury to believe his explanations of suspicious circumstances.

§ 1433. Considerable difference of opinion exists as to whether the proceeding detailed in the foregoing sections is fair to the prisoner. It is certainly most oppressive to subject accused persons to the inquisitorial and harassing examinations practised in some foreign courts. But so long as the procedure is conducted according to the law of this country, with perfect liberty to the prisoner to decline answering, and with the protection of a magistrate against importunity or cross-examination, there seems to be no good reason why it should be discontinued; for it is more likely to assist than to prejudice the innocent, while it often completes a defective proof for the Crown, and so prevents the guilty from escaping. No doubt, it admits of being abused in the hands of an over-zealous prosecutor and a weak or biassed magistrate with the connivance of witnesses equally unscrupulous. But the times when such improper practices could be successfully resorted to have gone bye, and the risk of them in modern procedure, although it may alarm the theorist, will not have any weight with persons acquainted practically with the administration of criminal law in this country.[13]

(*y*) Within a few hours after the mysterious murder of the bank porter Begbie in one of the streets of Edinburgh, the contents of most of the low gambling houses, and houses of bad fame of the city, were swept into the police office, when several citizens of good position, as well as many notorious criminals, emitted declarations as to their doings that afternoon. How many of these would on investigation have been found entirely free from falsehood and prevarication?

---

[13] The most recent writer on English Criminal Law is so impressed with the faultiness of the English system, which, by refusing to allow the prisoner to be interrogated, shows

CHAPTER IV.—OF USING IN ONE CAUSE JUDICIAL DECLARATIONS, ADMISSIONS, ETC., MADE IN ANOTHER CAUSE.

§ 1434. As no person has a just reason to complain of his deliberate statements being used in evidence against him, those which a party has made in one cause may in general be used against

---

an obvious neglect of the most natural and important way of obtaining information," that he comes to the conclusion that a modification of the French system (by which the prisoner is subjected to interrogations at the trial) might be advantageously introduced. It may be questioned however whether the Scotch system of taking declarations from prisoners be not safer and more satisfactory than the system which Mr Stephen advocates. At the same time, there can be little doubt that the Scotch practice, in certain particulars, is susceptible of improvement. Some assistance should be allowed the accused during his examination, for though the presence of the magistrate is generally sufficient to prevent the prosecutor from conducting the examination in an improper and inquisitorial manner, yet an accused person, ignorant of the law, and placed in a novel and difficult position, must be apt, when deprived of professional aid during, what is in effect, a skilful cross-examination, to expose himself to groundless misconstruction and suspicion. Nor does it appear reasonable that he should be prevented from submitting, if so advised, his declaration to the jury. At present the declaration is the property of the prosecutor, who has the exclusive right to determine whether it shall or shall not be employed as evidence in the cause,—the theory of the law being that the declaration may be used against, but not on behalf of, the panel. If it be held that the only duty of the prosecutor in all cases is to obtain a conviction, it may be expedient to allow him to exclude a declaration which does not aid the prosecution, but on no other ground can the practice be justified. The primary object of the examination is to obtain information from a person who is presumed to be acquainted with the circumstances under which a crime has been committed, and to give him an opportunity to explain his connection with them. It may be unadvisable to make him a witness in the cause, but if his explanation is to be admitted at all, it appears fair and calculated to aid the discovery of the truth that it should be admitted when it tells in his favour, as well as when it tells against him. The probative value of a declaration is, of course, a different question. But it is for the jury to say whether, taken in connection with the evidence laid before them, the explanation submitted by the panel is probable or improbable, is credible or incredible, and it appears unreasonable to prevent them from looking at the explanation simply because (whatever light it may otherwise throw upon the case) it is not calculated to assist the theory which assumes the guilt of the accused. Mr Stephen, though desirous to have the accused interrogated at a trial, would not admit him as a witness. "It is one thing to enable a man to be a witness on his own behalf, to tempt him to come forward and tell such a story as he thinks best for his own interest, and another thing to subject him to questions in the interest of the accuser. In the one case he comes forward to ask credit for his own account of the matter. In the other he is asked to admit or deny or explain particular circumstances, his ability to do so being a proof of innocence, his inability evidence of guilt. In the one case the man is tempted to invent a lie, in the other case he is probed for the purpose of discovering the truth."—A general view of the Criminal Law of England, by James Fitzjames Stephen, Barrister-at-law, 1863, pp. 189-203.

him in another cause, although with a different opponent, and involving a different issue. On this ground judicial examinations of the pursuers in a civil action on a policy of sea insurance, were held to be admissible against them in a criminal prosecution for sinking the ship to defraud the underwriters (a). So the declaration emitted by a party, when apprehended on a *meditatione fugæ* warrant, was received against him in a subsequent civil action relating to the same matter (b). An oath on reference emitted by a party in one cause is received against him in another, although with a different person (c). But admissions which it contains, however explicit, will not foreclose the party from leading contrary evidence, for such an oath is only conclusive in the cause in which it is emitted (d). It has been held competent to prove against a party in a civil cause that he was held confessed for not deponing on a reference to his oath in a previous action with the same party, and relating to the same matter (e). In like manner, an oath emitted by a party as to the value of his estate under an Income Tax Act was admitted against him in England in a subsequent suit regarding his qualification to kill game, leaving him to prove, if he could, that the valuation was erroneous (f). And the schedule given up by parties taking the benefit of an English Insolvent Act was admitted without objection in an action against them in the Court of Session for payment of the debt which the schedule stated to be due (g).

§ 1435. Declarations emitted by a prisoner, when examined on suspicion of a charge of reset, were admitted against her in a prosecution for having perjured herself in a trial for theft of the goods (h).

(a) M'Iver v. M'Callum, 1784, noted in 2 Hume, 326—Burnett, 495—2 Al. 557. In Humphreys' (*soi disant* Earl of Stirling) case, 1839, separate Report by Swinton, and Bell's Notes, 240, S. C., the judicial examination taken from the prisoner in a civil action relating to certain deeds was put in against him without objection in a trial for forgery of the documents. (b) Kitchen v. Fisher, 1821, 2 Mur., 588. It does not appear whether the parties to the respective proceedings were the same.

(c) Wright v. Lindsay, 1708, M. 14,033 (here the oath had been emitted in a reference which broke up without taking effect)—L. Advocate v. Home, 1711, M., 14,039—Innes v. Watson, 1712, M., 14,041—Hunter v. Nicolson, 1836, 15 S., 159. But see Brown v. Miller, 1828, 6 S. 561—Ersk. 4, 3, 36—Schaw v. Boswell, 1709, M., 14,034.

(d) Innes v. Watson, *supra*—Hunter v. Nicolson, *supra*. (e) Town of Edinburgh v. Lothian, 1677, M. 14,029. (f) R. v. Clarke, 1799, 8 Term R. 220.

(g) Ogilvie v. Taylor, 1849, 12 D., 266. See also Stockfleth v. De Tastet, 1814, 4 Camp., 11—Robson v. Alexander, 1828, 1 Mo. and Pa., 118. (h) Ross, 1836, Bell's Notes, 240.

But the decisions are conflicting as to the competency of using a declaration emitted before a magistrate on a criminal charge as evidence in a subsequent civil suit relating to the same matter In the first reported case on the point a declaration emitted by an apprentice in a charge of stealing his master's goods, was received as evidence for the master in an action against the apprentice and his cautioners for breach of indenture (*i*) Again, in an action against an insurance company for loss by fire the pursuer's declaration in a charge of wilful fire-raising, brought on the complaint of the fire office, was admitted (*k*) The point occurred also in a *cessio*, in which the brief report states that "the Court allowed a declaration emitted by the pursuer in a precognition taken before the Sheriff, with regard to an offence with which he was charged, to be produced in evidence against him" (*l*) These decisions are quoted by Lord Ivory in his Notes to Erskine, as fixing the law on the point (*m*) Declarations have also been admitted without objection in several civil cases (*n*), in one of which the Lord Chief-Commissioner charged the jury,—"There is no rule more clear than that the declaration of a party is evidence against him You will therefore take it as evidence" (*o*)

§ 1436 In a recent case, however, the Second Division of the Court unanimously held that the declaration emitted by a party charged with having forged a bill, was inadmissible in subsequent processes of suspension and reduction-improbation, founded on fraud in obtaining the document (*p*) The grounds of the decision were, that a prisoner has no legal adviser with him while he is making his declaration, and that his mind is directed to the criminal, not to the civil, consequences of the charge The document was also considered to be Crown property to which the private party had no legal right and the admission of which might encourage parties to bring criminal complaints in order to procure a declaration with a view to subsequent civil proceedings The Crown did not oppose the production, and the point was raised by the

(*i*) Maxwell *v* Buchanan, 1776, M, "Apprentice,' Appx, No 1

(*k*) Parker *v* Imperial Fire Office 29th November 1809, F C

(*l*) Alison's *Cessio*, 3d Dec 1814 F C

(*m*) Ivory's Ersk, 986, note 95

(*n*) Mackie *v* Wight, 1822, 3 Mur, 27—Hamilton *v* Maine 1823, 2 S, 356—Paterson *v* Houston 1837, 16 S, 225—Schaw *v* Wause, 1682, M, 9354—Miller *v* Moffat 1820 2 Mur, 316

(*o*) Mackie *v* Wight *supra* Here the action was for damages for assault and the declaration had been emitted with reference to a prosecution before the Sheriff for the offence

(*p*) Little *v* Smith 1845 8 D, 265—S C, 1847, 9 D 737

Court directing the declaration to be withdrawn from process, after both parties had treated it as admissible (r)

In this state of the authorities the point must be considered as still open

§ 1437 It was also held in this case that statements emitted by a party before a magistrate cannot be proved by parole in a subsequent civil suit, for if the written declaration was admissible, the rule which requires the best evidence makes it the only competent proof of its terms and the objections to production of it apply equally to proving its contents by parole (s)

§ 1438 The statements of parties examined (either on oath or declaration) under the Bankrupt Act are admissible against themselves in any subsequent proceedings (t)[1] This is also the rule as to admissions made by one when examined as a witness (u), or haver (w),[2] who will, however, be allowed to prove that his statement was made in error, or that he had not an opportunity of adding explanations or qualifications which might have materially

---

(r) Some of the *rationes decidendi* in this case are humbly thought to be questionable The objections that the prisoner has not a legal adviser with him during his examination and that his mind is not directed to the ulterior purpose for which the document is tendered, are equally applicable to extrajudicial admissions and the second of the objections referred to may be applied to all admissions except those made judicially with reference to the particular suit Besides the civil and criminal cases will almost always depend on the same question of fact, or, at least, the position of the party in them respectively will not depend on conflicting averments The objection to the production fixes the party in a dilemma, for the declaration must be either false or true A personal exception lies against his pleading the former alternative as a ground of exclusion while, if the latter is the fact, why should the declaration not be admitted? The chief difficulty lies in the character of the declaration as a document, which is taken for the single purpose of being used for the Crown in a criminal prosecution But should this be a sufficient reason for excluding it if the Lord Advocate is willing to give it up, or if there is no ground of public policy on which production of it should be withheld? On this point see the chapter on privileged communications, *infra*

(s) Little *v* Smith, 1847, 9 D 737 See also Craig *v* Marjoribanks, 1823, 3 Mur 347

(t) Dundas *v* Belch, 1806, 2 Bell's Com, 399, 482 See also Milward *v* Forbes, 1803, 4 Esp, 171—Smith *v* Beadwell, 1807, 1 Camp, 29—*Supra*, § 1131 (q)

(u) Collett *v* L Keith, 1803, 4 Esp, 212

(w) Boyd *v* Anderson, 1823, 2 S, 363—Thomson *v* Thomson, 1829, 8 S 156—Livingstone *v* Murray 1830, 9 S, 161—Home *v* Hardy, 1842, 4 D, 1181 See also Falconer *v* Stephen, 1849, 11 D, 1338—Paterson *v* Houston, 1837 16 S, 225 *Contra*, per Lord Chief-Commissioner in Clark *v* Spence, 1824, 3 Mur, 454, and Wight *v* Liddell, 1829, 5 ib, 39

---

[1] Emslie *v* Alexander, 1862, 1 Macph, 209

[2] This is thought to be law, but the cases quoted are chiefly cases in which the deposition of a haver, emitted under a commission, has been read at a subsequent jury trial in the same cause

modified its import (x) As it is irregular to examine a haver on the merits of the cause, any part of his deposition which lies under this objection may be deleted (y) If extant, it would rather seem to be admissible against him in subsequent proceedings (z)

In an action for aliment of an illegitimate child, the defender was allowed to prove that the pursuer had, on several occasions, when appearing before the kirk-session of her parish, declared that another person, and not the defender was the father (a)

§ 1439 It is not settled how far an admission in a closed record in one case is evidence in another case No doubt, if the admission is contained in a writing signed by the party, or otherwise authenticated as his own statement, it will be admissible but not conclusive, against him in another cause, either with the same or with a different party, because a person is responsible for his own statements on whatever occasion they may have been made (b) And the same rule will be applied to admissions made on record by the agent or counsel for a party who is proved to have expressly authorised or adopted them (c)

§ 1440 Again, where several actions, from being mutually contingent form one cause, admissions in record in one of them ought to be received (although not as excluding contrary proof), in any of the others without proof of special authority or adoption by the party, because the cases, although separate in form, are one in substance, they are conducted under mutual reference and dependence, and it would generally be inconvenient, if every fact founded on required to be either proved or admitted on record in each of the cases (d) If the actions have been formally conjoined, the two records will be regarded as one to the effect of importing into each of them any admissions appearing on record in the other (e)

§ 1441 But it is doubtful whether admissions in a record, which are not specially authorised or adopted by the party, can be

(x) Collett v Lord Keith supra—Milward v Forbes, supra—Taylor, 532 Of course the oath of a party examined as a haver cannot, like an oath on reference be treated as conclusive, Thomson v Thomson, 1829, 8 S 156 (y) Dye v Reid, 1831, 9 S, 342 See supra, § 1359 (z) See Stockfleth v De Tastet, 1814, 4 Camp, 11—Robson v Alexander 1828, 1 Moo and Pay, 118 (a) Greig v Morice, 1838 16 S, 338 See Baird v Baird, 1662, M, 12,630 (b) Cairns v Marianski, 1850, 12 D, 919, affd, 1 Macq 212—L Arran v Crawford, 1583 M, 14 023—Logan v Wallace, 1850, 1 B Sup, 461 (c) Smith v Puller, 1820, 2 Mur, 342 (d) See Andersons v Jeffrey, 1826 4 Mur 97, 100—Cook v Jeffrey, 1831, 4 De and And 358—See also Robertson v Hyndman, 1833 11 S 776—Fraser v Hill 1852 14 D 335—Falconer v Stephen, 1848, 11 D 220 (e) Shand's Pr, 502

used against him in an independent cause with the same or with a different adversary On the one hand, it may be argued that a record is prepared with a view to the conduct only of the individual cause, and facts which are not material to the issue depending in it are sometimes admitted in order to clear the case of unimportant matters of fact The counsel's mandate to bind his client by admissions is confined to the case in which he is employed while, if the second suit is with a different party, the admission lies under the additional objection of *res inter alios acta* On the other hand, it seems anomalous to hold an admission on record conclusive in one case, and to exclude it entirely as evidence of the same fact in another, since it will very rarely happen that the admission will be erroneous, and, if it is, the party will be allowed to prove that it was made in error The more recent Scotch decisions on the point (which are not uniform or clear), are unfavourable to the admission of the previous record (*f*) But in an old case it was held that where a party, pursued in a removing, declared that he was tenant of a third party, his admission was held to prejudge him, and to make up the pursuer's title, in a subsequent action at the instance of that party (*g*), and, in another case of old date, it was held that if a party in a criminal charge of theft pleads guilty, his confession may be used against him in a subsequent action for spuilzie unless he protested that it should not be so used (*h*) In England the rule seems to be settled that an admission on record in one case may be used as evidence (but not as conclusive) in another case, either with the same or with a different party (*i*) And, in a recent case, the Court of Session entertained considerable doubt as to the pur-

(*f*) In Wright *v* Liddle, 1827, 4 Mur, 327, Lord Mackenzie rejected the record in a previous case, where a different interest was at stake (The report does not state whether the parties are the same) And a similar ruling was given by the Lord Chief-Commissioner in a new trial of the same cause, Id *v* Eund, 5 Mur, 39 In M'Ghie *v* M'Kirdy, 1850, 12 D, 442 Lord Murray rejected a previous record between the same parties, relating to matters akin to those in issue in the second case and involving the same facts Mr Macfarlane, in his treatise on the Practice of the Jury Court (p 211), adopts the rule laid down in these cases But compare with them Anderson *v* Jeffrey, 1826, 4 Mur, 97, 100—and Cook *v* Jeffrey, 1831 4 De and And, 358, *supra*, note (*d*), where the admission of the previous record was not laid expressly on the contingency between the first and second actions See also, in favour of admitting the previous record, Mollison's Tr *v* Crawford, 1851 13 D, 1075, and the following cases, where it was received without objection, Robertson *v* Hyndman, 1833 11 S, 775—Mackenzie *v* J Dundas, 1835, 14 S, 144—Humphreys' (E of Stirling) case, 1839, Bell's Notes, 240—Burns *v* Burns, 1841, 3 D, 1273 (*g*) E Arran *v* Crawford, 1583 M, 11,023 (*h*) Grierson *v* L Zester, 1541, M, 11,021 (*i*) Tiley *v* Cowling, Bull, N P, 243—Starkie (Dowdeswell and Malcolm's ed), 362—2 Phil 25—Taylor 1115—1 Greenl, § 195

poses for which a record in one case could be used in another (*j*). The Committee of Privileges once held that an admission by a former Attorney-General of the pedigree founded on by a former claimant was "of no value" in the subsequent claim (*k*).

§ 1442. Where a party pleading guilty on record in a criminal prosecution, protested that his confession should not prejudice him in a subsequent civil case regarding the same matter, his protest was given effect to (*l*).

CHAPTER V.—EXTRAJUDICIAL ADMISSIONS IN CIVIL CASES

§ 1443. Statements made by a party extrajudicially to his own prejudice may be proved against him, and for the same reason as that which applies to the admissions already noticed, namely, that they are more likely to be true than false. This rule, for example, is applied to statements made by a party in conversation (*a*),[1] in correspondence (*b*), or in a placard or hand-bill issued by him (*c*), and statements made to an agent when the party was precognosced as a witness, with a view to another action, may be proved against him (*d*).[2] A statement made by a person, when not interested in the matter to which it refers, will be received against him after he has become interested in it (*e*), but its value will, of course, depend on his means of knowledge, and his object in making the statement, the prejudicial effect of which was probably unknown to him at the time. A statement which a party made as in his own

(*j*) Fraser *v.* Hill, 1854, 16 D., 789.

(*k*) Crawford and Lindsay Peerage Case, 1848, 2 Cl. and Finn., 553. The report implies that the evidence was rejected. (*l*) Grierson *v.* L. Zester, 1541, M., 14,021—Vicar of Kinghorn *v.* L. Seafield, 1541, M., 14,022—Same parties, 1542, M., ib.—Home *v.* Scott, 1552, M., 14,023. (*a*) See, *e.g.*, Gibson *v.* Kennedy, 1813, Hume D., 150—Hyslop *v.* Miller, 1816, 1 Mur., 53—Hay *v.* Boyd, 1822, 3 Mur., 14—Maclachlan *v.* Road Tr., 1827, 4 Mur., 218—Wilson *v.* Howden, 1829, 8 S., 230—Craig *v.* Hill, 1830, 8 S., 833—Same parties, 10 S., 219—Mack *v.* Cleland, ib., 850—Foggo *v.* Hill, 1840, 2 D., 1322—Fraser *v.* Wilson, 1842, 4 D., 1171—Gordon *v.* Stewart, 1842, 5 D., 8. (*b*) See, *e.g.*, Promoter Life Assur. Co. *v.* Barrie's Reps., 1830, 5 Mur., 136—Young and Co. *v.* Muir, 1824, 2 Sh. Ap., 25—Stewart *v.* Menzies, 1837, 15 S., 1198—Edmonstone *v.* Hamilton, 1842, 5 D., 414. (*c*) Anderson *v.* Anderson, 1848, 11 D., 118. (*d*) Fraser *v.* Wilson, 1842, 4 D., 1171. (*e*) Promoter Life Assur. Co. *v.* Barrie's Reps., 1830, 5 Mur., 136.

---

[1] But see H. M. Adv. *v.* Robertson, 1853, 1 Irv., 219, where admissions made in the course of conversation were not received.

[2] Morrison *v.* Somerville, 1860, 23 D., 233.

favour may be received against him on the fact turning out to his prejudice (*f*)

§ 1444 It has already been seen that entries in a party's cash-books are evidence against him (*g*) The books and balance-sheet of a company have been held conclusive of the interest of the partners respectively in the concern (*h*)

§ 1445 It is not settled how far admissions made by a person in a deed can be used in favour of one who is not a party to the document The rule in England is, that the admission is competent, but not conclusive, in favour of a third party (*i*) Yet if such an admission has been acted on by another, it is conclusive between that person and the maker of it (*k*) And this is the rule whether the admission is true or false, or whether it was made from carelessness or of design,—as the question is, whether it has been acted upon (*l*)

§ 1446 The rule which in consistorial causes, prohibits decree from passing on the party's admission on record does not prevent the Court from receiving extrajudicial admissions (*m*) These, indeed, "when perfectly free from all taint of collusion, and when confirmed by circumstances and conduct, rank amongst the highest species of evidence" (*n*) In actions of declarator of marriage the party may be judicially examined (*o*), and when the marriage is said to have been constituted by promise and subsequent *copula*, the promise cannot be proved except by the defender's writ or oath (*p*) So a letter by the defender to her husband admitting that she had been guilty of adultery, and stating that she made the confession freely and voluntarily, to put it in his power to procure a perpetual separation, was admitted, but held not sufficient to warrant divorce, without corroborating proof (*r*) The defender's

---

(*f*) See Cairns *v* Marianski, 1850, 12 D 919 1286, affd 1 Macq 225

(*g*) See *supra*, § 1183 (*h*) Blair *v* Russell 1828, 6 S 836, 8 ib, 72—Russell *v* Glen, 1827, 5 S, 221, where the contract of copartnery contained a provision to that effect (*i*) Wyatt *v* M Hertford, 1802, 3 East, 147—Graves *v* Kay, 1832, 3 Barn and Ald, 313, 8—Taylor, 573, and cases there cited (*k*) Wyatt *v* M Hertford, *supra*—Graves *v* Kay, *supra*—Heane *v* Rogers, 1829, 9 Barn and Cress, 586—Pickard *v* Sears, 1837, 6 Ad and Ell 474—Taylor, 564, and cases there cited—Best, Pr of Ev, 618 (*l*) Eyre *v* Lamby, 1798, 2 Esp, 635—Morgan *v* Bridges, 1818, 1 Barn and Ald, 650—Howard *v* Tucker, 1831, 1 Barn and Ald, 712—Note to Bacon *v* Chesney, 1816, 1 Stark R, 192—Taylor, 572—Best, Pr of Ev, 619 (*m*) 1 Fraser Pers and Dom Rel, 662—Bishop on Mar and Div, § 307

(*n*) *Per* Dr Lushington in Harris *v* Harris, 1829, 2 Hagg Eccles R, 109, 10

(*o*) *Supra*, § 1396 (*p*) *Supra* § 541 (*r*) E Egluntoune *v* The Countess, 6th Feb 1788, cited 1 Fraser, 662 See also Loveden *v* Loveden, 1810, 2 Hagg Con R, 23

letters in such cases are sometimes important links in the proof, and when they are addressed to the paramour, they are often real evidence on the question in issue, from containing expressions of attachment, appointing meetings, and the like (*s*) The defender's oral admissions of guilt may also be proved (*t*), and they are peculiarly trustworthy if made during severe illness, in order to unburden conscience in anticipation of death (*u*)

In England, the defender's extrajudicial admission has been received in an action of nullity of marriage on the ground of impotency (*x*), and it is also admissible, but of little value, when the ground of nullity is undue publication of banns (*y*).

§ 1447 In actions of divorce for adultery there is great risk of giving undue weight to supposed admissions by the defender (*z*) Expressions of attachment to the supposed paramour, and admissions of indiscretions or imprudent visits, if made to a person whose suspicions are roused, are apt to be exaggerated and misconstrued into acknowledgments of guilt, and even much less equivocal remarks sometimes have a meaning put on them which they do not fairly bear This is peculiarly the case if a considerable interval has elapsed since the supposed admissions were uttered.

§ 1448 A document will not be received as an admission if it has not been uttered, as, for example, a letter written but not dispatched (*b*), or a pleading prepared but not lodged in process (*c*) for such admissions may have been made hypothetically, or in anticipation, and they are like undelivered deeds or unuttered thoughts[2]

(*s*) See Don *v* Don, 1848 10 D, 1046—1 Fraser, Pers and Dom Rel, 662

(*t*) Springthorpe, 1830, 8 S, 751—Williams *v* Williams, 1798, 1 Hagg Con R, 304—Walton *v* Green, 1825, 1 Car and Pa, 621—Burgess *v* Burgess, 1817, 2 Hagg Con R, 226 (*u*) Mortimer *v* Mortimer, 1820, 2 Hagg Con R, 315, *per* Sir W Scott (*x*) Pollard *v* Wybourn, 1828, 1 Hagg Eccles R, 725

(*y*) *Per* Dr Lushington in Brealy *v* Reed, 2 Curt, 833—Bishop on Mar and Div, § 308 (*z*) See *per* Sir W Scott in Williams *v* Williams, 1798 1 Hagg Con R, 304 (*b*) Livingstone *v* Murray, 1831, 9 S, 757 (*c*) Gavin *v* Montgomerie, 1830, 9 S, 213

[2] No precise rule can be laid down as to the circumstances which import that a document has been uttered or delivered, to the effect of allowing it to be received in evidence as an admission or otherwise In H M Adv *v* Madeline Smith, 1857, 2 Irv, 696 a scroll of a letter, which it was not proved had been sent to any one was rejected, but the copy of a letter found in the depositories of the writer after his death, made by a copying-press, and connected by allusions to others which had been sent, was admitted, on the presumption that in these circumstances the original had been sent,—the presumption in the case of a scroll only being against delivery In Nathan *v* Jacob, 1859 1 F and F 452, Justice Crowder admitted a machine copy of a letter written

Yet the coincidence of statements in an undelivered document with the real facts may be material, as circumstantial evidence of knowledge. The objection that a document supposed to contain admissions has not been uttered does not apply to a party's private books (*d*).

§ 1449. It has repeatedly been held incompetent to prove against a party an admission which he has made in an attempt to compromise the case: for such transactions are commonly arranged upon mutual concessions, and the preliminary negotiations are carried on under the implied condition that they will not be evidence in the event of the attempt being unsuccessful (*e*). The Lord Chief-Commissioner, however, held that an offer of compromise by the defender was admissible for the pursuer in an action of damages for defamation (*f*), and in an action as to whether a bill was genuine, the same learned judge allowed the pursuer to found on letters from the defender to prove an attempt which he had made to compromise the case, as distinguished from an offer to buy his peace (*g*). These rulings are not consistent with the broad rule recognised in other cases (*h*).

§ 1450. In England it would seem that, while offers of compromise or pacification will be rejected, if they were made either expressly or impliedly "without prejudice" (*i*), yet in the absence of any express or implied restriction in an offer of compromise, it will be admitted as evidence of liability, its weight varying according

---

(*d*) *Supra*, § 1183.   (*e*) Smythe *v* Pentland, 20th May 1809, F C —Robertson *v* Baxter, 1821, 2 Mur, 427—Maclachlan *v* Road Tr, 1827, 4 Mur, 218—Wight *v* Ewing 1828, 4 Mur, 585—Fyfe *v* Miller, 1835, 13 S, 809—Williamson *v* Taylor, 1845, 7 D, 842.   (*f*) Keddie *v* Walker, 1822, 3 Mur, 38.

(*g*) Hepburn *v* Cowan, 1817, 1 Mur, 263.   (*h*) *Supra*, (*e*).

(*i*) Cory *v* Bretton, 1830, 4 Car and Pa, 462—Healey *v* Thatcher, 8 ib, 388—Jardine *v* Sheridan, 2 Car and Kir, 24—Underwood *v* L Courtoun, 2 Scho and Lef, 67, 68—Taylor Ev, 528.

---

by a plaintiff to a third party, not as a letter sent, but as a letter written, *i e*, as something in the handwriting of the plaintiff (or what was tantamount to it) amounting to an admission. A wrote a letter to the editor of a newspaper in reference to an article of which he complained. The editor agreed to insert it, and it was actually inserted in the newspaper, but, before it was published, A called at the office, and intimated that he did not wish it to appear. At a jury trial for libel against the proprietor of the newspaper at A's instance, the defender proposed to put in the letter as evidence of A's views upon the article at the time. It was held, (1) that the editor had not acquired the property in the letter, and was not entitled to publish it contrary to the wish of the writer, (2) that, in these circumstances, the letter was not admissible, Davies *v* Millar 1855, 17 D, 1166.

to the nature of the case (*k*) The limits of this distinction seem not to be well defined (*l*) The only cases where offers of compromise press against a party are where his character is involved in the issue But even in such cases many an innocent but weak person would make a pecuniary sacrifice, rather than undergo the vexation, exposure and risk of a trial (*m*)

§ 1451 The Court have reprobated attempts to draw a party into admissions (*n*) It cannot however, be said that an admission obtained by artifice must be excluded It would rather seem to be admissible, along with the circumstances under which it was obtained, for it is more likely to be true than false Thus where a wife had admitted adultery upon being falsely informed that the paramour had confessed, Sir William Scott observed, that the artifice would not detract from the effect of her confession, since if false, what would have been the language of an innocent and virtuous woman under such an accusation? She would not have pleaded guilty Would she not rather have repelled the charge, and inveighed against her traducer with animated indignation and not have admitted the truth of it?" (*o*).

§ 1452 No case seems to have occurred in this country as to the competency of admissions made under constraint It has been held in England that if obtained by means of illegal compulsion they are inadmissible, whereas they are admissible, if emitted when the party was under legal duress (*p*) This distinction is similar to that which prevails in Scotland as to the challenge of deeds on the head of force and fear, only illegal compulsion being a ground of reduction (*r*)

(*k*) Wallace *v* Small 1830 Moo and Mal, 446—Watts *v* Lawson 1830 ib, 447, note—Nicolson *v* Smith, 1822, 3 Stark R 129 (*l*) See Taylor, *supra*—Thomas *v* Morgan, 1835 2 Crom Mee and Rosc, 496 (*m*) It is said that some years ago, when the biography of a notorious person was in the course of preparation, several gentlemen of high respectability were informed that anecdotes regarding them would be inserted It is probable that some who "bought their peace" from such exposure and vexation were innocent victims of a disgraceful scheme of extortion

(*n*) Robb *v* Campbell 1824, 3 S, 301 Such attempts take a party at a disadvantage, and if they are proved by persons who were engaged in the plot, they come through a distorting and very untrustworthy medium (*o*) Burgess *v* Burgess 1817, 2 Hagg Con R 235—See also 1 Phillips, 405—Rosc Cr Ev 47, 8

(*p*) See Stockfleth *v* De Tastet, 1814, 4 Camp 11, per L Ellenborough—Robson *v* Alexander, 1828, 1 Moo and Pay, 448—Taylor, 531 (*r*) Stair, 1, 9, 8—Ersk 3 1, 16—Ib, 4, 1, 26—1 Bell's Com, 295—Bell's Pr, § 12 Illegal compulsion nullifies, although it was imposed by one for whom the party challenging the deed is not responsible for the rule is not designed for the punishment of the person who uses the

§ 1453 It seems not to be a ground for excluding an oral admission that the party was interrupted while making his statement But, of course, the fact of the interruption will go to the jury, because it may have prevented the party from adding qualifications or explanations which would have altered materially the effect of the words uttered (s)

§ 1454 An extrajudicial admission is not full proof of the issue, but must be corroborated by other evidence, varying in degree according to the natures of the admission and of the fact in dispute Some farther remarks on the probative value of admissions are made in a subsequent chapter (t)

CHAPTER VI —EXTRAJUDICIAL ADMISSIONS (USUALLY TERMED CONFESSIONS) IN CRIMINAL CASES

§ 1455 Extrajudicial confessions, whether made orally or in writing, are admissible in criminal cases, and for the manifest reason that they are far more likely to be true than false (a) This rule is observed in every-day practice, and applies in capital cases (b), and trials for treason (c), as well as in prosecutions for minor offences

§ 1456 It is essential to the admissibility of a confession that it should have been emitted voluntarily, without the influence of such feelings of hope or fear as tend to produce false confessions (d)

---

violence, but for the protection of him who suffers it, Pothier Tr des Oblig, i, 1, 1, 3, § 23 (s) Collett v L Keith, 1803, 4 Esp, 212—Milward v Forbes, 1803, ib, 172—Taylor, 532 (t) *Infra*, § 1489, *et seq* (a) 2 Hume, 333—Burnett, 439, 519—2 Al, 535, 579—1 Phill, 397—Taylor, 579—Best Pr of Ev, § 506—Rosc Cr Ev, 37 (b) 2 Hume, 333, 4 (c) 3 Trea Tr, 173—1 Al, 619—Foster, 241—1 Phill, 415

(d) 2 Al, 581—1 Phill, 407—Taylor, 580—Best's Pr of Ev, § 532—Roscoe's Cr Ev, 39, *et seq*—Wilson's case, 1820, 2 Trea Tr, 45, 170 186—Honeyman v Smith, 1815, 2 Hume, 335, note As to the ground for this exclusion, Lord Chief-Justice Eyre observed in Warrickshall's case, 1783, 1 Leach C C, 263, "It is a mistaken notion that the evidence of confessions, and facts which have been obtained from prisoners by promises or threats is to be rejected from a regard to public faith A confession forced from the mind by the flattery of hope or the torture of fear, comes in so questionable a shape, when it is to be considered as the evidence of guilt, that no credit ought to be given to it, and therefore it is rejected

Accordingly, a confession which the prisoner has made on being told by a magistrate, by the procurator-fiscal, or by any person authorised by the prosecutor, that his confessing would save him from prosecution, or procure him a lighter punishment, or might tend to produce such a result, will be rejected (*c*) The same rule will be applied to inducements held out by a superintendent of police or the governor of the jail in which the prisoner is lodged (*f*), for most prisoners are likely to rely on the assurances of such officials, and it would be both oppressive and dangerous to subject accused persons to their solicitations (*g*)[1] Sir Archibald Alison considers that a confession obtained upon inducements held out by a constable or sheriff-officer will be admissible because these subordinates have no power to tie up the hands of the public prosecutor (*h*) But it was held incompetent to prove that a prisoner gave an officer half-a-crown, being part of the money alleged to have been stolen by her, where the officer, without having made any promise, had used expressions intended to make the prisoner suppose that he would be thereby induced to hush up the offence (*i*) And it has been repeatedly held in England that promises or threats by a constable will vitiate a confession (*j*)[2] This is thought to be

(*c*) 2 Al, 581—Phill, *supra*—Taylor, 587—Best's Pr of Ev, *supra*

(*f*) Hope, 1845, 2 Broun 465 Here statements made to the keeper of the prison, who had acted as the prisoner's spiritual adviser and had communicated with her friends regarding her defence, were rejected The Court considered the case to be special (*g*) See M'Laren and Others, 1823 2 Al, 564 (*h*) 2 Al, 581

(*i*) Watt 1834, Bell's Notes, 244

(*j*) R *v* Morton, 1843, 2 Moody and Rob, 514—R *v* Mills, 1833, 6 Car and Pa, 146—R *v* Drew, 1837, 8 ib, 140 In this case the officer had stated that what the prisoner said "would be used for or against him at his trial," and Coleridge, J, considered that it was holding out a direct inducement to say that what the prisoner said could be evidence in his favour See also R *v* Enoch, 1833, 5 Car and Pa, 539, a confession obtained from a female prisoner by inducements held out by the female turnkey in whose charge she was, was rejected[2]

[1] See H M Adv *v* Mahler and Berenhard, 1858, 2 Irv, 634, where evidence of a confession made by a panel in consequence of inducements held out to him by a superintendent of police, was not admitted

[2] Though the precise extent to which the rule is carried in England is not very clear, it would seem that Justice Coleridge's view of an 'inducement' has latterly been held somewhat too strict In a recent case, decided in the Court for Crown Cases Reserved, Chief-Baron Pollock thus described the rule,—"The question now is, whether the words employed by the constable, 'He need not say anything to criminate himself, what he did say would be taken down and used as evidence against him' amount either to a promise or a threat We are not to torture this expression, or to say whe

correct (*k*) Nor is it inconsistent with the rule that inducements by subordinate officials do not vitiate a formal declaration, for they are not likely to disturb the prisoner's mind after he comes into the presence of the magistrate, whereas confessions wrung from a person while under the immediate influence of promises or threats from the officer in charge of him, cannot be regarded as voluntary

In one case where a marine was charged with having fired a loaded gun at a fisherman in a boat, where the prosecutor asked one of the officers whether the prisoner had made any statement to him regarding the occurrence, the Court expressed a doubt whether the evidence could be admitted, as the prisoner was bound to report to his commanding officer what had occurred when he was on duty, and therefore the statement was not voluntary (*l*) And in a case of incest, where the inspector of the poor of the parish deponed that he made a requisition to the male prisoner to support the child which had been born of the union, and gave the prisoner a number of advices, and spoke to him as to the heinous nature of the crime, telling him that if he persisted he would be punished, whereupon the prisoner confessed,—and that the confession was repeated six months afterwards,—Lord Justice-Clerk Hope refused to receive the acknowledgment, on the ground that it had been obtained by undue influence, which had continued to operate so as to render the second confession inadmissible, although the threats had not been repeated (*m*)

(*k*) See *infra*, § 1459 (*l*) Turner, 1853, 1 Irv, 285 (*m*) Robertsons, 1853, 1 Irv, 219

ther a man might not have misunderstood their meaning, for the words might, by ingenuity, be suggested to raise in the mind of the prisoner very different ideas from that which is the natural meaning The words are to be taken in their obvious meaning" It was important that a person charged with a crime should be told, when apprehended, the nature of the charge, and that attention should be paid to what he said in reply "It is proper that a prisoner should be cautioned not to criminate himself, but, I think, what he says ought to be adduced, either as evidence of his guilt or as evidence in his favour," R *v* Baldry, 1852, 2 Den C C, 430 By the law of England the inducement must be the prospect of temporal advantage, and confessions extorted by means of spiritual terrors are not excluded This was held in a case where a chaplain passed three hours and a-half with a man urging him to confess, and reading, amongst other things, the Commination Service,—the ground of the decision, it is thought, being, that religious considerations were not likely to induce a man to tell a lie, R *v* Gilham, Roscoe, Dig Crim Evid 41, 2 See also, as to recent English practice, R *v* Stripp, 2 Jur N S, 152—R *v* Parker, 1 L T, 151—R *v* Harriot, 8 Cox C C 375—R *v* Cheverton, 2 F and F, 833

§ 1457 But it would seem that inducements proceeding from private persons will not render inadmissible a confession emitted under their influence If they do not relate to the penal consequences of the charge, they will be disregarded on that ground (*n*), while if they were connected with it, they could only have been given by way of advice, not like promises on which the prisoner might rely (*o*) This rule holds where the inducements proceed from the person injured by the crime (*p*) The decisions in England as to the effect of inducements by persons not empowered to bind the prosecutor are conflicting (*r*)

§ 1458 Yet a confession will be excluded, if it was emitted in consequence of inducements held out by a private person in presence of one for whom the prosecutor is responsible, and who by his silence sanctioned or acquiesced in them (*s*)

§ 1459 The law is jealous of confessions made to criminal officers and persons connected with the prosecution, even where there is no proof that they were obtained by promises or threats Of late years the Court have excluded confessions elicited by the police questioning prisoners after they had been lodged in the police office (*t*) Nor will it render such examinations admissible that the prisoner was told he was at liberty to decline answering for the police authorities are not entitled to examine him without the protection of a magistrate (*u*) The Court have not extended the same

---

(*n*) Taylor 592 (*o*) 2 Al, 582 The value of such confessions is generally small

(*p*) In Honeyman and Smith, 1815, 2 Hume, 335 note, confessions made to the manager of a company from whom goods had been stolen, on his promise that the prisoners lives would be safe, and his subsequent recovery of the goods in consequence of directions received from the prisoners, were proved, and the prisoners were convicted on the capital charge, but recommended to mercy,—upon which they received a transportation pardon

(*r*) See the cases collected in Taylor, 588–590 The learned author thus concludes his summary of the cases (p 590)—"It is submitted that, without laying down any positive rule, whether of admission or rejection the judge should determine each case on its own merits, only bearing in mind that his duty is to reject such confessions only as would seem to have been wrung from the prisoner under the supposition that it would be best for him to admit that he was guilty of an offence which he really never committed" See also R *v* Court, 1836, 7 Car and Pay 487, per Littledale, J

(*s*) R *v* Pountney 1832 7 Car and Pay, 302, per Alderson, B—R *v* Drew, 1837, 8 ib 141 per Coleridge, J—R *v* Taylor 1839, ib, 734, per Patteson, J—R *v* Laugher 1846 2 Car and Kir 226, per Pollock C B—Taylor, 588

(*t*) Martin and Robb, 1842 1 Broun, 382, Bell's Notes, 245, S C—Wood 1842, 1 Broun 588 note, Bell's Notes ib See also Lowrie and Cairns, 1836 Bell's Notes, ib —Symon 1841 ib—Dowd 1852 1 Shaw, 575—Ker *v* Mackay, 1853, 1 Irv, 213

(*u*) Cases in preceding note

rule to confessions obtained in answer to questions from the police on apprehending the prisoner (*x*) or while conducting him to the police office (*y*) But they would certainly interpose if the officer importuned the prisoner by interrogations, because such unfair practices ought to be discouraged

§ 1460 There is no rule which excludes confessions made by a prisoner spontaneously to the procurator-fiscal or officers of police, either immediately on apprehension, or after having been lodged in the police cells (*z*) And confessions made by a prisoner to one confined along with him will be admitted (*a*), provided no person connected with the prosecution induced the fellow-prisoner to converse with him on the subject (*b*) Conversations between fellow-prisoners may also be proved by the jailor or turnkey who overheard them (*c*) But the Court will exclude such as were picked up by eavesdropping (*d*)[3]

(*x*) Christie, 1842 1 Broun, 388, Bell's Notes, 245, S C (*y*) Alexander and M'Court, 1831, Bell's Notes, 244 (*z*) Robertson, 1728, and Wilson and Hall, 1736, 2 Hume, 335 (*a*) Cases of Andrew and Others, 1774, Anderson and Marshall, 1728, noted in 2 Hume, 335, 6—Emond, 1830 Bell's Notes, 243—Wright, 1835, ib, 244—Miller, 1837 ib (*b*) Miller, *supra*—Emond, *supra*

(*c*) Brown 1833 Bell's Notes, 244—Miller, *supra* (*d*) Brown, *supra*—Tait and Stevenson, 1824 (not rep), noted in 2 Al, 585—M'Kinlay and Gordon 1829 2 Al, 537, reported on another point in Sh Just Ca, 225

[3] In H M Adv v Beaton, 1856, 2 Irv 455, where the statements were made to the keeper of a prison—H M Adv v Ross, 1859, 3 Irv, 434, where they were made to the chaplain—H M Adv v Hendry and Craighead, 1857, 2 Irv, 618 where they were made to the procurator-fiscal—H M Adv v Hay, 1858, 3 Irv 181, where they were made to a police officer before the warrant for apprehension had been issued—H M Adv v Millar, 1859 3 Irv, 406, and H M Adv v Smith and Campbell, 1855, 2 Irv, 17 where they were made to police officers—the evidence was disallowed In all these cases the statements made by the panels were made in answer to questions addressed to them but no inducements were offered to extract a confession In Hendry and Craighead, *supra*, a panel charged with forgery had, after his apprehension, at the request of the procurator fiscal, written his name on a slip of paper This was held to be, in effect an attempt by a police officer to elicit evidence by private interrogation In Hay, *supra*, the Lord Justice Clerk (Inglis) laid down generally that when a person is under suspicion of a crime, it is not proper to put questions to him and receive answers from him except before a magistrate This kind of evidence indeed, has been of late almost invariably refused, unless the case disclosed some very special feature In H M Adv v Wylie, 1858, 3 Irv, 218, it was proved that, shortly after the apprehension of the panel, a hat was brought into the police office, and the officer asked the panel if the hat were his The reply was received It was held in a suspension, in a case of theft, that an allegation, to the effect that the evidence consisted of statements made by the panel to detectives after his apprehension, was "too weak" to induce the Court to send for the Sheriff's notes, M'Rae v Blair 1856 2 Irv, 568 Where the questions, however, are such as may be properly put by a police officer in the discharge of his duty while engaged

These precautions are necessary to secure a prisoner against being unfairly wrought upon to make confessions, in the hope that they may be for his advantage They do not exclude credible evidence of guilt, for neither eavesdroppers, nor persons who win the confidence of their fellow-prisoners in order to betray them, are likely to narrate truly the conversations referred to[4]

§ 1461 Spontaneous confessions made in gaol to a magistrate or justice of the peace may be proved by the testimony of the persons in whose presence they were made (*e*). But in one case of this nature the propriety of sending the evidence to the jury was doubted, the magistrate having cautioned the prisoner not to say anything that would endanger himself, but not having taken down the statements in writing (*f*) The Court apparently considered that the magistrate should have had the statements repeated by way of formal declaration, instead of trusting to his recollection of them

§ 1462 It is settled in England that where in consequence of information improperly obtained from the prisoner, the stolen property, or articles of real evidence regarding the crime have been recovered the statement, as well as the circumstances attending the recovery, may be laid before the jury, because the ground on which admissions obtained by inducements are excluded in ordinary

(*e*) Ratcliffe, 1739 2 Hume, 336—Emond, 1830, Bell's Notes, 244
(*f*) Emond, *supra*

in apprehending and detaining a suspected person, and which are required to enable him to discharge that duty, it would appear that the answers will be received "If the officer goes out of his sphere altogether, such evidence would be rejected on the ground that his questions would then just amount to a precognition But when they are put with reference to the subject matter of the charge for which the prisoner is being apprehended under the warrant and are strictly confined to that charge, and not put *ex intervallo*, I think that the prisoner's answers ought to be admitted as evidence", *per* Lord Cowan in Lewis *v* Blair, 1858, 3 Irv, 16 See also H M Adv *v* Milne 1868, 35 Sc Jur, 470, where statements made in reply to a police surgeon, in presence of a police officer, by a prisoner whose sanity was doubted, were admitted,—the questions having been put for the purpose of ascertaining the panel's state of mind at the time

[4] Confessions obtained by means of fraud are admissible in England This was held where a person took an oath that he would not mention what a prisoner told him, where a turnkey promised to post a letter which contained a confession, and where a prisoner, while drunk, made a statement to a constable,—it being alleged that the liquor had been given him by the constable with the view of making him drunk, Roscoe Dig Crim Evid, 6th edit, 47, 8

cases is that they are probably untrue, whereas their truth in the cases supposed is established by the fact of recovery (*g*). And the same rule applies where the articles are produced by the prisoner himself (*h*). But, as the recovery or production only proves the party's knowledge of the place where the articles are the statement will only be admitted in so far as relates to that fact, and a collateral admission—as, for example, that the prisoner concealed them there—will be excluded (*i*).

These rules are both just and discriminating. It has, however, been held in this country to be incompetent to prove that a prisoner delivered to an officer part of a sum alleged to have been stolen, the officer having led the prisoner to suppose that he would thereby be induced to hush up the offence (*k*).

§ 1463. In England a confession uttered by a person when drunk has been admitted (*l*). A confession made by one talking in his sleep was once tendered, but was withdrawn, Lord Chief-Justice Tindal having doubted its admissibility (*m*). In this country the prosecutor was once allowed, without objection, to prove that the prisoner, when in gaol, had started up and made a certain ex-

---

(*g*) R v Gould, 1840, 9 Car and Pa, 364—R v Butcher, 1798, 1 Leach Cr Ca, 265, note—Per Le Blanc, J, in R v Grant and Craig, 1801, 2 East Pl Cr, 658—2 Stark Ev, 38—Taylor, 612—1 Phill, 411—1 Greenleaf, § 231. In some cases the Court only admitted the fact that the articles had been found, not the statement which had led to the discovery, R v Warrickshall, 1783, 1 Lea Cr Ca, 263—R v Mosey, 1784, note to ib, 265—R v Cain, 1839, 1 Craw and Dix, 36—R v Lockhart, 1785, 1 Lea Cr Ca, 386. (*h*) R v Griffin, 1809, Russ and Ry, 151. Here the prosecutor had told the prisoner it would be better for him to confess, whereupon he gave up some money as the stolen property. Mr Justice Chambre received this evidence, while holding that the confession was inadmissible, and a majority of the twelve judges adhered. See also R v Jones, 1809, ib, 152. (*i*) R v James *supra*—2 East Pl Cr, 658—Starkie, *supra*—Phill, *supra*—Taylor, *supra*.

(*k*) Watt, 1834, Bell's Notes, 241. (*l*) R v Spilsbury, 1835 7 Car and Pa, 187, per Coleridge, J—(*in vino veritas*).

(*m*) R v Sippet, 1839, noted in Taylor, 593, and in Best, Pr of Ev, 608, note.

Dark hints and suspicious conduct during sleep have been favourites of dramatists and writers of romance

"Foul whisperings are abroad unnatural deeds
Do breed unnatural troubles infected minds
To their deaf pillows will discharge their secrets."—*Macbeth*

"Nay, this was but his dream."
"But this denoted a foregone conclusion."
—"'Tis a shrewd doubt, though it be but a dream,
And this may help to thicken other proofs
That do demonstrate thinly."—*Othello*

clamation in his sleep (*n*) And if the property stolen, or the bloody knife with which a murder had been committed, were recovered in consequence of words uttered by the prisoner during sleep, these would be admitted as proving his knowledge Expressions indicating an intimate acquaintance with details connected with the crime would also be evidence of knowledge, if the prisoner had not an opportunity of hearing of them from unsuspicious quarters, and in any case, uttering such expressions during sleep would awaken suspicion and lead to investigation, although they might not be admissible in evidence (*o*)

§ 1464 In Scotland an extrajudicial confession is not full proof of guilt, but must be corroborated by other evidence, not merely to the *corpus delicti*, but throwing suspicion on the prisoner (*p*) It is not possible to lay down what amount of corroborative evidence should be required in order to warrant a verdict of guilty, because extrajudicial confessions admit of countless degrees of credibility, and it must therefore, lie with the jury in each case to say whether looking to the terms of the confession, the channel through which it comes, and the corroborating evidence—they are satisfied that the prisoner is guilty.

It has been repeatedly laid down in England that a confession made extrajudicially is sufficient, without any corroborating evidence, to warrant a conviction, if the jury believe it to be true (*r*)

(*n*) Emond 1830, Bell's Notes, 243

(*o*) A striking instance of crime discovered by expressions uttered in sleep occurred in the Court of Foujdaree, Udalut of Madras in September 1834, and is quoted by Mr Best (Pr of Ev, p 609, note) from Arbuthnot's Reports of Criminal Cases in that court, p 61 A person had been found murdered and mutilated, the head lying on an ant-hill, apart from the rest of the body Suspicion fell on one Venkatasami, with whom deceased had been on bad terms He was apprehended, along with Dasan, Nachan, Venkatachlam Tandanarayan and Chokan Venkatasami's answers, when questioned on the subject not having been satisfactory, he was watched, and during sleep was heard to say 'Dasan, catch hold of the hands Nachan, cut off the head Tandanarayan Chokan, and Venkatachalam, catch hold of his leg Come we may go home after we have deposited the head on the top of an ant-hill.' These words having been reported Venkatasami was arrested and charged with the murder, when he confessed, and criminated those whom he had named in his sleep, and they also, on being apprehended confessed It does not appear whether, before going to sleep, Venkatasami had been told of the position in which the body had been found

(*p*) 2 Hume 333—Burnett, 519—2 Al 582 The rule in the text follows *a fortiori* from that as to confessions in the prisoner's declaration, *supra*, § 1430

(*r*) R v Wheeling 1789 1 Lea, Cr Ca 311, note—R v Eldridge, 1821 Russ and Ry 440—R v White, 1823 ib, 508—R v Falconer and Bond, 1822, ib 481—R v Tippets 1823 ib 509—R v Stone, 1562, Dyer, 215, pl 50—2 Russell, 825—Best's Pr of Ev, 631

The point, however, has not been expressly decided (*s*), and it may still be doubted whether an extrajudicial confession is sufficient to found a verdict, when it is not supported by proof of the *corpus delicti*, if not also by circumstances implicating the prisoner (*t*)

Some further observations as to the probative value of confessions will be found in a subsequent chapter (*u*).

CHAPTER VII —HOW FAR ADMISSIONS OR CONFESSIONS MADE BY ONE PERSON ARE EVIDENCE AGAINST ANOTHER

§ 1465 In civil cases a party is often responsible for admissions made by other persons besides himself

Where several persons have full powers of administration over a common stock, *e g*, co-partners, admissions by any one of them on matters relating to the common estate may be given in evidence against the others (*a*) provided their mutual relation is admitted or proved (*b*) When that is the question in issue, the admission of one alleged partner will not be received against another (*c*) And, in an accounting between the heirs of two partners, entries in the private books of the one partner were held not to be evidence against the heirs of the other, there being no evidence that he had seen the books (*d*)

§ 1466 The admissions of any one of a body of trustees may be proved *valeant quantum* against the estate which he represents (*e*)

(*s*) See the cases analysed in 1 Greenleaf, § 217, note 3, and Taylor 585—Roscoe, Cr Ev, 38—Greaves' note to 2 Russell, 826 (*t*) See authorities in preceding note In R *v* Edgar, 1831 (not reported), cited in Greaves' note to 2 Russ 826 Patteson, J, observed "Could a man be convicted of murder on his confession alone, without any proof of the person being killed? I doubt whether he could"

(*u*) See *infra*, § 1489, *et seq* (*a*) 2 Bell's Com, 618—Nisbet's Tr *v* Morrison's Tr, 1829, 7 S 307, per L Glenlee—Grant *v* Jackson, 1793, Pen Ca, 203—Lucas *v* De la Cour, 1813, 1 Mau and Sel, 248—Wood *v* Braddick, 1808, 1 Taunt, 104 From Berry's Reps *v* Bogle, 1822, 1 S, 471, it would seem that books kept by one of two co-adventurers, as their joint accounts regarding the concern, would bind the other in a question with third parties (*b*) Grant *v* Jackson *supra*—Nicholls *v* Dowding, 1815, 1 Stark R, 81—See also Campbell *v* Macfarlane, 1840, 2 D, 663, Macf R, 200, S C (*c*) Dundas and Robinson *v* Belch 1806, 2 Bell's Com, 399, note 4—But see Smith *v* Fuller, 1820, 2 Mur, 342 (*d*) Smith *v* Logan, 1826, 5 S, 32, affd, 4 W S, 47 (*e*) E Fife *v* E Fife's Tr, 1816 1 Mur, 95—Young & Co *v* Muir, 1821, 2 Sh Ap Ca, 25—Graham *v* Graham 1827 5 S,

But, of course, where the interest of a trustee is antagonistic to that of the trust-estate, neither he nor any one interested along with him can found on his admissions (*f*)

§ 1467 Where parties have merely a common interest in a subject, the admission of one of them is not evidence against the others Thus the admissions of one owner of a ship do not bind the others (*g*), the admissions of one acceptor of a prescribed bill will not prove constitution or resting-owing of the debt as against another acceptor (*h*), and the admissions of one defender are not evidence against a co-defender, unless concert or conspiracy between them in regard to the matter is proved (*i*) It is held in England that, in an action against several joint makers of a note, the judicial admission of one of them that he subscribed, is not sufficient evidence of the fact against the others, as the plaintiff must prove against each that they all signed (*k*) So the admission of a widow, confirmed as executrix, will only affect her own interest, not that of the next of kin (*l*) And in an action of abstracted multures, the defender was not allowed to found on billets, which persons grinding at the mill had received from a previous miller, with whom the pursuer had no connection (*m*)

§ 1468 The admissions of a cedent are competent evidence against his assignee, if they were made before the assignation was granted, because *assignatus utitur jure auctoris*, and no one by merely assigning his right can deprive his debtor of the benefit of his admissions (*n*) So entries in the cedent's books, or writings

---

806—Nisbet's Tr *v* Morrison's Tr, 1829, 7 S, 307—Campbell *v* Cooper's Tr, 1829, 1 De and And, 169—Falconer *v* Stephen, 1849, 11 D, 1338 The admission ought to be held much less forcible evidence, when it is merely an inference deduced from facts patent to the court or jury, than when it is the result of personal knowledge, see M'Nicol *v* M'Neill, 1821, 1 S, 188—Hislop *v* Howden, 1843, 5 D, 507—Brown *v* Crawford, 1741 (Kilkerran's Rep), M, 9418—Compared with Dalziel *v* L Lindores, 1784, M, 10,994—Graham *v* Cochran, 1725, M, 10 992 See also Anderson *v* Jeffrey, 1826, 4 Mur, 111

(*f*) Murray *v* Lawrie's Tr 1827 5 S, 515 (*g*) Duncan *v* Forbes, 1831, 9 S, 540—Wight *v* Liddell 1829, 5 Mur, 42 (*h*) Allan *v* Ormiston, 1817, Hume D, 477—Houston *v* Yuill 1822 1 S, 449—M'Indoe *v* Frame, 1824 3 S, 295—M'Neill *v* Blair, 1823, 2 S, 174—See *supra*, § 459 (*i*) Campbell *v* Blackadder, 1839, Macf R, 200—2 D, 663 S C—South Metropolitan Gas Co *v* M Lothian 1838, Macf R, 13—Compared with Miller *v* Moffat, 1820, 2 Mur, 323—See also Combe *v* Hossack, 1826, 4 Mur, 54 (*k*) Gray *v* Palmer, 1794, 1 Esp, 135

(*l*) Dickson *v* M'Kalla 1681, 1 Fount, 145 (*m*) Clark's Tr *v* Hill, 1827, 4 Mur, 206 (*n*) Wright *v* Lindsay 1708 M, 14 033—Ramsay *v* Aitken 1826, 4 S, 390—Farquhar *v* Sloane, 1830, 9 S, 112—Finlayson *v* Murray, 1822 1 S 531

under his hand anterior to the intimation of the assignation, are admissible against the assignee, the cedent not being divested until intimation (*o*) But statements by the cedent, after the assignee's right has been completed, will not affect the latter, for, the cedent having been entirely divested, his statements were like those of a stranger (*p*) Again, where an executor-creditor sued a person for payment of rents due to the deceased, entries of payments holograph of the deceased and occurring in his account-books, were held to prove discharge of the debt (*r*) So a husband, sued for payment of debts contracted by his wife before marriage, will only be affected by such admissions as she made before that contract transferred to him all her rights burdened with all her obligations, whereas any admissions made by her subsequently will be excluded (*s*) In like manner the indorsee of a bill will not be affected by a previous holder admitting that it was not granted for an onerous consideration, yet, where the presumption in favour of the indorsation being onerous is overcome by proved or admitted facts, non-onerosity of the bill itself may be proved against the indorsee by the writ or oath of the previous holder (*t*)

§ 1469. The principle which those cases involve applies also in bankruptcy, so that while admissions made by a bankrupt before sequestration (if free from collusion) may be used against the general body of creditors (*u*), his statements in his examination taken before the Sheriff may not be founded on by individual creditors to the prejudice of the others (*x*), and this may be said also as to all other statements made by the bankrupt after sequestration, as they have not the essential element of being against interest (*y*). So, where the debt of the petitioning creditor in a sequestration was contained in a prescribed bill, it was held that the signature of the bankrupt to the petition recognising the debt, did not, as against

---

(*o*) Skene *v* Lumsden, 1662, M , 12,618—Currier *v* Halyburton, 1683, M , 12,625 See also Lawrie *v* Drummond, 1675, M , 12 622 (*p*) Stair, 3, 1, 18—Ersk , 3, 5, 9 , ib , 3, 6, 10 See sections on referring to oath of cedent, *infra*, § 1596, *et seq*

(*r*) Wardlaw *v* Gray, 1662, M , 12,620 (*s*) Kelly *v* Small, 1799, 2 Esp , 716, per L Kenyon—Urquhart *v* Nairn, 1688, M , 12,494—Morris *v* Monro, 1829, 8 S , 156—1 Fraser Pers and Dom Rel , 295 See also sections as to referring to wife's oath, *infra*, § 1576, *et seq* (*t*) Finlayson *v* Murray, 1822, 1 S , 531—Ramsay *v* Aitken, 1826, 4 S , 390—Innes *v* Lawson, 1828, 6 S , 513—Farquhar *v* Sloane, 1830 9 S , 112—Jameson *v* Grahame, 1832, 11 S , 80 (*u*) Anderson *v* Clouston, 1824, 2 S , 620

(*x*) Goddart *v* Brit Linen Co , 1806, 2 Bell's Com , 317, note See also Kirkland *v* Slater, 1831, 10 S , 169, where Lord President Blair's notes in Goddart *v* Brit Linen Co will be found (*y*) Cases in previous note See also Dyce *v* Paterson, 1846, 9 D 310—Adam *v* M'Lachlan, 1847 ib , 560

the general body of the creditors, amount to the writ of the debtor admitting the constitution and subsistence of the debt (z) [1]

§ 1470 A party is responsible for the admissions of those whom he has authorised to bind him by that means [2] It is in virtue of such authority that a counsel's admissions on record are binding on his client (a) and that not only on pure matters of fact, but also where law is involved (b) [3] Thus, also, where a debtor refers his creditor to another person thus, "If he says so and so, I will pay" such undertaking is obligatory (c) And where resting-owing of an account was referred to the debtor's oath, and he deponed that he believed his factor paid certain items, the Court ordered production of the factor's books, and on these not supporting the oath, decerned against the principal (d) In like manner, the creditors in a sequestration have been held bound by entries in a state of the bankrupt's affairs, made up by an accountant under their authority, admitting furnishings to the estate (e) So a party's cash and business books, prepared by his book-keeper, are in every-day practice received against him not merely as adminicles of evidence (f), but as his writ, proving facts which can only be established by writ or oath of party (g) And the same rule applies to books of a burgh, under the hand of the treasurer or other officer intrusted with the care of them (h)

(z) Lockhart v Mitchell, 1849, 11 D 1341 (a) See *supra* §§ 1386 7

(b) Royal Bank v Broughton, 1830 8 S, 424 (c) Burt v Palmer, 1804, 5 Esp, 145—Daniel v Pitt, 1807, 6 Esp 74—Lloyd v Willan 1794, 1 Esp 178—Williams v Innes 1808 1 Camp 365, and cases there cited—Hood v Reeve, 1828, 3 Car and Pa, 532 So held by the twelve judges in Warren Hastings trial noticed by Lord Ellenborough in Burt v Palmer *supra*, and Daniel v Pitt In the case last named the person to whom the party referred had died before the trial and his declaration made without an oath was allowed to be proved (d) Cooper v Hamilton, 1824, 2 S 728, affd, 2 W S, 59 See also Mackay v Ure, 1817 10 D 89—Same parties, 11 D 982, compared with Fyfe v Miller, 1837, 15 S 1188

(e) Buchanan v Mag of Dunfermline 1828, 7 S 35 (f) See *supra* § 1183, *et seq* (g) Black v Shand's Crs 1823, 2 S, 118—Knox v Martin, 1850, 12 D, 719—Berry's Reps v Wight 1822, 1 S 433 See *supra* §§ 342, 362

(h) Leslie v Mag of Brechin 15th Nov 1808 F C—Muirhead v Town of Haddington, 1748 (Kilkerran's Report), M 2507—Peebles v Town of Perth, 1626, M,

[1] Emslie v Alexander 1862, 1 Macph 209

[2] Hailes v Worman, 1861, 3 L T, 741—Baker and Adams v Scottish Sea Insurance Co, 1856, 18 D, 691

[3] The Royal Bank v Broughton, *supra* is to the effect that parties were held bound by an admission that "the Judges of the Court of Session considered that a certain question must be settled by the law of England," contained in a joint case But this was an admission of a matter of fact

§ 1471 When a person is liable for the dealings of another, as his agent, factor, or the like, he is also bound by whatever admissions or statements that person makes in so far as they form part of the *res gestæ* of his transactions (*i*) But he is not bound by the agent's subsequent admissions of what took place, so that, whenever a statement made by the agent, verbally or in writing, is a narrative *ex post facto* of the transaction in question, it will not be admitted as evidence against his principal (*k*) And, in like manner, admissions *ex post facto* by a principal do not bind his cautioner (*l*) This distinction is founded on the just principle that the party bound himself to implement whatever obligations his agent, or the person for whom he was cautioner, actually contracted, but not for those which he merely admitted that he contracted, and the rule is necessary in order to prevent collusion between the agent or the principal obligant and the party making the claim (*m*).

12,525—Mackenzie *v* Town of Elgin, 1693, 4 B Sup 54—Cases noted *supra*, § 1172, compared with Stuart *v* Mag of Edinburgh, 1697, M , 12 536

(*i*) So held as to an agent's admissions binding his principal, Reid *v* Stoddart, 1820, 2 Mur , 240—Mills *v* Albion Insur Co , 1826 4 Mur , 142—Aitchison *v* Robertson, 1846, 9 D , 15—Mackintosh *v* Pitcairn, 1851, 14 D , 187, see Clark's Trs *v* Hill, 1827, 4 Mur , 206, per L Ch -Com Adam ,—as to a letter by a money-broker being effectual against his employer , Mackintosh *v* Pitcairn, 1851, 14 D , 187 ,—as to a shipmaster's statements binding the owners, Cairns *v* Kippen, 1820, 2 Mur 250 ,—and the freighter, Wight *v* Liddell, 1829, 5 Mur , 43 ,—and as to statements of a messenger-at-arms binding his employer , Wight *v* Ewing, 1828, 4 Mur , 588 —a joint stock company being liable for their manager's admissions, National Exchange Co *v* Drew, 1850, 12 D , 950 (see also Ewing *v* Crichton, 1827, 4 Mur , 184),—a landlord being bound by his factor's admissions, contained in a fitted account delivered to the tenant , Ainslie *v* Chisholm, 1696, M , 12 626 ,—by the factor's books, Watson *v* Brown, 1710, M , 12,628, —and a state of rents prepared by him and delivered to the landlord , Mitchell *v* Berwick, 1815, 7 D , 382 But see *contra*, Ferguson *v* Bethune, 7th March 1811, F C , where entries of payments of interest by a factor in his accounts were held not to prove resting owing of a prescribed debt due by his employer The same principle holds in England , Howard *v* Tucker, 1831, 1 B and Ad , 712—Reg *v* Hall, 1838, 8 C and P 358—Emerson *v* Blonden, 1794, 1 Esp , 142—Fairlie *v* Hastings, 1804, 10 Ves , 123, and see *infra*, notes (*m*) and (*o*)

(*k*) So held as to admissions by an agent , Bruce *v* Beatt, 1765, M , 11,109—Fairlie *v* Hastings, 1804, 10 Ves , 123—Langhorn *v* Allnutt, *infra* (*m*)—Slimmack *v* Lock, 1825, 10 Moore, 39—Garth *v* Howard, 1832, 8 Bing , 451—Allen *v* Denstone, 1839, 8 Car and Pa , 760 ,—as to statements by a shipmaster tendered against the owners , M'Laren *v* Birk, 1829, 7 S , 483—Wight *v* Liddell, 1827, 4 Mur , 328 ,—statements by a ship's husband as against the owners , Duncan *v* Forbes, 1831, 9 S , 510

(*l*) Malvenius *v* Baillie, 1686, M , 12,161—Hunter *v* Carson, 1822, 3 Mur , 233—Evans *v* Beattie, *infra* (*m*)—Bacon *v* Chesney, 1816, 1 Stark R , 192—Longnecker *v* Hyde, 1813 (American), 6 Binney R , 1—*Contra*, Maxwell *v* Buchanan, 1776, M , "Apprentice," Appx No 1—Schaw *v* Wanse, 1683, M , 9351

(*m*) The distinction noticed in the text has been repeatedly stated by the English

The statement is also inadmissible from being hearsay evidence, whereas statements which form part of the *res gestæ* of the agent's or principal debtor's transactions do not lie under that objection (*n*)

§ 1472 In like manner, statements by a law-agent to the prejudice of his client cannot be used against the latter as admissions, unless they were connected with some act falling within the province of the agent (*o*)

§ 1473 But the distinction noticed in the preceding sections does not apply where a party intrusts the whole superintendence and conduct of a concern to a commissioner or general manager, the admissions of one who so fully represents his principal being evidence against the latter on matters relating to the concern (*p*)[3]

judges In Evans *v* Beattie 1803, 5 Esp 26, which was an action on a guarantee, Lord Ellenborough observed, "The engagement was to pay for such goods as should be delivered to Copper (the principal obligant), not what he should acknowledge to have received There might be collusion between the plaintiffs and Copper, the evidence offered is not the best the case is capable of" In Langhorn *v* Alnutt 1812 4 Taunt, 519, Gibbs, J, said, "When it is proved that A is agent of B whatever A does, or says, or writes, in the making of a contract as agent of B, is admissible in evidence, because it is part of the contract which he makes for B, and therefore binds B, but it is not admissible as his account of what passes The distinction is also stated in Wight *v* Liddell 1827, 4 Mur, 328, *supra*, and Fairlie *v* Hastings 1804 10 Vesey, 123—Taylor, 388 (*n*) See per L Ellenborough in Evans *v* Beattie, *supra* See also *supra*, § 92 (*o*) Forth Marine Insur Co *v* Burnes, 1848, 10 D 689, affd, 6 Bell's Ap Ca 564—Wallace *v* M'Kissock, 1829, 7 S, 542—Young *v* Wright, 1807, 1 Camp, 139—Wilson *v* Turner 1808, 1 Taunt, 398—Parkins *v* Hawkshaw, 1817, 2 Stark R, 239—Doe d Hulm *v* Richards 1845, 2 Car and Kir, 216, compared with Gellatly *v* Jones, 1851, 13 D 961, and *supra*, § 1388 (*p*) Smith *v* Falconer 1831, 9 S, 474 (see another branch of this case Smith *v* Maxwell 1833, 11 S, 323)—Campbell *v* Ballantyne, 1839, 1 D, 1061

[3] M'Grigor *v* M'Grigor, 1860, 22 D, 1264—where, in a question of prescription the writ of the debtor's factor was held to be the writ of the debtor The distinction is clearly stated in the opinion of the Lord President (M'Neill) 'It is not every agency or factory that will warrant us in holding that the party in whose favour the agency or factory is granted stands in the position of the debtor, or is entitled to make such an acknowledgment of liability as shall be binding upon the debtor It is settled that a general agency, and even that a factory in the ordinary sense of that term cannot confer a right to grant a writing which shall be held to be the writing of the original debtor On the other hand, if the debtor has put a certain party into his place—in his own position—as representative in the whole management of his affairs then that falls very much under the case of Campbell, which came to be a case in which that party is representative to the effect of being entitled to grant a writ which shall be held to be the writ of the principal" Lord Deas, referring to the case of Cullen *v* Smeal (1853, 15 D, 868, 1855, 17 D, 636) where his interlocutor as Lord Ordinary was acquiesced in, said that he did not hold there that the writ of a factor was, in the ordinary case, the writ of the party nor that the writ of an agent employed for general

§ 1474 A writing holograph of the creditor in a bill of exchange, acknowledging payment of interest, and found in the debtor's repositories was once regarded as equivalent to the debtor's writ under the act introducing the sexennial prescription, the Court considering that the debtor, by preserving the document, had made it his own writ (r) But although such a view might weigh with a jury in a case where presumptions and probabilities are admissible, it is, with deference, thought that the statute does not admit of such a construction of the words "writ of the debtor" (s)

§ 1475 The confession of one prisoner is not admissible as evidence against another (t)[4] This rule even applies to cases of theft and reset, where the confession by the thief is not an article of evidence against the resetter, and *vice versa* (v) Even in cases of conspiracy any statement by one prisoner which is either a narrative of measures already taken or a confession of the crime charged, cannot be used against a co-conspirator (x) On the other hand, all words uttered or documents issued by one conspirator in furtherance of the common design, and those which accompany acts of that description, and so form part of the *res gestæ*, may be used against all the other prisoners, provided there be *prima facie* proof that they engaged in the plot (y) The judge may also for the sake

(r) Wood v Howden, 1843, 5 D, 507—See also Scott v Douglas, 1737, M, 12,616 Elch 'Prescription,' No 12, S C (s) See this case noticed *supra*, § 450

(t) Milroy, 1839, Bell's Notes, 291—*Supra*, § 1428—1 Phill, 413—Taylor 613—Roscoe Cr Ev, 54 (v) R v Turner, 1832, 1 Moo Cr Ca, 347

(x) R v Hardy, 1794, 24 St Tr, 451—R v Blake, 1844, 6 Ad and Ell, N S, 126—Taylor, 383 But see per L Ellenborough in R v Watson, 32 St Tr, 352, where his Lordship said he would not consider himself concluded by the decision in Hardy's case (y) *Supra*, § 93—R v Stone, 1796 25 St Tr, 1277—R v M'Kenna,

purposes was the writ of the party, but that a party might give a written power, or delegate his power to another, in such terms as would make the writ of that other his or her writ The authority of the factor to act is to be deduced from the terms of the mandate, but in cases of nicety, the Court are not precluded from looking to the surrounding circumstances,—to the age and inability of the principal party to do anything and to the fact that the agent is allowed to do everything

[4] It was held, however, by a majority of the Court of Justiciary, that when a question is put by an officer to one of two persons at the time of apprehending them on a joint charge, the answer to such question may competently be put in evidence against the other when made in his hearing and without contradiction by him But Lord Handyside was of opinion seeing that the statements in question had been made after the apprehension of the other panel, that no obligation lay upon that panel to contradict them The statements stood substantially in the position of statements made in one prisoner's declaration—which could not be admitted as evidence against another, Lewis v Blair 1858, 3 Irv, 16 This view appears more consistent with the equitable rule adopted both here and in England, *infra* § 1483

of convenience, admit proof of statements by one prisoner as evidence against the others before the latter have been shown to be implicated in the conspiracy But this lies in the discretion of the judge, who will caution the jury that the evidence is received in anticipation of the prosecutor bringing the conspiracy home to the persons against whom it is adduced (*z*)

§ 1476 On the same principle, in the trial of Lord Melville for misapplying public money (*a*), a certificate and written acknowledgment by his Lordship's paymaster, having been tendered for the prosecutors, was admitted as evidence of the fact that the money had been drawn by that individual in the ordinary course of his business, but the Lord Chancellor (Eldon) observed, "But whether the money thus issued ever reached the noble Lord, or whether, having reached him, he made any criminal misapplication of it, is a question which it is impossible to suppose that the fact of this receipt by the paymaster can establish, and, therefore, in allowing this receipt to be read, nothing is proved but that this sum was issued out of the Exchequer to Mr Douglas (the paymaster), he having authority and power to receive it under the power of attorney from Lord Melville The receipt by the paymaster would in itself involve him civilly, but could by no possibility convict him of a crime"

§ 1477 In a case where two prisoners were tried for stealing bank notes, and a third, charged with resetting them was fugitated for not appearing, statements made by him, and a letter which he wrote in London in the act of passing one of the notes, were admitted to the effect of identifying the party as one whose house the panels used to frequent, and with the view of tracing the note from the possession of one of the panels to the writer of the letter (*b*)

§ 1478 The confession of one prisoner may always be read to the jury, however much it may implicate the others, but the Court will direct the jury to disregard it as evidence against any but the prisoner who emitted it (*c*)

1842, Irish Circ Rep, 461, per Pennefather, C J —Taylor, 381—1 Phill, 413 See also Hamilton, 1833 Bell's Notes, 291, where in a trial of a resetter the prosecutor was allowed to prove that the thief, in coming out of the prisoner's shop (where he had been with the stolen goods, for the purpose of selling them), had said that he had left them

(*z*) See Taylor 381 (*a*) Lord Melville's case, 1806, 29 St Tr 763

(*b*) Burnett, 1851 J Shaw, 497 (*c*) A striking illustration of this common practice occurred in R *v* Mannings, noted *supra* § 286

CHAPTER VIII.—IMPLIED ADMISSIONS AND CONFESSIONS

§ 1479. Admissions and confessions may be implied from a party's conduct, and they are sometimes involved in his pleadings. Those implied from conduct arise wherever a party, by either acting or abstaining, leads another to believe that he means to acknowledge a fact to his prejudice. They are therefore different from mere indications of a consciousness of such a fact, which often come involuntarily from those whose intention it is to deny it (*a*).

§ 1480. Admissions may be implied from a party remaining silent when statements to his prejudice are made in his presence (*b*). And a party has been allowed to put in a letter written by himself, in order to show that he made, without contradiction, the statements which it contains (*c*). In England, however, it has been held that not answering a letter is not an implied admission, as a person is not bound to reply to every letter written him (*d*).

§ 1481. Much caution and discrimination are required in regard to this kind of evidence (*e*). Thus, on the one hand, where a party to whom furnishings had been made had used the articles, and, on an account being rendered had made a partial payment, and had been repeatedly pressed to pay the balance without having objected to the rates of charge,—in an action raised two years and a half after the account had been rendered he was not allowed to object to the items (*f*). So where an account for work done in surveying

---

(*a*) Among inferences of the latter class are those springing from fear and attempts at flight (see *supra*, §§ 274, 5), from fabrication or suppression of documents, from falsehood and prevarication, or refusal to answer on examination before a magistrate (see *supra*, §§ 1417, 1428). The distinction noticed in the text has not been sufficiently adverted to by text writers. For example, both Mr Greenleaf (vol. i, § 196) and Mr Taylor (vol. i, p. 535) treat suppression of documents as an implied admission that their contents are deemed unfavourable by the party suppressing them; whereas such acts indicate only a consciousness or belief, not an admission, that the documents are of that nature.

(*b*) Mannel *v.* Fraser, 1818, 1 Mur., 389—Hall *v.* Otto, 1818, *ib.*, 444—Hay *v.* Boyd, 1822, 3 Mur., 13—Campbell *v.* Macfarlane, 1840 (2nd exception), 2 D., 663—Macf. Pr., 212. The same rule applies when the statement is in presence of the party's accredited agent; Mannel *v.* Fraser, *supra*—Smith *v.* Maxwell, *infra* (*g*)—Macf. Pr., *ib.*; see *supra*, § 1471, 3.

(*c*) Hamilton *v.* Hope, 1827, 4 Mur., 239, per L. Ch.-Commissioner.

(*d*) Fairlie *v.* Denton, 1828, 3 Car. and P., 103, per L. Tenterden—Short *v.* Stoy, 1836, per Alderson, B., noted in Rosc. Nisi Pr. Ev., 46—See also R. *v.* Plumer, 1814, Russ. and Ry., 265.

(*e*) See Taylor, 373, *et seq.*—Best's Pr. of Ev., § 503.

(*f*) George *v.* Scott, 1832, 10 S., 443.

operations in a stone quarry had been rendered to the factor for the proprietor and had been retained by him for seven years without any special objection and where the general facts of employment and attendance were admitted, the Court assumed that the particular items were correctly charged (*g*) In this case Lord Craigie observed, with the concurrence of the other judges, "It is a principle in mercantile practice and it should be extended to a case like this that if an account is rendered and retained for a long time without objection it is held to be right" This principle has been repeatedly followed in England (*h*) Thus, also, where a person had acted as attorney for a proprietor over his estate in Jamaica from 1803 to 1814, during which time he had transmitted to his principal monthly and annual accounts of his expenditure and drawn bills for balances due to him, which bills the principal had paid, in an action raised by the principal in 1815 the Court held him barred by acquiescence from investigating the items of the accounts (*i*) In another case the chief circumstances from which the Court inferred repayment of £1000 lent by one brother to another were that no claim for either principal or interest had been made for twenty years, and that the alleged creditor had made up or acquiesced in a state of accounts with his brother, which brought out a considerable balance against himself (*k*)

§ 1482 In like manner, when a person objects only to certain items of an account rendered, it will be presumed that he admits the others to be correct (*l*) But this inference will not be drawn where the objections are general, and certain items are specified by way of example (*m*) Again, in criminal cases the silence of a party, when charged directly with guilt is admissible, as indicating a tacit confession, the reason being that an innocent person would probably not permit such an allegation to be made in his presence without contradicting it (*n*) But the mere circumstance that a

---

(*g*) Smith *v* Maxwell, 1833, 11 S, 324 (*h*) Willis *v* Jernegan, 1741, 2 Atk, 252—Tickel *v* Short, 1751, 2 Ves Sen 239—Sherman *v* Sherman, 1692, 2 Vern, 276 It was here held that not objecting to an account by a second or third post implies an allowance of it This however, is too strong an inference for the facts to bear Nor is an Irish decision entitled to much weight in which it was laid down that, while not objecting to accounts delivered by hand implies acquiescence, it is otherwise when they have been sent by post, Price *v* Ramsay 2 Jebb and Symes, 338

(*i*) M'Arthur *v* M'Arthur, 1821, 1 S, 39 (Session Papers) See also Rose *v* M'Leay, 1830, 8 D, 1037, affd 2 Sh and M'L, 958 (*k*) Ryrie *v* Ryrie, 1840, 2 D, 1210 (*l*) Chisman *v* Count 1841, 2 Man and Gr, 307 (*m*) Phillpots *v* Lac 1847, 9 D, 1127 (*n*) Burnett 602—2 Al 518—Alexander, 1838, 2 Swin 110—Moran, 1836 1 ib, 231 See *supra* § 1451

person listens in silence to a conversation between two other persons in which his guilt is alleged, although it may be admitted as part of his conduct in relation to the charge (*o*), cannot be regarded as an implied confession by him, for one is not bound to interfere on such an occasion, and silence is not inconsistent either with a determination to deny the charge, or with a consciousness of innocence (*p*). In like manner, a party's silence during conversations between third persons in his presence will probably not be admitted against him in a civil case as an implied admission (*r*).

§ 1483. The principle adverted to in the preceding section, that silence does not imply assent, when contradiction is not fairly to be expected has been repeatedly recognised in England, where depositions taken in the presence of a party during a judicial examination, observations made by a magistrate to the parties before him, and confessions of an accomplice criminating his co-prisoner before the justices will not, in any subsequent trial, whether civil or criminal, be evidence against the party who heard in silence, because in judicial inquiries a regularity of proceeding is adopted, which prevents a person from interfering when and how he pleases, as he naturally would do in a common conversation" (*s*). A party's silence will be of no moment in a civil case when a statement to his prejudice is made by one who has no interest in the matter in dispute, and even in a criminal case the impertinent interference of a stranger may be best rebuked by silence (*t*). But it cannot be said that the circumstance is inadmissible in either case.

§ 1484. In all matters of this nature, however, much more depends on the disposition of the individual affected by the statement, than on the nature of the statement itself, or the circumstances under which it was made. Some persons will not hear any remark to their prejudice without being roused to an angry reply, while a far stronger statement would be received in haughty or indifferent silence by a man of cooler temper. Loquacity and reserve, courage

---

(*o*) Authorities in preceding note. (*p*) Taylor, 541.

(*r*) See Moore v. Smith, 1826, 14 Sergeant and Rawles R. 388, where in an action as to the boundaries of a certain property, the premises were viewed by the jury, on which occasion a neighbouring proprietor was one of the chain-bearers, and statements made in his presence by the litigants were not denied by him; it was held by the Supreme Court of Pennsylvania that these could not be used against the party as implied admissions, in a subsequent action regarding his own property. See also Taylor, 541.

(*s*) Taylor, 541—Melen v. Andrews, 1829, Moo. and Mal., 336—R. v. Appleby, 1821, 3 Stark. R., 33—Child v. Grace, 1825, 2 Car. and Pa., 193—Short v. Stoy, per Alderson, B., cited in Rosc. Nisi Pr. Ev. 46. (*t*) Child v. Grace, *supra*.

and timidity, love of display and modesty or pride, lead to such opposite conduct under similar circumstances, that guilt cannot be safely inferred from a person's silence on hearing a statement to his prejudice; for the jury almost never have sufficient information regarding his disposition, to enable them to judge what his conduct, if innocent or guilty, would likely be under the circumstances. In criminal cases, indeed, silence frequently proceeds from strong consciousness of innocence, while the most indignant and solemn denials are every day heard from the lips of the guilty.

§ 1485. The pleadings of a party sometimes involve an admission. In civil cases, for example, a defence of compensation or payment implies an admission that the debt was originally constituted. A denial that certain goods purchased were delivered, implies an admission that the price has not been paid (u). Homologation may imply an admission that the right was not valid in itself. And where a tenant claiming the value of ameliorations under a clause in his lease had got them valued on application to the Sheriff, and afterwards raised action in the Sheriff-court for the value of them, and where the landlord pleaded several grounds of defence but did not deny that the ameliorations had been made; in an advocation, in which the record was closed in the inferior court, he was not allowed to have the record opened up in order to add a new defence denying the ameliorations (x). But it is competent for a party to plead 1st, the triennial or sexennial prescription, which imports a denial of the constitution and subsistence of the obligation; and, 2d, compensation or discharge; the second defence being pleaded on the supposition that the party may fail in making good the first (y). And as already shown (z) a plea of homologation is not necessarily inconsistent with a denial of any defect in the right in question. The difficulty of dealing with such cases arises from a party having to plead all his defences at once. This not unfrequently requires a prejudicial and a subsidiary plea to be stated at the same time; the proper way to proceed in such cases being to dispose first of the former, and, only in the event of its being repelled, to enter on the consideration of the latter (a). If, however, a subsidiary defence, such as homologation, discharge

(u) Kidd v. Brown 1828 6 S. 825.

(x) Fraser v. Mackay 11 S. 391.

(y) See on this supra, § 108.

(z) See supra § 865.

(a) See this fully illustrated by Lord Just.-Clerk in Alcock v. Easson 1842 5 D. 366, supra § 108.

or compensation, is pleaded alone, the prejudicial fact of invalidity in the right homologated, or of constitution of the debt as the case may be, will be assumed

§ 1486 In criminal cases, also, a party may sometimes plead a defence which involves an admission In a charge of rape, for example, the defence that the woman consented, is an admission that connection took place, and in a charge of murder, the defence of accident provocation, self defence or acting in discharge of duty usually implies that the prisoner caused the death of the sufferer In such a case, however the prisoner might plead, 1st that death was not caused by the wounds inflicted on the occasion, or that the deceased injured himself in a scuffle between the parties and, 2d that any wound which the prisoner might have inflicted was justifiable And in a case of rape, the prisoner might deny the connection, but plead that the woman allowed him to use indecent liberties with her person The special defence ought therefore to be framed with caution so as to avoid any admission beyond what is necessarily involved in the plea, and it should be prefaced by a general plea of ' not guilty ' At the same time, the Court would not likely hold a prisoner foreclosed from his general defence, in consequence of an implied admission which may have been made by his counsel on an erroneous impression of what the witnesses for the Crown would establish

For further illustration of this subject reference must be made to works on pleading and practice, as a detailed commentary on it is beyond the scope of this treatise [5]

CHAPTER IX —QUALIFIED ADMISSIONS

§ 1487 When an admission is made under a qualification, the party who founds on it must take it as it stands and he may not adduce the portion which is favourable to him, and exclude the re-

[5] The effect of not calling a party as a witness at a trial was considered in M Ewan v Cotching, 1857, 27 L J (Exch), 42 It was there laid down that, although where there is no evidence to affect a defendant, the mere fact that he is not called as a witness will not be sufficient to sustain a verdict against him, yet if there is a certain amount of evidence against him (as an implied admission on his part), then the circumstance that he is not called to explain it may be enough to turn the scale, and sustain the verdict

mander (*a*) And this is the rule, although the qualification is one which, if occurring in an oath on reference, would be held to be extrinsic (*b*) [1] But the party founding on the admission is not tied down to the qualification No doubt where his only proof is the admission as qualified he will fail, if the qualification is an answer to his claim (*c*) But he may disprove the qualification, and found

(*a*) Anderson *v* Rintoul 1825, 3 S, 496, same parties 5 S, 741—Forbes *v* Milne, 1827 6 S, 75—Campbell *v* M'Cartney, 1843, 14 D 1086—Cases in following notes

(*b*) So held as to an admission that a debt was constituted qualified by an admission that it was paid, Gray *v* Monro 1829 8 S, 221—Grierson *v* Thomson, 1830, ib, 817,—and as to a qualification of compensation, Milne *v* Donaldson, 1852 14 D, 849 (But see *contra*, Sibbald *v* Fraser, 1837, 15 S, 591—Murray *v* Elliot, 1837, 15 S, 1141 The opinion expressed by Lord Jeffrey in the note to his interlocutor in this case would now be held erroneous) So held as to a qualification that the money of which repayment was claimed had been received to extinguish a debt Carnegy *v* Carnegy, 1825, 3 S, 366—See also Buist *v* Lyon, 1838, 1 D, 238—Chalmers *v* Chalmers, 1845, 7 D, 865 The difference in this respect between admissions and oaths on reference arises from the latter being conclusive not only against the deponent but also in his favour, and against the party referring Accordingly, this privilege of the deponent requires to be restricted to qualifications which are intrinsic to the question referred to his oath See the chapter on Qualified Oaths, *infra*

(*c*) As in Campbell *v* Scotland 1778, M, 9530—Hariot *v* Cunningham 1791, M

[1] The executor of a commission-agent after some correspondence with a party who had employed the deceased from time to time to sell potatoes, and who admitted and offered to pay a balance brought out in certain accounts rendered to him by the agent before his death, but only on condition of the executor's admitting that these accounts were correct and continued all the unsettled transactions between the parties as principal and agent, in reference to potatoes,—refused to accept payment on this footing and raised an action for payment of the admitted sum, reserving all other claims The Court found that he was not entitled to found upon the admission to the effect of obtaining decree, without acceding to the condition Had the action, indeed, been one of count and reckoning, in which the whole accounting between the parties would have come to be exhausted, and in which a judicial admission had been made similar to the extrajudicial admission here founded on the question would have arisen, Whether that admission was to be construed as virtually an admission that there would be, in any event, a balance due for which the pursuer was entitled to interim decree? Bilsborough *v* Bosomworth, 1861, 24 D, 109, and cases there cited A party deceased had entered in his ledger a sum of £50, as cash lent to William Dowdy His trustees having demanded payment received in reply a letter, saying, ' Whatever I got I received as a present, with a hearty welcome as a gift " The Court held that the writing did not instruct the subsistence of the alleged loan, the admission and qualification being read together Lord Ivory observed that there was this marked difference between writ and oath, " that the extrinsic qualities have been found to be necessarily adjected as part of the writ whereas they may be rejected in reference to oath You must take the writ as it is " But Lord Deas declined to give any opinion whether there might not be questions of extrinsic and intrinsic in writings " I rather think that such distinction has been given effect to in questions of prescription, but I do not wish to give any opinion upon the subject '—Dowdy *v* Graham 1859, 22 D 181

on the admission when freed from it (*d*) And if the qualifying statement is incredible, or improbable in the circumstances, the Court may disregard it, although the proof does not directly contradict it (*e*)

§ 1488 As already mentioned a party cannot found on entries on the debit side of his opponent's books, without taking also those on the credit side (*f*) But where the entries on the debit and credit side of the account kept by a bank with its customer were contained in different books, the Court held that while the former were evidence against the bank, the latter were not full proof in its favour of the advances a distinction being drawn between such a case and that of a continuous account containing opposite entries (*g*)

The effect of qualified admissions in proving debts which fall under the short prescriptions has been noticed in a previous chapter (*h*)

CHAPTER X —OF THE PROBATIVE VALUE OF ADMISSIONS AND CONFESSIONS

§ 1489 In probative value evidence of admissions and confessions admits of the greatest variety In estimating its weight two points require attention, viz —1st, the medium through which the supposed admission or confession comes before the jury, and, 2d,

---

12,405—Carnegy *v* Carnegy 1825, 3 S 566—Berry *v* Murdoch, 1822, 1 S, 828—Gall *v* Fordyce 1828, 6 S, 943—Gray *v* Monro, 1829, 8 S, 221—Grierson *v* Thomson, 1830, ib, 317—Kait *v* Galloway 1833, 12 S 131—Campbell *v* Arrott, 1835 13 S, 557—Lockerby *v* Stirling, 1835 ib, 978—Bust *v* Lyon 1838 1 D, 238—Chalmers *v* Chalmers 1845, 7 ib, 865—Scott *v* M'Cartney 1843, 14 ib 1086—Milne *v* Donaldson, 1852, 14 D, 849

(*d*) As in Anderson *v* Rintoul, 1827 3 S, 496, and 5 S, 744—Stephen *v* Pirie, 1832 10 S, 279—Miller *v* Oliphant, 1845, 7 D 283—Couper *v* Young, 1849 12 D, 190

(*e*) This seems to have been the ground on which the Court proceeded in Watson *v* Paul, 1831, 9 S 685, and Mag of Nairn *v* M'Intosh, 1830, 8 ib, 432—See also Sibbald *v* Fraser, 1837, 15 S, 591

(*f*) Sutherland *v* Johnstone, 1684, 2 B Sup 89, 4 ib, 74, S C—M'Kay *v* Ure, 1847, 10 D 89—Campbell *v* M'Cartney, 1843, 14 D, 1086—See also Lockerby *v* Stirling, 1835, 13 S 978

(*g*) British Linen Co *v* Thomson, 1853 15 D 314 This decision is thought to be questionable See Lord Fullerton's opinion

(*h*) *Supra*, §§ 408, 413, *et seq* 596 *et seq*

the motives which may have induced the party to make it, and the circumstances under which it may have been emitted (*a*)

§ 1490. When the admission or confession is made on record or in a document written by the party, there cannot, of course, be any doubt upon the first point Nor is there much risk of a judicial examination or a prisoner's declaration containing admissions which the party did not intend to make Yet it may happen that from his statement not having been taken down in the precise words in which he uttered it, its precise meaning may be misconceived and an intentional mis-statement of it is not impossible

§ 1491 There is, however, need of great caution in weighing evidence of *oral* admissions and confessions The jury ought always to be satisfied of the opportunity for observation, the accuracy and memory, as well as the veracity, of the witness testifying to the expression, before they attach any weight whatever to his evidence (*b*) It very frequently happens not only that the witness has misunderstood what the party has said, but that by unintentionally altering a few of the expressions really used he gives an effect to the statement completely at variance with what the party really did say" (*c*) A portion only of the statement may have been heard and important qualifications been unnoticed or forgotten And it sometimes happens that the party and the witness attached different meanings to an ambiguous or inaccurate expression, an accident of which there is considerable risk when either of them

---

(*a*) On this subject see Bentham Rat of Judic Ev, b v, ch 6, sect 2—Taylor, 477, 579—1 Phill 397—Best, Pr of Ev, 610, *et seq*—Wills on Circ Ev 61—Joy on Confessions (American) 100-9

(*b*) A good illustration of the inaccuracy of witnesses in repeating expressions occurred in R *v* Simons, 1834 6 Car and Pa 540 where a prisoner was indicted for arson, which was then a capital crime A witness swore to having overheard him say to his wife " Keep yourself to yourself and don't marry again " and another witness, called to corroborate the evidence stated the words to be ' Keep yourself to yourself, and keep your own counsel " Baron Alderson justly observed, ' One of these expressions is widely different from the other It shows how little reliance ought to be placed on such evidence "

(*c*) *Per* Parke in Earle *v* Picken, 1833, 5 Car and Pa, 542 note In Resp *v* Fields, 1823, Peck's (Tenessee) R, 140, it was observed by the Court, ' How easy it is for the hearer to take one word for another, or to take a word in a sense not intended by the speaker, and for want of an exact representation of the tone of voice, emphasis, countenance eye, manner, and action of the one who made the confession how almost impossible is it to make third persons understand the exact state of his mind and meaning For these reasons such evidence is received with great distrust, and under apprehensions for the wrong it may do —See also *per* L Ch-Commissioner in Hyslop *v* Miller 1816 1 Mur 53

understood it in a provincial sense (*d*). Another risk of error on this head arises from the witness stating his inference from the words used by the party, instead of repeating them *verbatim* (*e*). It is therefore always important to bring out as nearly as possible the very expressions which were used; and any such general statement as that the party confessed or admitted, ought to be disregarded.

§ 1492. Evidence of oral admissions is also easily fabricated, and the chance of detecting its untruth is small; for when all that a witness speaks to is an independent statement, his falsehood is almost beyond the reach of cross-examination and is seldom contradictory to the proved circumstances attending the crime. Peculiar caution is always necessary when the person repeating the supposed confession is an officer engaged in the pursuit of criminals, for such persons are apt to be biassed witnesses, and to attribute a guilty meaning to ambiguous and even to harmless acts and words, of persons whom they apprehend.

§ 1493. An admission when clearly proved to have been made, is in general good evidence, for it is more likely to have proceeded from the natural dictates of truth than to have been either an intentional fabrication, or an unfounded statement made at random. Its value will, of course, increase with the importance of the fact admitted, and of the occasion when the admission was made. And, for this reason, admissions on record are justly ranked as full proof, both in civil and criminal cases. Extrajudicial confessions also (if distinctly proved), are usually entitled to much weight, and strong

(*d*) See this illustrated in Bent Jud Ev, b 1, ch 10 (vol 1, p 172 ed 1827). In a case cited by him from Voltaire's 'Essai sur les Probabilités en fait de Justice" (Œuvres de Voltaire, tom 30, p 421, ed Gotha, 1786), a party was charged with murder and robbery and being confronted with one who had witnessed the murder the witness said that the prisoner was not the assassin. On this the accused cried out '*Dieu soit loué! en voici un qui ne m'a pas reconnu!*' The judge interpreted these words as a confession, thinking that they signified, *Je suis coupable, et on ne m'a pas reconnu*. The meanings of the expressions were very different; yet chiefly on this supposed confession the prisoner was condemned. Some days afterwards a felon, executed for another crime, confessed the act.

(*e*) For example, a woman was once indicted for stealing a shawl from her grandmother, and a policeman swore that on being apprehended and charged by him with the offence, "she confessed." But on cross examination he stated that the prisoner merely said "she had taken the shawl." The grandmother swore that the article was taken by the prisoner, but added that it was not stolen, and the prisoner was accordingly acquitted on the defence that she had not abstracted the article with the felonious intent, E Dow, Perth Spring Circuit, 1850, not reported.

corroborative evidence will not be required to complete the proof of guilt The peculiar value of confessional evidence lies in its furnishing the best proof of the intention, which constitutes the essence of most crimes

§ 1494 Yet admissions and confessions being, like other human actions governed by the laws of motive, are subject to the risk of intentional falsehood (*f*) and they sometimes arise from idiosyncracies of character or temporary aberration. There are several recorded instances of confessions made falsely, in the belief that the evidence of guilt was conclusive, and that a confession would procure a mitigated punishment (*g*) In a trial in England for setting fire to a stack of hay, when that was a capital crime, it was proved that the prisoner had been near the spot between two and three in the morning when the fire occurred, and had shortly afterwards stated to a policeman whom he met that he had raised the fire But on being taken before the magistrate, he exhibited appearances of derangement, and it was then ascertained that he had been pre-

(*f*) Yet false confessions have been emitted where no motive could be discovered See cases of Parry, 14 How St Tr 1312—Sharp Ann Reg for 1833 Chron 74—A B, in 1580 in Paris, Bonnier, Tr de Preuves § 256 These cases are all noted in Best Pr of Ev , § 540

(*g*) Sir Samuel Romilly (see his Memoirs, vol ii, p 182) mentions an instance of this in the trial of Thomas Wood on a charge of mutiny and murder aboard ship The case for the prosecution was proved by one witness, who swore positively to the prisoner's identity, but whose evidence could not have been of much value, as the prisoner had been only sixteen years old at the date of the alleged crime which occurred nine years before the trial The only other evidence against the prisoner was a written defence, which was a supplication for mercy, implying an admission of guilt The prisoner was convicted and executed, although, in the meantime, his brother and sister offered to prove by incontestable evidence that he had not been on board of the vessel at the time The youth had employed a person to write a defence for him, and had read it in the hope that it would excite compassion, and so serve him better than a denial of guilt In a case of murder which occurred in America, there was pretty strong circumstantial evidence against the prisoners, including proof of motive, of violence, of the absence of the person supposed to have been murdered, and of the discovery near the spot of some bones supposed to be those of a man On this proof, combined with a deliberate confession by the prisoners they were convicted and sentenced to death But a reprieve having been granted and a reward offered for the discovery of the missing person, he returned home in the interval He had fled for fear that the prisoners would kill him The bones were those of some animal The prisoners had been induced by misjudging friends to confess, in the belief that the proof would convict them but that a penitential confession might obtain a commutation of the capital sentence, case of Boorns, September 1819, mentioned in 1 Greenl , § 214, and in Wills's Circ Ev , 63 In another case a prisoner confessed a murder under the influence of a promise of pardon The confession was not received, and the supposed victim was afterwards found to be alive, Trial for murder of Mr Harrison noted in 1 Leach Cr Ca , 264

viously charged with some offence, and acquitted on the ground of insanity. On his trial he pleaded not guilty, and stated that he had been liberated about a year before, after two years' confinement in a lunatic asylum, that his mind had been wandering for some time, and that in a moment of delirium, he had made the groundless charge against himself. At the same time, he said, that rather than be acquitted on the ground of insanity, which would probably cause him to be immured in an asylum for the rest of his life, he would retract his plea of not guilty, and would plead guilty to the charge. Mr Justice Williams in summing up remarked, that there was no evidence against the prisoner except his own confession, and that it lay with the jury to say whether they believed that to be true, or to be the effect of aberration. The prisoner was acquitted (*h*).

§ 1495. Among motives which may induce false confessions are the desire to favour the escape of a friend (*i*), or to shield from punishment and disgrace a person of station in the hope of a reward (*k*).[1] In a French case, two women in great poverty falsely confessed a capital crime in order to obtain for the children of one of

(*h*) R. *v.* Wilson, 1844, noted in Will's on Circ. Ev., 67.

(*i*) In one case a party made a false confession in order to allow his guilty brothers to escape, and afterwards proved an *alibi*, case noted in Joy on Confessions (American), 107, and Taylor, 581, note.

(*k*) It is said that in China there are persons who will confess crime for this purpose on being sufficiently remunerated, Bonnier, Tr. de Preuves, § 256.

[1] One of the most remarkable cases of voluntary confession that have occurred of late years was that of William Roupell. Roupell, who was the illegitimate son of a gentleman of large property in England, occupied a fair position in society and was at one time Member of Parliament for a metropolitan burgh. At the trial of an action brought by the eldest legitimate son of his father, to recover a certain portion of his father's landed estate which had been sold, Roupell appeared in the witness-box and deponed that various deeds bearing to have been granted by his father in his favour, and under which the property in question had been conveyed by him to the purchaser were not the genuine writs of his father, but had been forged by himself. After his evidence had been given, a juror was withdrawn, and the case compromised. Roupell was immediately apprehended, was tried for the forgery, convicted on his own confession, and sentenced to a long period of penal servitude. In a subsequent action at the instance of his brother against a party who had purchased another part of the estate, and who held on the same title, Roupell was again adduced as a witness, and repeated the evidence which he had previously given. On this occasion the jury were discharged, having been unable to agree upon a verdict. Had they believed his evidence they would necessarily have returned a verdict for the pursuer, so that a certain number of the jurors must have been of opinion that the confession which he had emitted, and on which he had been convicted, was unworthy of credit.

them the provision secured by law to orphans (*l*) *Tedium vitæ* (*m*), love of notoriety, and personal vanity, have produced the same result (*n*) And it is easy to suppose that a felon or a conspirator might falsely boast of his crimes to his admiring associates, as licentious men sometimes narrate their imaginary triumphs of gallantry The risk of admissions being made falsely in order to annull or dissolve marriage is so great, that, as already noticed, admissions on record in actions for that purpose are disregarded and extrajudicial admissions require to be weighed scrupulously (*o*)

§ 1496 It is not necessary now, as it would have been a hundred and fifty years ago (*r*), to expose the utter worthlessness of confessions wrung from an accused person by the torture (*s*) Nor are the records of our criminal courts likely to be again darkened by charges of witchcraft (*t*), many of which were in olden times proved by the admissions of the accused—a striking illustration of the effect of excited imagination, and morbid desire of notoriety in producing false confessions

§ 1497 A person may make an admission or confession in consequence of error Of this nature was a case where a girl had died in convulsions when her father was beating her severely for a theft, and he fully believed he had caused her death but it turned out, on dissection, that she had poisoned herself on finding that she had been discovered (*u*) And a person may, by misuse of terms, confess that he committed robbery, when his crime only amounted to theft, or, in the agony of distress at having killed another through carelessness, might cry out "I have murdered him!"

(*l*) Case of Maria Schoning and Anna Harlin, *Causes Célebres Etrangères* (Paris 1827), vol i, p 200 One of the prisoners was executed The other died on the scaffold in grief and excitement at witnessing the death of her friend

(*m*) After the great fire in London a person named Hubert was convicted and executed on his own confession of having set the first house on fire The only way of accounting for his confession, which was believed by the Lord Chief-Justice to be false was to suppose him weary of life, Clarendon's Life (ed 1824) vol iii, 94, Wills's Circ Ev 63

(*n*) See Bent Jud Ev, b v, ch 6, § 2 (3)—Best Pr of Ev § 549

(*o*) See *supra* §§ 1391, 1446

(*r*) Torture was abolished in Scotland by 7 Anne, c 21 In 1628 it was held to be illegal in England, after having been often applied by eminent judges, including Lords Coke and Bacon, R *v* Felton 3 How St Tr, 371—Taylor 598

(*s*) On the use of torture see 2 Hume, 323—Taylor, 598, 9—*Supra*, § 288

(*t*) See some curious instances of this collected in Best Pr of Ev, 649 notes Those which occurred in Scotland (so late as 1678) are taken from the original trials in Arnot's Cr Tr 347, *et seq*, and Pitcairn's Cr Tr vol i, part 2, p 49, and vol iii, p 602

(*u*) Case mentioned in Beck's Med Jurisp 766

§ 1498 But while the possibility of falsehood in admissions and confessions, from the causes thus noticed, ought to make juries cautious in receiving such evidence, the risk of its being untrue ought not to be exaggerated That confessions have been discovered to be false in some exceptional cases, is no reason for an indiscriminate distrust of all evidence from this source The proper use of such cases is to point the judge and jury to the possible causes of danger, in order that the true character of the supposed confession in each case may be ascertained If, on careful investigation, the statement is found to be distinctly sworn to by an accurate and credible witness, to be free from any appearance of disturbing motive or misconception in the party, and to be in unison with the other evidence in the case, it ought to receive effect as evidence of a highly trustworthy character (*x*)

(*x*) See Taylor, 581—Best Pr of Ev, 656—Wills on Circ Ev, 64—1 Hoffman's Course of Legal Study, 367

TITLE III

GENERAL RULES AS TO THE OATHS OF THE PARTIES TO THE CAUSE

---

§ 1499 The broad rule which till recently excluded parties as witnesses was modified in some cases, so as to allow them to be examined on oath *in causa* The recent statute admitting party witnesses has not abolished any of these oaths, although it has in a great measure obviated the necessity for them

Oaths of parties (like statements by them without oath) may be divided into those which are emitted by a party in favour of himself, and those in which he is examined at the instance of his adversary The former class includes oaths *in litem*, oaths in supplement, and affidavits The latter includes oaths of calumny and oaths on reference Before discussing these kinds of evidence separately some rules applicable to them all will be considered.

§ 1500 It is, of course, essential to the competency of all oaths that the party be sane when he is examined Accordingly, although it is not a sufficient objection to a reference to oath that the party is advanced in life, and that age has impaired his understanding and memory, where it is not said that he is *non compos mentis* (*a*), yet if a party labours under such morbid delusions, or such loss of memory, that he is unfit to distinguish and remember facts, he will not be examined, or if examined, his deposition will be ordered to be withdrawn (*b*) The Court once allowed investi-

---

(*a*) Nicholson v. M'Alister, 1829, 7 S., 743 Here the Court repelled the objection that the party was "in an advanced stage of life, and his faculties so much impaired as neither to be distinct in recollection nor in apprehension of facts and their bearing"

(*b*) See Campbell v. Arrott 1836, 14 S., 505—See also M'Ilwham v. Kerr 1823, 2 S 240—Riley v. M'Laren 1853 16 D 323—See *supra* § 1407

gation where it was alleged that the commissioner appointed to take a party's oath on reference had collusively and falsely reported that the party was not in a fit state of mind to be examined and had refused to take down the answers which had been emitted (*c*)

§ 1501 The oaths of deaf and dumb persons may be taken, provided they understand the nature of an oath, and can observe, remember, and communicate facts They may be examined on written questions and answers or by a sworn interpreter through the medium of signs (*d*)

§ 1502 The oath of a minor *pubes* is admissible (*e*), and where a minor has curators, the reference will be to his oath, not to theirs (*f*) But the oath of a pupil is incompetent for he has not sufficient maturity of judgment to protect himself, and he has no *persona standi in judicio*, the cases in which he is interested not being carried on in his name (*g*) It would seem that in a reference to oath a minor *pubes* may not be examined on facts which occurred during his pupillarity (*h*). But cases may easily be conceived where the fact is so simple and where it occurred so recently before puberty, that the reason for this rule, namely the want of powers of observation when the fact occurred, would altogether fail

§ 1503 Quakers, Moravians, and Separatists, having by their respective creeds, religious scruples against taking oaths, may in place thereof emit declarations in the form prescribed by statute (*i*) [1]

(*c*) M'Laurin *v* Stewart, 1832, 10 S, 333—See also *supra*, § 1073

(*d*) See *supra*, § 1120—In Carnegie 1710 4 B Sup, 805 the oath of one who had become dumb from paralysis, was taken by his writing his answers to spoken questions See also as to deaf and dumb witnesses, *infra*, § 1686 (*e*) Maitland *v* Cashogsill 1623, M, 8917—Forbes *v* L Pitsligo, 1628, M, 8920, 12479, S C—E Mar *v* his Vassals, 1628, M, 8918, 1 B Sup, 265, S C—Somervell *v* his Debtors, 1670, 2 ib, 497 (*f*) Forbes *v* L Pitsligo, *supra* (*g*) Gordon's Tutors 1707, M, 8909 (*h*) Little *v* Graham, 1826, 4 S, 424, S C—Anderson *v* his Creditors, 4th Feb, 1826, F C—Somervell *v* his Debtors, 1670, 2 B Sup 497—See also Kinnear's Ex *v* Rae's Ex, 1623 M 8918—2 Fraser Pers and Dom Rel 69 177

(*i*) 1 and 2 Vict, c 5—Ib, c 77—See also ib c 15 The form prescribed by these acts has come in place of that by 9 Geo IV, c 17, and 4 and 5 Will IV, c 76 See the forms given in treating of affirmations by witnesses The statutory form must be accurately observed, and therefore the omission of the word "truly" was held fatal to a declaration appended to a claim in a sequestration, M'Cubbin *v* Turnbull, 1850, 12 D, 1123

---

[1] The act 18 Vict, cap 25, allows parties called as witnesses in any court of civil judicature in Scotland, who, from alleged conscientious motives, refuse or are unwilling to be sworn to make a solemn affirmation or declaration The act 26 and 27 Vict,

§ 1504 A Peer is entitled to give his word of honour, instead of his oath of calumny—in which except in certain consistorial cases (*k*), the party only states his belief that his action is well founded, but does not specify matters of fact (*l*) Peers have sometimes insisted that this privilege extends to all cases where their oaths are required judicially, but the Court has refused their claim, and has required peers to swear in a reference to their oaths (*m*), and in diligences against havers (*n*), as it is the practice for them to do when examined as witnesses

A peer's widow has in these respects the privileges of a peer (*o*)

§ 1505 The oath administered to a party is the same as that administered to a witness and the examination before the commissioner—when the oath is taken on commission, according to the common practice (*p*)—is conducted in the same way as examinations of witnesses (*r*) If the party can write, he must subscribe the report of his deposition If not his inability to do so must be set forth the report being subscribed by the commissioner and clerk in common form (*s*) If he refuses to sign a deposition really emitted by him the report should set forth that fact, whereupon he will be held as confessed (*t*)

(*k*) See *infra*, § 1535

(*l*) A S 25th Dec 1708, and 21st July 1711—Brysson *v* D Athol, 1710 M, 10,028—E Winton, 1711, M, 10,029—Ersk, 4, 2, 28, note—Tait Ev 289

(*m*) A S *supra*—Brysson *v* D Athol, *supra*—E Winton, *supra*—Ersk, *supra*—Tait, *supra* (*n*) A S, *supra*—D Montrose *v* M'Auley, 1714, M, 10 029—Young *v* E Bute, 1716, M, 10,030 (*o*) M'Donald *v* Widow of a Peer, 1756, M 10 081

(*p*) As to taking oaths before the jury see §§ 1513, 1523 (*r*) Tait 289, *infra*, chapter on swearing of witnesses, § 1986 The rules as to examining first on special interrogatories in reference to oath, are noticed afterwards (*s*) Carin *v* Wilson, 1672 M, 12,532 (*t*) Carin *v* Wilson, *supra*—See also § 1421

---

cap 85, contains similar provisions applicable to courts of criminal judicature in Scotland

TITLE IV.

OF THE OATH *IN LITEM*

§ 1506 A party whose goods have been lost or destroyed in consequence of the delict or *quasi* delict of another is entitled to prove their amount and value by his own oath in a civil action against the wrong-doer. This is termed the oath *in litem* It has been derived from the Roman law (*a*), and has in some respects more force than an oath of a party examined as a witness

CHAPTER I —OF THE COMPETENCY OF THIS OATH

§ 1507 The most favourable cases for admitting this oath are where the pursuer seeks restitution of property which the defender has taken from him by theft (*b*), robbery (*c*), or any other spuilzie (*d*) It is also received in actions laid on any wrongful or illegal act, although not of a criminal character *e g*, an action by a tenant against his landlord for the price of dung improperly carried off by the defender during a process as to his right to it (*e*)—an action by a tenant against his landlord for injury to furniture and for the expenses occasioned by an illegal ejection (*f*)—and an action of damages for illegal failure to enter the tenant to the subject

(*a*) Dig L xii, t 3, *de in litem jurando* (*b*) Forrester *v* Merstoun, 1684, M, 9357—M'Pherson *v* Auchlossin, 1680, M, 9370—Dean of Murray *v* L Coxton, 1580, M, 9360 (*c*) Gordon *v* Gordon, 1731, Cr and St, 60 Here it is erroneously called an oath in supplement (*d*) Ersk, 4 2, 18—Tait Ev, 280—Jardin *v* Ly Melgum, 1573, M, 9359—Brown *v* Murray, 1628 M, 9361—A *v* B, 1795 M 9362 (*e*) Lyle *v* Graham, 1821 3 S 125 (*f*) Douglas *v* Walker 1825, 3 S, 531

let, whereby he suffered loss in his cattle and sheep (*f*). This oath was also admitted in an action against the owners of the vessel, by a seamen whom the master had abandoned in a foreign port and who claimed the value of the clothes, &c., which he had left on board (*g*)—and in an action laid on failure to restore the subject of a depositation—the defender, by his failure to return it, having broken the faith and trust which the pursuer had placed in him (*h*). The Court also allow a party to prove by his oath *in litem* the tenor of documents which his opponent has wrongously abstracted or destroyed (*i*).

The oath *in litem* is admissible where the culpability of the defender is inferred by a presumption of law, without any express delict, as in an action of reduction and spuilzie by one whose goods had been poinded in mistake for those of another person of the same name (*k*). So where the defender had borrowed a disposition of goods and furniture, &c., but stated that he had lost it, the pursuer's oath *in litem* was admitted to prove what it contained (*l*). And where goods had been stolen from lockfast places in a house, and the owner raised an action for the value against the servant who had charge of the house-door, as *versans in illicito*, by lodging a travelling packman in the house one night, although it was not alleged that either the servant or the packman was implicated in the theft, which took place some time after the act objected to, the Court admitted the pursuer's oath (*m*). This decision may be questioned.

In contrast with these cases, the oath *in litem* was held inadmissible to prove the value of a watch which the defender had borrowed from the pursuer, and had handed to a third party in his presence, there being no delict or *quasi* delict involved in such an act (*n*).

§ 1508. The oath is competent in an action against one responsible for the actual wrong-doer, as where they are master and ser-

---

(*f*) Elliot *v.* Scott, 1693, 4 B. Sup. 95. (*g*) Gowans *v.* Thomson, 1844, 6 D. 606. (*h*) Stair, 1, 13, 10—Bell's Pr., § 212. In Lyell *v.* Brand, 1667, M., 9362, 2 B. Sup. 128, the oath was admitted against one who had improperly intromitted with a pack of goods which the pursuer had deposited with him as security for a debt. (*i*) Dougal *v.* Murdoch, 1684, M., 9370—Calder *v.* Calder, 1825, 4 S. 331 (*infra* § 1510)—Buchanan *v.* Baillie, 1696, 4 B. Sup., 311—Compared with Sinclair *v.* Sinclair, 1830, 9 S., 28 (*infra* § 1510). But see M'Pherson *v.* Auchlossin, 1688, M. 9370—and Mein *v.* Gray, 1699, 2 Fount. 53. (*k*) Henderson *v.* Dunbar, 1706, M. 9353. (*l*) Dougal *v.* Murdoch, 1684, M., 9370, compared with cases *supra* (*i*). (*m*) Campbell *v.* M'Laren, 1734, M., 9352.

(*n*) L. Coupar *v.* L. Pitsligo, M. 5626, 9349, S. C.

vant (*o*) owners and shipmasters (*p*), or the cautioners and apprentice in an indenture (*r*) But where the apprentice of a bookseller had been imprisoned on a complaint by his master for stealing books, and had escaped from prison after having in his declaration before a magistrate admitted the theft of certain of the books,—in an action at the instance of the master against the magistrates of the burgh for the value of the missing articles, the Court refused to admit the pursuer's oath *in litem* as to the value of the books, which the apprentice had stolen, besides those admitted in the declaration (*s*)

§ 1509 Important applications of the oath *in litem* have occurred in cases founded on the edict *nautæ caupones stabularii*, under which ship-owners, innkeepers, and stablers, are responsible *quasi ex delicto* for loss or damage to luggage, goods, &c, intrusted to their care, whether the real culprits are their servants or strangers (*t*).[1] In such cases the pursuer's oath is received to prove the number and value of the articles destroyed or amissing (*u*), and at one time it was held to be the only competent mode of proving them (*x*)

§ 1510. This oath has been refused where proof from the ordinary sources was accessible to the pursuer, because in such cases there is no necessity for admitting the exceptional and make-shift evidence of the party's own statement Thus in an action against ship-owners for the value of lint which had been unskilfully stowed by the ship-master, and which, owing to its position in the vessel, had been damaged by water from a leak sprung during a storm, the pursuer's oath *in litem* was refused, because the amount of the goods could be proved by the bill of lading, and their value by ordinary witnesses (*y*) So in a case of spuilzie it was considered

(*o*) See notes (*u*), (*x*) (*p*) Gowans *v* Thomson, 1844, 6 D, 606—Cracour *v* St George Steam Co 1842, 5 D, 10 (*r*) Forrester *v* Merstoun, 1684, M, 9357 (*s*) Schaw *v* Wanse, 1683, M, 9354 The *rationes decidendi* are not reported Nor do the different reports agree as to what the oath *in litem* was tendered to prove The text is taken from Home's report (M, 9356), which is the most precise upon the point (*t*) As to this edict being founded on *quasi* delict see Inst Justin, L iv tit 5 (*de oblig quæ ex delicto*), 1, 3, and Dig L xliv, tit 7 (*de oblig et act*), 1, 5, *ult* (*u*) Ersk, 3, 1, 29—Ib 4, 2, 18—1 Bell's Com, 471—Bell's Pr, § 242—Tait, 283—Scott *v* Gillespie, 1827, 5 S, 669—Cracour *v* St George Steam Co, *supra* (*x*) Bell's Pr, § 242 (*y*) Carnegie *v* Napier, 1672, M 9349

[1] Innkeepers are not now liable for loss except to a certain amount, unless in certain cases, 26 and 27 Vict c 41, § 1

that if there be "a concurring probation agreeing on the quantity" of the articles abstracted, the oath is inadmissible (*z*). And where a party founding on entries in a certain account-book, traced it into the hands of the agent for his opponent, who was unable to produce it, and where, without leading any further evidence either as to the *casus amissionis* or the contents of the book, the pursuer tendered his own oath *in litem* to prove that it contained certain entries, the Court held that that mode of proof was premature (*a*). On the other hand, where the defender had unwarrantably intromitted with a pack of goods which the pursuer had left with him as a security for a certain debt, but before doing so had got the contents inventoried and valued by four neighbours on a warrant from a magistrate, the Court held that that *ex parte* proceeding did not deprive the pursuer of his right to depone *in litem* (*b*).

§ 1511. This kind of evidence being only admissible to prove the extent of the loss, a foundation must be laid for it by such proof as the case admits of, to show that a loss to some extent occurred (*c*). In a case of spuilzie, for example, the fact of a spoliation must be proved, before the pursuer is entitled to depone (*d*); and, in an action laid on the edict *nautæ caupones*, &c. the pursuer must first show that he had in his possession the missing articles, or a trunk or travelling-bag in which they might have been contained, and that the trunk or bag disappeared, or was found broken open, at a time when the defender was responsible for it (*e*). So, when the claim is for a considerable sum of money, or for articles of value, alleged to have been abstracted from the pursuer's clothes or travelling-bag, there must be *prima facie* proof that he had such articles in his possession (*f*). And a similar rule applies where the articles of value are alleged to have been abstracted from a parcel intrusted to a carrier (*g*). If, however, spuilzie of certain of the articles li-

(*z*) Fea *v* Elphinston 1697, M., 9367—Ersk., 4, 2, 18. It is otherwise if the witnesses differ as to quantity, Tait Ev. 282. (*a*) Sinclair *v* Sinclair, 1830, 9 S., 28. With this case compare Calder *v* Calder, 1825, 4 S., 331, *infra*, § 1517.

(*b*) Lyell *v* Brand, 1667, M., 1817, 9362, 2 B. Sup., 428. The Court appointed the oath to be taken in presence of the persons who had valued the goods.

(*c*) Stair, 4, 30, 2—Ib. 4, 44, 4—Ersk., 3, 1, 29—Ib., 4, 2, 18—Tait's Ev., 284.

(*d*) Stair, *supra*—Ersk, *supra*—Tait, *supra*—Forrester *v* Merstoun, 1684, M., 9357—Jardine *v* Ly. Melgum, 1573, M., 9357—Dean of Murray *v* L. Coxton, 1580, M., 9360—Brown *v* Murray, 1628, M., 9361. (*e*) Ersk. 3, 1. 29—Tait Ev., 284—Cases in Mor. 9233–41—Williamson *v* White, 21st June 1810, F. C. (*f*) White *v* Crockat 1661 M. 9233—Hay *v* Wingate, 1691, M. 9236—Gooden *v* Murray 1700, M. 9237. (*g*) Williamson *v* White *supra*.

belled on is proved, the oath *in litem* will be admitted as to the whole (*h*)

CHAPTER II.—OF THE EFFECT OF THE OATH *IN LITEM*.

§ 1512 The oath *in litem* (as already noticed) is admissible both upon the quantities and the values of the articles which have been abstracted and, being received *in modum pœnæ*, it seems originally to have been regarded as conclusive on both these points (*a*) In later practice it has been held that the pursuer's valuation of his goods, being the opinion of one subject to great bias, may be taxed or modified by the Court (*b*) But the oath as to the number or quantity of the articles, being on a specific matter of fact, has hitherto been sustained without modification (*c*) There seems, however, to be good ground for holding that the court or jury are not bound to give this effect to the oath where they believe it to contain falsehoods or exaggerations, for not only would it be against justice and common sense to receive as true, evidence which is believed to be the reverse, but, moreover, the chances of falsehood would be greatly increased if the party understood that his statement would be conclusive in his own favour (*d*) The Court once refused to allow the defender a conjunct probation in an action of spuilzie, holding that the pursuer's oath *in litem* was the only competent mode of proof (*e*) This decision would not be repeated

---

(*h*) Authorities in note (*d*)

(*a*) See argument in Man *v* Campbell, 1737, M, 9362, 9371, S C

(*b*) Stair, 4, 44, 4—Ersk, 4, 2 18—1 Bell's Com, 471—Tait's Ev, 286—Gordon *v* ——— 1579, M, 9369—Brown *v* Murray, 1628, M, 9361—Forrester *v* Merstoun, 1684, M, 9357—Dougal *v* Murdoch, 1684, M, 9370—Elliot *v* Scott, 1693, 4 B Sup, 95—Buchanan *v* Baillie, 1696, 4 ib, 311—Brouster *v* Lees, 1707, M, 9239—Man *v* Campbell, *supra*—Scott *v* Gillespie, 1827, 5 S, 669—Gowans *v* Thomson, 1844, 6 D, 606

(*c*) Ersk, *supra*—Tait Ev, *supra*

(*d*) Professor Bell seems to hold that the claim might be modified by the Court as to both quantity and value, 1 Com, 471, 2, and the terms of the reservation to modify in the cases in the preceding note (*b*) favour the same view But see *contra*, Douglas *v* Walker, 1825, 3 S, 531 A striking illustration of the untrustworthiness of this kind of evidence occurred in Brouster *v* Lees, 1707, M, 9239, where, after the Court had given decree to the pursuer in terms of his oath, it was discovered that he had got back the articles and fraudulently concealed them

(*e*) Man *v* Campbell, 1737, M, 9371

On the other hand where one who had been unlawfully ejected by her landlord raised an action of damages against him for 1*st*, destruction to her furniture, 2*d* expenses which the ejection had occasioned to her in rent of lodgings, &c, 3*d*, loss of trade, and, 4*th*, *solatium*—the Court admitted the oath *in litem* as to the two first items, but rejected it as to the others, which, not being matters exclusively within the pursuer's knowledge, did not require to be proved in that way (*f*)

§ 1513 The oath may be taken before the jury when the case is tried by that tribunal, provided a foundation be laid for it by proof of the spuilzie (*g*)

§ 1514 In all the cases in which the oath *in litem* is admitted, the pursuer may now adduce himself or his adversary as a witness (*h*) But there is this important difference between the evidence of a party as a witness and his oath *in litem*, that the one is not legal proof on any issue unless it is corroborated, whereas the other is full proof alone The existence of such an anomaly suggests the question Whether the oath *in litem*, with its artificial rules as to admissibility and effect, should not be abolished? for it is difficult to see what peculiar virtue the statement of a party in his own favour—a questionable kind of evidence—has from being emitted in this form The original object of the proceeding was to provide a remedy where the exclusion of the evidence of a party in his own favour was peculiarly unjust, but the occasion for it has been obviated by admission of party witnesses, under the ordinary rules as to the mode of ascertaining the truth of their depositions —a mode of investigation more likely to elicit the truth than is the oath of one of the parties deponing *in litem*

(*f*) Douglas *v* Walker 1825 3 S 531

(*g*) Cracour *v* St George Steam Packet Co, 1842, 5 D, 10—See also § 1402

(*h*) 16 Vict, c 20

TITLE V.

OF THE OATH IN SUPPLEMENT

§ 1515 Another of the expedients by which the old exclusionary system was modified, was the oath in supplement This mode of proof was admitted in certain classes of cases where full proof from ordinary sources was likely to be awanting It was only received where there was *semiplena* proof of the fact in issue from other sources It is still competent, but its importance has greatly diminished since parties were made competent witnesses in favour of themselves

There are only two classes of cases in which the oath in supplement is admissible, namely, 1*st*, actions for payment of furnishings in a course of dealing, and analogous cases, and, 2*d*, actions for the aliment of illegitimate children

CHAPTER I —OF THE COMPETENCY OF THE OATH IN SUPPLEMENT TO PROVE FURNISHINGS BY A MERCHANT

§ 1516 As a merchant cannot be expected to preserve full proof upon every article furnished by him during a course of dealing, his oath is admitted in supplement of a *semiplena probatio* of his furnishings (*a*) The rule holds primarily as to sales of merchandise It has also been applied in an action for tolls incurred

(*a*) Ersk, 1 2, 14—1 Bell's Com 331 Tait, 273—*Supra*, § 1180 during a period by the tacksman of an adjoining iron mine, for passage of his carts along the road (*b*). So, in a question between a factor or steward and his constituent, Mr Erskine considers that the factor may prove disbursements by his oath in supplement (*c*) But such proof would not be allowed in regard to those more important disbursements, for which written vouchers ought to be taken In an action at the instance of a law-agent against his client for payment of his business account, the pursuer's oath will be admissible to prove such professional charges and disbursements as do not admit of more formal evidence (*d*) Thus, also, where a party who had been employed for some years as a concurrent by his late brother who was a sheriff-officer, raised action against his brother's heir for payment for his services and offered to prove his claim from the books of the deceased, and, where one of these books had disappeared a few months before the action was raised, and no satisfactory explanation of the disappearance was given, the Court allowed the pursuer to depone to the amount of his claim, in support of evidence appearing from the remaining books Their Lordships were mainly moved by the suspicious disappearance of the book, which made the case like one of spuilzie, where the pursuer might emit his oath *in litem*, but they gave to the oath the effect of one in supplement, by admitting it in support of the evidence appearing from the other books Lords Justice-Clerk Boyle and Glenlee considered that the books were to be regarded as those of both parties (*e*) In another case, where a party claiming repayment of £100 sent in bank notes by post to the defender, proved that he had been in the course of transmitting money in that way to his correspondents, and especially to the defender, that on the date in question he drew the proper sum from the bank, that his cash was found to be correctly balanced in the evening, and that the post-bag, in which the letter and notes should have been, had been broken open, the Court were of opinion that his books and oath in supplement would be sufficient proof that the money had been dispatched (*f*)

§ 1517 In general the oath is competent only where the arti-

(*b*) Balfour *v* Sharp, 1833, 11 S, 784 (*c*) Ersk, 4, 2 14—Tait, 275

(*d*) See Limond *v* Reid, 1821, 1 S, 232 Law-agents accounts are included under the term "merchants' compts, and the like debts" in the Act 1579, c 83, introducing the triennial prescription See *supra*, § 184 (*e*) Calder *v* Calder, 1825, 4 S 331 See *supra* § 1507 (*f*) Cumings *v* Marshalls, 1752, M, 10 095 12,366, S C See also Buchanan *v* Buchanan 7th Feb 1812 F C *infra*, § 1517 (*i*)

cles in question were furnished during a course of dealing between the parties, and it is usually refused in actions laid on isolated transactions,—*e g*, the sale of a horse, or of a quantity of goods purchased at one time (*g*) So in an action against an alleged guarantee for the price of cotton which the pursuer alleged he had furnished to another person on the defender's credit, a previous furnishing having been made to the same person on the defender's credit, and paid for by him, the pursuer tendered his oath in supplement of entries in his books, and his salesman's oath to the order, but the Court held that the oath was not a lawful course of evidence in such a case' (*h*) The Court, however, allowed an oath in supplement in some old cases, where the transaction in issue was isolated (*i*) The circumstances of these cases made it probable that proof from the ordinary sources would have been deficient, and this seems to have induced the Court *ex officio* to admit an exceptional kind of evidence, according to a practice not uncommon at the time (*k*) The oath of the agent of a bank, and of the cashier of a trading company (neither of whom was admissible as a witness on the point), has been received to complete the proof of the respective companies having intimated dishonour of a bill (*l*)

§ 1518 What amount of evidence is *semiplena*, entitling the pursuer to depone in supplement, must, of course, depend on the nature and circumstances of each case It may be defined as that amount of evidence which, if corroborated by a credible oath in supplement, would prove the fact in question (*m*) In actions for furnishings, the evidence of one witness with the merchant's books,

---

(*g*) Cameron *v* Anderson 1815, Hume D, 421—Tait Ev, 276

(*h*) Buchanan *v* Scott, 1816, noted Hume D, 422

(*i*) In Buchanan *v* Buchanan, 7th Feb 1812 F C, the oath in supplement of a party was admitted, where he alleged that he had sent certain bank notes by post, the only other evidence adduced by him being a letter from his correspondent calling on him to make the remittance, and proof that he had employed a person to write letters inclosing the notes, that he had inclosed them in these letters, and had set out for the post office for the purpose of dispatching them The Court regarded the case as special See also Cumming *v* Marshalls, 1752, M, 10,095, 12,366, *supra* (*f*) In the case of Begg *v* Nicol, 1666, M, 9372, the elements of spuilzie appeared, and the oath was as much an oath *in litem* as one in supplement See also Cairns *v* Hunter, 1628, M, 9371, where the defender's oath in supplement was admitted to prove his plea in an action of spuilzie

(*k*) See Tait Ev, 277 The cases referred to are analogous to those in which witnesses usually inadmissible were received where there was a *penuria testium* See chapters on admissibility of witnesses, *infra*, § 1791

(*l*) Colebrook *v* Douglas 1780 M, 1605, 9371—Douglas, Heron, & Co *v* Alexander 1781 M 1606 9371

(*m*) See *infra*, § 1620

if regularly kept will suffice for this purpose (*n*) and it is not necessary that the witness should depone to the articles specifically, if his evidence fairly corroborates the books (*o*) The evidence of one witness speaking distinctly to the several articles, without entries in the books, would also be held *semiplena probatio* And in an action against the customer's heir, where the merchant's apprentices proved delivery of the goods, the Court ordained the merchant to give his oath with regard to the furnishings and prices (*p*). Proof of a course of dealing, combined with entries in the merchant's books seems to be *semiplena* proof (*r*) But neither the books, nor general evidence of a course of dealing, unless corroborated, would be held to be *semiplena* (*s*) And if the books have not been regularly kept, little or no regard will be paid to them in determining whether the pursuer's oath in supplement should be admitted (*t*)

CHAPTER II —COMPETENCY OF THE OATH IN SUPPLEMENT IN ACTIONS OF ALIMENT OF NATURAL CHILDREN

§ 1519 In actions for aliment of natural children the pursuer's oath in supplement has from an early period been admitted, on account of the secrecy usually attending illicit intercourse, and because the action is in a manner instituted on behalf of the child (*a*) The oath is only competent where there is a *semiplena probatio* from other evidence (*b*)

§ 1520 It is in this class of cases that most difficulty has been felt in defining ' *semiplena probatio* " It is ' something less than

---

(*n*) Ersk , 4, 2 14—1 Bell's Com , 331—Wood *v* Kello 1682 M , 12,728 See also ——— *v* Forrest, 1630, M , 12 725—Lawson *v* Fairie, 1832, 5 De and And 307

(*o*) Cases in preceding note

(*p*) Braidfoot *v* Elphinston 1697, M , 9373

(*r*) Tait, 273—Balfour *v* Sharp, 1833, 11 S , 784 Here in an action by a toll-keeper for dues during a considerable period, his oath in supplement, and his books proved by two witnesses to have been prepared daily from jottings made as each cart passed were held full proof See also Tait's Justice of the Peace, p 421 but see Thomson *v* Carnegy, 1695, M , 9373, 1 Bell's Com , 331

(*s*) Thomson *v* Carnegy, *supra*—Tait *supra*

(*t*) Ersk , 4, 2, 4—Tait Ev , 274—Ivory *v* Gourlay, 1816, 4 Dow, 467, noted *supra*, § 1181 (*n*)

(*a*) See per L Just -Cl Hope in Hill *v* Fletcher, 1847, 10 D , 7

(*b*) Bell's Pr § 2061—Tait's Ev , 277—Shand's Pr 782

proof and more than suspicion" (*c*), and may perhaps be described as that amount of evidence which, if corroborated and supplemented by the oath of a party interested and open to suspicion, as is the pursuer of such an action, would prove the libel (*d*). Lord President Blair, in an opinion which has often been quoted, observed that "a *semiplena probatio* does not mean merely a suspicion" but that it "must amount to such evidence as induces a reasonable belief although not complete evidence" (*e*). But Lords Mackenzie and Jeffrey have shewn that this definition is incorrect, since evidence which "produces a reasonable belief" is full proof, not merely in civil, but even in criminal cases (*f*).

§ 1521. Many cases will be found in the books (*g*) illustrating what the Court regard as *semiplena* proof; but as every question of this nature must be decided on its own circumstances, no decision in one case can be a ruling precedent for another. It may, however, be observed that the result sometimes depends on the status of the parties, as considerable suspicion might be raised by familiarities between persons in the upper classes of society or between persons whose respective ranks are different, whereas the same kind of behaviour on the part of persons of the lower orders would only indicate coarse frolic, or rough but not indecent courtship (*h*). It will be a circumstance in favour of the defender that he bears a good moral character, or that he is a married man (*i*). His conduct after the date of the alleged connection may turn the scale against him, as where he purchased medicine for the pursuer to procure abortion (*k*) (which is a very suspicious circumstance), or where he assisted her with money, after knowing that she had charged him with the paternity (*l*). An admission or proof of connection not much within or beyond the usual period of gestation, combined with proof of opportunities about the supposed time of conception, has often been regarded as *semiplena* proof (*m*).[1] It is doubtful if,

(*c*) Per L. Gillies in M'Crowe *v.* Bell, 1831, 9 S., 692—Per L. Moncreiff in Bruce *v.* Petrie, 1841, 4 D., 49. (*d*) Per Lords Mackenzie and Jeffrey in M'Laren *v.* M'Culloch, 1844, 6 D., 1133. (*e*) Craig *v.* Creighton, 14th June 1809, F. C.

(*f*) Per Lords Mackenzie and Jeffrey in M'Laren *v.* M'Culloch, *supra*—Mason *v.* Forrest, 1850, 12 D., 1090, per Lord Mackenzie. (*g*) Sh. Dig., vol. ii., p. 1074, vol. iii., p. 374—Shand's Pr., 786. (*h*) See Binney *v.* Kennedy, 1821, 1 S., 134—Aitken *v.* Neill, 1822, 1 S., 559—Boyd *v.* Kerr, 1842, 4 D., 1424—Bertram *v.* Steel, 1829, 7 S., 431. (*i*) See Martin *v.* Smith, 1834, 12 S., 604.

(*k*) See Lowe *v.* Bayne, 1840, 2 D., 470. (*l*) See Mackenzie *v.* Smith, 1826, 5 S., 190—Compared with *supra*, § 1150. (*m*) Compare Brown *v.* Smith, 1799,

[1] An admission of connection by the defender within the usual period of gestation,

in determining whether the proof is half-full, the Court will pay regard to the character of the pursuer, which of course materially affects the credibility of her oath in supplement (*n*) The fact that she stated that other men had connection with her about the time of conception will not render her oath incompetent, since either the defender or any one of them might have been the father, and the pursuer is likely to know which of them was so Such a statement, however, will be an important circumstance against her case (*o*)

Some observations as to the usual and possible periods of gestation will be found in a previous chapter (*p*)

§ 1522 It is only the mother of the bastard who is entitled to depone in supplement, because the oath is admitted as that of one who is personally familiar with the facts as to her supposed connection not only with the defender but also with other men,—matters regarding which, of course, no one else can give similar information Accordingly, where the mother died after an interlocutor had been pronounced finding that there was a *semiplena probatio* the oath of her mother, who was thereupon sisted as pursuer in her room, and who was adduced to prove statements by the deceased, was considered to be inadmissible as an oath in supplement (*r*)

Hume D 32—Leckie *v* Lindsay ib, 33—Hunter, 24th May 1814, F C—Paul *v* Gilmour, 1824 3 S, 368—Robertson *v* Petrie, 1825, 4 S, 333—Burns *v* Cumming, 1846 8 D, 916—Foley *v* Douglas 1848 10 D, 1424 *et seq* (*n*) *Per curiam* in Foley *v* Douglas, *supra*—and in Mann *v* Forrest 1850 12 D 1090 (*o*) Martin *v* Smith, 1834, 12 S, 604—Greig *v* Morice, 1838 16 S, 338—Lowe *v* Bayne 1840, 2 D, 470—Simpson *v* Ross, 1841, 3 D, 984 (*p*) *Supra*, § 314, *et seq*

(*r*) Dobie *v* Gaff, 1843 5 D, 1385, observed by Lords Justice-Clerk Hope and Meadowbank The grandmother's oath had been taken in the Sheriff-court where her compearance as pursuer had been sustained, but in the Court of Session it was held that she was not entitled to be sisted

combined with proof of opportunities about the time of conception along with the pursuer's deposition that connection had taken place at the period of conception, was held sufficient to instruct the pursuer's case But there is no legal presumption applicable to these circumstances,—it is in each case a question of the preponderance of evidence, Ross *v* Fraser, 1863, 1 Macph 783 See also Lawson *v* Eddie, 1861 23 D, 876

CHAPTER III —OF THE MODE OF TAKING THE OATH IN SUPPLEMENT, AND OF ITS EFFECT

§ 1523 In cases in the supreme court, oaths in supplement are usually taken on commission If the case is tried by jury, however the oath should be taken before the jury like that of a party witness (*a*) The practical effect of the admission of the parties as witnesses (*b*) will probably be to abolish oaths in supplement, because there is no occasion to consider a part of the proof, in order to determine whether an oath in supplement should be allowed, when the pursuer is entitled, even at the outset of the case, to depone as a witness [1]

(*a*) See Cracour *v* St George Steam Packet Coy, 1842, 5 D, 10—See also *supra*, § 1402 (*b*) By 16 Vict, c 20

---

[1] It has not been expressly decided whether, in actions of filiations, since the admission of the parties as witnesses, the pursuer is still entitled to emit her oath in supplement, and conflicting opinions have fallen from the bench The Lord President (M'Neill), in an opinion formerly quoted (*supra*, § 1401, note [3]), held that the old system was not abolished, and that (at least where a judicial examination of the defender was sought) "it is still quite competent to order his judicial examination, to hold him as confessed if he fails to appear and thereupon, with the oath in supplement of the pursuer, to hold the paternity as proved ', M Kellar *v* Scott, 1862, 24 D, 499 The question directly before the Court related to the competency of a judicial examination of the defender, but the observation appears to apply indifferently to any case where under the old practice, the pursuer's oath in supplement was admissible In a previous case, decided in the Second Division, the Lord Justice-Clerk (Hope) and Lord Murray thought that the provisions of the former law (allowing the pursuer the benefit of giving her oath in supplement when she had made out a *semiplena* proof) were no longer in force Actions of filiation were not reserved from the operation of the Evidence Statutes It could not be in the option of the woman (according as she might think it for her advantage) to make herself either a witness, or a party entitled to give an oath in supplement "Her oath in supplement was allowed because she could not be a witness, while the nature of her case, implying secret matters required that her oath should be allowed But now she is allowed to be a witness, and what can she require more?" But Lords Wood and Cowan doubted whether the old law had been wholly abrogated "If the pursuer does not offer herself as a witness, and the defender does not put her into the witness-box, I am not sure that we might not have to proceed upon the old law, and to consider whether or not a *semiplena probatio* had been made out without her evidence, and if satisfied that it had, then to admit her oath in supplement," *per* Lord Wood, Scott *v* Chalmers, 1856, 19 D, 119 In practice, however, the old method is no longer in use It is believed that since the change in the law the pursuer's oath in supplement, in an action of filiation, has never been taken Her evidence, therefore, is now liable to be tested in the same way as that of any other witness She is open to contradiction under the proof allowed to the defen-

§ 1524 The party emitting an oath in supplement commences by making his own statement, after which the defender is entitled to cross-examine him (*c*) If the deposition is in general or doubtful terms, a re-examination will be allowed with a view to clearing it up (*d*) But this, it seems, will be refused where the oath is clear (*e*)

§ 1525 The oath in supplement is the evidence of one acquainted with the facts, but subject to great bias Being only admissible as in supplement of the other evidence, it must be corroborative of that evidence, in order to raise the proof from *semiplena* to *plena* Accordingly, although slight inconsistencies in details will not materially impair the credibility of the whole proof, yet contradictions in essential particulars will be fatal (*f*) The oath may also fail to complete the proof in consequence of its intrinsic improbability In these respects, therefore, the oath in supplement differs from the oath on reference, where the only question is *quid*

(*c*) MacNaughton *v* Glass 1838 16 S, 611—*Contra*, Jameson *v* Barclay, 14th Jan 1820 F C (*d*) Ersk 4 2 15—Tait's Ev 239 (*e*) Ersk, *supra*—Tait *supra* (*f*) See Foley *v* Douglas, 1848, 10 D, 1424—MacNaughton *v* Glass 1838 16 S, 1103—Greig *v* Morice, 1838, ib, 1132

der, as well as by the cross-examination of her own witnesses "Filiation cases have no longer the peculiarity that the evidence of one of the witnesses is received as conclusive evidence after a *semiplena probatio* has been made out The evidence is to be dealt with as in other cases, the parties are the principal witnesses, they know the facts which lie at the bottom of the case and what the Court has to consider is, on the whole evidence, on which side is the balance of credibility," *per* Lord Justice-Clerk (Inglis) in M'Bayne *v* Davidson, 1860 22 D 738 It may, perhaps admit of argument whether the admission of parties as witnesses in filiation causes has been attended with much advantage The admission of parties has unquestionably in most cases proved of signal service in ascertaining truth and administering justice, but the testimony of parties must be comparatively worthless in those cases where, from the secret nature of the transactions, independent evidence is scarcely to be looked for, and the witness cannot be contradicted except by his opponent The consequence has been that in filiation causes the change in the law has been productive of perjury on a somewhat extensive scale, as few cases occur in which the pursuer's testimony is not directly contradicted by the defender's The change in the law, by which the pursuer is relieved from the burden of establishing a *semiplena probatio* as the initial step of her case, but is on the other subjected to contradiction and to a searching cross-examination, has had some rather curious results In Scott *v* Chalmers, *supra*, Lord (Ordinary) Handyside, while holding that the pursuer had failed to instruct the paternity, thought that the evidence (apart from her own) which had been adduced would have been sufficient to establish a *semiplena*, while in M Bayne *v* Davidson, *supra* where the paternity was found proved, Lord Benholme remarked that it was abundantly clear that, under the old law requiring a *semiplena* in the first instance the pursuer would have had no case at all

juratum est on matters intrinsic to the reference Again, the oath in supplement differs from the oath *in litem*, which is full, and not merely supplementary, proof of the number and value of the articles deponed to, a foundation being first laid for it by proof of the spuilzie, whereas the oath in supplement is not full proof on any matter, but must be weighed along with the *semiplena* proof, in order to ascertain whether they together establish the fact in issue.

TITLE VI.

OF THE OATH OF CALUMNY

CHAPTER I.—COMPETENCY AND EFFECT OF THIS OATH IN ORDINARY CAUSES

§ 1526. To prevent parties from wittingly maintaining groundless suits, the Scottish Legislature—following the Roman law (*a*)—required that both of the parties, if present, and their advocates, should at the outset depone "that the cause he trowis" (believes) "is gud and leil" (just and true) (*b*). The Act of Sederunt, 13th Jan. 1692, afterwards made it competent for any party for whom an allegation has been proponed and found relevant to require the other party to depone "whether he does not know the same to be true," and also for one against whom an allegation has been made to inquire of the party making it "whether he knows that it is not true."

§ 1527. This oath, called the oath of calumny, although much used at one time, has been seldom required since the Act of Sederunt 1st February 1715, § 6, by which either party might be compelled to admit or deny (but not on oath) matters of fact stated against him, under the penalty of the expenses occasioned by a ca-

---

(*a*) See Dig. L. xii. tit. 2 (*de jurejurando*) 1, 34, § 4, and L. ib. tit. ib. 1. 37. Lord Stair (4, 44, 16) finds difficulty as to the meaning of "*calumnia*." It is evidently used in the sense of quirk or quibble; see Facciolatus' Dic. and Riddle's Dic., *voce* "*Calumnia*." (*b*) 1429, c. 125. This statute concludes thus:—"And gif the principal partie be absent, the advocate sall sweare in the saule of him, after as is contened in thir meters:

"Illud juretur, quod lis sibi justa videtur,
Et si quæretur verum, non inficietur,
Nil promittetur, nec falsa probatio detur,
Ut lis tardetur, dilatio nulla petetur."

In practice the oath was only applied at the instance of the other party. Ersk. 4, 2, 16.

luminous denial (*b*) It fell still more into desuetude under the modern system of records and judicial examinations, and will now be rarely used in practice—at least in those cases in which a party may examine his opponent as a witness (*c*) This oath, however, may be advantageously used for stopping an unjust cause at the outset, or where legal evidence cannot be got, as where one claims a debt which he has discharged by an unstamped deed (*d*), or where allegations or denials are made in the name of a party which he is likely not to adopt

The practice of making counsel emit an oath of calumny is obsolete (*e*)

§ 1528 This oath may be put to either party in any civil cause, except where the ground of action is a matter which may be prosecuted criminally, in which the defender is not obliged to swear, *ne detur occasio perjurii*, and because *nemo tenetur jurare in suam turpitudinem* (*f*) Still less can a party prosecuted criminally be called upon to emit this oath (*g*) It may be required from a private person insisting in a criminal prosecution (*h*), but not from the Lord Advocate or his depute (*i*) In a declarator pursued by Weir "as procurator-fiscal for the manufactories," to have certain contraband goods confiscated and burnt, conform to act of Parliament, the Court held the pursuer bound to give his oath of calumny whether he had just reason, and believed that he had cause, to pursue the libel (*k*) The same rule does not seem to have ever been applied to a procurator-fiscal prosecuting an ordinary criminal complaint

§ 1529 The oath of calumny is not competent, unless the averments on which it is craved have been found relevant, or at least have been remitted to probation by an interlocutor before answer (*l*) At one time the oath was allowed at any subsequent stage of the cause, even after the party had led a full proof of his allegations (*m*) [1] But more recently it has not been granted after

(*b*) Ersk, *supra*—Tait Ev 215 (*c*) Under 16 Vict, c 20

(*d*) Duguid *v* Mitchell, 1824, 3 S, 96, affd, 1 W S, 203 (*e*) M'Queen, 1764, 5 B Sup, 902—More's Notes, 416—Shand's Pr, 385 The counsel's oath was ordered in Houston *v* Shaw, 1726, Rob Ap Ca, 561, and Baird *v* Leslie, 1629, M, 9381 (*f*) Stair, 4, 41, 15—Tait Ev, 215—Shand's Pr, 386—A B *v* Master of Grey 1583, M, 9376, see *infra* § 1540, *et seq* (*g*) See *supra*, § 1412, and *infra*, § 1548, *et seq* (*h*) 2 Hume 128—2 Al, 114 (*i*) 2 Hume, 132—2 Al, 92 (*k*) Weir *v* Simpson 1702, 4 B Sup 523 (*l*) Stair 4 44 17—But see *infra* § 1533 (*d*) (*m*) Ersk, 4, 2, 16—Fount, vol 1, p 5 (3 B Sup

[1] If applicable at all to the present form of process the most proper time for putting

a proof had been led, unless that proof was deficient (*n*), because, where a party has proved his case fully he is entitled to decree, and he should not be forced to depone except on a reference (*o*) The Court refuse the oath where the evident object of the party requiring it is to create delay, as where the other party is abroad at the time (*p*) In actions of reduction-improbation the pursuer's oath of calumny cannot be required before the production has been satisfied, because falsehood in the writings called for in these actions is libelled on *fictione juris*, in order to force their production, and the pursuer, although he may not believe that the writings are forged, may have good reason to insist on their being produced with a view to reduction (*r*) Where the defender in an action of reduction-improbation consented to allow the deeds to be reduced for non-production, but called for the pursuer's oath as to the conclusion for improbation, the Court refused to divide the libel, and held that the pursuer was only bound to depone generally that he had just cause to insist in it (*s*)

§ 1530 The oath of calumny may be taken not only on the original statements in the summons or defences, but also on any additional statements made in later pleadings (*t*) With this exception, however, a party will not be required to emit a second oath of calumny (*u*)

§ 1531 As this oath is one of credulity and not upon specific facts, a party is not bound to swear *in facto proprio et recenti*, because a deposition on such a matter would be equivalent to an oath of verity, which cannot be required from a party except on a reference to his oath (*x*) On the same principle, a party is only bound to depone generally that he believes his cause to be just and true, and he is not bound to answer interrogatories on individual facts (*y*)

---

240)—Ker *v* Ker, 1582 M 9375—L Duffus *v* Monro, 1625, M, 9379—L Drum *v* Tenants of L Lesmore, 1628, M, ib—See Murray *v* Burnett, 1695, 4 B Sup, 277

(*n*) Stair, 4, 44 19—Ersk 4, 2, 16—Graham *v* Logie, 1699, M 9382—See also L Drumquhassil *v* L Glenhegies, 1558 M, 9374 (*o*) See *infra*, § 1554, *et seq*

(*p*) Byron *v* Craw, 1760, M, 9384—Tait's Ev, 216—Shand's Pr, 386

(*r*) Ersk, 4 2 16—Home *v* E Home, 1716 M, 9383—Elliot *v* Elliot 1698 4 B Sup 425—Tait, *supra*—Shand *supra* (*s*) E Galloway *v* Maxwell, 1629, M, 9381 (*t*) Stair 4 44, 15 (*u*) L Drumquhassil *v* L Glenhegies 1558, M 9374 (*x*) A S, 13th Jan 1692—Stair, 4, 44, 20—Ersk, 4, 2 16—Dunn *v* Dunn 1835, 13 S 590 (*y*) Dunn *v* Dunn, *supra*—L Drumquhassil *v* L

---

the oath of calumny is when the averments of both parties are before the Court on a closed record, *per* Lord President M'Neill in Paul *v* Laing 1855 17 D 604

§ 1532 The oath of calumny must be emitted by the party in person (*z*) And even where his advocate's oath had been taken (according to an obsolete practice), the party himself might be called on to depone, because, although it is enough for an advocate to proceed upon the information of his client it may happen that the client wittingly misinformed him (*a*)

§ 1533 The consequence of a party deponing against his allegations is to exclude him from insisting in them (*b*) But his deposition in support of his case is not conclusive against the other party, who may, thereafter, adduce contrary proof, and may even call for a second deposition on a reference to oath (*c*) It was once held that objections to the relevancy of allegations of compensation might be proponed after an oath of calumny had been emitted, the Court treating the oath as if it had been taken before answer (*d*)

§ 1534 A party failing to appear and depone when duly cited may be held as confessed (*e*), in the same manner, as when the cause is referred to his oath (*f*) If the private prosecutor in a criminal case refuses to depone, the Court will desert the diet, and in Baron Hume's opinion such desertion will bar the party from insisting in another libel for the same crime (*g*)

It has already been seen whether the oath of peers, minors, and quakers, and some others, can be called for (*h*) [2]

Glenhegies, 1558, M. 9375—L. Gadzeard *v* Sheriff of Ayr, 1582, M., 9377—Mommusk *v* Kincusky, 1611, M., 9378—Elliot *v* Elliot, 1698, 4 B. Sup., 425

(*z*) Lovat *v* L. Lovat, 1575, M., 9374 (*a*) Stair, 4, 44, 18

(*b*) Stair, 4, 44, 20—Ersk., 4, 2, 16—Tait Ev., 216—Shand's Pr., 386—Duguid *v* Mitchell, 1824, 3 S., 96, affd., 1 W. S., 203 (*c*) Stair, *supra*—Ersk., *supra*—Tait, *supra*—Cooper *v* Hamilton, 1849, 12 D., 190 (*d*) Ly. Craigforth *v* Murray, 1710, M., 9382 But see *supra*, § 1529 (*e*) Stair, 4, 44, 15, 21—Ersk. 4, 2, 17—2 Al., 115 (*f*) See the chapter on holding as confessed, *infra*, § 1657, *et seq* (*g*) 2 Hume, 129—2 Al., 115 (*h*) See *supra*, § 1502 *et seq*

---

[2] In a late case, where the question was elaborately argued, the Court, without expressly deciding that the oath of calumny was in desuetude, refused to allow the oath to be tendered to the pursuer, in respect that it was tendered *de facto proprio et recenti* The view which the Court adopted as to the scope and application of the oath came substantially to this,—That the oath of calumny, in consistorial causes at least, was known to the common law prior to the statute 1429, c. 125, that the statute was not intended to apply to consistorial causes, and that, in so far as regulated by the statute, it could not be held that the oath had maintained its existence in the Civil Courts through use in the Commissary Court, that the cases and Acts of Sederunt did not show that the statute was obsolete, but that its application had been modified and was now to be measured by the practice which had followed upon it, which left the law very much in

CHAPTER II.—OATH OF CALUMNY IN CONSISTORIAL CAUSES

§ 1535 The object of the oath of calumny, considered in the preceding chapter is to protect a party against groundless litigation An oath bearing the same name is required in certain consistorial causes, in order to prevent them from being carried on collusively. This used to be the practice in the Commissary Court in actions of divorce and declarators of nullity of marriage in both of which there is considerable risk of collusion (*a*) And the oath was also administered in actions of separation *a mensa et thoro*, although collusion is unlikely in these cases (*b*) The act of Parliament which transferred the jurisdiction of the commissaries to the Court of Session ordains 'that the Lord Ordinary shall, in all actions of divorce, administer the usual oath of calumny to the pursuer' (*c*) From this provision it may, perhaps, be inferred that the oath is not necessary in the other consistorial causes above referred to In practice it is not required in actions of separation (*d*)

§ 1536 This oath is emitted in Court before the Lord Ordinary, when the case first appears in the rolls (*e*) But a commission to take it will be granted on special cause shown *e g*, where the pursuer is abroad or in bad health (*f*) Where a party who

(*a*) Fraser Pers and Dom Rel 701—Shand's Pr 421, 430

(*b*) Fraser *supra*—Shand, *supra*

(*c*) 11 Geo IV, and 1 Will IV, c 69 § 36

(*d*) 1 Fraser, 702

(*e*) Shand's Pr, 433, 437

(*f*) A B *v* C D, 1838, 16 S, 1143—Murray *v* Murray, 1846, 8 D, 535—M'Laren *v* M'Donald, 1849 22 Sc Jur, 46

the same position as if it rested on the practice without the statute, and fell to be enforced, like other judicial regulations, in so far only as necessary for accomplishing its original purpose, having regard to other and more recent regulations introduced for the same purpose, that the new forms of pleading, to a great extent, obviated the use of the oath, that, consequently, the oath could no longer be demanded as matter of right, but that it might be within the discretion of the Court to allow it to be put when, from peculiar circumstances, it seemed necessary for the ends of justice that it should be allowed, that the Act of Sederunt 13th January 1692 had regulated the later practice, in so far as it bore upon the nature of the oath, that this act expressly provided that a party should not be compelled to give his oath *de facto proprio et recenti*, and implicitly that the oath was to be administered in very general terms,—not for the purpose of ascertaining specific facts but as "the test of a good conscience, to prevent rash and needless litigation and to avoid proof, in matters of dispute where proof might be avoided See the opinions of Lord President M'Neill and Lord Deas in Paul *v* Laing 1855 17 D 604

had raised and executed a summons of divorce for adultery was about to sail on a protracted voyage, the Court, on a petition duly intimated to the defender, allowed his oath of calumny to be taken, to lie *in retentis* till the summons should be called and enrolled (*g*) [3]

§ 1537 In an action of divorce raised against a sequestrated bankrupt on the head of adultery, where the pursuer had emitted her oath of calumny, and the adultery had been proved, the trustee for the defender's creditors was not allowed to prove that the action had been carried on between the spouses collusively in order to defeat the rights of the creditors (*h*)

(*g*) Potts, 1839, 2 D, 248

(*h*) Greenhill *v* Ford, 1822, 1 S, 296, affd, 2 Sh Ap Ca, 435

---

[3] In an action of divorce the jurisdiction was objected to by the defender, but sustained by the Lord Ordinary After argument on this plea had been heard in the Inner House, and avizandum made, the Court, on a note stating that the pursuer, who was a soldier, was obliged to return to India administered the oath of calumny,—although it was maintained by the defender that the note should be refused, in respect that the jurisdiction had not been sustained, and was disputed Hook *v* Hook, 1862, 24 D, 488

TITLE VII

OF THE OATH ON REFERENCE

§ 1538 Before the recent Law of Evidence Amendment Act, the only way in which a party could obtain the deposition of his opponent on the facts of the case was by a reference to his oath This proceeding was competent on the simple and just ground that no person, however strong might be his own evidence, or however weak that of his opponent, is entitled to a judicial sentence contrary to the truth as revealed by his own conscience on matters within his knowledge (*a*) The characteristic feature of this proceeding is, that the party referring stakes the issue upon his opponent's oath, which is therefore received as the only evidence on the point referred, and as conclusive, whether it be against or in favour of the deponent's interest It was borrowed from the Roman law (*b*), and, notwithstanding recent changes, retains a prominent place in the Scotch law of evidence (*c*) It stands alongside of the party's writ as the only admissible proof on many matters, on others, it is received as well as writ and parole evidence (*d*), and in general, it is competent to an unsuccessful litigant, as an appeal from the courts of law to the *forum conscientiæ* in his adversary's bosom

(*a*) This principle is well stated by Lord Moncreiff in Pattinson v Robinson 1846, 9 D, 229 and in Adam v Maclachlan, 1847, ib, 576 (*b*) Dig L xii, tit 2

(*c*) By 16 Vict, c 20 § 5, it is declared that the right of reference to oath shall remain as then established by the law and practice of Scotland (*d*) As to the competency of this oath to prove different issues, see *supra*, § 539, *et seq* How far it is admissible to modify writings is noticed *supra* 239, *et seq* Its admissibility to prove prescribed debts and to redargue presumptions, has been noticed in the chapters on these subjects

CHAPTER I.—COMPETENCY OF THE OATH ON REFERENCE

I. *The right to refer to an Opponent's Oath is subject to the discretion of the Court.*

§ 1539. Reference to oath is not so much a species of evidence, as a mode of supplying the want of evidence, and preventing unjust consequences, *ubi non deficit jus sed probatio* (*a*). It is accordingly settled that a party has not an absolute right to call for his opponent's oath; but that the Court, in the exercise of its discretion, may refuse the reference, if they consider that it would not aid the justice of the case (*b*). Lord Chancellor Lyndhurst stated this rule in the following terms:—"It is not imperative upon the Court under all circumstances to allow the oath to be put; but the Court, this being an appeal to the equitable consideration of the Court, has a right to exercise a discretion upon the subject; and if they see reason to believe that justice is likely to be perverted by the administration of an oath of that description, they will not give authority for the oath to be administered" (*c*).

This opinion was expressed in a case where a bill accepted by a person in favour of his brother, had been taken up (after having been past due) by a creditor of the drawer, and where the acceptor, when charged by the creditor, offered to prove by his brother's oath that the bill had been accepted without value. But the Court of Session refused to allow the reference, because the brother had been rendered infamous by a conviction for a crime. On appeal, the House of Lords waived deciding the general question as to the effect of infamy but held that the reference had been properly refused in the circumstances. The doctrine that the Court has a discretion to grant or refuse a reference to oath, was given effect to in a subsequent case of special circumstances, where a party having been allowed to refer to his opponent's oath on condition of consigning a certain sum, and having, on a change of circumstances, tendered a reference of new, but without consignation, the Court refused to sustain it (*d*). But while these cases show that a party cannot insist on referring to his opponent's oath where doing so

(*a*) See per L. Just. Clerk Hope in Adam v. Maclachlan, *supra*.

(*b*) Bell's Pr., § 2264. See *infra* § 1607 *et seq*.

(*c*) Bruce v. Mackay, 1829, 3 W. S. 190, affirming 4 S., 531.

(*d*) Pattison v. Robertson, 1846, 9 D. 226.

would be unjust or improper, the Court will not exclude a reference to oath except for strong and special reasons (*e*) A recent statute, indeed, speaks of the "right of reference to oath" (*f*)

II *As to Reference to Oath in incompetent and irrelevant actions, and Reference before Answer*

§ 1540 The ordinary rule, that averments made in an incompetent action cannot be proved, applies where the proof tendered is a reference to an adversary's oath This rule was applied in an advocation of a judgment of an inferior court, where the original action involved a challenge of a written discharge which could not be set aside without a reduction (*g*) So, in a suspension of a charge on a bill, where the holder, who kept a public-house but had not a spirit license, admitted that the bill had been granted for payment of wine and the hire of a prostitute in his house, and offered to prove the debt by the debtor's oath, the Court, holding that the bill was utterly vitiated, and could not warrant summary diligence, refused the reference (*h*)

§ 1541 In like manner reference to oath is incompetent where the averments have been held not to be relevant to infer decree (*i*), or not to be sufficiently specific (*k*) And, where the revised condescendence contains facts not within the *media concludendi* of the summons, a reference of the whole cause to oath will not be granted (*l*) So, where a bankrupt had been discharged on a composition-contract, on the footing that a certain debt ranked in the sequestration was due, in a suspension at his instance on the ground that the debt was not due, but had been fraudulently reared up to defeat the rights of his creditors, the Court would not allow him to prove his averments by reference to the charger's oath (*m*) Thus, also, in an action for fulfilment of an obligation, founded on a deed deficient in the statutory solemnities, the reference must embrace the obligation, and not merely the genuineness of the subscription, because proof merely of the latter fact would not validate the deed or warrant decree (*n*)

(*e*) Cases *supra*, (*c*) and (*d*) (*f*) 16 Vict, c 20, § 5

(*g*) Macfarlane v Watt, 1828 6 S, 1095 (*h*) Hamilton v Main 1823, 2 S, 356 Action for the debt was reserved (*i*) Maclaren v Buik, 1829, 7 S, 780 (*k*) Phœnix Ins Co v Young 1834, 12 S 921

(*l*) Thomson v Simpson 1844, 7 D 106 (*m*) Gordon v Glen 1828, 6 S 393 (*n*) See *supra* § 813

§ 1542. Nor will the oath on reference receive effect on any matter on which it contradicts the deponent's statements or admissions on record, because he may not contradict these by evidence of any kind (*o*) And for the same reason a party may not call for his opponent's oath to prove a fact inconsistent with his own record

§ 1543 Reference to oath is also incompetent while questions prejudicial to the merits of the cause are undisposed of Thus, in a suspension, the Court would not allow reference to the charger's oath, under reservation of objections to his title (*p*) It follows from this rule that if the party depones without reservation, he will be held to have waived his preliminary defence Accordingly, where, in an action in the inferior court by Turnbull, as partner of Armstrong, for payment of work done by Armstrong, where the defender objected to Turnbull's title, and the Sheriff, without disposing of that defence, allowed reference to the defender's oath, as to whether the debt was due to Turnbull, and the defender deponed without reservation, he was not allowed, in an advocation by Turnbull (against whom the Sheriff had decided) to recur to his preliminary plea (*r*)

§ 1544 On account of the peculiar character of this mode of proof, it ought not, except in very special circumstances, to be allowed before answer as to the relevancy of the allegations on which it is tendered It was allowed, however, in the following case, which was regarded as special. The debtor in a bill presented a suspension on the ground of no value, and the creditor in his oath on reference stated that it was agreed the money should be repaid by instalments when the debtor could, and that on the bill falling due it should be renewed This oath having been held negative of the reference, the debtor was incarcerated, whereupon he presented a suspension and liberation, on the ground that payment was to be made in the manner formerly stated by the creditor, and he offered to pay a sum to account and grant a new bill for the balance, and craved leave to prove the alleged condition by the creditor's oath The creditor pleaded that the ground of suspension had been com-

(*o*) Darnley *v* Kirkwood, 1845, 7 D, 595—Noble *v* Scott 1843, 5 D, 727—Thomas *v* Dunbreck, 1834, 12 S, 285—*Supra*, § 107—But see Younger *v* Pollock, 1832 10 S, 570—M'Donnell, *v* Rankin, 1830, 8 ib, 815—*Supra*, § 56—M'Millan *v* Stewart, 1815, Hume D, 924 In the last two cases slight inconsistencies between the party's statements on record and his oath were overlooked (*p*) Henderson *v* Smith, 1850, 14 D, 583 (*r*) Turnbull *v* Borthwick 1830 8 S, 735—See also M'Donald *v* Burden 1829, 7 S, 306

petent and omitted in the previous suspension, and that a second reference to his oath on the same subject matter was incompetent But the Court before answer sustained the reference (*r*) In another case, where the pursuer, before the record was closed, tendered a reference to the oath of the defender, who was above seventy years old, the Court, feeling great doubt as to the competency of a reference on an open record suggested that the oath might be taken to lie *in retentis*, before answer as to the defender's prejudicial pleas And this was agreed to (*s*)

§ 1545 The Court have allowed reference to the oaths of tutors and curators, before answer as to the competency of that mode of proof (*t*) And where reference to the oath of trustees (*u*), and of a party's wife (*v*), was objected to, the Court allowed the oath to be taken reserving all questions as to its effect Reference to a bankrupt's oath has also been allowed, before answer as to whether it was competent evidence against his creditors (*w*). But, in commenting on the case last mentioned, Lord Justice-Clerk Hope observed, that a reference before answer seems to be repugnant to the very foundation of the proceeding (*x*), and, in a case in 1829, where written pleadings had been ordered as to the competency of a reference to the oath of one of several defenders, the Court refused to allow the oath to be taken to lie *in retentis* till the question of competency should be decided, although it was stated, and not denied, that the party was in a very precarious state of health (*y*) It is not likely that a reference to oath will again be granted before answer as to the competency of that mode of proof

III *Reference to Oath is incompetent on matters of law*

§ 1546 Oath on reference being only admitted for the purpose of ascertaining disputed matters of fact, is incompetent on matters of law (*z*). Accordingly, the Court refused to allow a reference as to whether the defender was jointly liable with another party in the price of a purchase of soap, holding that the reference should have

---

(*r*) Grant v Marshall, 1851 13 D, 500 (*s*) Riley v M'Laren, 1853, 10 D, 323 (*t*) L Fairney v L Melville, 1662, M 12,308—Hay v Ogstoun, 1666, M, 16,276—See Bruce v Jack, 1670, 1 B Sup, 609 (*u*) Murray v Laurie's Tr, 1827, 5 S, 515 (*v*) Marshall v Forrest, 1676, M, 5851

(*w*) Blair v Balfour, 1745, M 12,473 Elch, "Arrestment," No 25, S C—Sinclair v Johnston, 1749, M, 12 475 (*x*) Adam v Maclachlan, 1847, 9 D, 568 572 (*y*) Bell v Syme's Tr, 1829 7 S, 893—See *contra*, E Melvil v E Perth 1693 4 B Sup, 171 (*z*) Bell's Pr, § 2269

been as to the facts on which the liability was maintained (*a*) So a party was not allowed to refer whether he had been relieved of a certain guarantee (*b*) "A reference, however, is not necessarily objectionable because it involves a question of law, for law cannot always be separated from fact before a proof, as long experience has shown But the party to whom a reference is made seems entitled to insist that the separation shall be made, in so far as it can be clearly done, that he may not be called on to give an opinion on what he is not supposed to understand" (*c*)[1] A reference to oath of resting-owing is a familiar example of this principle In interpreting such an oath, however, the Court will separate the law from the facts deponed to, and will not sustain a general denial of resting-owing, unless that be the proper legal inference from the facts appearing in the oath (*d*)

§ 1547 In like manner "usage of trade," or the custom of a district, is thought not to be a proper subject of a reference to oath, especially as (if it exists) it may easily be proved by persons in the trade or locality (*e*) But the practice or usage on a person's own estate, or in his business transactions, being a *factum proprium*, may be referred to his oath (*f*)

IV *Reference to Oath is incompetent on matters involving Crime or Infamy*

§ 1548 The examination of a party on oath as to serious crimes charged against him is opposed to the fair spirit of our jurisprudence, and would, in general, be more likely to elicit falsehood than truth The defender's oath is therefore incompetent in criminal prosecutions, where his "life, limb, or liberty," is at stake, or where

(*a*) Taylor *v* Hall, 1829, 7 S, 565 (*b*) Conacher *v* Robertson, 1829 8 S 141 (*c*) Per Lord Corehouse (Ordinary) in Lawson *v* Murray, 1829 7 S, 380 See also Grubb *v* Porteous, 1835, 13 S 603 (*d*) See *supra* § 453 *et seq*—515 *et seq* (*e*) See Ewing *v* M'Eachern, 1824, 3 S, 9—*Contra*, F Galloway *v* Telzifer, 1627, M, 7193, 12,421 (*f*) See L Rowallan *v* Muir, 1626, M, 12419

[1] In Anstruther *v* Wilkie, 1856, 18 D, 422, the Court pronounced this interloctor, —"Sustain the reference reserving all questions as to the relevancy and sufficiency of the averments offered to be proved" The reference was sustained after parties had renounced probation, and after judgment in favour of the pursuer had been given The action had been decided apparently on a pure point of law, but the interlocutor on the merits bore to have been pronounced "in the circumstances of the case" The oath when taken was admitted to be negative

the conviction infers infamy (*g*) But it has repeatedly been received in cases punishable only by fine (*h*), and it was allowed in one case where the prisoner was to be fined and sent abroad as a recruit, which was said to be "only a useful disposal of such as would not live regularly at home" (*i*) None of those cases, however, are of recent date and it may be doubted whether reference to the panel's oath would now be allowed in any criminal prosecution (*k*)

§ 1549 In a civil action for reparation of the damages occasioned by criminal acts, referring to the defender's oath is also incompetent, because, even although the oath taken in the former were not to be used in the latter, the party might be greatly prejudiced on his trial by having emitted it (*l*) Accordingly the reference has been held inadmissible in an action of damages for a serious assault punishable by imprisonment (*m*), and in an action of damages for sending a threatening letter, as that inferred a similar penalty (*n*), whereas in civil actions laid on assaults which merely inferred a fine, the oath was received, when it was the practice to take it in the criminal courts in such cases (*o*) Of late, the point seems not to have occurred purely in a civil suit regarding such slighter offences, but the leaning of the Court, as indicated in several cases, is against allowing reference to oath in

---

(*g*) Stair 4, 44, 5—Ersk, 4, 2, 9—Ib, 4, 4, 94—2 Hume, 337—Tait Ev, 233

(*h*) Authorities in preceding note It has been received in prosecutions for smuggling Irish grain, Boswell *v* Gray 1712, M, 9398—Hamilton *v* Boyd 1742, M, 7335 9402,—in offences against the game laws, Proc-Fisc of Edinburgh *v* Wilson 1787, M, 12,442—and against the monopoly of the post-office, Proc-Fisc of Edinburgh *v* Murray 1787 (not rep), noted in Ersk 3 1 29, note *,—in prosecutions for conduct inferring a challenge to fight a duel, Proc-Fisc of Edinburgh *v* Campbell, 1736, M, 9400, Elch, "Proof" No 3,—and for prosecutions for cutting down another person's trees, Burnett, 1637, 2 Hume, 337 (*contra* Stirling *v* Christie, 1762 M, 9403, which is said to be misreported, see Logan *v* Howatson, 1775, M, 10 492) In prosecutions for usury, which were of a *quasi* criminal kind, and inferred nullity of the obligation and security, the oath of the accused was admissible by 1597, c 251, explained by 1600, c 7—2 Hume 336—See *infra*, § 1549 (*p*) But this was rather an oath in supplement than on reference, as the act 1597 c 251, allowed the oath of party and all other lawful probation conjoined therewith See also 2 Al 587

(*i*) Boswell *v* Irvine, *supra*—but see Proc-Fisc of Edinburgh *v* Wilson, *supra*

(*k*) See 2 Hume, 337—2 Al, 586, 7—Shand, 395, and cases noted *infra*, § 1549 (*p*)—*Contra*, Tait Ev, 233

(*l*) Ivory's note (15) to Ersk 4, 2, 9 See *supra*, § 1412

(*m*) Brown *v* Miller, 1828, 6 S 561

(*n*) M'Callum *v* M'Call, 1825, 3 S, 551

(*o*) Edgar *v* Darling 1634, M, 9393 1 B Sup 349—Gordon *v* Cruickshanks, 1678, M, 9397 See also Elphinstone *v* Elphinstone, 1609, M 9389

actions of this kind (*p*). In actions of reduction-improbation, forgery is usually alleged only *fictione juris*, in order to compel production of the writings called for, and the conclusion to have the defender punished as accessory to forgery is merely a clause of style, which has no practical effect. Accordingly, the libel may be referred to the defender's oath (*r*) unless the ground of action is a forgery for which he might be responsible criminally. The defender's oath on reference may also be taken in actions of damages for defamation, unless where the slander is one which may found a criminal prosecution (*s*).

§ 1550. It seems never to have been decided whether reference to oath on a matter inferring penal consequences is competent if the party has been secured against the risk of a criminal prosecution by a verdict of acquittal, or by having turned Queen's evidence, or if he has been already convicted and punished for the offence (*t*).

§ 1551. The oath of a party may be taken on averments which cast a stain on his moral character, but do not infer legal infamy or liability to criminal prosecution (*u*).

§ 1552. Reference to oath in a civil case on a matter inferring criminality is not incompetent in itself, but from privilege of party, which may be waived either expressly or by implication (*v*).[2]

Some further illustrations on this subject will be found in the chapter on the examination of witnesses on matters inferring infamy.

§ 1553. It is incompetent in any criminal proceeding, whether

(*p*) Thomson *v* A B, 1828, 7 S, 32—Ewing *v* M'Eachern, 1824, 3 S, 9—Roger *v* Cooper, 1823, 2 S, 444, *infra* (*s*). In Ritchie *v* Lyall, 15th Feb 1810 (not rep, noted in Gordon *v* Campbell, 22d Dec 1809, F C), it was considered to be incompetent to refer usury to the oath of the pursuer in an action for payment of the debt, the act 1600, c 7, making it competent to take only the defender's oath in cases of usury. See *supra* (*h*). (*r*) Clark *v* Hyndman, 20th Nov 1819, F C Session Papers. See also Thomson *v* Ross, 1677, M, 9397. (*s*) M'Callum *v* M'Call, 1825, 3 S, 551. In Roger *v* Cooper, 1823, 2 S, 444, where a slander was prosecuted for fine and palinode (according to a practice now obsolete), reference to the defender's oath was not allowed, but in the subsequent case of M'Callum *v* M'Call it was mentioned from the bench that there were "other peculiar circumstances which weighed with the Court in rejecting the reference." (*t*) The competency of the oath in such cases is favoured by Jantzen *v* Easton, 3d Feb 1814, F C, *supra* § 1396. See also Gordon *v* Gordon, 1731, Cr and St, 60. (*u*) Cameron *v* Armstrong, 1851, 13 D, 1256—*Supra*, § 1396. (*v*) Gordon *v* Gordon, *supra*. From this case it would seem that if a party has waived his privilege, he cannot retract and refuse to be examined, or resist a judgment holding him as confessed for not deponing.

[2] Conacher *v* Conacher, 18[illegible], 21 D, 597.

at the instance of the public or of a private prosecutor to refer the libel to the prosecutor's oath (u)

V. At what stage of the process Reference to Oath may be made

§ 1554. It is doubtful whether reference to oath is competent on an open record (x). In older practice one who had adduced parole or written evidence could not refer to his opponent's oath, because he was held to have elected his mode of proof (y), and the reference might have inferred perjury in the witnesses or party (z). But it has now been settled for a long time, that even if a party has succeeded in a proof led by himself or by his adversary, he will not be entitled to decree unless he can stand to his case on oath (a). The reference may be made after the verdict of a jury has been returned against the party referring (b) and even after the verdict has been applied, provided the decree following upon it has not been extracted (c). The Law of Evidence Act of 1853 makes it incompetent for one who has called and examined his opponent as a witness, to refer the cause or any part of it to his oath (d).[3]

§ 1555. The cases in which the reference has been allowed at the end of the cause proceed on the footing that it is competent any time before the action is taken out of Court by extracting the decree (e). One learned judge, however, considered that even after extract the case might be opened up by suspension, in order to allow reference to the successful party's oath (f). But this does not

---

(u) Cameron v. Paul, 1853, 1 Irv. 316—2 Hume 403—3 Al. Cr. Law, 623.

(x) See Riley v. M'Laren, 1853, 16 D., 323—*Supra* § 1541—*Infra* § 1565.

(y) Cases in Mor., 12,123, 12,135, 9, 12,136, 12,449. (z) Irvine v. Irvine, 1676, M., 12,112, 12,143—Duff v. Keith, 1624, M., 9389. (a) Law v. Lundin, 1747, M., 12,158, Elch. "Oath of Party," No. 2, S. C.—Dalziel v. Richmond, 1792, M., 9407—Fleming v. Simpson, 1798, Hume D., 412—Grey v. Leny, 1801, Hume D., 414—Campbell v. Turner, 1822, 1 S., 538—Cameron v. Armstrong, 1851, 13 D., 1256.

(b) Clark v. Hyndman, 20th Nov. 1819, F. C.—Murray v. Murray, 1839, 1 D., 484—Wallace v. Robertson, 1839, 2 D., 204—Binnie v. Willox, 1844, 6 D., 520. But the Court will not delay applying the verdict on the ground that the losing party contemplates referring the whole cause to his adversary's oath, Sheriff v. Sheriff's Tr., 1836, 15 S., 115. (c) Sheriff v. Sheriff's Tr., *supra*. (d) 16 Vict., c. 20, § 5.

(e) Cases in notes (a), (b)—See also M'Lennan v. Reid, 1826, 4 S., 781.

(f) Per L. Balgray in Clark v. Hyndman, 20th Nov. 1819, F. C.

---

[3] See Rutherford v. Marshall, 1861, 23 D., 1276, and Renny v. Will, July 18, 1863, not yet reported. These cases are noted *infra* § 1711, note.

seem to have ever been attempted and it would probably be held inadmissible on the ground of competent and omitted [4]

Reference to the oath of a party seems to be competent where the Court of Session had decided the case against him, but the House of Lords had reversed the judgment, and remitted to the Court to proceed with the cause (*g*)

§ 1556 In Bill Chamber cases the suspender may refer to the charger's oath, after the note of suspension has been refused, provided the certificate of refusal has not been issued (*h*) And the reference was allowed after the issuing of the certificate, where the case had been kept in Court by a reclaiming note, on which the Inner House had adhered to the Lord Ordinary's interlocutor, and remitted to him to decern for expenses (*i*) [5]

§ 1557 Lord Stair (*k*) lays down that one may not be forced to depone on reference unless the party referring renounces all other probation, and depones that he has none, especially that he has no probative writ on the point, "because the malice of some in small matters may be so great as to be content to lose the point referred so that they might make the swearer infamous by reserving his writ to the contrary" Mr Erskine (*l*) and Professor Bell (*m*) state the same rule, but no modern case has been found in support of it [6]

(*g*) Reid *v* Hope, 1826 4 S, 402 (*h*) A B 1843 16 Sc Jur 86—Macdonald *v* Cooper, 1848, 10 D 740—See Aitchison *v* M'Donald, 1823, 2 S 329 *contra*, Young *v* Patton, 1826, 5 S 151 (*i*) Brown *v* Ferguson, 1852, 14 D, 841

(*k*) Stair 4, 44, 2 (*l*) Ersk, 4, 2, 8 (*m*) Bell's Pr, § 2264

---

[4] So long as the case remains in Court to any effect a reference is competent Thus a reference to the oath of the pursuer was sustained after a decree on the merits had been extracted, but before approval of the auditor's report and decerniture for expenses, Drew *v* Drew, 1855, 17 D, 784—See also Bannerman *v* Melville, 17 D, House of Lords 6—Conacher *v* Conacher, 1859, 21 D, 597,—where after the verdict a reference to the oath of a party in Australia was sustained of consent, the party referring finding caution for the sum found due by the verdict, and paying expenses In Scott *v* Livingstone, 1831, 10 S, 107 and 174, after an interlocutor, which sustained the defence and assoilzied the defender had been pronounced, the pursuer put in a minute of reference to the defender's oath, but the Court held, that after a cause had been decided, an incidental petition craving the Court to allow the reference, was requisite The principle of this decision was recognised in Winton & Co *v* Thomson & Co, 1862, 24 D, 1094, but it was there held that a note addressed to the President of the Division, accompanying the minute of reference and craving that it should be sustained, was equivalent to an incidental petition

[5] Winton & Co *v* Thomson & Co, 1862 24 D, 1094

[6] Although parties have renounced probation, a reference to oath is competent after judgment is pronounced, Anstruther *v* Wilkie, 1856 18 D 405

§ 1558 There is not any general rule that the party referring after verdict or decree must pay the previous expenses, and this will be required or not according to the circumstances (*n*) Where the reference seemed to be made in order to create delay, as where the party was abroad at the time, the Court allowed it only on consignation of sums which had been previously decerned for (*o*) [7]

Where, after a party had obtained a verdict his oath, emitted on a reference of the whole cause was found to be affirmative of the reference the other party was held entitled to the expenses of the trial, as well as the other expenses in the case, because they had been occasioned by the deponent's improper conduct in maintaining pleas contrary to equity and truth (*p*)

§ 1559 Where the interlocutor of a Lord Ordinary has become final but has not been extracted, the motion for a reference to the successful party's oath must be made before the Lord Ordinary (*r*), in the same way as after final decree in the Inner House the motion is made to the Court without an appeal to the House of Lords

VI *When may only a Part of the cause be referred?*

§ 1560 When the reference is made during the progress of the cause, it may be confined to individual points of fact (*s*) But, when tendered after decree, it must embrace the whole libel or defence, or at least such facts as will be conclusive of the cause, otherwise it would open up the litigation, instead of ending strife (*t*)

(*n*) See Campbell *v* Turner, 1822, 1 S 538—Wallace *v* Robertson, 1839 2 D, 204—Nisbet *v* Taylor's Exec 1840 3 D, 332—Sayer's Assignee *v* Haldane ib, 1005—Binnie *v* Willox 1843 6 D 520 (*o*) Mainwaring *v* Baxter, 4th Feb 1812, F C—M'Kenzie *v* M'Intosh, 1828, 6 S 1057—Pattinson *v* Robertson, 1846, 9 D 226—Compared with M'Ewan *v* Muirhead 1852, 15 D 16 (*p*) Murray *v* Murray 1839, 1 D 484 (*r*) M'Lennan *v* Murray 1826, 4 S, 781

(*s*) Cowan *v* M'Cormack 21st Nov 1811 reported in note to White *v* Murdoch, 9th June 1812 F C—Welsh *v* Ker, 1823, 2 S, 126—Moore *v* Young, 1843 5 D, 494—Tait Ev, 235—Shand Pr, 389 (*t*) White *v* Murdoch, *supra*—Butters *v* Loch 1830, 8 S, 843—Ogle *v* Smith, 1824 3 S, 629—Rowland *v* Stevenson, 1827 6 S, 272—Thomson *v* Paterson 1830, 2 De and And, 177 But it is not necessary that the conclusiveness of the reference be manifest from the terms of the minute In Broom *v* Edgley, 1843, 5 D, 1093, Lord Justice-Clerk (Hope) observed, ' The reference may not lead at once to judgment against the defenders, but if it shall be sufficient to overturn the defence, upon which alone the defenders were assoilzied, it will destroy that judgment I need not enter into the question raised by the defenders, whether, after final judgment a reference to oath must always be in terms which lead, of necessity to a decree for payment I am aware of no such inflexible rule ' The proper form for the reference after a verdict is of the issues in the ' cause, and all relevant

7 Conacher *v* Conacher, 1859, 21 D, 597

But a party may refer one part of a case without abandoning a decree in his favour on another part which is independent of the point referred (u) In an action of aliment of a bastard child, where the Sheriff found that the birth of the child was proved, but that there was not a *semiplena probatio* of the paternity, and assoilzied accordingly, the pursuer was allowed, in an advocation, to have a finding of the fact of the birth, and to refer only the question of paternity to the defender's oath, although the latter contended that that did not exhaust the cause (x)

As already noticed, a reference of the whole cause will not be allowed where there are irrelevant or incompetent allegations, because these would be embraced by such a reference (y)

§ 1561 Where a party in the inferior court objected to a reference after decree as not exhausting the cause and, on the Sheriff repelling his objection, acquiesced and deponed, the Court of Session held him barred from insisting in the objection in an advocation (z)

§ 1562 If a party makes a reference of more than is necessary to entitle him to judgment he is not bound to prove such surplus matters of fact, but he will succeed if the oath is affirmative of the facts which are necessary to sustain his libel or defence (a)

VII *The oath must be emitted on a Judicial Reference in causa*

§ 1563 As afterwards more fully illustrated reference to oath is a *quasi* contract, by which the parties agree to determine finally, by a particular mode of proof, the truth or falsehood of certain allegations It is therefore indispensable that a party should depone under a judicial reference to his oath in the individual cause (b), otherwise statements would be held as conclusive which the parties

---

facts", Binnie v Willox, 1841, 6 S 520 In Clark v Hyndman, 20th Nov 1819 F C, Sess Papers, the reference was of "the facts admitted to probation as contained in the issues sent to the jury" (u) Campbell v Turner, 1822 1 S, 538 Here, in a suspension of charges on two bills, and a reduction of the bills the Court having suspended and reduced as to one of them the suspender was allowed a reference to the charger's oath as to the other without giving up his partial decree

(x) Cameron v Armstrong 1851 13 D 1256 This seems to be the farthest length the Court have gone in allowing a partial reference after decree It appears to conflict with the general rule laid down in previous cases (y) Phoenix Insur Co v Young, 1834, 12 S, 921 Thomson v Simpson 1841, 7 D 106—*Supra*, § 1511

(z) Brown v Edgley, 1843 5 D 1087 (a) Per L Mackenzie in Hoddle v Baker, 1841 3 D, 376—See also *supra*, § 15 *et seq* (b) Tait Ev 236 Shand's Pr, 390—Lord v Ins Co 1828, 6 S, 969

did not agree to abide by, and which may have been made erroneously, without sufficient information on the one part, or sufficient interrogation on the other. Accordingly, statements which a party may have made on the merits of the case when examined as a haver will not be evidence in his own favour (*c*), and if they are to his prejudice, they will not be final against him, as if they had been made under a reference to his oath (*d*). It is doubtful indeed if they will be admissible against him to any effect (*e*). In like manner, the deposition of a party examined as a witness under the Law of Evidence Amendment Act has not the effect of an oath on reference (*f*), but is subject to be redargued by contrary evidence and to be weighed like any other part of the proof (*g*).

On the same principle the oath on reference in one cause, although it will be received in another cause as an admission by the party, will not be conclusive against him, because it was not emitted on a reference in the cause in which it is afterwards founded on (*h*).

§ 1564. Again, where a summons for payment of a debt referred its constitution and subsistence to the defender's oath, and the will of the summons contained a certification that, if the defender failed to appear and depone he should be held as confessed, and where decree in absence was pronounced thereupon, the defender having died his representatives were reponed against the decree, which was held not to have proceeded as on confession, since the libel had not been referred to the oath of the deceased under judicial authority (*i*).

§ 1565. At one time it was the practice to insert in summonses a reference to the defender's oath (*k*); but the case just noticed shows that a decree in absence on such a summons has not any peculiar virtue, while, if the defender appears, the reference can be made without the summons concluding for it. The practice has therefore become obsolete. It is irregular to refer to a party's oath in a plea in law (*l*), or in any other part of the record which ought only to set forth the averments and pleas of the parties, not their mode of proof. The proper practice is to lodge a minute stating

(*c*) Elliots *v.* Ainslie, 1740, M. 9363.—Yule *v.* Robertson, 1788, M. 9419. See *supra*, §§ 1359, 1138. (*d*) *Supra*, § 1438. (*e*) *Supra*, § ib.

(*f*) 16 Vict. c. 20, § 5. (*g*) See chapter on the Evidence of Party Witnesses, *infra*. (*h*) See *supra*, § 1134. (*i*) Nicholson *v.* M'Leod, 23d November 1810, F. C.—*Contra*, 1 Ivory's Form of Process, 239.

(*k*) Shand's Pr., 387. See a curious instance of this, *infra*, § 1567 (*e*).

(*l*) Thomson *v.* Wyld, 1840, 3 D. 150.

the matters to be reserved to which the Court or Lord Ordinary interpones authority if, after hearing parties, they approve of the reference In one case, the Lord Ordinary on the Bills, erroneously supposing that the suspenders had referred to the charger's oath, appointed him to depone, and his oath was accordingly taken in presence of the suspenders, who put some questions to him On the oath (which was negative) being reported, the suspenders pleaded that it was inept, as no reference had been made, but the Lord Ordinary and the Court held that it was binding, as the facts and circumstances implied a reference on the part of the suspenders, who might have founded on the oath if it had been favourable to them (*m*) [S]

§ 1566 It may be added that a procurator in an inferior court requires special authority to enable him to refer to the oath of his client's adversary (*n*) whereas this power is embraced by the general mandate to a party's advocate (*o*)

CHAPTER II —OF RETRACTING A REFERENCE TO OATH

§ 1567 A party who has referred to his opponent's oath is usually entitled to retract the reference at any time before the oath has been emitted provided no change of circumstances has occurred whereby the retractation would place the other party in a worse position than he held previously (*a*) But where, after a defender

---

(*m*) Hewitt *v* Pollock, 1821, 1 S, 178 (A note of the Judges speeches is given in 1 S, new ed, 159) See also Hamilton *v* Lindsay, 1852, 14 D, 841

(*n*) A S, 10th July 1839, § 84—Hardy *v* Allan, 1709, M, 12,248—Inglis *v* Fuller 1712, M, 12,249—Grahams *v* Ferguson, 1775, M, ib (*o*) See Gilfillan *v* Brown, 1833 11 S 518—Currie *v* Glen 1816, 9 D, 308—Forbes *v* L Duffus 19th January 1837, F C—Shand's Pr, 151 (*a*) Chalmers *v* Jackson, 18th February 1815, F C—Hall *v* Hardie 18th March 1810, reported in note to Chalmers *v* Jackson—Houlditch *v* Johnston, 20th December 1809, also there noted—Binnie *v* Mack, 1832, 10 S, 255—Leitches *v* Locheads 1676, M, 16,676—Bowsie *v* Harvey, 1832, 5 Dc and And, 125 See also Jameson *v* Wilson, 1853, 15 D, 111—Tait's Ev, 237—Shand's Pr, 396

[S] The terms of a minute of reference to oath should be precise and definite, and a minute which embraces different lines of examination is irregular *per* Lord Justice-Clerk (Hope) in Lindsay *v* Outram, 1851 14 D 53 had referred to the oath of the pursuer, who thereupon deferred back to the defender, and where the defender died before the oath was emitted and his heir on being sisted in his room, sought to retract the original reference the Court held that to be incompetent, because the heir's object evidently was to take advantage of his ancestor's death whereby the deference had been rendered inoperative (*b*) A party will not be allowed to retract a reference after the other party has deponed to certain of the articles referred (*c*) Nor will a retractation be allowed where the object of the party is merely delay (*d*) In one case, where a summons was referred to the defender's oath, and he gave in a qualified oath, whereupon the pursuer attempted to resile, being willing that the defender should take out protestation against him, the Court held that the pursuer must either accept the oath, or be excluded from taking it at a subsequent stage of the cause (*e*) If the Court had interponed authority to the reference, the pursuer would not have been allowed to resile from it on any terms

§ 1568 The party retracting must bear the expense which the reference has occasioned to his opponent, and in unfavourable cases the Court inflict on him a farther payment of expenses (*f*)

CHAPTER III —OF DEFERRING TO THE OATH OF THE PARTY WHO MAKES THE REFERENCE

§ 1569. When a party, to whose oath reference has been made, is not in a position to speak distinctly upon the facts, he may defer to the oath of his opponent, and the Court will require that party to depone whom they consider to have had the best opportunities of knowing the facts (*g*)

(*b*) Galbraith *v* M'Neill, 1828, 7 S, 63 (*c*) Henry *v* Lyon 1681 1 B Sup, 321, 881, S C (*d*) Chalmers *v* Jackson *supra*—Tait's Ev 237—Shand's Pr, 396 (*e*) L Torrie *v* Wardlaw 1627 M 9391

(*f*) Chalmers *v* Jackson *supra* (*g*) Stair, 4 44, 13—Ersk 4, 2, 8—Tait Ev 237—Oliphant *v* Ker 1627 M 9391—Galbraith *v* M'Neill *supra*

CHAPTER IV.—OF REFERRING TO THE OATH OF ONE PERSON AS REPRESENTING OR BINDING ANOTHER

§ 1570 In general, the appeal to an adversary's conscience, which is involved in a reference to oath, can only be made by referring to the oath of the party who has the substantial interest in the cause There are cases, however in which one person so fully represents another, or a number of others, that a reference to his oath is competent where they are interested. On these points some illustrative cases will be found in the corresponding chapter upon admissions (*a*) But in regard to such cases it will be observed, that the power to make a simple admission in the name of a person may be conferred, where authority to bind him absolutely by an oath on reference would be withheld

§ 1571 No clearly defined rule can be laid down as to the nature and extent of the authority which allows one person to bind another by his oath on reference In general, the Court rejected the oath of a person who was not excluded as a witness under the old objection of interest, and this was sometimes regarded as testing the competency of the reference (*b*) But it does not meet the case of reference to a party's wife (*c*), while it is only a very few of the persons who came within the class of interested witnesses, whose oaths would be competent against those associated with them The rules on the point must therefore be examined in detail, with reference to the different modes in which one person may represent another

I *Reference to Oaths of Co-Partners and Joint Adventurers*

§ 1572 During the subsistence of a copartnery each of the partners has full powers of administration, and can bind the others in all matters connected with the common business But it does not seem to have been settled whether this principle allows a person litigating with a company on a matter within the copartnership

(*a*) *Supra* § 1465, *et seq*

(*b*) See Kirkwood v. Wilson, 1823, 2 S. 125—Moir v. Towers, 1829, 7 S. 902—Cromar v. D. Gordon, 1820, 8 S. 353—Ferrier v. Graham, 1831, 9 S., 419—Borthwick v. Christie, 1838, 16 S. 1136—Adam v. Maclachlan, 1817, 9 D., 560

(*c*) *Infra*, § 1576 *et seq*—See also *infra*, § 1590. It is to the oath of a general manager or commissioner for a party which seems to be competent, although he would not have been excluded as a witness

to refer to the oath of any one of the partners whom he may select instead of referring to the oaths of them all. Deponing on a reference to oath not being an ordinary act of administration, can hardly be said to be embraced by the copartnership; and the leaning of the Court is against allowing a reference to the oath of only one partner (*d*). There are many cases, indeed, where such a reference would leave a *hiatus* in the proof; as, for example, where resting-owing being referred to the oath of one partner, he deponed that he did not pay. Such an oath would by no means infer that the debt was subsisting, as it might have been paid by another partner or discharged in some transaction between such other partner and the creditor (*e*). Yet if one partner admitted the constitution of a proper company-debt, it would be difficult to refuse effect to his oath as against the others, since the partner might have bound them effectually by a written acknowledgment, and then oaths denying the constitution could not countervail his admission of it.

§ 1573. At all events it seems to be clear, that if the whole business transactions of a company have been intrusted to one of the partners as general manager, the reference may be confined to his oath (*f*).

If, however, reference has been made to the oaths of all the partners, it will not be held to be exhausted by the deposition of one of them (*g*).

(*d*) In M'Nab v. Lockhart, 1843, 5 D. 1014, which was an action against the partners of a dissolved company, Lord Medwyn observed that "in the ordinary case of partners, all acting in the business of the company, he thought one partner cannot be selected to whom the reference is to be made, but the reference must be made to the whole defenders;" and the other judges seemed to adopt this view. Again, in Broom v. Edgley, 1843, 5 D. 1094, Lord Justice Clerk Hope observed: "It is very true that in the first instance the deposition of one partner, either before or still more after dissolution, may not be sufficient to constitute liability against the others without also a reference to their oaths. Thus it is not enough to single out a partner who may know of the constitution of the debt, but may not from his situation in the company have had any means of knowing or attending to the pecuniary affairs of the concern; and so we found, after very full consideration, in a recent case in this division" (M'Nab v. Lockhart, *supra*). Mr Tait (p. 265) lays down that the oath of one partner may bind the company; but although this may be correct, it is not borne out by the cases on which he founds, viz., Stewart v. Stewart, 5th December 1823, 2 S. 558, and Nisbet's Tr. v. Morrison, 23d January 1829, 7 S. 307. The view in the text is supported by the rule that a reference to arbitration by one partner will not bind the company unless they assent to or homologate it; Ersk. 3, 3, 20; 2 Bell's Com. 618.—Lumsden v. Gordon, 1728, M. 14,567.

(*e*) Broom v. Edgley, *supra* (*d*).—But see Stewart v. Stewart, 1823, 2 S. 558, as noted *supra* § 455.

(*f*) See Gow v. M'Donald, 1827, 5 S. 472; *infra* §§ 1576, 1579; compared with Kendall & Co. v. Campbell, 1766, M. 12,351.

(*g*) Cleland v. M'Cleland, 1851, 13 D. 504.

§ 1574 After a partnership has been dissolved, the oath of any of the partners will not affect the interests of the others (*h*)

§ 1575 The contract of joint adventure does not embrace a liability by one adventurer for statements made by another on a reference to his oath (*i*)

II *Reference to Oath of Opponent's Wife*

§ 1576 A wife is presumed to be *præposita rebus domesticis* of her husband and as such to be intrusted with ordering and paying for all furnishings required in his family (*k*) On this account one who sues the husband for the price of such furnishings may prove his claim by the oath of the wife, not as a witness, but as representing and deponing for her husband on a reference to oath (*l*) And the reference may comprehend the subsistence as well as the constitution of the debt (*m*).

§ 1577 Reference to a wife's oath is also competent on matters relating to any business over which the husband may have placed her—*e g*, to prove furnishings for an inn or shop intrusted to her care (*n*)—provided a foundation for the reference is laid by proof of such special *præpositura* In like manner, where a wife was cited in an action of exhibition *ad deliberandum* of deeds belonging to her, but in which her husband had an interest *jure mariti* and where he had left Scotland and intrusted her with his charter-chest reference to her oath was allowed, under certification that if she did not depone she would be held as confessed (*o*) Here the wife had the substantial interest in the cause and, in so far as her

(*h*) Nisbet's Trs *v* Morrison's Trs 1829 7 S 307 —Easton *v* Johnston, 1831, 9 S 419—M'Nab *v* Lockhart *supra* (*d*)—Per L Just Clerk in Broom *v* Edgley *supra* (*d*)—Neill & Co *v* Campbell and Hopkirk, 1849 11 D, 979

(*i*) Duncan *v* Forbes, 1831 9 S, 541 See also Kerr *v* Lawson, 1747 M, 14,567—Tait Ev, 260—*Supra*, § 1467

(*k*) The rules as to the extent of this *præpositura* will be found in 1 Fraser Pers and Dom Rel 298, *et seq* As to its termination by inhibition or separation see ib, 318, *et seq*

(*l*) Ersk, 3, 7 18, note —Tait's Ev, 263 4—1 Fraser Pers and Dom Rel, 312—Dick, 1672, 2 B Sup 615—Dalling *v* Mackenzie, 1675 M, 6005, 12,480, S C—Lauder *v* Chalmers, 1685 M 12,481—Cochrane *v* Lyle 1740, M, 6018—Paterson *v* Taylor 1771, M, 12,485, Hailes 391, 5 B Sup 474 S C—Young & Co *v* Playfair, 1802, M 12,486

(*m*) Young & Co *v* Playfair *supra*—1 Fraser Pers and Dom Rel, 312 See also Calhoun *v* Stewart's Reps 1797 M, 12,042

(*n*) Barclay *v* Binnie, 1630 M 12,479—Cochrane *v* Lyle 1740 M 6018

(*o*) L Cunninghame *v* L Cardross, 1680 M 12,495 3 B Sup, 389 S C See also L Swinton *v* L Westnisbet 1633 (Spottiswood Rep), M 1000

husband was concerned, she had been specially intrusted to act in his absence. On the other hand, where a husband, when sued for repayment of money alleged to have been advanced to his wife as *institoria* in his shop, admitted that she acted in that capacity but denied that the money was *in rem versum* of him, the Court were of opinion that the latter fact could not be proved by her oath, as her *præpositura* did not embrace borrowing money (*p*). Again, in an action of reduction-improbation of an inhibition, where the pursuer having failed in his proof, alleged that the wives of the inhibitors had corrupted his witnesses, and that the circumstances inferred that the husbands were accessory to their acts (which however, was not proved), the Court would not allow the allegations to be established by the wives' oaths on reference (*r*).

§ 1578. It might be thought that, as a husband is liable for personal debts contracted by his wife before marriage, the creditor would be entitled to prove them by her oath, because she has an interest like that of a partner in the common stock, and because she should not be allowed by marrying to prejudice the rights of her creditors. But it has been settled that a wife's oath on reference cannot be taken on such claims, to the effect of making her husband liable (*s*); and in like manner, her oath is inadmissible against her husband suing on personal obligations, which were granted to her before marriage, and passed to him *jure mariti* (*t*). Nor will the husband be held as confessed upon his wife's failure to appear and depone in either of these cases (*u*).

§ 1579. A learned judge has observed that "the principle of these decisions is this and it is a correct one. If a creditor who suffers his claim of debt against a woman to lie over unconstituted until after her marriage, were to be permitted then to bring it forward, and prove it by her oath, so as to affect the husband's estate, the consequence would be that whenever a dispute took place be-

(*p*) M'Intyre *v.* Graham, 1795, Hume D., 203.

(*r*) Renton *v.* L. Wedderburn, 1632, M., 6787, 12,480, 12,488, S. C.

(*s*) Ersk., 4, 2, 10—Heriot *v.* Watson, 1613, M., 5850, 12,489—Ker *v.* Ly Covington, 1627, M., 12,489—A. B., 1628, 1 B. Sup., 259—Stirling *v.* ——— 1630, M., 12,490—Graham *v.* Stirling, 1631, 1 B. Sup., 73—Temple *v.* Ly Whittinghame, 1636, M., 12,490—Crichton *v.* Logan, 1682, M., 6006—Urquhart *v.* Nairn, 1688, M., 12,491—Monro *v.* M'Leod, 1809, Hume D., 215—Morice *v.* Monro, 1829, 8 S., 156—1 Fraser, Pers. and Dom. Rel., 295—*Contra*, Brunton *v.* Maxwell, 1830, M., 12,490—Wilson *v.* Robinson, 1688, M., 12,493. The wife's oath of calumny is also inadmissible on such claims, Paton *v.* Pitcairn, 1676, M., 12,491—Bruce *v.* Alexander, 1676, 2 B. Sup., 193.

(*t*) Bruce *v.* Alexander, *supra*—Reid *v.* Barnes's Heir, 1682, 2 B. Sup., 50.

(*u*) Urquhart *v.* Nairn, 1688, M., 12,494—Paton *v.* Pitcairn, *supra*. See also Graham *v.* Tours, 1688, M., 12,491.

tween the married parties the whole substance of the husband might be carried off by false claims, which could always be easily made" (x) But with deference it is thought that the risk of an improbable fraud and perjury in a very few cases is no ground for rejecting in all cases the evidence of the person most familiar with the fact in issue The correct principle seems to be, that as the husband comes in place of the wife, both as to her debts and rights, her oath is incompetent, on the ground that the cedent's oath cannot be taken against the assignee (y)

§ 1580 But the oath on reference of a wife as to her antenuptial debts has repeatedly been admitted during the marriage with the view of affecting her share of the goods of communion on the marriage being dissolved (z), and it is also competent in order to give the creditor a claim against any estate belonging to the wife, from which the *jus mariti* is excluded (a) Moreover, when the subject of the action is estate of this nature, reference to the wife's oath is competent for she is the real party to the cause And therefore where a wife with consent of her husband, had instituted legal proceedings in relation to an alimentary fund, from which the *jus mariti* was excluded, and the agent who had conducted the proceedings sued the wife for payment of his business account, her oath (to which reference seems to have been made without objection) was held to prove both constitution and resting-owing of the account after it had incurred the triennial prescription (b)

§ 1581 The question was once raised, but not decided whether a husband is liable for his wife's antenuptial debt, where the only proof of it is her oath on reference, and he declares that he believes her deposition to be true (c) At all events the husband cannot be called on to confess or deny, in an oath of calumny or otherwise, whether he believes his wife's oath (d) Yet in an action against a husband and wife for payment of her antenuptial debt it was held competent to refer to her oath the existence of the debt and her promise to pay and to the oath of her husband whether he

(x) Per L Balgray in Morris v Monro, *supra* The reason stated by his Lordship would apply with equal force to the wife's oath on matters within her *præpositura*, which as already noticed, may be taken against her husband (y) Bruce v Alexander, *supra*—See *infra* § 1596 (z) Ersk 4, 2 10—Ker v Ly Covington 1627, M 12 189—A B, 1628, 1 B Sup, 259—Graham v Stirling 1631 1 B Sup, 73—Temple v Ly Whittinghame 1636, M, 12 190—Graham v Tours, 1668 M, 12 191—Reid v Barner's Heir, 1683, 2 B Sup, 50 (a) Graham v Tours, *supra*—1 Fraser Pers and Dom Rel, 296 (b) Gifford v Rennie, 1853, 15 D, 451 See also Macara v Wilson, 1848 10 D, 707 (c) Young v Young 1667 M, 5851 (d) Graham v Tours, 1668 M, 12 191

knew of the promise before the banns of their marriage were proclaimed (*e*) And where a widow had been appointed tutrix to her son and had entered into a second marriage in an *actio tutelæ* at the son's instance against her and her husband, the Court sustained reference to her oath as to her intromissions, on the ground that the husband, before marriage, knew that she was tutrix, and, therefore liable to account (*f*) *A fortiori*, if action of diligence on the wife's antenuptial debt was raised before the marriage, her oath on reference will be received as against her husband, the matter having become litigious before his interest arose (*g*)

III *Reference to Oath of Opponent's Child*

§ 1582 In an action against a party for furnishings to his son *in familia*, the Court once admitted the son's oath, apparently on reference, to prove the libel (*h*) But this is thought to be erroneous because the father's obligation for needful furnishings to his child arises *ex lege*, and not from any actual or presumed *præpositura* and to hold a father bound as under a reference to oath for whatever articles (not being improper or extravagant) his children might admit having received, would be a fruitful source of fraud The child may be examined as a witness to prove the furnishings, which was not competent at the date of the case referred to (*i*)

IV *Reference to Oath of Opponent's Tutor or Curator*

§ 1583 Actions by or against a pupil are conducted in name of his tutor, whose admissions on record are conclusive Reference to the tutor's oath is also admissible on matters which fell under his official administration (*k*) But, as to facts which occurred before he took office, his knowledge is non-official, like that of an ordinary

(*e*) Wemyss *v* Christison, 1606 M, 12 489 (*f*) Marshall *v* Basil 1676, M 5851, 12 492 (*g*) Bankt, vol 1, p 125—Davie *v* Johnstone, 1649, 1 B Sup 429—1 Fraser Pers and Dom Rel, 296—See also *infra* § 1596—But see *contra* Crichton *v* Logan 1682, M 6006 (*h*) Lauder *v* Chalmers, 1685, M, 12 481 cited, without being questioned by Mr Tait, Ev 263 See also Hopkirk *v* Deas 1698, M, 12,482 (*i*) See on Admissibility of Relations as witnesses, *infra*, § 1714, *et seq* (*k*) Stair, 1, 6 20—Ersk, 1, 2 10—Tait Ev, 262, 4—2 Fraser Pers and Dom Rel, 118 134—Gaut *v* Loch 1665, M, 12 029—In Hepburn *v* Hamilton 1761 M, 8465, 12 480 the tutor's oath was taken *ex officio* In L Fairnie *v* L Melville, 1662 M 12 308, and Bruce *v* Jack 1670 1 B Sup, 609 it was taken before answer In Mulloch *v* Graham 1673, 1 B Sup 681 the admissibility of the tutor's oath was considered "very difficult to be determined

witness, and reference to his oath is incompetent (*l*) It seems however, not to render the tutor's oath incompetent on matters within his administration, that, at the date of the action, he had become *functus officio* (*m*) But where this was the case, and where the tutor was brother-in-law to the party calling for his oath the Court refused to allow the reference (*n*) Where, on a reference to the oath of a tutrix she refused to depone on account of having forgotten the matter, the Court would not hold her as confessed, but found that she might be forced to depone by horning and caption, as other witnesses' (*o*).

§ 1584 A curator is only a counsellor to assist the minor in managing his affairs the minor being the chief party in causes in which he is interested Accordingly, reference can only be made to the minor's not to the curator's oath (*p*)

§ 1585 The Court refused a reference to the oath of a judicial factor *loco tutoris* on matters which occurred before his appointment (*r*) Nor is it likely that they would allow such a reference even on matters of his individual administration

V Reference to Oath of a Trustee

§ 1586 Trustees appointed by a party to administer a certain estate, or to manage his whole affairs, are in the same position as tutors with regard to their admissions on record, and their control over processes relating to the trust-estate It has not been settled, however, that the trustee's oath on reference, like that of a tutor (*s*), is admissible in regard to matters in which he acted officially, but inadmissible in all other cases, nor are the authorities on the point either uniform or satisfactory Mr Erskine observes, incidentally, that no "debt can be fixed against a truster by the oath of the trustee" (*t*), and this seems to be the rule where the radical right and interest remain in the truster, as for example, where he has exe-

---

(*l*) Stair, *supra*—Ersk, *supra*—1 Fraser Pers and Dom Rel 118, 131—Eccles v Eccles, 1664, M, 16,270—Gordon's Tutors, 1707, M, 8909—See also *supra* § 1502 (*h*) and *infra*, § 1586 (*m*) Tait Ev 262—Johnstone v Dean of Guild of Aberdeen, 1676, M 12,480—But see Waddell v Wadderstoun, 1707, M, 12,484

(*n*) Waddell v Wadderstoun *supra*—See also *supra*, § 1539 and *infra*, § 1607-8

(*o*) Caunt v Loch, 1665, M, 12,029 (*p*) Forbes v L Pitsligo, 1628 M, 8920, 12,179—E Mar v his Vassals, 1628, M, 8918, 1 B Sup, 265 S C—Maitland v Cashogill 1623, M, 8917—Somerville v his Debtors, 1670, 2 B Sup, 197—*Supra* § 1502—See *contra* Hay v Ogstoun 1666, M, 16,276 (*r*) Stewart v Syme 12th Dec 1815 F C (*s*) See *supra*, § 1583 (*t*) Ersk 4 2, 10

cuted a trust-deed for behoof of his creditors. But the Court drew a distinction between such a trust and one where the trustee takes up the *universum jus* of the truster on his decease, and accordingly, under a trust-deed of this kind their Lordships sustained reference to the oaths of the trustees as to resting-owing of the debt in a prescribed bill to which the truster had been a party (and which, therefore, did not become known to the trustee officially), all questions as to the effect of the oath being reserved (*u*). There seems however to be a conflict between this case and one in which a party suing road trustees on a prescribed account for various pieces of work, having, without objection, referred his claim to their oaths, it was held incompetent to examine one of them on matters which had come to his knowledge, not *qua*-trustee, but when acting in another capacity (*v*). In another case, considerable discussion arose as to whether the oath on reference of the trustee of one deceased partner could be available against the representatives of the other, to prove the debt in a prescribed account said to have been incurred by the company; but the Court seem to have entertained no doubt that the oath (which had been taken without objection), was effectual against the trust-estate of the partner whom the deponent represented (*x*). In an action at the instance of two statute-labour trustees, the defender was allowed to refer to their oaths whether they had the statutory qualification for the office (*y*).

VI. *Reference to Oath of an Executor.*

§ 1587. In actions where a party appears as executor of another, reference to his oath will not be allowed except with the view of affecting his own interest in the executry estate (*z*). And this rule has been applied not only to executors-dative (who hold the office *ex lege*) but also to those who (like trustees) are nominated to it by the deceased (*a*). The reason for the rule is, that the office of an executor extends only to realising and distributing the estate under his charge, and that in accounting with the creditors

---

(*u*) Murray *v.* Laurie's Trs., 1827, 5 S. 515. (*v*) Hotson *v.* Threshie, 1833, 12 S., 57. (*x*) Nisbet's Trs. *v.* Morrison's Trs., 1829, 7 S., 307. The trustees of the latter partner had compromised the case before the question noticed in the text was brought before the Court. (*y*) Moore *v.* Young, 1843, 5 D., 494.

(*z*) Ersk. 4, 2, 10—Monteith *v.* Smith, 1624, M. 12,477—Scott *v.* Cockburn, 1627, M. ib.—Ker *v.* Ly. Covington, 1627, M. 12,478—Dickson *v.* M'Kalla, 1681, 3 B. Sup., 407—See Hay *v.* Ogstoun, 1666, M. 16,276. (*a*) Cases in preceding note.

and legatees of the deceased, he would not be allowed credit for debts proved only by his own oath The Court have sometimes allowed the executor s oath to be taken on the libel, declaring that the decree should only affect his own interest, and with this view requiring the party who made the reference, to find security to repay the sum decerned for, in the event of the executor being called to account for it by other persons interested (*b*)

§ 1588 Any one of a number of executors may emit the statutory oath of verity to a debt due to the estate, with the view of voting for the trustee in the debtor's sequestration (*c*)

VII *Reference to Oaths of Magistrates, Agents Factors, &c*

§ 1589 In a suspension at the instance of a party charged by the dean of guild of a burgh, on the ground of a promise by the provost and magistrates who had previously been in office the suspender was allowed to prove his averment by the oaths of these magistrates (*d*), which seem to have been taken as on a reference Whether this decision be right or not it is thought that in an action with a burgh, reference may be made to the oaths of the magistrates (who are the *domini litis*) provided the matter referred fell within their official knowledge (*e*)

§ 1590 Where the tacksman of a toll, suspending a charge by the clerk of the road trustees, offered to prove by the clerk's oath one of his grounds of suspension, namely, partial payment to the clerk's partner, the Court sustained the reference (*f*) And reference to the oath of the agent of a branch bank seems to be competent in regard to his agency transactions (*g*)

§ 1591 On the other hand reference to the oath of a factor has been held incompetent as a mode of proof against his principal (*h*) The oath of a ships-husband, who was also a part owner, was held not to bind the other owners (*i*), and reference to the oath of the law-agent and mandatory of a person abroad, was held to be incompetent (*k*) It is rather thought, however, that if a

---

(*b*) Ker *v* Ly Covington, *supra*—Scott *v* Cockburn, *supra* (*c*) Watson *v* Morrison, 1848, 10 D, 1414 (*d*) Johnston *v* Dean of Guild of Aberdeen, 1676 M, 12,480 (*e*) See *supra* §§ 1583, 6 (*f*) Dykes *v* Hill, 1828, 6 S, 479, and Session Papers (*g*) See Dickson *v* Ker, 1830, 9 S, 125—See also Colebrook *v* Douglas, 1780, M, 9371—Douglas, Heron, & Co *v* Alexander, 1781, M, ib (*h*) Cromar *v* D Gordon, 1830, 8 S, 353—Mackay *v* Ure, 1849, 11 D, 982—But see *contra*, Hunter *v* Dun, 1809, Hume D, 584 (*i*) Duncan *v* Forbes, 1831, 9 S, 510 (*k*) Stein's Assig *v* E Mar, 1827, 6 S, 1 The principle of

party intrusts the whole conduct of a concern to a general manager or commissioner, transactions which such a functionary has entered into may be proved by reference to his oath, as binding upon the person whom he so fully represents (*l*)

§ 1592 Where a party on reference to his oath depones that he believes that a certain thing was done (as, for example, that payment was made) by his clerk or servant, such deposition does not imply a devolution of the reference to the clerk or servant, whose oath, therefore can only be taken as that of a witness (*m*)[1]

VIII *Reference to Oaths of Co-Debtors and Co-Creditors*

§ 1593 In actions at the instance of a creditor against parties bound to him as principal and cautioner, the principal's oath denying the debt, frees both himself and the cautioner because a cautionary obligation cannot stand alone (*n*) But if the principal obligant depones affirmatively on a reference to his oath, that will not affect the cautioner, whose obligation bound him to pay what the principal owed, not what he merely admitted that he owed (*o*) Still less will the oath of a cautioner admitting the debt render the principal obligant liable for it (*p*)[2]

§ 1594 The oath of one of several *correi* will not bind any of the others, but reference must be made to the oath of each of them in so far as it is intended to affect his individual interest (*r*) Lord Stair lays down that the oath of one co-obligant denying the debt frees all the others (*s*) But Mr Erskine sees "great reason to doubt" that opinion (*t*) There cannot be any question, however,

the cases in this and the two preceding notes is supported by Bruce & Co *v* Beatt, 1765, M 11,109—Kendal *v* Campbell 1766, M, 12 351—Kirkwood *v* Wilson, 1823, 2 S, 125—But see *contra*, Mowat *v* L Southesk, 1673, M, 9421 (*l*) In support of this view see *supra*, §§ 1473, 1576, 7, 1583, 1590 (*m*) Mackay *v* Ure, 1849, 11 D 982—Cochrane *v* Ferguson 1831, 9 S, 501 (*n*) Stair, 4, 44, 8

(*o*) Malvenius *v* Baillie, 1686, M 12,465—*Supra*, § 1471—See *contra*, Porteous *v* Fordyce 1716, Rob Ap Ca, 183 (*p*) Cochrane *v* Ferguson, 1831, 9 S 501

(*r*) Ersk 4 2 10—Cases noted *supra*, §§ 459, 460 (*s*) Stair, 4, 44, 8

(*t*) Ersk, 4, 2 10

[1] A party alleged that he had, by verbal agreement, entered into a lease of certain subjects for three years, and that the verbal agreement had been followed by *rei interventus* It was held that the verbal agreement could not be proved by parole, but that a reference to the oath of the alleged lessor was competent, Walker *v* Flint, 1863, 1 Macph, 417 Unless *rei interventus* be relevantly averred, a reference to the oath of the lessor as to the terms of a verbal lease is incompetent See opinion of Lord Deas, Cowan's Trustees *v* Carstairs, 1862 24 D 1382

[2] Cautionary obligations must now be in writing, 19 and 20 Vict c 60, § 6

that if one of the debtors (as, for example in a prescribed bill or account) swore that he paid it, or that the creditor discharged the debt on any other ground, such oath would liberate the others, because it would render it impossible for the creditor to prove resting-owing by their oaths The result would be different if in a reference both of constitution and resting-owing, one of the joint obligants merely deponed *non memini*, or denied the constitution, because another obligant might, on a reference to his oath admit both of the facts in question, and so prove the debt as against himself (*u*)

§ 1595 In like manner, where there are more creditors than one in an obligation, the oath on reference of one will not bind the others (*x*), unless they are connected in some of the modes noticed elsewhere, in which the oath of one person is available against another (*y*)

IX *Reference to the Cedent's Oath in actions with the Assignee*

§ 1596 In general, a person litigating with an assignee cannot refer to the oath of the cedent, for the obvious reason that the assignation divested the cedent of his interest (*z*) [3] It is otherwise if the assignation has not been intimated, because, in that case, the real right has remained in the cedent, and, as he might discharge the debt or assign it anew, he may extinguish it by an oath denying its constitution or subsistence (*a*) Reference may also be made to the cedent's oath, if the subject of the assignation was made litigious before intimation, *e g*, by an action raised by the debtor against the cedent to extinguish the debt (*b*) But where the debtor in a bond, after having executed a summons to reduce it, suffered the action to fall by lapse of year and day without any judicial act having followed, the Court held that the matter had

---

(*u*) See *supra*, § 1586 (*y*) (*x*) Tait Ev, 261—Bell *v* Gib, 1619, M, 12,477—L Kenton *v* L Wedderburn, 1632, M, 6787, 12,480, 12,488, S C

(*y*) *Supra*, §§ 1572, 1596, 1601 (*z*) Stair, 3, 1, 18—Ersk, 3, 5 9—Ib, 3, 6, 10—Stewart *v* Baillie 1617, M, 828—Monypenny *v* Black, 1622, M, 829—Cunningham *v* Ross, 1627, M, 12,453—Chancellor *v* Seltzer, 1692, 4 B Sup, 3

(*a*) Stair, *supra*—Ersk, 3, 5, 9—L Pitfoddles *v* L Glenkindy, 1662, M, 12,451—Fraser *v* Fraser, 1678, M, 844 (*b*) Stair, *supra*—Ersk, *supra*—L Pitfoddles *v* L Glenkindy, *supra*—Aitchison's Assignee *v* Drummond 1737, Elch, "Assignation," No 3, and ib, Notes "Adjudication," No 10

[3] Held, in a question with an assignee, that it was not competent for a third party to refer to the oath of the cedent, Campbell *v* Campbell, 1860, 23 D, 159

not been rendered litigious, so as to make the cedent's oath admissible in a question between the debtor and an onerous assignee whose right had been acquired after the summons had fallen (*c*)

§ 1597. Where it is proved that an assignation has been granted in trust for behoof of the cedent, reference to the cedent's oath will be allowed in an action for payment of the debt for he is the person really interested and he may not deprive the debtor of a good defence by assigning the ground of debt to a friend in trust for his own behoof (*d*) The cedent's oath has also been received where it was probable, from his relationship to the assignee, that the assignation was either in trust or gratuitous (*e*)

§ 1598 Again (as indicated by the case just noticed) reference to the cedent's oath is competent, as against the assignee, where the assignation is gratuitous, because a creditor may not prejudice his debtor in order to favour his friend, and it is not likely that in such a case the cedent will swear falsely to the prejudice of his assignee (*f*) If the assignation is partly onerous and partly gratuitous, the cedent's oath will be admitted to affect the assignee, in so far as the right is gratuitous (*g*) But "the Lords thought that the cedent's oath was not competent" as against an onerous purchaser from an assignee whose right bore to be for "love and favour" (*h*)

§ 1599. The same principles apply in regard to bills While reference to the oath of the drawer will not be admitted, as against an onerous indorsee to prove a defence by the acceptor, it will be received if there be proof from the indorsee's writ or oath that he merely holds for the drawer's behoof (*i*) And this will also be

---

(*c*) Houston *v* Nisbet, 1708 M, 8329 (*d*) Ersk, 3, 5, 10—Arrat *v* Lindsay 1664, 2 B Sup, 358—Barnes *v* Hamilton 1677, 3 ib, 130—Innes *v* Lawson, 1828, 6 S, 513 (*e*) White *v* Brown, 1665, M, 12,455—Wardlaw *v* Pittello 1671, M, 12,456, 2 B Sup, 613 S C (*f*) Stair 3 1, 18—Ersk, 3, 5, 10—Barnes *v* Hamilton, *supra*—Arrat *v* Lindsay, *supra*—Cases in preceding note—Wright *v* Shiel, 1665, M, 12,455—Jack *v* Mouatt, 1666, M, 12 456—Telfer *v* Spence, 1749, M 12 461—Elch, "Assignation," No 7 (*g*) Elch, *supra*—Steil *v* Orbiston, 1679 M, 8467 But compare Barnes *v* Hamilton, 1677 3 B Sup 130, from which it appears that non onerosity is not inferred from the consideration being inadequate, provided the right was not granted *ex gratia* (*h*) Aitchison's Assignee *v* Drummond, *supra* (*i*) See *supra* § 336 *et seq*—Jameson *v* Grahame, 1832, 11 S, 80—Innes *v* Lawson, 1828, 6 S, 513—Compared with Boys *v* Gillies 1685, 2 B Sup 69—Thomson & Co *v* Sharp *infra* In Pringle *v* Campbell, 1731, M, 12,461, an indorser's oath was received against an onerous indorsee to prove that the bill had been granted for a gambling debt the *ratio* being, that the indorser was liable in warrandice and therefore was the party really interested But this decision may be questioned the rule where the presumption in favour of the onerosity of the indorsation is overcome by the admitted or proved facts (*k*) Where suspension of a charge was raised on the ground that the bill had been granted for the accommodation of a person not named in it, and that the charger was not an onerous holder, and where the charger admitted that he held as trustee for a prior indorsee the Court passed the note on caution, and Lord Moncreiff observed that non-onerosity must be proved by the oaths of all the indorsees (*l*)

§ 1600 If a party, when sued by the assignee of his creditor pleads that the debt has been extinguished by compensation, and the assignee replies that the compensating debt was recompensated, the debtor is entitled, as against the assignee, to prove by the cedent's oath that the recompensating debt was paid or discharged (*m*) The reason is that that debt being in the person of the cedent unassigned, the debtor would be entitled, as in a question with the cedent, to prove any defence to it by the cedent's oath and the assignee may not prejudice the debtor in his defence

X *To whom Reference may be made in cases of Arrestment*

§ 1601 Arrestment, until completed by furthcoming, is inchoate diligence and corresponds to an assignation which has not been intimated As the arrester has only right to the subject of his diligence *tantum et tale* as it stood in the common debtor, the arrestee is entitled to prove, by the common debtor's oath on reference, any defence he may have to payment of the debt arrested (*n*) In one case, where Johnston had arrested a quantity of spirits belonging to Vallange, and where Sinclair, who resisted his claim to have them made furthcoming, offered to prove by the oath of Vallange that they had been sold to him (Sinclair) before the date of the arrestment, the Court allowed the oath to be taken before answer although Vallange was said to be "bankrupt, or at least insolvent," and, upon advising the oath, they preferred

(*k*) See *supra*, § 357, *et seq* (*l*) Thomson & Co *v* Sharp, 1849, 11 D, 887

(*m*) Boyd *v* Story, 1674, M, 12,456—Crawford *v* M Carter, 1675, M, 12,458

(*n*) Ersk, 3, 6, 16—Tait Ev, 257—Horn *v* L Murray, 1711, M, 12,464—Forbes *v* Forbes' Crs 1711, M ib—Nairn *v* Ogilvie, 1725, M, 12,468—Moodie's Crs *v* Broomfield, 1736, M, 12,471, Elch, "Qualified Oath," No 3, S C—Pringle *v* Biggar, 1711, M, 12,473—Blair *v* Balfour, 1715, M, 12,473, Elch, "Arrestment," No 25—Hogg *v* Low, 1826, 4 S, 702 As to the competency of this reference when the common debtor is bankrupt (which was the fact in several of these cases), see *infra* § 1603

Sinclair's claim (*o*) So in a competition between an assignee in security and an arrester where the assignee was preferred in regard, 1st, to debts and obligations specified in the assignation, 2d, to debts incurred and payments made for the common debtor before the arrestment and 3d, to payments after the arrestment, but applicable to obligations incurred before it,—the common debtor's oath on reference was admitted to prove against the arrestor what debts fell under these heads (*p*) But where Isles and Gill were competing creditors of Duncan who was a creditor of Reid, and Isles having arrested in the hands of Reid, Gill alleged that before the arrestment Duncan verbally ordered Reid to pay to him which Reid promised to do, whereupon he (Gill) made farther furnishings to Duncan, the Court would not allow Gill to prove his averments by Duncan's oath (*r*) There were several specialties, however, in this case

§ 1602 The arrester may, of course, refer to the oath of the arrestee, whether the debt intended to be attached is resting-owing But the arrestee's oath denying the debt will not affect the common debtor (*s*), or an assignee of the common debtor (*t*), because it was not emitted on a reference by them Yet where an arrester referred to the arrestee, whether the debt was owing at the date of the arrestment, and the arrestee having deponed *negative* was assoilzied, and where the arrester afterwards received from the common debtor an assignation to the same debt in security, and for payment of the debt upon which the arrester's diligence had proceeded, the Court held that the oath which the arrestee had emitted was *res judicata* as against the assignee, and repelled his plea that as it could not bind the common debtor it was ineffectual against him when suing in right of that party (*u*)

XI *Reference to the Oath of a Bankrupt in questions with his Creditors*

§ 1603 By the present Sequestration Act, the bankrupt's estate is vested completely in the trustee, and the bankrupt is divested absolutely and irredeemably' as at the date of the sequestra-

(*o*) Sinclair *v* Johnston 1749, M 12 475 See this case noticed *supra* § 1545 and see *infra*, § 1604 (*p*) Gordon *v* Dunnet 1839 M L and Rob 28

(*r*) Isles *v* Gill 1837 9 Sc Jur 489, 1 D, 380, note—See a similar case, Elphinstone *v* Home 1674 M 12 462 (*s*) Fisk 3 6 16—Tait Ev, 257—*Contra* L Palmerino *v* Lochinvar 1627, M, 970 (*t*) Elies *v* Watson 1712 M 11,041 (*u*) Ferguson *v* Maitland, 1722 M, 11 012

tion (x)[4] The bankrupt has thus no interest in the estate, except in the improbable event of its yielding a surplus after paying all the creditors and the expenses of sequestration, and therefore (except in that case) his oath admitting any individual debt would not affect himself, but would merely favour one creditor to the prejudice of another, whereas the policy of the bankruptcy law is to fix the rights of the creditors in the state in which they were at the date of the sequestration, without any additional security or proof flowing from the bankrupt

On these grounds it is incompetent for an individual creditor to refer to the bankrupt's oath as conclusive evidence of his claim (y) Nor will the bankrupt's oath on reference be admitted as a part of the claimant's proof, because reference to oath is incompetent except on a *quasi*-contract by which the parties stake the issue on the deposition (z) On the same principle it is incompetent for a party sued by the trustee in the sequestration to refer to the bankrupt's oath (a)[5]

§ 1604 It is not necessary now to detail the cases on this subject which occurred under the former bankrupt law They seem to have established the practice of admitting the bankrupt's oath before answer (b), or *ad remandam veritatem* (c) The oath was not regarded as full proof of the creditor's claim (d), and was refused where there was risk of collusion e g, where the claimant was related to the bankrupt (e), or where the claim had a suspicious ap-

---

(x) 2 and 3 Vict, c 41, §§ 78, 83

(y) Dyce v Paterson, 1846, 9 D, 310—Adam v Maclachlan, 1847, ib, 560

(z) Adam v Maclachlan, *supra*—Dyce v Paterson, *supra*

(a) See Shepherd v Campbell, 1823, 2 S 346 517, where the reference was refused, *supra*, (y)—*Contra*, Halkerston v Lindsay, 1783, M 12,476

(b) Blair v Balfour, 1745, M, 12,473, Elch "Arrestment," 25 S C—See Sinclair v Johnstone, 1749, M, 12,475

(c) Selkrig v Somerville 1804, Hume D 500—Halkerston v Lindsay, 1783, M, 12,476—2 Bell's Com, 484

(d) Cases in preceding note—Bell's Com, *supra*—Tait Ev, 268 In some cases it does not appear what effect was given to the oath Grant v Grant's Crs, 1788, M, 12 476—Forbes v Forbes' Crs, 1711, M, 12 464—Moonie's Crs v Bloomfield, 1736, M 12,471, Elch, "Qualified Oath" No 3—Pringle v Biggar, 1741, M, 12,473—Buchan v Robertson Barclay, 1787, M, 11 128

(e) Spalding v Shaw, 1805, Hume D, 501—Moir v Towers, 11th July 1829, F C, 7 S 902—Johnstone v Grant, 1835, 13 S, 606—Compare with Nairne v Ogilvie 1713 M, 12,468—See *contra*, Selkrig v Somerville, 1804 Hume D 500

---

[4] 19 and 20 Vict, c 79, §§ 12, 102

[5] Reference to bankrupt's oath refused as incompetent, Thomson v Duncan 1855 17 D 1081

pearance (*f*) The want of correct principle which pervades these decisions has been exposed in a recent case (*g*)

§ 1605 Reference to the oath of a bankrupt who had been discharged on a composition was refused in a question between a debtor to the estate and the trustee for the creditors, because the discharge having extinguished the bankrupt's interest, he was thereby rendered admissible as a witness (*h*)

§ 1606 It is not settled whether the oath of one who has granted a trust-deed for behoof of his creditors will be admitted on a reference by one of them If his estate turns out to be more than sufficient to pay them all he has a manifest interest to exclude any person from ranking to whom he is not indebted, whereas, if his debts exceed his assets, his oath would only affect the ranking of the creditors The proper course seems to be to refuse the oath unless there is reason to expect a surplus after paying the debts (*i*) [6]

XII *Of the effect of interest, relationship, &c, in excluding Reference to the Oath of one party as representing another.*

§ 1607 In the different cases in which reference is competent to the oath of one person as representing another connection between these persons, or their unity of interest, will of course not exclude the oath. But it is otherwise where reference is proposed to the oath of a tutor, trustee, magistrate, or the like, whose individual interest is opposed to that of the persons whom he represents It is incompatible with the idea of the judicial compact which every reference to oath implies, to suppose that a party would consent to be bound conclusively by the statement of one who has a conflicting interest to him, and, as already observed (*j*), an oath on reference cannot be taken merely as an adminicle of evidence Accordingly, where resting-owing was referred to the oaths of the trustees of the acceptor of a bill, one of them was not allowed to depone, because he was a co-acceptor, and had an interest to

(*f*) Nairne v Drummond 1725 M, 12,468 (*g*) Per L Just-Clerk (Hope) in Adam v Maclachlan, 1847 9 D, 560 (*h*) Ferrier v Graham, 1831, 9 S, 419 See *supra* § 1571 (*i*) Robertson v Thom 1848, 21 Sc Jur, 96 interlocutor of Lord Wood Ordinary, acquiesced in (*j*) See *supra* § 1603

[6] In the case of Renny v Will 18th July 1863 (not reported) a reference by a creditor to the oath of a party who had granted a trust-deed for behoof of his creditors was refused but it was observed that such a reference might be competent in certain circumstances

render the trust-estate liable in order to free himself from part of the debt (*k*)

§ 1608 In several cases, also, the Court refused to admit the oath of a bankrupt, upon the ground that he was related to the party who tendered the reference (*l*). And where a party, as assignee to a bond granted to his tutors for his behoof, used diligence against the granter of it, the latter was not allowed to refer his allegation of payment to the oath of one of the tutors, who was his brother-in-law (*m*)

Again, where the drawer and acceptor of a bill were brothers, and the drawer, having become bankrupt, executed a trust-deed for behoof of his creditors, and was afterwards convicted of a crime (fraud and wilful imposition) inferring infamy, and where one of the creditors of the drawer, having paid the bill and taken an assignation to it used diligence against the acceptor, and afterwards carried on the case on behalf of all the creditors of the drawer—the acceptor, in a suspension of the charge, was not allowed to prove his averment of no value by the drawer's oath In the Court of Session the reference was disallowed on the ground of infamy, but the House of Lords waived deciding that point, and held that, under the circumstances, the oath had been properly rejected, because the admission of it was more likely to defeat than to promote the justice of the case (*n*)

§ 1609 Upon this broad principle, reference to oath should be refused wherever the person to whom it is tendered, as representing the party really interested, is so connected by relationship common interest, or otherwise, with the party who proposes the reference, that its admission would not be consistent with truth and equity And, if the person whose oath is called for has been convicted of a *crimen falsi*, the risk of his emitting a false deposition where contrary proof is inadmissible (as it is in cases of reference to oath) will probably induce the Court to reject the reference

§ 1610 Where James raised reduction on the ground of compensation of bonds which he had granted to his brother John and Nairn, a creditor of John, used arrestments in the hands of James, James was allowed to prove the compensation by John's oath, on

(*k*) Murray v Laurie's Tr, 1827, 5 S, 515

(*l*) Spalding v Shaw, 1805, Hume D, 501—Mein v Tovey, 11th July 1809, F C, 7 S, 902, S C—Johnstone v Grant, 1835 13 S, 606—Compared with Selkirg v Somerville, 1801 Hume D 500—See *supra*, § 1601

(*m*) Waddell v Madderstoun, 1707, M, 12,184 The other tutor had died

(*n*) Ritchie v Mackay 1826 4 S 531, affd, 3 W S, 181—See *supra* § 1539

account of litigiosity having arisen before the arrestment, but he was required to report the oath although John was abroad, because there would have been risk of collusion if he could have succeeded on John being held as confessed for not deponing (*o*)

CHAPTER V.—OF THE EXAMINATION AND RE-EXAMINATION.

§ 1611. In the Court of Session oaths on reference are emitted before a Commissioner of Court. They may also be taken by the judge and minuted by the clerk (*a*). But an oath on reference ought not to be emitted before a jury, because jurors would be apt to weigh it along with the other evidence in the cause, instead of receiving it as full and conclusive proof, and because its application raises only questions of construction and law, which are for the Court, not for a jury (*b*). Yet an oath which before the trial has been emitted on special facts, may be used (like an admission on record) as full proof of these facts.

§ 1612. In several older cases parties whose pleadings were not candid were examined in presence of persons who were acquainted with the facts (*c*). But this useful check against falsehood has not been applied recently.

§ 1613. The oath is the same as that which is administered to a witness, and the examination is conducted by the party who makes the reference (or his procurator) putting to the deponent the questions which the reference embraces. But it is not necessary for him to examine upon the whole of these, as it lies with him to determine whether the oath emitted as to a part of them is sufficient for his purpose (*d*). The commissioner ought to put any questions which he deems proper for eliciting the whole truth upon the matter deponed to, whether these questions are agreeable to the

(*o*) Nairn *v* Ogilvie, 1725, M., 12,468. See *infra*, § 1661.

(*a*) See Gordon *v* Gordon, 1731, Cr. and St. 60. The oath is taken in this way in the Sheriff-court, unless where the party resides out of the county.

(*b*) See Bell's Pr. § 2268.—Allan *v* Thomson, 1822, 3 Mur., 3.

(*c*) Williamson *v* Tennant, 1627, M., 12,305—Carmichael *v* Dempster, 1676, 1 B. Sup. 770—Weir *v* Russell, 1703, M., 12,331—Bett *v* Hardie, 1759, M. 13,217. See also Lyell *v* Brand, 1667, M., 1817, 9362, 2 B. Sup., 128, S. C. *supra*, § 1510, (*b*).

(*d*) Observed by Lord Mackenzie in Heddle *v* Baikie, 1841, 3 D., 370.

parties, or not (*e*) This is especially his duty where the deponent is an ignorant person (*f*)[1]

§ 1614 Documents may be shown to the party in order to refresh his memory, or to obtain from him explanations as to discrepancies between them and his oath (*g*)

§ 1615 When the deponent is known to be a man of honour, an examination as to the details of the case is unnecessary the simplest course being to ask him at once the main question referred But if his veracity is doubtful, the examination should be commenced with those questions regarding the history and circumstances of the transaction which only bear upon it indirectly, and these ought, if possible, to be put in such sequence that a foundation of probability will have been laid for the truth of the main fact before it comes to be examined upon When the examination is skilfully conducted in this way, the result sometimes is that the party inclosed in a net of circumstantial evidence formed out of his own answers, is forced to admit the main fact referred Or it may happen that, in attempting to deny circumstances which only bear indirectly on the issue and in extemporising explanations to make his deposition seem consistent he involves himself in contradictions, the consequence of which may be that his answer, negative of the main question is disregarded from not being borne out by the rest of his deposition (*h*)

§ 1616 The party cannot escape from an interrogation of this kind by refusing to answer except upon the main question referred He is bound to answer all special questions which are relevant to that matter, and if he refuses, he may be held as confessed (*i*)

§ 1617 Special interrogatories, however, must usually be put before general ones, for if a general question has been put and answered, any questions which infer contradiction of the answer are incompetent, as involving the party in risk of perjury (*j*) If

(*e*) Soutar *v* Soutar, 1851, 14 D, 140 (*f*) Soutar *v* Soutar, *supra*

(*g*) Boyd *v* Ker, 1843, 5 D, 1213—Heddle *v* Baikie, 1847, 9 ib, 1254—*Infra* § 1631—See also § 1628, *et seq* (*h*) See Murray *v* Murray, 1839, 1 D, 484

(*i*) A B, 1751, M 12475—A B, 1756, 5 B Sup, 842—Callander *v* Wallace, 1717, M, 9416—Swan *v* Swan, 1736, M, 9418, Hailes, 998—*Supra*, § 453

(*j*) Ersk, 4, 2, 15—More's Notes 417—Tait Ev, 238-9—Husband *v* Blair, 1678 M, 9422—Aitken *v* Finlay 1702, M, 9423—Callander *v* Wallace *supra*

[1] A party who is under examination on a reference to oath is entitled to the assistance of counsel to suggest questions to the Commissioner or to refer to documents Blair *v* M'Phun 1856, 18 D 1202—See also Cooper *v* Hamilton 1824 2 S 610 affirmed, 1826 2 W S 59 referred to in Blair *v* M'Phun by Lord President M'Neill

however, a general answer contains inferences the grounds of these may be investigated by special questions, because such a mode of examination involves only error in judgment not falsehood, in the party deponing (*k*) This is often illustrated in references of resting-owing and of non-onerosity of bills, in which the general denial is an opinion founded on facts, which come out in a detailed examination, and bear a different inference (*l*) Accordingly, where the holder of a bill after having deponed "that he paid value for the indorsation and was an onerous indorsee," refused to specify what the value was, the Court found that his heir was not entitled to the privileges of an onerous indorsee (*m*)

§ 1618 It is also competent to put special interrogatories after the deponent has given a general answer to a question which did not infer one, otherwise the party making the reference would, without any fault on his part, be deprived of his right to examine in detail And where special questions have been put irregularly after more general ones, the Court will give effect to the answers, because the objection to that mode of examination is personal to the party, and may be waived by him (*n*)

§ 1619 Where an oath on reference is in general or doubtful terms, the Court will allow a re-examination in order to clear it up, provided the questions do not involve the party in perjury (*o*) This, for example has been allowed where the first oath did not exhaust the reference (*p*), and where in a reference of resting-owing of the debt in a prescribed bill, the party deponed generally that it was compensated, and that he did not consider himself indebted to the pursuer (*r*), and again in a reference as to the existence of a trust, where the alleged trustee deponed generally *negative* and specified certain facts, but it was not clear whether he meant to deny that the right was intended to be held by him for behoof of the alleged beneficiary (*s*) Thus, also, in a reference of the onerosity of an indorsation, where the oath (which referred to

(*k*) See Fotheringhame *v* Mauld, 1679, M, 16,179—Heddle *v* Baikie, 1841, 3 D, 370 (*l*) Callander *v* Wallace, *supra*—Turnbull *v* Borthwick, 1830, 8 S 735—Per L Gillies in Heddle *v* Baikie, *supra*—See *supra*, § 453, *et seq*

(*m*) Swan *v* Swan, 1786, M, 9418, Hailes, 998 (The session papers show that the general answer was given to a general question of onerosity) (*n*) Heddle *v* Baikie, *supra* (*l*)—See also Fotheringhame *v* Mauld 1697, M, 16,179

(*o*) Ersk, 4, 2, 15—Tait Ev, 289—Cases in following notes, and A B, 1666, M, 9421—Ker *v* Ker, 1667 M 3874, 9421—Forbes *v* Forbes' Crs, 1711, M, 12,464—Mowat *v* E Northesk, 1673, M, 9421 (*p*) Thomson *v* Thomson, 1830, 8 S, 571—See also Johnstone *v* Law, 1843, 5 D, 1373 (*r*) Fraser *v* Fraser 27th June 1809, F C (*s*) Fotheringhame *v* Mauld 1679 M, 16,179

certain books and to other bills) was unsatisfactory and partly unintelligible, the Court allowed a re-examination (*t*) And where the creditor in a bill being examined three years after its date on a reference whether the bill had been granted for value deponed that he had had numerous bill transactions with the suspender's father (who was a co-obligant in the bill) and that the consideration of the bill was cash, but he could not remember how much, the Court allowed him to be re-examined, on the understanding that in the interval he should consult his books and other documents as to the transactions in question (*u*)

A re-examination has also been allowed where the oath had been emitted in absence of the party who had made the reference, and whose failure to attend had arisen from want of proper notice of the diet (*x*)

§ 1620 On the other hand, wherever a deposition is full and specific, the re-examination will be refused, "otherwise an oath, in place of being the end, might be more properly called the beginning of strife" and the re-examination would be useless unless it brought out a contradiction, which would involve the party in perjury (*y*) Accordingly, where the defender in an action laid on (*inter alia*) a loan of money, admitted that he received the sum, but added that it was in re-payment of a debt, and where the pursuer thereafter alleged that the only debt due by him to the defender had been under a condition which had not been fulfilled the Court would not allow a re-examination on that fact, because it might have involved the party in perjury (*z*) In another case, where, in answer to a general interrogatory, the defender in an action for payment of an account deponed that he was not resting-owing the sum claimed, the Court for the same reason refused to allow him to be re-examined as to whether he had not received a parcel of lint, and in what way he had paid for it (*a*)

(*t*) Young *v* Pollock, 1832 10 S, 570 (*u*) Anstruther *v* Lewis, 1851, 13 D, 841 (*x*) Peacock *v* Smiles, 1828, 6 S, 1081—Hill *v* Cameron, 1835, 13 S, 764—Compared with Ker *v* Hopkirk and Imlack, 1833, 12 S, 272

(*y*) Ersk 4, 2, 15 (*z*) Aitken *v* Finlay, 1702, M, 9423

(*a*) Campbell *v* Tait, 1677, M, 9422—Compare cases noted *supra*, § 1617

CHAPTER VI.—OF THE INTERPRETATION AND EFFECT OF THE OATH ON REFERENCE

§ 1621 The oath on reference is conclusive of the matter referred, whether it be favourable or adverse to the deponent's interest, so that in applying the oath, the point is not *quid verum est*, but *quid juratum est* (*b*) This rule does not flow from the superior credibility of the oath (for an unsupported statement in a party's own favour is doubtful evidence) but from the reference being a *quasi* contract by which the parties are supposed to stake the result on the oath (*c*)

§ 1622 An oath on reference is conclusive both in the action in which it is emitted, and in all subsequent proceedings involving the same matter, and depending on the facts deponed to (*d*) And accordingly, an oath on reference emitted in the Bill Chamber by the charger will exclude farther proof at the instance of the suspender, on the case coming into the Court of Session on the passed note (*e*) But the oath admitted in one action will not exclude a new action for the same debt, if laid on different *media concludendi* (*f*)

§ 1623 The party wronged by a false oath, however, has an indirect means of redress, by prosecuting the deponent criminally for perjury (*g*), and if he proves his libel, the Justiciary Court may sentence the perjurer to pay to him such a fine as will cover what he lost in the civil suit (*h*) But this is a cumbrous remedy, and very far from adequate, for it is much more difficult to establish perjury in a criminal prosecution, than it would be to contradict the party's oath in the civil suit in which it is emitted

---

(*b*) Stair, 4, 44, 8—Ersk, 4, 2, 8—Tait Ev, 256—The oath may not be contradicted by the deponent's bond Rule *v* D Hamilton 1623, M, 13,231 or by his letter, Kincaid *v* Dickson, 1673, M, 12 143—Young *v* Pollock, 1832 10 S, 571, per L Craigie—See also Thomson *v* D Hamilton, 1688, 2 B Sup, 121 The defender's oath was held conclusive where it had been emitted under an erroneous decision in the inferior court sustaining a plea of prescription in which decision the pursuer had acquiesced, M'Donalds *v* Burden 1829 7 S 306—See also Turnbull *v* Borthwick, 1830, 8 S, 735

(*c*) Ersk *supra*—Tait, *supra*

(*d*) Stair, *supra*—Tait *supra*

(*e*) Wyllie *v* Latta 1832 11 S, 151

(*f*) Stair, 4 44, 8—Tait Ev 256

(*g*) 1 Hume, 373—Th Somerville, 1813, there noted—See also Stewart *v* M'Whirter 1713, 4 B Sup, 914, 5 ib, 99

(*h*) Where an indorsee on a reference of value for a bill of £43 deponed that he gave full value, and the oath was held conclusive of the civil interest, and the acceptors

§ 1624. When a party depones *non memini*, his oath is commonly held neither to admit nor to deny the fact referred, which may therefore be proved by such other evidence as its nature and the stage of the cause admit of (*i*). But if the matter is a *factum proprium et recens*, which the party cannot be supposed to have forgotten, his oath of *non memini* will show an attempt to evade or shirk the reference, and he will be held as confessed, in the same way as if he had refused to depone (*k*). This effect, however, will not follow where, owing to the number of transactions of the same kind which the party entered into, the unimportant nature of the fact referred, or any similar cause, an oath of *non memini* only indicates a not unnatural obliviousness (*l*).

§ 1625. Contradictions frequently occur in oaths on reference, and create considerable difficulty in ascertaining whether the party admits or denies the fact referred. Every such case must be decided on the terms of the individual oath; and it is only necessary to keep in view that the question is not whether there are discrepancies which throw doubt on the credibility of the statement, but *quid juratum est*, truly or falsely, on the matter. It may be observed, however, that if the contradiction is between specific facts, and facts which the party has inferred from these, the Court will disregard the inferences and give effect to the direct statements (*m*). This is often seen in references of onerosity of bills and resting-owing, where, notwithstanding the party's general denial, the Court deduce from his specific statements an inference to his prejudice.

§ 1626. As already observed, a party who states that a certain transaction was conducted, a certain payment made, or the like, by

---

paid, on a libel at their instance against the indorsee in the Justiciary Court, concluding for the pains of law, damages and expenses, they were allowed to prove *prout de jure* that the oath was false. They succeeded in doing so, whereupon the pannel was sentenced to imprisonment for six months, and to the pillory, and was fined £150 in payment of damages. "In this shape of an award of a large sum of damages, the Court substantially, though indirectly, corrected the iniquity of the civil decree proceeding on the false oath, which decree could not be directly set aside either in the criminal or civil court." Baron Hume's note of Th. Somerville, *supra*.

(*i*) Ersk., 4, 2, 11—Tait, Ev., 240—Fisher *v.* Lithgow, 1672, M., 12,142—Melvil *v.* E. Perth, 1693, 4 B. Sup., 171—See also Gow *v.* M'Donald, 1827, 5 S., 472. But see *contra* Thomson *v.* D. Hamilton, 1688, 2 B. Sup., 121.

(*k*) Ersk., *supra*—Tait, *supra*—Irvine *v.* Carruthers, 1675, M., 12,031—Littlegill, 1682, M., 12,035—Ly. Aboyne *v.* her Tenants, 1710, M., 10,145.

(*l*) See Wemyss *v.* Maitland, 1630, M., 9393—Thomson *v.* D. Hamilton, *supra*.

(*m*) See *e.g.*, Hunter *v.* Geddes, 1835, 13 S., 369—Grubb *v.* Porteous, 1835, ib. 603—Murray *v.* Murray, 1839, 1 D., 484—Gifford *v.* Rennie, 1853, 15 ib. 451—See *supra* § 153 *et seq.*, and § 515 *et seq.*

another person on his behalf, neither imports into his oath the statements which that person may have made, nor devolves the reference to him (*n*) In dealing with oaths of this kind, the Court will distinguish between cases in which the party states, from his own knowledge, that the individual acted in the way supposed, and cases in which the party merely infers from certain circumstances that such is the fact and they will not allow the deponent, by drawing an erroneous inference in his own favour, to deprive the other party of the proper legal effect of the facts admitted (*o*) [1]

CHAPTER VII —OF CONTRADICTING AND EXPLAINING THE OATH BY DOCUMENTS TO WHICH IT REFERS

§ 1627 It has already been seen that an oath on reference will receive effect, although it should contradict a writing under the party's own hand This is the rule where the oath refers to the document, but denies the statements which are therein contained (*a*), for the written statements may be untrue and the question whether it is true or false would involve a proof incompatible with the conclusive character of an oath on reference

§ 1628 But if an oath stating certain facts refers to documents as the source from which the party derived his information, the Court will hold the documents to be imported into the oath, and will judge for themselves whether the party's account or construction of them is correct (*b*) Thus in an action for payment of a

(*n*) *Supra*, § 1592 (*o*) See *supra*, §§ 455, 516, *et seq* —Gordon *v* Christie, 1678, M, 13,203—Hay *v* Fulton 1786 M, 13,220, Hailes, 995, S C

(*a*) *Supra* § 1621 (*b*) —Opinions in Hunter *v* Geddes, 1835, 13 S 369, *infra* (*d*), and per Lord President (M'Neill) in Nicol *v* Law, 1852, 14 D, 1044—Gibb *v* Winning, 1829, 1 De and And 97 In a reference to oath of the debt in a prescribed bill, bearing value received, the debtor may admit that he signed the document, but deny that he received value, see *supra* § 443, *et seq* (*b*) This is analogous to the rule stated *supra*, §§ 1625, 6

[1] On a reference to oath a defender deponed that he had paid to a relative with whom he had other pecuniary dealings, money to discharge the claim sued for, but had never seen a discharge, nor been told that the debt was paid His relative had left the country, and had died without a final settlement of their accounts having been made It was held that resting-owing was proved Crichton *v* Campbell, 1857, 19 D, 661

prescribed account, where the defender swore that he believed the account had been paid by his factor, and was certain of this from having settled accounts with the factor and otherwise, and from the receipts in process the Court granted diligence to recover the factor's accounts, and finding that these did not instruct payment, held that the account was resting-owing, and the House of Lords affirmed the judgment (*c*). In another case of this nature, where the defender deponed that the debt had been settled in terms of certain accounts, the Court held these to be imported into the oath and drew their own inference from them (*d*).

§ 1629. The same rule applies *a fortiori* where the oath involves an opinion in point of law as to the construction or effect of the documents to which it refers. Accordingly, where an arrestee deponed that he paid the debt under a former decree of furthcoming obtained by a creditor of the common debtor, the Court would not sustain the payment unless the decree was produced (*e*). So, where the debtor in a prescribed bill deponed not resting-owing, because he had assigned his effects to his creditors according to the law of England (where he resided at the time) and the assignment cleared him of all his debts, Lord Fullerton (Ordinary) required the deed to be produced, as the discharge was matter of law, depending on the construction and effect of the deed; and the Court afterwards gave effect to the judgment,—in which the defender had acquiesced (*f*). Again, in an action on a prescribed bill, where the defender deponed not resting-owing, as the pursuer had acceded

(*c*) Cooper *v.* Hamilton, 1824, 2 S., 728, affd., 2 W. S., 39.—See an analogous case, Mackay *v.* Ure, 1847, 10 D., 89.

(*d*) Hunter *v.* Geddes, 1835, 13 S., 369. Lord Glenlee observed: "No doubt the defender was bound to produce the account mentioned in his oath, and if the Court put a different construction on it from what he does, we are bound to give effect to it, and we did so in a late case." Lord Medwyn said, "I know that if a party refers to documents as confirming his oath, they may be produced, and his inference from them overruled, if not supported by them." Lord Justice-Clerk Boyle said, "When a party refers in any way to documents as grounds of his deposition, they become truly parts of it. . . . It was right to have the account produced, and it becomes necessarily part of the oath to which we are entitled to refer, as was decided in the case of Cooper, *supra* (*c*), affirmed in the House of Lords." Lord (Ordinary) Jeffrey took the same view, and after showing that the documents referred to did not prove payment, observed (note to his last interlocutor), "If this be the true result of the facts established by the oath, it is supposed to be plain enough that the defender could not alter or at all affect that result by swearing that in his opinion the debt was not resting-owing. This is a conclusion of law over which he has no control."

(*e*) Blair *v.* Balfour, 1748, M., 13,217.

(*f*) Stevenson *v.* Stevenson, 1838, 16 S., 1088.

to a composition-contract, and the composition money had been consigned the Court held that it lay with them and not with the deponent, to determine what was the legal effect of the composition-contract (*g*) It was probably on the same ground that in an action against Finlay on account of intromission with Aitken's sheep, where Finlay deponed that under warrant from the Laird of Cardross he had taken away nine ewes as Aitken's proportion of a levy for the militia, the Court held the quality extrinsic, unless the warrant was produced (*h*) And where Kilpatrick, being sued by Irvine for vitious intromission with goods *in bonis defuncti* of Clacherie, his (Kilpatrick's) father-in-law, deponed that ten days before Clacherie's death he bought the goods from Craik, to whom Clacherie had disponed them but he did not produce the conveyance the Court decerned against him (*i*).

§ 1630 There seems, however, to be some conflict between these cases and one in which the defender in an action laid on his having vitiously intromitted with his predecessor's writings, deponed that he only meddled with such as were his own by assignation of all his predecessor's personal estate and the Court, with hesitation and by a bare majority, assoilzied him, although (as Lord Fountainhall observes) the oath made the deponent "himself judge of what belonged to him" (*k*) Their Lordships probably considered that the oath took away the element of *culpa* on which the action was laid In another case, of old date and very doubtful authority, where the defender in a count and reckoning for his intromissions with certain crop, deponed that he had lawfully poinded them the Court refused to divide the oath, or to require him to produce the document of debt, decree, or warrant to poind upon which his defence was founded (*l*)

§ 1631 A late case, depending chiefly on specialties, seems to have qualified to some extent the rule in question In a claim by a landlord against his tenant for arrears of rent, the tenant (who pleaded the quinquennial prescription) deponed on a reference to his oath that the arrears had been partly extinguished by sales of sequestrated crop and the Court sustained this oath as negative of resting-owing, although an examination of the proceedings in the processes of sequestration seemed to show that the oath was erro-

---

(*g*) Brown v M'Intyre, 1828 6 S 1022 (*h*) Aitken v Finlay 1702, M, 9423 (*i*) Irvings v Kilpatrick, 1679, M, 13,229 (*k*) E Airley v Sharp, 1698, M, 9673, 13,205 See also Donaldson v Cunningham, 1694, 4 B Sup 136 (*l*) L Fenton v Drummond, 1632 M, 13 228

neous (*m*) The ground of decision was, that the party had not been properly examined on the processes of sequestration, so as to have made them part of his oath, the Court considering that if the examination had been complete, he might have explained the apparent contradiction The oath, also, had been emitted at the end of a long litigation and the landlord's mode of dealing with it involved a protracted investigation as to the disposal of the proceeds of the sequestrations. This case, therefore, does not come into conflict with the principles established by Cooper *v* Hamilton and kindred decisions (*n*) [2]

CHAPTER VIII —OF QUALIFIED OATHS ON REFERENCE

§ 1632 When a party, instead of answering categorically the questions referred, makes a partial admission, and adds an explanatory statement in his own favour, he is said to emit a qualified oath, and the question arises whether effect is to be given to the qualification Such cases depend on whether the qualification is *intrinsic* or *extrinsic* to the reference, or (as Dirleton defines these terms) whether or not it is "inherent in the act and matter in question" (*a*) Such questions have been frequently before the Court,

(*m*) Heddle *v* Baikie, 1847 9 D, 1254 *dissentiente* Lord Medwyn See also Cochrane *v* Ferguson, 1831, 9 S, 501 (*n*) *Supra*, § 1628 (*a*) Dirle Doubts and Stew Ans, p 214 This is adopted by Erskine, 4 2, 11

[2] When a person under examination on reference to oath has been previously examined as a haver, and excerpts from his books have been taken it is competent to show him the deposition, and to ask him if the excerpts contain a true account of the transaction to which they refer, Blair *v* M'Phun, 1856, 18 D, 1203 A deponent in a reference to oath produced documents on the defender's call, and deponed that all of them had relation to the matter referred, and were genuine It was held that they were not imported into the oath so as to form part of it Lord Justice-Clerk (Inglis),—"What the oath on this point has proved is, that they are genuine documents and relate to the matter referred, but I do not know that anything results from that but that they would be admissible in evidence if we were in a proof *prout de jure* Now we are in a case of proof by the oath of party It seems to me to be an insuperable obstacle to giving effect to these documents that we are in a case where the proof is limited to what is deponed under the reference It is not difficult to make writings available in an examination on reference, if what is necessary is done—that is, placing the writings in the hands of the deponer, and interrogating him in reference to them, his answers to which interrogatories are part of the evidence But all that is evidence is what the defender says on his oath," Gordon *v* Pratt, 1860 22 D, 903 See also Hamilton's Executors *v* Struthers, 1858, 21 D, 51

and there are few points attended with more difficulty, and on which the decisions have been less uniform or less based on principle.

1. *Of Intrinsic and Extrinsic Qualifications in regard to the Constitution of Obligations.*

§ 1633. When the constitution of an obligation is referred to oath, it will only be proved if it is admitted expressly, or is the proper legal inference from admitted facts. Accordingly, any statements incompatible with the constitution of the obligation are intrinsic, because an oath so qualified denies the obligation.

Thus in an action for repayment of an alleged loan, it is an intrinsic quality that the money was received as a gift (*b*) or to extinguish a debt due to the deponent (*c*). And in a reference to oath of a verbal agreement, it is an intrinsic fact that the parties agreed that its terms should be committed to writing, and that the deponent resiled without having executed the relative deed; because where writing is stipulated for, there is *locus pœnitentiæ* until it has been interponed (*d*). Thus also in an action on a prescribed bill, it is intrinsic to state that the deponent signed it in mistake for a receipt (*e*); or that he received the amount in payment of a previous bill due to him by the pursuer's father, and granted the bill sued on as the receipt for that payment (*f*); or that he signed the bill on an agreement that it should not constitute a debt against him (*g*); or that he accepted it blank for the purpose of retiring another bill with the proceeds, but that the payee applied them to a different purpose, which was not for the deponent's benefit (*h*).

§ 1634. Again, in a claim for wages, it is intrinsic that the services were agreed to be given for board and maintenance with-

(*b*) Stewart *v.* Walpole, 1804, Hume D., 416. With this case compare Taylor *v.* Crichton, 6th Dec. 1854, 27 Sc. Jur. 85, where the debtor's oath that he received the money, but that nothing was said about repaying it, and he considered he was not bound to repay, was held to prove resting-owing. See also Meikle *v.* Stewart, 1737, M. 13,225.

(*c*) Aitken *v.* Finlay, 1792, M., 9423, 13,205, S. C. So in Minty *v.* Donald, 1824, 3 S., 394, where the defender swore that he received the money as payment of a debt due to himself by one to whom the pursuer advanced it for that purpose, and that he never undertook to repay it. See also Sinclair *v.* Sinclair, 1703, M., 13,205.

(*d*) Campbell *v.* Douglas, 1676, M. 8470, 13,203, S. C.—*Supra*, § 603.

(*e*) Agnew *v.* M'Rae, 1782, M., 13,219.

(*f*) Fraser *v.* Fraser, 27th June 1809, F. C., decided by a bare majority.

(*g*) Little's Trs. *v.* Baird, 1827, 5 S., 820.

(*h*) Drummond *v.* Crichton, 1848, 10 D. 340.—*Supra*, § 443.

out wages (i) and that the pursuer claiming wages as first mate, was hired and served as second mate during part of the term libelled (k)

§ 1635 Where the claim is for the price of goods, it is held to be an intrinsic qualification that they were not furnished on the defender's credit (l), or that they were furnished to extinguish a counter claim (m) or as the consideration under an agreement that the defender should teach the pursuer to play the violin, and should paint pictures for the pursuer's wife, all which the defender was ready to do (n) In an action for the price of wine, it is intrinsic that the defender refused to receive the wine, because it was spoiled (o) and that the wine was sent with directions that it should not be sold till farther order, in consequence of which the defender kept it until it was in danger of spoiling and then sold it at a certain rate per tun (p) [1]

§ 1636 Thus, also an action laid on the defender's wrongful intromission with moveables or money belonging to a deceased person will fail, if the defender depones that he received them from the deceased as a gift, because such an oath negatives the allegations that they were *in bonis defuncti*, and that the intromission was wrongful (r) In all claims, indeed, for restitution of moveables, the deponent's admission that he received them from the other party will be intrinsically qualified if he adds that they were gifted (s) and in cases laid on wrongful intromission, the intromitter may add that he acted by judicial authority, or with the consent of the other party (t) So in an action by an heir against a debtor for exhibition of the bond which he had granted to the ancestor, where the debtor deponed that the deceased redelivered the deed to him on deathbed as a *legatum liberationis*, on his under-

(i) Alcock v Easson, 1842, 5 D 356—Anderson v Halley, 1847, 9 D, 1222, per Lord Ordinary Cunninghame, acquiesced in—*Supra*, § 506—*Contra*, M'Naughton v M'Naughton, 1813, Hume D, 396 (k) Paden v Govan, 1751, M, 13,207, Elch, "Qualified Oath," No 7, S C (l) Meyer and Mortimer v Leonard, 1851, 14 D, 99 (m) Campbell v Grierson, 1848, 10 D, 361

(n) Lauder v M'Gibbon, 1727, M, 13,206 (o) Trotter v Clark, 1667, M, 13,204—Stair, 4, 44, 14 (p) Learmonth v Russell, 1661, M, 13,201 With this case compare Robertson v Clarkson, 1784, M, 13,211, noted *infra*, § 1655.

(r) Howies v Wyllie, 1765, M, 13,208, 5 B Sup, 913—Mortimer v Archibald, 1710, M, 13,230, 4 B Sup, 777, S C—Donaldson v Cunningham, 1691, 4 B Sup, 136—L Airley v Sharp, 1698, M, 9673, 13,205 (*supra*, § 1630)—Mitchell v Wright, 1759, M, 8082 (s) Scott v Elliot, 1672, M, 13,228—L Fenton v Drummond, 1632, M, 13,228 (t) Stair, 4, 44, 14.

[1] Thomson v Duncan, 1855, 17 D, 1081, *infra*, § 1655 note 7

taking to pay the expense of the burial, the Court sustained the qualification, but required the deponent to prove that he had fulfilled his undertaking (*u*). And where Edgar sued Ewing for money which Ewing had uplifted under Edgar's verbal order, and Ewing deponed that "he lifted it for his own behoof Edgar being owing him as much," the qualification was held to be intrinsic (*x*).

§ 1637. Looking to the principles which these cases establish, there is room for questioning a decision, where in an action by a master against the cautioners in an indenture for the damages caused by the apprentice's desertion, the Court held as extrinsic the defender's oath that the pursuer had beaten and put away the boy (*y*). This oath, it is thought, negatived the averment of desertion, on which the action was laid. In another case where reference was made to the oath of the charger in a bill, whether it was for value, and he deponed that it was granted by the suspender (who was his father-in-law) some time after his marriage, and that it was in implement of a promise of tocher to him by the suspender, the Court held the quality to be extrinsic (*z*). But as this oath negatived the averment of no value, which was the point referred, it seems to have been qualified intrinsically.

§ 1638. Where a party admits that he undertook the obligation libelled on, but under a condition which has not been fulfilled, his oath is held to be qualified intrinsically, for it denies that under existing circumstances the obligation has arisen (*a*). But where a party, in a reference by his brother as to whether he signed a certain deed regarding their father's estate, swore that he did so under a verbal condition that the parties should execute mutual tailzies in each other's favour, under which condition he stated that he would implement the deed in question, the Court held the quality to be extrinsic (*b*). The reason probably was that the deed had been set up by the admission that it had been validly executed, and a condition could not be adjected to it except by the writ or oath of the party who founded on it.

§ 1639. Qualifications as to the terms or stipulations of the obligation deponed to are intrinsic, being inherent in the matter referred. This principle was applied in a process of removing,

---

(*u*) Walker *v* Clerk, 1702, M., 13,230. See also Mortimer *v* Archibald, *supra*—Brown *v* Mitchell, 1669, M., 13,202.

(*x*) Edgar *v* Ewing, 1677, M., 13,229.

(*y*) Fife *v* Daw, 1667, M., 13,233.

(*z*) Halliday *v* Halliday, 1826, 5 S., 116.

(*a*) Dirleton, p. 298—Stair, 4, 44, 14—Ersk. 4, 2, 11—More's Notes, 418—Tait Ev. 244—Meikle *v* Tennant, 1737, M. 13,225—Greig *v* Boyd, 1830, 8 S., 382—*Contra*, L. Torsons *v* Pringle, 1611, M. 13,247.

(*b*) Christies *v* Christie, 1745, M. 8437, 13,225.

where the tenant having averred that he possessed under a lease, the landlord deponed that it was one of the stipulations of the agreement (which was verbal) that the defender should remove, if the deponent wished to pull down the house or use it himself (*c*). And in a reference as to the existence of a certain partnership, the qualification that the deponent did not contract for the time libelled, or for any definite time, and always understood that it was in his power to dissolve the contract when he pleased, was held to be intrinsic (*d*). In an action of mails and duties, where the defenders deponed that they possessed under verbal leases at certain rents, but that the pursuer agreed to make a certain abatement, the Court held that if the abatement was made before warning time of the year to which it applied, the quality was intrinsic, because it was part of the contract on which the tenants agreed to take their possessions for the year; but that, if the abatement was agreed to after the warning time, the qualification was extrinsic, because the tenants having become bound to possess at the old rents by tacit relocation, the abatement was not a condition of the contract, but a subsequent agreement engrafted upon it (*e*).[2]

§ 1640. The distinction taken in this case would show that an extrinsic qualification in regard to the constitution of an obligation arises where the party admits that the obligation was undertaken, but adds that it was annulled or modified by a subsequent transaction; the reason being that the burden of proving that fact falls on the deponent (*f*). Accordingly, where a shipmaster being sued by a seaman for payment of wages, qualified his admission of the contract by stating that the pursuer was unfaithful and undutiful

(*c*) Thomson v. Robertson, 1824, 3 S. 186. (*d*) Ewing v. Dundas, 1749, M., 13,226. See this case again noted *infra*, § 1640 (*h*). (*e*) Montgomery v. Baillie's Tenants, 1676, 2 B. Sup., 202. (*f*) See More's Notes, 419.

[2] A defender deponed that a deceased offered to assist him with funds to take a farm; that if he was successful in the farm, repayment was to be made, but that he was not to repay if unsuccessful. He further deponed that advances were made,—that improbative acknowledgments were granted for these,—that he was unsuccessful in the farm,—that the subject of repayment was not resumed,—but that, on his deathbed, the deceased said the acknowledgments would never come up against him. It was held that the oath was affirmative, the constitution of the debt being proved, but not the alleged condition, nor any subsequent extinction. The majority proceeded upon the view that it did not appear from the oath that there was an express obligation that the money was not to be repaid if the party was unsuccessful; but Lord Curriehill thought the oath, being to the effect that the money was not simply borrowed, but was advanced under a condition which had not been purified, was negative of the reference. Hamilton's Executors v. Struthers, 1858, 21 D., 51.

during the service, and embezzled part of the cargo, the Court held that the qualification was extrinsic (*g*) And in a case already noticed, where a party deponed that the contract of copartnery libelled on was not meant to be binding longer than he chose, his additional statement that he had intimated his intention to put an end to the contract was held to be extrinsic (*h*) Farther, in an action of exhibition and delivery of a marriage-contract, where the defender deponed that he executed it in minority and without consent of his curators, and that he had therefore cancelled it, the Court held the qualification to be extrinsic, because it did not amount to a denial of the constitution of the obligation, but merely to a ground for reducing it, the burden of proving which lay on the deponent (*i*) Opposite decisions have been pronounced as to whether, in a reference to oath of the debt due under a prescribed bill it is an intrinsic or an extrinsic qualification that the bill was granted for an illegal consideration or purpose (*k*) It is thought to be intrinsic,—the Court, however judging for themselves whether the facts specified by the deponent involve an illegality fatal to the bill[3]

II Of Oaths admitting the Constitution of Obligations, but denying their subsistence

§ 1641 In cases falling within the sexennial, quinquennial, and triennial prescriptions the pursuer must prove the subsistence as well as the constitution of the obligation, and therefore in all these cases, its discharge is intrinsic to the reference (*m*) The reason is, that these prescriptions are partly founded on a presumption of payment during the statutory periods[4] On the other hand,

(*g*) Workman *v* Young 1699, M, 13,234 (*h*) Ewing *v* Dundas, 1719, M 13,226 (*i*) Carse *v* Kennedy 1714 M 13 247 (*k*) M Neill *v* M Kissock, 28th Feb 1805, F C—*Contra* Clarkson's Tr. *v* Gibson, 8th June 1820, F C—Campbell *v* Scotland 1778 M 9530 These cases are noted *supra*, § 445

(*m*) See this fully considered *supra* § 142, *et seq* §§ 473 503, *et seq*

3 The holder of a bill deponed that the consideration for which it was granted was partly payment of a debt and partly payment of a sum which the acceptor, his father-in-law had promised him if he would take back his wife from whom he had been divorced, and in repayment of expenses connected with the divorce The Court held that, except the direct debt there was no consideration, there being no liability on the father-in-law for the expenses of the divorce, and the alleged consideration of taking the woman who had been his wife to live with him being extrinsic They were further of opinion that this consideration would in any view, have been *turpis causa*, Graham *v* Kennedy 1860 22 D 560

4 But it was laid down in Cullen *v* Smeal, 1853 15 D 868 with regard to the

the object of the vicennial prescription of holograph writs being to guard against forgery, the party's oath admitting that the writing is holograph, restores its character as a valid and subsisting deed, and it is extrinsic to state that it has been discharged (*n*).

§ 1642. With regard to cases not falling within these statutes, it depends on the nature both of the obligation, and of the alleged extinction, whether the latter will be held intrinsic or extrinsic.

If the oath admits that an obligation was constituted by writing, the qualification that it has been discharged is extrinsic, because a written contract infers a written discharge, and the admission sets up the deed, like a proving of its tenor, whereupon the obligant must prove its discharge by proper evidence (*o*). This rule has been applied to an oath admitting that a debt was due by bond or "ticket," but adding that it was paid in money (*p*), or grain and a horse (*r*). So where Hume arrested in the hands of Taylor as a debtor of Seaforth, and referred the debt to Taylor's oath, and Taylor deponed that he agreed in writing to purchase cattle from Seaforth, that he advanced 14,000 merks in part-payment, that a large proportion of the cattle were not delivered, that no more were delivered than the advance covered, and that, after the arrestment, he and Seaforth cancelled the agreement, the Court rejected the qualification of the advance, but allowed Taylor to prove the tenor of the contract, that it might be seen if it set forth that matter. They also allowed Hume to prove that more cattle were delivered than Taylor admitted (*s*).

§ 1643. There seems to be an exception to this rule where a party depones that he granted a document of debt but that the creditor cancelled or re-delivered it on discharging the debt, because that coincides with the presumption *chirographum non extans presumitur solutum* (*t*).

§ 1644. *E converso* of the same rule when the obligation does

(*n*) See *supra*, § 422. (*o*) Ersk., 4. 2, 13. See § 1638 (*b*).

(*p*) Barrens *v.* Hutchison, 1631, M. 13,232. The document was subscribed with initials, which the defender admitted to be his. (*r*) Allan *v.* Young, 1677, M., 13,223—See also Blair *v.* Balfour, 1748, M., 13,217—*Infra*, § 1652, *et seq.*

(*s*) Hume *v.* Taylor, 1679, M. 8352. (*t*) Brown *v.* Mitchell, 1669, M., 13,202—Walker *v.* Clerk, 1702, M., 13,230—*Supra*, §§ 382, 1636 (*t*).

triennial prescription, that the statute 1579, c. 83 (properly c. 21, see Thomson's ed.) introduced no presumption of payment but merely enacted a certain specific and imperative rule on the subject of probation. So that a creditor must prove the subsistence of his debt, because the statute provides that, after the three years, he shall have no action, except he either prove by writ or oath of his party."

not infer a written discharge, its extinction is intrinsic to an oath admitting its constitution. This generally holds in regard to obligations not constituted by writing, because *unumquodque eodem modo dissolvitur quo colligatur* (u). Accordingly, where, in an action of accounting by a member of parliament against his agent, the defender deponed that he had received a sum to employ in bribing town councillors at an election, and that he had so spent it, the quality was held intrinsic (x). And where a corporation had money in loan from Hepburn which was claimed by Home as executor of Stewart, for whom Hepburn was said to have been trustee, and by Colt as representing Hepburn, Hepburn's oath (taken on deathbed to lie *in retentis*) that Stewart had once deposited money in his hands, but that he had afterwards called it up, was held to be qualified intrinsically (y). But payments for which there ought to be written vouchers are extrinsic to the oath, although the obligation was only verbal (z), and therefore, where a tutor admits articles of charge, articles of discharge (except on trifling incidents) are extrinsic (a).

§ 1645. It seems still to be an open question whether payment is intrinsic to the defender's oath in an action for an open account which has not prescribed. Mr Erskine (b) holds it to be extrinsic, because a party is generally understood to refer those facts which he must bear the burden of proving, and it lies on the defender to prove payment unless the account is prescribed. But Professor Bell (c) considers, that although the defender must prove payment where the pursuer has proved constitution of the debt by parole or written evidence, yet if the pursuer has no proof of the constitution except the defender's oath, the whole debt must be referred, and therefore its subsistence is an intrinsic quality. This view—which is adopted by Lord Ivory (d) and by another of Erskine's annotators (e), as well as by Mr Tait (f)—is supported by several older cases (g). It is clear that an admission of furnishings may

(u) Ersk., 4, 2, 13—Tait, 246—See Kay's Reps. v. Cleghorn, 1678, 3 B. Sup., 266.

(x) Campbell v. Scotland, 1776, M., 9530, Hailes, 812, S. C. The question arose on the defences, but was treated as if it had occurred in an oath on reference.

(y) Home v. Colt, 1685, M., 13,204.

(z) Ersk., 4, 2, 13—See Walker v. Clerk, 1702, M., 13,230, and Ewing v. Dundas, 1749, M., 13,226, *supra*, § 1640.

(a) Ersk., ib.—Cant v. Lochs, 1665, M., 13,222—Compared with Jack v. Robertson, 1699, 4 B. Sup., 445, and Brown v. Dow, 1707, M., 13,224.

(b) Ersk., 4, 2, 11. In support of this view see Maitland v. Baillie, 1707, M., 13,212.

(c) 1 Bell's Com., 333.

(d) Ivory's Note, 52, to Ersk., 4, 2, 11.

(e) Gillon's (4th) ed. of Ersk., *supra*. The note is given in Ivory's Ersk., p. 970.

(f) Tait Ev., 246.

(g) Gordon v. Cusigne, 1674, M., 13,234—Kay's Reps.

be qualified by stating that payment was made at the time of purchase or delivery, because in that case the constitution and extinction of the debt were *partes ejusdem negotii*

In an action for re-delivery of the pursuer's watch, where the defender deponed that the pursuer handed it to him that he might take it to a watchmaker to be repaired, and that he saw the watchmaker return it to the pursuer, the Court held the re-delivery to be extrinsic (*h*) But this decision has been questioned (*i*)

§ 1646 In one case the following distinction between extrinsic and intrinsic qualities in regard to the constitution of obligations was laid down by Lord Pitfour, and adopted by the Court — "Payment or performance, by which the obligation is dissolved in the natural way, is always held to be *partes ejusdem negotii*, though it did not happen at the same time that the obligation is entered into For example, if the defender swears that he got from the pursuer a loan of so much money, and repaid it at any distance of time, that quality will be intrinsic, but if he says that he did not pay the money, but that it was compensated by a debt which the pursuer owed him, or that he paid him not in money but by delivery of goods, which the pursuer accepted in place of payment, that is *aliud negotium*, therefore extrinsic, and to be proved otherwise than by the defender's own oath '(*k*) But, as already noticed, payment *ex intervallo* will be held extrinsic to an oath of constitution if the debt is one for payment of which a written voucher should have been taken, while the distinction between payment in money, and payment in goods accepted in lieu of money, is thought to be erroneous If the discharge of the debt is intrinsic to the reference (*e g*, where prescription has run on it), then it is no matter whether the extinction was by a money payment, by acceptance of goods in discharge of the debt, by agreeing to hold it compensated by a counter claim, or by voluntary cancellation, for all these equally import discharge On the other hand if the discharge of the debt by one of these modes is extrinsic, it is thought that discharge by any other of them is equally so The real distinction lies between a discharge by agreeing to hold the debt compensated, or accepting goods as payment of it on the one

v Cleghorn, 1678, 3 B Sup, 266—Crawford *v* Boyd, 1765, 5 ib 911—Forbes *v* Forbes' Crs, 1711 M, 12 464—and opinions, particularly that of L President Campbell (A), in Douglas *v* Grierson, 1791, Bell's Fo Ca 97, M 11,116, S C

(*h*) Boyes *v* Abercromby 1687, M, 12,731

(*i*) Tait Ev, 251

(*k*) Wylie, 1765, 5 B Sup, 913 This doctrine is said to have been 'confirmed in Crawford *v* Boyd 1765, ib 914

hand, and simple set-off or delivery of goods as payment on the other; statements of the latter kind being extrinsic to an oath of resting-owing (*l*).

III. *Of Qualified Oaths as to the extinction of Obligations.*

§ 1647. Reference to oath as to the extinction of an obligation may be made either by the debtor, where the *onus* lies on him, and he has no other mode of proof; or by the creditor, where from the debt having prescribed, from the debtor having possession of the document of debt, or of a written discharge, or from any other cause, the creditor requires to refer resting-owing to the debtor's oath. The same principle applies to both these classes of oaths;—the question in each case being, whether the qualification is consistent with a discharge of the debt, or resolves into an independent transaction, which it falls upon the deponent to prove.

§ 1648. Accordingly, it is intrinsic to the oath of the creditor that money or goods which the debtor alleges were delivered in payment of the debt, were gifted (*m*). And where a debtor referred to his creditor's oath, whether he had not conveyed certain shares of a vessel to him in payment, the oath admitting the conveyance was held to be qualified intrinsically by statements as to the price received for the shares after deducting expenses (*n*).

§ 1649. This principle ought also to be applied to an oath by the creditor stating that the money or goods which he received from the debtor, were meant by both parties to be in discharge of a different account or obligation from the one in question, because that is a denial that the latter has been paid (*o*). But where the pursuer of an action on a bill deponed that £5 which he received was in payment of a separate account, the Court held that it must be applied to the bill, "unless the pursuer would instruct the open account otherwise than by his own oath" (*p*). This decision, however, seems to be doubted by Lord Kames who reports it.[5]

(*l*) See *supra*, § 156, *et seq.*, and *infra*, § 1650, *et seq.* (*m*) Ersk., 4, 2, 12—M'Lean *v.* Ogilvie, 1700, 4 B. Sup., 487—Forbes *v.* Shaw, 1688, M. 12,733.

(*n*) Stewart *v.* Telfer, 1821, 1 S., 101. (*o*) Ersk., *supra*—Sinclair *v.* Sinclair, 1705, M., 13,206—M'Lean *v.* Ogilvie, *supra*—Pringle *v.* Manderston, 1708, M., 13,230.

(*p*) Cameron *v.* Dunskine, 1730, M., 13,207.

[5] In an action by an indorsee on a bill of exchange against the acceptors, they pleaded non onerosity. In an oath on reference the indorsee deponed that the bill was handed to him by the drawer for negotiation; that he failed to get it negotiated, and

In a suspension, where the creditor deponed that an alleged partial payment was received by him in satisfaction of several particulars not relating to the bond charged upon, the Court refused to sustain the qualification (r). The ground of judgment was that the debtor might have ascribed the payment to the bond if he got a receipt for an indefinite payment. This decision indicates a distinction which was justly applied in another case (s). If the creditor depones generally that the payment is applicable to a different debt, his oath involves matter of law, which is extrinsic to the reference, as it lies with the Court to determine to which of two debts an indefinite payment shall be imputed. But if he depones that the sum was both given and received as payment of a different debt from the one in issue, that is matter of fact and intrinsic, because denying payment of the latter debt.

In one case (t), where the suspender of a charge on a bond produced a ticket for 100 merks and 10 dollars in part-payment of a larger sum, and the creditor deponed that it applied to a different debt from the one in issue, the Court held that he must prove that debt. Here however the "ticket" was a written voucher, which was presumed to apply to the debt in question, and it lay with the creditor to prove that it related to another obligation.

§ 1650. There is sometimes difficulty where, in a reference of resting-owing to the oath of the debtor, he depones that the debt was not paid in money, but was extinguished in some other way

(r) Reid v. Binning, 1670, M., 13,202. (s) Sinclair v. Sinclair, 1703, M., 13,205. (t) Burnside v. Bruce, 1672, 2 B. Sup., 157.

that the drawer desired him to keep it as security for money which had been lent by the indorsee to the drawer, and was still unpaid. The Court held that the statement, that the drawer was indebted to the indorsee when he told him to retain the bill in security, and that the debt was still due, was intrinsic, and that the oath was negative of the reference. The bill had, no doubt, been put into the indorsee's hands for one purpose, and had been left with him ultimately for another. "But a bill may be put into a party's hands for a particular purpose, and there may be engrafted on his title of possession a different purpose." The ultimate purpose was a most natural use of a bill, for bills are constantly transferred in security of previous advances. Had the money been advanced of the date of the bill, the statement would have been clearly intrinsic, and it made no difference that the money had been previously advanced, and that the bill was afterwards granted as a security. "I can see no principle for applying a different rule as to the legal effect of an oath when the value deponed to is of earlier date than the bill, which is a common case where the bill is pledged as a security, and where it is of equal date with the bill itself, consisting of money then advanced or otherwise," *per* Lord Wood. But Lord Cowan held that the pursuer was not entitled to prove by his own oath that the prior debt was owing to him,—that being a separate transaction, and requiring to be proved *aliunde*, Gordon v. Pratt, 1860, 22 D. 903.

The rule in such cases seems to be that if the debtor depones that the creditor discharged the debt in consideration of a counter claim, or of a transaction of any kind (*e g* compromise or receiving goods in satisfaction), the oath imports a denial of resting-owing for the consideration which induced the creditor to hold the debt extinguished is immaterial to the real point referred Every statement of this kind, therefore, is intrinsic to an oath of resting-owing, whereas the statement of a counter claim, delivery of goods, or the like without adding that in consideration thereof the creditor agreed to hold the debt extinguished, is extrinsic, for it is merely the allegation of an independent transaction, which is not inconsistent with the subsistence of the debt The following decisions have occurred on the point[6]

§ 1651 In a reference of resting-owing the debtor's oath was held to be negative, where it stated that the parties agreed to a compromise of the claim, and that the commuted sum was paid (*u*) And where Clerk referred to the oath of Dallas, whether certain prescribed rents were resting-owing and Dallas deponed that Cockburn, who was both debtor to him (Dallas) and creditor to Clerk, had, in accounting with Clerk, deducted the amount for which Dallas gave Cockburn credit in their accounting, the Court held that the qualification was intrinsic, as it imported payment by delegation (*x*) And a similar decision was pronounced where the debtor deponed that the debt was settled by the creditor retaining the amount from wages due by him to the deponent's son, who consented to the arrangement (*y*) In a recent case, however, the debtor in a prescribed bill to his brother for £200, deponed that he had purchased certain heritable property from his brother by verbal bargain at the price of £600, and had afterwards sold the same property on his own account to a third party for £900, that he paid his brother the £600 as the price of the property, and £200 to extinguish the bill, and that the balance of the purchase money (which amounted to about £70) was also paid to his brother who said it was all one which of them got it, as the deponent's family would succeed to all that the brother left The Court held this quality to be extrinsic, upon the ground that it imported a separate transaction, which, from its nature (being a sale of heritage), re-

(*u*) Napier *v* Graham, 1829, 1 De and And, 218 (*x*) Clerk *v* Dallas, 1711, M 13213 (*y*) Law *v* Johnstone, 1843, 6 D, 201

6 Thomson *v* Duncan 1855, 17 D 1081 *infra* § 1665, note 7

quired to be proved by writing (z) Lord Cockburn however considered that the debtor's deposition that he paid the amount due by the bill was negative of the reference and was not rendered extrinsic by statements as to the purchase and second sale of the property This case is very special, and the decision is narrow

§ 1652 It has been repeatedly held that deponing that the debt was discharged by the creditor accepting goods in satisfaction of it, and that that mode of settlement was agreed to at constituting the contract, is intrinsic to an oath of resting-owing (a) And it is thought to be intrinsic, although it should not have been *pars contractus*, for a debt cannot be considered resting-owing which the creditor has held to be discharged (b) But some cases are against this view (c)

§ 1653 Again, it has been held that an oath that the debt sued for has been compensated is extrinsic (d), but that deponing that the creditor discharged the debt in consideration of the counter claim is intrinsic (e), in a reference of resting-owing The reason

---

(z) Stewart v Robertson, 1852, 15 D, 12

(a) Maitland v Baillie, 1707, M, 13,212—Johnston's Assignee 1687 M, 13,241—Gordon v Cusigne, 1674, M 13,234—Forbes v Craigie's Crs, 1711, M, 12,464, 13 212—1 Bell's Com, 334—See also Lauder v M Gibbon, 1727, M, 13,206—Thomson v Thomson 1830, 8 S, 571

(b) See *infra* § 1653, (e)

(c) Wylie, 1765, 5 B Sup, 913 (*supra*, § 1646) In Forbes v Craigie's Crs, *supra* the Court held that delivery of goods in payment is extrinsic unless it was *pars contractus* In Gilchrist v Murray, 1675 M, 13,210, the Court sustained an oath as to payment in money, but not as to delivery of goods But the report does not bear that the deponent stated that the goods were accepted as payment In Gordon v Cusigne, 1674, M 13,234 Lord Stair's report bears that in a claim for the price of a horse, the defender's oath that the pursuer accepted a cow in lieu of it was extrinsic because it was not *pars contractus* But Lord Kames (2 Folio Dic 299) observes that the ground of the decision was, that the exception was not proponed at litis contestation, and that if it had there can be no doubt that effect would have been given to the qualification Professor Bell (1 Com, 334) seems to take the view recognised in Forbes v Craigie's Crs, *supra*

(d) Ersk, 4, 2 11—Simpson 1628, M, 12,450—Learmonth v Russell, 1664, M 13,201, 13 241—Johnston's Assignee, 1687, M, 12,732, 13,241—Borthwick v Ramsay, 1697, M, 4981—Workman v Young, 1699, M, 13,231—Fincham v Muirhead, 1707, 4 B Sup 665—Maxwell v Herries, 1712, M, 11 218—Milne's Crs v Broomfield, 1736, Elch "Qualified Oath" No 3, and Elch Notes, "Arrestment," No 6, S C—Mitchell v Mackinlay, 1761, M, 13,241—Rankine v Adan, 1799, M, 13,245—Sinclair v Sinclair, 1703, M, 13,205—Stevenson v Campbell, 1803, Hume D, 115—Hepburn v Hepburn, 1806, ib, 117—Wright v M Farlane, 1837, 16 S, 67

(e) In an action on a prescribed bill, the defender swore that the bill was originally binding, but that both he and the creditor had overlooked a counter claim of his, which was equal to it on discovering which the creditor agreed to cancel the bill The Court held this to be intrinsic, Grant v Grant's Cr, 1793, M 13 221 In a similar action

is, that compensation does not extinguish *ipso jure* the debt to which it applies, but is an independent defence, which the debtor must bear the burden of proving, whereas discharge by the creditor must necessarily import not resting-owing, whatever was the consideration which induced him to grant it

§ 1654 Deponing that the debt was compensated, and that the parties, at contracting, had agreed to its extinction in this way, is also an intrinsic qualification being *pars contractus* (*f*) But, in order to its being held intrinsic that the creditor and debtor agreed that their counter claims should be mutually compensated and discharged, it is not necessary that that should have been originally stipulated for, provided it was agreed to at the settlement (*g*)

§ 1655 A transaction of this kind, however, will not be held intrinsic, unless the oath bears distinctly that the creditor agreed that the debt should be extinguished in that way If the oath merely imports intention by the debtor, or a half promise, or expression of probable intention on the part of the creditor, it will not suffice (*h*) [7]

---

deponing that the pursuer had, at a meeting with the defender admitted counter claims, had promised to give up the bill whenever he had an opportunity and stated that he would have given it up then if he had had it with him, was held not to prove resting-owing, L Forrester v L Elphinstone 1742, M 13,215, Elchies' Notes, "Qualified Oath," No 6 So, where a defender deponed that the sum sued for was lent him by the pursuer on his ticket, but that the ticket was re-delivered on account of a compensating claim for the price of goods furnished to the pursuer's wife to whom it had been granted, this was held intrinsic, Brown v Mitchell 1669, M, 13,202 In Hepburn v Hepburn, 1806, Hume D, 417, Baron Hume states, "It is a settled point that claims of compensation in an oath of reference of a claim of debt are extrinsic, unless the mutual claims of parties have been applied to each other by some regular settlement or transaction of parties" This principle is farther supported by Gall v Eviot, 1629, M, 13,240 —Clark v Dallas 1711, M, 13,213, *supra*, (*x*)—Law v Johnston, 1843, 6 D, 201, *supra*, (*y*)—Maxwell v Herries, 1712, M, 11,218 (*ad fin*)—Hunter v L Kinnaird, 1830, 9 S, 154—and per Lord Kames *supra*, (*c*)

(*f*) 1 Bell's Com, 331—Irvine v Dickson, 1733, Elch "Qualified Oath," No 1—Thomson v Thomson, 1830 8 S, 571—Maitland v Baillie, 1707, M, 13,212—Lauder v M'Gibbon, 1727 M 13,206

(*g*) Cases noted *supra*, (*e*)—Professor Bell seems to have overlooked this class of cases when he laid down (1 Com 334), "If the import of the oath is only that the defender has, on account of something collateral a defence against the debt, as compensation, the quality is not intrinsic, unless it was *pars contractus* originally that there should be such set-off"

(*h*) Hunter v L Kinnaird, 1830 9 S, 154—Mitchell v Mackilnay, 1761, M 13,241 In Rankine v Adair, 1799, M, 13,245, where the oath bore that the counter claims had

---

7 A sum of £500 was lent by A to B On A's bankruptcy his trustee sued B for the

§ 1656 When the debtor in a prescribed account admits the constitution of the debt, but adds that the items are overcharged,

---

been allowed to stand over on assurances that they would be deducted at the settlement of the bill sued for, the qualification was held extrinsic but it did not appear that there had been a specific promise to deduct The case of Robertson v Clarkson, 19th Nov 1784, F C, as appearing in the Session Papers, also illustrates the text It was an action on a prescribed bill, where the defender swore that the bill had been granted for the price of wine which turned out to be inferior that the defender acquainted the pursuers of this, "and desired them to take it back and deliver up the bill, but they begged he would do the best he could to dispose of it as it was worth nothing to them, adding that in any event the defender should be no loser" The quality was held to be extrinsic It did not come up to a distinct agreement to quit the debt on account of the bad quality of the wine In the Fac Coll the defender is reported to have sworn that the pursuers had said that the price "would not be demanded" But this is incorrect See also Williamson v Peacock, 11th Dec 1810, F C

---

sum It was pleaded in defence, that at the time the debt was incurred it was agreed that A's son should board with B, and that the board should be imputed in extinction of the loan It was further alleged that, sometime afterwards A came to reside with B, and that it was then agreed that the balance of the loan should be held to be discharged —the amount of A's board being taken to represent the balance On a reference to oath, B deponed substantially in terms of his defence The Court held that the first allegation—in as much as it went into the very bargain between the parties—was intrinsic, but that the second was extrinsic It was held to be extrinsic by reason chiefly of the vague and confused account of the transaction which had been given by the defender Lords Murray and Cowan, indeed, founding upon the case of Gordon v Cusigne, 1674, M, 13 234, reported by Lord Stair, were disposed to hold that the allegation was extrinsic on the ground that the arrangement deponed to, being an *ex post facto* arrangement, entered into at a date subsequent to the constitution of the loan, could not be proved by the oath of the defender The case referred to by Lord Stair can scarcely be considered an authority in support of this view seeing that Lord Kames, in his report of the case, states that the defence was repelled, because it had not been proponed at litis contestation, and that, had it been so, it would undoubtedly have been given effect to (2 Fol Dic 299) and Lord Cowan admitted that the view taken by Lord Mackenzie in Mitchell v Ferrier 1842 5 D, 169, might be well founded when parties came together and agreed distinctly on the terms of a settlement Lord Wood, while holding that the allegation of an *ex post facto* agreement was too vague and general to be given effect to, took care to guard against the supposition that he decided the point on the ground that such an agreement could, in no circumstances, become an intrinsic quality of the oath "It must, I conceive, be conceded in principle that the admission upon oath of the constitution of a debt may be so qualified by statements in regard to the mode of solution other than payment in cash (which is the natural mode of liquidation), agreed to at the time of its contraction, and of the debt having been so extinguished, entirely or partially, as to require these statements to be taken as part of the admission and to render them as available to the debtor as the admission is to the creditor Not only so but I am not at all prepared to say that similar statements may not be entitled to the same effect, although they refer to an agreement entered into subsequent to the constitution of the debt, if they are clear and explicit, and of that business sort of character which gives them the form of a definite transaction, which might properly take place in reference to the debt admitted to have been then due, Thomson v Duncan, 1855, 17 D, 1081

and that he made payments which extinguished all that was justly due, the qualification will be held extrinsic, for, being matter merely of opinion, it is not involved in the reference. The Court will therefore remit the accounts to persons of skill, or will take some similar means for ascertaining whether their just amount is covered by the partial payments sworn to (*i*) [7]

The rules as to oaths that the debt was paid through the medium of a third person have been noticed already (*k*)

It has also been seen, in a previous chapter, whether a party with whom a deed had been deposited may qualify his admission of the depositation, by swearing that the granter of the deed directed him to cancel it (*l*) [8]

(*i*) *Supra*, § 519 (*k*) *Supra*, § 454 *et seq* § 516 *et seq*, § 1626
(*l*) See *supra*, § 971, *et seq*, and § 1306

[7] Fife *v* Innes 1860 23 D, 30—M'Gregor *v* M'Gregor, 1860, 22 D, 1264

[8] A quality is intrinsic of the oath when the condition deponed to is *pars ejusdem negotii* it is extrinsic when the condition does not expressly and directly enter into the substance of the agreement This rule (the most explicit perhaps which can be laid down in regard to qualified oaths on the constitution of obligations) applies *mutatis mutandis* to qualified oaths on the extinction of obligations The obligation is discharged whenever payment, in whatever form made is *pars ejusdem negotii*, but payment, in whatever form made if not imputed to the obligation is *aliud negotium*, and extrinsic of the reference Of course the rule presumes that the condition was adjected with the full consent of the contracting parties a mere belief, supposition, or conjecture, on the part of the person emitting the oath not being enough According to this view it is of no consequence that the condition was not a condition of the contract when first entered into if it was subsequently imported into it by the express consent of each of the parties The parties were entitled to agree to a reconstitution of the contract and it is not the terms of a superseded and extinct contract which are referred, but the terms of that subsisting contract of which implement is sought So, also, of the extinction of obligations The qualification is not to be considered extrinsic, although the party depone that payment was not made in money, but in some other way to which the parties agreed A money payment is the most natural solution of a debt but it may be discharged by payment in goods or in service, and if the mode alleged be a sufficiently natural mode of liquidation and if it was adopted with clear and express reference to the prior obligation, there seems no reason why the qualification should not be dealt with as an intrinsic part of the oath Nor is it necessary that the parties should have contracted, if they ultimately agreed to settle, on that footing Even if the goods or service were originally given without reference to the prior debt, it is thought that they will be held to be in payment of it, if the oath bears that at a subsequent settlement the parties agreed that the counter claims should be set against each other and thus discharged Lord Mackenzie in Mitchell *v* Ferrier, 1842, 5 D, 169, states the proposition clearly and briefly —' A defender may say that, although a debt was once due by him yet it was long ago actually settled between the parties, having been set-off against a debt due to the defender It would be difficult to hold that this is not intrinsic" See also opinions of Lord Wood in Thomson *v* Duncan, *supra*, and Gordon *v*

CHAPTER IX.—OF HOLDING AS CONFESSED AND REPONING

§ 1657. Interlocutors ordering parties to depone always imply, and sometimes express a certification that if they fail they will be held as confessed (*a*) The consequence is, that if a party cited under such an interlocutor disobeys, he will be held as confessed,—

(*a*) Stair, 4, 44 21—Ersk, 4, 2 17—Tait Ev, 287

Pratt, 1860 22 D, 903, both of which deserve attentive consideration as sound and consistent expositions of difficult questions which arise in regard to qualified oaths It has been said, indeed, that when the *onus* of proving the condition lies upon the person emitting the oath, or when the condition resolves into a separate transaction, the quality must be considered extrinsic, Ersk 4 2 11 Mr Erskine's illustration of the doctrine has been repeatedly challenged, and is thought to be erroneous The *onus* of proving that a condition has been adjected to a contract lies, as a general rule, on the party who founds on the condition, it being a part of his case which he is bound to instruct But of that burden he is discharged if his opponent undertake to refer the matter to his oath, and if, on construing the oath, it appears that the qualification was truly a qualification of the contract assented to by both parties, it is difficult to see why that part of the oath should be cut off from the rest It may be called a separate transaction, but it is a separate transaction which the contracting parties have agreed to affiliate with the contract, and thus, whatever character it may have borne originally, it becomes, as at the date of settlement, *pars ejusdem negotii* These observations might be variously illustrated One of the prestations of the contract of employment, for instance, is remuneration, and a defender who alleges that service was given gratuitously can prove his allegation only by the writ or oath of the person employed, Taylor *v.* Forbes, 1853, reported 24 D, 19 This, therefore, is a case where not only the *onus probandi* rests on the defender, but where he is strictly limited in his mode of proof But if the pursuer refer the matter to the defender's oath, it is thought that it would be held an intrinsic quality of the oath if the defender deponed that it was agreed that the service should be rendered gratuitously, see Knox *v.* M'Caul, 1861 24 D 16 Thus the *onus probandi* furnishes no test which admits of definite or invariable application It may be said, no doubt, that in the case supposed the condition enters into the substance of the contract, and that it cannot be considered a separate transaction But, as already observed, it is obvious that the expression "a separate transaction" can have little meaning in cases where the essence of the averment is, that the transactions were not separate but identical,—identical in respect that they were brought together by consent of the contracting parties, and such cases as Gordon *v.* Pratt, 1860, 22 D, 903, seem to show that the Court is not inclined to give effect to distinctions which are chiefly technical Whether, indeed, the technical rules of evidence can be properly applied to the construction of the oath on reference, is a question that has not been sufficiently considered The oath on reference, strictly regarded, is not a mode of probation, it is an appeal which a litigant, whose evidence is exhausted, makes to the conscience of his adversary, and, as such, any condition whether affecting the constitution or the extinction of the obligation, which is distinctly deponed to should be liberally construed, and only rejected when not fairly referable to the transaction which is the ground of action There appears, at least, to be no reason in principle why any matter relevant to the question which is put in the minute of reference should be separated from the oath

that is, as having constructively admitted the fact referred to his oath, because it may be fairly presumed that his failure arises from his knowing that the truth is against him (*b*) But effect will not be given to this certification, unless the party's appearance on a day named was required by personal citation if he is in Scotland, or by edictal citation if he is out of the kingdom or has no fixed or known residence (*c*) As already observed, the practice of embodying in the summons a reference to oath, with a relative certification is now obsolete (*d*)

§ 1658 A party will be held as confessed not only if he fails to appear but also if he refuses to answer competent questions (*e*) or if he depones *non memini* on a *factum proprium et recens* (*f*), or refuses without good cause, to sign a deposition which he has really emitted (*g*).

§ 1659 This presumptive confession, however has not the same conclusive effect as the party's oath admitting the fact in question The party will be reponed against it, if he shows good reason for his non-appearance (as, for example, detention abroad or illness), and offers to depone (*h*) If he applies *de recenti*, he will be reponed on slighter excuses, under penalty of the expenses caused by his non-appearance (*i*), and payment of the whole expenses in the cause was required where the party had been contumacious (*k*) One who was only cited edictally, will be reponed on pleading ignorance of the order, and offering to depone (*l*) A party will not, except upon very special grounds, be reponed *ex intervallo* against a decree proceeding on his constructive confession, because the delay may have caused the other party to lose evidence by which he might have confirmed the decree (*m*) But even in that case it is thought that the party will be reponed if he offers to prove by referring to the oath of his adversary (*n*)

Where reference to the defender's oath had been made in an inferior court, and he failed to obey the order to depone, and en-

(*b*) Stair *supra*—Ersk, *supra*—Tait Ev, *supra*—Gordon *v* Gordon, 1731, Cr and St, 60—Cases in following notes

(*c*) Ersk, *supra*—Tait, *supra*—M'Kewar *v* Vernon, 1676, M, 12 031—Buchanan *v* Logie 1676, M 12 034—Kinloch *v* Forbes 1704 M 12,038

(*d*) *Supra* § 1565

(*e*) Murray *v* Murray, 1839, 1 D, 484

(*f*) *Supra*, § 1624

(*g*) Carin *v* Wilson, 1672, M, 12,532

(*h*) Stair, 4, 44, 22—Ersk 4, 2 17—Tait Ev, 288

(*i*) Ersk, *supra*—Miller *v* Cooper, 1835, 13 S, 369

(*k*) Drummond *v* Gilmour 1832, 10 S, 266

(*l*) Buchanan *v* Logie, 1676, M, 12,034—Kinloch *v* Forbes, 1704 (M, 12 038) as in 2 Folio Dic, 184—Ivory's Ersk, p 974 note 56

(*m*) Stair, 4 44 23—Ersk 4 2 17

(*n*) Stair, 4, 44, 22

cumduction passed against him, and where he thereafter led proof of an averment inconsistent with the fact referred to his oath, and was of new allowed to depone, but suffered the term to be again circumduced, and decree to be pronounced against him, and where he afterwards presented a bill of advocation, in which he did not pray to have the circumduction opened up, the Court refused to open it up (*o*)

§ 1660 Where a party having been duly cited, has failed to appear, and has died without being reponed against a consequent decree holding him confessed, the Court will not restore his heir against it (*p*) And if one who has been reponed *ex gratia* has died without swearing, the decree which proceeded on his constructive confession will revive and be effectual against his heir (*r*), unless the failure was occasioned by obstacles or improper litigation raised by the party who made the reference (*s*) Where a party was entitled to be reponed *ex debito justiciæ* (as, for example, on account of defect in the citation), the decree holding him confessed will fall entirely, and his heirs will be restored against it (*t*)

§ 1661 Holding as confessed is not appropriate to cases where reference is made to the oath of one person as representing another, for the party really interested ought not to lose his case on account of the non-appearance of such a person, as if he had himself refused to depone Accordingly, where one brother, as arrestee, referred to the oath of another, as common debtor, in a question with the arrester, the Court required the oath to be reported, because there would have been risk of collusion if the party referred to had been held confessed for not deponing (*u*) And where reference was made to the mother and tutrix of the party really interested, the Court found that she could not be held as confessed, not being the party but the tutrix, but that she might (like a witness) be forced to depone by diligence (*x*)

(*o*) Buchan *v* Boyd, 1828, 6 S, 1025—Compare Drummond *v* Gilmour, *supra* (*k*)

(*p*) Grant *v* M'Gregor, 1839, 1 D, 1048

(*r*) Ersk, 4, 2, 17—Wright *v* L Rutherford, 1686, M, 12,036

(*s*) Gilmour *v* Stewart, 1797, M, 12 042—Tait Ev, 288

(*t*) Ersk, *supra*—Wright *v* L Rutherford, *supra*—Tait Ev, *supra*—See also M'Laurin *v* Stewart, 1832, 10 S, 333

(*u*) Nairn *v* Ogilvie, 1725, M 12,168

(*x*) Cant *v* Loch, 1665 M, 12,029

TITLE VIII.

OF AFFIDAVITS

§ 1662 An affidavit is a written *ex parte* statement, affirmed on oath by the person who emits it, before one having authority to administer oaths

It is required by statute as *prima facie* proof on some matters, the most important of which are, applications under the Entail Amendment Act of 1848, in which the petitioner must lodge an affidavit stating whether there are any and if so, what debts affecting the estate (*a*),—sequestrations, in which the creditors must make oath to the verity of their debts (*b*),[1]—and certain motions in jury causes (*c*) At common law affidavits are required in applications for *meditatione fugæ* warrants, the creditor having to make oath to his claim, and to the circumstances which induce him to believe that his debtor means to abscond (*d*) The judicial ratification of deeds by married women is also made on oath (*e*)

§ 1663. An affidavit is not admissible evidence on the merits of any issue, because it is emitted *ex parte*, and without the person against whom it is used having an opportunity to cross-examine (*f*)

(*a*) 11 and 12 Vict, c 36, § 6 (*b*) 2 and 3 Vict, c 41, §§ 9, 10 The rules as to these affidavits are given at length in Burton on Bankruptcy, p 285, § 338, *et seq*, and p 480 § 599, *et seq* (*c*) Affidavits are required in applications to examine witnesses who reside beyond the jurisdiction of the Court, or who cannot attend on account of age or infirmity, A S, 10th Feb 1841, § 17, and in applications to put off the trial on account of the absence of a material witness, or other sufficient cause, Ib, § 25 (*d*) Ersk, 1 2, 21, and Ivory's Notes—2 Bell's Com, 559

(*e*) *Supra* § 737 (*f*) Mag of Aberdeen v More, 1813, Hume D, 502—Simpson & Co v M'Farlane, 1822, 3 Mur, 194—Glyn v Johnston, 1834, 13 S, 126—See the chapters on examining witnesses, *infra*

---

[1] 19 and 20 Vict, cap 79 §§ 21 22 As to affidavit of domicile under Confirmation of Executors Act, see § 17 of 21 and 22 Vict c 56

It is even excluded where the person who emitted it has died (*g*) and where he is abroad and refuses to depone before a commissioner of court (*h*) Nor does the oath made by a creditor in a sequestration "supersede production of legal evidence, where required in any judicial discussion before the Court of Session, the Lord Ordinary, the Sheriff, or the trustee" in the sequestration (*i*)[2] Affidavits laid before the Commissioners of Inland Revenue, as to any facts which may regulate the stamp-duty payable on any deed or instrument requiring to be stamped *ex post facto* cannot be used against the party in any proceeding whatever except an inquiry as to the stamp-duty chargeable on the document (*k*)

§ 1664 At one time the use of affidavits had become so common, that oaths had lost much of their value as safeguards against falsehood It was accordingly enacted by 5 and 6 Will IV, c 62 that "from and after the commencement of this act, it shall not be lawful for any justice of the peace, or other person, to administer or cause or allow to be administered, or to receive or cause or allow to be received, any oath, affidavit, or solemn affirmation touching any matter or thing, whereof such justice or other person hath not jurisdiction or cognisance by some statute in force at the time being Provided always that nothing herein contained shall be construed to extend to any oath, affidavit, or solemn affirmation before any justice in any matter or thing touching the preservation of the peace or the prosecution, trial or punishment of offences, or touching any proceedings before either of the Houses of Parliament, or any committee thereof, respectively nor to any oath, affidavit, or affirmation which may be required, by the laws of any foreign country to give validity to instruments in writing, designed to be used in such foreign countries respectively" (*l*) It is also provided that nothing contained in the act shall extend or apply to any oath or affidavit in any judicial proceeding in any court of justice (*m*) And a subsequent statute declared that the prohibitory enactment does not apply to judicial ratifications by married women (*n*)

§ 1665. An affidavit may be taken by any magistrate, judge ordinary or justice of the peace Justices may take affidavits be-

(*g*) Mag of Aberdeen *v* More, *supra*—See also *supra*, § 106 (*h*) Glyn *v* Johnston, 1834, 13 S, 126 (*i*) 2 and 3 Vict, c 41 § 43 (*k*) 17 and 18 Vict, c 83, § 18 (*l*) 5 and 6 Will IV, c 62, § 13 (*m*) Ib, § 7 (*n*) 6 and 7 Will IV, c 43

[2] 19 and 20 Vict c 79, § 58

yond the county to which their commissions apply (*o*), and a Scotch justice may act in this matter in England (*p*), as an English or Irish justice may officiate either in his own country or in Scotland (*r*) But Professor Bell considers that the jurisdiction o a judge ordinary in this matter is confined to his own territory (*s*). An affidavit may be validly emitted before a baron bailie (*t*) And an affidavit taken before one of the magistrates of Aberdeen, described as one of Her Majesty's Justices of the Peace for that city, was sustained, because the magistrates of Aberdeen are empowered by royal charter to exercise the functions of justices within the burgh (*u*) An affidavit has been sustained, where the justice before whom it had been emitted was erroneously described as in the commission of the peace of an adjoining county (*v*) In a case under the Entail Amendment Act an affidavit taken before one who was called as a respondent was objected to But it was sustained on the ground that the party was only called as the husband of an heiress, and had no personal interest, his *jus mariti* having been excluded (*w*) The point is still open whether a justice of the peace can act in a matter where he is interested personally (*x*)

§ 1666 Affidavits under the Sequestration Act by creditors who are out of Great Britain or Ireland may be emitted before "a magistrate, or justice of the peace, or other person qualified to administer oaths in the country where he resides (he being certified to be a magistrate, or justice of the peace, or qualified as aforesaid by a British minister, or British consul or by a notary public)" (*y*) [3] This is a good course to follow in regard to other affidavits emitted abroad, at a distance from a British consulate. Where there is a "consul-general or consul appointed by Her Majesty at any foreign port or place," affidavits may be emitted before him (*z*) And

---

(*o*) 2 Bell's Com , 336—Turnbull *v* Smellie, 1828, 6 S, 676—Kerr *v* M Ailsa, 1852, 14 D , 240 , affd on appeal, 1854, 1 Macq , 736

(*p*) Kerr *v* M Ailsa *supra* (*r*) Taylor *v* Little, 1822, 1 Sh Ap Ca , 254 affirming 22d May 1819, not reported—Kerr *v* M Ailsa, *supra* (*o*)—But see Place *v* Dennison, 2d July 1814, F C (*s*) 2 Bell's Com , 336 (*t*) Murray *v* Philips, 1821, 1 S , 81 (*u*) Paterson *v* Duncan, 1846, 8 D , 950—So, as to the Magistrates of Edinburgh , Mackay & Co *v* Bond, 19th Nov 1818, F C

(*v*) Turnbull *v* Smellie, 1828, 6 S , 676 (*w*) Kerr *v* M Ailsa, *supra* (*o*)

(*x*) See *supra*, §§ 1191, 1215 (*y*) 2 and 3 Vict , c 41, § 10

(*z*) 6 Geo IV , c 87, § 20

---

3 19 and 20 Vict , c 79, § 23—24 and 25 Vict c 134 (English Bankruptcy Act 1861) §§ 207 208

every such oath or affidavit has the same force and effect as if it had been taken before any justice of peace in Great Britain or before any other legal or competent authority (*a*) An affidavit of this kind, therefore does not require to be verified, but proves itself, like one emitted before a magistrate or justice of the peace in this country

§ 1667 Every affidavit should bear, that at the place and on the day named, in presence of the magistrate, who should be correctly named and designed (*b*) appeared the party, correctly named and designed (*c*) "who being solemnly sworn, depones," &c , and it should conclude thus "all which is truth as the deponent shall answer to God" It must be signed by the deponent (if he can write) and by the magistrate (*d*) If the deponent cannot write, the affidavit should state so, and should be signed by the magistrate, notarial subscription for the party being unnecessary (*e*) If the affidavit extends to more than a single sheet the number of pages should be mentioned, and each page should be subscribed A marginal note not signed by either the deponent or the magistrate (*f*), or signed only by one of them (*g*), will be disregarded And erasures or deletions *in essentialibus* will be fatal, if the affidavit does not bear that they were made before subscription (*h*) But a mere error in grammar, or a trifling inaccuracy in filling up a printed form of affidavit, will be overlooked (*i*). An affidavit by the creditor in a sequestration was held not to be vitiated by a clerical error in describing the date of the document of debt (a bill) as 14th, instead of 4th, March 1848, the rest of the description being correct, and sufficient to identify the writing (*k*)

§ 1668 This is not the place to discuss the details which must be set forth in the different affidavits The rules on the subject

---

(*a*) 6 Geo IV c 87, § 20 (*b*) But see § 1665 (*c*) But see Murray *v* Phillips, 1821, 1 S, 81 (*d*) In Perryman *v* M'Clymont, 1852, 14 D, 508, it was held not to vitiate an affidavit in a sequestration that the deponent's signature had been written over some other name and could hardly be deciphered See *supra*, § 664 (*e*) Paul *v* Gibson, 1831, 12 S, 131 (*f*) Mackersey *v* Guthrie, 1829, 7 S, 556 (*g*) Miller *v* Lambert, 1848, 10 D, 1419

(*h*) White *v* Girdwood, 1846, 9 D, 283—Jardine *v* Harvie, 1848, 10 D, 1501 With these cases compare Dyce *v* Paterson, 1846 9 D, 310 where the oath of a creditor in a sequestration was sustained, although the amount of the debt had been scored out, and a different sum had been interlined, the alteration being evidently in the hand of the justice who subscribed, and corresponding with the relative account which was annexed (*i*) Hart *v* Berwick, 1830, 8 S, 671—Taylor *v* Manford 1848 10 D, 977 (*k*) Foulds *v* Meldrum, 1851 13 D 1357 In Anderson *v* Monteith 1847 9 D, 1432, a question of *falsa demonstratio* was raised, but not decided

will be found in books upon forms and practice The most frequent questions on this head used to occur in competitions for trusteeships in sequestrations But these will now be comparatively rare, as the creditor is entitled to rectify his oath when it is not framed according to statute, unless where the failure to comply with the statutory rules shall appear to have been made for some improper or fraudulent purpose or where injury can be qualified by the other creditors or any of them in respect thereof" (*l*)

§ 1669 Merely technical objections to affidavits lodged under the Entail Amendment Act have been rendered harmless by a clause in a subsequent act (*m*), which provides that "no interlocutor, judgment, or decree following, or that has followed, upon any petition presented, or which shall be presented, under the said recited act or this act shall be questionable or reducible upon the ground of any want of compliance with the provisions of the said recited act and of this act, and of any relative act or Acts of Sederunt in so far as such provisions regard applications or petitions to the Court of Session under the authority of the said recited act, or of this act, . the making and producing of affidavits therein, the matters to be set forth in such affidavits, Provided always that no injury shall have been suffered by any person through such want of compliance"

(*l*) 16 and 17 Vict, c 53, § 7

(*m*) 16 and 17 Vict, c 94, § 1

BOOK THIRD.

OF TESTIMONY, OR THE EVIDENCE OF PERSONS EXAMINED AS WITNESSES

TITLE I

OF THE ADMISSIBILITY OF WITNESSES

CHAPTER I.—GENERAL RULE AS TO ADMISSIBILITY

§ 1670. The spirit of the old Scotch law was to exclude the evidence of every person whose character, whose connection with the parties, or whose interest in the cause, raised a doubt as to the trustworthiness of his evidence. It was then more difficult to discover who were admissible, than who were incompetent, witnesses (*a*). For a number of years, however, the prevailing spirit

(*a*) The statute, 2 Rob. I, cap. 34 (appended to Reg. Majest.), contains the following list "of them quha are repelled from pruife, acquitance, and testimonie."

Item, from probation, acquitance, and testimonie, sould be repelled ane bairn being minor, quha hes not compleited the age of fourtene zeires; forouse men, bondmen (or slaves), women, adulterers, theifes, pure men, men sworne and perjured men, men scurged about the kirk or throw the town, infamouse men, convict and redemed fra the justice, men sib in blude, compinions and partakers of the samme crime, native bondmen, clerks agains laicks, and laicks agains clerks.

"2. Mairover, from acquitance, inquisition, probation, and ane assise sould be repelled the father, the sonne, the brother, the father brother, and they quha are in blude

both in the Courts and in the Legislature has been to sweep away the grounds for excluding witnesses—leaving to the old objections whatever effect they ought to have upon the credibility of witnesses who are open to them[1]

Now, therefore, the general rule is, that the evidence of every person is admissible, and this applies in most cases to the parties themselves, their relations, and law-agents and in all cases to witnesses merely interested in the result of the cause, and those who have been convicted of crime Some witnesses are still excluded, either on account of their evidence being entirely unworthy of credit or on grounds of public policy

---

CHAPTER II —OF WITNESSES OBJECTED TO ON ACCOUNT OF NON-AGE

§ 1671 Only those persons ought to be admitted as witnesses whose powers of observation and memory and whose knowledge of

---

or affinitie within the fourt degree, the Lord (or maister) the maister s baillie the man wearand his maister's cleathes and he quha is of his counsell or retinew and haldand of him land for ferme or for zearlie rent, and he quha is partaker of the accusation, and enemie or evill-willer to the partie, and he quha is conduced be prayer or be price, and he quha is cursed and excommunicat, or imprisoned, or in bands, and all they quha are repellit as unworthie from accusation, all they quha are outlawes, all they quha are accused criminallie and are not lauchfullie clenzed be reason their accusation as yit depends not discussed"

[1] Lord Mackenzie in noticing the operation of the recent statutes abolishing most of the disabilities which formerly affected witnesses, observes — Great apprehensions were entertained that these changes might open the door to perjury, but experience has demonstrated that the latitude allowed under the new system all objections to credit being duly weighed, is, on the whole, highly beneficial, by enabling courts of law to reach the truth in a multitude of cases where the ends of justice were formerly defeated by excluding the testimony of the parties best acquainted with the facts in dispute," Studies in Roman Law by Lord Mackenzie, 1862 This passage may be contrasted with a passage in Sir George Mackenzie's works, in which the views then current are rather quaintly expressed,—"It is very observable, that the longer the world lasts, probation by witnesses lessens always in esteem, because men grow always more wicked In our Saviour's time out of the mouth of two or three witnesses every word was to be established Thereafter by our law, and by the laws of other nations, nothing above an hundred pounds could be proven by witnesses" Observations upon the Third Parliament of King Charles II

the duty to speak the truth, are so far developed that they will be likely to give trustworthy evidence. To comprehend and undertake the obligation of an oath requires more maturity of intellect and some education, and is not so essential.

§ 1672. Accordingly, in criminal cases, where the facts are usually simple, and justice requires a full investigation, children, however young, may now be examined on facts within their comprehension (*a*), although they may not be old enough to understand the nature of an oath. Under this rule children of four and five (*b*), six (*c*), and seven (*d*) years of age have been admitted, and it is the daily practice to examine witnesses who are still in pupillarity.

§ 1673. At one time pupil children were inadmissible in criminal cases against their parents (*e*). A recent statute is held to have rendered them admissible (*f*).

§ 1674. But while these liberal and just rules are fixed in the criminal code, it has hitherto been laid down, that as pupils (*i e*, boys under fourteen and girls under twelve) are incapable of the obligation of an oath, they are inadmissible in civil cases, except on facts regarding injuries or crimes (*g*). The authorities on this point, however, are inappropriate in a system where exclusion is the exception, not the rule, and in an age when the education of youth is well cared for. It is therefore thought that in civil as well as criminal cases, a witness in pupillarity should be admitted, if he

---

(*a*) 2 Hume, 341, 2—Burnett, 391—2 Al, 433—Bell's Pr § 2240.

(*b*) In the trial of Buchan (1833, Bell's Notes, 246) for assault with intent to ravish, the injured party, who was between four and five years old, was examined. In the trial of Hempsen (1839, ib, 247) for stealing clothes from three children described as about four, and one child of three, years old respectively, the three older were examined. In Mary Sherift (1837, ib, 247), tried for the same crime, the child, between three and four years old, was produced to the jury, the Lord Justice-General (Hope) observing that that was necessary, but she could not be induced to speak. In Collins (1834, ib, 247), for the same crime, the child was examined after having stated she was three years old, her actual age, as specified in the indictment and mentioned by her mother, having been five years. It does not appear from the reports that the admission of witnesses of such tender years has been extended beyond cases where they were the persons on whom the crime had been committed, see Burnett, 391.

(*c*) White, 1782, 2 Hume, 341, and Burnett, 393—Price, 1830, Bell's Notes, 246.

(*d*) Low, 1827, 2 Hume, 342—Baillie, 1830, Bell's Notes, 246.

(*e*) 2 Hume, 347, note—Burnett, 392—2 Al, 465.

(*f*) 3 and 4 Vict, c 59—Purves *v* Carns, 1811, 2 Sw, 531.

(*g*) Ersk, 4, 2, 22—Bell's Pr, § 2240—More, 411—Tait Ev 342—1 Fount, 92, 3 B Sup, 341—Douglas *v* Graham, 1694, 4 B Sup, 180—Bannatyne *v* Charteris, 1691, ib, 620—Davidson *v* Charteris, 1738, M, 16,899, Elch, "Witness," 12, S C—*Contra* Home *v* Home, 1582, M, 8906—D Queensberry *v* Barker, 7th July 1810, F C.

has sufficient intelligence and education to observe, remember, and speak the truth upon the facts on which he is tendered (*h*)

The old rule, however ought to be applied to instrumentary witnesses (*i*), because, while there is no danger in laying the evidence of a child before a jury, who will give it such weight as in the circumstances it deserves, some intellectual maturity in the witnesses is essential to secure against the fraudulent concoction or impetration of formal deeds Nor is there any necessity for a different rule, as the witnesses to a deed are chosen by the maker of it

§ 1675 Except in the case last noticed, the admissibility of witnesses depends on their age when tendered, not when the facts to which they speak occurred (*k*) What weight is due to a narrative of events in the early life of a witness must be determined by the jury with reference to his age at that time, the period which has elapsed since, the apparent accuracy of his recollection, and, still more, the nature of the fact as likely (or not) to make an impression on the mind of one so young

§ 1676 The competency of a young witness has to be determined by the judge, after a preliminary examination of the child, and other evidence (if necessary) as to his intelligence If he appears to be altogether uneducated, and not likely to feel the obligation of truthfulness, he ought to be rejected (*l*), whereas it is not necessary to his admissibility that he should understand the nature of an oath, and witnesses have been admitted who had some elementary knowledge, but did not know that it is a sin against God to tell a lie (*m*) These cases seem to be of doubtful authority.

(*h*) See D Queensberry *v* Barker, *supra*—Home *v* Home, *supra*—2 Fraser Pers and Dom Rel, 67 (*i*) See *supra* § 689

(*k*) Stair, 4, 43, 7—2 Hume, 342—Ersk, 4 2, 22—Douglas *v* Graham 1694, 4 B Sup, 180—Bannatyne *v* Charteris, 1705 4 ib, 620 Lord Stair mentions (*supra*) that "when march stones are solemnly set boys used sometimes to be laid down upon them and sharply whipped whereby they will be able to remember and be good witnesses as to these marches when they are very old that impression on their fancy lasting long" In cases of pedigree and prescriptive possession witnesses often speak to what happened in their early childhood But see Love 1687, Hume, *supra*

(*l*) In M Carter (1831, Bell's Notes 247), a boy nine years old who knew he ought to tell the truth but did not know where liars go to, could not read, had never been taught to read the bible or to know the catechism and who had "gotten no instruction at all," was held inadmissible even on declaration

(*m*) In Sinclair (1822, Sh Just Ca, 75) a boy twelve years old who could read, but did not understand the nature of an oath, or that God would be offended with him if he told untruths, was examined on declaration and this was also done in Galloway (1836 1 Swin 239 corrected in Bell's Notes, 247) as to a boy nine years old, who had

§ 1677 An oath, however, can only be administered to a witness who is of sufficient age and intelligence to comprehend and undertake its obligations Accordingly, children under twelve years of age may not be sworn (*n*), in general children above fourteen may (*o*), while an oath should not be administered to a witness between these ages, unless the judge is satisfied that he understands its nature (*r*) A young witness to whom the oath is not administered is examined on "declaration," that is, an affirmative answer to the judge's injunction that he should "tell the truth, the whole truth, and nothing but the truth."

---

been at school and knew he should not tell lies but had not been taught the bible or catechism and did not know that it is an offence against God to tell a lie In Buchan (1819 Sh Just Ca 35) a boy fourteen years old, who had not been at school, and did not understand the nature of an oath, was examined on declaration In Howison (1831, Bell's Notes, 247) a boy eight years old, who could not read, had not been at school or learned the catechism, but knew who created him, and that he should tell the truth in court, and that it is a great crime to tell a lie, was examined in the same way See also M Carter, 1832, Bell s Notes, 247—Collins, 1834, ib —and cases noted in Burnett, 391, 2 Hume 341, and 2 Alison 433

(*n*) 2 Hume, 341—2 Alison, 433—Bell's Notes, 246 In Clydesdale (1804 Burnett, 393), a boy of ten years old was sworn But this appears to be the only case where the general rule in the text was departed from Burnett s opinion (p 394), that children under twelve should be sworn if they understand the nature of an oath, has not been followed in practice

(*o*) Hume, *supra*—Burnett *supra*—Alison *supra*—Bell s Notes, *supra* In Miller (1781 Burnett, 393, note), and Brown (1811 2 Hume, 341) boys fourteen years old were examined on declaration, and in Adam and Scott (1805, Burnett, ib) an opinion was expressed that a boy of that age should not be sworn, if he did not fully understand the effect and import of the oath These however are exceptional cases The rule may, therefore, be stated thus —That boys and girls of fourteen are presumed fit to be sworn, until a special examination (which will only be made if called for) shows that they do not understand the nature of an oath, that it is *pars judicis* to examine witnesses between twelve and fourteen on that point and only to put them on oath if they are qualified, and that children below twelve ought in no case to be sworn, however precocious they may be

(*r*) Hume (vol ii p 341) states it as doubtful whether a boy of fourteen can be sworn, if he appears to understand the nature of an oath But the text is fully borne out by the following authorities —2 Al, 433—Bell s Notes, 246 In Holmes (1799 Burnett, 392), it was held fixed that a boy nearly fourteen might be sworn, if he understood the nature of an oath In Main and Aitchison (1818, 2 Hume, 341 2), a boy between thirteen and fourteen years was sworn, after some preliminary questions to that effect In M Quarry (1817, 2 Hume, 212), the oath was administered to a boy under fourteen, and in Neill and Bruce (1827, Syme, 187, Hume ib) and Mellen (1837 1 Swin, 527), it was administered to girls between twelve and fourteen The reporters in these cases do not mention whether the witnesses were examined as to their understanding of the nature of an oath On the other hand in Buchan (1819, Sh Just Ca 35) and Sinclair (1822 ib 77) boys between twelve and fourteen were examined on de-

§ 1678 In England the admissibility of children depends on whether they can comprehend the nature of an oath, and if they cannot, the Court may in criminal cases delay the trial until they shall have been instructed (*s*) A child having the necessary knowledge is admissible, and will be sworn, although under seven, and perhaps if only five years of age (*t*) But Mr Justice Park rejected the dying declaration of a girl four years old (for the murder of whom the prisoner was tried), because, however precocious she might be, she could not have an adequate idea of a future state (*u*) In a recent case (*x*), Chief Baron Pollock refused to postpone a trial till a child of six years old should be instructed as to the nature of an oath, and observed, that "where the infirmity arises from no neglect, but from the child being too young to have been taught, I doubt whether the loss in point of memory would not more than countervail the gain in point of religious education" The Scotch rule avoids this dilemma, by admitting the evidence without an oath, and leaving to the jury to give to it what weight it deserves in the circumstances

§ 1679 An intelligent child is generally a good witness in matters within his comprehension Being accustomed to observe more than to reflect, he tells what he has seen or heard without colouring from inferences or preconceived opinions The solemnity of the examination has a strong influence on his mind, while one who is daily examined at school is in good training to answer distinctly as a witness In cross-examination a young witness generally tells ingenuously whether he has been tutored, and (if so) what he was desired to say [2]

---

claration, not understanding the nature of an oath, as was also a girl of similar age and equal ignorance in Lang (1764, Burnett, 393, note) The same rule seems to have been applied in Findlater (1749, Burnett 392, note)—Adam and Scott (1805, ib, 393)—Young (1738, 2 Hume, 312)—Reid (1774, ib) as to boys of that age The notes of these cases do not state whether the witnesses underwent a preliminary examination

(*s*) Starkie (4th ed) 117—1 Phill 5—2 Taylor 920 (*t*) Starkie, *supra*—Phill *supra*—Taylor, *supra*—Buller's Nisi Pr, 293—Brasier's case 1779, 1 Leach, 199

(*u*) Pike's case, 1829 3 Car and Pa 598 (*x*) R v Nicholas 1846, 2 Car and Kir 246

---

[2] At the trial of John Stewart for murder, 1855, 2 Irv, 166, a boy of about seven years of age, who said that he had witnessed the assault was examined It was afterwards proposed to prove by some of the subsequent witnesses what the boy had said to them with reference to it, immediately or shortly after the occurrence The Court admitted the evidence, chiefly for the purpose of ascertaining whether or not *de recenti* the child gave the same account of the occurrence, and thus testing the value of his evi-

CHAPTER III.—OF THE ADMISSIBILITY OF PERSONS LABOURING UNDER MENTAL DISEASE.

§ 1680. Mental derangement admits of infinite degrees and varieties from nervous excitability to mania, and from extreme stupidity to idiotism. Its intellectual and moral obscuration is sometimes intermittent, sometimes continuous, and varies in nature and extent, not only in different persons, but in the same person at different times. The admissibility of a witness alleged to be of unsound mind must therefore depend on the character and strength of his individual malady.

§ 1681. An idiot, or a person insane at the time of trial, must of course be rejected (*a*). But a witness will not be excluded because his memory and faculties are impaired by age, provided he is *compos mentis* (*b*), for his appearance under examination is sufficient to enable the jury to judge whether he can be relied upon. In one case, however, it was considered sufficient to exclude a witness that she was unable to take the oath from being weak in intellect, and, when agitated, imbecile (*c*).

§ 1682. One who is subject to occasional fits of derangement is admissible during lucid intervals (*d*). Some authorities entitled to

---

(*a*) Stair, 4, 43, 7 (2)—2 Hume, 340—Burnett, 390—2 Al. 436—Tait, 342. In M'Namara, 1848, Arkley, 521, the medical officer of the asylum where a witness had resided, on whom an assault with intent to ravish was alleged to have been committed, deponed that she was far from being a perfect idiot, and was not insane, but that if examined in Court upon what had happened to herself, she would get stupified; that she had no notion of a future state, and could not (he thought) understand the nature and obligation of an oath, but that she knew she should not tell a lie. The Court would not admit evidence of her statements made *de recenti* to a neighbour. The Crown counsel then pleaded that they could be proved, not as statements, but like a scream from one of the lower animals, but the Court held that they must be connected by other evidence with the act libelled, and the examination was not prosecuted.

(*b*) Nicholson *v.* M'Alister, 1829, 7 S., 743—Riley *v.* M'Laren, 1853, 16 D., 323.

(*c*) M'Gilvray, 1830, Bell's Notes, 261. The note of the case states that the witness was "dismissed," but it does not appear whether this was the act of the Court or of the prosecutor *proprio motu*.

(*d*) In Love (1687, 2 Hume, 340), a witness who had frequently been insane, but had not been so for four years previously, was admitted *cum nota*, and in Meldrum (1826, Syme, 31, 2 Hume, 340), note, a witness who was proved to have been insane from the effects of liquor was admitted, and the Court refused to mark him *cum nota*.

---

dence. In a later case the Court refused to admit the evidence of a child three years of age. H. M. Adv. *v.* Thomson, 1857, 2 Irv. 717.

high respect, lay down that a witness of this kind is incompetent, if a fit has intervened since the date of the circumstances on which he is to be examined, because he would be apt to confound his delusions with his sane recollections (e) But this will only hold where the violence of the frenzy leaves his mind distorted to a corresponding extent on return to sanity (f) And, accordingly the rule is thus stated by Lord Stair that fatuous and furious persons are inadmissible "except they had long lucid intervals, for short intervals are hard to be known" (g) In England and America the return of a lucid interval restores the competency of the witness (h)

§ 1683 In some cases the monomaniac is sane beyond the sphere of his delusions, while in others he sees everything distorted by them It seems to be only in cases of the latter description that he is inadmissible A case in which a monomaniac was able to observe remember, and testify, occurred recently in England, where in the trial of an attendant in a lunatic asylum for manslaughter of one of the patients, another patient tendered as a witness for the prosecutor, was admitted by Mr Justice Coleridge, a case being reserved for the Court of Criminal Appeal as to his competency (i) According to the evidence adduced (see foot-

(e) 2 Hume 340—Burnett, 390—Tait 342

(f) See 2 Al, 436

(g) Stair, 4, 43, 7 (2)—See also Bell's Pr, § 2241

(h) 1 Phil 4 2 Taylor 919—1 Greenleaf 168

(i) Reg v Hill 1851 1 Temple and Mew 582 From the reserved case it appeared that the witness laboured under the delusion of having a number of spirits about him, who were always talking to him The medical superintendent of the asylum stated on oath "I believe him to be quite capable of giving an account of any transaction that happened before his eyes I have always found him so It is solely with reference to the delusion about the spirits that I attribute to him the being a lunatic When I have had conversation with him on ordinary subjects I have found him perfectly rational, but for this delusion I have seen nothing in his conduct or demeanour in answering questions, otherwise than the demeanour of a sane man" The former medical officer of the asylum corroborated this evidence and stated generally with regard to such cases "that in monomania the mind is unsound, but unsound on one point only There is no doubt, however, that all the mental faculties are more or less affected, but the affection is more strongly manifested in some than in others In ordinary cases there is no particular difference between a monomaniac apart from his particular delusion, and an insane person in a lucid interval During the lucid intervals of the insane person he is well but a monomaniac is a monomaniac all the time In the instance of a monomaniac you produce the insanity the moment you touch the particular chord It is possible that you might revive insanity in a madman during a lucid interval by touching on the same subject if it is but recent" The witness himself having then been called in and examined before being sworn, stated that he had twenty thousand spirits which ascended from his stomach and head and were also in his ears &c that they

note) the witness believed he was surrounded by thousands of spirits, who were constantly speaking to him, but he understood perfectly the meaning and obligation of an oath, and the consequences of perjury, and he gave an intelligible account of the affair in issue, with only a slight reference to his spiritual attendants. After a full argument, the Court of Appeal unanimously held that the witness had been properly admitted, and that it lay with the jury to give to his evidence what weight they thought it deserved. Lord Chief-Justice Campbell observed, 'Various authorities have been cited to show that a person *non compos mentis* is not admissible. But the question is, in what sense is *non compos* used? If a man is *non compos mentis* so as not to know the nature of an oath, he ought not to be admitted. If he is aware of the nature of an oath he ought to be admitted. I think that is the proper line to be pursued.' 'The state of the witness' mind may be brought out on cross-examination, to show that no confidence can be given to his statements.' Barons Alderson and Platt took the same view, while Mr Justice Coleridge, confining himself to the particular case, observed, that the witness' 'examination showed he was a man with a diseased mind, but the disease was of such a character as not to operate upon the matter in question. With regard to memory, he was in the state of most other persons and with regard to the nature of an oath, he was unusually competent."

Mr Justice Talfourd remarked, that 'it would be very disastrous if mere delusions were held to exclude a witness. Some of the greatest and wisest of men have had particular delusions." And Lord Campbell added, 'The rule which has been contended for would have excluded the testimony of Socrates, for he had one spirit always prompting him."

§ 1684. A more humble illustration occurred in the person of a practitioner in the Court of Session, who believed he was in daily communication with the spirits of Plato, Burns, and others of the

---

spoke to him incessantly, and were speaking to him at the time of his examination — that he was a Roman catholic, and knew that when he swore he appealed to the Almighty, and that one who breaks an oath will go to hell for all eternity. He was then sworn, and gave a "perfectly connected and rational account of a transaction which he reported himself to have witnessed. He was in some doubt as to the day of the week on which it took place, and on cross-examination said, 'These creatures insist upon it it was Tuesday night, and I think it was Monday,' whereupon he was asked, 'Is what you have told us what the spirits told you, or what you recollect without the spirits?' to which he answered, 'No, the spirits assist me in speaking of the date, I thought it was Monday, and they told me it was Christmas eve, Tuesday, but I was an eye witness, an ocular witness to the fall to the ground.

mighty dead Yet he attended the Court, and conducted rationally the few processes which were intrusted to his care until his death, in 1854

§ 1685 The competency of a witness objected to as insane is usually ascertained from the evidence of physicians and persons acquainted with him And it is not uncommon to examine the individual in court (k)

The investigation should take place before the witness commences his deposition His incompetency, however, may be manifest from his own manner when under examination In a trial for robbery, where the Crown had closed its case, including the evidence of the injured party, proof that he was "of weak intellect, and incapable of giving rational evidence," was admitted on behalf of the prisoner (l) The result is not reported

CHAPTER IV — OF THE ADMISSIBILITY OF DEAF AND DUMB WITNESSES

§ 1686. Before modern science had proved that the deaf and dumb could be educated, they were regarded as in a mental condition not many degrees above idiotcy and were inadmissible as witnesses The old rule remains to this effect that a party adducing a deaf and dumb witness must prove that he is fit to give evidence (a) It is necessary that such a witness should not only be able to observe and remember but also that he should know right from wrong and believe in a God who punishes evil-doers (b) It

(k) Reg v Hill *supra*, § 1683, (i)—Love, 1687, 2 Hume 340,—Reid, 1835, Bell's Notes 245 But see M Namara, 1848, Arkley 521, where after medical evidence on the sanity of a witness had been led the Court would not allow her to be brought before them in order that they might judge from their own observation

(l) Adams v Macintosh, 1829 Bell's Notes, 245

(a) Cases in following notes —1 Phill, 4– Taylor, 919—1 Greenl, 469—Best Pr of Ev, § 144 So the Court refused to appoint a judicial factor to a deaf and dumb person who was able to manage her own affairs, Kirkpatrick 8th June 1853 15 D, 731

(b) White, 1812 1 Broun, 228, Bell's Notes, 246 S C—Martin, 1823 Sh Just Ca, 101—2 Hume, 340, S C—Wintrup, 1827, Sh Just Ca 211—Gibb, 1835, Bell's Notes, 245 From these authorities it appears that the Court went wrong in the case of Farquhar, 1833 (house breaking), Bell's Notes, 245, where they allowed a deaf and dumb girl (whose age is not mentioned) to be examined by signs through an interpreter

would also seem that a deaf and dumb adult is inadmissible unless he comprehends and believes in the obligation of an oath (*c*) In two cases, however, the Court appear not to have considered this to be necessary (*d*)

§ 1687 Deaf and dumb witnesses are usually examined by signs through a sworn interpreter But, if they can write it is generally better to take their written answers to written questions(*e*) In every case that mode of examination should be adopted which the education and habits of the witness show to be the best mode of eliciting a distinct statement from him (*f*).[1]

CHAPTER V —OF THE EXCLUSION OF WITNESSES ON ACCOUNT OF ATHEISM

§ 1688 Law, in its jealous fear of false evidence, refuses to admit the testimony of persons who—influenced though they may be

without being sworn, although a teacher of the deaf and dumb swore that she was totally uneducated, and that it was impossible to convey to her the idea of an oath

(*c*) See Martin, *supra*—Gibb, *supra*—See *infra*, § 1688

(*d*) Farquhar 1833 Bell's Notes, 215 This decision is questioned *supra*, (*b*) In Wintrup, 1827 Sh Just Ca 211 the chief witness in a case of rape was examined without an oath The occult nature of such crimes, and the difficulty of investigating them without the evidence of the injured party, may require them to be an exception to the general rule In neither of these cases is the age of the witness mentioned in the report

(*e*) Reid, 1835, Bell's Notes, 246—See also Carnegie, 1710, 5 B Sup, 805—Smith, 1841, 2 Swin, 517 Bell's Notes 242, S C —*Supra* §§ 1420 1501—Morrison *v* Lennard, 1827, 3 Car and Pa, 127—Taylor, 919—1 Phill, 4—Best Pr of Ev, § 144

(*f*) In a case of seduction before Lord Campbell the seduced party was deaf and dumb, but could write very well Her examination was carried on by signs, and, when these were not understood, by writing, Bartholomew *v* George, 1850 (not rep) noted in Best Pr of Ev § 144

[1] In H M Adv *v* Thomas O'Neil, 1858, 3 Irv 93, a witness for the Crown who was unable to speak articulately, was disallowed In a case of assault with intent, the injured party, who was deaf and dumb, who had not been educated, and who could converse by means of arbitrary signs and gestures only, was examined on declaration not on oath The Court considered that the witness was in the situation of an ideot to whom an oath ought not to be administered, but whose evidence was admissible if it appeared that she understood the obligation of telling the truth, H M Adv *v* Montgomery, 1855, 2 Irv, 222

by a sense of honour, regard to character and fear of punishment by man—have not the higher rectitude which springs from religious belief (*a*) This rule is only directed against atheists It does not exclude Jews, Mahomedans, or Pagans, or witnesses of any creed, provided they believe in a God who enjoins truth and punishes falsehood (*b*) In this country it has generally been considered that a witness will not be admitted unless he believes in a future state of rewards and punishments (*c*) But there is no express decision on the point, while in England, belief in a God whose rewards and punishments extend only to this life seems to be considered sufficient (*d*)

A striking exception to this rule was recognised recently by a statute (*e*), which allows various tribes of barbarous and uncivilised people in the colonies and plantations who are "destitute of the knowledge of God and of any religious belief," to be examined, without any oath, before courts and magistrates within the colonies in or adjacent to which such persons reside [2]

(*a*) Bankton, 4, 30, 4—Burnett 395—Bell's Pr, § 2242—Ivory's Note to Ersk 4 2 22—Tait Ev, 347—2 Al 437 The rule in the text existed at a time when no witness, whatever might be his religious scruples against swearing, could be examined without an oath, see 2 Hume 376—22 George II, ch 46, § 37 An atheist, of course, could not be sworn and therefore was inadmissible

(*b*) Authorities in preceding note—Jews were admitted in Ryan, 1764, 1 Lea Cr Ca, 64 cited in 2 Hume, 376 note 1—Horn *v* Maclaren, 1831, Bell's Notes, 265—Menzies *v* Morrison, 1712 M, 16 732 (see next note) In Nicolson *v* Nicolson (1770, M, 16,770, aff'd on appeal, ib), a negro who believed in God and in a future state, but was not a christian was admitted So a unitarian who had used impious language against christianity was admitted in Macfarlane *v* Young, 1824, 3 Mur, 411 See also Starkie (4th ed) 116—1 Phill, 11—Taylor, 922—Best's Pr of Ev, § 159 Fountainhall states (vol ii, p 908, M, 16 732) that in the trial of Captain Green, in 1705, for piracy, two heathen boys were examined But the reports (14 How St Tr 1261 6—Arnot's Crim Tr 248) show that both of them professed christianity—See also (*g*)

(*c*) Bell's Pr § 2242—Tait Ev, 347—2 Al, 437 In Menzies *v* Morrison, *supra* the Lords admitted a Jew, "because his religion doth not hinder him to swear our formula by God himself unless he were a sadducee, who denies the resurrection"

(*d*) Starkie (4th ed) 116—Taylor 922 In America the rule stated in the text is settled, 1 Greenl § 369, Taylor ib, and cases there cited

(*e*) 6 and 7 Vict c 22

[2] In Suttar *v* The Aberdeen Arctic Co an Esquimaux was examined not on oath, but on his declaration to speak the truth On his examination *in initialibus* he deponed that he did not know that there was a God but that he believed in a future state after death, and that a man would be liable to punishment in that future state for crimes committed in this world, Suttar *v* Aberdeen Arctic Co 1861, 23 D, 465 The mode in which his examination was conducted does not appear from the report, but the examination will be found at length in the Session Papers (Pursuer's Proof, p 35) An

§ 1689 In this country the objection of atheism may be proved by examining the witness (*f*), as well as by evidence of his previous declarations regarding his opinions (*g*) Nor will it be easy by evidence of the latter kind, to exclude a witness who states, in his initial examination that he believes in God, for no one except himself can know whether he believes or not and he may have abandoned his former opinions, or his declarations regarding them may have been untrue (*h*)

§ 1690 The English authorities are not agreed as to the mode in which this objection to a witness may be proved According to one view the witness may be examined on his opinions (*i*), and it has been said that this is the only competent mode of proof (*k*), whereas other authorities entirely reject it considering the examina-

---

(*f*) The witness was examined on this point (but apparently without being sworn) in Nicolson v Nicolson 1770, M, 16,770 In Captain Green's case, 1705, 14 How St Tr, 1261, the witnesses objected to were sworn, and then examined *in initialibus* as to their belief in God and in the effect of an oath See next note

(*g*) In Henry, 1842, 1 Broun 221, the prisoner proved by other witnesses that a witness tendered for the Crown had often denied the existence of God or Devil, as well as the truth of the holy scriptures Having then been examined by the Court, he stated that he believed in a Supreme Being, and in a future state of rewards and punishments, upon which he was put on oath and examined more fully on the grounds on which his admissibility was objected to He contradicted the evidence of the witnesses as to his declarations, admitting that he said he did not believe the whole of the bible, but adding that he did believe in the existence of a God, in the sanctity of an oath, and a future state of rewards and punishments and that he attended the Established Church every Sunday The Court held that he was admissible, but recommended to the prosecutor not to press the examination The prisoner thereupon pleaded guilty to a part of the charge, and the Advocate-Depute stated that, if the case had gone on, he would have withdrawn the witness

(*h*) See on this Best Pr of Ev § 157 Yet this mode of investigation involves a paradox For if the witness is an atheist and *ex hypothesi* one who will swear falsely on the merits of the cause, is it to be presumed that he will speak the truth in his initial examination? On the other hand, if he candidly admits that he is an [illegible]ist, does that circumstance indicate such a reckless or intentional disregard of truth, that his evidence on the facts must be excluded? Or again, may not the case be figured of a witness tendered for the prosecution in a criminal trial, endeavouring to save his friend from the damaging effect of his evidence, by pretending a scepticism he does not feel, and declaring, both before the trial and in his initial examination, that an oath has no influence on his mind?

(*i*) 1 Phill, 11—Starkie (4th ed), 115, 6—Rose Cr Ev (3d ed), 132—Best Pr of Ev, § 157—R *v* Serva, 1845, 2 Car and Kir, 53—R *v* Taylor, 1790, 1 Peake Ca, 11—See 1 and 2 Vict, c 105

(*k*) Phill, *supra*—Rose, *supra* See also Starkie, 116

appeal against the deliverance admitting him as a witness taken at the time, was ultimately fallen from

tion of a person as to his religious opinions to be inquisitorial (*l*) Professor Greenleaf takes the latter view (*m*)

§ 1691 It is hardly necessary to add that the creed of a witness is matter for the jury to consider in weighing his credibility, as the high precepts of the christian faith, and the loose doctrines of many other creeds, differ very widely in their tendency to produce truthfulness

§ 1692 The unqualified exclusion of witnesses on the ground of atheism is of very doubtful expediency Cases may easily be figured where it would produce fatal consequences, while observation shows that sceptics are often as truthful and honourable men as those who profess religion It is believed that admitting the testimony of persons of this class, their credibility being left to the jury would be more likely to promote than to defeat the ends of justice The only cases, indeed, in which opinions as to religion ought absolutely to exclude are, where the creed of the witness ordains or allows perjury (*n*) [3]

(*l*) Professor Christian in note 11 to his ed of Blackstone vol iii, p 369—Taylor 923 (*m*) 1 Greenl, § 370 (*n*) See Benth Jud Ev vol i, p 235, vol v, p 184, and Best's Pr of Ev, § 161 These writers cite several instances in which the Hindoo creed declares false testimony to be allowable Nay are there not many circumstances in which the casuistry of one christian church permits, and even enjoins, false testimony?

---

[3] In Maden v Cattanach, 1861 7 Hurl and Nor Exch Rep 361, Sarah Maden one of the plaintiffs, was called as the first witness her evidence being essential to the establishment of the claim The defendant's advocate proposed to interrogate the witness with regard to her religious belief before she was sworn This was objected to and it was contended, (1) that defective religious belief ought not to be treated as a ground of incompetency, (2) that, if such defect should be held to render the witness incompetent, it ought to be proved, like any other fact, by independent evidence, and not by interrogating the witness (3) that in any case, as the witness did not object to take the oath, she was not compellable to answer any questions until she had been sworn The judge overruled the objections, and the witness was sworn on the *voir dire*, when having deponed that she did not believe in a God, or in a future state of rewards and punishments, but that she considered herself morally bound to tell the truth, the judge refused to allow her to be examined The Court of Exchequer were unanimously of opinion that the course of procedure adopted by the judge was in accordance with the law and practice of the Courts in England and they dismissed the appeal The propriety of this disqualification has been lately challenged by several legal writers, on the following, among other grounds —(1) That it proceeds on a theory of evidence which does not now obtain,—a theory which overlooks the fact that the great security against judicial errors lies in the power of exposing or contradicting false evidence, not in preventing false evidence from being given, (2) that it proceeds upon the erroneous assumption that a man is solely induced to tell the truth by the fear of future punishment whereas the motives which induce him to do so are much more intimate and compli

CHAPTER VI.—OF THE EXCLUSION OF WITNESSES ON THE GROUND OF OUTLAWRY.

§ 1693. One who lies under sentence of fugitation or outlawry has forfeited his person in law, and is inadmissible as a witness (*a*). His competency can be restored by the Court of Justiciary, on application by the public prosecutor, or on his giving himself up to justice (*b*). But where the objection of outlawry was stated to a Crown witness, the Court of Justiciary refused to repone him at the trial, as they considered that the application should have been made previously (*c*). The ground of this exclusionary rule is not the untrustworthiness of the witness. It is a penalty directed apparently against the outlaw, but really punishing the innocent party who requires his evidence, and who, from want of that proof, may lose his case. Fortunately this rule has very seldom to be applied in practice.

(*a*) 2 Hume, 270—2 Al., 350—Hunter, 1838, 2 Swin., 181; Bell's Notes, 228, S. C.
(*b*) 2 Hume, 272—2 Al., 352. (*c*) Hunter, *supra*.

cated, and are motives which influence men who do not believe in a supreme being or future punishments as well as those who do; (3) that a man who has the courage and honesty to avow himself an atheist in a public court gives the strongest possible proof of his truthfulness; (4) that seeing that cases may arise where the testimony of atheists is indispensable, their exclusion is a public injury, and hurtful to the administration of justice; (5) that it is unjust to any class of the community to deprive them of the protection of the law by attaching a civil disability to religious opinion. After the decision in Maden *v.* Cattanach, *supra*, it would appear that the Courts in England now hold (it had been previously doubted, and the institutional writers had indicated a different view), that a witness, whether he be or be not a party to the cause, may be competently examined on his religious belief. Baron Bramwell, indeed, put in a strong light the inconsistency which the admission of this evidence involves. 'A singular state of things arises in cases of this description. The presumption of law is, that a man is qualified by his religious belief to take an oath. Then, what are the materials by which his capacity is judged? His own statement. Then, by the hypothesis, he is made incredible by a statement which is not to be believed.' But if a witness refuses to answer questions as to his religious belief on the ground that the answers may tend to discredit him, can the Court compel him to answer, or infer, from his refusal, that he is incompetent? It would appear that the point has not been decided. Stephen on Criminal Law, p. 289. A bill has been repeatedly introduced into Parliament for the purpose of removing this disability, but it has not yet been passed.

CHAPTER VII.—OF THE ADMISSIBILITY OF ACCOMPLICES.

§ 1694. In order to secure the detection and punishment of crimes which have been committed with secrecy, our law permits the public prosecutor to adduce one *socius criminis* as a witness against another (*a*). But as it would be highly dangerous to leave a witness of this kind at the mercy of the prosecutor, and as a full disclosure could not be expected from one who might afterwards be tried for his own share of the crime, it has long been settled in this country that the public prosecutor, by adducing a *socius criminis*, discharges him from all the penal consequences of his offence, whatever may be the result of the trial in which he is examined (*b*). The Court explain this to the witness before his examination begins.

§ 1695. This rule applies only to prosecutions by the Crown where one of the offenders turns 'Queen's evidence.' A private prosecutor cannot tie up the hands of the public authorities by examining a *socius criminis* (*c*).[1]

(*a*) 2 Hume, 367—Burnett, 417—2 Al., 452. This frequently occurs in practice. See next note.

(*b*) In the trial of Stewart of Dunearn for killing Sir Alex. Boswell in a duel, a difficulty occurred to the Court in regard to Lord Rosslyn, who had been one of the seconds, but who, as a peer, was beyond the jurisdiction of the Court, and therefore (in strict law) beyond its protection. His Lordship, however, considered himself protected, and was examined. See separate rep., p. 17, and 2 Al., 19. In Dreghorn, 1807, 2 Hume, 367, Burnett, 419, and ib. App. No. 21, S. C., where it was pleaded that the Court could not protect a *socius criminis* who was a soldier liable to trial by court-martial for his share in the offence (murder), and who was then in confinement on that account, he was admitted, the Court holding that they could interfere to prevent his being endangered by his evidence. A detailed statement of the rules as to the protection of the *socius* is beyond the scope of this treatise. They will be found in 2 Hume, 367—Burnett, 417—2 Al., 452—Bell's Notes, 261. See also the law on this point fully discussed in the successful objection to the indictment of Hare, who had been examined as *socius* in the trial of Burke and M'Dowall in 1829, Sh. Just. Ca., 205, Syme, 373, and separate report of trial of Burke and M'Dowall.

(*c*) Per L. Mackenzie in Hare's case, 1829, Bell's Notes, 261; Syme, 373, S. C.

[1] After the trial of Jessie M'Lauchlan for murder, 1862, 4 Irv. 229, 35 Sc. Jur., 50, the question whether a witness who had been examined at a trial could be afterwards tried for the same offence, was much discussed. During a debate which took place in the House of Commons (see Appendix to vol. iv. of Mr Irvine's Reports) the Lord Advocate (Moncreiff), after reviewing the authorities, stated that he was of opinion that the trial of a person who had been examined as a witness in such circumstances was not a competent proceeding by the law of Scotland. There can be no doubt that a *socius cri-*

§ 1696 In England, accomplices are admitted on application to the Court in whose discretion it lies to determine whether their

---

minis who is adduced as a witness by the public prosecutor, and who is admonished in the usual way by the presiding judge cannot thereafter be brought to trial for the same offence The law appears to presume that when the prosecutor adopts a *socius* as a witness, he enters into a compact or agreement with him, whereby, as the price of his evidence he undertakes to protect him from the penal consequences of the offence The understanding on which the rule is founded might, perhaps, be held to cover the case where, when suspicion attaches to two parties the prosecutor, without entering into an agreement with either, determines to try the one, and to put the other in the witness box But it can scarcely be said that any such implied contract arises where at the time when a person is examined as a witness in a criminal cause the prosecutor is ignorant that any suspicion of complicity attaches to him or where the witness has only been called to speak to an incidental and collateral matter,—as in the instance, suggested in the House of Commons by Mr Muir, of an architect brought to prove plans of the house where the offence was committed The compact cannot be presumed to extend, either expressly or by implication to such cases, and if it is held that a witness in these circumstances is protected it can only be on the general ground that by the law of Scotland, a person who has been examined on oath at a criminal trial cannot afterwards be indicted for the offence regarding which he was examined But, notwithstanding some remarks in the latest work on criminal law, 2 Al, 568, it is thought that no such absolute rule obtains in the law of Scotland and if it do not, then it is clear that the principle which protects the *socius*, whose evidence has been bought by the prosecutor cannot include the case of a witness who, at the time when he was examined was supposed by the prosecutor to be unconnected with the crime or who was examined on an incidental or collateral matter This opinion is supported by the view which was expressed by several of the judges in Hare's case, and which was to the effect that the judicial arrangement, or *quasi* contract, between the prosecutor and the *socii* was not perfected until the witness had given his evidence If after being sworn, he refused to give his evidence he lost his protection,—the refusal to give his evidence being equivalent to a refusal to appear as a witness and a breach of the condition on which indemnity had been granted, see the opinion of Lord Mackenzie—Separate Report, p 105 (The question directly in issue in Hare's case was whether a *socius* who had been adduced by the public prosecutor could afterwards be indicted at the instance of a private prosecutor and the opinions of the judges are directly applicable only to the case of a witness who is known to be a *socius* at the time when his evidence is given) It has been argued indeed that though the rule contended for may not be absolutely inflexible and that though it may be relaxed to meet certain cases where it could not reasonably be insisted in yet that it applies whenever a witness is examined upon the substantial and material parts of a cause But even this position does not seem tenable It is obvious that the Court would be called upon to discharge a very anomalous and perplexing duty were it required to discriminate between the formal and the substantial parts of a proof Apart, however, from any technical difficulty suppose that during the investigation into a case of murder, a person appeared and stated that, about the time when the crime was committed he saw the accused at or near, the place where the body was found Such evidence might be of material importance —might be sufficient to ensure a conviction But if, after he had been examined as a witness at the trial it appeared that his story was false and that he himself was implicated in the offence could it be maintained that the public prosecutor was prevented from indicting him, and bound on the contrary to protect him from prosecution? It is thought, therefore, that evidence is required (*d*) And the examination only gives the witness an equitable right to a recommendation to royal pardon if he makes a full and fair confession (*e*) He is therefore more subject to bias against the prisoner than is the *socius criminis* in this country where his freedom is matter of legal right (*f*) Still more objectionable was the old English law of "approvement," under which the pardon of the witness depended on the prisoner being convicted (*g*)

§ 1697 In England it is competent in point of law for the jury to convict, even in a capital case, on the evidence of an accomplice alone, if they believe him, but the practice is to require corroboration of his testimony (*h*)[2] In this country the evidence of one witness is not legal proof, even where he is untainted, and, of course, it is insufficient, if he is a *socius criminis* (*i*) Baron Hume mentions a case of housebreaking, in which a verdict of guilty was found, and followed by capital punishment, on the evidence of two *socii*, whose depositions formed the entire proof (*k*)[3]

§ 1698 In point of credibility the evidence of accomplices stands very low. To the original offence of which they are guilty (whether the panels are so or not), they have added treachery to their comrades, and, in general, it is the worst of the gang who turns Queen's evidence. No doubt their freedom does not depend on the nature of their evidence, but it is the reward of disclosures true or false made on precognition under a tacit compact that they would be repeated at the trial There is, especially, a risk of their transposing the persons to the scene, and thereby shifting the guilt from themselves, or a favourite comrade, to another prisoner, a de-

(*d*) 2 Russell 959—1 Phill, 29 (*e*) 2 Russell 957—1 Phill, 28 (*f*) *Supra*, § 1694 (*g*) 2 Russell, 957 (*h*) 2 Russell, 960—1 Phill, 30 (*i*) 2 Hume, 367—2 Al, 452 See chapters on the number of witnesses required, *infra* (*k*) Smith's case, 1693, Hume *supra*

there is no authority which can force the Court to put other than a moderate and reasonable interpretation upon the rule in question, and it must be kept in mind that the *onus* of adducing authority lies upon those who maintain an exception to the general principle, that a person who commits an offence becomes amenable to the penalties which the law inflicts

[2] In England it is not a rule of law, but of practice only, that a jury should not convict on the unsupported testimony of an accomplice, R *v* Stubbs, 1855, 25 L J M C 16

[3] In the case of H M Adv *v* Campbell or Brown, 1855 2 Irv 232, Lord Cowan, with the concurrence of Lord Handyside, laid down, that the general rule is, that the evidence of accomplices must be, to a greater or less extent, corroborated by unsuspected testimony

vice which can sometimes be carried through without destroying the coherence or credibility of the narrative At the same time, the presence of the prisoners, and the witness knowledge that he cannot benefit himself by swearing falsely to their prejudice, tend to produce truth, while a skilful cross-examination will probably involve the witness in prevarication or inconsistencies, if his evidence is not candid The jury ought therefore to examine with care and suspicion the evidence of an accomplice, and ought not to believe it, unless it hangs well together and is amply corroborated It is chiefly useful in filling up the gaps and binding the threads in cases of circumstantial evidence, where, if the *socius* admits his own share in the crime (*l*), and if his story is consistent and tallies with the rest of the evidence, it may complete a proof which would otherwise have been defective [4]

The admissibility of the evidence of informers is noticed afterwards (*m*)

§ 1699 As injustice might frequently arise if the prosecutor in a criminal trial could deprive the accused of exculpatory witnesses, by including them in the libel it is in the power of the Court, on special cause shown, to separate the trials of prisoners lying under the same charge, in order that one of them may be adduced as a witness for the other (*n*) No rule can be stated as to the circumstances in which this should be done, as it is in the discretion of the Court, to say whether it is necessary or proper with a view to the ends of justice It may be observed, however, that if the counsel for one prisoner states on his professional responsibility that he believes the evidence of another prisoner to be important to the defence of his client, the trials ought to be separated, for that could only create inconvenience or delay, whereas refusing the motion would limit the investigation, and might occasion an erroneous verdict of guilty [5]

(*l*) See Grant, 1820, Sh Just Ca, 50 where a *socius criminis* denied his participation in the crime (*m*) *Infra* § 1742 (*n*) 2 Hume, 175, 402—2 Al 241—Bell s Notes, 182

---

[4] Evidence of statements made by a *socius* who had died was received in H M Adv *v* Reid, 1858 3 Irv 235 Had the *socius* been alive he would have been a competent witness, and, by the law of Scotland, statements made by a person deceased are admissible

[5] In H M Adv *v* Jane M'Pherson or Dempster and Others, 1862 4 Irv, 113 the Court refused a motion to separate the trial of one panel from that of four others,—the Lord Justice Clerk (Inglis) observing "that some special cause must be shown where

§ 1700 Formerly the proposed witness was tried first, and only in event of his acquittal was admitted for his fellow prisoner (*o*) But as infamy is not now a ground of exclusion (*p*) he will be equally admissible whether he is convicted or acquitted If each of the prisoners applied to have the other examined as a witness for him, the Court would probably refuse the motion on account of the risk of a preconcerted story, which each should tell on behalf of his friend Yet if there were no reason to suspect collusion, it would be competent to try the prisoners separately the one to be tried last being examined as witness on the first trial, and adducing his fellow prisoner when he is afterwards put on trial himself[6]

§ 1701 In a recent case on circuit two prisoners were tried on the same libel for assault, and were defended by the same counsel, who after the case for the Crown was closed, proposed to examine one of the prisoners as a witness for the other But the Court held this to be incompetent being of opinion that the proper course was to have moved for a separation of the trials, and that the statute 16 Vict c 20, § 3, did not make any alteration in this respect (*r*)

(*o*) 2 Hume, 175, 402—2 Al, 212 (*p*) 15 Vict c 27, § 1

(*r*) Hagan 1853 1 Irv, 342

the justice of the case requires the separation' before the Court will entertain the motion In an indictment charging murder against two panels and concealment of pregnancy alternatively, against one of them it was held competent to separate the trials to the extent of dealing with each charge separately, so that in the event of the charge of child-murder breaking down, one of the panels might be adduced as a witness on behalf of the panel against whom the alternative charge of concealment of pregnancy was libelled H M Adv v Duncan and Brechin, 1862, 4 Irv 206 The separation of trials is a matter within the discretion of the Court, and refusal to separate trials is not a relevant ground of suspension except when it amounts to oppression, Law and Turner v Linton 1861 4 Irv, 106 A motion that two keepers of an asylum, charged with assaulting a patient should be tried separately was refused by Lord Deas in H M Adv v Coupland and Beattie 1863, 35 J, 454

6 Where one of several panels pleads guilty, the other panels are entitled to the benefit of his evidence In general the following is the order of procedure adopted — the prosecutor accepts the plea of guilty the Court pronounces an interlocutor delaying sentence, and the panel is removed to and kept in, the witness-room until he is recalled and examined H M Adv v Brown and M'Leish 1856 2 Irv 578—H M Adv v Wilson and Others, 1860 3 Irv 624 After evidence had been led in a case of uttering, the prosecutor departed from the charge against Mary Beattie, one of three panels The Court was then moved by the counsel for the other panels to direct the jury to find a verdict acquitting Mary Beattie, so that she might be removed from the bar and examined as a witness The Court refused the motion holding that the proper course was to have moved for a separation of the trials H M Adv v M'Fadyen and Others 1857, 2 Irv, 599 See also Fitzsimmons v Linton, 1861, 23 D, 1301

CHAPTER VIII.—OF THE ADMISSIBILITY OF THE PARTIES TO THE CAUSE.

§ 1702. So long as interest and partial counsel were objections to the competency of witnesses, the evidence of the parties to the cause was, of course, inadmissible in their own favour. This rule excluded not only the parties who were really interested, but those who appeared *virtute officii*, without having any personal interest in the issue (*a*).

§ 1703. Nor could one party adduce his adversary as a witness; the rule being, that a party in a civil case was not bound to depone against himself, except on a reference to his oath (*b*). In criminal prosecutions the examination of the prisoner on oath is justly considered an inquisitorial and cruel proceeding, which the fair principles of our law forbid (*c*).

§ 1704. Recent legislation first limited (*d*) and then abolished (*e*), the exclusion of parties as witnesses either for or against themselves in all civil cases, except "any action, suit, or proceeding, instituted in Scotland in consequence of adultery, or for dissolving any marriage, or for breach of promise of marriage, or in any action of declarator of marriage, nullity of marriage, putting to silence, legitimacy, or bastardy, or in any action of adherence or separation." In these cases the parties are still inadmissible as witnesses.[1]

(*a*) Among many cases on this point see Smeal *v.* Wilson, 1821, 1 S., 231—Watson *v.* Hamilton, 1824, 3 Mur., 483—Smith *v.* Robertson, 1832, 10 S., 829.

(*b*) See Wallace *v.* Robertson, 1838, 16 S., 1065—Per Lord Colonsay in Wilson *v.* Glasgow and S. Western Ry. Co., 1851, 14 D., 6, and case of Mackenzie *v.* Bathurst (not reported) mentioned by his Lordship.

(*c*) See *supra*, §§ 1411, 1548.

(*d*) 15 Vict., c. 27, § 2.

(*e*) 16 Vict., c. 20, §§ 1, 4.

[1] The 5th section of 24 and 25 Vict., c. 86 (Conjugal Rights Act) provides that an order of protection under the act shall have the effect of a decree of separation *a mensâ et thoro* in regard to the property, rights, and obligations of the husband and of the wife, and in regard to the wife's capacity to sue and be sued. The act 16 Vict., c. 20, which allows the parties to a cause to be examined as witnesses, continues, by § 4, to exclude the parties in actions of separation. In Walker, petitioner, 1862, 24 D., 300, the question arose, whether a wife petitioning for an order of protection under the Conjugal Rights Act was a competent witness. The Court held that the 16 Vict., c. 20, was an enabling act, which allowed the examination of the parties, except in certain cases; that among the excluded cases were actions of separation; that if the Conjugal Rights Act had declared that an order for protection was to have the same operation as a decree of separation the evidence might have been excluded; that the act did not declare that an order was

§ 1705. The tutors and curators of parties interested in these cases are equally inadmissible with the parties themselves. This arises from the clause in the act of 1852 (*f*) which admitted the parties to the record (if not substantially interested), having been repealed absolutely by a subsequent statute, which while making the parties admissible, whether they are really interested or not, declares that nothing contained in it shall apply to the causes above enumerated (*g*).

§ 1706. In a question of succession, where the summons concluded for reduction of the service of a competing heir, and for declarator that the pursuer was the lawful son procreated of the marriage between the ancestor and his wife, and as such was heir of entail to the ancestor, it was held that the pursuer could not adduce himself as a witness, because the conclusion for declarator of legitimacy brought the case within the exceptional clause of the statute above quoted (*h*). The Court, however, felt that difficult cases might arise on this head, where the real question between competing heirs involving marriage or legitimacy, without the action being one of those enumerated in the statute.

(*f*) 15 Vict. c. 27, § 2. (*g*) 16 Vict., c. 20, §§ 1, 4.
(*h*) Sandilands *v.* Nimmo, 14th Feb. 1855, 27 Sc. Jur. 178.

---

to have the same operation, but only to certain effects; that, in point of fact, the act applied only to the patrimonial rights of the husband; that, in these circumstances, a petition for protection was not one of the excluded cases under the Evidence Act, and that the petitioner was a competent witness. In England the parties are inadmissible in this class of actions, only in actions instituted in consequence of adultery, and in actions for breach of promise of marriage. But in England a wife cannot obtain a divorce *a vinculo* solely on the ground of the adultery of the husband, but the adultery must be conjoined with cruelty, desertion, &c., 20 and 21 Vict. c. 85, § 27. In the case of Pyne *v.* Pyne, 1858, 1 Swab. and Trist., 178, the Court of Probate and Matrimonial Causes held that the wife was not a competent witness even to prove the fact of desertion. In consequence of this decision the act 22 and 23 Vict. c. 61, § 6, was passed, which provides that "on any petition presented by a wife praying that her marriage may be dissolved by reason of her husband having been guilty of adultery coupled with cruelty, or of adultery coupled with desertion, the husband and wife, respectively, shall be competent and compellable to give evidence of, and relating to, such cruelty and desertion." In the same way the Scotch Courts have held that, in an action of divorce for adultery, the husband is not admissible as a witness, even in regard to the proof of an incidental matter, such as the question of domicile with reference to the jurisdiction of the Court, Tulloch *v.* Tulloch, 1861, 23 D. 639. The expediency of making the parties in actions of divorce on the ground of adultery competent witnesses to establish the incidental or formal matters which require to be proved in such actions, and in actions of divorce on the ground of desertion, of receiving their evidence to establish the fact of desertion, has been recently advocated in a Report on the Law of Evidence by a Committee of the Faculty of Advocates, and seems manifest

§ 1707 In criminal causes, the public or private prosecutor is admissible as a witness on either side (*i*).[2] But the statute which rendered party-witnesses admissible, expressly declared that "nothing herein contained shall render any person who in any criminal proceeding is charged with the commission of any indictable offence, or any offence punishable on summary conviction, competent or compellable to give evidence either for or against himself or herself" (*k*).[3]

(*i*) 16 Vict c 20 § 3 (*k*) Ib The clause quoted in the text continues thus, "excepting in so far as the same may be at present competent by the law and practice of Scotland" This, however, is not meant to qualify the provisions above quoted, but other enactments of the section in which it occurs

[2] It is incompetent in a prosecution under the 4 Geo IV, c 34 § 3 "Master and Servants Act," to refer the matter to the oath of the prosecutor, Cameron v Paul 1858, 1 Irv, 316, but the prosecutor may be examined as a witness for the defence Paul v Barclay and Curle, 1856, 2 Irv 537

[3] This provision has given rise to much discussion In all the cases, however, in which the point has been raised in Scotland, it has been held that the parties were inadmissible So it was held in Stevenson v Scott, 1854 1 Irv, 603, which was a prosecution for penalties under the Tweed Fisheries Act, in Watson v Simpson, 1857, 19 D, 380, which was a prosecution in the Court of Exchequer under the Excise Act 18 and 19 Vict, c 94, § 36 in Bruce v Linton, 24 D, 184 which was a prosecution for penalties under 16 and 17 Vict c 67 (the Forbes Mackenzie Act), in Alison v Watson, 1862, 1 Macph, 87, which was a prosecution for penalties for selling spirits without a license under the statutes, 6 Geo IV, c 81 § 26, and 7 and 8 Geo IV c 53 Upon the effect of the corresponding provision in the English Evidence Act (14 and 15 Vict, c 99, § 3), the Court of Exchequer, in Att-Gen v Radloff 1854, 23 Law Journ (Exch), 240 (which was a prosecution for penalties under the Smuggling Act, 8 and 9 Vict c 87, § 46), were equally divided but in an information before justices, under one of the statutes inflicting penalties for pursuing or taking game 1 and 2 Will IV, c 32, § 23, it was held that the party was not a competent witness, Cattell v Ireson, 1858, 4 Jur N S, 560 The grounds on which, in all the cases, the Courts proceeded, were these:—The Evidence Act admitting parties to be witnesses did not extend to any criminal proceeding for an offence punishable on summary conviction, the illegal transactions in question were, in the sense of the Evidence Act, offences, they were punishable on summary conviction and the proceedings resorted to for imposing the punishment were criminal proceedings They were criminal proceedings, because the character of the proceeding did not depend upon whether it was instituted in a civil or criminal court—(most of the courts in this country exercise both a civil and criminal jurisdiction and a court is, for the time, a civil or criminal court according to the nature of the cause which it is trying White v Simpson 1862, 1 Macph 72, where the Lord Justice-Clerk (Inglis) divided courts into civil, criminal, and fiscal),—but upon the nature of the action, and the action, in each instance, was of a criminal nature, because it was an action, not for recovering a debt to be ranked for, or enforced by ordinary diligence, but for imposing a punishment which might take the form, either of a penalty to be paid, or of imprisonment to be suffered Section 13 of 19 and 20 Vict, c 56 (Court of Exchequer Act) provides that section 3 of 16 Vict, c 20, shall not be deemed to apply to any cause to be instituted under that act relating to the customs and inland revenue

§ 1708 It has been held that this exceptional provision includes a prosecution for penalties under the Tweed Fisheries Act, in which, therefore, the prisoner is not admissible as a witness either for or against himself (*l*)

§ 1709 In such civil actions as are laid on delicts which may be prosecuted criminally, both the defender and the pursuer may be adduced as witnesses on either side, but the defender is not bound to answer any question tending to criminate himself (*m*) This privilege indeed extends to all cases where parties are examined as witnesses (*n*)

§ 1710 The Evidence Act of 1853, provides that "the adducing of any party as a witness, in any cause or proceeding by the adverse party shall not have the effect of a reference to the oath of the party so adduced (*o*).

§ 1711 The statute also provides "that it shall not be competent to any party, who has called and examined the opposite party as a witness, thereafter to refer the cause or any part of it to his oath, and that, in all other respects, the right of reference to oath shall remain as at present established by the law and practice of Scotland" (*p*) This provision, it will be seen, does not exclude reference to the oath of one who having adduced himself as a witness, has been cross-examined by his adversary but only where he has been both 'called and examined' by that party[1] And where there are several parties having separate interests in a cause, the right of one of them to refer to the oath of the opposite party will not be cut off by another having called and examined that party as a

(*l*) Stevenson *v* Scott, 1854, 1 Irv, 603, per Lord Ivory The main grounds of judgment were that the proceeding was instituted, not *ad civilem effectum*, but *ad vindictam publicam* that the mode of prosecution was that used in criminal matters, and the analogous rule that reference to the prisoner's oath is inadmissible in this class of cases With this case compare Att Gen *v* Radloff, 1854, 23 Law Jour (Exch) 210

(*m*) 16 Vict, c 20, § 3 See this noticed fully in the chapters on examining witnesses § 2016, *et seq* (*n*) Ib (*o*) Ib § 5 (*p*) Ib, § 5

[1] In Rutherford's Executors *v* Marshall which was an action for repayment of a loan, the Sheriff allowed a proof *prout de jure* and the defender was examined as a witness for the pursuer On the cause being advocated, the defender maintained that the proof was incompetent He further stated that he would not object to a reference to his oath, although it might be argued that, under section 5 of the Evidence Act (16 and 17 Vict), a reference was now incompetent The Court held that the debt could be proved only by writ or oath, recalled the interlocutors allowing a proof, but allowed the pursuer to lodge a minute of reference to oath, Rutherford's Executors *v* Marshall, 1861, 23 D 1276 In a later case the Court held that the Evidence Act excluded a double examination If a party was examined as a witness by the opposite party, he could not subsequently have the case referred to his oath, Renny *v* Will, 18th July 1863 (not reported)

witness. The Court, however, may exclude the reference in either of these cases (r), if it is against the spirit of the statutory rule, which refuses to allow to a party a sworn precognition of an adversary, previous to referring the cause to his oath. Or the Court may limit the reference, so that it shall not embrace matters on which the party has been already examined as a witness.

§ 1712. In an English case upon the corresponding statute admitting party witnesses, Lord Campbell told a litigant who conducted his case in person that if he addressed the jury as an advocate, he could not thereafter give evidence as a witness, and that he must therefore make his election. He thereupon elected to act as his own advocate, and the verdict having been against him, he obtained a rule (which was afterwards made absolute,) for a new trial, on the ground that Lord Campbell's decision was erroneous. The reason why it was overturned was, that before the act admitting party-witnesses was passed, every party was entitled to conduct his own cause; and the statute did not make an exception in the case of a party who did so. Accordingly, the Court held that whatever views they might have of the expediency or propriety of the proceeding, they could not deprive a party of his right to act in both capacities.

Lord Campbell, however, in delivering the judgment of the Court, observed, "we may hope that, without any positive rule against a party addressing the jury, and being examined as a witness on oath on his own behalf, a practice so objectionable is not likely to spring up; for it is not only contrary to good taste and feeling, but as it must be revolting to the minds of the jury, it will generally be injurious to those who attempt it." (s)

Both the decision upon the right, and the observation upon the propriety, of a party appearing as advocate and witness, apply to this country as well as to England. In small debt courts, however, where parties usually conduct their own causes, there is no impropriety in their acting in both capacities.[5]

Whether a party can adduce himself as a witness after having heard the evidence of other witnesses, is noticed afterwards.

§ 1713. Under the rule that "the adducing of any party as a

(r) The Court has a discretionary control over references to oath. See *supra*, § 1539.
(s) Cobbett *v.* Hudson, 1852, 1 Ell. and Black., 11, 14. See also *infra*, § 1731 (*j*).

[5] It is not sufficient that the papers in a cause are signed by the parties themselves where the Act of Sederunt, 11th July 1828, § 112, requires the signature of counsel. Watt *v.* Johnson, 1863, 1 Macph., 260—Denny *v.* Macnish, 1863, 1 Macph., 268.

witness by the adverse party shall not have the effect of a reference to the oath of the party so adduced ' (*t*), statements by a party-witness in his own favour may be contradicted by his opponent Even if they are not expressly disproved, they should be received as the evidence of one subject to the bias of self-interest, and the excitement of litigation, influences which too often produce both distorted perception and false narrative regarding the facts in issue

The evidence of a party witness against himself comes under the ordinary rule that the testimony of one witness is not full legal proof But it will always be possible to obtain such corroboration as will make the proof sufficient in point of law, and if it is, the jury will have little doubt as to their verdict In general, the party leading the proof will be able to complete it by adducing himself as a witness [6]

CHAPTER IX —OF THE EXCLUSION OF WITNESSES ON THE GROUND OF RELATIONSHIP TO THE PARTIES

§ 1714 As the law formerly stood, the near relations of a party were inadmissible as witnesses for him, on the presumption that they would be too much biassed to give credible evidence Under this rule, husband and wife were inadmissible for each other in all civil (*a*), and almost all criminal (*b*), cases The exclusion of other relations and connections in civil cases was fixed at the same limits as the incompetency of judges in cases of their relations (*c*) But in criminal cases all the relations of the prisoner were admitted, except his or her wife or husband (*d*)

§ 1715 The wife of a prisoner was once admitted without objection as a witness for him in a charge of murder, where the de-

(*t*) 16 Vict c 20, § 5 (*a*) Stair, 4 43, 7 (4)—More's Notes, 412—Tait Ev , 363—1 Fraser Pers and Dom Rel 506 The Court ordered the deposition of a wife, which had been taken on commission without objection, to be expunged from the proof, Bannerman *v* his Crs , 5 De and And , 375 See also Brown *v* M'Kie, 1801, Hume D , 896 (*b*) 2 Hume, 400—Burnett 429—2 Al , 461—Todd, 1835, Bell's Notes, 251 (*c*) Ersk , 4, 2, 24—Bell s Pr , § 2251—More s Notes, *supra*—See *supra*, § 1670, (*a*) (*d*) 2 Hume, 400—Burnett, 392—2 Al 461

[6] See as to effect of not calling the party where there are adverse circumstances, *supra* § 1486, note [5]

fence was, that the prisoner had found his wife and the deceased in the act of adultery, and that, in the rage naturally excited by the discovery, he had inflicted the fatal wound (*e*) Here, it will be observed, the fact was of so occult a nature that it could not have been proved without the wife's evidence, while the motive to save her husband was not likely to have induced her to perjure and disgrace herself by a false confession of adultery.

Mr Burnett considers that where the charge is one in which the prisoner's wife or husband (as the case may be) would be admitted as a witness for the Crown under the rule noticed afterwards (*f*), the same evidence is admissible for the prisoner (*g*) This seems to be the rule in England (*h*)

§ 1716 The fear of producing perjury, and destroying domestic peace and confidence led to a limited exclusion of witnesses who were related to the party *against* whom they were adduced In civil cases, husband and wife were always inadmissible under the former law (*i*) But, with that exception, the nearest relations of a party could be adduced against him (*k*) In criminal cases the prisoner's nearest relatives were admitted as witnesses for the Crown (*l*), husband and wife, however, being inadmissible (*m*)

§ 1717 But there is one class of cases where either spouse may be adduced against the other, namely, criminal trials for injuries inflicted by the prisoner on the witness (*n*) In these cases the evidence of the injured spouse is often indispensable to complete the proof, and, if the general rule were applied in them, it would

(*e*) Christie, 1731, Maclaurin's Cr Ca, 632, 2 Hume, 400, Burnett, 434 2 Al 464 With this case compare Goldie 1804, 2 Hume, 400, Burnett, 434, where, in a trial of a man for murder, the prisoner alleged that in retorting an assault made on, or an insult offered to, his wife by the deceased, he had killed him, and the Court refused to admit her as an exculpatory witness, but allowed the prisoner to prove that she had shown marks of violence upon her person, and "any account thereof connected therewith"

(*f*) *Infra* § 1717, *et seq*

(*g*) Burnett, 433

(*h*) Per Abbot in R *v* Sergeant 1826, Ry and Moo, 352—2 Russ, 986 See Taylor, 902

(*i*) Erskine *v* Smith, 1700, M, 16,703—M'Intosh *v* Blair, 1737, Elch, "Witness," No 8—Campbell *v* Crawford, 1744, M, 16,749, Elch "Husband and Wife" No 20, S C—Cameron *v* Lawson, 1744, M, 16,753, Elch, ib, No 21, 1 Fraser Pers and Dom Rel 506 Tait Ev, 387—*Contra*, Gavin *v* Montgomerie 1830, 9 S 213

(*k*) Cameron *v* Lawson, *supra*—Cowie *v* Fleming, 1828, 7 S 146—Tait Ev, 389—*Contra*, Drummond *v* Alexander, 1700, M, 16 703

(*l*) 2 Hume 346—2 Al, 460—Tait Ev, 390

(*m*) 2 Hume, 349—Burnett, 432—2 Al, 461—Tait Ev, 387—1 Fraser Pers and Dom Rel, 506 The wife of a prisoner was rejected as a witness for her husband in a case of theft although her name was included in the list of witnesses for the Crown, Clark and Greig, 1842, 1 Broun 250

(*n*) 2 Hume, 349—Burnett 433—2 Al, 461—Tait Ev, 388—1 Fraser Pers and Dom Rel 506—Bell's Notes 252

conceal and foster oppression, whereas its object is to promote the mutual confidence and comfort of the spouses. The most common application of this principle is in cases of personal violence (*o*). It has also been applied in trials of a husband for a forgery, conspiracy, and attempt to poison directed against his wife and her sister (*p*), and for having falsely accused his wife before the authorities of an attempt to poison him (*r*). But in a trial for bigamy, the first husband or wife (as the case may be) of the prisoner is inadmissible; because the crime does not, either from its secrecy or from the nature of the personal injury to the witness, come within the exceptional principle (*s*). The other party to the second marriage, however, is admissible upon the first marriage being proved to the satisfaction of the Court, for such proof shows that the witness is not the husband (or wife) of the prisoner (*t*).

In a case where a party was charged with two assaults, one on his wife and the other on his infant child, Lord Justice-Clerk Boyle, with concurrence of Lord Medwyn, expressed an opinion that the wife could only be examined as to the assault upon herself. Lord Mackenzie, however, entertained doubts of the propriety of the limitation, "regarding it as extremely dangerous to families if the mother's testimony were inadmissible in such cases" (*u*).

§ 1718. In England, also, the injured spouse is admissible in cases of personal violence (*x*), and in prosecutions of abduction, whether forcible (*y*) or fraudulent (*z*); whereas, in a prosecution of a prostitute for conspiracy in entrapping a minor into marrying her, the husband was held inadmissible as a witness for the prosecution (*a*).

(*o*) Hume, *supra*—Al., *supra*. (*p*) Elliot *v.* Nicolson, 1693, 2 Hume, 350. In Graham, 1827, Syme, 151; Hume, 349, where a wife was tried for an attempt (which was nearly successful) to hang her husband during his sleep, his evidence against her was admitted, although he swore that he would not object to take her home to live with him again, if she were at liberty. (*r*) Miller, 1847, Arkley, 355.

(*s*) Roger, 1813, 2 Hume, 349—Armstrong, 1841, 2 Broun, 251—1 Fraser Pers. and Dom. Rel., 507—2 Al., 162. But see Macdonald, 1832, 1 Broun, 238. This is also the rule in England. 1 Hale, 693—Taylor, 900. In Fagan *v.* Mackenzie, 1849, J. Shaw, 261, the question was raised, but not decided, whether a husband could be admitted as a witness against his wife on a charge of having forged his signature. On a suggestion from the Court, the Crown counsel did not press for a decision on the point.

(*t*) M'Lean, 1836, 1 Swin., 278—Thorburn, 1844, 2 Broun, 4.

(*u*) Loughton, 1831, Bell's Notes, 252. (*x*) Taylor, 908—1 Phill., 79.

(*y*) R. *v.* Wakefield, 2 Lewins Cr. Ca., 279—Taylor, *supra*—Phill., *supra*.

(*z*) R. *v.* Gore, 1 Jebb and Symes, 363; Taylor, *supra*. It seems not to exclude the evidence of the wife in these cases, that she cohabited voluntarily with the prisoner after the marriage. (*a*) R. *v.* Sergeant, Ry. and Moo., 352.

§ 1719 The former criminal law, in consideration of the pain to the feelings of the witness, and of the risk of perjury, consequent upon forcing a child to give evidence against his parent, allowed a witness so situated to decline being examined for the Crown (*b*), and if the witness was in pupilarity, the law, exercising that option for him, refused to admit his evidence (*c*) But this declinature or inadmissibility, as the case might be, did not exist in a trial of the parent for injury to the child (*d*)

It was doubtful whether parents had a reciprocal right to decline giving evidence against their children (*e*)

§ 1720 Recent legislation greatly limited the old objection of relationship By one statute the relations of a party were made admissible as witnesses for him, the only exception being in the case of husband and wife (*f*) The same act abolished the privilege of the children of prisoners to decline giving evidence against them in criminal prosecutions (*g*), and by a corollary rendered the pupil-child of a prisoner a competent witness against him (*h*)

§ 1721 In all criminal proceedings in which a person is charged with the commission of any indictable offence, or any offence punishable on summary conviction, it is still incompetent to examine the husband or wife of the prisoner as a witness on either side, except in so far as that was competent before the passing of the Law of Evidence Amendment Act (*i*)

It is also incompetent to adduce the husband or wife of a party to " any action suit, or proceeding instituted in Scotland in consequence of adultery, or for dissolving any marriage, or for breach of promise of marriage, or in any action of declarator of marriage, nullity of marriage putting to silence, legitimacy, or bastardy, or in any action of adherence or separation " (*k*)

But in any action or proceeding not coming within these exceptions, it is competent to adduce and examine the husband or wife of a party, either for or against that party (*l*) [1]

(*b*) 2 Hume, 346—Burnett, 432—2 Al, 446—Tait Ev, 390 (*c*) 2 Hume, 346, note—Burnett, *supra*—2 Al, 464 (*d*) Lundie, 1824, Sh Just Ca, 126—2 Hume, 348—See also Blair, 1840, 2 Swin, 196—Commelin, 1836, 1 Swin, 291—*Infra*, § 1723 (*e*) See 2 Hume, 348—Burnett, 432—2 Al, 468—Tait Ev, 391—Bell's Notes, 250 (*f*) 3 and 4 Vict, c, 59, § 1 (*g*) Ib

(*h*) Cairns and Others, 1841, 2 Swin 531, Bell's Notes, 249, S C

(*i*) 16 Vict, c 20, § 3 The exception noticed in the text refers to the class of cases considered *supra*, § 1717 (*k*) Ib, § 1 See *supra*, § 1701 *et seq*

(*l*) Ib, § 3

[1] Anon v Anon, 1856, 22 Beav, 481, 23 Beav 273—Selfe v Isaacson 1858, 1 F and F, 194

§ 1722. In all cases it is competent for a party against whom a witness is tendered, to examine the husband or wife of the witness, in order to prove an objection of enmity or the like (*m*)

§ 1723 A husband or wife adduced to prove personal injury by the prisoner has not a privilege to decline answering (*n*) If it were otherwise the law would afford only a delusive protection to the injured spouse, whom the prisoner would in general be able to coerce or importune into remaining silent.

§ 1724 The Act of 1853, however, declares that nothing contained in it "shall in any proceeding render any husband competent or compellable to give against his wife evidence of any matter communicated by her to him during the marriage or any wife competent or compellable to give against her husband evidence of any matter communicated by him to her during the marriage" (*o*)

§ 1725 The exclusionary rules in regard to husband and wife apply whether the marriage was in *in facie ecclesiæ* or irregular (*p*) But it is thought that a promise of marriage with a subsequent *copula* will not exclude, unless decree of declarator of marriage has been pronounced thereupon (*q*) In an English case the defendant's wife was held admissible as a witness for the plaintiff The marriage took place after she had been cited to give evidence (*r*) [2]

(*m*) Heidie, 1831 Bell's Notes, 252, (*n*) Commelin, 1836, 1 Swin, 291, Bell's Notes, 252, S C—A B, 1824, Bell's Notes, ib See also *supra*, § 1719

(*o*) 16 Vict, c 20, § 3 In Becket, 1831 Bell's Notes, 251 where the prisoner in a case of theft objected to the admissibility of the first witness for the Crown on the ground that she was his wife by acknowledgment and cohabitation, the Advocate Depute admitted the relevancy of the objection, and the Court allowed a proof before answer After the examination of two witnesses, the prosecutor gave up the case without asking judgment (*q*) See Glen, 1827, Syme, 267—1 Fraser Pers and Dom Rel, 164, *et seq* (*r*) Pedley *v* Wellesley, 1829, 3 Car and Pa 558—1 Phill, 70—Taylor, 900

[2] In support of a plea of *alibi*, a panel proposed to examine as a witness a woman who, on examination *in initialibus* deponed that she considered the panel as her husband, on the ground that she had lived with him and that he had acknowledged her as his wife In the special circumstances of the case the evidence was disallowed, the Court holding, apparently, that the witness had no motive to disqualify herself (having been called on behalf of the panel) and that her statement ought therefore to be received It might have been different had she been a witness for the Crown, "the inducement of the witness to disqualify herself being different in the two cases," and the prosecutor would have been entitled to prove *aliunde* that she was not the wife of the panel It may be doubted, however, whether there is any solid distinction between the two cases The probability is that a woman who has lived with a prisoner as his mistress will state when publicly examined in Court that she believed herself to be his

§ 1726 Where the party adducing the witness denies the alleged marriage, the other party may prove his objection by examining the witness *in initialibus* (s), as well as by other evidence (t), the proof in either case having no effect on the status of the parties, but being adduced merely to satisfy the Court whether the objection is well founded

§ 1727 In consistorial causes, and trials for bigamy, and other cases where necessary, it is competent to exhibit to the witnesses and jury for the purpose of identification or the like, a husband or wife whose evidence on the merits of the cause is inadmissible (u)[3] Attendance for this purpose may be enforced by the citation of the spouse as a witness and by second diligence if required (x)

The admissibility of the husband or wife of one of several parties to a cause, where inadmissible so far as that party's interest is concerned, is noticed afterwards (y)

§ 1728 With regard to credibility, it may be said that the tendency in a witness to being biassed in favour of a relative will usually bear some proportion to the closeness of the connection and consequent intimacy, and to the extent of the interest at stake But if the witness and party have quarrelled, the bias will usually be the other way because considerable bitterness usually springs out of quarrels among near relations In all cases, however, so much depends on the character of the individual witness, that these external circumstances furnish but a faint and doubtful index to

(s) In Muir, 1836, 1 Swin, 402 where the prisoner was charged with assaults on G M, his wife or reputed wife, and on another person, and G M deponed that she was not his wife, but only cohabited with him, she was admitted as a witness for the Crown on both charges See also Innes v Innes, 1837, 2 Sh and M L, 417—Scott v M'Gavin, 1821, 2 Mur, 490 (t) Becket, *supra* (o) (u) Laig, 1817, 2 Hume, 349, note—Bryce 1841, 2 Broun, 119—Bell's Notes, 253, S C—M'Lean, 1836, Bell's Notes, 252—2 Al, 463 (x) Bryce, *supra* (y) *Infra* chapter xvi of this title

wife Even should she happen to be acquainted with the rule of evidence which excludes a wife, she will endeavour to protect her character, without considering what effect her answers may have on her position as a witness, H M Adv v May and Others, 1856, 2 Irv, 179

[3] The question has been raised whether a husband is a competent witness to prove an incidental fact in a trial for bigamy He would not be competent as a witness on any point bearing directly on the question of his wife's guilt Can he be admitted to prove an incidental fact without reference to the object for which it is required at the trial? In a case on circuit Lord Ivory after consulting with Lord Cowan remarked that the point was new and doubtful, he therefore gave the prisoner the benefit of the doubt, and refused the evidence, H M Adv v Paterson 1860, 3 Irv 619

his trustworthiness. It must be with the jury in each case—from these circumstances, from the manner in which the witness gives his evidence, and from a comparison of his statements with the rest of the proof—to determine how far he can be credited.

This is peculiarly the case when the evidence is tendered to prove a defence of *alibi* where, by transferring to the date of the alleged crime, circumstances which really happened on a different day the prisoner's relations often succeed in telling a consistent story, which if true would establish the defence.* No general rule can be laid down for such cases. It may, however, be observed that if the alleged *alibi* is true, it could probably not be proved by other or better evidence, and therefore it should receive effect unless the jury, after examining it carefully, and weighing it against the evidence for the Crown, do not entertain a reasonable doubt of the prisoner's guilt.

§ 1729. In civil cases the evidence of the husband or wife of a party will usually be strong proof, if it is unfavourable, whereas the double taint of interest and affection materially impair its credibility, when it is favourable to the other spouse. In the criminal trials in which such evidence is admitted, the offence has more frequently arisen from drunken or temporary rage than from continued ill usage which subsequent kindness will not atone for. Accordingly it often happens that the witness denies or mitigates the injury, and this is almost always the case where the spouses have lived together in the interval. Indeed juries frequently convict against the testimony of the injured spouse, whose account recently after the offence is more likely to be true than her evidence given under the dictates of affection and marital influence. On the other hand the unfavourable testimony of a husband or wife, whose mind is filled with jealousy or resentment is about the worst kind of evidence, as no hatred is more bitter and blind than that of a mismated pair.

CHAPTER X.—OF THE EXCLUSION OF WITNESSES ON THE GROUND OF AGENCY.

§ 1730. A common objection to the admission of witnesses under the former law of evidence was "agency and partial counsel", under which was included all advice or assistance towards the preparation of the case which had been given by the witness to the party who adduced him (*a*) The Law of Evidence Amendment Act of 1852 abolished this ground of exclusion, provided always "that it shall not be competent to adduce as a witness in any action or proceeding any person who shall, at the time when he is so adduced as a witness be acting as agent in the action or proceeding in which he is so adduced, excepting in so far as the same may be competent by the existing law and practice of Scotland" (*b*) A subsequent statute repealed this exceptional provision (*c*) and thereby rendered admissible even the agent conducting the cause in which his evidence is tendered But this statute declares that nothing contained in it shall apply to any of the consistorial causes enumerated above (*d*) Accordingly, in these cases the *proviso* of the act of 1852 remains, whereby a party may not adduce the evidence of his law-agent conducting the individual cause The old objection of agency and partial counsel has been abolished in all other respects [1]

§ 1731 The act of 1852, however, reserved entire the right of a party to adduce his agent in so far as competent before the passing of the act This reservation pointed at the rule whereby the law-agent of a party was admissible to prove all matters upon which he was a necessary witness, as for example, the circumstances attending the execution of a deed written or prepared by him or to which he was an instrumentary witness (*e*) and the granter's state of mind at the time of subscription (*f*) So, the law-agent of a party has been admitted to prove delivery of a deed

(*a*) Ersk 4 2 25—Bell's Pr § 2253—Tait Ev 367, 8 (*b*) 15 Vict, c 27, § 1 (*c*) 16 Vict, c 20 § 2 (*d*) Ib, § 4—See *supra*, § 1721

(*e*) M'Clatchie *v* Brand 1773 2 Pat Ap Ca, 312, reversing, M 16,776—Halliday *v* Laub 1822 3 Mur 120—M'Neill *v* M'Neill, 1822 ib 150—Andersons *v* Jeffrey 1826 4 ib. 202—Mason *v* Merry, 1830, 5 ib 310—See also Elder *v* Smith, 1827 Syme 115 (*f*) M'Clatchie *v* Brand *supra*—Scott *v* Caverhill, 1786 M 16,977—Andersons *v* Jeffrey, *supra*

[1] A clerk of the panel's agent was called to speak as to the state of a house (where a murder had been committed) at the time when he was conducting the precognition but on Lord Deas doubting how far the matter of the precognition for the prisoner was evidence and whether if part of it was given, the Court might not be entitled to have it all, the counsel for the prisoner, although contending that the evidence as to the facts regarding the state of the house was quite competent, withdrew the witness, H M Adv *v* Davidson Aberdeen 1857 Irv, ii p 168

to which he was an instrumentary witness (*g*), and to prove that documents produced by his client were *noviter venientes ad notitiam* (*h*) And an agent has also repeatedly been admitted to prove transactions into which he had entered on behalf of his client (*i*) There will seldom be occasion for applying this principle in the consistorial causes above noticed

It is held in England that in a case conducted by an attorney he may address the Court or jury for his client, and then adduce himself as a witness (*j*)

§ 1732 The credibility of witnesses who were subject to the old objection of agency and partial counsel is now left to the jury (*k*) It admits of as many degrees as there are between gentlemen of high honour and truthfulness, and pettifoggers who lead a life of quirk and quibble, and who to the zeal of the agent often add the interest of the party, from their remuneration depending on success The jury ought therefore to scrutinize this kind of evidence carefully and give to it such weight as it deserves, looking to the known character of the witness, his appearance under examination, and the corroboration or contradiction of his statements by the rest of the proof

§ 1733 When the witness is not the professional adviser of the party, the taint to his credibility will vary with the extent of his gratuitous interference Such a witness is more subject to the bias of partisanship and zeal than is the professional man to whom it is usually a matter of indifference whether he is employed for the one or the other party

§ 1734 Agency, even under the former law, was a one-sided objection, a party being entitled to adduce the legal adviser of his opponent to prove any facts which were not privileged as confidential (*l*) The rules as to this privilege are noticed afterwards (*m*)

(*g*) E March *v* Sawyer, 1750 Cr and St, 479 reversing, M, 16,757 Elch, Witness No 21 S C (*h*) Wilkie *v* Jackson, 1834, 12 S 520

(*i*) Wardrop *v* Dickie, 1805, Hume D, 899—King *v* Stevenson, 1807, Hume D, 344—See also Macalpine *v* Macalpine 2d Dec 1806 F C (*j*) De Rely 28th Feb 1852 18 Law Times, 293 See also *supra*, § 1712 (*k*) 15 Vict, c 27, § 1 (*l*) Stair 4 43, 9 (8)—2 Hume, 350—Tait Ev, 384

(*m*) See Chapter on Confidential Communications, § 1861 *et seq*

CHAPTER XI.—OF THE EXCLUSION OF WITNESSES ON ACCOUNT OF BRIBERY AND PROMISE OF REWARD.

§ 1735. For manifest reasons, one who has been bribed by the party who adduces him, or with his authority, is inadmissible as a witness for that party (*a*). Even an unsuccessful attempt to bribe will disqualify,—not because the witness is unworthy of credit, for his refusal indicates the reverse,—but *in odium corrumpentis* (*b*).

§ 1736. A witness however, will not be rendered inadmissible by such proceedings, unless they can be traced to the party who adduces him, or to some one acting with his authority; otherwise a party might lose the evidence of his best witnesses through the ill-judged interference of a friend, or the dexterous plot of an adversary (*c*). Accordingly, a promise by a third party of a sum sufficient to pay the witness' house-rent and travelling expenses was held not to disqualify (*d*). So two witnesses, to each of whom an unknown person had given a half-dollar, saying he wished well to the party and hoped they would do the same, were admitted, because the sum was small, and might have been given by the opposite party in order to exclude the witnesses (*e*). In like manner, a witness for the public or private prosecutor in a criminal trial will be received, although he received promise of pardon from a magistrate, for the prosecutor is not bound by such interference (*f*). And the same principle applies to the governor of the jaol in which the witness was confined (*g*) and *a fortiori* to police officers, turnkeys, and other subordinates. Mr Burnett considers that a witness who has been offered a bribe by an unauthorised person will only be admitted if he has not courted and solicited the interference, or received the bribe, or agreed to the corrupt proposal (*h*). But no

(*a*) Ersk., 4, 2, 28—2 Hume, 377—Burnett, 414—2 Al., 497—Tait, 379.

(*b*) Ersk., *supra*—Hume, *supra*—Burnett, 415—Al., *supra*—Tait, *supra*. In this way the evidence of a witness likely to speak the truth is excluded, and the party may lose his case (perhaps in a trial for murder) in consequence; whereas, if his other evidence is sufficient, his attempt to bribe will go unpunished. Would it not be better to admit the witness, and punish the party by fine or imprisonment?

(*c*) Hume, *supra*—Burnett, *supra*—Al., *supra*—Tait, *supra*. See § 1711.

(*d*) M'Donald, 1754, Burnett, *supra*—Al., *supra*.

(*e*) Erskine *v.* Erskine, 1701, M. 16,701. The witnesses were imprisoned for their conduct.

(*f*) 2 Hume, 377—Case of Brodie, 1788, there cited—2 Al., 497.

(*g*) M'Kinlay, 1829, Sh. Just. Ca., 224—Bell's Notes, 266, S. C.

(*h*) Burnett, 415. In Smith, 1832, Bell's Notes, 265, the prosecutor withdrew a witness who stated that a third person gave him £1 to get the prisoner convicted.

other authority has been found to support this view which is opposed to one of the cases above noticed (*i*) In joint prosecutions at the instance of the Crown and a private party Baron Hume considers that it is doubtful whether the latter can disappoint the course of public justice by an unauthorised attempt to bribe a witness, but that if the witness received the reward, or seriously promised to comply in the hope of it he is certainly disqualified whether the proffer came from one or other of the prosecutors (*k*)

§ 1737 The exclusion of witnesses on this head applies to every benefit, pecuniary or otherwise, which, looking to the circumstances of the witness, may be fairly considered as placing him under an obligation to give evidence favourable to the adducer (*l*) Nor is it necessary that the premium shall have been given or received expressly with a view to buying the evidence, for the most dangerous kind of bribery is where the party and witness understand each other so well that no agreement to that effect is made between them Accordingly, a witness in humble life was rejected after having deponed *in initialibus* that the pursuer offered her £2 to swear to things she had never seen, that she replied she would not do that for either of the parties, but took the money, saying she would return it if she could (*m*) And a deposition was set aside because the witness, before deponing, had received a promise of good deeds from the party, which were performed to him after his deposition, for the Lords found it not necessary, and would not restrict the pursuer to libel or reply that the good deed was given *specifice ad hunc effectum* to depone (*n*) So a witness was excluded in an important case of status, because, after his citation, the adducer had indorsed for him, without value, bills for several hundred pounds and the party's plea, that he had for a number of years been in the habit of assisting the witness with his credit, was disregarded, because the witness was bankrupt and indebted considerably to the party at the time (*o*) Giving a witness an extravagant sum for travelling expenses may also cause him to be excluded, although the party may not have had a corrupt intention (*p*) But neither the admissibility nor the credibility of a

---

(*i*) Erskine *v* Erskine *supra* (*e*)

(*k*) 2 Hume 377, 8

(*l*) Burnett, 416, 2 Al 497

(*m*) Crichton *v* Fleming, 1840 3 D, 313

(*n*) Geelin *v* Cochrane 1624, M, 12,099

(*o*) Farquharson *v* Anderson, 1800, M, 'Witness' Appx No 2

(*p*) Compare L Milton *v* Ly Milton, 1671, M, 12,105 16,674—Chalmers *v* Monro 1587, M, 16,653—and Forbes *v* Ly Udny 1699, M, 16,702, where the Lords thought there was no design of corruption but judged it of a bad preparative to engage the

witness will be impaired by his having received a fair consideration for expenses and loss of time and if he resides abroad, a liberal allowance may be made to him on account of the trouble and annoyance attending a journey, which he could not be forced by the diligence of the law to undertake (r)

§ 1738 It was laid down in a case of shopbreaking that although a promise of reward "if the witness would speak out" will not disqualify him yet if the promise were that "if he gave such and such evidence when brought before the Court and examined upon oath," and if this were agreed to by the witness, it would exclude his evidence as it is not only a bribe, but an instruction how to depone (s)

§ 1739 It sometimes happens, as in cases of combination, that a witness exposes himself to peril by giving evidence for the Crown One so situated is under the strongest temptation to perjure himself as the only way to escape martyrdom The question therefore arises, whether the prosecutor can save the witness from this dilemma, by promising to convey him to a safe place abroad In one case (t), a Crown witness deponed, *in initialibus*, that being afraid of evil consequences to himself and his wife, and even of assassination or torture, if he remained in Britain after giving evidence, he had declined to appear unless he could get a passport and means to convey him to the Continent, that the prosecutor thereupon undertook to provide for his safety in that way, but that "there was no attempt to instruct him as to what he should say in giving evidence" The prisoner having objected that the witness was under the influence of a bribe the Court "seemed to be of opinion" that

---

affections of poor folk by too much entertainment and allowance for their journey, and remitted to the Lord Ordinary to investigate whether there was an excess allowing for the risk of detention at sea, and to receive the witnesses if there was not

(r) In the trial of Humphreys for forging titles to the Stirling peerage, 1839, 2 Swin, 356, and separate rep, 143, 7 the Justiciary Court repelled the objection stated to two French witnesses, the one a print-seller and the other a house-porter that they had each a bond from the prosecutor for £40 per month, which was much more than they would have earned in their ordinary occupations at the time It was observed on the Bench that there is a great difference between a witness in this country, who is accessible to diligence, and one abroad, whose attendance, unless procured by remuneration might indicate improper zeal for the party who advances him Yet the Court considered that an excessive premium would cut a foreign witness

(s) Holmes, 1799, Burnett, 116

(t) M'Kinlay, 1817 2 Hume, 377 A letter had been written by the witness, seemingly with the insidious design of inducing the Advocate Depute to give him such assistance as would render his evidence inadmissible he was equally disqualified whether his statement were true or false, as in the one case he was bribed, and in the other he was perjured. Upon this the Lord Advocate stated that he would withdraw the witness, whatever might be the result of the proof regarding the objection; but that he wished the proof to be led in order to ascertain the facts. In these circumstances the Court refused to go into the investigation,' and the witness was dismissed.

Although in this case the Court merely refused to investigate the competency of a witness whom the prosecutor did not intend to examine, the opinions which their Lordships entertained involve an important principle. It is thought, with deference, that they are erroneous. If the witness had been intimidated, the undertaking on the part of the Crown was not a bribe to induce perjury, but merely the protection required for enabling the witness to give truthful evidence, and it was necessary in order to restore his mind to the balance which the intimidations of those acting with the prisoner had disturbed. To exclude witnesses so situated would encourage actual intimidation, as well as produce a pretence of it on the part of unwilling witnesses (*u*), and would render doubly successful those combinations which too frequently conceal and encourage crime.

The view that the witness must be rejected, because if he spoke truth he was bribed—if falsehood, he was perjured—is also thought to be erroneous, for it implies that a friend of the prisoner may escape from giving evidence for the Crown by falsely admitting bribery or enmity or any other ground of exclusion, a result for which there is no authority either in law or practice.

§ 1740. Accordingly, these views were departed from in the Glasgow cotton-spinners case (*v*), where it was held to be no objection to witnesses for the Crown that they had been promised full protection both before and after the trial. Sir Archibald Alison (*x*) also challenges the views expressed in the case of M'Kinlay, and in a trial in 1820, where the counsel of a prisoner argued upon the authority of that case, that if a witness states in his initial examination that he has been bribed, he must be excluded, as being either bribed or perjured, the Advocate-Depute answered (apparently without contradiction from the Court) that the opinion referred to 'was utterly unfounded in the principles of the law of

---

(*u*) See *supra* (*t*).

(*v*) Hunter and Others, 1838, Bell's Notes 267.

(*x*) 2 Al., 500.

Scotland was contrary to former precedents, and had been considered erroneous and frequently disapproved of from the Bench" (*y*)

At the same time, the Court will not countenance an unnecessary or injudicious exercise by the public authorities of the right (supposing they possess it) to afford to their witnesses the protection referred to The Court will probably interfere, wherever they consider that the circumstances did not render that extraordinary course necessary for the ends of justice

§ 1741 It has been seen that *socii criminis* are admissible, although all such witnesses obtain their freedom by agreeing to give evidence for the Crown (*z*) And when infamy was a ground of exclusion, witnesses were admitted who had obtained a royal pardon in order to remove the objection (*a*) But in these cases the witness would have been excluded, if his pardon or liberty had been granted on a promise to depone in a certain way, or had been conditional on his deposition tending to produce a conviction (*b*)

§ 1742 Witnesses who give their evidence under the influence of a reward to which they have right by statute or proclamation, are extremely apt to be biassed against the prisoner (*c*), the tendency being of course strongest where the reward is only payable in the event of conviction In the common informer this influence combined with a life of skulking and treachery, renders his evidence almost worthless Witnesses who had such an interest on the side of the Crown seem formerly to have been excluded, as in a prosecution of a creditor for usury, where the debtor and informers were held inadmissible (*d*) Baron Hume notes a subsequent case, where there is reason to believe that a witness was rejected on the ground that he would have been entitled as informer to a reward of £50, in the event of a conviction (*e*) And that eminent lawyer considered it doubtful whether a promise of reward, which depended on conviction, "should not serve to exclude, or at least to discredit the evidence of the informer" (*f*)

(*y*) Grant, 1829, Sh Just Ca, 50—2 Al, 502 (*z*) *Supra*, § 1691

(*a*) 2 Hume, 377—2 Alison, 351—Tait 346 (*b*) 2 Hume, 377—Burnett, 417 One of the reasons on which Fletcher of Saltoun's forfeiture was rescinded was, that the principal witness had been under terror of death as charged with the same crime, and had not been pardoned till after his deposition Burnett ib

(*c*) In Scott *v* Crown Agent, 1797, Burnett, Appx No 20, the late Lord President Campbell expressed a strong opinion that rewards tend to corrupt evidence and his Lordship "seemed to think" they had been attended with that result in one case which he mentioned (*d*) Wilson, 1667, 2 Hume, 363 (*e*) Coulton, 1738, 2 Hume 364 Burnett, 417, † The record, however, only shows that the witness was not examined, not that he was rejected (*f*) 2 Hume 364

§ **1743** It is now settled that a promise of reward, even of this objectionable character, affects merely the credibility, not the competency, of the witness who in order to earn it gives evidence for the Crown In an old case of house breaking, the Court admitted a *socius criminis* who earned a certain reward by every felon whom he served to convict (*g*) Again, in a prosecution of a Roman catholic for having altars, crucifixes, &c, in his house, certain constables were held to be competent witnesses against the prisoner, the objection being overruled that "they were entitled to a premium and reward for the discovery, and so were parties that could tine (lose) or win' (*h*) Thus, also, in the year 1780 a witness for the prosecutor was admitted by Lord Kennet, on circuit, in a trial for assault and deforcement, although he was entitled to a reward on the prisoner's conviction (*i*) And a witness in the same situation was admitted, on circuit, by Lord Hermand in a case of wilful fire-raising (*k*) These decisions have been followed by a unanimous and authoritative judgment of the High Court of Justiciary, deciding that a witness is not disqualified by a proclamation in which the Sheriff of the bounds, acting under authority of the Crown, offered a reward to any person "who shall give such information and evidence as shall lead to the discovery and conviction of the murderer" (*l*) In this case it was admitted at the Bar, and argued from as a clear principle by the Bench, that a witness is not rendered inadmissible by a statute giving right to a reward on the offender's conviction

It has also been held that the objection to a Crown witness that he had said he would swear anything to hang the prisoner so that he might get the reward offered for the prisoner's apprehension, and that he had taken active measures towards the apprehension, went only to the credibility of the witness and was not a ground of exclusion (*m*)

The mode in which the objection of bribery is proved, is noticed afterwards

---

(*g*) Smith, 1693, 2 Hume, 352 (*h*) Mackie *v* Town of Edinburgh, 1711, 4 B Sup, 850 (*i*) Norman, 1780, Burnett 447 (*k*) Crossan, 1817, 2 Hume, 364, note (*l*) Hunter, 1838, 2 Swin, 1, Bell's Notes, 259

(*m*) Little, 1831, Bell's Notes, 253—2 Al, 484—See *infra*, § 1763

CHAPTER XII.—OF THE EXCLUSION OF WITNESSES ON ACCOUNT OF THE PARTY HAVING TUTORED THEM

§ 1744. As the value of testimony depends on each witness speaking from his own observation and recollection, it is fatal to the admissibility of a witness, that the party adducing him has "tutored" or instructed him how to depone (*a*), and conduct which tends indirectly to the same result will impair the witness' credibility. Here, however, as in the case of bribery, a witness is not excluded unless the tampering was by the adducer, or those acting with his authority (*b*), any officious or improper interference by other persons affecting the credibility of the witness, but not excluding him (*c*). In one case, where a number of exculpatory witnesses for one of the prisoners had conversed together regarding his defence of an *alibi*, and signed a joint certificate regarding the facts, they were admitted *cum nota*, the prosecutor not being able to connect their proceedings with the prisoner to whom their evidence immediately applied. The Court expressed a unanimous opinion that if the witnesses had been inadmissible for him, they could not have been examined for the other panels (*d*). With regard to prosecutions at the joint instance of the Crown and a private party, the acts of one of the prosecutors will have the same effect upon the instance of the other as in cases of bribery (*e*).

§ 1745. If the acts complained of manifestly tend to tutor the witness, they will render him inadmissible, although they may have been the result of carelessness or ignorance, and not of improper intention, because evidence which has become tainted in consequence of the blunder of one party should not be used against the other. Thus in a question regarding the amount of certain rents, the Court rejected witnesses whom the party had called to his chamber, and shewed an unsubscribed rental of the lands (*f*). So a witness was excluded in consequence of the party who adduced him having, apparently from carelessness, and not with an im-

(*a*) Ersk. 4, 2, 28—2 Hume, 378—Burnett, 415, 9—Tait Ev., 380—2 Al., 502.

(*b*) 2 Hume, 379—Burnett, *supra*—Al., *supra*—Mackay *v.* Wight, 1822, 3 Mur., 23—Farquharson *v.* Anderson, 1800, M., "Witness," App. No. 2—Hunter, *infra* (*d*)—*Contra* Spalding, 1673, noted in 2 Hume, 378, and Baxter, 1803, noted in Burnett, *supra*. See also *supra*, § 1736.

(*c*) Preceding note.

(*d*) Hunter and Others, 1838, 2 Swin., 1, Bell's Notes, 267, S. C.

(*e*) See *supra*, § 1736.

(*f*) Ly. Crumstane *v.* Cockburn, 1682, M., 16,683.

proper object, sent to him the depositions of other witnesses in the case (*g*) And a witness, adduced to prove the value of certain improvements on an entailed estate was rendered inadmissible by the adducer's agent having told him the estimates of other witnesses, although there did not appear to be any intention to tutor him (*h*) In another case it was found to be "illegal and unwarrantable" to show to a witness "a paper upon which he was adduced to depone," and the party was fined for doing so but no decision was pronounced on the point of admissibility (*i*)

Where a witness being objected to upon a ground which affected his character, and his examination having been delayed in order to allow time for inquiry the agent for the adducer told him in the interval that the objection had been stated, and also held some conversation with him on the subject of the cause, the Court, while acquitting the agent of all bad intention held that the witness was inadmissible (*k*)

§ 1746 On the other hand, where the agent for the party adducing a witness had, after citation, conversed with him on an unimportant point of the case, and had shown him some documents, but from the station of the witness (who was a clergyman) there was no reason to suppose that his mind would have been influenced by these acts the Court by a narrow majority held him admissible (*l*) And it was held not to exclude a witness that he had been shown the pleadings in the cause, where these were not calculated to tutor him, and there had been no intention to do so (*m*)

§ 1747 Where the conduct of the party has evidently proceeded from an intention to tamper, the witness will be excluded *in odium corrumpentis* although he refused to comply (*n*), whereas the cases above cited show that if there was no improper intention, the Court will admit the witness, provided the information he acquired is not likely to have confused his own recollection of the facts (*o*)

(*g*) Wight *v* Liddell, 1829 5 Mur, 46 (*h*) Fraser *v* L Lovat, 1841 3 D, 1132 (*i*) Geddes *v* Parkhill 1741, M, 16 744 (*k*) Caddell *v* Morthland and Johnstone, 1799, M., 16,789 The report bears that the Court "had no doubt of the objection," but, somewhat inconsistently they only found that the witness could not be examined *hoc statu* (*l*) Farquharson *v* Anderson, 1800, M, "Witness," Appx No 2 (*m*) Donaldson *v* Stewart, 1842, 4 D, 1215—Kirk *v* Guthrie, 1817, 1 Mur, 275 compared with Bertram *v* Milne, 1805, Hume D, 905 note

(*n*) Ersk, 4, 2, 28—Burnett, 419—Tait Ev 380—2 Al, 503—L Milton *v* Ly Milton, 1671 M 12,105, 16 674—See *supra* § 1735 (*o*) See *supra*, § 1746, and *infra*, § 1753

§ 1748 A case cannot be properly prepared for trial, unless the party has, by a preliminary examination, or 'precognition,' of the witnesses, ascertained what evidence they are likely to give Such a communing therefore, is not only harmless but necessary and proper, so long as it is conducted fairly (r) But it is liable to be abused, in attempts both to tutor the witnesses (as noticed in the preceding sections), and to tie them down to statements which they have made *ex parte*, and perhaps incautiously, on precognition (s) On this account, it was held to impair the credibility of a witness in a civil case that the party had precognosced him on oath or affidavit (t), and the Court disapproved of this practice (u), which is now prohibited by act of Parliament (x) It is also improper in a party who has been injured by the delict of another, to lodge a criminal information and get the witnesses examined before a magistrate, with a view to subsequent civil proceedings (y) And it is irregular, in civil cases, either to get the witnesses to sign their precognitions, or to take written statements under their hands regarding the matter in issue (z)

§ 1749 In criminal investigations, however, where the witnesses are often unwilling to speak out, and where their statements made without an oath cannot be relied upon, they may be precognosced on oath before the judge ordinary or a magistrate, and their attendance for that purpose may be enforced by diligence (a) If it were not so, the authorities would often be thwarted and deceived in their attempts to detect and punish crime But the law prohibits the prosecutor from taking sworn precognitions without the presence of a magistrate, to secure fairness in the examination (b) And, accordingly, witnesses were excluded where the prosecutor had collected them in a tavern, and taken from them

(r) Ersk 4, 2, 28—Tait Ev, 382 (s) In A B, 1679, M, 16,681, the Court found that witnesses may be asked what they know of the matter, provided that no paction be made with them to adhere to their statements (t) Mackenzie v Henderson, 1820, 2 Mur, 217—Mackay v M'Leods, 1827 4 Mur 279—Russell v Crichton, 1838, Macf R, 185 (u) Mackenzie v Henderson, *supra*—In Sundius v Sheriffs, 1811, Hume D 902 the Court of Session rejected a witness on this among other grounds, but the House of Lords remitted the case for reconsideration and (as the reporter understood) it was afterwards compromised (x) 5 and 6 Will IV, c 62, § 13, quoted *supra*, § 1661 (y) Wemyss v Wemyss 1793, M, 16,782—Boyle v Yule, 1778, M, 1899—Little v Smith, 1815, 8 D, 265, 9 ib 737, *per curiam*

(z) See Ellis v D Hamilton, 1681, M, 16,682 3 B Sup 165, S C—Durham v Mair, 1698, M 16,786—Duncan v Thomson 1831, 12 S, 935 (a) 2 Hume, 82—2 Al 137, 504 This power is reserved in the act 5 and 6 Will IV c 62 § 13 quoted *supra* § 1661 (b) 5 and 6 Will IV *supra* 2 Hume 378—2 Al, 504

signed declarations upon oath, which he had kept in his own or his agent's custody, in order to overawe the witnesses (*c*)

§ 1750 A witness who has been precognosced (however regularly) on oath before a magistrate is entitled to have his previous statement cancelled before he begins his evidence at the trial, otherwise he would likely feel trammeled by it, and would try to make his evidence at the trial agree with his previous *ex parte* statement, instead of speaking freely from his recollection at the time (*d*)

§ 1751 A common, but highly reprehensible, practice is to precognosce witnesses in each other's presence, by which means the recollection of one is refreshed and eked out by the statements of another, and a story more consistent than true, is sometimes patched up among them Where an improper purpose of this kind appears, the witnesses will be excluded, because their evidence has become tainted by the party's attempt to tutor them, and if the irregularity arose from gross carelessness and ignorance, without an improper intention, it will be fatal, where, from the delicate nature of the question in issue, or the information which the witnesses may have received, that course is necessary for the justice of the case

§ 1752 On this ground, where an agent in precognoscing the witnesses collected them in a room, took down the statement of each in writing, read it over to him, and got him to sign it, and all this was done in the presence and hearing of them all, the Court rejected the first witness, and, the party not tendering other evidence, the jury found a verdict against him (*e*) In an action of proving the tenor of a will alleged to have been destroyed by the maker when insane (a case of peculiar delicacy), it was held to be a fatal objection to the pursuer's witnesses, that his law-agent had precognosced them in presence of each other, although it was not said that he intended to tutor them (*f*) It was also held fatal to

(*c*) Maccaul, 1714, 2 Hume 378, 2 Al, 504 —See also Mackay *v* M Leods, 1827 4 Mur 279

(*d*) 2 Hume, 381—2 Al, 504

(*e*) Duncan *v* Thomson, 1834, 12 S, 935

(*f*) Reid *v* Duff, 1843, 5 D, 656 The law on the point noticed in the text is stated by Lord Jeffrey thus,—"Precognoscing witnesses in presence of each other used to be a peremptory objection It is now necessary, however, to make out a case of such gross imprudence and mismanagement, as to bring it to a case of peril to the other party, not of tampering, that is not requisite There is quite enough in this case to make us hold that the party is not entitled to the testimony of the witnesses In questions of opinion as in this case, of the unsoundness of a person's mind, we all know the

the admissibility of witnesses in a civil action of damages, that the agent of the pursuer had transmitted to each of them a copy of precognitions, which had been taken from them all on oath with a view to a criminal prosecution (*g*) And, in a criminal trial, thirteen exculpatory witnesses were rejected, because they had assembled at the desire of the prisoner's agent, and had their declarations taken down and read over in presence of each other (*h*)

§ 1753 On the other hand, where it was objected to the admission of a husband and wife, that each had been present when the other was precognosced, the objection was overruled, because the attendance had taken place casually, and not from any improper motive (*i*) And where in an action for the price of ale and porter, two witnesses had been precognosced in presence of each other, and their statements had been read over before them both, but there had not been any intention to tutor them, the objection to their admissibility was overruled (*k*) In a criminal case, the Court admitted a Crown witness who had been present at the precognitions of some other witnesses, but without any improper motive on his part or that of the prosecutor (*l*) And one of the grounds on which the Justiciary Court repelled the objection, that a Crown witness had heard another precognosced, was that he had not thereby become aware of any fact which he had not known before (*m*)

§ 1754 The objection, that a witness heard other witnesses precognosced, had been disregarded where he had attended in consequence of official duty, as procurator-fiscal, town-clerk, or police-officer,—provided he could distinguish between what he had observed himself, and what he heard other witnesses state upon the matter in issue (*n*) Nor will it render the evidence of a party inadmissible under the Law of Evidence Amendment Act, that he

---

force of the feeling *defendit numerus* Is it fair, moreover, that a party should be allowed to bring to his witnesses knowledge of circumstances, not falling under their own observation, in support of the judgment they had formed? Their opinion is then derived, not *ex propria scientia*, but from the evidence of others In the proceeding here, there was such a total disregard of the interest of the antagonist, that with the greatest unwillingness to exclude testimony, I think the witnesses so dealt with cannot be received '

(*g*) Fall *v* Sawers, 1785, M, 16,777 (*h*) Lindsay, 1791, 2 Hume, 379 See also Hunter and Others, noted *supra*, § 1741 (*i*) Kerrs *v* Penman, 1830, 5 Mur, 145 (*k*) Aitken *v* Weir, 1840, 2 D, 1029—See also Millar *v* Fraser, 1826, 4 Mur, 120 (*l*) Macleod, 1801, 2 Hume, 380, 2 Al, 142

(*m*) Mitchell, 1850, J Shaw, 293—See *supra*, § 1746 (*n*) Anderson *v* Sproat, 1793, M, 16,783—Begrie, 1820, Sh Just Ca 8, 2 Hume, 380—Smith, 1837, Bell's Notes 270, 2 Al, 141—Compared with Stephens, 1839 2 Swin, 348

had taken or seen the precognitions of other witnesses in the cause, the statute not making any such exception in opening the door to party-witnesses (*o*)

§ 1755 Witnesses on matters of opinion (*e g*, medical men and engineers) must of course, know the facts upon which their opinions are required, nor can they be prepared to give evidence at the trial unless they have been previously informed what facts the party expects to prove Accordingly, it is not in general a ground for excluding such witnesses that they have either seen the precognitions of the party who adduces them, or heard the witnesses precognosced (*p*), provided they have not seen or heard the precognitions of other witnesses on matters of opinion (*r*) The consequence of this may be, that a scientific witness gives evidence on hypothetical views of the facts, which are materially different from those proved to the jury And where the evidence is contradictory, or comprehends inferences and presumptions, he may draw from it a different conclusion from that which the jury arrive at and consequently may found his opinion on erroneous *data* In general, however a skilful cross-examination will discover such discrepancies and will enable the witness to adapt his opinion to the facts really proved as well as to different hypothetical views of the case

§ 1756 But this practice must be kept within such limits (at least in cases of complexity) that the evidence of the scientific witnesses shall not involve an inference in point of fact from the whole evidence, for such inferences as do not require scientific or technical knowledge should be drawn by the jury themselves from the facts proved, and it is doubly objectionable to lay before them, as matter of evidence, inferences from facts which one of the parties merely expected to prove Accordingly where in a trial of several persons for neglect of duty in constructing and working a railway, whereby a fatal accident had been occasioned, the prosecutor tendered an eminent engineer to speak to the strength of the rails and the rate at which they should have been travelled on, the Court sustained the objection that the witness had seen the precognitions of several other Crown witnesses and the declarations of the prisoners with a view to giving his opinion on the whole circumstances (*s*)

(*o*) See *supra*, § 1730, *et seq*

(*p*) Harkness, 1797 2 Hume, 380—Richardson 1824 Sh Just Ca 125—Mitchell 1850 J Shaw, 293

(*r*) Fraser *v* Lovat, 1841, 3 D, 1132, *supra*, § 1745

(*s*) M'Lure, 1848, Arkley 448 See this case noticed by Lord Just-Clerk Hope in Mitchell, 1850, J Shaw, 293

§ 1757 Precognoscing a witness after his citation used to be a ground of exclusion, for what reason does not precisely appear (*t*) It no longer disqualifies (*u*)

The mode of proving the objections noticed in this chapter is considered afterwards

---

CHAPTER XIII.—OF THE EXCLUSION OF WITNESSES ON THE GROUND OF HAVING HEARD THE EVIDENCE OF PREVIOUS WITNESSES

§ 1758 Until within the last few years a witness was excluded if he had been in court during the examination of any of the previous witnesses lest his own recollection of the facts should have been disturbed by what he had heard them say (*a*) But this has not been applied to the attendance of scientific witnesses during evidence upon the facts on which their opinion is required, their absence being only necessary during the evidence of other scientific witnesses (*b*) Nor was it a ground for excluding a witness that he had heard the depositions of witnesses in a previous trial involving the same facts, as the party adducing him ought not to be held responsible for such attendance (*c*)

§ 1759 A recent statute enacts that "in any trial before any Judge of the Court of Session or Court of Justiciary or before any Sheriff or Stewart in Scotland, it shall not be imperative on the Court to reject any witness against whom it is objected that he or she has without the permission of the Court and without the consent of the party objecting, been present in court during all or any part of the proceedings, but it shall be competent for the Court, in its discretion to admit the witness where it shall appear to the Court that the presence of the witness was not the consequence of culpable negligence or criminal intent, and that the witness has not been unduly instructed or influenced by what took place during his or her presence or that injustice will not be done by his or her examination" (*d*)

(*t*) See Ersk 4 2 28, note—2 Hume, 378—Macf Prac, 114—Hinshaw *v* Hinshaw, 1846, 9 D, 251 (*u*) 15 Vict c 27, § 1 (*a*) 2 Hume, 379—Tait Ev 420—Macf Prac 150—2 Al, 512 (*b*) 2 Hume, 380, notes—Macf Prac, *supra*—Tait 421—Al, *supra* On this subject see the section on examining scientific witnesses, *infra*, and see *supra*, § 1755 (*c*) 2 Hume, 380 not

(*d*) 3 and 4 Vict c 59 § 3

§ 1760 Where the law-agent of one party was cited as a witness by the other, the Court refused to require him to be inclosed, in order that he might not hear the evidence of the other witnesses, because that would have deprived his client of his professional assistance (*e*) In like manner, a party would be entitled to remain in court, in order to assist in conducting his case, although he had been cited as a witness by his adversary But it is thought that a party who intended to give evidence as a witness for himself could not successfully resist a motion by the other party to have him ordained to leave the court-room At least if he remained, his evidence might be excluded, if the Court considered that his presence during the examination of other witnesses had arisen from an improper motive, or had "unduly instructed" him (*f*) [1]

CHAPTER XIV —OF THE EXCLUSION OF WITNESSES ON ACCOUNT OF ENMITY TO THE PARTY AGAINST WHOM THEY ARE ADDUCED

§ 1761 Trustworthy evidence cannot be expected from one who hates the party against whom he is adduced, for although comparatively few men will intentionally state falsehood in order to gratify malice, yet to most men facts appear distorted and discoloured when viewed through such a medium Accordingly, bitter and deep-rooted malice (*malitia capitalis*) will exclude the witness who entertains it, and a less violent dislike will impair his credibility In determining such questions the Court have to estimate the strength of the feeling by examining its supposed cause,

---

(*e*) Fullerton, 1768, 2 Hume 380, I—Mackenzie *v* Roy, 1830 5 Mur, 257
(*f*) 3 and 4 Vict c 59, § 3

---

[1] In Selfe *v* Isaacson, 1858, 1 F and F, 194 it was held that the plaintiff was entitled to be present at the trial of a cause, and the same was held in Constance *v* Brain 1856, 2 Jur N S, 1145,—but it was remarked from the Bench that the fact of a party being in court might tend to affect his credibility as a witness In H M Adv *v* Montgomery, 1855 2 Irv 226, a witness was permitted to remain in court during the examination of another witness, but the circumstances of the case were special

and the overt acts by which it is manifested The mere language of the witness is an inadequate guide, for many persons use violent expressions when they do not entertain real hostility, while the friends of a party (especially in criminal trials) sometimes attempt by this device to escape from giving evidence against him

§ 1762 In some cases, chiefly of old date, the use of malicious expressions was considered sufficient to exclude a witness, where they had been violent and frequently repeated (*a*) But it has for a long time been settled law that a witness is not rendered inadmissible by expressions of enmity, however pointed and violent unless they have been accompanied by some malicious act, or have sprung from some cause likely to create hostility (*b*) Indications of ill-will coming short of this affect the credibility of the witness, but not his competency

It is not likely that the Court would, in any criminal case, reject a witness for the panel on the ground of malice to the prosecutor (*c*)

§ 1763 The first branch of this rule has been often applied Thus a witness for the Crown was admitted, although he had used strong expressions of malice, one of which was that he would do all in his power to hang the prisoner, and if the city of Glasgow wanted an executioner, he would himself put the rope round the prisoner's neck and hang him (*d*) In another case, a Crown witness was admitted, who had said he would do all in his power to have the prisoner hanged (*e*) Again, where a witness had threat-

---

(*a*) 2 Hume, 358, 9 In Spalding, 1673 2 Hume 358 a witness for the Crown was excluded, in consequence of having repeatedly said that he wished to wash his hands in the prisoner's heart's blood A proof of malicious expressions has repeatedly been allowed (but without success) on their being stated as an objection to the admission of the witness as in Davison, 1786 2 Hume 359—Strong *v* Stewart, 1811, ib—Macbain 1812, ib—Hardie 1831 Bell's Notes, 258—See also Mackenzie *v* Roy, 1830, 5 Mur, 259—Rose *v* Junor, 1846 9 D, 12—Crubb, 1827, Sh Just Ca, 208—Williamson, 1837, Bell's Notes, 258

(*b*) Stair, 4 43, 7 (6)—Ersk 4, 2, 28—2 Hume 360, 3—Burnett 412—Bell's Notes, 258—2 Al, 480 1—Tait 370 The law on this point is well summed up in Thomas *v* Pinkston, 1796, Hume D, 894, where it was observed on the Bench, in regard to malicious expressions used by a witness, "It will be presumed that these were rash and heedless words, or perhaps she may have spoken so with a view to disqualify herself as a witness She can only be set aside on the ground of *inimicitiæ capitalis* for acts of enmity proved against her, or in respect of such a situation and circumstances as may naturally have bred a hostile disposition to the party"

(*c*) 2 Hume, 402 (*d*) Miller, 1818, 2 Hume, 369, note

(*e*) Muir 1793, 2 Hume, 363

cried that, right or wrong, she would bring the prisoner to the gallows, but neither any overt act indicating malice nor any cause for such feeling appeared, the Court would not allow a proof of the allegation (*f*) So the objection was overruled that on a petty provocation two witnesses had conspired to swear falsely in order to inculpate the prisoner, and had mentioned this agreement in the hearing of third parties, but without demonstrating it by any overt act (*g*), and the objection, that the witness had said he would swear anything to hang the prisoner and get the promised reward, and that he had taken active measures towards his apprehension, was admitted only to affect the witness' credibility (*h*) Thus also, in a reduction of a deed on the ground of the granter's incapacity, where the defender's mother-in-law was adduced against him, and he alleged that on many occasions she had used strong expressions of malice and most horrid imprecations towards him, had repeatedly accused him openly of having killed her daughter, had instigated the pursuer to raise the action, and signified her wish that the defender might fail in it, the Court refused to allow a proof of these allegations as a ground for excluding her, and it was observed from the Bench, that it is not enough that a cause for the ill-will be assigned in the expressions themselves, but there must be a cause distinct from them, *e g*, that the party should be proved to have done some heinous injury to the witness, or the like (*i*)

§ 1764 Where both malicious expressions by the witness and a supposed cause for them appear he will only be rejected if the cause is sufficient to have provoked strong and deep-rooted malice (*malicia capitalis*), or if by overt acts the witness has evinced such feelings, although springing from some slighter provocation (*k*)

Thus, on the one hand, it was held sufficient to exclude a witness that he had indulged in vindictive expressions against the prisoner, had been engaged in various feuds with him, and had once been present at an assault on him by a party of men in arms (*l*) And in a trial of mutual libels for murder and hame-sucken, the Court rejected a witness who was a near relation of the person killed, and who had been wounded in the broil which gave occasion to the homicide and had threatened to take personal revenge on the pri-

(*f*) Brown and Wilson 1773 2 Hume, 362 (*g*) Clark and Greig, 1842, 1 Broun, 250, Bell's Notes, 258 (*h*) Little, 1831, Bell's Notes, 253—2 Al, 481 —See § 1743 (*i*) Irving *v* Ly Saphock, 1751, M 16 762, 5 B Sup, 230, S C

(*k*) 2 Hume, 360—Burnett 411—2 Al, 484—Tait Ev, 379 (*l*) Spalding, 1673 2 Hume 363

soner if he did not get justice otherwise (*m*) In several older cases, injuries by the prisoner, and even by one of his relations to a relation of the witness were held sufficient to raise deadly malice, and to exclude the individuals as witnesses (*n*) But although these decisions may have been just in an age when most men adopted their kinsmen's and even their clansmen's quarrels the Court would not now exclude a witness on this head, except in extreme cases as, for example where the party against whom he is adduced had inflicted a serious injury on a parent, child brother, or sister, of the witness, who had thereupon evinced a determination to be revenged (*o*)

In a criminal case a witness was rejected because recently before the date of the alleged crime (fire-raising) he had had a quarrel ending in a fight with the witness in which they had violently beaten and drawn blood from each other (*p*) It does not appear whether the witness had thereafter expressed malice against the prisoner

§ 1765 Lord Stair lays down that enmity arising from ' any atrocious injury done or attempted against life or fame will render a witness inadmissible ' (*r*) But no case has been found of exclusion on account of the enmity raised by an unsuccessful attempt to injure

§ 1766 On the other hand the witness was admitted reserving his credibility to the jury, where the cause assigned for his malicious expressions was, that the party had dismissed him from his service (*s*), had caused him to be apprehended on a caption (*t*) and had lodged information of his having been art and part in a theft of money from a third person in consequence of which the witness had been apprehended and brought to much trouble (*u*) So a witness will be admitted although the party has sworn a law-bur-

(*m*) Master of Tarbet and Porsset, 1691 2 Hume 358, 9 (*n*) See Master of Jedburgh *v* Elliot, 1623 M , 16,659—Muirhead *v* Clelland, 1616, M , 16,658—Aitchison *v* Sinclair, 1589, M , 16,653 (*o*) See Tait Ev 371

(*p*) Cunningham, 1677 2 Hume, 363 (*r*) Stair 4, 43, 7 (6)—See also Tait, 370 (*s*) Sheddan, 1752, 2 Hume, 362—Nairn and Ogilvie, 1765 ib

(*t*) Niven, 1680, 2 Hume, 360 Here the witness had threatened to be revenged on the party, but fourteen years had elapsed since, and they had conversed together in the witness' house in the interval See also Drummond 1736, 2 Hume, 361 where the witness deponed that the prisoner's father had poinded his effects and "harried him," but that his malice would not induce him to swear falsely against the prisoner, whereupon his evidence was remitted to the jury

(*u*) Crawford, 1818, 2 Hume, 359 Here the witness had repeatedly said she would swear away the prisoner's life for a farthing

rows against him, or *vice versa* (x), and although they have mutually sworn law-burrows against each other (y) unless the ground of the proceeding was "deadly feud and blood" (z) In such cases, the person adopting the measures in question merely availed himself of his legal right, a course which, if taken by the witness, does not indicate deadly malice on his part, and, if adopted by the party against him, does not necessarily raise such feelings (a)

§ 1767 Again, in a trial of a man for the murder of his illegitimate child, the mother was held to be admissible as a witness against him although she had said to several persons that she "would hunt him like a dog to the gallows," and although she was then pregnant of another child to him after promises of marriage, which he had broken (b) And it was held not relevant to exclude two witnesses (who were husband and wife) against the prisoner, that recently before the trial he had taken away furniture from them, in consequence of which it was alleged that they had conceived deadly malice against him, and had entered into a conspiracy to swear falsely to his prejudice (c)

§ 1768 It has long been settled law that the person upon whom a crime has been committed is admissible against the prisoner charged with it, although he may not only have used expressions inferring malice and a wish that the prisoner should be convicted, but may also have aided in conducting the inquiries preparatory to the trial The reason is, that some irritation on his part is natural if not also justifiable, and usually springs from the strength of his belief in the prisoner's guilt, while moreover, he is in general a necessary witness (d) But the existence of strong malice in that party anterior to the act charged may cause him to be excluded (e) This view seems to have been taken where a person charged with assault on his father, and rape and incest on his mother-in-law objected to the admission of the latter on the ground that she had expressed inveterate malice against him be-

(x) Armstrong *v* Johnston, 1544, M 16,619—L Salton (or Halton) *v* Hepburn, 1610, M, 16,655 (y) Carnegy, 1672, 2 Hume, 360—Armstrong *v* Sharp, 1711, M, 16,731 (z) L Salton *v* Hepburn, *supra* (a) But see Innes 1833, Bell's Notes 258, where a proof was allowed of the allegation by a prisoner that a Crown witness had a quarrel with him about the letting of a toll-bar in consequence of which the witness entertained malice against him had said he would have his life, and used other malicious expressions (b) Glen, 1827 Syme, 207

(c) Clark and Greig, 1812, 1 Broun, 250 (d) 2 Hume, 357—2 Al 477—Burnett, 428—Scott 1816 2 Hume, 362—See also *infra*, § 1770 (e) Burnett, 413 4—2 Al, 485

fore the date of the acts libelled, and (as he alleged) had instigated the prosecution through gross falsehood and malignity, because she wished to prevent him from bringing a wife into the father's family, in order that she might continue to embezzle the father's effects. Lord Kames, holding these allegations relevant to cast the witness, allowed a proof of them, and on considering the proof, held the witness to be inadmissible (*f*). His Lordship's decision, however, has been questioned by Baron Hume and Sir Archibald Alison (*g*), and it is not unlikely, as the learned Baron observes, that the proof of the objection was treated in a great measure as an exculpatory proof, and one which utterly subverted the charge; for the depositions showed that to be a foul contrivance to ruin the panel and drive him from home.

It will, however, be kept in view that where the witness and the prisoner have entertained animosities, and had mutual quarrels or bickerings, there is the more reason to expect that one of them will break out into some violent or malicious act against the other, and therefore the testimony of the one who complains of such an injury should not be rejected, except in an extreme case (*h*).

§ 1769. Farther, a witness will be excluded on the ground of malice where, without any known provocation, there is enough in his overt acts (not his mere words) to show that he entertains a deep-rooted hostility to the party against whom he is adduced.

Thus, on the one hand, a witness for the Crown was excluded, because he had fired a pistol at the prisoner, with the intention of killing him (*i*). And in a trial for housebreaking and wilful fire-raising, where a Crown witness had inserted in the newspapers an advertisement, directly asserting that the prisoner was guilty, and called on the clergymen of all the parishes in the district to give warning against him from the pulpit, and had offered a reward of £50 for the prisoner's apprehension, which sum he had either paid, or obliged himself to pay to the authorities—the Court held that he had evinced so much zeal for the prosecutor as to have rendered himself inadmissible (*j*). But this decision has been questioned, on the ground that the acts of the witness were only directed towards bringing the prisoner to justice (*k*).

(*f*) Burnett, 1768, noted in 2 Hume, 358, Burnett, 114, and 2 Al., 485.
(*g*) Hume, *supra*.—Al., *supra*.
(*h*) See 2 Hume, 358.
(*i*) Wright, 1788, 2 Hume, 363.
(*j*) Ross, 1821, Sh. Just. Ca., 10; 2 Al., 485; per Lords Hermand and Succoth. It does not appear whether the witness was the person against whom the crime had been committed.
(*k*) Al., *supra*.

§ 1770 On the other hand, where the counsel for a prisoner proposed to ask a Crown witness *in initialibus* if he harboured malice against the prisoner, and if on an occasion (not involved in the indictment) he had struck the prisoner the Court held that the assault could not be proved as inferring malice, "unless at least it were first shown to have originated in declared malice on a special cause" (*k*) Here the overt act did not indicate inveterate malice Again, in the trial of the factor of the Marquis of Stafford for culpable homicide the admission of the Sheriff-substitute of the county as a witness for the Crown was resisted on the ground that he had imprisoned the panel on a warrant which was afterwards set aside as illegal—had unlawfully refused to allow him bail—had without complaint or trial struck him off the roll of procurators in the county—had written a partial and inflammatory account of his conduct to the Marquis of Stafford—and had dissuaded those who wished to be bailsmen for him, and said that the prisoner should be hanged, and that Botany Bay was too good for him To this it was answered, that the warrant had fallen in consequence of a mere informality, that on this account alone the Court of Justiciary had admitted bail (the charge being of a capital crime)—that the prisoner might have been properly struck off the roll—that it depended on the terms of the communication to the Marquis of Stafford what effect it might have on the question—and that the prosecutor only intended to examine the witness as to the practice of the county in removing tenants The Court, after allowing a proof of the objection by examining the witness *in initialibus* and by other evidence (which supported the statement of the prosecutor as to the warrant and bail), held that the witness might be admitted *cum nota*, but recommended to the counsel for the prosecutor not to press his examination, whereupon he was withdrawn (*l*) In some other cases witnesses who had manifested undue zeal for the prosecution (*m*), and had accused the prisoner of the crime in the public journals (*n*), were held to be admissible their credibility being left to the jury

Where a witness was objected to on the ground that he had shown ill-will to the prisoner, and among other malicious acts had tried to buy up one of the prisoner's debts in order to ruin him, the object of the witness being (it was said) to get possession of a valu-

(*k*) Specks 1835, Bell's Notes 258 (*l*) Sellar, 1816, 2 Hume, 350—2 Al 485 (*m*) Harkness 1797 2 Hume 362—See Scott, 1816, ib

(*n*) Mitchell and Miller 1803, Burnett 414—Cuddie 1821 2 Al, 486

able grazing, for which the prisoner had successfully competed with him, the Court after hearing evidence (the result of which is not mentioned) held that the objection affected only the credibility of the witness, not his competency (*o*)

§ 1771. Malice which, if caused by recent injuries, or indicated by recent conduct, would exclude the witness, will only affect his credibility if there is reason to believe the feeling has become deadened by lapse of time (*p*), or been removed by a reconciliation between the witness and party (*r*)

§ 1772 The objection of malice is not unfrequently concocted between the witness and the party against whom he is adduced, in order to save that party from the damaging effect of his evidence In criminal cases this is usually the secret history of the objection, when stated against a relation or acquaintance of the prisoner (*s*) The risk of such collusion is great, when the acts and expressions founded on to support the objection occurred after the cause of action arose, and still more so if they happened after the witness had been cited (*t*)

§ 1773 Where a witness has been detected in a plot of this kind, his statements in favour of the party adducing him may safely be credited, whereas those of an opposite tendency should be viewed with suspicion, on account of the strong and unfair bias which the witness has manifested

§ 1774 In a case of divorce for adultery it was alleged that one of the witnesses for the pursuer entertained malice, not against the defender, but against the alleged paramour As the objection

(*o*) Kennedy, 1822, Sh Just Ca, 81

(*p*) See *e g*, Henry *v* Evans, 1820, 2 Mur 330—Niven, 1680, 2 Hume, 360

(*r*) Stair, 4 43, 7 (6)—Burnett, 412—Niven *supra*

(*s*) 2 Hume 360—Burnett, 413—2 Al, 481—In Dean, 1720, 2 Hume, 361, a Crown witness, on being examined *in initialibus*, stated that he bore malice to the prisoner, and had threatened to do all in his power to get him hanged The witnesses to whom he had uttered these threats, having been examined, admitted that the whole was a plot to get the witness excluded, and he on being placed in the custody of a macer, became alarmed and admitted that such was the fact In Clark, 1790, 2 Hume, 363, a Crown witness was objected to on the ground that she had repeatedly threatened to swear away the prisoner's life, and had asked money from him to buy off her evidence but her initial examination showed that she was a friend and confidant of the prisoner with whom she had concerted the device in order to disqualify herself See also Ross and Ward, 1819, 2 Hume, 360, note, and Crabb, 1827, ib Sh Just Ca, 208 in both of which cases the malicious expressions which had been used by the witness were a device of this kind See also *supra*, § 1739 (*t*)

(*t*) An objection founded on malicious expressions was disregarded, because they had been uttered after citation, in Harkness, 1797, Burnett, 413, Tait Ev, 371 was only stated to affect the credibility of the witness (to which extent proof of it was allowed) the question did not arise whether a witness could be excluded on such a ground And the Court avoided indicating an opinion on that point (v)

The rules as to proving the objection of enmity are noticed afterwards

---

CHAPTER XV —OF CERTAIN GROUNDS OF EXCLUSION OF WITNESSES EXISTING FORMERLY, BUT NOW ABOLISHED

In the preceding chapters a number of instances are given in which the old exclusionary rules have been either abolished or limited[1] The other grounds of inadmissibility under the former law, and their abolition, will now be noticed

§ 1775 At one time *women* were generally rejected, both in civil and criminal cases (a), and Erskine writing in the year 1754, enumerates as exceptional the cases in which they were then received Their exclusion, which is now matter of history, was borrowed from the canonists, and is believed to have arisen more from the fancied indecorum of their appearing in court, than from doubts as to their trustworthiness (b) There is still some doubt whether women may be instrumentary witnesses (c)

§ 1776 *Poverty*, as laying witnesses open to corruption, was a ground of exclusion under the old Scotch law, which admitted no one who was not worth the "Kings unlaw," (£10 Scots, or 16s 8d sterling) (d) For a long time the poverty of a witness has ceased to be a ground for excluding him

§ 1777 Until recently a witness was rejected, if he had been convicted of a *crime inferring infamy* (e) Such convictions created

(v) King v King, 1841, 4 D, 124

(a) Stair, 3, 43, 9—2 Hume, 339—Ersk 4, 2, 22—*Supra* § 1670 (a) The last instance of exclusion on this ground seems to have occurred in Wiseman v Morrison, 1736, M, 16,743 (b) Compare Burnett, 388—Ersk *supra*—More's Notes, 409 (c) See *supra* § 689

(d) Stair, 4, 43 9 (1)—Tait 348—*Supra*, § 1670 (a)

(e) The rules as to this objection will be found in 2 Hume, 353—Bell's Pr, § 2243—Burnett, 400—Tait Ev, 345—2 Al, 440 The crimes which inferred infamy were

[1] In H M Adv v M Guire, 1857, 2 Irv, 620, the subject of a nation with which this country was at war was held a competent witness in a criminal trial

infamia juris, to which this ground of exclusion was limited *Infamia facti*—that is, infamous character or criminality, without conviction—however great and notorious, did not create inadmissibility (*f*)

At common law the competency of the witness could be restored by royal pardon (*g*) Consequently, the Crown had an exclusive privilege of adducing a numerous class of witnesses, who were considered so unworthy of credit as to be inadmissible for any other party

§ 1778 After much inconvenience and some injustice had been occasioned by this ground of exclusion, especially in criminal cases, a statute was passed, whereby the admissibility of one who had been convicted of any crime except perjury or subornation of perjury was restored on his having undergone punishment (*h*)

A subsequent statute abolished the objection of infamy as a ground for excluding witnesses, reserving its effect as regards their credibility (*i*) Now, therefore, inadmissibility does not arise from conviction of any number of crimes, however heinous, perjury and subornation not excepted

The rules as to proving conviction of a crime, and as to its effect on the credibility of the witness are noticed afterwards

§ 1779 The *servants* and *retainers* of a party, and his *tenants*

---

perjury and subornation of perjury, forgery coining, fraudulent bankruptcy, swindling, theft, and robbery, all of which (except the last) involved a *crimen falsi* But none of these crimes created infamy unless the offender had been convicted in a trial by a jury, or had confessed on a libel for such a trial, 2 Hume, 354—Tait Ev, 346—Aitchison v Patrick, 1836, 15 S, 360 And accordingly, deposition of a clergyman by the General Assembly on a charge of theft did not brand him with *infamia juris*, but only affected his credibility, Thomson, 1842, 1 Broun, 413

(*f*) Bell's Pr, *supra*—Tait Ev 346—Al, *supra*—Armstrong's Assignees v Leith Bank, 1834 12 S, 440 The text is illustrated by the rule of common law under which a *socius criminis* was admitted, see § 1694, *et seq* So a witness against whom an indictment for a crime inferring infamy had been raised was admissible as a witness, Hannah, 1836, Bell's Notes, 256—Liddell, 1838, ib and in the trial of a woman for having instigated boys to steal, they were admitted as witnesses for the Crown, although theft, if followed by conviction (which it had not been as to them), inferred infamy, Fairlie, 1775, 2 Hume, 351 So it went only to the credibility of a witness that he had perjured himself in his initial examination, M'Ghie, 1832, Bell's Notes, 256—Hepburn, 1836, ib—Mochrie, 1844, 2 Broun 293—But see *supra* § 1739

(*g*) Bell's Pr, § 2243—2 Hume, 356—Burnett, 404, *et seq*—2 Al, 451—Bell's Notes, 257—Johnston, 1815 2 Broun, 101

(*h*) 11 Geo IV and 1 Will IV, c 37, § 9

(*i*) 15 Vict c 27 § 1 This act provides that "no person adduced as a witness in Scotland shall be excluded from giving evidence, by reason of having been convicted of or of having suffered punishment for, crime"

possessing from year to year, used to be inadmissible as witnesses for him, being supposed incapable of giving independent and trustworthy evidence (*k*) It has for a long time been the practice to examine such witnesses, leaving the jury to judge whether their situation impairs their credibility (*l*)

§ 1780 The *tutors* and *curators* of a party were formerly incompetent witnesses in his favour on account of their supposed partiality (*m*) But this objection came in course of time to be limited to cases where the witnesses were parties to the record, or were open to the objections of interest and partial counsel (*n*) Recent legislation has abolished the remains of this ground of exclusion, except where the tutor or curator is a party to the record in certain consistorial causes above enumerated (*o*)

§ 1781 The circumstance of the witness having a *pecuniary interest* (*p*) in the issue used to be a fruitful source of disqualification (*r*) For a number of years the tendency of the Courts, and especially of the House of Lords, had been to limit this objection by only applying it where the witness would have been directly benefited by a verdict in favour of the adducer (*s*) If he would, he was inadmissible, however slight the benefit might be (*t*) and even where it would only have accrued to a joint stock company in which he was a shareholder (*u*) Such a state of the law in a con-

---

(*k*) Ersk, 4 2 25—Tait Ev 370—*Supra*, § 1670 (*a*)

(*l*) 2 Hume, 343—Ivory's Note to Ersk *supra*—Tait, *supra*

(*m*) Ersk, 4, 2, 25

(*n*) Ivory's Note to Ersk, *supra*—Tait Ev, 366

(*o*) 15 Vict, c 27, § 1—16 Vict, c 20, § 3, 4—*Supra*, §§ 1704 5, 1730

(*p*) In several cases witnesses were held disqualified by interest to preserve character, as where they were adduced to contradict allegations of fraud by themselves, Glendinning *v* Brown 8th December 1814, F C—Williamson *v* Corrie, 1833, 12 S 562 and in cases of divorce Carruthers, 1742, and Bell *v* King, 21st January 1797 (not rep) noted in Tait 361, where the alleged paramour was adduced to prove that he had not committed the adultery libelled on But this ground of objection to admissibility was overruled in the more authoritative decisions of the House of Lords in Marshall *v* Anderson, 1798 M 16,787 (reversing), and of the Second Division of the Court in Russell *v* Liston's Tr, 1844, 6 D, 1098

(*r*) The former law on this subject will be found in Bell's Pr, § 2244, *et seq*—More's Notes, 413—Tait, 349, 360—Br Synop, p 1040—Sh Dig, vol ii, p 1047, and vol iii, p 366

(*s*) The progress of the law to this result will be seen from comparing the rules stated in More Bell, and Tait *ut supra* with the judgments in the House of Lords in Ralston *v* Rowat 1833 6 W S, 468, and Wood *v* Young, 1847, 6 Bell's Ap, 89, in both of which cases the decision of the Court of Session was reversed

(*t*) Bell's Pr, 2246—Tait, 357

(*u*) As in National Bank *v* Forbes 1849, 12 D 437—Houston *v* Aberdeen Bank 1849 12 D, 407

mercial country often obstructed and defeated justice It was therefore, altered by a recent act (*x*), which provides that no one adduced as a witness in Scotland, before any court or any person authorised to take evidence, shall be excluded on account of interest

§ 1782 This enactment does not embrace the objection of interest in regard to instrumentary witnesses The reason seems to be, that while little or no evil, and much good, are likely to arise from laying the evidence of interested witnesses before the jury, to be weighed along with the rest of the proof, there would be considerable risk of impetration and fraudulent concoction of deeds, if the attestation of them by persons materially interested were sufficient A deed so witnessed could not be received without additional evidence of its authenticity, and this would conflict with the useful principle, that attested deeds are probative It is, therefore both just and expedient that the party making a deed should select as witnesses to it persons who are *omni exceptione majores* No inconvenience is occasioned by this rule, which, indeed, would be followed in practice by all respectable and judicious conveyancers, even if it were no longer compulsory

§ 1783 It has already been seen that instrumentary witnesses are not rendered incompetent by interest which is not both direct and considerable (*y*)

§ 1784 The remarks made in a previous chapter (*z*) as to the credibility of party-witnesses apply, in a great measure, to those who have a material interest in the issue The latter, however, are not subject to the bias which litigation produces, especially in persons of keen or obstinate temperament

§ 1785 Witnesses used also to be rendered inadmissible by *ultroneousness*,—that is, appearing to give evidence without having been cited by the proper officer, which was supposed to indicate partisanship in favour of the person adducing (*a*) This objection is now abolished as regards the admissibility of witnesses, any effect it may have on their credibility being left to the jury (*b*) There is no reason whatever to suppose that a witness is biassed because

(*x*) 15 Vict, c 27, § 1 The exclusionary rule had been slightly modified by 3 and 4 Vict, c 26, and 8 and 9 Vict, c 83, § 83 (*y*) See *supra* § 690

(*z*) *Supra*, § 1713 (*a*) Stair, 4, 43, 9 (5)—Tait Ev, 369—Brown's Synop, p 1958 (*b*) 15 Vict c 27 § 1 The objection had been abolished in criminal cases by 9 Geo IV c 29 § 10 before these statutes there had for some time been a tendency to confine it to the credibility of the witness, Bell's Pr § 2253 (1)

he appears in Court without a citation, which in most cases is an unnecessary piece of form

CHAPTER XVI —OF WITNESSES DISQUALIFIED AS TO ONE OF SEVERAL PARTIES

§ 1786 When several parties are associated on the same side of a cause, a witness disqualified as to one of them is inadmissible as regards all the others, on every part of the cause in which they are mutually interested (c) The reason is, that the interests of parties on the same side are usually so interwoven, that it is impossible to estimate what effect circumstances which render a witness inadmissible as to one of them might have on his statements in regard to the others Accordingly, where several prisoners are tried together on the same indictment, the wife of one of them is inadmissible, either for or against the others, in any charge in which her husband is involved (d) In one case, where one of two panels charged on the same libel had been fugitated for failing to stand trial, it was proposed, on the part of the Crown, to adduce his wife as a witness against the other prisoner, but the Lord Justice-Clerk Boyle said that she ought not to be called, and the other judges were rather of the same opinion (e) An opposite decision was pronounced a few years afterwards (f) and seems to be correct, because the absent husband could not be affected by the verdict in the case where his wife was tendered

(c) 2 Al, 533—Tait Ev 372

(d) Wilson 1826 Syme 40—Clark and Greig 1842, 1 Broun 250—Law and Others 1817 (not rep), noted in 2 Al 533—Burnett, 607—See also Fagan v M'Kenzie, 1819, 1 Shaw, 261—M'Manus, 1833 Bell's Notes, 251—*Contra*, Hutchison and Others 1814, 2 Hume, 347, Burnett *supra* where the wife of one of several prisoners was adduced for the Crown without objection, the questions put to her relating chiefly to the guilt of the other prisoners In Smith and Brodie 1768, 2 Hume 349 the Court were understood to be of opinion that while the wife of one of two prisoners could not be allowed to give evidence against her husband she was a competent witness against another panel tried along with him on the same indictment In a subsequent case, however (Gavin v Montgomerie, 1830 9 S 217 note), great doubt was expressed from the Bench as to the authority of this case, and it has been said to be erroneous Todd, 1835 Bell's Notes 251 It is challenged by Mr Burnett p 607

(e) Todd 1835 Bell's Notes 251 (f) Clark and Greig 1842 1 Broun, 250

§ 1787 Again, a witness, inadmissible on the ground of agency for one of several prisoners, was rejected as to them all (*g*) And where witnesses tendered for one of the panels to prove an *alibi* were challenged as having been tampered with by persons acting under his authority, the Court "expressed a unanimous opinion that if the witnesses had been inadmissible for him, they could not have been examined for the other panels" (*h*)

§ 1788 It follows from this rule, that if one of several prisoners indicted on the same charge wishes to adduce his fellow-prisoner's wife (or any witness inadmissible for a fellow-prisoner), he ought to apply to the Court to have the trials separated (*i*) ,—a motion which will not likely be refused So if, in the course of a trial of several prisoners, a Crown witness is objected to on a ground which directly applies only to one of them the prosecutor may abandon the case as regards that prisoner, and proceed with it against the others (*k*) If the objection is known to the prosecutor before the trial begins, he may try the prisoners separately, and adduce the witness against the prisoner to whom the objection does not apply

§ 1789 In civil cases Lord Kilkerran lays down, that ' where more persons pursue or are pursued *super eodem medio concludendi*, an objection made to a witness of any one of the defenders is likewise sustained to cast him from being a witness for any of the rest ' (*l*) Accordingly, the relations of one of the parties have repeatedly been excluded as to all the others who were interested along with him on the matter in issue (*m*) Nor was the objection removed by the name of the pursuer, to whom the witness was related, being withdrawn before the trial commenced , because he remained liable with the others for the expenses incurred during his compearance (*n*) But where a witness is incompetent as regards one of several defenders, the pursuer may consent to decree of absolvitor in favour of that defender, and adduce the witness against the others, provided the instance as against them would be good

---

(*g*) O Neills, 1801, Burnett, 607 , 2 Al , 535 (*h*) Hunter and Others, 1838 2 Swin , 1 , Bell's Notes, 267, S C —*Supra*, § 1711 (*i*) M'Manus, 1833 Bell's Notes, 251—See *supra*, § 1699 (*k*) Rutherford, 1838, Bell's Notes 251—Fagan *v* Mackenzie, 1849, J Shaw, 261 (*l*) Gray *v* ———, and Barony of Tillibole *v* ———, 1752, both reported in M 16,761 (*m*) Gray and Barony of Tillibole, *supra*—Erskine *v* Robertson, 1684 M , 16 692—Hunter *v* Robb, 1766, M , 16,769—Angus *v* Mag of Edinburgh 1827, 1 Mur , 341 (*n*) Angus *v* Mag of Edinburgh *supra*

§ 1790. A point of some nicety on this head occurred in an action of reduction-improbation raised by Miss Gavin, of a bill bearing to be drawn by Crawford on, and accepted by her and to be indorsed by Crawford to Montgomerie, the action being laid against both Crawford and Montgomerie, on the ground of fraud and forgery of Miss Gavin's signature. Crawford gave in defences, stating that his pretended signatures were also forged, and consenting to decree of reduction, which however Miss Gavin did not take against him. The case having then proceeded to trial, on a record between Miss Gavin and the trustee on Montgomerie's bankrupt estate who denied the forgery, Crawford's wife was held admissible as a witness for Miss Gavin on the ground that as any interest which Crawford might have had was against that party, and as the verdict could not be used in his favour in any subsequent proceedings he would have been admissible, and consequently there was no reason for excluding his wife (*o*). This case, it will be observed, occurred before the statute admitting party-witnesses was passed, and therefore the Court must have regarded Crawford as in effect not a party to the cause although, in point of form, his name still appeared on record.

It has already been seen how far improper proceedings by persons for whom one of the prosecutors is responsible will render witnesses incompetent in criminal trials at the joint instance of the Crown and a private prosecutor (*p*).

CHAPTER XVII.—OF ADMITTING EXCEPTIONAL WITNESSES WHERE THERE IS *PENURIA TESTIUM*.

§ 1791. The exclusionary rules of the old law were relaxed where the only evidence of which the case admitted was of a kind generally incompetent (*a*). Under this rule the near relations and servants of a party were admitted, *cum nota* to prove facts which

---

(*o*) Gavin *v.* Montgomerie, 1830, 9 S. 213. With this case compare Rankin *v.* Dickson, 1847, 9 D. 1048—Chalmers *v.* Borthwick, 1848, 10 ib. 1544, 1570.

(*p*) See *supra*, §§ 1736, 1744.

(*a*) The rules on this point will be found in Stair, 4, 43, 8—Ersk. 4, 2, 26, 7—Tait Ev. 373 *et seq.* As to the effect of *penuria testium* on the admissibility of judges see *infra*, § 1831.

occurred in his family, as better evidence of them could not be expected In one case, even the wife of a party charged with murder was admitted as a witness for him, to prove a fact which, from its occult nature, was not likely to admit of better evidence (b) And as already seen, the law-agent of a party could be adduced to prove the execution and delivery of deeds which he had prepared or attested and other matters upon which he was a necessary witness (c) This is also the ground upon which the oath *in litem* (d), and the oath in supplement (e), are admitted

§ 1792 This principle was necessary in order to prevent injustice in cases where, if such exceptional evidence had not been competent, the discovery of truth would have been often defeated It demonstrated the erroneousness of the exclusionary system for if a witness of doubtful credibility was justly received leaving his credibility to the jury, when his trustworthiness could not be tested by other evidence, what good reason could there be for excluding him in other cases where falsehood was much less likely to escape detection, and, consequently, less likely to be attempted (f)?

A detailed notice of the rules as to *penuria testium* is now unnecessary, as they had reference to a system of evidence which modern legislation has almost entirely abolished [1]

(b) Christie, 1831, noted *supra*, § 1715 (c) *Supra*, § 1731

(d) *Supra* §§ 1506, 1510 (e) *Supra* § 1515, *et seq*

(f) Lord Cockburn observed in Murray *v* Sinclair, 1847, 9 D, 598 'With regard to *penuria testium*, I always thought it a good reason for excluding a baddish witness that there was no other person who could speak to the facts, giving him thus an opportunity of saying what he liked without fear of contradiction '

[1] In H M Adv *v* Smith and Campbell, 1875, 2 Irv 40, a witness, whose name was not included in the list of witnesses, either for the prosecution or the defence, was examined at the desire of the Court, his evidence being considered necessary to explain certain delusions under which the panel was said to labour

TITLE II.

OF OBJECTIONS TO THE CREDIBILITY OF WITNESSES

§ 1793 Many circumstances in the situation and character of a witness and his connection with the cause or with the parties, although they would not be good grounds for excluding him, may materially impair his credibility These considerations are for the jury in weighing the evidence By estimating the probable strength of the biassing influence, and observing the manner of the witness when under examination, the intrinsic probability and consistency (or the reverse) of his statements, and their corroboration or contradiction by the rest of the proof, an intelligent jury will usually form a correct opinion how far such evidence is credible.

§ 1794 As to impugning the character of a witness an important distinction exists in Scotland between doing so on the ground that he has committed a specified crime, and alleging generally that he is disreputable and unworthy of credit

At a time when the *infamia juris* consequent upon conviction for the more heinous crimes was a ground of exclusion, conviction of the witness for slighter offences which indicated a disregard of truth or honesty, might be proved as affecting his credibility (*a*) This is now the rule also as to the crimes which formerly disqualified infamy being no longer a ground of exclusion (*b*) But when the offence pointed at does not indicate either disregard of truth or general depravity of character (*e g*, a breach of the peace, trifling assault, and most police offences), the Court are in the practice of stopping inquiry regarding it, as being irrelevant

(*a*) 2 Hume 354—2 Al 440—Tait Ev, 346, 402—Donald, 1831 Bell's Notes, 250—Thomson and Martin, 1832, 1 Broun, 413

(*b*) 15 Vict, c 27, § 1—*Supra* § 1778

§ 1795 If the witness has not been convicted of the alleged offence, the party may not lead proof of it in order to impair his credibility, because a person ought not thus to be put on his trial incidentally when he could not be prepared with a defence and because, in general, the party who states the objection has no title to prosecute for the crime Besides, if such an inquiry were competent, there might often be several incidental trials of witnesses in the course of the trial in which they are tendered, the consequence of which would not only be to produce confusion and delay, but also to disturb the attention of the jury in judging of the case before them, thereby producing the risk of an erroneous verdict (c)

§ 1796 But it is competent to ask any witness if he has committed a crime which affects his credibility, whether he has been tried for it or not the witness, however, being entitled to decline to answer the question (d) This point was deliberately settled in the trial of Burke and Macdowall for murder, where the counsel for the prisoners were allowed to ask Hare (who was tendered as a *socius criminis*) whether he had been engaged in any other murders besides the one then before the jury, the Court, however, warning him that he had right to decline answering (e) Since that decision, witnesses have repeatedly been asked whether they had committed perjury (*f*), theft (*g*), and other crimes affecting their credibility, and in one case a witness was asked whether he had been engaged in lifting dead bodies, that being supposed to indicate a desperate and degraded character (*h*)

§ 1797 Where a witness had given a negative answer to a question of this kind, it was held incompetent to interrogate him upon specific facts, with the view of inferring his guilt, for that is an underhand way of criminating him (*i*) Nor is a party entitled to ask an adverse witness if when he gave evidence on a previous trial the presiding judge expressed an opinion that he had perjured himself (*j*) But a witness may be asked whether, at the time of

(*c*) 2 Hume 358—Burnett 397—2 Al, 445—Macl Pr 162—Tait Ev 346 182—and cases cited in these works (*d*) Tait Ev, 428—2 Al 527—Bell's Notes 255-6 (*e*) Burke and Macdowall, 1828, Syme 361

(*f*) Pendar, 1836 1 Swin 25—Bell's Notes, 255—Brown and Others *infra* (*j*)

(*g*) Miller 1837 1 Swin 189 See also Blair, 1844 2 Broun 167

(*h*) Ferguson and Others 1829 (not reported) 1 Al, 216, and 2 ib 527

(*i*) Miller 1837 1 Swin 189 (*j*) Pendar 1836 1 Swin 25 Bell's Notes, 255, S C But see Brown and Others Bell's Notes, ib where a question of this nature was put without objection

examination he stands indicted for a crime (k). This, indeed, is more fair to the witness than to ask whether he committed the offence and leave him to decline answering, because his declinature might prejudice him in his own trial. A witness is bound to answer whether he has been convicted of a specified crime (l).

§ 1798 It is also competent, with the view of discrediting a witness to ask him whether he committed an offence which, although not indictable, manifests a want of truthfulness. Thus, in an action of divorce for adultery, where the pursuer adduced a former servant of the defender, the latter was allowed to ask her in cross-examination whether "she had been frequently found fault with, by various persons in whose service she was, for listening at doors and windows and telling lying stories,"—it being explained to the witness that she was entitled to decline answering (m).

§ 1799 But while the credibility of a witness may be impugned on the specific grounds thus noticed, it is firmly established in this country that (except in one class of cases) the party against whom a witness is adduced may not assail his character by alleging or proving generally that he is a dissolute and base person or one who cannot be believed on his oath (n). The reason is, that a sweeping and summary impeachment of a witness on such grounds would be unfair, not only to the party adducing him, who is not likely to be prepared with evidence to meet such aspersions, but also to the witness, as it might seriously injure his character, without his having had any warning of the challenge, or any opportunity to vindicate himself. Moreover, such investigations would burden and prolong the trial, while they would seldom aid in discovering the truth, owing to the rashness and lubricity usually exhibited in such general evidence, and to the wide field which they would open to the indulgence of bad passions.

§ 1800 The only exceptions to this rule are prosecutions for rape and assault with intent to ravish. It is the constant practice

(k) Hannah and Higgins, 1836 Bell's Notes, 256 (l) Johnston, 1845 2 Broun, 401 (m) King v King, 1842, 4 D 590

(n) 2 Hume 352—2 Al 527—Tait Ev 402—Bell's Notes, 251—E Fife v E Fife's Tr, 1816, 1 Mur, 131—Baillie v Bryson 1818, ib 319 332—Wight, 1836, 1 Swin 47. The rule in the text was applied in regard to two witnesses who were respectively nine and twelve years old, the Court refusing to allow a subsequent witness to be asked whether from her knowledge of them she could place any reliance on their recollection of stories" or "whether they were veracious boys," Galloway, 1836, 1 Swin, 232, Bell's Notes 254 S C

in criminal trials for such offences to allow a full investigation as to the character for chastity of the alleged sufferer, because proof that she is unchaste is circumstantial evidence to rebut the charge while so much depends on the truth of her statements, and there is so great risk of her story having been concocted in a fit of jealousy or with the view of extorting money, or covering her shame when discovered in a voluntary connection that a full inquiry into her character is requisite to enable the jury to estimate her credibility

The authorities on this point are cited in a previous chapter (*o*), where the competency of proving the woman's character in civil actions laid on seduction, and kindred cases is also noticed (*p*)

§ 1801 It has been held that in a trial for forgery of a bill, the witness whose name was alleged to have been forged might be asked whether he was in embarrassed circumstances, and that he was not entitled to decline answering the question, as it involved merely his mercantile credit, and not his general character (*r*)

§ 1802 The law of England differs widely from our system as to challenging the character of a witness, for, while it does not allow a party against whom the witness is adduced to prove particular facts or transactions which tend to discredit him, it admits proof that the general character of the witness is such that he is unworthy of belief when on his oath The reason is, that, although one cannot be expected to be prepared with evidence to rebut specific charges (the proof of which also involves a collateral issue), it is likely that every respectable man will be able to support his general character when it is attacked

§ 1803 The credibility of a witness is often impaired by circumstances which tend to bias him in the particular cause, or which indicate a leaning to favour one of the parties Each case of this kind must be determined by its own circumstances, nor can any precise rules be laid down upon the subject It has been well observed that, "generally, any feeling or purpose in the mind, from whatever motive, which may dictate false or prompt exaggerated and highly coloured statements in the cause, and so render reliance on the purity of the evidence either unsafe or questionable is material to be known, and may affect the credibility of the witness" (*s*)

(*o*) *Supra*, §§ 23 29 (*p*) *Supra*, §§ 23, 26, 27 (*r*) Pender 1836, 1 Swin, 25 Bell's Notes, 258 S C (*s*) Per L Just -Clerk Hope in King v King 1841 1 D 128

§ 1804. The case in which these observations were made, is a good illustration of the general doctrine. It was an action of divorce for adultery, where the credibility of a witness for the pursuer was impugned on the ground of malice to the alleged paramour, and the Court allowed the objection to be proved, because if such malice existed the witness had a bias to criminate the alleged paramour and, as a consequence, to prejudice the defender.

As already observed, the old objections of relationship, interest and agency and partial counsel, although no longer existing as grounds of exclusion, remain in so far as they may affect the credibility of the witnesses who are subject to them (*t*) and, of course, the credibility of party-witnesses is still more open to question (*u*).

§ 1805. Nothing is so fatal to the credibility of a witness as contradictions in his statements to the jury; for while other objections are founded on the probability of his emitting false or partial testimony, in this case his untrustworthiness is proved out of his own mouth. At the same time, evidence so tainted ought not to be cast aside under the old maxim *falsum in uno falsum in omnibus*, for perjury seldom or never extends over the whole statements of a witness and the contradictions may have arisen from thoughtlessness rather than from an intention to deceive. It often happens, also, that the motive to falsehood is limited to one branch of the case, as where the witness desires to favour one of several prisoners, or to prevent some bad consequence to himself; while (as already noticed) he may have attempted, by pretending bribery or malice, atheism, or some other ground of exclusion, to escape from giving evidence against a friend. It is peculiarly the province of the jury to examine and weigh such evidence. No doubt the presence of a single falsehood taints the whole of the witness' statement; yet if parts of it appear to be emitted with candour, if they are beyond the scope of the biassing influence, and if they are probable in themselves, or are corroborated, they ought to receive from the jury that effect which they produce in an intelligent mind. This is the view which a late eminent judge, remarkable for his knowledge of human character and his almost intuitive perception of truth, used to take even in cases where falsehood was so manifest that the witness was committed on the spot on a charge of perjury (*x*). It is

(*t*) 15 Vict. c. 27, § 1.—See *supra*, §§ 1728-9, 1732, 3, 1781.

(*u*) See *supra*, § 1713.

(*x*) In M'Ghie and Others, 1832, the short note of the case preserved in Bell's Notes

still more appropriate in the common case of a witness prevaricating or giving evasive answers, for the skilful and sifting examination to which such a witness is subjected from the Bar and the Bench seldom fails to extract more truth than falsehood from him

§ 1806 It used to be incompetent to prove, either by the examination of the witness himself, or by other evidence, that he had previously made a different statement from that admitted by him in the witness-box (*y*) The reason for this rule was, that what a witness states on oath ought not to be contradicted by hearsay of loose statements which he has made without that solemn sanction and that if one party were allowed to discredit the deposition by proving such contradictory statements, the opposite party should be allowed to prove other statements by which the deposition might be corroborated, whereby much loose hearsay proof would be introduced on both sides of the case A recent statute abolished this old rule, and enacted, that "it shall be competent to examine any witness who may be adduced in any action or proceeding, as to whether he has, on any specified occasion, made a statement on any matter pertinent to the issue differing from the evidence given by him in such action or proceeding, and it shall be competent in the course of such action or proceeding to adduce evidence to prove that such witness has made such different statement on the occasion specified" (*z*) There can be little doubt of the justice of this new rule, which proceeds on the principle that a witness who has previously made statements contradictory of his deposition is not so worthy of credit as one whose statements have been consistent

§ 1807 By limiting the inquiry to a 'specified occasion,' the statute prevents witnesses from being annoyed by such examina-

---

256, bears, that Lord Justice-General Boyle (then Lord Justice-Clerk) observed to the jury, "I do not say that their committal (on a charge of perjury) excludes the evidence of these two women, but only that the jury must attend to the matter contained in their depositions, and the manner in which it was delivered" And in Hepburn, 1836, Bell's Notes, ib, it is said that his Lordship "held that the correct course for the jury to pursue in judging of the evidence of the witness, which was opposed to that of others in the case, was to recollect the whole of his demeanour and the way in which he delivered his testimony, and then to determine which was to be believed" The view taken in these cases is more correct than that adopted in Muir, 1793, 2 Hume, 378, and separate report, p 62, 3, where, on a witness for the prisoner having prevaricated in his initial examination, the Court committed him to prison without examining him *in causa*

(*y*) 2 Hume, 481, 409, note—Burnett, 463—2 Al, 522—Tait Ev 403—Compared with Mills, 1841, 2 Broun 275 where the previous statements of the witness were proved as part of the *res gestæ* (*z*) 15 Vict, c 27 § 3 See *supra* § 101

tions, where there is no ground for supposing that their statements have been contradictory.[1] The statute also requires the witness to be cross-examined on the point, before other evidence upon it is adduced, because apparent contradictions in a person's statements often arise from the individual to whom they were addressed having misunderstood or misremembered them; and justice both to the witness and to the party who adduces him, requires that he should have an opportunity to explain himself.[2]

§ 1808. There is no limitation as to the nature of the previous occasions on which the inconsistent statements are supposed to have been made. If, however, they were made on oath, the witness may decline answering whether he emitted them, as such a question involves a charge of perjury (a).[3] But whether he declines or gives a negative answer, the party against whom he is adduced may prove the statements founded on. Nor is there an exception of previous statements made by the witness on precognition. But the Court would likely discourage a lengthened inquiry as to such statements, otherwise the solemn deposition of a witness might, in

(a) See sections on witnesses declining to answer questions which tend to criminate them, *infra*, § 2016 *et seq.*

[1] See as to construction of the words in the statute "a specified occasion," H. M. Adv. v. Wilson, 1861, 4 Irv. 46. The case was special.

[2] In Ross v. Fraser, 1863, 1 Macph., 783, Lord Cowan observed, that where in a case of filiation it was proposed to contradict the principal witness by other evidence to be afterwards led upon matters which, if true, she must be acquainted with, it was only fair and just that she should be cross-examined upon the points on which it was proposed to contradict her. Where, however, evidence comes out suddenly and unawares tending to affect the credibility of a previous witness (as, for instance, evidence of malicious feeling), it is not incompetent to receive the evidence although the previous witness was not examined on the matter, Robertson v. Mackenzie, 1856, 2 Irv., 411. The 4th section of the Evidence Act, 15 Vict., c. 27, provides for such a case by allowing the judge to recall the previous witness.

[3] An action was raised by the trustee on a sequestrated estate for reduction of an assignation granted by the bankrupt before his sequestration. After the adjustment of issues the defender moved the Court for a diligence to recover the deposition emitted at his examination by the bankrupt. The Court granted the diligence on the ground that it was possible that the deposition might be used as evidence in the case. "If the bankrupt is examined as a witness, and gives an account of the transaction referred to in the action different from what he gave in his examination under the Bankrupt Act, the defender's counsel would be entitled to ask whether he had not given a different account of the matter on that occasion; and if the bankrupt did not answer that question honestly, it would then be competent to adduce evidence to prove that he had made such a statement. Now the proper evidence of that, because the best, is the authentic statutory record of what he said," *per* Lord Justice-Clerk (Inglis), Emslie v. Alexander, 1862, 1 Macph., 209.

effect, be contradicted by proving what an unscrupulous agent extracted from him by leading questions, suggested answers, and other unfair devices in precognition [4]

§ 1809 In the great majority of cases, the credibility of witnesses is impugned by the party against whom they are adduced But a party is sometimes disappointed by finding that his own witness gives evidence against him; and the question therefore arises, whether one can discredit a witness adduced by himself There is very little authority on this point in Scotch law In England it is settled that a party may not impeach the credibility of his own witness by general evidence tending to show that he is not worthy of belief (*b*) The reason is, that the party by adducing the witness represents him to the Court as deserving credit, and to allow him thereafter to attack the general character of the witness for veracity would enable a party to maintain the credibility of the witness if he spoke in his favour, and to destroy his credit if he gave unfavourable evidence the party having thus the means of injuring the character of the witness if the evidence was not satisfactory to him (*c*) It would seem that this rule does not apply in England to witnesses whom the law obliges the party to call (as, for example, the subscribing witness to a deed) because such witnesses are not of the party's own selection (*d*) Nor does it exclude a party from showing, by other evidence, that statements

(*b*) Bull, Nisi Pr, 297—2 Phil, 448—1 Greenleaf, § 442—Taylor, 948—Best Pr of Ev, § 615 (*c*) Authorities in preceding note (*d*) Taylor, 949—1 Greenl, § 443

[4] It has been held incompetent, under the Evidence Act, 15 and 16 Vict, c 27, § 3 to prove that a witness had, when examined on precognition by a procurator fiscal, made a statement different from that given by him in the witness-box In a criminal trial a prisoner's counsel stated that he proposed to ask a witness whether he had said on precognition that a different person had inflicted the wound (the case being one of stabbing under 10 Geo IV c 38) and that he afterwards proposed to examine the procurator fiscal so as to contradict the witness Lord Justice Clerk Hope held the evidence inadmissible under the section of the act H M Adv v O Donnel, 1855, 2 Irv, 236 In Emslie v Alexander, 1862, 1 Macph 209, Lord Neaves observed that he wished to guard against giving countenance to the opinion that under the 3d section of the Evidence Act of 1852, it was competent to lead evidence of a witness's precognition His own impression was, that it was not competent to contradict a witness by proof of what he said on precognition The Lord Justice Clerk (Inglis) added, that he had rejected such evidence in criminal cases But as it was competent before the Evidence Act to ask a witness whether he had on precognition made a different statement, the case of O Donnel where the question to the witness was not allowed to be put, seems to go further than

made by his own witness are untrue or erroneous, although he may thereby discredit his witness collaterally for a witness does not represent the party who adduces him (e)[5]

§ 1810 Bankton (who frequently founded his opinions upon the analogous rules of English law) lays down "As to the question how far one can insist in a reprobator against the witnesses produced by himself, it is very plain that, regularly, he cannot upon grounds that were competent and known to him at the time of the citation or examination, but if such witnesses have taken bribes from the other party, and which, at the time of examining them was unknown to the producer, I do not see why he may not reprobate their testimonies on that ground, or in any such case' (f)

(e) 2 Phill, 448—1 Greenl, § 443—Taylor 949—Best's Pr of Ev, 615
(f) Bankt iv 31, 6 See also Macf Pr, 164—Burnett, 465 note

[5] The English Common Law Procedure Act, 1854 17 and 18 Vict c 125, provides by § 22, that a party producing a witness shall not be allowed to impeach his credit by general evidence of bad character, but he may, in case the witness shall, in the opinion of the judge, *prove adverse*, contradict him by other evidence, and, by leave of the judge, prove that he has made at other times a statement inconsistent with his present testimony, but before such last mentioned proof can be given, the circumstances of the supposed statement, sufficient to designate the particular occasion, must be mentioned to the witness, and he must be asked whether or not he has made such statement Section 23 provides, further, that if a witness upon cross-examination as to a former statement made by him relative to the subject-matter of the cause, and inconsistent with his present testimony, does not distinctly admit that he has made such statement, proof may be given that he did in fact make it but before such proof can be given, the circumstances of the supposed statement, sufficient to designate the particular occasion, must be mentioned to the witness, and he must be asked whether or not he has made such statement In Dear v Knight, 1859, 1 F and F, 433 the defender proposed to examine one of his witnesses to show that he had, at a previous time, made a statement inconsistent with the evidence he had then given It was objected that it must be first shewn that the witness was adverse but Justice Erle remarked, that he was prepared to hold the witness adverse *quoad* the particular statement —holding probably, that the words "an adverse witness" meant a witness who had given unfavourable evidence, though he had not shown a hostile mind But the Court of Queen s Bench has held that to be ' adverse' within the meaning of the section, so as to entitle the party calling him to prove that he has made, at another time a statement inconsistent with his present testimony, such witness must be, in the opinion of the judge, 'hostile,' Greenough v Eccles, 1859, 28 L J C P 160 It is not necessary that the statements should be directly or absolutely at variance Jackson v Thomson 1861, 31 L J Q B, 11 Where a party is tendered as a witness for examination, but not examined in chief he cannot be cross examined to discredit him, Bracegirdle v Bailey, 1859 1 F and F, 536 The 24th section of the act provides for the cross-examination of a witness as to previous statements made by him in writing, see Smith v Prickett, 1861 7 Jur N S 610—Sladden v Sergeant 1858 1 F and F 322

This seems to be a just distinction, for while it is improper to leave it in the power of a party to discredit his witness or not, upon grounds known to him when the witness was tendered, there is no good reason why one who has been deceived or betrayed by a witness, whom he believed to be credible, should be prevented from laying before the jury circumstances, *noviter venientes ad notitiam*, which will prevent them from forming an erroneous estimate of the witness' credibility

§ 1811 Whatever may be said upon this point, it is plain that a party who adduces an unwilling witness may use a rigid examination in order to extort from him answers which he attempts to withhold, although by such a proceeding the candour and impartiality of the witness are impugned (*g*) Examinations of this kind are frequently required in criminal cases, when the Crown has to adduce the friends and relations of the prisoner They are also allowed in civil cases where witnesses exhibit reluctance to answer Thus in an action of damages for illegal use of diligence, the pursuer, when examining in chief the messenger by whom the diligence had been executed, peremptorily called on him to give an explicit answer to a question, whereupon the defender objected to that mode of examination, but the Lord Chief-Commissioner repelled the objection, and observed, "If this was not a person who had been employed by you, and if he had not shown him a very unwilling witness, I would have checked this style of examining A party cannot discredit his own witness, but if a witness turn out adverse and unwilling to speak the truth, justice may require a relaxation of this rule" (*h*) In another case, where the counsel for a party examining one of his own witnesses insisted that he should answer a question, otherwise he would move the Court to send him to prison whereupon the opposite party objected, the Lord Chief-Commissioner refused to interfere, observing "I feel a difficulty in allowing you in this manner to discredit your own witness . It is a very delicate matter to allow a party to discredit his own witness, but an unwilling witness must be treated in some respects as one from the enemy's camp" (*i*)

§ 1812 It is also competent in this country, as in England (*k*), for a party to shew that statements made by one of his own witnesses are untrue, although he may not be entitled either to attack

(*g*) See M'af Pr, *supra*—Burnett *supra* (*h*) Manuel v Fraser 1818 1 Mur, 390 (*i*) Smith v Fuller, 1820, 2 Mur, 346

(*k*) See *supra* § 1809

the credibility of the witness on any general ground, or to plead that he was inadmissible (*l*)

§ 1813 Where a party avails himself of his right to adduce his opponent, the Court will not interfere to prevent him either from forcing out answers which the witness would fain withhold, or from freely criticising the statements of the witness as emitted by one who is peculiarly subject to bias against the adducer

---

(*l*) See Keddie *v* Christie, 1848 11 D. 150, per Lord Mackenzie (*primus*)

TITLE III.

OF STATING AND PROVING OBJECTIONS TO WITNESSES

Several of the rules as to stating and proving objections to witnesses have been noticed in the two preceding titles These points will now be treated in connection

---

CHAPTER I —OF THE TIME FOR STATING AND PROVING OBJECTIONS TO WITNESSES

§ 1814 In both civil and criminal cases, the proper time for objecting to the admissibility of a witness is, when he appears in Court and before he is sworn (*a*) It is incompetent to state objections of this kind after the examination *in causa* has commenced, for a party is not entitled to keep up his objection until he shall have seen whether the witness is favourable or adverse to him (*b*) An exception, however, exists in regard to the husband or wife of a party in cases where their evidence is still inadmissible, for it is *pars judicis* to stop the examination of such witnesses at whatever stage the fact of marriage appears (*c*)

(*a*) 2 Hume 376—2 Al, 429—Macl Prac, 130—Tait Ev, 398

(*b*) Robertson v D Athol, 10th Feb 1810 F C—Elder v Jack 1827 5 S, 791 Adams and Reid 1828 2 Hume 376 —Forrester v Forrester, 1837, 15 S 690 Wilson v Glasgow and S Western Railway 1851 14 D, 2 (*c*) In Bannerman v In Cro, 1832, 5 Dea and And, 375 the Court ordered the deposition of a party's wif

Where an objection to admissibility is meant to be proved from the initial examination of the witness, it is, of course, not necessary to state it before the oath is administered But an objection which goes to the administration of the oath, *e g* when the witness is said to be an atheist, must be stated before he is sworn

§ 1815 Commissions to take depositions to lie *in retentis* are granted under express or implied reservation of all lawful objections to the evidence, and therefore the proper time for objecting to the competency of witnesses so examined is when their depositions are tendered at the trial, or when they are founded on in evidence, if the whole proof is on commission (*d*) For the same reason objections to parts of the deposition may be stated when the clerk of court is reading it to the jury (*e*)

§ 1816 In proofs on commission, and proofs before the Sheriff in his ordinary civil court, objections to the admissibility of witnesses should be stated at the same stage as when the witness is adduced before a jury But if the party is not then prepared to prove his objection, he may keep matters open by protesting for reprobators, and a reprobatory proof is sometimes allowed, although it has not been protested for The rules on these points are noticed afterwards (*f*)

§ 1817 A reprobatory proof is evidently incompetent in jury trials as in them the diets are peremptory and the functions of the jury cease on their verdict being returned (*g*) Accordingly, objections to witnesses in such cases can only be determined upon the proof led at the time There may, however, be cases in which great injustice would arise from enforcing this rule. Baron Hume considers that there is difficulty as to whether it should not be relaxed where the ground of objection amounts to a fundamental vice in the process and an imposition on all concerned He observes, 'Put the case (if such a thing could happen) that some one personates a witness, and is examined instead of him It may at

---

which had been taken on commission without objection to be deleted from the proof This was also done as to the deposition of a party's nephew when so near a relative was inadmissible, Brown *v* M'Kie, 1801 Hume D, 896 (*d*) A S, 16th Feb 1841 § 17—Macf Pr, 188—Paul *v* Old Shipping Coy 1816 1 Mur 68—Downie *v* Burgan & Co 1817 ib, 221—Hunter and Dodds 1832 10 S 833—Paul *v* Commercial Ins Co 1832, ib 496—See also *supra* § 1361, and chapter on taking depositions to lie *in retentis infra* (*e*) A S, *supra*—Haddoway *v* Goddard, 1816, 1 Mur, 151—Morgan *v* Hunter 1817, ib, 258—and see authorities in preceding note

(*f*) See *infra* § 1829 (*g*) Per L Cringletie in Mackay *v* M'Leods 1827 4 Mur, 283

least be plausibly maintained that, like a similar mistake in the case of a juryman, this is an absolute and incurable nullity of the whole trial" (h) The same view is taken by Mr Burnett (i) and Sir Archibald Alison (k) If this be sound law in criminal cases where the prisoner gets a list of the Crown witnesses fifteen days before his trial it seems to hold with at least as much force in civil jury trials, in which neither party knows what witnesses are to be adduced against him until they appear in the witness-box, and where, consequently, a party who has a good objection to a witness is sometimes unable to prove it at the time Where there is reason to believe that the admission of a witness so situated has led to an erroneous verdict in favour of his adducer the Court will probably grant a new trial, as being "essential to the justice of the case" (l)

CHAPTER II —OF THE MODE OF PROVING OBJECTIONS TO WITNESSES

§ 1818 At one time every witness after being sworn, and before commencing to depone *in causa*, was examined *in initialibus* (a) In this examination he was "purged of malice and partial counsel," that is, he was asked whether he had been instructed what to depone, whether he had received any good deed or promise for what he was to say, and whether he bore malice to the party against whom he was adduced The witness had also to answer any other questions inferring objections to his admissibility (b) The initial examination does not now require to be applied to every witness but it is still competent, if required by the judge or commissioner taking the proof, or by the party against whom the witness is adduced (c) It is the most common but not the only, means of proving objections to witnesses Some objections, however, cannot be established by it

§ 1819 It is inappropriate where the objection is that the wit-

---

(h) 2 Hume, 376 (i) Burnett 455 (k) 2 Al., 430

(l) See 55 Geo III, c 42, § 6 compared with 13 & 14 Vict, c 36, § 15

(a) Stair, 4 43 11—Ersk., 4 2 28 9—Tait Ev., 399 (b) Ersk., 4 …; Tait Ev., 424—Macf Pr., 130, 160 (c) 3 & 4 Vict, c 59, § 2

ness cannot be sworn, *e.g.*, in consequence of nonage, insanity, or atheism. These objections have therefore to be established by other evidence. In the case of children, however, the procedure is similar: the child being exhibited in Court and examined in order to ascertain his fitness to give evidence.

The objection of insanity is proved by persons acquainted with the witness, and by medical evidence (*d*), and it may be apparent from the manner of the witness himself when put in the box. It is competent, also, to interrogate him in order to see if he is fit to be sworn (*e*). But after the prosecutor in a trial for rape had examined a medical witness, who deponed that the injured party was incapable of giving evidence (the object being to get in proof of a statement she had made to a neighbour *de recenti*), the Court would not allow the prosecutor to produce the girl herself, in order that they might judge whether she ought to be examined as a witness (*f*).

The proof as to a deaf and dumb person is the same as where the witness is said to be insane. Such a witness has been excluded upon a sworn interpreter stating that she could communicate with persons accustomed to her manner, but did not understand the nature of an oath, or the obligation to speak truth (*g*).

§ 1820. It has already been seen that the objection of atheism may be proved both from the mouth of the witness and by evidence of his declared opinions (*h*). The proper course seems to be to admit proof of his declarations, and then to examine him whether he believes in a Supreme Being who punishes vice. If his own statement, agreeing with the proof of his declaration, shows him to be an atheist, he will be excluded; whereas if he states that he is a believer, he may be put on oath and examined more fully as to his views upon religion, his admissibility being determined from the whole of the proof (*i*). As already observed, if the witness repudiates atheism it will be very difficult to cast him on account of his previously declared opinions (*j*).

§ 1821. The objection of infamy, when stated to the admissibility of a witness under the former law could (according to strict rule) be proved only by an extract of the conviction, with parole evidence to identify the witness as the person to whom it ap-

(*d*) See *supra* § 1683 *et seq*.

(*e*) Reg. *v.* Hill, noted *supra* § 1683 (*e*).

(*f*) M'Namara, 1848, Arkley, 521.

(*g*) White, 1842, 1 Broun, 228.

(*h*) *Supra*, § 1689.

(*i*) This was the course adopted in Henry, 1842, 1 Broun, 221; *supra* § 1689.

(*j*) See *supra ib.*

plied (*k*) As an objection to credibility, it may be proved either by an extract conviction, or by cross-examination of the witness himself (*l*) but not by parole from other witnesses (*m*)

Outlawry, like infamy under the former law, being an objection to admissibility, can only be proved by an extract of the sentence with at least one witness to identification (*n*)

§ 1822 The objection that the witness is the husband or wife of one of the parties may be proved by the initial examination, as well as by other evidence (*o*)

§ 1823 Bribery and tutoring are most commonly proved from the mouth of the witness, and when he admits facts relevant to exclude him, further evidence is seldom adduced on the point (*p*) Yet the party tendering him may prove that he attempts to exclude himself by a false admission (*r*) And if the witness denies the ground of objection other evidence may be adduced to prove it (*s*)

§ 1824 The objection of malice must be established by some evidence besides the initial examination, for either a cause for the alleged animosity, or overt acts to indicate it, must be proved independently of the witness (*t*) But witnesses have been cast upon their statements *in initialibus* (*u*) Mr Burnett considers that the witness's denial of deadly malice ought in general to exclude all farther proof on the point (*x*) This, however, is stated too broadly for, if the objection is well founded the witness is not likely, by an admission of his enmity, to deprive himself of the opportunity of gratifying it (*y*)

(*k*) 2 Hume 355–8 Al 443, 600–1 But this strict rule was not always enforced, see Scott *v* M'Gavin 1821 2 Mur 490—Smith 1829 1 De and And, 183—Liddell 1838 Bell's Notes 257

(*l*) Cases of Douglas 1830 Blackwood 1831, Watson 1831 Sweeny 1832, and Docherty, 1838 noted in Bell's Notes 255 Thomson 1842, and Henderson, 1838, ib 256 In Johnston, 1845 2 Broun 401 it was held that a witness is not entitled to decline answering whether he has been convicted of theft

(*m*) Thomson 1839, Bell's Notes 256—See also Blair, 1844 2 Broun 167

(*n*) Hunter, 1838 2 Swin, 181, Bell's Notes, 257 2 Al, 600-1 *supra*, (*k*)

(*o*) See *supra* § 1726

(*p*) See, for example Crichton *v* Fleming, 1840, 3 D 313—Fraser *v* L Lovat, 1841, ib, 1132—Farquharson *v* Anderson, 1800 M "Witness," Appx, No 2

(*r*) See Burnett 457—*Supra* § 1772, compared with §§ 1739, 1740

(*s*) Stair 4 43, 11—Ersk 4 2 28—Macl Pr 160—King *v* King 1841 4 D, 130—Mackay *v* M'Leods 1827, 1 Mur 279, 283 Kirk *v* Guthrie 1817, 1 Mur 272

(*t*) See *supra* § 1762, *et seq*

(*u*) M'Killop, 1831, Bell's Notes, 258 Hog, 1720 2 Hume 363

(*x*) Burnett, 414—See also Tait Ev 401

(*y*) In Ross *v* Jenn 1846 9 D, 12 n proof of enmity was allowed after the witness had denied having used malicious expressions But it was unsuccessful

§ 1825 Proof of enmity in a witness almost always includes evidence of malicious expressions which he has uttered, these being the ordinary indications of his feelings But evidence that the witness had stated he had been bribed or tutored is hearsay and inadmissible (z), except when tendered, under the recent Law of Evidence Amendment Act, to impugn his credibility after he has denied that he made the statement (a)

§ 1826 In proving enmity bribery, tutoring, and most other objections to witnesses, the practice is to commence by examining the witness himself In the case of enmity indeed his examination seems to be indispensable because, while other evidence can only show previous acts or expressions from which enmity may be inferred, he can himself swear directly to the present state of his feelings and besides, he ought to have an opportunity of explaining conduct or expressions which other witnesses may have misunderstood The general rule, therefore is that the party must examine the witness on this ground of objection, before leading other evidence of it (b) This, however, does not seem to be necessary where the objection admits of evidence equal in degree to that of the witness himself, as in the case of tutoring and bribery both of which may be proved by other persons who were present It has already been seen that previous statements made by the witness cannot be proved by other evidence, without first examining him regarding them (c)

(z) Donaldson v Stewart, 1842, D, 1215—See also Mackay v M'Leods, 1827 4, Mur, 281—*Supra* § 88

(a) See *supra*, § 1806 (b) In Clark and Greig 1842 1 Broun 250, where the credibility of a witness was challenged on the ground of enmity, the Justiciary Court refused to admit other evidence of the objection until the witness had been cross-examined upon it In King v King, 1841, 4 D, 130 (noted *supra* § 1774), where the objection was enmity, Lord Justice-Clerk Hope observed, that in some cases objections to the credibility of witnesses may be proved by other evidence, the party who adduced the witness being entitled to recall him whereas in other cases, the party stating the objection must examine the witness— And why? Because the witness' own explanation of his feelings and intentions is most material, and the whole case would not be raised if these were not brought out Now in the common and larger class of cases there is no option as to putting the matters on which the objection to credibility is to raised to the witness You must examine him on them, and then if he fails you other evidence is admissible This view is in accordance with the opinion of the twelve judges in the Queen's Case where the credit of a witness was impugned on the ground that he had endeavoured to procure persons corruptly to give evidence on the same side, and the judges thought that other evidence of the fact was inadmissible without first cross-examining the witness upon it, Queen's Case, 1820, 2 Brod and Bing 311 And the law is so stated as to other objections in 2 Phill, 435—Taylor, 981

(c) *Supra*, § 1806–7

§ 1827 Any objection to a witness may be proved by the oath on reference of the party who adduces him (*d*), and, under the recent Evidence Act the party may, in most cases, adduce himself, or be examined by his opponent, as a witness to prove such objections (*e*)

CHAPTER III —OF REPROBATORS

§ 1828 A reprobator is a proof which a party against whom a witness has been examined adduces afterwards in support of an objection which he was not prepared to prove at the time of examination

Under the old system of proofs on commission a decree which had proceeded on incompetent testimony could be set aside in an action of reprobator, but more frequently the decision in the principal cause was postponed until the objection to the evidence had been investigated in an incidental reprobatory proof (*a*) Actions of reprobator are unknown in modern practice Incidental reprobators, also, are falling into desuetude, but are still competent, provided decree in the cause has not been pronounced (*b*) As already noticed, they are incompetent in jury trials (*c*)

§ 1829 Reprobators have generally been used for proving objections on which the witness had been examined *in initialibus* (*d*) They are competent, however, as to all other objections, either to admissibility (*e*), or to credibility (*f*) But a deposition on the merits of the cause cannot be contradicted by a reprobatory proof (*g*)

§ 1830 In general, it is necessary for the reprobator, if stated to admissibility, to be protested for before the witness begins to depone *in causa*, in order that the adducer may have an opportunity

---

(*d*) Stair, 4, 43 11 (*e*) See § 1704, *et seq* (*a*) Stair, 4, 16, 16 — Ersk, 4 2, 29—Tait Ev 399 (*b*) See Monro *v* Crawford, 1822, 2 S (new ed), 95—Innes *v* Innes, 1835, 13 S 1050, affd 2 Sh and M'L 417—Lowrie *v* Mercer 1840 2 D, 959—King *v* King, 1841, 4 D, 124 (*c*) See *supra* § 1817 (*d*) Stair 4, 1 15—Ib, 4, 12, 18, and 4, 16, 16

(*e*) Stair 4 43 11—Ersk, 4 2 29 (*f*) Innes *v* Innes *supra* Monro *v* Crawford, *supra*—King *v* King, *supra* (*g*) Stair, 4, 1 15 Ib, 4, 12, 18, and 4, 16, 17

of proving his case by other evidence, and because the opposite party is presumed to acquiesce in the examination, if he does not protest for reprobators (*h*) A protest is usually required at the time of examination, in order to entitle the party to a reprobatory proof of an objection to credibility (*i*) But the want of a protest will be overlooked if the objection is one which a party using proper vigilance might not have discovered in time to protest (*k*) A reprobator was also received without a previous protest where the party had been prevented by a storm from attending the proof (*l*) In older practice, the want of a protest was overlooked if decree had not been pronounced on the proof, and if other evidence open to the adducer had not been lost in the interval (*m*) Protests for reprobators require to specify the grounds of objection, general protests being incompetent (*n*)

§ 1831 The same proof is admissible to support a reprobator, as when the objection to the witness is verified at the time of examination (*o*)[1]

§ 1832 If the objection is to the witness' competency, proof of it in a reprobator will cause the deposition to be cast, but the adducer will be entitled to decree, if the rest of his evidence proves his case (*p*) If the objection is merely to the witness' credibility, proof of it will cause the deposition to be received *cum nota*

(*h*) Stair 4 1 45—Ib, 4, 43, 11—Ersk, 4, 2, 29—Tait Ev, 398—E Tweeddale v L Drummelzier 1676, 2 B Sup, 209—Irving v Irving, 1676, M, 12,112—Paip v Newton 1683, M 9012—Glass v Christison, 15th May 1819, F C In Monro v Crawford, 1822 2 S (new ed), 95, where a witness after being purged of malice and partial counsel, was examined for Crawford, and then cross-examined for Monro both on matter affecting his credibility, and on the merits of the cause, and where Monro then protested for reprobators, but afterwards cited the witness on his own side the Court refused to allow Monro a reprobatory proof (*i*) Innes v Innes, 1835, 13 S, 1059, affd, 2 Sh and M L, 417—Monro v Crawford, *supra* (*k*) Stair 4, 43 11—Observed *per curiam* in Glass v Christison *supra*—Monteith v Henderson, 1677 2 B Sup 219—Milton v Milton, 1668, M, 12,104—Robison v White, 1635, M, 12,100, 1 B Sup, 209, S C—Compared with Innes v Innes *supra*

(*l*) Gooden v Murray 1700, M 12,118 (*m*) Ersk 4, 2, 29

(*n*) Wright v Din, 1737, M, 12,119—Lowrie v Mercer, 1840, 2 D 959, Note of Lord Moncreiff Ordinary (*o*) Ersk, 4 2, 29 (*p*) Stair 4, 46 15

[1] A witness, who was objected to as partial was examined *in initialibus*, and the objector protested for reprobator before his examination *in causa* It was held incompetent to adduce evidence of what the witness had said subsequent to his examination *in causa* Anderson v Gill, 1858, 20 D, 1326

TITLE IV

OF THE EXCLUSION OF WITNESSES ON THE GROUND OF JUDICIAL AND OFFICIAL SITUATION,—AND OF EVIDENCE EXCLUDED FROM REGARD TO THE PUBLIC SERVICE

— —

CHAPTER I.—OF THE EXCLUSION OF JUDGES ON MATTERS WHICH OCCURRED BEFORE THEM JUDICIALLY

§ 1833 Judges, like other members of the community must give evidence on matters which happened in their presence as ordinary observers (*a*) But there is considerable doubt whether judges of the Supreme Courts can be examined on matters which occurred before them judicially as parts of civil or criminal process (*b*)

§ 1834 The point arose so early as the year 1685, where, in an action to reduce a decree on the ground that the judges had been concussed into pronouncing it, the pursuer having tendered some of the judges to prove the concussing, and the defender having objected, the Lords "demurred" to their admissibility (*c*)

The question was again raised in 1821 in an action of damages for causing the pursuer to be tried for reset (*d*) The pursuer having called Lord Justice-Clerk Boyle who had presided at the criminal trial, the Lord Chief-Commissioner expressed a strong opinion against the competency of examining his Lordship on facts

(*a*) A judge may be examined as to a riot in court, per L. Ch.-Commissioner in Harper *v* Robinson 1821, 2 Mur 390—per Lord Moncreiff in Mackenzie *v* Wilson noted in Tait Ev, 393 (*b*) See on this point Tait Ev 392

(*c*) Gray *v* E Lauderdale 1685 M 16,497 16,501 (*d*) Harper *v* Robinson 1821 2 Mur 38[illegible]

which occurred before him judicially, when several other persons were present, but as both the witness and the party against whom he was adduced consented to the examination, the Court did not interfere His Lordship was accordingly examined as to what the defender had stated as a witness on the criminal trial, but objections were sustained to the questions, whether the Court had concurred in the propriety of abandoning the prosecution, and had made observations on the conduct of the party on whose complaint it had been brought A few years afterwards, a party was indicted before the High Court of Justiciary for perjury when deponing as a witness in a civil trial, and the names of two judges of the Supreme Court (Lords Justice-Clerk Boyle and Mackenzie), who had tried the case, were in the list of witnesses for the prosecutor, evidently with a view to their examination on the evidence which had been emitted before them On a motion by the pursuer for diligence to cite the witnesses, Lords Gillies, Moncreiff, and Medwyn, who formed the Court intimated strong opinions against the competency of such an examination where there is no *penuria testium*, Lord Moncreiff observing, that the consent of parties or of the judge himself would not remove the objection, for it is against the proper administration of justice" Their Lordships opinions, however, seem to infer that in a case of *penuria* the evidence would be received The Lord Justice-Clerk and Lord Mackenzie expressed their concurrence in these views, and the former stated that Lord Meadowbank entertained the same opinion The diet in the case was afterwards deserted, and the question therefore, did not arise either for debate or decision (*e*) In a subsequent case as to the competency of examining jurors, Lord Pitmilly observed, *obiter*, that a judge of the Supreme Court "is not to be called on or permitted to give evidence" (*f*).

The ground of these opinions is, that "the dignity and success of the administration of justice require the exclusion," as it would prove prejudicial to the administration of justice, if the judge were to be cross-examined and to be contradicted by other evidence (*g*)

§ 1835 But there are cases of an opposite tendency In an incidental proving of the tenor of a bond, which was alleged to have been lost in the office of one of the clerks of court, pending

(*e*) Muckarsie *v* Wilson 24th Feb 1824 (not reported) The opinions are given in Bell's Notes, 99 and Tait Ev 393 (*f*) Stewart *v* Fraser, 1830, 5 Mur, 188

(*g*) Per L Ch-Commissioner in Harper *v* Robinson, 2 Mur, 385—and per Lord Pitmilly in Stewart *v* Fraser 5 ib 188

proceedings of which it was the subject, the oath of the Lord Ordinary "who had perused the bond in process and heard the case" was taken and considered by the Court, without any doubt being suggested as to the competency of the examination (*h*) So Mr Burnett, after laying down generally that the judge before whom a false oath has been emitted ought to be cited as a witness to prove it in a trial of the witness for perjury, mentions a case in 1792, in which the judges of a Circuit Court of Justiciary were cited (*Query*, Were they examined?) in a case of this kind (*i*) Again, in an action of damages in the Jury Court against the publisher of a newspaper, for having published a statement that the pursuer had by false representations obtained a confession of guilt from a panel tried in the Justiciary Court, Lord Pitmilly, one of the Justiciary Judges, was examined without objection from any quarter, as to whether the prisoner had pleaded guilty whether the pursuer had acted as his agent, and on several other matters which occurred before his Lordship judicially (*k*) And in a prosecution for perjury, Lords Meadowbank and Hermand, who had sat with the Lord Justice-Clerk (Boyle) in the case in which the false oath had been emitted, were adduced to prove that the panel knew what he was about when he emitted his deposition, and that he was not an idiot, but the Lord Justice-Clerk, who had presided at the trial, seems not to have been adduced (*l*) This seems to be one of two cases, Morrison and Watt, mentioned by Lord Pitmilly, in which judges were admitted to a limited extent, but which his Lordship hoped would not be followed as precedents (*m*)

The point was again mooted in the Justiciary Court in a prosecution for perjury in a small debt case before the Sheriff who was held competent to prove the terms of the oath which had been emitted before him, but the Court abstained from giving any opinion as to the admissibility of a judge of the Supreme Courts on a similar matter (*n*) It may be added that this point is not adverted to by Lord Stair, Lord Bankton, Mr Erskine or Baron Hume (*o*)

(*h*) Calderwood *v* Comrie, 1681, M 15,800 See also Brown *v* Wilson, 1680, M, 12,267, where the incompetency of such an examination seems not to have occurred to the Court, the proof having been refused on another ground (*i*) Durham 1792 Burnett, 563 See also 1 Hume, 376 (*k*) Gibson *v* Stevenson, 1822, 3 Mur 208, and separate report, 32 This was one of the "Beacon" newspaper cases

(*l*) A B, noticed in 2 Mur, 389, 105 (*m*) Per L Pitmilly in Harper *v* Robinson, 1821, 2 Mur, 105 (*n*) Monaghan, 1844 2 Broun, 131

(*o*) A passage in the learned Baron's Commentaries (vol i p 376) seems to infer that no doubt of the competency of a judge's evidence had occurred to him

§ 1836 Accordingly, the opinions above quoted, while they are not supported by any Scotch decision or institutional writer, are opposed to the previous practice of our courts Still less do modern views of evidence favour the exclusion of witnesses of the highest class on account of jealousy of their judicial dignity

§ 1837 Judges of inferior courts are admissible on matters which occurred before them judicially (*p*)

§ 1838 In England, judges of courts of record cannot be called upon to state what occurred before them in court (*q*) and on this ground the grand jury were advised not to examine the chairman of the Quarter Sessions as to what a person had testified in a trial in that court (*r*)

CHAPTER II —OF THE EXCLUSION OF JURORS ON MATTERS WHICH OCCURRED AMONG THEM IN THAT CAPACITY

§ 1839 It has already been seen that although the recorded verdict of a jury may not be impugned on account of mere informalities in the procedure, it is open to challenge on grounds which strike at its essential justice *e g*, that the jury cast lots for it, or that they had been tampered with, and had misconducted themselves (*a*) The law is settled, however, that in such investigations the evidence of the jurymen is inadmissible to prove any proceedings or communings which took place among them in that capacity

§ 1840 This principle may be seen in an early trial for rape and abduction, where the day after a unanimous verdict of guilty had been returned, a large majority of the jurymen gave in to the Court when about to pronounce sentence, a paper declaring that they understood that certain mitigated findings in their verdict would have saved the prisoner from capital punishment But the Court ' absolutely refused to receive" the document and signified their disapprobation of the jury in submitting it They considered

(*p*) Walker 1838 Bell' Notes 99—Monaghan *supra* See also Gibsons *v* Marr 1823 3 Mur , 268—Robertson *v* Dunbar 1730 M , 12 338—Philp *v* Heir of Cruden, 1724 M 12 539 (*q*) 1 Greenl , § 249—Taylor, 634 But see Best's Pr of Ev § 182 (*r*) R *v* Gazard, 1838, 8 Car and Pa , 595 per Patteson, J

(*a*) See *supra* §§ 48 1068

that the reception of it would be opposed to the jealousy with which law guards against tampering with juries, and that it would be a dangerous practice in the country, especially if under an arbitrary government, to allow recorded verdicts to be altered by such means (*b*) In another case where, in the interval between recording a verdict of guilty and pronouncing sentence the prisoner offered to prove that a majority of the jurors had not agreed to the verdict, and proposed to examine them on the point, the Court held that the investigation was incompetent (*c*) Again, where after a verdict of guilty had been returned and recorded, the prisoner moved in arrest of judgment that five of the jurors had not been sworn, the judges, in the hurry of circuit, and not deeming the inquiry to be altogether incompetent, examined four of the five jurors (the fifth having left the place), and certified the case for decision by the High Court of Justiciary The result was a unanimous judgment that the objection was incompetent Here (as in the two previous cases) no express decision was pronounced as to the examination of jurors, but from the note of the case preserved by Mr Burnett it appears that Lords Justice-Clerk Hope (*primus*) and Meadowbank (*primus*) entertained doubts upon the point (*d*) Lord Pitmilly, in noticing the case, observes that the Court disapproved of the examination (*e*)

§ 1841 The point arose purely in a civil case, where a party alleged that a verdict which had been returned against him had been the result not of deliberation but of chance, as the jury had cast lots for it, and the Court, while admitting the relevancy of the objection, and allowing it to be proved by other evidence, held that the jurors themselves could not be examined upon it (*f*) The ground of judgment was, that such an examination involves a violation of the confidence which is essential for enabling persons unaccustomed to debate to commune together, in order that their views may be mutually compared and rectified It was considered that the utmost danger and uncertainty would arise, if an examination of jurors as to the mode in which they had arrived at their verdict were competent, after they had deliberately announced it in open Court, and had been discharged and exposed to the external influences which are so jealously guarded against so long as their

(*b*) M'Gregor, 1752, Maclau Cr Ca, 119 (*c*) Mill *v* Nicol, 1767 Maclau Cr Ca, 372 (*d*) Hunny, 1809, 2 Hume 316, Burnett, Appx 70

(*e*) Per L. Pitmilly in Stewart *v* Fraser, 5 Mur 190 (*f*) Stewart *v* Fraser, 1830, 5 Mur 166, Adam on Jury Tr, p 209, and ib, Appx No 11

functions continue. The Lord Chief-Commissioner, in a full commentary on the English cases showed that they came to the same result (*g*).

The authority of this decision was recognised in a subsequent case, where, on a motion for a new trial on the ground that the jury had been tampered with and had misconducted themselves, the party moved for a proof of the allegations by other witnesses than the jurymen and the Court, before answer, granted a commission for the purpose (*h*).

These cases render it unnecessary to notice one or two instances in which the evidence of jurors was admitted without objection, and apparently *per incuriam* (*i*).

§ 1842. The incompetency of jurors, however, does not apply to matters which, although they occurred in course of the trial were observed by them as ordinary witnesses (*j*). The deposition of a witness who had been examined before them may be proved by their evidence in a prosecution of him for perjury. And it is held in England that the jurors may be examined upon matters which occurred in Court at taking down the verdict, or to rectify a mistake in the minutes (*k*).

§ 1843. Baron Hume (*l*) notices the question whether the allegation that the clerk of court had made an essential error in recording a verdict—as, for example, missing out the word 'not' in a verdict which the jury announced as "not guilty"—could be proved by their evidence. As an inquiry into such an averment can hardly be deemed incompetent (*m*), neither does there appear to be any good reason for refusing to examine the jurors upon it, for they are likely to have the best knowledge upon the fact, and their examination does not involve any breach of the confidentiality with which law guards their deliberations.[1]

(*g*) The rule in England will be found in 1 Phill., 182—Taylor, 639—1 Greenl., § 252—Best's Pr. of Ev. § 585. (*h*) M'Whir *v.* Maxwell, 1836, 15 S., 299.

(*i*) Menzies, 1790, 2 Hume, 469—Sharpe, 1820, ib.—Graham *v.* Newlands, 1825, 3 Mur., 531, as these cases are noticed by Lord Pitmilly in 5 Mur., 191, 3.

(*j*) See *supra* § 1833. (*k*) R. *v.* Woodfall, 1770, 5 Burr., 2667.

(*l*) 2 Hume, 430—See *supra*, § 1072. (*m*) See § 1065, *et seq.*

[1] In Dobbie *v.* Johnston and Russell, the pursuer moved for a new trial in respect, *inter alia*, that the whole verdict as returned by the jury, including a general finding for the pursuer, was not entered up, that the jury intended to find for the pursuer and that, in point of fact, although it was not stated by the foreman, the jury had determined the amount at which the damages should be assessed. The motion was sup-

CHAPTER III —OF EXAMINING WITNESSES AS TO DELIBERATIONS IN PARLIAMENT

§ 1844 In the case of Plunkett against Cobbett for publishing a libel which reflected on the conduct of the plaintiff as a member of the Irish House of Commons, the Speaker of that House having been asked as to expressions and arguments which the plaintiff had used in the course of debate, Lord Ellenborough, while allowing the question whether he had spoken upon particular questions, stopped the detailed examination and observed "It would be a breach of the witness' duty and his oath to reveal the councils of the nation" (*n*) This principle has been extended by text writers to the examination of other witnesses on these matters (*o*) The rule is required for securing the freedom of discussion which is essential to parliamentary deliberations

---

(*n*) Plunkett *v* Cobbett 1804 29 How, St Tr 71 2, 5 Esp 136

(*o*) Starkie (4th ed) 193—Taylor, 640—1 Greenl , § 251

---

ported by affidavits by the foreman and nine of the jurymen The Court, while holding that the affidavits could not be received to contradict the notes of the presiding judge of what took place in Court did not consider that they were absolutely inadmissible to any effect Lord Cowan observed that with respect to occurrences not in presence of the Court, and which might affect the regularity of the procedure and conduct of the jury, the affidavits tendered might be legitimately considered, subject to this observation, that jurymen could not be allowed, either directly by themselves or through their foreman, to impugn what passed in their presence and in open court, in reference to the verdict returned and recorded with their consent and acquiescence as then return on the issues When the foreman has committed a mistake as to the views of the jury this had been allowed to be the subject of inquiry by affidavit tendered immediately on discovery of the error, as in the case of Cogan *v* Ebden, by Lord Mansfield 1757 (1 Burrows 383) But it was different when affidavits were offered to instruct misconduct on the part of the jury, in such a case the evidence of persons other than the jury who could swear of their own knowledge to the alleged misconduct could alone be received Lord Benholme said,—"With regard to the affidavits of the jury as to what took place during their inclosure, and as to their actual intention of giving their verdict, and their probable intentions had they foreseen what they came afterwards to know, I must observe, that had these affidavits been intended directly to impeach the verdict to which they had assented in open court as not being their true verdict I should have hesitated to admit the competency of such documents For as a general principle I consider it would be a dangerous example to admit of such *ex post facto* impeachment of their own solemn and public declaration on oath But I am relieved from the necessity of considering such a question, for, admitting all that the jurymen say, I see no reason to disturb the verdict." Dobbie *v* Johnston and Russell 1861 23 D 1139

CHAPTER IV.—OF OFFICIAL COMMUNICATIONS WITH, AND INVESTIGATIONS BY, PUBLIC FUNCTIONARIES

§ 1845 Reasons of public policy require that evidence should be excluded upon matters, the disclosure of which would be prejudicial to the public service This privilege extends to communications, whether written or verbal, with public functionaries relative to the administration of government and, in a limited degree, to such as relate to the investigation of crime The ground of it is, that if such matters were divulged, investigations important to the State might be frustrated, while they could not be carried on with that secrecy and freedom which are necessary for success (*a*)

§ 1846 On this principle the Court refuse to order production of communications between persons in the public service regarding the conduct of functionaries under their official superintendence (*b*) This includes official communications between the East India Company and Board of Control (*c*) and between the governor of a colony and his attorney-general (*d*), or the military officers under his authority (*e*) Under the same rule, communications between a sheriff and his predecessor as to the character of the procurator-fiscal of the county were protected (*f*) And the Lord Chief-Commissioner held it "impossible for the Court to interfere," where the Lord Advocate declined, unless ordered by the Court, to disclose communications made by him officially to the Secretary of State as to a pardon (*g*). So, in an action of damages at the instance of a parish schoolmaster against the kirk-session, for defamation and improper proceedings to his prejudice, the Court refused an unopposed motion to enable the pursuer to recover excerpts from a report by the Government Inspector of Schools, because it was a re-

---

(*a*) See Tait Ev, 180, 394—1 Phill, 181—1 Greenl, § 251—Taylor, 640—Best's Pr of Ev, 584 (*b*) Young & Co *v* Commissioners of Excise 27th Feb 1816, F C (approved of in 1 Sh Ap, 206, per L-Ch Eldon in reversing the case on another point)—Edwards *v* Mackintosh, 1823, 3 Mur, 371—Home *v* Bentinck, 1820, 2 Brod and Bing, 130, *infra*—See also Craig *v* Marjoribanks, 1823, 3 Mur, 343 351—Tytler *v* Mackintosh, 1823, 3 Mur, 244—Boyd *v* Reid, 1801, Hume D, 610 But the person making such an investigation may go beyond his privilege, as by openly charging a subordinate with crime, see, *e g*, Blackell *v* Lang, 1854, 16 D, 989

(*c*) Smith *v* East India Co 1841, 1 Phillip's C C 50—3 and 4 Will IV, c 85 §§ 29, 30, 35 (*d*) Wyatt *v* Gore, 1816, Holt's Nisi Pr Ca, 299

(*e*) Cooke *v* Maxwell 1817, 2 Starkie R, 183 (*f*) Greig *v* Edmonstone, 1820, 4 Mur, 70 per L Ch Commissioner (*g*) Gibsons *v* Stevenson 1822 3 Mur, 220

port to government, of which the Court had not power to order production (*h*) But in an action of damages for a slanderous complaint, in consequence of which the pursuer had been deprived of an office in the Excise —one of the alleged slanders being that he had not accounted for his intromissions,—where an order for production of the accounts of payments made by the pursuer's successor was opposed by the Board, on the general ground that a public board is not bound to give up its papers, the Lord Chief-Commissioner, seeing no detriment to the public from their production, and none being alleged, was disposed to overrule the objection, whereupon it was withdrawn, on a suggestion from the Court (*i*)

§ 1847 On the same grounds of public policy, the minutes of investigations by a public board (*e g*, of Excise) regarding charges against one of its officers, cannot be recovered in an action of damages by him against the private complainer (*k*) The principle also protects information on such matters, and on the fitness of candidates for office, when furnished by persons out of the department on solicitation of the Board (*l*) So in an action of damages for defamation, contained in certain letters addressed to the Lord-Lieutenant of the pursuer's county, the Lord-Lieutenant was allowed to be asked whether he had taken the opinion of counsel as to the propriety of communicating the letters without consent of the writer, but it was held that he was not bound, and not entitled, to disclose the terms of the opinion (*m*) And where the Commander-in-Chief had appointed a commission to inquire into the conduct of an officer, who afterwards sued the president of the commission for a libel contained in his official report the Court held that that document could not be produced at the trial (*n*).[1]

(*h*) Sturrock *v* Greig, 1849, 12 D, 166 (*i*) Leven *v* Young, 1818, 1 Mur, 356 (*k*) Young & Co *v* Commissioners of Excise, *supra*

(*l*) Earl *v* Vass, 1822, 1 Sh Ap Ca, 229, reversing, 20th Feb 1818, F C

(*m*) Edwards *v* Mackintosh, 1823, 3 Mur, 369, per L Ch Commissioner See also Cooper *v* Mackintosh 1823 ib, 358 (*n*) Home *v* Bentinck, 1820, 2 Brod and Bing, 130

[1] Some important observations on the confidentiality of communications with public boards fell from the judges in The Rajah of Coorg *v* The East India Company, and Beatson *v* Skene An independent sovereign prince was possessed of two promissory-notes of the East India Company In the course of a war between this sovereign and the company the notes were taken as spoils of war The prince filed a bill against the company for the recovery of the notes and moved for the production of certain documents, which were described by the defenders as documents of a political nature The Master of the Rolls decided, that when a government is properly made a defendant to a

§ 1848. But where a stranger has officiously or from improper motives volunteered information to public functionaries impugning the conduct of their subordinates, the communication, if written, may be recovered, and, if verbal, may be proved orally in an action of damages by the party slandered against his accuser; otherwise persons in the public service would have neither protection nor redress against unfounded and calumnious statements made in the quarter where they were calculated to do them most serious injury (*o*).

(*o*) Leven *v.* Board of Excise, 8th March 1814, F. C. (The documents so recovered

---

suit in which its acts can be impeached, it cannot refuse to produce relevant documents on the ground that they are political communications between itself and its agents; but upon appeal to the Lords Justices, it was held that the plaintiff was not entitled to production, the documents being political communications passing between the Company and its agents relating to matters of government and state affairs. Lord Justice Turner said that he could not give his assent to the proposition that, in previous cases where the privilege had been sustained, it had been sustained in respect that the public boards were not parties to the actions. The principles on which they had been decided were more important. In the first place, the refusal to compel the production of such documents was grounded on the principle that production would be prejudicial to the public interests, and was therefore against public policy. "I am satisfied that there is in this Court a further principle applying to cases of this description—namely, that with matters of political relations between state and state this Court, as I take it, has nothing whatever to do. They are matters which are exempted from municipal jurisdiction; and when therefore this Court is called upon to order the production of documents relating to such matters it is, in truth, called upon to order the production of documents relating to matters which, in their nature, are not subject to the jurisdiction of the Court;" The Rajah of Coorg *v.* The East India Company, 1856, 25 L. J., 345. In a later case Chief-Baron Pollock, delivering the judgment of the Court of Exchequer, observed, that he and his brethren were of opinion that if the production of a state paper would be injurious to the public interest, the general public interest must be considered paramount to the individual interest of a suitor in a court of justice. The question then arose, How was this to be determined? It was manifest that it must be determined either by the presiding judge or by the responsible servant of the Crown in whose custody the paper was. The judge could not do so without ascertaining in public what the document was and why the publication would be injurious—an inquiry which would do all the mischief which it was proposed to guard against; so that the question fell to be determined, not by the judge, but by the head of the department having the custody of the paper. If he was in attendance and stated that, in his opinion, the production of the document would be injurious to the public service, then the judge ought not to compel the production of it; Beatson *v.* Skene, 1860, 6 Jur. N. S., 780. But see Dickson *v.* The Earl of Wilton, 1 F. and F., 419, and Dickson *v.* General Peel and Others, reported in *The Times* newspaper, 9th May 1863, in the latter of which the Court of Queen's Bench allowed certain interrogatories, which were objected to on the ground that they were calculated to disclose state matters of a confidential nature, to be put to a late Secretary of State, in respect that it was obvious that they might be answered without prejudice to the public interests.

§ 1849 In like manner, as persons against whom groundless and malicious accusations of crime have been made to the public authorities are entitled to reparation from their calumniators, the Lord Advocate is in general, bound to name his informer (*p*), persons who make complaints erroneously, but in *bona fide*, being protected under the issue of malice and want of probable cause, which the party suing them must take (*r*) The same principle applies to the recovery of the written information lodged by the party who made the complaint (*s*)

§ 1850 But the Lord Advocate will not be required to divulge the name of his informer, where that would be prejudicial to the public service This is the rule in prosecutions for treason and similar state crimes, and for frauds on the revenue, because, if it were otherwise, fear, shame, or the dislike of being mixed up with the prosecution would deter most persons from giving information as to such crimes, and the consequence would be, that the detection of them would often be frustrated (*t*) For the same reason it is held in England that a witness may not be asked if he was the informer (*u*), and that all questions tending to the discovery of the channels by which the information was conveyed to the public authorities are incompetent, every person connected with the discovery of the crime being protected (*x*)

---

were referred to by Lord Eldon in the House of Lords in reversing a judgment on another branch of the case, 1 Sh Ap Ca, 179)—Tytler v Mackintosh, 1823, 3 Mur, 244—Blake v Pilford, 1832 1 Moo and Rob, 198—1 Greenl, § 251—Taylor, 641—See also Warrand v Falconer 1771 M, 13 933—Thomson v Gillie, 16th May 1810, F C—*Contra*, James v Watkins, 1708, M, 3432

(*p*) 2 Hume, 135—Burnett, 313—2 Al, 94—Tait Ev, 395—*Per curiam* in Henderson v Robertson, 1853, 15 D, 292—Arbuckle v Taylor, 1815, 3 Dow, 160 (as noticed by L Just-Clerk in Henderson v Robertson)—Boag v Gillies, 1832 5 De and And, 434 per L President Hope—*Contra*, Mackenzie's Obs on Stat 1425, c 50 (Works, vol ii p 177) In M'Donald, 1751, noted in Burnett, 313, 1, where a panel having been tried on circuit on a charge of murder, and acquitted, applied by petition to the two judges of the Circuit Court to ordain the Lord Advocate to name his informer, their Lordships refused to interfere, apparently from doubts as to their jurisdiction

(*r*) Arbuckle v Taylor, *supra*—Henderson v Robertson, *supra*—Sheppeard v Fraser, 1849, 11 D, 446 (*s*) Steven v Dundas, 1727 M, 7905, also noted in 2 Hume, 135, 6—Arbuckle v Taylor, *supra*—Henderson v Robertson, *supra* (*t*) Per L Ch Eldon in Earl v Vass, 1822, 1 Sh Ap Ca, 237—Per L Just-Clerk Hope and Lord Rutherfurd (Ordinary) in Henderson v Robertson, 1853, 15 D, 292 (But the Lord Justice Clerk observed in this case, that whether information as to the Customs and similar cases "would now be surrounded with the same degree of inviolability as they seem to have been is questionable These stand upon statutory authority")—See also per L Ch Just Dallas in Home v Bentinck, 1820, 2 Brod and Bing 130—Muirhead, 1681, 2 Hume, 135—1 Greenl, § 250—Taylor, 636 (*u*) M'Gorn v Briant 1846, 15 Mee and Wel, 169 (*x*) R v Hardy, 1821, 24 How St Tr, 808 820

It would also seem that the Court would refuse to interfere in a case not within this exceptional rule, if the Lord Advocate stated, on his official responsibility, that there were special reasons for withholding the information, for it might defeat his object if the reasons had to be divulged (*y*).

§ 1851 In general the investigations at the instance of the Crown with a view to criminal prosecution are privileged, because secrecy in them is usually essential to success, and, if they could be recovered criminal complaints would often be made with a view to ulterior civil proceedings (*z*) Plans, reports by persons of skill, and similar documents prepared on the employment of the public prosecutor, are privileged on the additional ground of being Crown property (*a*)

§ 1852 But the Court will order production of precognitions taken by the Crown authorities, where withholding them would manifestly cause injustice and where no special reasons of state require them to be protected (*b*), as, for example, where a procurator-fiscal is sued for damages on account of having maliciously conducted a groundless prosecution and taken down false statements of what the witnesses said on precognition (*c*).

§ 1853 As the exclusionary rule thus noticed proceeds on reasons of public policy, and not upon any interest personal to the witness or haver, the Court will interpose, although neither he nor the party against whom the evidence is meant to be used opposes the disclosure (*d*) In some cases it would seem that they will do

---

(*y*) Per Lords Cockburn and Rutherfurd in Henderson *v* Robertson, *supra*—Leven *v* Young, 1818, 1 Mur, 356, per L Ch-Commissioner (*z*) So held as to precognitions taken by the Crown authorities in Boag *v* Gillies, 1832, 5 De and And, 434—Donald *v* Hart, 1844, 6 D, 1255—Hill *v* Fletcher 1847 10 D, 37—See also Craig *v* Marjoribanks, 1823 3 Mur 343-7 As to whether a declaration emitted before a magistrate can be recovered in order to be used in a civil action, see *supra*, § 1435, 6 (*a*) M'Glashan *v* H M Adv, 1848, Arkley, 500—Hill *v* Fletcher, *supra* (*b*) Per Lords Corehouse and Craigie in Boag *v* Gillies, *supra*, and see cases in next note (*c*) Harper *v* Robertson, 1821, 2 Mur, 383—Per Lords Just Clerk Hope and Cockburn in Donald *v* Hart 1844, 6 D, 1255—Per Lord Cockburn in Little *v* Smith 1847, 9 D, 743—But see Craig *v* Marjoribanks, 1833, 3 Mur, 342, where, in an action of the kind referred to in the text, raised against a justice of the peace, the Lord Chief Commissioner refused to order production of the precognitions and letters transmitting them to the Lord Advocate because the precognitions had been followed by a trial before the Sheriff and a verdict of guilty, and the Lord Advocate had not taken any steps upon the communications made to him This case shows that the Court will exercise a discretion in granting or refusing such motions (*d*) Earl *v* Vass, 1822 1 Sh Ap Ca, 237, per L Ch Eldon—Edwards *v* Mackintosh, 1823 3 Mur, 369—Little *v* Smith 1847, 8 D, 265, and 9 D, 737—

so although the privilege is waived by the public officer or board entitled to it (*e*)

§ 1854 When an original information or precognition is excluded on this ground, secondary evidence of its contents is inadmissible for the same reason, and also under the rule which requires the best evidence (*f*)

Sturrock *v* Greig, 1849, 12 D, 166—Home *v* Bentinck, 1820, 2 Brod and Bing, 130—Plunkett, *v* Cobbett, 1820, 29 St Tr, 72, 3, 5 Esp, 136, S C (*e*) Compare Leven *v* Young, 1818 1 Mur 356—Earl *v* Vass, *supra*—and Little *v* Smith, 9 D, 740 per Lords Justice-Clerk and Cockburn (*f*) Little *v* Smith, 1845, 9 D 737—Craig *v* Marjoribanks, 1823, 3 Mur, 347—Home *v* Bentinck, *supra*—Taylor, 641

TITLE V

OF EVIDENCE PRIVILEGED ON THE GROUND OF CONFIDENTIALITY.

CHAPTER I — OF CONFIDENTIALITY IN COMMUNICATIONS BETWEEN PARTIES ON THE SAME SIDE OF THE CAUSE

§ 1855. Where several parties are engaged on the same side of a cause, it is essential to the success of their prosecution or defence that they be able to communicate with each other upon the subject of the suit without fear of their communings being divulged Such communications, therefore, whether verbal or written, are privileged Thus where the heirs of a party who, shortly before his death, had transacted with the local agent of an Assurance Company for a policy on his life, sued the company and the agent for payment of the sum alleged to have been insured, and called for written communications which had passed between the company and the agent after intimation had been made that the action was about to be raised, and in which mutual advice was given and facts were stated with a view to the defence, the Court held that the communications could not be recovered (*a*) [1]

(*a*) Rose *v* Medical Invalid Insur Co, 1847, 10 D 156

[1] But it has been held, in England, that communications made by one defendant to another, to enable them to defend a suit are not privileged Vice-Chancellor Wood — 'It is necessary for carrying on business in courts of justice and therefore for the interests of society, that communications with or by the solicitor of a party should be protected But it is not necessary for the interests of society that two defendants should be at liberty securely to concert together measures of defence It would open a new

§ 1856 The same principle protects communications between the counsel and agents of the respective parties on the same side And therefore, where the law-agents acting for different creditors on a bankrupt estate had held certain conversations as to opposing the bankrupt's discharge, and the bankrupt thereafter raised action against one of them on the ground that, in these conversations, he had maliciously represented him to be a fraudulent bankrupt, the Court held the action to be irrelevant, considering that to abridge the liberty of such statements, 'either while used in pleadings before the Court, or in private conversations between men of business, would be highly unwise, and would too much fetter the proceedings in the management of business" And this decision was affirmed on appeal (*b*)

§ 1857 Where one of several parties is adduced as a witness under the Law of Evidence Amendment Act, he will be entitled to decline answering questions as to such communings with a co-pursuer or co-defender, nay more, he will be bound to do so, unless the privilege is waived by the party so united with him

---

CHAPTER II.—OF CONFIDENTIALITY IN COMMUNICATIONS BETWEEN HUSBAND AND WIFE

§ 1858 The Law of Evidence Amendment Act of 1853, while making husband and wife admissible for and against each other in most civil cases (*c*), provides that nothing contained in it "shall in any proceeding render any husband competent or compellable to

(*b*) Stein *v* Marshall, 1864, M, 12 413, affd, M, 'Proof,' Apps, No 1

(*c*) See *supra*, § 1721, *et seq*

and very dangerous ground of protection to hold so No authority has been cited, and it would be very dangerous to hold that, when two co-defendants choose to communicate (each of them being at liberty to communicate with a common solicitor or with separate solicitors, as they may think fit) their communications are not to be disclosed", Betts *v* Menzies, 1857, 3 Jur, N S, 887 But the sounder view appears to be that taken by Lord Jeffrey in the case of Rose, *supra* "A party identified *ab initio* is more nearly connected with the defender than his law-agent, and to force a communication between such parties to be produced would be going further than to force communications between a law agent and his client They are conjunct—they are one person, like husband and wife"

give against his wife evidence of any matter communicated by her to him during the marriage, or any wife competent or compellable to give against her husband evidence of any matter communicated by him to her during the marriage"(d) It is also incompetent to examine third persons as to communications which may have passed between husband and wife in their presence (e). The principle of both these rules is the same, namely, that unlimited confidence between husband and wife is essential to the happiness of the married state, and this confidence the law secures by keeping perpetually inviolable whatever has been confided by one of the spouses to the bosom of the other (f)[1]

Accordingly, the confidentiality of such communications remains although the marriage has been dissolved by death or divorce (g)

§ 1859 This rule, however, does not prevent conversations or correspondence between married persons from being proved as part of their reciprocal conduct where the action involves the terms upon which they lived (h) But in an action of damages for adultery with the pursuer's wife, letters which she had written to him during the period when the adultery was alleged to have taken place, and when he was necessarily absent from home were held to be inadmissible as evidence for him on account of the risk of collusion and fabrication which could not be guarded against by oath, or be detected by cross-examination, as in the case of parole proof of the conduct of the spouses (i) This decision coincides with the rule in England that, in actions of this kind, the terms on which the husband and wife lived before the adulterous intercourse commenced, may be proved in order either to increase or diminish

(d) 16 Vict, c 20, § 3 The corresponding English statute (16 and 17 Vict, c 83, § 3) only provides that husband or wife shall "not be compellable" to disclose any communications, &c (e) In Lougton, 1831, Bell's Notes, 251, Lord Justice-Clerk Boyle would not allow the public prosecutor to ask a witness what she had heard the prisoner's wife say in his presence as to an assault committed by him on his child

(f) 1 Greenl, § 254—1 Phill, 75—Taylor, 900 (g) Monro v Twistleton, 1803, Pea Add Ca, 219, as explained by L Ellenborough in Aveson v Lord Kinnaird, 1805, 6 East, 192—1 Phill, 75—1 Greenl, § 254—Taylor, 901

(h) See *supra*, § 89 This sort of evidence is constantly used in actions of divorce and separation as well as in criminal prosecutions of one spouse for ill-treating the other (i) Kirk v Guthrie, 1817, 1 Mur, 276

[1] Ford v De Pontes, 1859, 5 Jur, N S, 993—Anon v Anon, 22 Beav 481, 23 Beav 273—Selte v Isaacson, 1 F and F, 194

the damages, and that the wife's letters to her husband are admissible for this purpose, provided they were written before her criminality or misconduct commenced (*k*)

§ 1860 The Sequestration Act makes it competent to examine the bankrupt's wife on matters relating to his estate (*l*) But this is thought not to destroy the privilege of communications which he made to her (*m*) [2]

CHAPTER III —OF CONFIDENTIALITY IN COMMUNICATIONS BETWEEN A PARTY AND HIS LEGAL ADVISER

§ 1861 By a sacred and settled rule of law, communications between a party and his legal adviser regarding the subject of a suit depending or threatened are secure from disclosure (*a*) "The

---

(*k*) See *supra*, § 89 (*l*) 2 and 3 Vict, c 41, § 68 (*m*) See ib, § 69, where the persons examined are required to answer "all lawful questions" But see against this view in the text, Mackersie *v* Mackenzie, 1828, 2 S, 256 noted *infra*, § 1877 (*a*) Stair, 4 43, 9 (8)—Ersk 4, 2, 25—2 Hume 350—Burnett 435—Bell's Pr, § 2254—More's Notes, 415—Tait Ev, 384—2 Al, 469 An interesting case (E Dunfermline *v* Callender, 1675, 3 B Sup, 469), which reflects honour on the Scottish Bar may be mentioned here A party having appealed to the King and Par-

---

[2] A different view of the law was adopted in Sawers *v* Balgarnie, 1858, 21 D, 153 It was there held that, in investigations in bankruptcy, communications made by the husband to the wife during the marriage are not privileged and that, when under examination, she is bound to answer any pertinent question, although her knowledge may have been derived from her husband Antecedent to the Evidence Act, the wife had been made a competent witness in investigations in bankruptcy, and she might then have been examined on any subject pertinent to the investigation, whether her knowledge had or had not been derived from her husband The Evidence Act made the wife a competent witness in cases where she could not previously have been examined, but under the condition that she was not to be permitted to disclose matters communicated to her by her husband during the marriage This privilege of confidentiality was the provision of statute, and was not a principle of the common law for the old objection to the admissibility of the wife's evidence was grounded on the relationship of the parties The Evidence Act was an enabling act, but it did not require the Evidence Act to make the wife a competent witness in proceedings in bankruptcy and the limitations which an enabling act contained could apply only to the cases with which it dealt, and could not have the effect of excluding any evidence which, before its passing, was admissible To do so an express provision would have been required

foundation of this rule, Lord Chancellor Brougham observes, "is not on account of any particular importance which the law attributes to the business of legal professors, or any particular disposition to afford them protection But it is out of regard to the interests of justice, which cannot be upholden, and to the administration of justice, which cannot go on, without the aid of men skilled in jurisprudence, in the practice of courts, and in those matters affecting rights and obligations, which form the subject of all judicial proceedings" (*b*) His Lordship observed on another occasion, that if a party could force production of cases laid by his opponent before counsel with reference to the proceedings, no man would dare to consult a professional adviser with a view either to the defence or to the enforcement of his rights, and without such communication, no person could safely come into Court, either to obtain redress or to defend himself (*c*)

§ 1862 This privilege is perpetual, the communications which it embraces being secured from publicity after the termination, as well as during the subsistence of the employment (*d*) Nor does it matter whether the communications were made under an express promise of secrecy, for that is implied in all such communications (*e*) On the other hand, such a promise will not protect communications which in their own nature are not privileged (*f*)

§ 1863 This privilege extends only to professional legal advisers, that is to say, counsel and law-agents, with their several clerks (*g*) It does not apply to communications between a party and his factor (*h*), or a general agent whom he employed in negotiating loans (*i*) And a banker is bound to answer as to the state

---

liament against a decision of the Court of Session the King by letter commanded inquiry to be made as to the advisers of the appeal, whereupon the four advocates for the appellant were called but refused to give any answer regarding their accession, and protested that the appeal was legal This was followed by a peremptory letter from the King commanding these advocates to disown appeals and, on their refusing to do so, they were deprived of office Nearly fifty of their brethren from resentment of the injury done to the profession, deserted it, and were also debarred This case raised some interesting discussion as to the confidentiality of communications between counsel and client (*b*) Per L Ch Brougham in Greenough *v* Gaskell 1833, 1 My and Kee 103 (*c*) Bolton *v* Corp of Liverpool 1833, 1 My and Kee, 94 5

(*d*) Ly Bath's Ex *v* Johnston, 12th November 1811 F C—Hyslop *v* Staig, 1816 1 Mur, 17—Wight *v* Ewing, 1828, 4 Mur, 587—Macf Pr 166

(*e*) Leslie *v* Grant 1805 5 B Sup 874 (*f*) Per L Pres Blair in Bower *v* Russell, 28th May 1810 F C (*g*) Burnett, 436 8—2 Al 470, 1—More's Notes, 415—Tait Ev 386—Ker *v* D Roxburghe, 1822, 3 Mur, 126—Taylor *v* Foster 1826 2 Car and Pa 195—Taylor, 262 (*h*) Mitchell *v* Berwick 1843 7 D 382—Kinloch noted *infra* (*i*) Humphrey's case 1839, sep report p 165; Bell's Notes 253, S C

of a customer's account at a certain date (*k*) Information acquired by a professional accountant employed to inspect a party's books is not protected (*l*) Nor are communications which a party made to his friend, although under a promise of secrecy (*m*). In like manner communications made to a lawyer who is not employed professionally by the party in the matter, are not privileged, as, for example, where they were made after the employment had been declined (*n*)

A non-professional person employed in the capacity of a law-agent may be compelled to divulge facts which the party confided to him (*o*),—except, perhaps, in criminal prosecutions, as it is common for prisoners to intrust the preparations for their defence to private friends instead of professional lawyers, and there is no reason why they should not be able to do so confidentially (*p*) But communications between a party and his mandatory, and between the mandatory and the party's agent are protected (*r*) And a similar extention of the privilege seems warranted where the client from illness or absence, is obliged to communicate with his legal adviser through the medium of a third person, if not, also wherever the client communicates with his law-agent in this way (*s*) Of

---

(*k*) Loyd *v* Freshfield 1826 2 Car and Pa, 329 (*l*) Wright *v* Arthur 1831, 10 S, 139 (*m*) Burnett, 438—2 Hume, 350—2 Al, 471—More's Notes, 415—*Per curiam* in Stuart *v* Miller 1836, 14 S 837 (*n*) Burnett, 435 6—Per L Ch Brougham in Greenough *v* Gaskell 1833, 1 My and Kee, 104

(*o*) Stuart *v* Miller, *supra*

(*p*) In Gavin *v* Montgomerie, 1830 9 S 213, Lord President Hope, in speaking of the confidentiality as between a prisoner indicted for crime and one who had acted as his agent, observed, "It is not necessary that he be a law-agent It is sufficient that he acts in that capacity The correspondence clearly related to the impending criminal proceedings, and a person in this position may employ any one, even a country gentleman, to take evidence or to do other confidential acts, and that confidence will be protected" This opinion (which was *obiter* to the question decided) is challenged by Lord Just-Cl Boyle, but approved of by Lord Medwyn, in Stuart *v* Miller *supra* In Hope, 1815, 2 Broun 465, one of the grounds on which the Court excluded proof of a confession alleged to have been made by the prisoner to his jailor was that the jailor had acted as an agent in carrying communications between the prisoner and his friends regarding his defence

(*r*) Campbell *v* Campbell, 1823, 2 S, 139 See Hope, *supra*, and next note

(*s*) In Jarvis *v* Anderson, 1811 3 D, 990, the interlocutor bears, that the pursuer was "not entitled to recover any letters or correspondence that may have passed betwixt the defender or others on his behalf and Mr Cullen or others his law-agents" But it does not appear at whom the interlocutor pointed as the "others on his behalf The text is also supported by the case of Hope, *supra* Conflicting views on the point were entertained by the Court in Stuart *v* Miller, *supra* (*m*), while in the trial of Sir A Kinloch in 1795 for murder, as noted in Burnett, 438, 9 one [illegible] whom the prisoner had occa-

course where a party employs a solicitor to take the chief conduct of a cause, and another to manage some subsidiary branch of it, communications passing between these persons in fulfillment of their client's directions are privileged (*t*)

§ 1864 Farther, communications with persons not in the legal profession will be protected, if they formed part of the preparation or preliminary investigation which the party made with reference to the cause Thus, in an action by a proprietor against his mineral tenants, to put a stop to certain operations as being in violation of the lease, the defenders having obtained a diligence to recover (*inter alia*) plans, sections, and drawings of the workings and reports letters, memoranda, and other documents relative to the coal workings, and having called upon an engineer to produce drafts of reports and correspondence falling under the specification, the pursuer objected to their production on the ground of confidentiality, as they had been prepared at the request of his counsel, in terms of special instructions and with immediate reference to the action; and the Court, without calling on the pursuer's counsel, held them to be privileged, observing that the defender was really asking to get access to the preparations which the pursuer had made with a view to the action, and that such documents were in a high degree privileged (*u*) [1]

§ 1865 On the other hand, the legal adviser of a party must disclose facts of which he became aware from other sources than employment by his client, because his doing so does not involve a breach of professional confidence, and a party should not be de-

---

sionally employed as his factor or otherwise, and who had written to him about retaining counsel for his defence, was not only without objection examined by the prosecutor, but was called upon to produce letters written by the prisoner both before and subsequent to the fatal event"

(*t*) Mackenzie *v* Yeo 1841 2 Curteis' Ec Ca, 866 (*u*) Wark *v* Bargaddie Coal Co, 27th Feb 1855, 27 Sc Jur 221 The Lord Justice-Clerk also observed that the documents even if recovered, could not be used, not being evidence

---

[1] In Wark *v* Bargaddie Coal Co 1855, 17 D 526, the reports of an engineer prepared in the circumstances noticed in the text, were held by the Second Division to be privileged But the Lord Ordinary (Handyside) held that reports prepared by an engineer more than a year before the raising of the action were not privileged and the judgment on this point was acquiesced in by the parties The Lord Justice-Clerk (Hope), however observed — 'The party has acquiesced in the interlocutor up to a certain point But I wish to state that I am not prepared to say that the objection might not have been carried further" The judgment was affirmed on appeal, Bargaddie Coal Co *v* Wark, March 15 1859 3 Macq, 467

prived of evidence, in consequence of his witnesses being employed by his opponent professionally in the cause (*x*). Thus the agent conducting the defence of a prisoner has been examined upon matters known to him otherwise than as agent (*y*). So, in the prosecution at the instance of the Lord Advocate and the Duke of Roxburghe against Chatto for forgery, where one of Chatto's lawyers was asked whether his client had shown him the writing in question, and what was its tenor and date, and what conversation he had with his client and with the Duke's lawyer about it, he was required to answer as to having seen the deed, as to its tenor and date, and his conversations with the Duke's lawyer; but not whether the prisoner showed it to him, or what conversation he had with the prisoner regarding it (*z*). In reporting this decision Lord Elchies mentions that it was in accordance with the previous case of Wamphray (*a*), where, in an action of proving the tenor of a marriage-contract, which the defender had fraudulently destroyed, the defender's advocate was examined for the pursuer as to whether he had seen the deed and what was its tenor; but was not required to divulge anything as to its existence or tenor communicated to him by his client at consultation, and which did not appear from the writ itself. So, in a declarator that a bond had been granted in trust, the Court allowed the defender's counsel to be examined for the pursuer on such matters relating to the conveyance as he knew from other persons, but not as to any information derived from his client (*b*).

§ 1866. It has been "determined that a man who was agent in a cause, cannot be called by the other party as a witness to declare upon oath such things as he learned in the course of that employment without distinction whether they were told him by his client or not; for the Lords were of opinion that everything he was informed of as agent, belonged to the secrets of the cause . . . And the same decision will, no doubt, apply to a lawyer, or any other man employed in law business in the way of his profession" (*c*). Under this rule information which the agent has derived from communications with the client's relations or witnesses,

---

(*x*) 2 Hume, 350—Burnett, 435, 6—More's Notes, 415—2 Al. 469.

(*y*) Wilson, 1790, Hume, *supra*.

(*z*) D. Roxburghe *v.* Chatto, 1758, Elch., "Witness," No. 37—See also A. B. 1675, noticed by L. Fountainhall in 3 B. Sup., 173, and see *infra*, § 1875.

(*a*) Wamphray's Crs. *v.* Wamphray, 1675, M., 347.

(*b*) E. Northesk *v.* Cheyne, 1680, M., 353. This occurred at a time when trusts were allowed to be proved by parole.

(*c*) Leslie *v.* Grant, 1760, 5 B. Sup., 874. See *supra*, § 1863 (*t*).

or from inspection of his papers in relation to the cause, are protected (*d*) In an English case, where the plaintiff called for production of letters written by the defendant's solicitor to one of the witnesses, and the defendant declined to produce them on the ground that they 'related to, and were connected with, the matters in question in the suit, and were prepared and written after the institution of it, for the purpose of the defendant's defence to the suit and for the purpose of the action between the parties," they were held not to be sufficiently characterised as privileged (*e*). The question seems never to have been raised in Scotland, whether statements made, either in writing or verbally, by the agent of one party to the witnesses in the course of precognoscing them, could be put in evidence by the other party, except in support of an objection that the witness had been tutored, for which purpose they are admissible

In an English case, the Atlas Insurance Company sought to set aside as fraudulent a policy which the Eagle Company had taken out from the Atlas Company on the life of Cochrane, and they stated that an officer of the Economic Company, with which the Eagle had previously tried to take out a policy on the same life, had come into the office of the Eagle Company and stated that a medical report on the life was unfavourable The solicitor of the Eagle Company was required to mention what occurred at the conference, although he stated that he was present as the confidential professional adviser of the Company (*f*)

§ 1867 There is some conflict of authority as to whether it is essential to the privilege of confidentiality that the communications shall have been connected with legal process Certainly communications between a party and his legal advisers with reference to proceedings threatened, as well as depending, are protected (*g*) [2] And the Court have sometimes admitted the privilege

---

(*d*) 2 Hume, 350—2 Al 470—Ker *v* D Roxburghe, 1822, 3 Mur, 126—But see Mackenzie *v* Yeo, 1821, 2 Curteis' Ec Ca 866 where information derived by a party's solicitor from a witness in the course of investigations in the cause was held by Sir Herbert Jenner Fust not to be privileged It was however, rejected as hearsay

(*e*) Mayor of Dartmouth *v* Houldsworth 1840, 10 Simmon's C C, 476—See also Mackenzie *v* Yeo *supra*

(*f*) Desborough *v* Rawlins 1838 3 My and Craig, 515

(*g*) Campbell *v* Campbell, 1823, 2 S, 139 and cases in following notes

---

[2] In Hay *v* The Edinburgh and Glasgow Bank, 1858, 20 D, 701, it was laid down that the plea was not limited to documents passing subsequently to the raising of the action, and documents of a confidential nature relating to the subject-matter of the

where there was a very slight connection between the evidence sought to be recovered, and the subsequent proceedings. Thus in an action by the heir of a creditor, against the representative of a debtor, where the question was whether a service expede by the intermediate ancestor of the pursuer had created a general representation, the defender was held not to be entitled to recover correspondence between that ancestor and his law-agent at the time of the service, although long before the action in which they were required had been thought of. One of the judges considered that, under the rule recognised in the previous case of Bower *v.* Russell (*h*), the correspondence was not privileged, as it did not relate to a depending cause. But the other judges entertained a different opinion, and Lord President Blair observed, "A confidential correspondence has passed between client and agent remotely indeed, connected with his cause, but still sufficiently connected with it to bar production of it being compelled. The whole question turns upon the design and intention of Sir W. Pultney in the general service he exped to his brother Sir James Johnston, and any confidential correspondence as to his views at that time is sufficiently connected with the present question to come under the rule regarding confidential correspondence between client and agent. Suppose a person brings an action of debt on a bond or bill, would he be entitled to call for letters between his alleged debtor and his agent previous to the action being raised, in which the debtor acknowledged the existence of the debt, and authorised him to buy him off as cheaply as possible? I apprehend not." (*i*)

The authority of this decision was recognised in a subsequent case, where correspondence which had passed between certain parties and their agents with reference to contemplated actions of relief against them were held to be privileged in a subsequent action of reduction-improbation of the bond of caution (*j*). Lord Moncreiff observed, "I think the distinction was properly drawn in the case of the executors of Lady Bath (*k*),—where a demand was made for correspondence prior to the institution of the process,—that no correspondence which had relation to the institution of the process,

(*h*) *Infra*, § 1869 (*m*). (*i*) Ly. Bath's Exrs. *v.* Johnstone, 12th Nov. 1811, F. C. (*j*) Jarvis *v.* Anderson, 1841, 3 D., 990. (*k*) *Supra* (*i*).

action in the hands of the law agent of the bank, and of dates considerably prior to the raising of the action, but subsequent to the time when the bank had reason to expect legal proceedings, were held to be protected; see also the English cases noticed *infra*, § 1879, note [8].

although previous in date thereto, should be compelled to be produced" Lord Medwyn concurred, observing, that "the principle applies to every communication connected with the institution of the action"—Both of these cases, therefore, recognise the principle that documents are only privileged when they have some connection with a depending or anticipated suit

§ 1868 In like manner, communications are privileged which were made with reference to proceedings contemplated at the time but never instituted, as was held in an action of reduction-improbation of a bill on the ground of forgery, where the pursuer moved for production of correspondence between the defender and his agent with reference to a criminal prosecution for the forgery, which had been abandoned (*l*)

§ 1869 But in a question as to the terms of the contract between the seller and purchaser of a superiority, the Court granted diligence to recover correspondence which had passed between the purchaser and his confidential agent in the transaction; and Lord President Blair observed, that communications being made to an agent, and confidentially, was no sufficient reason why production of them should not be called for and that it was only communications *in causa* which had any privilege in this respect' (*m*) Again in the trial of Sir A Kinloch for the murder of his brother, the advocate who had been consulted by the deceased with regard to certain family settlements in which the grudge between the brothers was said to have originated, was examined as to the conversations he had had professionally with the deceased (*n*)

§ 1870 It has, however, been settled in England that the privilege of confidentiality "is not qualified by any reference to proceedings pending or in contemplation,"—for "if it were confined to proceedings begun or in contemplation, then every communication would be unprotected which a party makes with a view to his general defence against attacks which he apprehends, although at the time no one may have resolved to assail him" (*o*) —and "it would be most mischievous if it could be doubted whether or not an attorney, consulted upon a man's title to an estate, were at liberty to divulge a flaw" (*p*) In the case of a party consulting a counsel or solicitor as to a defect which he may have discovered in

(*l*) Gavin *v* Montgomerie, 1830, 9 S, 213 (*m*) Bower *v* Russell, 28th May 1810, F C See also Ivory's Note to Ersk, 4, 2, 25 (*n*) Kinloch, 1795, 2 Hume, 350—Burnett, 436—2 Al, 469 (*o*) Per L Ch Brougham in Greenough *v* Gaskell, 1833, 1 My and Kee, 102 The whole cases on the point are reviewed by his Lordship (*p*) *Per curiam* in Cromack *v* Heathcote 1820, 2 Brod and Bing 6

his titles, it is said that the party takes preliminary steps to protect himself against the attacks of an apprehended adversary, and that there is no solid reason why he should not be entitled to do so in as complete safety as if the apprehended adversary had put forward his claim in the shape of a threatened suit (*r*) [3] Accordingly, it seems to be the rule in England, that the privilege extends to attornies consulted on title as well as those employed in a cause (*s*)

§ 1871 The rule of English law thus noticed, especially as it is recognised in the case of Cromack *v* Heathcote (*t*), was considered by Lords Alloway and Pitmilly to be founded on principles equally applicable to the law of Scotland (*u*) In a recent case also, the Lord Justice-Clerk observed, "I am ready to give full effect to the views stated by Lord Brougham in Greenough *v* Gaskell, in the class of cases to which that opinion, as I understand it, is applicable Indeed our courts adopted the same views in the case of Lady Bath's Executors, long before the English Courts got rid of a limitation which in principle was indefensible" But his Lordship observed that the English law as to recovering documents differs from ours in many important particulars. In this case also, Lord Wood observed, "According to the law of Scotland, communications between clients and their legal advisers are privileged, although they may not relate to any suit depending or contemplated or apprehended, and so it was substantially decided in the case of Lady Bath's Executors in 1811 (*x*) It therefore required no authority from the law of England to support that proposition" (*y*)

In this state of matters the law upon the point must be held as not settled

§ 1872 Professor Bell lays down that a party cannot call for a memorial laid by his opponent before counsel, with the relative opinion (*z*). But it has not yet been determined that this privilege extends beyond consultations in regard to a pending or anticipated suit (*a*)

(*r*) Per Knight Bruce, V C, in Pearse *v* Pearse, 11 Eng Jur, 52

(*s*) Per Richardson J, in Cromack *v* Heathcote, *supra*, approved of by Lord Brougham in Greenough *v* Gaskell, *supra*, 1 My and Kee, 107

(*t*) *Supra* (*p*)

(*u*) Lumsdaine *v* Balfour, 1828, 7 S, 7

(*x*) Noted *supra*, § 1868

(*y*) Per L Wood in M'Cowan *v* Wright, 1852, 15 D, 237

(*z*) Bell's Pr, § 2251 See also Denholm *v* Balcarras, 1695, 4 B Sup, 73

(*a*) A memorial and opinion of this nature were held to be privileged, although they were referred to by the party on record as containing a true

[3] But see the English cases—Lafone *v* Falkland Islands Co, Hampson *v* Hampson Desvaynes *v* Robinson, Bluck *v* Galsworthy—noted *infra* § 1879, note [8]

§ 1873 There are certain exceptional cases to which the privilege of confidentiality does not extend

The law-agent of a party, when cited in an action of exhibition, or under a diligence against havers, must answer all questions pertinent to the discovery of the documents (*b*), although his knowledge may have been derived from his client (*c*), because the client himself is bound to depone in such inquiries, and his agent cannot be in a more favourable situation On the other hand one whose acquaintance with a party's titles is only derived from his agency is not bound or entitled to answer questions regarding them, which could not be put to the client himself (*d*)

In the analogous case of a proving of the tenor the counsel or agent of the defender will be bound to depone whether he ever saw the lost document, and what was its tenor, but will not be required to divulge any fact on these points which he obtained in consultation with his client, otherwise than from inspection of the document (*e*)

§ 1874 Where a counsel or law-agent has entered into a transaction for his client in the course of legal proceedings, he may be examined upon it, in order to ascertain if the party authorised or homologated his acts, and to throw light on the terms of the transaction The reason is, that such an examination does not involve a disclosure of the measures taken by a party for his success in a cause, but is designed for investigating the terms and effect of a transaction which, although made by a lawyer and relating to a lawsuit, does not in principle differ from ordinary contracts made by procuration On this ground, where one of two defenders in an action, having paid the sum sued for called on his co-defender to relieve him of one-half of it, in terms of an alleged arrangement between their respective agents, the Court allowed him to recover letters between the co-defender and the agent who had acted for that party at the time (*f*) So in an issue whether a case had

statement of the facts, and although they had been communicated to the opposite party in the course of an attempt to compromise the case, Thomson's Tr *v* Clark, 1823, 2 S, 262—Clark *v* Spence (same parties) 1824, 3 Mur, 455

(*b*) As to what questions may be asked see *supra* § 1357 *et seq*

(*c*) Ersk 4, 2, 25—Tait Ev, 386—Macf Prac, 79—Betson *v* L Grange, 1628, M 342, 1 B Sup 159—A B, 1628, M, 16,663—Bathgate *v* Armstrong, 1666, 1 B Sup 521—A B *v* Rollocks, 1666 M 344 (*d*) Scott *v* L Napier, 1637, M 358 Elch, "Witness," No 7 Cr and St 441 S C—Fisher *v* Bontine 1827, 6 S 330 noted *supra* § 1311—Macf Pr *supra* (*e*) Crs of Wamphray *v* Ly Wamphray, 1675 M, 347—Ersk 4, 2, 25 See § 1864 (*f*) Kid *v* Bunyan, 1842 5 D, 193

been compromised by a private friend of one of the parties acting with her authority, her counsel were examined without objection as to whether they had entered into or sanctioned the arrangement (*g*) The same principle is supported by the case of Bower *v* Russell, already noticed (*h*) Thus, also, in a question whether the pursuer had by his mandatory agreed to discharge a certain claim on a composition-contract, the Court ordered the pursuer's agent to give up all correspondence between the pursuer and the mandatory tending to show the instructions under which the latter had acted, and whether the pursuer had homologated his proceedings (*i*), although, as already noticed, communications between a party and his mandatory in relation to the conduct of a suit are privileged (*j*) [4]

§ 1875 One who consults a legal adviser, with a view to committing a fraud or other crime makes him either an innocent instrument of his guilt or an accomplice In neither case will so important a part of the history of the crime be excluded on account of confidentiality, for the ground of policy on which the privilege is founded in ordinary cases must give way, where preserving it would prevent crime from being detected (*k*) Accordingly, the conveyancer who has been consulted by a party with a view to the fabrication of writings, is bound to disclose such communications (*l*), provided they do not involve him in a criminal charge, and he may be examined as to his preparation of a deed to which his client is said to have adhibited forged signatures (*m*) So in

(*g*) Jaffray *v* Simpson, 1835, 13 S, 1122, noticed by Lord Ordinary Cunninghame in his note to Kid *v* Bunyan, *supra* (*h*) See *supra*, § 1869 (*m*)

(*i*) Campbell *v* Campbell, 1823, 2 S, 139 (*j*) See *supra*, § 1863

(*k*) Burnett, 437—Tait Ev, 384, 5 See D Roxburghe *v* Chatto, *supra* § 1864 (*z*)

(*l*) See Burnett, 436, 7—*Per curiam* in M'Leod *v* M'Leod, *infra*—Per L Mackenzie in Kid *v* Bunyan, 1842, 5 D, 193 (*m*) M'Lean, 1838, 2 Swin, 183, Bell's Notes, 253

[4] See as to circumstances in which the Court allowed a correspondence between defenders and their law-agents, relating to the subject-matter of an action to be recovered under a diligence, Anderson *v* E Elgin's Trustees, 1859, 21 D, 654 Two actions, involving several parties, referred to the same subject-matters of dispute The pursuer and defender in the one action were both called as defenders This last action was at the instance of a public company, and was settled The defender in the other action averred that it was settled by collusive arrangement for the purpose of defeating his rights The Court held that he was entitled, for the purpose of proving this arrangement, to recover from the agent of the company excerpts from the minutes of the company, and also letters between himself, as country agent, and his correspondent in Edinburgh, so far as these related to the alleged arrangement Miller *v* Small 1856, 19 D 112

the celebrated trial of Humphreys for forging documents to support his claim to the Earldom of Stirling, the law-agent whom he had employed in the civil proceedings where the forged documents were used was examined as to what he had done in the course of his agency, no objection being stated to the examination although the prisoner was defended strenuously by eminent counsel (n).[5]

§ 1876. In like manner in an action against a bankrupt by the trustee in his sequestration to set aside a composition-contract on the ground that the bankrupt had procured the consent of a creditor by promising him a premium, letters between the creditor and his agent were held to be recoverable, partly on the ground that "the objection of confidentiality can have no operation in a question of fraud" (o). So where it was alleged that an arrestee had fraudulently got arrestments laid in his hands, his law-agent was held to be examinable as to all he knew regarding the party's attempts to procure the arrestments, the examination being confined to the time before the arrestments were moved in Court, as the agent had acted in the legal proceedings relating to them. The Court expressly refused to limit the examination to information which he had derived from other sources than his client (p). It has also been held that although advocates are not bound to discover the secrets of their clients concerning the point of right, they are obliged to depone in the expiscation of private fraudulent conveyances (r). And where conveyances by a bankrupt to his brother-in-law were sought to be reduced on the ground of fraud at common law and contravention of the act 1621, c. 18, the Court held that correspondence between the brother-in-law (who was defender in the action) and his agent relating to the state of the bankrupt's affairs at the dates of the deeds under reduction, and as to measures for paying or securing a debt by the bankrupt to the defender, were

(n) Humphreys, 1839, separate report by Swinton, and Bell's Notes, 253.

(o) Inglis v. Gardner, 1843, 5 D. 1029.

(p) M'Leod v. M'Leod, 1744, Elch. "Witness," No. 26, M. 16,751, S. C.

(r) Keith v. Purves, 1684, M. 354.

[5] In Morrison v. Somerville and Others, 1860, 23 D., 232, the pursuer tendered in evidence a "Case" which a witness deponed that he had prepared as agent for one of the defenders, with a view to an action which that defender subsequently raised, and that it consisted of statements made by that defender to him. It was objected that the case was inadmissible because it was a confidential communication between agent and client, and because it was secondary evidence, and the defender was alive. The objections were repelled on the ground that the action was based on fraud, and that it was competent to adduce secondary evidence to prove the statements of a party as against himself.

not protected (s) The ground of decision was that the object of such actions, especially when laid on the statute 1621 is to defeat the bankrupt's attempts to give fraudulent preferences to conjunct and confident persons under the mask of onerous transactions, and that this necessarily involves an exposure of the confidential communications which he and the party he meant to favour may have had with their respective agents, for these are part of the *res gestæ* of the transactions in issue The authority of this decision, however is impaired by the fact that the case was compromised on an appeal, which embraced this point as well as the judgment on the merits

§ 1877 By a clause in the Sequestration Act (t), the bankrupt's law-agent may be examined, and is bound to answer all lawful questions relating to the estate [6] It was considered by a majority of the Court, that a corresponding provision in the former act superseded the common law rules as to confidentiality, but the decision was that, in respect of the special circumstances, the agent might be examined upon his knowledge of the bankrupt's affairs, whether derived from the bankrupt or not (u) Such an examination seems to be competent both because its object is to ascertain if the bankrupt has improperly concealed or made away with his funds, and because, the creditors having succeeded him in all his rights, he has no interest to which the privilege could properly be referable [7]

§ 1878 It need hardly be added that the principle thus noticed

(s) M'Cowan v Wright, 1852, 15 D, 229, 494—See also Grant v Grant, 1748 M, 949, Fich, "Fraud," No 19, S C (t) 2 and 3 Vict, c 41, §§ 68, 69
(u) Mackenzie v Mackenzie, 1823, 2 S 256

[6] 19 and 20 Vict, c 79, § 90 It was held in Paul v Laing's Trustees, 1855 17 D, 457, that an agent who had been agent for a partner of the bankrupt firm long prior to the bankruptcy, but who was now an agent for a claimant on the estate (whose claim was resisted by the trustee), could not be examined as a witness for the trustee under the statute, and that confidentiality applied See also A B v Binny, 1858 20 D, 1058

[7] Section 84 of 19 and 20 Vict, c 79, enacts that the trustee shall record in the Sederunt Book all minutes of accounts reports, and other documents relating to the sequestration, "Provided always, that when any document is of a confidential nature (such as the opinion of counsel on any matter affecting the interest of the creditors on the estate), the trustee shall not be bound to insert it in the Sederunt Book, or to exhibit it to any other person than the Commissioners" The prior act, 2 and 3 Vict, c 41, § 63, contained the proviso, "unless he be ordered by competent authority to do so" By the omission of these words it is now left wholly to the discretion of the trustee, acting with the advice of the Commissioners, to grant or refuse inspection of confidential documents

does not apply to communications which passed between a party and his legal adviser, after investigation of the alleged fraud had been commenced or threatened Nor is there any doubt that a bankrupt, like persons accused of crime may safely take legal advice when he gets to issue with his creditors on allegations of embezzlement, fraudulent preferences, and the like

§ 1879. Confidentiality is the privilege of the client, not of the agent, who is bound not to disclose, without his client's authority, any privileged communication (*x*) And, on the other hand, the privilege is at an end if the client waives it (*y*) Upon this principle, also, in a question between a trustee and beneficiaries, the former may not plead against the latter confidentiality in regard to his communications with the counsel or agent for the trust on matters in which the estate generally is concerned, because they were made on behalf of the beneficiaries themselves, not of the trustee (*z*) [8]

(*x*) Bell's Pr § 2254—More's Notes, 415—Tait Ev, 180—Macf Pr, 166—Hyslop v Staig 1816 1 Mur, 17—Edwards v Mackintosh, 1823, 3 Mur, 371—Ker v D Roxburghe, 1822 3 Mur, 141 (*y*) Bell's Pr *supra*—Tait Ev, 180—Macf Pr, *supra*—Forteith v E Fife 1821, 2 Mur, 467 (*z*) Provan v Telfer's Tr, 1830 8 S 797 See also D Hamilton v Hamilton, 25th May 1819 F C, where the decision proceeded on the ground that the letters sought to be recovered had been written to the agent of one of the parties by the factor on the lands which were claimed by the parties respectively, and that it depended on the result of the action, whether he had acted for one or the other party at the time But, *query*, Were the letters admissible evidence, not being either on oath or admission of party ?

---

[8] The following cases have been decided in England since the first edition of this work was published Cases and opinions of counsel taken by trustees, as such merely, are not entitled to protection in a suit by the *cestuis qui trust* against the trustees or their representatives, the real interest being in the trust, Devaynes v Robinson 1855, 20 Beav, 42 The same was held as to a communication by a trustee to an attorney, Sncan v Philips 1859, 1 F and F, 149, see also Wynne v Humberston, 1859, 27 Beav, 421 Before the institution of a suit, but in expectation that proceedings would be taken against them, the defendants, acting on the advice of their solicitor, employed an agent to collect evidence at a great distance from this country The communications made by the agent were held to be privileged Protection will not be withheld from communications made in apprehension of litigation, on the ground that the precise form which the litigation afterwards assumed was not foreseen, Lafone v The Falkland Islands Company, 1857 27 L J (Chan), 25 Letters written two years before the institution of a suit by a country solicitor to a firm acting as his London agents, were held not privileged, though the firm afterwards acted as his solicitors in a suit which involved the subject-matters of the letters, Hampson v Hampson, 1857, 26 L J (Chan), 612 Cases and opinions taken before the time when the party first heard of the questions in the suit being raised were held not privileged, Devaynes v Robinson, *supra* The pri-

§ 1880 The Law of Evidence Amendment Act of 1852 provides, that "where any person who is or has been an agent shall be adduced and examined as a witness for his client, touching any matter or thing, to prove which he could not competently have been adduced and examined according to the existing law and practice of Scotland, it shall not be competent to the party adducing such witness to object, on the ground of confidentiality, to any question proposed to be put to such witness on matter pertinent to the issue (*a*) It had been previously laid down by the Lord Chief-Commissioner, that a party by calling his agent waives the privilege of confidentiality (*b*)

The rules as to the proper time for objecting to the production of documents on this ground have been noticed already (*c*)

CHAPTER IV —ARE COMMUNICATIONS MADE BY A PARTY TO A CLERGYMAN OR PHYSICIAN PRIVILEGED?

§ 1881 Confessions which a criminal makes to a clergyman to relieve his burdened conscience have the highest intrinsic trustworthiness, and the more heinous and dark the crime, the more valuable would such a confession be in proving it On the other

(*a*) 15 Vict c 27, § 1 (*b*) Forteith *v* E Fife, 1821, 3 Mur 467—Mact Pr, 166 (*c*) See *supra*, §§ 1345, 1362

vilege of not disclosing communications between solicitor and client belongs to the client and his representatives as against third parties alone, not *inter se*, Gresley v Mousley, 1856, 2 Jur N S, 156 Where fraud was alleged in a purchase by a solicitor from his client at an undervalue, it was held that title-deeds and documents were not privileged *Ibid* The communications between a Scotchman residing in Scotland and his Scotch solicitors residing in London have the same privilege as if the solicitors were English, Lawrence v Campbell, 1859, 5 Jur N S, 1071 A communication to be privileged must have been made by the client to the solicitor, or by the solicitor to the client, Marsh v Keith, 1860, 6 Jur N S, 1182 See also Reg *v* Leatham, 1860–61 7 Jur N S, 674 Where communications and statements are made by a client to his confidential adviser touching the matter before any suit has been instituted, they are not entitled to protection except there be some extraordinary circumstances But the Court will not order the production of documents which contain advice given confidentially to a client upon these occasions Block *v* Galsworthy 1860 7 Jur N S, 91 Several of these decisions seem inconsistent with the rules as to confidentiality that had been laid down in prior cases

hand, if communications between clergymen and prisoners were not protected, the reforming agency of religion would not prosper where it is most required, for how could a clergyman give spiritual advice to a prisoner, when he might neither urge him to confess nor converse with him unreservedly, lest he should afterwards be forced to betray the trust reposed in his sacred office, by repeating the prisoner's confidential statements to him?

§ 1882 The law is not yet settled as to whether such communications are privileged In one case a parish clergyman, for whom the prisoner had sent to disburden his conscience to him, was allowed to give evidence respecting a confession made in his presence and that of two magistrates of the burgh (*d*) But this case (in which the question of competency does not seem to have been raised) may perhaps come within a rule noticed afterwards (*e*) In a recent case (*f*), which favours the confidentiality of this class of communications, Lord Justice-Clerk Hope declined giving an opinion on the general point.

Nor are the text writers agreed upon it. Baron Hume in one passage (*g*) observes, that "there is room to question the propriety of allowing such a disclosure" as that made in Anderson and Marshall's case (*h*) In another place (*i*), after laying down that communications to clergymen are not privileged, he adds, 'It is true no call will probably ever be made on a clergyman to disclose any confession of guilt however spontaneous, which the panel may have made to him when in jail, and preparing for his trial, to relieve his mind, and with a view to spiritual consolation Such a conference is a separate and a later incident, and no part of the story of the man's guilt But put such a case as this—that a man has attempted to poison his wife, that, being in bad health and seized with compunction, he has disburdened himself of this load on his conscience to the clergyman of his parish and that afterwards, having recovered, he returns to his cruel practices, and, in the end, dispatches the woman In such a case the interests of justice and humanity will not suffer the clergyman to suppress this confession, which is a fact in the history of the murder, and a strong circumstance in the train of the evidence against the panel Certainly it is desirable that all should receive who truly stand in need of spiritual consolation, but it is not expedient to hearten criminals

(*d*) Anderson and Marshall, 1728, 2 Hume, 335

(*e*) See *infra*, § 1885

(*f*) Hope, 1845, 2 Broun 465, *infra* § 1884

(*g*) 2 Hume, 335

(*h*) *Supra*, (*d*)

(*i*) 2 Hume, 350

in the prosecution of their crimes, or to nourish them in the hope of impunity and peace of mind, by securing the secrecy, in every event of such communications."

Sir A. Alison, conceiving (not quite accurately) that Baron Hume holds communications to be privileged if they were made after, but not if made before, the prisoner's incarceration, observes that it may reasonably be doubted whether there is any good ground for this distinction (*k*). He would extend the privilege to confessions made to a clergyman at any time, in order to unburden conscience and obtain spiritual consolation. Mr. Tait, founding on the learned Baron's authority, lays down, that where a prisoner in custody and preparing for trial confesses his crimes to a clergyman, the statement is privileged; but he repeats as exceptional the case already noticed, in which the communication is said to form part of the history of the crime.

§ 1883. In England it has been ruled that confessions to clergymen are not privileged (*l*). But Lord Kenyon observed that he would have paused before he admitted such evidence (*m*). And Lord Chief-Justice Best has said, "I for one will never compel a clergyman to disclose communications made to him by a prisoner; but if he chooses to disclose them, I shall receive them in evidence" (*n*).

In this state of the authorities the point must be considered as open in this country. It is not likely that the Court will refuse to protect communications of this nature, unless in some extreme case, such as that put by Baron Hume.[1]

(*k*) 2 Al., 471. See also ib., 537, 586. (*l*) R. *v.* Sparkes, cited in Du Barre *v.* Livette, 1791, 1 Peake, 77—Butler *v.* Moore, MacNally's Ev., 253—Wilson *v.* Rastall, 1792, 4 Durf. and E., 753—1 Phill., 165—1 Greenl., § 247—Taylor, 665—Best Pr. of Ev., § 587. (*m*) Du Barre *v.* Livette, *supra*.

(*n*) Broad *v.* Pitt, 1828, 3 Car. and Pa., 519. This view is, with deference, thought to be erroneous. If the privilege exists at all, it is for the protection of the prisoner, and the clergyman ought not to be allowed to waive it. See *supra*, § 1879.

[1] In R. *v.* Griffin, 1853, 6 Cox's C. C., 219, Baron Alderson expressed an opinion that communications made by a prisoner to a spiritual adviser ought not to be disclosed. In a trial before Justice Hill a Roman Catholic priest was asked from whom he received a watch, which was produced at the trial. The witness declined to answer the question, on the ground that he had received it in connection with the confessional, and that, if he were to answer the question, it would implicate the person who gave him the watch. He was held guilty of contempt of court, and committed to jail; R. *v.* Hay, 1860, 2 F. and F., 4; and see the authorities there quoted in note (*a*) on the privilege which at common law, in England, attaches to confession, and in Best's Pr. Ev., § 612 *et*

§ 1884 The protection will not in general be extended to communications made to a lay friend when acting as spiritual counsel-

---

seq In H M Adv *v* David Ross, 1859, 3 Irv, 434, the Court refused to admit a statement made by a prisoner in answer to a question put to him by the prison chaplain The point was fully argued in M'Lauchlin *v* Douglas and Kidston, 1863, 35 Sc Jur 322, 4 Irv, 273, but the Court avoided giving a decision upon the general question The circumstances were similar to those in Hay, *supra* and the question, which the clergyman declined to answer, did not relate to statements made in confession by the prisoner, but to facts which took place in connection with, and following upon, the confession The Lord Justice General (M'Neill) in delivering the judgment of the Court observed, "It appears to me to be unnecessary to inquire into, or to pronounce any opinion upon, either the existence or the scope of the principle contended for as to penitential confessions of criminals to clergymen, because I am very decidedly of opinion that there is neither authority nor principle for holding that the question which the complainer refused to answer comes within the operation of even the widest range of any rule of confidentiality recognised in our law, or suggested anywhere by our law writers Assuming though not asserting, that the law may regard as confidential and therefore not to be disclosed a confession made by a criminal to his spiritual adviser, to ease his conscience and obtain consolation and advice, and even that it protects from disclosure the whole of what I may call the spiritual intercommuning between them no one has ever said that it goes further, and extends, not to anything said by the penitent to the priest, or by the priest to the penitent in the course of that spiritual intercommuning but extends to every act afterwards done by either of them if it can be regarded as a consequence of the confession made" The distinction is probably sound, at the same time it is easy to figure cases in which it would be as truly a breach of the secrecy of confession to reveal circumstances following upon, and arising out of confession, as to repeat the exact words of the penitent's communication, and a communication can scarcely be regarded as protected in the proper sense of the term if the law insist on the disclosure of facts and circumstances which indirectly, but in effect, disclose the substance of the communication The policy of protecting communications of this nature appears to be now generally admitted There is undoubtedly a strong disinclination on the part of the ministers of religion to disclose communications which have been made to them in their spiritual capacity, while, by the law of his church, the Roman Catholic priest who violates the secrecy of the confessional may be punished by deprivation of office Were it to be held that such communications are not privileged, the position of a Roman Catholic priest would become one of peculiar difficulty But as that communion is in this country a protected and tolerated communion, it would seem that its members are entitled to practise any of the rites of their religion which are not *contra bonos mores*, or inconsistent with the provisions of the law Nor can any strong expediency be shewn for refusing to tolerate a fundamental institution of that religion For it is to be recollected that the information which the Roman Catholic priest receives under the seal of confession would not be obtained by him if the confessional did not exist So that, were the confessional abolished, either directly or indirectly, the priest, having nothing to communicate, would no longer be available as a witness The secrecy, therefore which the church law enjoins does not diminish the area from which evidence may be obtained The evidence in question is of an exceptional kind, created so to speak, by the machinery of the church itself, and ceasing to exist when that machinery is dissolved So that the law cannot be said to suffer any injury by the exclusion of this kind of evidence The same observation applies in some measure to the ministers of lor But in a special case the Justiciary Court excluded proof of a confession said to have been made to a jailor, who had been the medium of communication between the prisoner and her friends in regard to her defence, and had communings with her on religious topics when she was under depression Their Lordships considered that he had made himself both the legal and spiritual adviser of the prisoner, whereby he had so completely secured her confidence that she had been "disarmed of any feeling of self-protection or reserve" (*o*)

§ 1885 Confessions made by a prisoner to a third person in consequence of the advice of his clerical counsellor are not privileged, for they are dictated by the hope of spiritual advantage to be derived from disclosing the truth, and such a hope has no tendency to produce a false confession as in the case of inducements which vitiate confessions (*p*)

§ 1886 Communications made by a person to his medical attendant are not privileged, for the discovery of truth is in general more important than the preservation of the confidence which has often to be reposed in a physician or surgeon (*r*) At the same time, good feeling should induce a party not to force a medical man to disclose communications of a confidential nature, unless the interests of justice make that really necessary (*s*).

(*o*) Hope, 1845, 2 Broun, 465 (*p*) R *v* Gilham, 1828, 1 Moody's C C, 186—2 Al, 472, 586—1 Greenl, § 229—Taylor, 591—Best Pr of Ev, 587 See Anderson *v* Marshall, 1728, 2 Hume, 335, *supra*, § 1882 (*r*) 2 Hume, 350—Burnett 438—2 Al 470—Tait Ev, 387—Christian *v* L Kennedy, 1818, 1 Mur, 421—R *v* Duchess of Kingston, 1776, 20 St Tr, 572—1 Phill, 164—Taylor, 618 The rule in the text was fully recognised in A B *v* C D, 1851, 14 D, 171, where, however, the Court sustained as relevant an action of damages against a medical man, laid on his having disclosed facts communicated to him under the seal of professional confidence (*s*) See Christian *v* Kennedy, *supra* In several American States information acquired by physicians and surgeons, when acting professionally, is privileged, 1 Greenl, § 248, note

---

every communion for it is impossible to doubt that, were the privilege of confidentiality withdrawn, confessions (which might be repeated in the witness-box) would cease to be made by penitents to their spiritual advisers

TITLE VI.

OF THE PROCEDURE FOR COMPELLING WITNESSES TO ATTEND AND DEPONE.

§ 1887 Every court of law has power to compel the attendance of witnesses residing within its jurisdiction, for it is a public duty in all persons to give evidence in judicial investigations. In Scotland this attendance is enjoined by citation, and may be forced by personal apprehension upon letters of diligence, and, in some cases, upon a certified copy of an interlocutor of the Court in which the investigation takes place The witness is bound to obey a citation, although his doing so may cause him personal inconvenience Nor may one disregard a citation on account of there being a good objection to his admissibility, for it lies with the Court, and not with him, to determine that question (*a*) Indeed, a citation may be used for compelling the attendance of one who is incompetent as a witness, but who may be exhibited to the jury as a production (*b*)

§ 1888 It was at one time doubtful whether the privilege of peers of exemption from imprisonment did not render incompetent second diligence for forcing their attendance (*c*). And the Court, to avoid the difficulty, sometimes ordered peers to attend, under a penalty equal to the damage which their failure might have caused to the party (*d*) In a recent case, however, where Lord Lovat had, without any assigned reason disobeyed a citation as a witness in the Court of Session, the Court on an unopposed motion by the party,

---

(*a*) See Bryce, 1844, 2 Broun, 119—Collins v N British Bank 1851, 13 D, 541

(*b*) Bryce, *supra*—See *supra* § 1727

(*c*) See A S, 25th Dec 1708, and 27th July 1711—Tait Ev 183

(*d*) Young v E Bute, 1716 M, 10,030—and case of E Kincardine there cited granted letters of second diligence, and their Lordships expressed a unanimous opinion that the privileges of the peerage do not protect against the consequences of such disobedience (*e*) This is the rule *a fortiori* in the Justiciary Court, where the prisoner's life may depend on the evidence of a peer (*f*) So, in England, a peer may be imprisoned for contempt of court if he refuses to attend or take the oath (*g*)

There seems to be no authority as to whether a similar power resides in inferior judges (*h*)

The widow of a peer is in the same position, in these respects, as a peer (*i*)

§ 1889 In those cases in the Court of Session in which the proof is taken on commission, the interlocutor ordering the proof "grants diligence" for citing witnesses to attend Formerly this had to be followed by taking out letters of diligence, which were writs running in the Sovereign's name, ordering the witnesses to attend, and were signed by the extractor, and passed the signet If the witness failed to attend, the Lord Ordinary or Court, on application, granted letters of second diligence which were writs of the same nature, concluding with warrant for apprehension of the refractory witness (*k*) Sometimes first and second diligences were granted at the same time, the latter being only intended to be put in force in case of the witness failing to attend on the first citation (*l*) The formal extracts have been practically abolished by a recent statute, which provides that a copy of the interlocutor granting a diligence, certified by the clerk to the process, or his assistant, shall have the same effect as the extract according to the former practice (*m*) Under this provision it was held that if a party, cited on an interlocutor of a Lord Ordinary granting a first diligence fails to attend, second diligence may issue against him, although he has intimated his intention to reclaim (but has not actually reclaimed) against the interlocutor, and although the reclaiming days have not expired (*n*)

§ 1890 In jury causes witnesses may be cited on letters of

(*e*) Fraser *v* Nicholl, 1840, 2 D 1254

(*f*) Burnett, 451—L Mackenzie (*primus*) in Fraser *v* Nicholl, *supra*

(*g*) R *v* L Preston, 1691, 1 Salk R 278—Starkie (4th ed), 33—Taylor, 917

(*h*) It will, however, be competent to obtain the authority of the Supreme Civil or Criminal Court (as the case may be) to compel a peer to attend before an inferior judge

(*i*) Macdonald *v* Widow of a Peer, 1756, M, 10,031

(*k*) Shand's Pr, 351—Beveridge's Forms of Proc 607

(*l*) Shand *supra*—Beveridge, *supra*

(*m*) 13 and 14 Vict, c 36 § 25

(*n*) Collins *v* N Brit Bank, 1851, 13 D, [illegible]

first and second diligence, which are issued by the clerk of court, and pass the signet, the practice being to issue both sets at once, in order that the party may at his discretion force attendance (o) A copy of the interlocutor fixing the trial, certified by the clerk to the process or his assistant, is a good warrant for citing witnesses to the trial (p), but it does not empower the messenger to apprehend them, and therefore the practice is to take out letters of diligence as formerly In trials before the Lord Ordinary without a jury, under the late Court of Session Act (r), witnesses are cited on a certified copy of the interlocutor ordering the trial

§ 1891 In the Court of Justiciary, letters of diligence for citing witnesses for the Crown used to be issued under the seal of court, upon a warrant from one of the judges, which was granted of course on petition or bill at the instance of the Lord Advocate (s) A recent statute dispenses with such petitions, and ordains that letters of diligence shall be issued by the clerk of court to the Lord Advocate on exhibition of the indictment on which such letters of diligence require to be raised, or a copy thereof signed by the Crown Agent for the time being (t) "Letters of exculpation,' for citing exculpatory witnesses, are issued on application by the prisoner at the justiciary office They are signed by the clerk of court, and if taken out at the office of the Justiciary in Edinburgh, bear the seal of court, which is not impressed on such letters when issued on circuit, or on letters of diligence for the Crown (u)

§ 1892 In civil causes before the Sheriff, a certified copy of the interlocutor fixing the diet of proof, or of the portion of the interlocutor relating to that matter, is a sufficient warrant for citing witnesses and havers within the Sheriff's county and if a witness, duly cited on at least forty-eight hours' notice, fails, without a reasonable excuse, to appear, he forfeits a penalty not exceeding forty shillings to the party for whom he was cited and the Sheriff may grant second diligence for compelling his attendance, the expense whereof falls upon the witness, unless a special reason to the contrary be sustained by the Sheriff (x) Witnesses and havers residing beyond the Sheriff's jurisdiction used to be cited on letters of supplement obtained from the Court of Session (y) But now

(o) Macf Pr, 111. (p) 13 and 14 Vict, c 36, § 43
(r) 13 and 14 Vict, c 36, §§ 46, 48 (s) 2 Hume, 154, 398—11 and 12 Vict, c 79, § 2 (t) Ib § 2 (u) Ib (x) 16 and 17 Vict, c 80 § 11 (y) A B, 27th Feb 1813, F C—Cameron 1826, 4 S 617

a warrant issued by the Sheriff of any county is effectual for citing witnesses residing in any other county, on being indorsed by the sheriff-clerk of the latter county (z) And the same rules apply to the failure of witnesses to obey such citations, as where they are cited under warrant of the Sheriff of their own county (a)

§ 1893 In criminal cases warrants issued by the Circuit Courts of Justiciary and the several Sheriffs, used not to be effectual for the citation of witnesses beyond their several bounds, and such witnesses were therefore cited on letters of supplement issued by the High Court of Justiciary, whose jurisdiction embraces the whole of Scotland (b) The delay and expense occasioned by this practice were remedied by an enactment, "that when the attendance of any person shall be required as a witness in any criminal cause or proceeding, or in any prosecution for a pecuniary penalty, before any court or magistrate in Scotland, such person, although not residing within the jurisdiction of the court or magistrate granting the warrant of citation, may be cited on the warrant of such court or magistrate, and this either by a messenger-at-arms, or by an officer of the court or magistrate granting the warrant, or by an officer of the place in which such person may be for the time and such citation shall be sufficient to enforce the attendance of such person as a witness in all respects as if such person had been resident within the jurisdiction of the magistrate by whom such warrant shall have been granted" (c)

§ 1894 Considerable inconvenience used to be occasioned by there being no means of compelling witnesses residing beyond Scotland to attend trials in this country, or depone before a commissioner of court As a partial remedy of this evil, in so far as regards witnesses in England and Ireland, it was first enacted that a writ of subpœna or other process issued for citing witnesses in any criminal prosecution in one part of the United Kingdom, shall be effectual in any other part of it, and that in case of the witness so cited failing to appear, and of his failure being certified from the court to which he was cited, he may be proceeded against and punished in the country of his residence in like manner as if the citation had issued from one of the supreme courts therein (d) —provided it were shown that at the time of serving the subpœna or citation, a sum sufficient for defraying the expense of coming

(z) 16 and 17 Vict, c 80, § 11 (a) Ib (b) 2 Al 100, [illegible]
(c) 11 Geo IV, and 1 Will IV, c 37, § 8 (d) 45 Geo III, c 92 § [illegible]

and attending to give evidence, and of returning, had been tendered to the witness (*e*)

This proviso impeded the practical working of the act A subsequent statute provided that "all warrants issued in England, Scotland, or Ireland, respectively, may and shall be indorsed, and executed, and enforced, and acted upon, in any part of the United Kingdom in such and the like manner as is directed by the said recited act of the thirteenth year of the reign of his present Majesty (*f*), in relation to warrants issued or granted in England and Scotland respectively, as fully and effectually to all intents and purposes as if all the provisions of the said act were in this act repeated and re-enacted" (*g*) "And that it shall be lawful for any judge of any of his Majesty's Courts of Record in Westminster, of the Court of Session in the county palatinate of Chester, or of any of the Courts of Great Sessions in Wales, or for any judge in any of his Majesty's Courts of Record in Dublin, to indorse any letters of second diligence issued in Scotland, for compelling the attendance of any witness or witnesses resident in England, Wales, or Ireland, upon any criminal trial in Scotland, and such letters shall, upon such indorsement have the like force and effect as the same would have in Scotland, and shall entitle the bearer thereof to apprehend the witness or witnesses mentioned therein and to convey such witness or witnesses to Scotland, for the purposes of the trial, or trials, in respect of which such letters shall have been issued, without any tender of any expense or expenses of any such witness or witnesses, anything contained in the said last recited act of the forty-fifth year aforesaid notwithstanding" (*h*)

§ 1895 In civil cases commissions for examining witnesses abroad could only flow from the Supreme Court, on application by the party, swearing that they were necessary witnesses (*i*) And the Court were in use to interpone authority to commissions for this purpose from inferior courts (*j*) But attendance of the witnesses before the commissioner could not be enforced (*k*) In the year 1843 an act was passed, which made it compulsory on witnesses and havers in England and Ireland to attend before a commissioner or commissioners appointed by any of the courts of law

(*e*) 45 Geo III c 92 § 4

(*f*) 13 Geo III, c 31 This statute allowed criminals to be brought for trial from any part of England to Scotland and *vice versa*

(*g*) 54 Geo III, c 186, § 2

(*h*) Ib, § 3

(*i*) Town of Irvine, 1627 M, 16,664, 1 B Sup, 167—E Mar *v* his Vassals 1630, M, 16,665

(*j*) Town of Irvine, *supra*

(*k*) Izatt, 13th June 1809, F C—Glyn *v* Johnstone, 1834, 13 S, 126

in Scotland the havers being also required to produce the writings or documents mentioned in the rule or order of the Scottish court For this purpose it is necessary that the witness or haver shall have been served with a written notice to attend at a specified time and place, such notice being signed by the commissioner or commissioners If he refuse or fail to appear and be examined such refusal or failure must be certified by the commissioner or commissioners, whereupon it is competent to, or on behalf of, the party suing out the commission, to apply to any of the superior courts of law in that part of the Kingdom within which the commission is to be executed, or to any one of the judges of such courts, for a rule or order to compel the witness or haver to attend and be examined before the commissioner or commissioners, and the court or judge to whom the application is made, may by rule or order command the attendance of any person to be named, or the production of any writings or documents to be mentioned in such rule or order (*j*) If, upon the service of the rule or order, the witness or haver does not appear or produce the documents, his disobedience renders him subject to such pains and penalties as he would be subject to by reason of disobedience to a writ of subpœna in England or Ireland, as the case may be (*k*) It is also provided that every person so cited shall be entitled to the like conduct-money and payment of expenses and for loss of time, as if he had attended at a court of law, and that no person shall be compelled to produce any document which he could not be compelled to produce at a trial, or to attend on more than two consecutive days to be named in such rule or order (*l*)

§ 1896 There are reciprocal provisions as to commissions issued from the courts of law and equity in England and Ireland to be executed in this country If a person refuses or fails to obey a written notice, in the form above mentioned, to attend upon a commission from any of these courts, his refusal or failure shall be certified by the commissioner or commissioners, whereupon the party may obtain from any of the superior courts in Scotland, or any judge thereof, an order to compel such person to attend and be examined, and to produce the writings called for, and if he does not obey such order, the party, upon proof of such disobedience, may obtain from the Lord Ordinary on the Bills second diligence in common form (*m*) These enactments are subject to the provi-

(*j*) 6 and 7 Vict, c 82 § 5 See Appendix (*k*) Ib, § 6
(*l*) Ib § 7 (*m*) Ib, §§ 5, 6

sions already noticed as to the expenses of the person cited, the documents which he must produce, and the time during which he is bound to attend (*n*).[1]

§ 1897. By a recent statute (*o*) witnesses in any part of the United Kingdom can be forced to attend personally in any trial in any action or suit depending in any of the superior courts of common law at Westminster or Dublin, or the Court of Session or Exchequer in Scotland. If it shall appear to the court in which the suit is pending, or if such court is not sitting, to any judge thereof, that it is proper to compel the personal attendance at any trial of a witness who may not be within the jurisdiction of the court, such court or judge may order a writ of *subpœna ad testificandum* or of *subpœna duces tecum* (*p*), or a warrant of citation, respectively, to issue in special form, commanding the witness to attend the trial, wherever he shall be within the United Kingdom, and the service of such writ is as valid in any part of the kingdom as if it had been served within the jurisdiction of the court from which it issued (*r*). It is enacted that every such writ shall have at the foot a statement or notice that it is issued by the special order of the court or judge, and that no writ shall issue without such special order (*s*). If the person so cited fails to appear, the court out of which the writ issued may, upon proof of the service and the default, transmit a certificate of the default under the seal of the court, or under the hand of one of the judges or justices thereof, to any of the superior courts of common law at Westminster, if such service was in England,—if it was in Scotland, to the Court of Session or Exchequer in Edinburgh,—or if in Ireland, to any of the superior courts of common law in Dublin, and the court to which such certificate is sent shall thereupon proceed against and punish the person in default, in like manner as if he had neglected or disobeyed a writ of

(*n*) 6 and 7 Vict. c. 82, § 7.

(*o*) 17 and 18 Vict., c. 34. See Appendix.

(*p*) The former of these writs is a citation to attend as a witness; the latter is a writ of the same nature, and includes a requisition to produce the documents specified in it. Tomlin's Law Dic. art. *Subpœna*.

(*r*) 17 and 18 Vict., c. 34, § 1.

(*s*) Ib., § 2.

[1] The act 22 Vict., c. 20, provides facilities for taking evidence in, or in relation to, actions, suits and proceedings, pending before tribunals in Her Majesty's dominions, in places in such dominions out of the jurisdiction of such tribunals. The Court, having jurisdiction in the place where the witness resides is empowered by § 1 to issue an order for the examination of the witness. The act will be found in the Appendix to this volume.

subpœna or other process issued out of such court (*t*) But none of the said courts shall proceed against or punish any person so in default, unless it be made to appear to such court that a reasonable and sufficient sum of money to defray the expenses of coming and attending to give evidence, and of returning from doing so, had been tendered to the person at the time of serving the writ or citation (*u*) This statute does not curtail the power of any of the courts above specified to issue commissions for examining witnesses beyond its jurisdiction (*x*) Nor does it alter or affect the admissibility of any evidence at a trial, which before the passing of the act was receivable on the ground of a witness being beyond the jurisdiction of the court (*y*) The deposition of such witnesses taken on commission is therefore equally admissible with their evidence before the jury [2]

§ 1898 Arbiters, being private persons, have not power to compel witnesses or havers to appear and give evidence, or produce documents, before them The defect is supplied by the courts of law interponing their authority to injunctions from the arbiter (*z*) The application for this interposition may proceed either from the party leading the proof (*a*) or from the arbiter (*b*) and is usually at their joint instance (*c*) It may be made to the Judge Ordinary of the bounds (*d*), or to the Court of Session (*e*), but not to the Lord Ordinary on the Bills (*f*) The Court have refused to com-

---

(*t*) 17 and 18 Vict, c 34, § 3 (*u*) Ib § 4 (*x*) Ib, § 5 (*y*) Ib, § 6 (*z*) Ersk 4, 3, 31—Tait Ev 418 (*a*) Stevenson *v* Young, 1696, M, 634 (*b*) Ker *v* Scott, 1670, M, 634 (*c*) Blaikie *v* Aberdeen Ry Co 1851, 13 D, 1307, same parties, 14 ib 590 (*d*) Harvey 1826, 4 S, 809 (*e*) Cunningham *v* Chalmer 1733, Cr and St, 367 —Harvey, *supra*—Ersk 4, 3, 31—Tait Ev 418 (*f*) Harvey *supra*

---

[2] The act 19 and 20 Vict, c 113, proceeding on the preamble that it is expedient that facilities should be afforded for taking evidence in Her Majesty's dominions in relation to civil and commercial matters pending before foreign tribunals, provides, that the Court, having jurisdiction where the witness resides, may order the examination of the witness upon oath upon interrogatories, or otherwise before any person or persons named in such order By § 2 it is provided, that a certificate under the hand of the ambassador of the foreign power that such a suit is in dependence, and that the evidence of the witness is necessary shall be taken as sufficient evidence of these facts A witness giving false evidence is, by § 3 declared guilty of perjury A commission to individual commissioners to examine witnesses at Pesth was sent back unexecuted through the Austrian Embassy,—on the ground that that government did not permit any but the tribunals of the country to examine witnesses in Hungary The Court thereupon issued a commission, directed to the Imperial Royal Provincial Court at Pesth, to examine the witness, Fisher *v* Izataray, 1858, El Bl and El, 321

pel witnesses or havers to leave the county in which they reside, in order to appear before an arbiter, the proper course, when they are in a different county, being for the arbiter to go there, or to grant a commission for examining them (*g*).

When a party to an arbitration has obtained from the arbiter a commission for examining of witnesses in England or Ireland, with the authority of the Court of Session interponed thereto, he may enforce their attendance before the commissioner, under the 6 and 7 Vict., c. 82, already noticed (*h*).

§ 1899. If the witness refuses to depone, or the haver to produce the document called for and persists in his refusal after the arbiter has overruled his objection, the party may, without any recommendation from the arbiter, apply by summary petition to the Sheriff of the bounds or to the Court of Session to interpone authority to the order, and, on failure, to grant warrant of incarceration (*i*). This order, however, ought only to be granted on the judge to whom the application is made being satisfied that the witness or haver's objection is bad (*j*).

§ 1900. Church courts, like arbiters, have no power to compel the attendance of witnesses or the production of documents in cases before them, their compulsitors being limited to ecclesiastical censures, which only affect persons within their communions. It is not settled whether the courts of the established church differ from those of dissenting churches in being able to obtain the aid of the civil courts for this purpose. It is considered in some quarters that such a power is implied in an act passed in the year 1693, which (*ad finem*) statutes and ordains that "all magistrates, judges, and officers of justice give all due assistance for making the sentences and censures of the church and judicatories thereof to be obeyed, or otherwise effectual as accords" (*k*). A subsequent act (*l*), which prohibits civil magistrates from enforcing or compelling "any person or persons to appear when summoned" in prosecutions with a view to excommunication, is said to imply that in other prosecutions the intervention of the civil magistrate is available. The books upon process in the church courts (*m*) and an act of the

(*g*) Gordon v. Nielson, 1741, M., 634.

(*h*) Blaikie v. Aberdeen Ry. Co., 1851, 13 D., 1307. The diligence was enforced in England by Mr. Justice Patteson, after a hearing of parties at chambers. The provisions of the act will be found *supra*, § 1895.

(*i*) Blaikie v. Aberdeen Ry. Co., 1852, 14 D., 590.

(*j*) Ib.

(*k*) 1693, c. 22.

(*l*) 10 Anne, c. 7, § 7.

(*m*) Stuart's Forms of Process (4th ed.), vol. i, p. 145.—Cook's Forms, p. 20.

General Assembly (*n*), direct that application be made to the Judge Ordinary to secure the attendance of witnesses who disregard the citations of the church judicatories. But, of course, these are not authorities upon the legal question

§ 1901 In an old case where the presbytery of Dunse applied to the Court of Session by bill for letters of horning against witnesses who had failed to appear on citation, "the Lords did demur, in respect letters of horning ought not to be direct, but either by consent of parties, or by warrand by acts of Parliament ordaining horning to be direct upon sheriff's and commissioner's decreets, and decreets within burgh, and admiral's decreets" (*o*) This decision, although pronounced when letters of horning were used against witnesses and havers in civil cases (*p*), seems only to have determined that they were inappropriate in cases before the church courts,—thus leaving the general question undecided

The point was raised in a recent case, where the presentee to a parish applied to the Sheriff to interdict certain persons from putting away or destroying a letter, which he alleged contained statements injurious to him and which he expected to require in proceedings before the presbytery as to his induction The Court refused the application, on the ground that the petition did not set forth any proper title or interest in the document, and that the petitioner had not raised, or stated that he intended to raise, any civil action in which the document might be required (*r*) The decision, however, proceeded upon the opinions of two judges to one, and, as it altered the interlocutor of the Lord Ordinary, it cannot be held as authoritative Their Lordships' views were conflicting as to the competency of the civil courts aiding those of the church in ecclesiastical investigations Lord Justice-Clerk Hope's opinion was against such a power, which, his Lordship observed, was not matter of statutory jurisdiction, and against which he thought there were reasons affecting the peace and well-being of society Lord Meadowbank entertained an opposite opinion, and observed that it is in being able to obtain such aid to explicate their jurisdictions, that the courts of the established church differ from those of dissenting bodies, and that Lord President Blair stated, in the case of Bullock (*s*), that this constituted the great

(*n*) Assembly, 1707, act 2, § 9 (*o*) Presbytery of Dunse, 1675, M, 6740

(*p*) Stair 4, 20, 13—Ib, 4, 41, 9 (*r*) Barclay *v* Gifford, 1843, 5 D, 1136

(*s*) Bullock *v* Smith, 31st January 1809, F C The report does not mention this dictum

difference between them Lord Medwyn considered that if the document in question were required in a process in a church court, the machinery of ecclesiastical censure should be first used, and that no other court could interfere, unless there was a competent process in which the document was required for evidence and unless the custodier of it was either not subject to the orders of the church, or defied them, to the defeating of justice Lord Cockburn's interlocutor implies that, in his opinion, the civil courts have the power in question

The point must be considered as still open (*t*)

§ 1902 By the Annual Mutiny Acts witnesses civilians as well as military men, who refuse to attend courts-martial, or to be sworn or answer questions, or to produce documents in their possession or under their control are liable to be apprehended on diligence issuing from the Court of Session or Sheriff-court of the bounds in the same manner as witnesses who neglect to attend trials in these courts respectively (*u*)

§ 1903 As already mentioned, a witness who refuses to appear may under the second diligence be apprehended, and brought before the court or commissioner for examination He ought to have an opportunity of obeying a citation in the usual way, before this extreme measure is resorted to Yet if it is manifest that he will not obey the first citation the compulsitor may be applied, the means of conveyance to the place of examination, or money sufficient for that purpose being first tendered (*x*) If the witness has not a good excuse for having disobeyed the first citation, he may be kept in custody until the next diet of proof, or until he finds caution to appear when required (*y*) The Court may also proceed against him for contempt which they do by subjecting him in a fine (*z*), and the cost of the second diligence and depriving him of

(*t*) The late learned procurator of the church (Mr R Bell) informed the author that he was directed by the General Assembly of 1846 to try this question on the first favourable opportunity (*u*) The enactments for the year 1855 are in 18 Vict c 11 (Army), § 15—and ib c 12 (Navy) § 17 (*x*) Macf Pr, 113

(*y*) 2 Al 397—Adams 1829, Bell's Notes 262 (*z*) 2 Hume, 378—2 Al, 397—Macf Pr, 113 In criminal cases the witness incurs a fine of 100 merks Scots (£5 11 $1\frac{4}{12}$ sterling) 2 Hume, ib —2 Al, ib See also Brownhill, 1831, Bell's Notes, 262 In a civil case the Court imposed a fine of £20 and expenses, Donald *v* Hart, 1844 7 D, 273, and in Mackenzie *v* Henderson, 1820, 2 Mur, 216, a fine of £5 See 8 and 9 Vict, c 83, § 84 as to the fine for failure to attend before the Sheriff under the Poor Law Amendment Act

the usual allowance for expenses and loss of time (*a*) These consequences are incurred whether the witness was cited personally or at his dwelling-place, provided he was aware of the citation (*b*)

§ 1904 In civil cases where it is expected that a witness will leave the United Kingdom before the trial, his deposition should be taken on commission to lie *in retentis*, there being no means of compelling him to remain in the country Such commissions are not granted in criminal cases, but if either the prosecutor or the prisoner has reason to believe that one of his witnesses means to abscond, to the disappointment of justice, he may apply to the Justiciary Court to have the witness apprehended and imprisoned until he find caution to appear at the trial, and on the application being supported by proof to the satisfaction of the judge, it will be granted (*c*) And if there is ground to expect that the witness would forfeit his bail-bond rather than appear, the Court may refuse to allow caution (*d*) In criminal cases, where a witness cannot be safely allowed to remain at large, from being exposed to intimidation, tampering, or other improper influences, and more especially if there is risk of his being carried off or personally injured, the Court, on being satisfied of this, may, upon an application by the party who intends to adduce him, grant warrant for committing him to a place of safety to remain till the trial (*e*) This proceeding is peculiarly necessary in political cases and trials arising out of combinations among workmen, and the like, where the feelings of a number of persons are excited, and a considerable organization is kept up in order to carry out some illegal object

§ 1905 As it is an extreme and delicate measure thus to interfere with the liberty of innocent persons, the proceeding should only be adopted where it is evidently necessary for the ends of justice And if the application comes from a private prosecutor, or from the panel, care should be taken lest its object be to gratify malice against the witness (*f*) On account of its delicacy this proceeding has hitherto been confined in practice to the Justiciary Court But in urgent cases the Sheriff may in the course of a pre-

(*a*) Ersk, 1 2, 30—A S 21st December 1765—Town of Fraserburgh *v* L Saltoun 1707, M 16,712—Donald *v* Hart, *supra*—Tait Ev, 418 (*b*) 2 Hume 374 5—2 Al, 397 (*c*) 2 Hume, 375—Burnett, 469—2 Al, 399

(*d*) 2 Hume, ib—Per L Royston in Smith, Brodie, and Others, 1788 there cited 2 Al 400 (*e*) 2 Hume, 375, and cases there cited—Burnett 469 2 Al 399

(*f*) If this is done maliciously and without probable cause the witness will get redress in an action of damages see 2 Al, 399

cognition, and much more while an accusation is pending before him, adopt a similar precaution for securing witnesses, at least until more formal proceedings can be adopted (*g*)

§ 1906 It would seem that the witness must maintain himself during his confinement, if he is able to do so If he is not, the Court will assign him a suitable aliment, which the party making the application must supply (*h*)

§ 1907 It almost always lies with the party who requires the evidence of a witness, to cite him, and secure his attendance But if the usual compulsitors are ineffectual, *e g*, from the witness being abroad or his residence not being discoverable, and if the Court are satisfied that the other party could, without difficulty, obtain his attendance, they may ordain that party to produce the witness (*i*) Thus in an old case where one party had used all competent diligence against the servants of the other, but they refused to attend from fear of their master, the Court granted an application for letters to charge him to produce them (*k*) And where a witness was abroad, between whom and the party against whom he was to be adduced there was great intimacy, if not also collusion the Court ordained that party to produce him (*l*) The attendance of one party as a witness or haver for the other, may be secured by an order in the cause, in place of diligence, wherever that may be expedient, *e g*, from the party's residence not being known (*m*) [3]

In case of alleged impetration of a deed, where there was risk of some important witnesses for the pursuer, who were servants and tenants of the defender, being put out of the way by him before the proof, the Court allowed their depositions to be taken to lie *in retentis*, unless the defender would find security for their attendance (*n*)

(*g*) 2 Hume, 375—Burnett, 469—L Just -Clerk Hope (*primus*) in M'Dougal, 1805, there noted—2 Al 399 (*h*) Hume, *supra*—2 Al, 399

(*i*) Tait Ev 418 (*k*) L Carnousie *v* L Meldrum, 1629 1 B Sup, 172

(*l*) E Londonderry's Exec *v* E Stair, 1748, M, 16 748 (*m*) Newry, &c, Ry Co *v* Graham 1851 14 D, 297 (*n*) L Castlemilk *v* Whiteford 1676, M, 12,092

[3] In an action against a witness for non attendance at a trial the plaintiff was held entitled to substantial damages, Yeatman *v* Dempsey, 1860 6 Jur N S, 778

TITLE VII.

OF THE PERSONAL PROTECTION OF WITNESSES

---

§ 1908 Where a debtor who is attempting to evade the diligence of his creditors by concealment or remaining in the sanctuary, is required as a witness, a protection, in certain cases, may be obtained to enable him to attend in safety (*a*) This practice, in consequence of abuses, had to be regulated by statute and act of sederunt (*b*). Under these the Courts of Session, Justiciary and Exchequer are prohibited from granting protections, except for the purpose of enabling debtors to obey citations to appear before these courts respectively (*c*) Such protections are issued upon the party or his tutors or curators, if he is a minor, giving their oaths of credulity or subscribing a certificate under their hands upon oath (*i e*, an affidavit) that those who are cited are material witnesses (*d*) A protection cannot be granted under such application, unless the creditor has been cited on an *induciæ* of fifteen days, to show cause why it should not pass (*e*), and it must be limited to such few days, not exceeding a month in all, as will enable the witness to appear in court and return to his former place of security (*f*) All protections so granted must be recorded in the books of the courts from which they issue (*g*) Any judge granting a protection, except under the rules prescribed by the acts 1663 and 1681, is liable as a cautioner for the debt (*h*) The statutes imply that inferior

---

(*a*) Ersk, 4, 3, 21—2 Hume, 374, 5—Burnett, 171—Tait Ev, 418

(*b*) Statutes noted *infra*—A S 1 Feb 1676 (*c*) 1663 c 1—1681, c 9—1698 c 22 The powers under these Acts were extended to the Jury Court by 59 Geo III, c 35 § 28 (*d*) 1681, c 9 (*e*) 1698 c 22

(*f*) 1663, c 1—1681, c 9 (*g*) 1681, c 9 (*h*) 1663, c 1—1681, c 9

courts cannot grant protections and this power is not exercised by them in practice.

§ 1909 Protections may be granted under these statutes where the proof is taken on commission (*i*) And the Court also allowed to a haver, who was in the sanctuary, protection for the purpose of going to his repositories, in order to obtain the writs called for, and produce them at the several diets of examination (*k*) But where protection was sought for a witness who had gone abroad to escape the diligence of his creditors the Court, partly on the ground that the protection was not necessary, and partly influenced by doubts as to whether it would avail the witness against third parties, refused to grant it, and allowed him to be examined on commission (*l*). In an old case, also, a commission was granted to take the oath on reference of a party who was under diligence, "which the Court used rather to do than grant a protection" (*m*) It may be added that the Court refused to allow a party protection to enable him to attend a commission in his own cause, although he alleged that it could not be properly conducted without him (*n*)

§ 1910 Under the Annual Mutiny Acts, persons are secured against arrest while they are going to, attending and returning from, courts-martial as witnesses, and the procedure is defined by which their release may be obtained if they have been unduly arrested (*o*)

As already noticed, witnesses who are in danger of intimidation or personal injury from the persons against whom they are to be adduced, may be committed to a place of security before the trial (*p*), and furnished with means to leave the country after giving evidence (*r*)

§ 1911 As a counter-part of these rules the attendance of a witness who is in prison may be obtained under warrant from one of the supreme courts to have him taken to court in charge of a proper officer, whose duty is to see that he is safely returned to custody (*s*) In examinations on commission, the common practice is to examine such witnesses in prison

---

(*i*) Paton, 1836 11 S 679 (*k*) Paton, *supra*

(*l*) M'Culloch *v* Babington, 1851 14 D, 172 (*m*) Durham, 1628 1 B Sup 257 (*n*) Cockburn, 1700, 4 B Sup 497 But compare cases noted *infra*, (*s*) (*o*) The enactments for 1855, 6, are in 18 Vict, c 11 (for the Army), § 15 and Ib c 12 (for the Navy), § 17 (*p*) See *supra* § 1904

(*r*) See *supra*, § 1740 (*s*) Tait Ev, 419—See also Moodie 18th May 1819, F C—Alison, 9th July 1814 F C—Hope *v* Prosser, 11th Dec 1816 F C—Presbytery of Dumfries 7th July 1818, F C—Presbytery of Stirling, 8th July 1818 F C note—Menzies *v* Barry 1826, 4 S 829—But see *contra* Duncan *v* Rordanz, 25th June 1817 F C

TITLE VIII

OF THE EXAMINATION OF WITNESSES

CHAPTER I.—BEFORE WHOM THE EXAMINATION IS CONDUCTED

§ 1912 Witnesses are examined before judges, one or more, sitting either with or without a jury, before a magistrate or justice of peace before a commissioner of court, or before an arbiter chosen by the parties or a commissioner appointed by him

§ 1913 Legal antiquarians consider that jury trial was originally the prevailing mode of investigation in civil causes in Scotland (*a*) Long ago, however, it had become limited in the civil courts to certain classes of cases, the chief of which were cognitions of insane persons, services of heirs, kennings of the widow's terce, and divisions of property among heirs-portioners,—these cases relating merely to matter of fact without the questions of law which are almost always involved in ordinary actions

§ 1914 In the Court of Session it became the practice to take all proofs in writing, in order to their being submitted to the court as judges both of law and fact The examination, which was formerly conducted before one of the Lords Ordinary (who sat in weekly rotation), as "Ordinary on oaths and witnesses" (*b*), was made competent before the Lord Ordinary in the cause (*c*) But for a long time the judges have discontinued taking such proofs personally, and have been in the practice of appointing a commissioner in each case to perform the duty (*d*) It is still competent,

---

(*a*) Kames' Law Tracts (4th ed), 291—Swinton on Court of Session and Revival of Jury Trial, 79—6 Bell's Styles, 1 *et seq* —2 Ivory's Forms of Process, 259

(*b*) 1537, c 53—A S, 5th June 1711

(*c*) 1 and 2 Vict c 118 §§ 3 4.

(*d*) The A S, 11th March 1800 directs that, in proofs to be reported to the whole

however for either the Court or the Lord Ordinary in the cause to direct witnesses to be examined before themselves, whenever that may be expedient (*e*)

§ 1915 The cumbrous machinery of written proofs was in daily use when the Jury Court was instituted, in the year 1815 (*f*) At first it was not imperative to send any class of actions to trial by jury But certain causes were afterwards appropriated to that tribunal (*g*) and these are almost always tried in this way, although a recent statute made it competent for either Division of the Court of Session (with which the Jury Court was amalgamated in the year 1830) to allow proof on commission in any of the enumerated causes where the action is not an action for libel or nuisance, or properly and in substance an action of damages (*h*) [1]

Court, the commissioner shall be a practising advocate of at least five years' standing, and resident in Edinburgh, or a sheriff-depute unless where the Court, on special cause shown, name some other person In proofs ordered by a Lord Ordinary to be reported to himself, the commissioner may be any of these persons, or any sheriff-substitute, or the clerk or assistant-clerk of any court the parties not being allowed to name their own commissioners These regulations are not strictly observed They do not apply to consistorial causes, see *infra*, § 1916 (*e*) Craigie *v* Croll, 1832 10 S, 315 —See also Officers of State *v* Alexander, 1839, 1 D 1188—*Supra*, § 1402

(*f*) 55 Geo III, c 42 (*g*) Certain causes were first appropriated to jury trial by 59 Geo III c 35 § 1 The provisions of that act on the subject were repeated by 6 Geo IV, c 120, under which (§ 28) the causes so appropriated are ' all actions on account of injury to the person whether real or verbal as assault and battery, libel or defamation, all actions on account of any injury to movables or to land, when, in this last case the title is not in question all actions for damages on account of breach of promise of marriage, or on account of seduction or adultery, all actions founded on delinquency or *quasi* delinquency of any kind, where the conclusion shall be for damages only and expenses, all actions on the responsibility of shipmasters and owners, carriers by land or water, innkeepers or stablers for the safe custody and care of goods and commodities, horses, money, clothes jewels, and other articles, and, in general, all actions grounded on the principle of the edict *nautæ caupones stabularii*, all actions brought for nuisance, all actions of reduction on the head of furiosity and idiotcy or of facility and lesion, or on force and fear, all actions on policies of insurance, whether for maritime, or fire, or life insurance, all actions on charter parties and bills of lading, all actions for freight, all actions on contracts for the carriage of goods by land or water and actions for the wages of masters and mariners of ships or vessels "

(*h*) 13 and 14 Vict c 36, § 49

---

[1] It has been lately laid down that where matters of fact are in dispute, the rule is that they must be tried by jury unless special cause be shewn why there should be a proof on commission In Cameron *v* Kerr, 1861, 23 D, 1257, where there were few matters of fact in dispute—the principal point regarding the usage of trade,—both parties were desirous to have the proof taken on commission But the Court refused the motion for a commission the Lord Justice-Clerk (Inglis) observing— *Prima facie*, every question of disputed fact should go to a jury No doubt there are many exceptions to the rule, as when the fact and law are so mixed up that it seems difficult to

In cases which are not specially appropriated to trial by jury (except consistorial causes), that mode of investigation is usually adopted for trying either the whole cause or special issues of fact but it is competent to the Lord Ordinary, with consent of both parties, or on the motion of one party with leave of the Inner House obtained on report, or to the Court when the cause comes into the Inner House, to appoint the evidence, or any portion of it, to be taken by commission (i)

§ 1916 The proof in consistorial causes is almost always taken on commission before one of the Sheriffs appointed to discharge that duty, and who alone are qualified to act as commissioners (k),[2] except in the case of witnesses "furth of the kingdom," who may be examined before any commissioner appointed by the Lord Ordinary or the Court (l) It is also competent to either Division of the Court, or to a Lord Ordinary, after advising with the Inner House, to direct that any consistorial cause, or any issue or issues

(i) 13 and 14 Vict c 36, § 49 (k) 6 and 7 Will IV, c 41, § 2—11 Geo IV, and 1 Will IV, c 69, § 41 The sheriffs are appointed to this office by the Home Secretary in such number as he shall think fit In Shaw v Shaw, 1850, 12 D, 1239, a remit was made to the Judge Ordinary of the bounds to take the proof as to a question of domicile, on which the defence depended (l) 13 and 14 Vict c 36, § 26

extricate them before a jury, or when the questions of fact in the case are so slight as compared with the questions of law that it is not worth while to send the case to a jury, but the general rule is, that cases involving questions of fact should go to a jury And parties who wish a proof on commission, instead of a jury trial, will need to show special cause to induce the Court to allow it" Where there is a necessity for taking a great deal of evidence abroad thus rendering a commission necessary at any rate, that has been held a good ground for allowing the whole proof to be so taken, Wemyss v Australian Co of Edinburgh 1857, 19 D, 400 But see Watt v Watt, 1859, 19 D, 787, where, although it was stated that the pursuer resided in New York, and that much evidence would require to be taken abroad, the Court sent the case to a jury Where the subject in dispute is of small value, the Court have granted a commission, Jack v Jack, 1857 19 D, 862 There is no absolute rule that cases of deathbed must be tried by jury, and, when strong grounds for a proof on commission are shewn, it is open to the Court to grant commission, Fairholme v Fairholme's Trustees, 1856, 19 D, 178 Actions of damages for breach of promise to marry are invariably tried by jury, Sinclair v Rowan, 1861 23 D, 1365 In a recent case, which involved the question of the legitimacy of the pursuer, the Lord President (M'Neill) observed, that though in the statutes appropriating cases to jury trial cases of legitimacy were not included, yet that not being excluded, it was open to the Court to say whether they should be sent to a jury but that he knew of no case in which that question had been submitted to a jury, and that he did not consider such a course advisable A proof on commission was granted, Swinton v Swinton, 1862, 24 D, 833

[2] Proofs in consistorial actions are no longer taken by the Sheriffs, 24 and 25 Vict, c 86, § 13 (Conjugal Rights Act) See next note

of fact connected therewith, be tried by jury (*m*) This form might often be adopted with a saving both of time and expense [3]

§ 1917 A new mode of trying causes was introduced by the Court of Session Act of 1850 If the parties in any cause before the Court of Session in which an issue has been adjusted, shall consent to the Lord Ordinary before whom the cause depends trying it without a jury the cause may be so tried, unless the Court, on report of the Lord Ordinary shall deem it inexpedient and improper (*n*) It is also competent for the Lord Ordinary in a cause without adjusting an issue, to appoint questions of fact to be tried by himself without a jury, where he considers they should not be investigated either by jury trial or by proof on commission, and such questions shall be tried by the Lord Ordinary accordingly, unless the Court shall deem that course to be inexpedient, or shall otherwise alter his Lordship's interlocutor (*o*) In both of these cases the decision of the Lord Ordinary on matters of fact is final, but he may within a certain period review and correct his findings or order a new trial, as he may think fit (*p*) [4]

§ 1918 The Court of Session Act also enables litigants in that

(*m*) 11 Geo IV and 1 Will IV c 69, § 37 (*n*) 13 and 14 Vict c 36 § 46 (*o*) Ib, § 48 (*p*) Ib, §§ 47, 48

[3] The Conjugal Rights Act, 24 and 25 Vict, c 86, § 13 provides that proofs in consistorial actions (except when a witness is beyond the jurisdiction of the Court, or unable to attend by reason of age, infirmity, or sickness) shall be led before the Lord Ordinary The Lord Ordinary is authorised either to take and write down the evidence with his own hand or to dictate it to a clerk, "or the Lord Ordinary shall cause it to be taken down and recorded in short-hand by a writer skilled in short-hand writing, and the Lord Ordinary may if he think fit dictate to the short-hand writer the evidence which he is to record, and the said short-hand writer shall afterwards write out in full the evidence so taken by him, and the notes of the judge, or the extended notes of such writer, certified by the presiding judge to be correct shall be the record of the oral evidence in the cause" This provision has worked remarkably well, the evidence in consistorial causes being now taken very expeditiously

[4] In Hood *v* Williamson the Court intimated an opinion that the causes to which the act of 1850 was intended to apply were not ordinary jury questions "It was thought by the framers of that act that there was a class of cases in use to be tried by jury in which the jury might well be dispensed with—cases involving questions of law and likely to issue in special verdicts—cases in which special verdicts are the best mode of raising the questions of law between the parties, and in which though it might be necessary to take evidence the parties and the judge would probably adjust a special verdict the presence of the jury being a mere matter of form For such cases this section (the 46th) was intended, but to hold it as providing for the trial of what are ordinary jury questions is an entire mistake," *per* Lord Justice-Clerk (Inglis) in Hood *v* Williamson 1861 23 D 496 Cases tried before the Lord Ordinary under this section should proceed continuously, and in the same way as jury trials, Hood *v* Williamson *supra*

court, by mutual consent, to refer the issues in any cause to one, three, five, or seven arbiters by whom the cause is tried as by jury, the verdict, whether pronounced unanimously or by a majority, being final, so as to exclude a new trial on the ground of its being against evidence, or on any other ground implying miscarriage on the part of the jury alone (*q*)

§ 1919 In the Court of Exchequer, where the procedure is conducted in the antiquated English form directed by the act 6 Anne, c 26, questions of fact are always investigated by jury, and the English rules of evidence are to some extent applied (*r*)[5]

§ 1920 Till recently the depositions of witnesses in civil causes in the Sheriff-court (except small debt cases) were taken in writing before the Sheriff or Sheriff-substitute like proofs on commission, a too common practice of granting commissions for the purpose having been prohibited, except where neither the Sheriff nor his Substitute could personally perform the duty, without interfering with other and more important official duties (*s*) By a recent statute the old form of written proofs is abolished in ordinary Sheriff-court cases, except in examining witnesses who reside beyond the jurisdiction of the court in which the cause is tried, and those who from infirmity or illness are unable to attend in court (*t*) The Sheriff or Sheriff-substitute has now to take the proofs personally, and to make a note of the evidence, by way of narrative, in his own handwriting, or to dictate it to any competent person where he is unavoidably prevented from writing it with his own hand (*u*) There is no general system of civil jury trials in the Sheriff-courts But a few cases are tried by Sheriffs in this way both by common law—as brieves of idiocy and kennings of the terce, and by statute—as claims for compensation against railway companies on account of land taken or injured by railways (*x*)

(*q*) 13 and 14 Vict, c 36, § 50 (*r*) Adv -Gen v Sinclair, 1855 17 D, 290

(*s*) A S, 10th July 1839, § 68—A S, 10th March 1819, § ii, 2

(*t*) 16 and 17 Vict, c 80, § 10 (*u*) Ib (*x*) 8 Vict, c 19, § 36, *et seq*

It was observed by Lord Deas, in Kerr v Hamilton, 1857, 19 D, 322, that the Judicature Act had been held to discountenance proofs before answer, but that this objection was removed by the act of 1850, by which a proof could be led before the Lord Ordinary without delay or much expense The mode of trial provided by the act has never, however become popular, and comparatively few causes are tried under either the 16th or 48th section

[5] It does not appear that any change in this respect has been effected by the Court of Exchequer Act, 19 and 20 Vict cap 56

In Small Debt Courts Sheriffs and Justices of the Peace decide both on law and fact, without having to record or note the evidence

§ 1921 For time immemorial all trials in the Justiciary Court for crimes, small as well as great, have been by jury (*y*) [6] The numerous cases which are too important for summary trial, and not sufficiently so for prosecution in the supreme criminal court, are tried by the Sheriff or Sheriff-substitute of the bounds with the aid of a jury, while police offences petty thefts, and other minor cases are tried summarily without a jury by Sheriffs, Magistrates, and Justices of the Peace Proofs on commission are unknown in criminal causes, the only procedure analogous to them being that by which the declarations of witnesses supposed to be dying are taken before one of the officers just referred to, in order to be given in evidence at the trial, if the witness has died in the interval (*z*)

§ 1922 In cases submitted to arbitration the proof is led before the arbiter, witnesses who reside at a distance being examined on commission (*a*) There is no law prohibiting arbiters from ordering the whole proof to be taken in this way

---

CHAPTER II—OF THE RULE THAT WITNESSES MUST DEPONE *IN CAUSA* AND OF TRANSFERRING DEPOSITIONS FROM ANOTHER CAUSE

§ 1923 It is a fundamental rule that witnesses must be examined judicially as such in the particular cause in which their testimony is required The reason is, that an examination and cross-examination in open court under the solemn sanction of an oath, are the best means of securing truth and detecting falsehood, while the demeanours of the witnesses greatly assist the jury in estimating contradictory or questionable evidence Personal attendance is not less necessary in depositions on commission, in order

(*y*) 2 Hume, 138 (*z*) See *infra*, § 1965 (*a*) See *supra*, § 1898

[6] In Scotland an alien cannot insist on being tried by a jury composed partly of aliens and partly of British subjects H M Adv *v* Itansen, 1858, 3 Irv, 3—See also H M Adv *v* Cavalan, 1854, 1 Irv, 564

that the truth may be brought out by cross-examination, and that the commissioner may observe and report anything in the conduct or appearance of the witnesses which may impair their credibility

§ 1924 This rule excludes written statements of fact under the hand of witnesses who are still alive—as, for example, certificates (*b*) (except in the cases noticed *infra*, § 1933), reports (*c*), although made on soul and conscience (*d*), or even by way of affidavit (*e*) And although the commissioner before whom a witness has been examined may embody in his report any observations upon the behaviour of the witness (*f*), a letter written by him *ex intervallo*, containing a statement of that nature, will be disregarded (*g*) The same rule (as already noticed) excludes notarial instruments (*h*), and messengers executions (*i*), respectively, on matters for which law has not prescribed these official narratives And the probative quality of judicial records suffers a similar limitation (*j*) For the same reason, works upon medical or other science are not evidence, the proper mode of proving the matters set forth in them being by the examination of scientific witnesses (*k*)

§ 1925 Even regular examinations on oath, taken with reference to other proceedings, are inadmissible (under certain exceptions noticed afterwards),—as, for example, the depositions of a bankrupt, of the members of his family, and other persons, examined under the Sequestration Act, which are taken in order to ascertain the condition of the bankrupt estate for the creditors generally, and are not competent evidence in favour of individual claimants (*l*)[1] So the deposition of a haver in the cause, being designed for securing production of documents, cannot be used as

---

(*b*) Skene *v* Lumsden 1662, M, 12,618—Wishart *v* Davidson, 1670, M, 12,630—Bell *v* Robertson, 1676, M, 12,631—Kirk *v* Guthrie, 1817, 1 Mur, 275—Ure *v* Pollock, 1832, 10 S, 450—Humphreys' case, 1839, separate rep 128—Stalker, 1844, 2 Broun, 79—Cavalari 1854, 1 Irv 561 (*c*) Sturrock *v* Greig, 1849, 12 D, 166—Per L Just-Clerk in Wark *v* Bargaddie Coal Co, 27th Feb 1855, 27 Sc Jur, 224 (*d*) Stothert *v* Johnstone's Tr, 1821, 2 Mur, 541

(*e*) Mag of Aberdeen *v* More 1813, Hume D, 502—Simpson & Co *v* M'Farlane, 1822, 2 Mur, 194—Johnston *v* Scott, 1829 7 S, 235—Glyn *v* Johnston, 1834, 13 S, 126 (*f*) See sections on commissioner's report of proof, *infra*

(*g*) Cowper *v* Marq of Bute, 1828, 4 Mur, 551 (*h*) *Supra*, § 1188

(*i*) *Supra*, § 1227 (*j*) *Supra*, § 1077 (*k*) See *supra*, § 1178

(*l*) 2 Bell's Com, 399, 400, 482—Robb's Sequestration, 26th May 1809, noted in ib, 399—Dundas and Robinson *v* Belch, 10th June 1806, ib

---

[1] But see Emslie *v* Alexander, 1862, 1 Macph, 209

the evidence of a witness on the merits (*m*) The same incompetency exists in regard to depositions emitted in another cause, relating to the same matter but with a different party, because the party against whom they are tendered had not an opportunity of protecting his interest during the examination, and every witness should be examined with reference to the issue in the individual cause, and the other parts of the proof therein (*n*) For the latter reason depositions in a previous suit, even between the same parties, are generally inadmissible (*o*) It is also irregular for the counsel conducting the second or third trial of a cause to refer to evidence emitted by witnesses in a previous trial (*p*) Where a witness whose deposition had been taken to lie *in retentis* at the commencement of a cause was prevented by illness from attending the trial, the Court refused to admit that deposition on the ground that he should have been examined on adjusted interrogatories with a view to the trial (*r*)

§ 1926 From these authorities, and the rules of modern practice, it is plain that the Court would not now follow some older decisions, in which the depositions in one case were admitted in another case both with the same and with a different party (*s*) It is not necessary to consider the value, as precedents, of some instances in which the depositions taken in a criminal case were imported into a civil prosecution for damages against the wrongdoer, the evidence in criminal cases not being now taken at length in writing (*t*)

§ 1927 In an old case where a submission had been allowed to expire without a decree-arbitral, whereupon an action was raised regarding the same matter, the depositions which had been emitted in the submission were received in the action reserving to both parties to re-examine the witnesses and lead additional proof, and also reserving all objections to the depositions of witnesses already

---

(*m*) See *supra* § 1359 (*n*) L Gadgirth *v* L Auchinleck 1631, M 14,027 —Broomhall *v* M Douglas 1665, M, 14,028—Glendinning *v* E Nithsdale, 1675, M, 14,031, 12 226—A B, M 14,032—Anderson *v* Murray, 1695 4 B Sup, 297—Montgomery *v* L Cassilis, 1711 M 14,041—Macdonald 1721, Rob Ap Ca 307

(*o*) Cases in two next notes (*p*) Hallam *v* Gye, 1835, 14 S, 199—E Fife *v* E Fife's Tr 1816, 1 Mur 125 See *supra*, § 1086 (*r*) Watson *v* Glass 1837, 15 S 754 See *infra*, § 1953 (*s*) Whitelaw *v* Ruthven, 1630 M, 14 026—Finlayson *v* Lookup 1628, M, 14,024—Ramsay *v* L Craigie, 1565 M 12 447 (*t*) Bontein *v* Buchanan's Crs, 1739, M, 14 043, Elch, 'Proof,' No 5 S C—Machargs *v* Campbell, 1767 M 12 541, Hailes, 192 S C—2 Hume, 179, 480—Bell's Pr, § 2216—See *supra*, § 1082, 3

examined (*v*) Again in a modern case, where after an action had proceeded some length, and a proof had been taken in it, an objection to the pursuer's title was sustained, the Court reserved to the pursuer to use the proof in any other competent action (*x*), which from the nature of the case (a reduction on the head of deathbed) could only have arisen with the same defenders The principle of these decisions is that the second process was truly a continuation of the first, which had been rendered abortive by an objection in point of form, and that it would have been a useless expense to repeat the proof Of course, the witnesses would have been examined of new, if the second case had been tried by jury

§ 1928 Mr Erskine lays down that where a purchaser of heritable property, after having been evicted sues the seller upon the warrandice, he may found on the proof led in the action against himself, reserving all objections to its validity (*y*) In like manner where the heir of a debtor, having been defeated in an arbitration with the creditor, raised action of relief against the ancestor's executor, the Court sustained the claim as determined by the decree-arbitral, unless the executor could prove collusion in taking the proof, or could show any good ground for lessening the sums decerned for, reserving to the defender to re-examine such of the witnesses as were yet living (*z*) The same principle would apply to actions of relief at the instance of a cautioner against the principal debtor (*a*)

§ 1929 Again where the proof is on commission, it is competent to the parties, of consent, to import into the case depositions taken in another case (*b*). But this will not be allowed in jury trials except in regard to witnesses who are dead or unable to attend the trial from illness or the like (*c*) The proper course, if parties are agreed on certain facts, is to admit these by minute If they are not agreed, the jury must see the witnesses examined

§ 1930. Under the rule which admits secondary evidence where

(*v*) Chalmers *v* Cunningham, 1733, Elch, 'Proof, No 1 affd Cr and St 267 (In noting this case Lord Elchies observes *Sed vide* if the judgment of the House of Lords be not founded on some specialty, not noticed in their interlocutor" It appears that their Lordships went in some measure on the circumstance of the party having acquiesced for six years in the interlocutor admitting the proof) See also Ersk , 4, 3, 36

(*x*) Macindoe *v* Lyon, 7th December 1826, F C (*y*) Ersk 2, 3 32

(*z*) D Gordon *v* Lv H Gordon, 1718 M 14,015 (*a*) See a case illustrative of the same doctrine Struthers *v* Dykes, 1817, 9 D 1137 affd 7 Bell's Ap Ca 290.

(*b*) Lack *v* Lyall 1833 11 S 711 affd on merits, 1 Sh and McL , 77

(*c*) Mackellar *v* Lambert 1828 4 Mur 515

witnesses have died (*d*), their depositions, when taken in a previous case between the parties regarding the same matter, are admissible being more trustworthy than hearsay of their statements (*e*) This holds where the adverse party allowed the previous case to proceed in absence for if evidence so taken were not admissible, a party who has a good case depending on parole proof could not secure his rights against an opposition, which his adversary has reserved until the witnesses shall have died (*f*) Of course, testimony emitted by a witness in a former trial of the same cause will be admitted if he has died in the interval (*g*) And in like manner, the depositions of persons examined under the Bankrupt Act seem to be admissible in any subsequent question relating to the bankrupt estate, if they have died in the interval (*h*)

§ 1931 But even the death of a witness will not render his deposition in another cause admissible as substitutionary evidence, "if it has been emitted under circumstances which raise a presumption that it does not give a proper reflex of the mind of the party who made the statement" (*i*) On this account it is thought that depositions emitted in a previous suit with a different party should be excluded, although the witnesses have died, for it is impossible to calculate how far the aspect of such evidence would have been altered, if the party against whom it is tendered, had examined the witnesses with reference to the subsequent case (*k*) But this rule will probably be relaxed in questions of pedigree, ancient boundaries and the like, where the proof is almost always of a makeshift character (*l*) Even in this favourable class of cases however, depositions in a previous process will be rejected, if they were not taken and recorded by a court or judge competent to give them a character of credence for the end for which they are tendered (*m*)

(*d*) See *supra*, § 102, *et seq* (*e*) Mackenzie *v* Ross 1818, 2 Mur, 17—Henderson *v* Gardyne, 1820 2 Mur, 337—Smith *v* Knowles 1824 3 Mur, 429, 431—Mackellar *v* Lambert, *supra*—Oswald *v* Laurie, 1828, 5 Mur, 10—Watson *v* Glass, 1837, 15 S 753—Cleland *v* Fleming, 1847 10 D, 40 (*f*) *Per curiam* in Watson *v* Glass, *supra*—See also M'Lean *v* Sibbald, 1819 2 Mur, 122—Douglas 1855, 17 D, 431 (*g*) Robertson *v* Allardice, 1830, 5 Mur, 330—Cleland *v* Fleming 1847 10 D, 40—Willox *v* Farrell, 1848 10 D, 807 (*h*) 2 Bell s Com 482

(*i*) Per L Pres M'Neill in Geils *v* Geils 1855, 17 D, 404

(*k*) A B, M 14,032—Anderson *v* Murray 1695 4 B Sup, 297 But such depositions will be admitted of consent, Cochrane *v* Wallace, 1820, 2 Mur, 299 In one case a deposition taken in a different suit between the same parties was rejected but its terms were afterwards proved by one who had been present and the case does not seem to deserve much weight, Smith *v* Knowles, 1824 3 Mur 421 compared with ib, 430

(*l*) Per L Moncreiff in Gordon *v* Grant, 1850 13 D, 1—See *supra*, § 1174, *et seq*

(*m*) Per L Moncreiff in Gordon *v* Grant, *supra*

Accordingly, depositions which had been taken in a proceeding before justices of the peace were rejected in a process of division of commonty in which the same question was involved, because one of the justices was interested as a party in the cause while one of the proprietors had not been called for his interest (*n*). In like manner, depositions in previous proceedings between the same parties will be rejected if they were taken by one of them *ex parte* at a diet which the other was not called to attend (*o*).[2] The reason why such depositions are rejected, while hearsay of the casual statements made by a deceased witness are admitted, is, that the former are taken for a special purpose to bring out only certain facts by a one-sided interrogation; whereas the statements which a witness makes casually and spontaneously are usually a fair reflex of his mind upon the facts to which he speaks, the whole circumstances attending the conversation being laid before the jury (*p*). Depositions of persons who had been examined as havers in the same cause were once rejected as evidence on their death (*r*). This decision may perhaps be defended on the ground that it is irregular to ask a haver any questions upon the merits of the cause (*s*). But there is room for questioning it,—at least in so far as it would exclude such parts of the deposition as were relevant to the recovery of the writings to which the haver referred.

§ 1932. In a recent case the following point occurred. A suit for restitution of conjugal rights having been raised by a husband against his wife before the Arches Court of Canterbury, she met it by a responsive allegation of cruelty and adultery, and, in the course of the suit, several witnesses were examined for her and then de-

(*n*) Gordon *v.* Grant, *supra*. (*o*) Carleton *v.* Strong, 1821, 1 Mur., 28. (But see Lord Chief Commissioner's remarks on this case in 2 Mur., 299.)—Macl. Pr., 191—M'Lean *v.* Sibbald, 1819, 2 Mur., 124. In Scott *v.* Wilson, 1829, 5 Mur., 53, depositions were rejected because they were not on stamped paper, in terms of a statute existing at the time they were emitted. (*p*) See *per curiam* in Grant *v.* Grant, *supra*, and in Geils *v.* Geils, 1855, 17 D., 397. (*r*) Campbell *v.* Davidson, 1827, 4 Mur., 178. (*s*) See *supra*, § 1359.

[2] A husband raised an action of divorce on the ground of adultery. The summons was personally served on the wife when within Scotland, but she did not lodge defences. Intimation was made to her of the diets of proof, but she did not appear at any of them. Decree of divorce was pronounced, but within a year and day she raised a reduction of the decree. It was contended by the pursuer that the Court could not look at the evidence taken in the action of divorce, which had been led *ex parte* and in another action, but it was held that it was competent for the Court to consider the proof so led; Stewart *v.* Stewart, 1863, 1 Macph., 449.

positions were recorded according to the ordinary mode of taking proofs in the Court of Arches. The wife having afterwards raised an action of divorce in the Court of Session on the ground of adultery, and tendered the depositions of certain of the witnesses who had died in the interval, the husband objected to their admissibility. It appeared that in the Arches Court witnesses are examined by an officer of court (called an Examiner), who receives a copy of the libel, and who is instructed by the proctor of the party who produces the witness, upon what allegations the witness is to be examined. The examination is taken down in writing, and after having been read over to the witness in order that he may correct it where necessary, it is signed by him. The cross-examination is conducted by the same officer, who is furnished with interrogatories framed by the counsel and proctor for the opposite party after being informed of the articles upon which the witness is to be examined in chief. The whole examination is conducted out of the presence of the parties, their counsel and proctors.—It was strongly urged by the counsel for the husband that these were in fact *ex parte* depositions, taken in a manner which was inconsistent with the principles of the Scotch law of evidence, and was not calculated to bring out the truth. But the Court held that the depositions were admissible, because they had been taken according to a mode of investigation which, although not the best for eliciting the truth, was yet a fair procedure, and was the regular mode of proving facts in the court where the examination was conducted. Their Lordships did not, however, decide that depositions taken in a foreign court according to the forms there recognised will, in every case, be admitted in this country, if the witnesses so examined have died in the interval (*t*). On the contrary, their opinions show that in determining such questions the Court will pay regard to the mode of investigation adopted in each individual case, and will reject the depositions if they are taken in a way which is not likely to elicit a fair statement from the witness. Slighter defects in the procedure will go merely to the credibility of the depositions.

§ 1933. Again, the death of a witness does not render admissible an affidavit (*u*), or certificate (*x*) under his hand; for such documents are more frequently one-sided stories dressed up for the

(*t*) Geils *v.* Geils, 1855, 17 D. 397.

(*u*) Mag. of Aberdeen *v.* More, 1813, Hume D. 502.—See *supra* § 1663.

(*x*) Humphreys' case, 1839, separate report by Swinton, 197, and Appx. 86.—See also Wilson *v.* Kirkwood, 1822, 3 Mur. [illegible]

occasion, than fair substitutes for the witness' deposition before the jury [3] Still less will affidavits (*y*), or certificates (*z*), be rendered admissible by the person who emits them being out of the country, and so inaccessible to second diligence. Yet in ancient matters such evidence will be admitted if it is free from appearance of concoction (*a*)

An exception from the general rule against certificates is also recognised in criminal cases, a prisoner who pleads guilty being allowed to use, in mitigation of punishment certificates of previous good character But the Court refuse to admit such evidence either in exculpation or in mitigation of the punishment when the case goes before a jury (*b*)

§ 1934 When a deposition made in a previous case is admissible, it is usually proved by the commissioner's report, if it was taken on commission (*c*), and by the judge's notes, if it was emitted before a jury (*d*) If the witness was examined on adjusted interrogatories before a first trial, but attended that trial of the case, his evidence, on his having died before the second trial, may be proved either from the deposition, or from the judge's notes of the trial (*e*) Any person who was present at the first trial, also may prove the deposition (*f*) [4]

(*y*) Glyn *v* Johnston 1834, 13 S 126 (*z*) Skene *v* Lumsden 1662 M, 12 618—Wishart *v* Davidson 1670, M, 12,630—Cavalan, 1854, 1 Irv, 564—See also Rouat 1853, ib, 79—But see Ranking of Cleland's Crs, 1708 M 12 634—*Supra* § 104 (*a*) Stair 4, 43 5—See *supra*, § 107, and § 1174 *et seq*

(*b*) Rosenberk 1842 1 Broun, 367—Stalker 1844, 2 ib, 81

(*c*) Mackenzie *v* Ross 1813, 2 Mur, 17—Henderson *v* Gardyne, 1820 2 Mur 336 *Supra* § 1939, *et seq*—But see *contra*, Smith *v* Knowles 1824, 3 Mur 421 compared with ib, 430 (*d*) Cleland *v* Fleming 1847, 10 D, 40—Mackellar *v* Lambert, 1828, 4 Mur 545—Robertson *v* Allardyce 1830, 5 Mur, 330 In this case the judge's notes were not in Court but the evidence was read from a bill of exceptions, in which the notes had been engrossed (*e*) Willox *v* Farrell 1848 10 D, 807

(*f*) *Supra*, § 117

---

[3] On this principle, in a criminal trial, the pocket-book of a deceased person, containing entries, alleged to go directly to the essential parts of the charge, and tendered as secondary evidence of the events to which the entries related, was rejected H M Adv *v* Madeline Smith, 1857, 2 Irv, 618 Another ground of judgment was that the entries were made in pencil, but it is not thought that there is any difference in the value of pencil and of ink see opinions of Lord Justice-Clerk (Hope) in Williamson *v* Kennedy, 1857, 19 D, 413, and of Chief-Justice Abbot in Geary *v* Physic 1826 5 Barn and Cres, 234 But Lord Cowan was not prepared to say that looking to the facilities with which forgery might be made a document in pencil was in the same position as if written in ink, Williamson *v* Kennedy *supra*

[4] When a new trial is granted, and witnesses who were examined at a previous trial

Some of the points noticed in these sections have been treated at length in the chapter on hearsay (*g*). The competency of depositions as proof of admissions by the persons examined has also been considered (*h*) The rules as to taking depositions to lie *in retentis* will be found below (*i*)

CHAPTER III.—OF EXAMINATIONS BEFORE AND AFTER ANSWER AS TO THE RELEVANCY OF THE AVERMENTS ETC

§ 1935 In general, the proof in a cause should not be allowed until all questions as to the relevancy of the respective averments, to infer a ground of action or defence, have been disposed of, because *frustra probatur quoad probatum non relevat*, and an opposite practice would often cause a useless investigation, with its consequent expense and delay (*a*) This rule is observed strictly in criminal prosecutions, where all objections to the relevancy of the libel must be disposed of before the case is remitted to an assize (*b*) In civil cases tried by jury the relevancy of the ground, both of action and defence, is almost always settled before fixing the issues And this is also commonly done before allowing a proof when it is taken on commission [1]

(*g*) *Supra*, § 103, *et seq* (*h*) *Supra*, § 1438 (*i*) *Infra*, § 1939, *et seq* (*a*) Stair, 4, 39 4—Ib , 4, 45, 10 (*b*) 2 Hume, 284—Bell's Notes, 234—See also *supra* § 46

---

have died or cannot attend, it is competent for the presiding judge to certify his notes of the evidence of such witnesses (although no bill of exceptions has been tendered)—such signature certifying the correctness of the notes, Bell *v* Reid, 1862, 24 D , 1428 See also M'Intosh *v* Great West Ry Co 1855 7 De Gex Mac and G , 737

[1] Lord Curriehill, in Millar *v* Small observed that when a question of relevancy is raised, and judgment asked upon it before the facts are ascertained, it requires the exercise of the sound discretion of the judge whether he shall comply with that demand, or whether he shall have the disputed matters of fact investigated in some proper manner before answer "There has prevailed, however, a notion in the Outer House for some time, that a judge is bound to give the parties a judgment upon the question of relevancy if they ask it My experience, since I have had the benefit of sitting in the Inner House, has taught me that that is a mistake, and that in the Outer House the judges should apply their minds more to the matter of discretion than they do" The other judges concurred , Millar *v*. Small, 1856, 18 D , 492 In Dobbie *v* Johnston, the

§ 1936 In civil cases, however, where the questions of fact seem to admit of easy solution, while the question of relevancy is difficult, the Court have sometimes reserved the latter till the former should have been investigated by a "proof before answer" And where the case embraces averments both relevant and irrelevant, a proof of this kind is not unfrequently allowed, leaving the points of law to be determined afterwards with reference to the facts as proved, and not upon hypothetical views of them This course is more frequently adopted where the proof is on commission than when it is by jury trial But cases are sometimes sent to a jury before answer, or under reservation of all question as to the relevancy of the averments (*c*) This course, also, is sometimes adopted where the case contains matter of law independent of the point of relevancy (*d*)

Without attempting to lay down a definite rule as to the cases in which this order of procedure is advisable, it may be said generally, that wherever a case involves questions of law, the decision of which in a certain way would supersede the necessity for a trial, or proof on commission, as the case may be, these should be first disposed of (*e*), and that it is not a sufficient reason for reserving them that their solution is attended with difficulty

§ 1937 As a proof before answer is adduced under reservation

(*c*) 59 Geo III, c 35, § 3—Aikman *v* D Hamilton, 1829, 8 S, 54—Anderson *v* Blair, 1836, 14 S, 972—Devon Iron Co *v* F Mansfield, 1839, 2 D, 268—Shaw Stewart *v* Walker & Co, *infra*, (*e*)—Compared with Braidwood *v* Braidwood, 1835, 13 S, 419 See also per L Ch Cottenham in Duncan *v* Finlater, 1839, 1 M'L and Rob, 934, Macf Pr, 52—Cullen *v* Ewing, 1832, 10 S, 497, rev on merits, 6 W S, 566

(*d*) Authorities in preceding note

(*e*) Macf Pr, *supra* Some important views on this subject were thrown out in the House of Lords in the case of Shaw Stewart *v* Walker & Co, 1855, 4 Macq, 424

---

pursuer, after issues had been adjusted, moved the Court to dispose of the question of relevancy before the trial took place, but the Court, in the circumstances, refused to do so Lord Justice-Clerk (Inglis)—"It seems to me that, by the Jury Court Act it is left to the Court to arrange, as a matter of expediency, whether they shall at once determine questions of law or relevancy arising on the face of the record or send the case to a jury, leaving such questions to be raised at the trial That discretion is expressly given to the Court by the statute, and it is in the exercise of that discretion that we are now acting" And his Lordship added, "I cannot help thinking, that to decide questions of relevancy or law before the trial is a practice which the Court ought, in the general case, to be very slow to adopt", Dobbie *v* Johnston, 1859, 21 D 624 See also Priestnell *v* Hutcheson, 1857, 19 D, 495—Earl of Galloway *v* Grant, 1857, 19 D, 865—Ker *v* Hamilton, 1857, 19 D, 322—Swinton *v* Swinton, 1862, 24 D, 833

of the relative point of law the result may be that the party proves all his averments, and yet loses his case, in consequence of the question of law being decided against him (*f*)

§ 1938 In like manner, although questions as to the mode of proof are seldom disposed of before remitting the case to trial, yet where the party against whom an averment is made, pleads that it can only be proved by his writ or oath, it is not unusual first to decide that point, because a jury trial is improper where the proof is so limited (*g*) The point is also usually disposed of before allowing a proof on commission Such a proof, however, is sometimes allowed "before answer" on the point, and the consequence may be that it is ultimately disregarded as incompetent (*h*) When a case is sent to a jury, the party against whom the issue is taken is not foreclosed from pleading that it can only be proved by his writ or oath (*i*),—unless that point has been previously determined against him.

CHAPTER IV —OF TAKING DEPOSITIONS TO LIE *IN RETENTIS*

§ 1939 The general rule, that witnesses cannot be adduced until the record has been closed, yields where there is risk of evidence being lost, if it is not taken at an earlier stage In civil causes which are not matured for leading the whole proof, witnesses who are of great age, or in bad health, or who are expected to leave the country, may be examined on commission their depositions being sealed up to lie *in retentis* until the other evidence in the cause shall be led (*a*) This rule may be noticed somewhat in detail

§ 1940 Witnesses seventy years old and upwards may always

(*f*) See, *e g*, M'Rostie *v* Halley 1850, 12 D, 124, 816 (*g*) See *e.g*, Law *v* Gibsone 1835 13 S, 396—M'Lean *v* Richardson, 1834, 12 S, 865

(*h*) See *e g*, Fotheringham *v* Hunter, 1708, M, 12,414—Alcock *v* Fasson, 1842, 5 D, 356 noticed *supra*, § 111—Wodrow *v* Paterson, 1845, 7 D, 385—Little *v* Smith, 1845 8 D, 265 (*i*) Clark *v* Callender, 9th March 1819, F C, 2 Mur, 87, affd 16th June 1819, 19 F C, 772—M'Lean *v* Richardson, 1834, 12 S, 865

(*a*) Stair 4, 41, 7 (3, 5)—Ersk, 4, 2 31—Macf Pr, 88—Tait Ev, 112, *et seq*—Shand's Pr, 362—A S, 11th July 1828, § 117, noticed *infra*, § 1947

be examined in this way, however healthy they are at the time (*b*) [1] If they are within that age, then depositions will not be taken except on special cause shown, as, for example, that they are infirm, or that there is *penuria testium* (*c*) [2]

The examination of a witness who is pregnant will be allowed, if the trial is to come on after or about the time of her expected delivery (*d*)

§ 1941 Commissions have been granted for examining a soldier who had suddenly received orders to leave the country on foreign service (*e*), a witness about to emigrate to America (*f*), and a carpenter in the Royal Navy, who might be sent on foreign service at any time (*g*) But the application was refused where the party merely stated that the witness "intends to go abroad" (*h*) And where a commission was granted during the preparation of the record for examining a seafaring witness temporarily resident in England, the Court refused to include in it witnesses who resided there permanently, the proper time to examine them being after the case had been matured for proof (*i*) In a case of alleged impetration of a deed, where important witnesses for the pursuer were in the defender's service, and there was risk of his putting them out of the way, the Court allowed him the alternative of finding caution to produce them, or having their depositions taken to lie *in retentis* (*k*)

§ 1942 Where the evidence of a witness is vitally important to the case, his deposition has been taken to lie *in retentis*, lest by his death the party's rights should be imperilled This, for example, was done in regard to the instrumentary witnesses to deeds challenged on the ground of impetration from a person of unsound

---

(*b*) Forbes *v* Smith, 11th March 1820, F C—Harvey's Tr *v* Leslie, 1827, 5 S 896—Morrison *v* Watson, 1828, 6 S, 1082—Watsons 1829, 8 S 261—A S 11th July 1828, § 117 (*c*) Authorities in preceding note (*d*) Gordon *v* Orrok, 1849, 11 D 1558 (*e*) A B, 1831 1 Dea and And, 252

(*f*) Monro *v* Mackenzie 23d June 1831 F C (*g*) Clouston *v* Morris 1848, 20 Sc Jur, 228 (*h*) Ferrier *v* Berry 1822, 1 S 560

(*i*) Gray *v* Sutherland, 1849, 11 D 1189 (*k*) L Castlemilk *v* Whitefoord, 1676, M, 12092—See *supra*, § 1907

---

[1] In Ross *v* Forbes, 1856 18 D, 986, the Court granted commission to take the deposition of a witness, to lie *in retentis*, in a declaration of right to salmon-fishings although it was not alleged that he was seventy years of age, the party applying for the commission paying all expenses

[2] Hay *v* Dunney, 1859, 22 D, 183 Here the witness was said to be upwards of sixty years of age, and to have gone to Canada The application was refused

mind (*l*), and on the ground of fraud (*m*), falsehood (*n*), and informality in the execution (*o*). It was also allowed in older practice where there was no occasion for it beyond the risk which always exists to some extent where a case depends on parole testimony (*p*). But these cases would not now be followed (*q*). In a case of death-bed, however, where before the record was closed, both parties were desirous to have the depositions of witnesses who were abroad taken to lie *in retentis*, a commission was granted for the purpose, although there was no special ground for apprehending loss of their evidence (*r*).

The Court have refused to grant commission to examine seamen in the employment of the party making the application, but who were about to be sent abroad, as he could secure their attendance at the trial, or get it postponed until their return (*s*).[3]

§ 1943. Where a party had taken out a brieve for service before the macers of the Court of Session (according to the former practice), the Court granted him a commission for examining one of the only two surviving witnesses to the marriage of the applicant's father and mother, but who was not expected to live till the inquest should be held; and on account of the urgency of the case the Court dispensed with intimation, and the same day dispatched two macers and one of the clerks of court to take the deposition (*t*). This case presents the peculiarity of the Court of Session lending its aid to preserve evidence in a case not depending before it (*u*).

§ 1944. As to the stage of the cause at which depositions may be taken to lie *in retentis*, there does not seem to be any limit. In one case indeed, where during the dependence of a multiplepoinding a claimant announced his intention to raise a reduction of his

(*l*) Copland *v.* Bethune, 1827, 5 S., 272. (*m*) E. Lauderdale *v.* Duchess Lauderdale, 1696, M., 12,095. (*n*) F. Annandale *v.* Dalziel, 1696, M., 12,095. (*o*) E. Fife *v.* E. Fife's Trs., 11th March 1815, F. C. (*p*) L. Balmerino's Crs. *v.* Ly. Coupar, 1669, M., 10,421, 12,091.—E. Southesk *v.* L. Stormonth, 1696, M., 12,091. (*q*) See Tait, Ev., 410. (*r*) Malcolm *v.* Stewart, 1829, 7 S., 715. (*s*) Munn *v.* M'Gregor, 1854, 16 D., 385. See *infra*, § 1950. (*t*) E. Winton *v.* Kingston, 1710, M., 12,096. (*u*) See a corresponding power in regard to documents, *supra*, § 1350.

[3] In a jury cause the defenders, after the record was closed, but before issues were adjusted, applied for a commission and diligence to examine seamen in their employment, who were going on a voyage to Greenland. The Court granted the application,—the examination, on the suggestion of the Court, being taken on adjusted interrogatories, to obviate the necessity for re-examination after the adjustment of issues; Sutter *v.* Aberdeen Arctic Co., 1858, 30 Sc. Jur., 300.

competitor's title, the Court granted his application for an examination of old witnesses with reference to that intended process (*x*) The action of reduction, however, was merely required for enabling the party to plead an objection which was stated in the multiplepoinding, but could not be raised formally without reduction In general the examination is incompetent until the summons or petition in the case has been executed, because till then there is no dependence (*y*) Formerly it was refused unless the summons had been called, because a case is not in court until the calling (*z*) But now it is allowed in cases of urgency before the calling (*a*)

§ 1945 Under the Court of Session Act of 1850, a case which has been taken to the House of Lords on appeal from a judgment of the Court of Session remains before the Court for procedure in any matters not necessarily dependent on the interlocutor appealed from (*b*) The Court may therefore grant commission to take depositions to lie *in retentis*, while an appeal from a judgment which they have pronounced on the case is pending (*c*) In like manner, the Lord Ordinary in a cause may grant commission for this purpose after an interlocutor pronounced by him in it has been reclaimed against (*d*) [4]

(*x*) Johnston *v* Keyden 1824 3 S, 238 (*y*) Cranston *v* Ker, 1657, M, 12,091—Carlton *v* Strong 1816 1 Mur, 29—Tait Ev, 415 (*z*) Hamilton *v* Master of Balmerino, 1695, M, 12,091—Grant *v* Grant, 1745 M, 9596—Mag of Glenbervie, 1804, M, 12,097—Tait, *supra* (*a*) A S, 11th July 1828, § 117—Balmerino's Crs *v* Ly Coupar, 1669, M, 10,421, 12,091—Smith 1802, M, Appx "Process," No 5—M'Neill, 11th March 1819 (not rep) noted in Tait Ev, 417—Blair *v* Mag of Brechin, 1825 4 S 98—Monro *v* Mackenzie 23d June 1831, F C—Clouston *v* Morris, 1848, 20 Sc Jur, 228 (*b*) 13 and 14 Vict, c 36, § 13

(*c*) In Rose *v* Mackenzie, 1830, 3 De and And, 198, the Court did so before the act above cited was passed (*d*) 13 and 14 Vict, *supra* As to the former practice see Brown *v* Gilfillan, 1825, 3 S, 475

---

[4] The words of the act are, that no reclaiming note shall be held to remove the process from before the Lord Ordinary "as regards any point or points not necessarily dependent on the interlocutor so submitted to review," 13 and 14 Vict, c 36, § 13 In Swan *v* Carruthers, after a reclaiming note against an interlocutor of the Lord Ordinary repelling the plea that the action was irrelevant, had been presented, a motion was made before him for a commission to take evidence to lie *in retentis* The Lord Ordinary having doubts whether he could grant the commission (in respect that if the defender succeeded in his reclaiming note there was an end of the case, so that the taking of evidence was "necessarily dependent" on the interlocutor), and having reported the matter to the Court, "the Court waived deciding the point whether the Lord Ordinary had power or not, but themselves, on the Lord Ordinary's report, granted the motion," Swan *v* Carruthers, 1857, 19 D, 1015 An application for a commission to take evidence to lie *in retentis* should be made to the Lord Ordinary, before whom the case depends, and not to the Inner House, Hunt *v* Commissioners of Woods and Forests, 1856, 18 D, 317

§ 1946 In a case standing on summons and defences where an order to sist a mandatory had been pronounced, but before it had been implemented, a commission to examine aged witnesses was granted, on the understanding that no step would be taken under it until a mandatory had been sisted (*e*) And a commission for the same purpose was granted to the pursuer in an action against an heir, who pleaded the *annus deliberandi* (*f*), and where the defender was a minor who pleaded *non tenetur placitare super hæreditate paterna* and so brought the process to a stand until his majority (*g*) The pursuer has also been allowed a commission to take depositions to lie *in retentis* in the interval between the defender's death and the calling of his representative (*h*)

In such cases the party against whom the proof is taken will be allowed to attend the examination without prejudice to any plea competent to him (*i*)

§ 1947 At one time there was no means of taking depositions in the Court of Session when the Court was not sitting But that has been remedied by Act of Sederunt, which provides that, in order to prevent the loss of evidence by the death of witnesses, it shall be competent, during vacation or recess, to apply to the Lord Ordinary on the Bills on an application duly intimated forty-eight hours before to the known agent of the opposite party, and, on production of a depending process or of a summons before the Court of Session duly executed, or of letters (now of a note) of suspension or advocation duly executed or of the copy of such summons or letters served on the defender or respondent, or of an extract of such letters under the hand of the extractor of the signet, the proper legal evidence of execution being also produced —his Lordship, after hearing objections and on being satisfied that the application could not have been made to the Court or to the Lord Ordinary in the cause during session, may grant commission and diligence for examining "witnesses whose evidence, owing to great age (not under seventy years), or to severe indisposition, or to their intending to go abroad and to remain abroad for a considerable period, is in danger of being lost, such examinations to be sealed up by the commissioner and to lie *in retentis* subject to future orders of Court, provided always that such examinations

(*e*) Sandilands v Sandilands 1848, 10 D, 1091 (*f*) Moreton v Macdonald 1849, 11 D, 1417—*Contra* Duff v Innes, 1683, 2 B Sup, 37 (*g*) Kellie v Home, 1665, M 9063, 12 090—Kello v Kinnear, 1671, M, 9066

(*h*) Corbets v Love 8th July 1815, F C (*i*) Moreton v Macdonald, *supra*

shall be limited to matters of fact to be set forth in a correct condescendence for the party making the application, with or without answers thereto" (*k*)

§ 1948 These regulations apply to all causes in the Court of Session, whether the proof is ultimately taken on commission or before a jury, provided issues have not been ordered If they have, the case comes under the Act of Sederunt relating to jury trials (*l*)

§ 1949 Under the Act of Sederunt of 1828 (*m*), the application for a commission, if made in recess or vacation, must be intimated forty-eight hours before to the known agent of the opposite party A similar rule is observed in applications to the Court or Lord Ordinary during session But in the latter cases this is dispensed with where there is great urgency, as where the object is to examine a witness under orders to leave on foreign service (*n*) or where the state of the witness' health renders dispatch necessary to prevent his evidence from being lost (*o*)

§ 1950 The petition ought to set forth the names of the witnesses to be examined But the Court have granted commissions to examine witnesses named, and such other witnesses as should be proved to the commissioner to be at least seventy years old, or in bad health, or about to leave Scotland (*p*)[5] Commissions have been granted without the names of any witnesses being mentioned, the party leading the proof being required to furnish his opponent with a list of them a few (usually six) days before the examination (*r*) Formerly the applicant had to satisfy the Court that the witnesses were old, or infirm, or about to leave the country (*s*) But the practice now is to produce proof on the point to the commissioner (*t*).

§ 1951 A condescendence of the facts on which the examination is required, must be given in when the application is made to the Lord Ordinary on the Bills, in vacation or recess (*u*) This

(*k*) A S 11th July 1828, § 117

(*l*) See § 1954, *et seq*

(*m*) *Supra* (*k*)

(*n*) A B, 1831, 4 De and And, 252—See also Blyth *v* Trotter, 1629

(*o*) E Winton *v* Kingston, 1710, M, 12,096

(*p*) Morrison *v* Cowan, 1828, 6 S 1082—Watson, 1829, 8 S, 261

(*r*) Oswald *v* Lawrie, 1824 3 S, 381—Gardner *v* Mag of Kilkenny, 1825, ib, 613—Ramsay *v* Cochrane, ib 613—Mag of Glasgow *v* Dawson, 1827, 5 S, 915

(*s*) Mag of Aberdeen, 11th July 1811 F C

(*t*) Livingston, 10th March 1813, F C—Harvie's Tr *v* Leslie, 1827 5 S, 896—Cases in notes (*p*) and (*r*), *supra*

(*u*) A S, 11th July 1828 Under the present practice, the condescendence appended to the summons, if precise, will be sufficient

[5] Hunt *v* Commissioners of Woods and Forests, 1856, 18 D, 317

used also to be the practice when the examination was craved *in initio litis* during time of session (x) But in a later case the Court ordered a condescendence which had been appended to the petition for the diligence to be withdrawn as irregular (y)

§ 1952 It is not in general a good ground for opposing the application, that the witnesses will be inadmissible at the trial or that the line of proof is irrelevant as all such objections may be pleaded when the deposition is tendered in evidence (z) And objections to parts of the deposition may be pleaded when it is read in Court (a) Objections on the ground of confidentiality, and the like may be stated before the commissioner It is not now (as it used to be) the practice to insert in the interlocutor allowing the examination, a reservation of all competent objections The Court however, sometimes dispose of such questions when the examination is moved for (b)

§ 1953 As the sole object of allowing depositions to be taken to lie *in retentis* is to prevent evidence from being lost, they are not admissible at the trial, unless where the death of the witness or his absence from the country is proved (c) A deposition so taken will be excluded, if the witness is alive, but unable to attend the trial in consequence of illness, as he should have been re-examined on adjusted interrogatories (d) But in practice the party against whom the witness is examined often agrees by minute to receive the deposition at the trial, as if it had been taken in the latter mode In strict form, also, a witness examined *in initio litis* ought to be re-examined where the whole proof is taken on commission. But this is not the practice [6]

(x) Livingstone, 10th March 1813 F C—Copland *v* Bethune, 1827 5 S, 272

(y) Watsons, 1829 8 S, 261—Approved of in Cameron, 1830 ib, 435

(z) *Supra* §§ 1815 1963—Macf Pr, 91 (a) Haddoway *v* Goddard, 1816, 1 Mur 151—Morgan *v* Hunter, 1817, ib 258—*Supra*, §§ 1815, 1963

(b) Macf Pr 91—See *supra* § 1361 (c) Watson *v* Glass, 1838, 15 S 753 It is not enough that there are circumstances which render the death of the witness merely probable, and that a search for him has been unsuccessful, Aitchison *v* Patrick, 1836, 15 S, 360 But see Ewing *v* E Mar 1851, 14 D, 314, and Harvey, 1835 Bell's Notes, 292 *Query*, Would a deposition be admissible where the witness had become insane since it was taken? See *supra* § 104 (d) Watson *v* Glass *supra*

---

[6] At a jury trial there was tendered in evidence the deposition of a foreign seaman, taken, under the Act of Sederunt, to lie *in retentis*, before the adjustment of issues The other party objected to the evidence being admitted but did not aver or prove that the witness could have been examined on interrogatories, or could have been adduced at the trial The party tendering the deposition deponed that he had not heard of the witness

CHAPTER V.—OF TAKING DEPOSITIONS IN CIVIL JURY CAUSES, WHERE ATTENDANCE AT THE TRIAL CANNOT BE OBTAINED

§ 1954 The rules noticed in the preceding chapter apply equally to cases in which the whole proof is on commission and to those which are to be tried by jury, but in which issues have not been ordered (*a*) After the issues have been ordered, the case comes within the Act of Sederunt applicable to jury causes, which provides "that when it shall be made out upon oath, to the satisfaction of the Court that a witness resides beyond the reach of the process of the Court, and is not likely to come within its authority before the day of trial, or cannot attend on account of age or permanent infirmity, or is labouring under severe illness, which renders it doubtful whether his evidence may not be lost, or is a seafaring man, or is obliged to go into foreign parts or shall be abroad and not likely to return before the day of trial, it shall be competent to examine such witness by commission, on interrogatories to be settled by the parties, and approved of by one of the Principal Clerks of Session or record clerk" (*b*)

(*a*) Macf Pr, 88, 9 An order for issues has come in place of the remit to the issue clerks under the former practice Formerly the procedure in the early stages of cases specially appropriated to jury trial was peculiar But this distinction was abolished by 13 and 14 Vict, c 36, § 36

(*b*) A S, 16th Feb 1841, § 17

---

since his deposition was taken The Court held that it was not necessary, in order to render the deposition available, to prove that the witness could not have been adduced at the trial, or examined on adjusted interrogatories after the issues had been approved. The Lord Justice-Clerk (Inglis), who presided at the trial, observed, that the witness being a foreigner and a seaman, "and it being, as I agree, presumable that he has not been within the jurisdiction of the Court after the issues were adjusted, I do not think that any duty was laid on the party proposing to use his deposition No doubt he was bound to produce the best evidence accessible But was it within the power of the party to obtain the deposition of the witness on interrogatories in the fair meaning of these words? No application to the Court could secure it, because the witness was not within the jurisdiction of the Court The party could only have asked a commission to examine the witness in a foreign country, and under that commission he could not be certain of examining him, because he had no legal *compulsitor* which he could bring to bear on the witness," Boettcher v Carron Co, 1861, 23 D, 322 See this case, also, for remarks by Lord Justice Clerk (Inglis) on A S 9th December 1815,—not contained in printed collection of Acts of Sederunt The act will be found in Lord Ivory's Forms of Process, ii, 339 It appears to be competent to examine a witness on adjusted interrogatories before the adjustment of issues, see Sutter v Aberdeen Arctic Co, 1858, 30 Sc Jur, 300

§ 1955 If the motion has to be made during vacation, it comes within the rule that all motions necessary to the trying of causes "shall be heard before the judge who is to preside at the trial if in Edinburgh or by a judge who is appointed to be upon the circuit on which the cause is to be tried, if the trial is to be on the circuit and in case of the absence of either of them respectively, by the Lord Ordinary on the Bills, it being shewn to the satisfaction of the judge before whom the motion is made, that it could not have been made during the session" (c)

§ 1956 The Court will not grant commission to examine witnesses where such a step is obviously unnecessary (d) On this ground an application (made under the corresponding provisions of a previous Act of Sederunt) for a commission to take the depositions of two old witnesses, to lie *in retentis*, in an action of damages for slander from the pulpit, was refused, because there was no occasion in so public a matter to preserve the evidence of persons who, in consequence of age, were likely not to be good witnesses, and whose death could not place the party's interests in jeopardy (e) The Court also refused to grant commission for taking the opinion of English counsel on questions of English law, because there could not be any difficulty in getting such witnesses to attend the trial (f)

§ 1957 Where a witness whom a party intended to produce has become suddenly ill, and the illness has not been known to the party until after the commencement of the trial, a commission will be granted during the trial for his examination (g) If, however, a party is aware before the jury are impannelled, that a material witness is unable to attend on this account he should move to have the trial put off (h) [1] If he does not do so, a commission to examine the witness will not be granted (unless of consent) during the trial (i)

(c) A S, 16th Feb 1841 § 21 (d) Macf Pr 92 See *supra*, § 1942 (e) Dudgeon v Forbes 1832, 10 S 810 (f) Maberly & Co, 1834, 12 S 902 (g) Stone v Aberdeen Ins Co, 1849, 11 D, 1041—Morrison & Co v Reid & Co July 1853, not reported—Macf Pr 89 (h) A S, 16th Feb 1841 § 27—Gordon v Orrok 1849 11 D, 1358—Paul v Old Shipping Co 1816, 1 Mur, 66—Macf Pr, *supra* (i) White v Clark 1817, 1 Mur 284—L Forbes v Leys, 1830 5 Mur, 289—Macf Pr *supra*

[1] After a case was put out for trial, the pursuer moved that a witness unable to attend on account of the dangerous illness of his wife should be examined on commission But on the defender agreeing to delay trial the motion was refused Lord Deas— I do not wish to go upon the position of the witness being insufficient to excuse his attendance but upon the inexpediency of taking proof by commission where there is consent

§ 1958 In applications under the Act of Sederunt above cited the names of the witnesses to be examined must be given, and the Court refused to dispense with this where it was stated that the names would be given as soon as known, although the other party said that he did not object to the commission being granted (*k*) The examination is taken on interrogatories (*l*) adjusted by the parties with the assistance of the Court, if necessary, the object being to prevent an answer to an incompetent question from going to the jury, as well as to guide those who conduct the examination, when it is taken abroad or by persons not familiar with such matters In cases of great urgency the Court may dispense with interrogatories, and allow the examination to be conducted as in a proof on commission (*m*) In other cases also, this is frequently done of consent. In a case already noticed, where the deposition of a witness which had been taken on commission in the ordinary form, to lie *in retentis*, was tendered at the trial, on the ground that the witness was too infirm to attend, the Court held it inadmissible, on the ground that she should have been re-examined on interrogatories (*n*)

Even where adjusted interrogatories are not used all the important parts of the deposition should be taken down in the form of question and answer in case of any questions as to the competency of the examination being raised at the trial

§ 1959 Wherever a commission, under the Act of Sederunt above cited is granted upon the application of one party, "it shall be competent to the other party to have a joint commission, or to propose cross-interrogatories to such witnesses to be settled as aforesaid, and in addition to the interrogatories so settled, it shall be competent to the commissioner to put such additional questions to the witnesses as may appear to him to be necessary, taking care to mark the question so put as put by him (*o*) In practice the commissioner puts any relevant questions suggested by either party ' When one party obtains a commission to examine witnesses, and does not use the evidence obtained under the commission, the other

(*k*) Gray *v* Sutherland, 1849, 11 D, 1023 (*l*) *Supra*, § 1951

(*m*) In A B, 1831, 4 De and And, 252, this was done under the corresponding provisions of a previous Act of Sederunt (*n*) Watson *v* Glass, 1838, 15 S 753

(*o*) A S, 16th Feb 1841 § 17

—

to postpone trial," Dobie *v* Aberdeen Railway Co, 1856, 19 D, 195 In two recent cases, the evidence of witnesses labouring under serious illness was, of consent of the parties, taken down by a short-hand writer,—the parties dispensing with the signature of the witnesses

party may use the evidence given under it at the trial, provided he satisfies the Court at the trial that he could not bring the witness or witnesses whose evidence he proposes to read, in which case he shall be liable for the expense of the commission" (*p*)

§ 1960 Where a witness who had been examined on adjusted interrogatories attended and was examined in the first trial of the cause but died in the interval before the second trial, the party who adduced him may at that trial put in his previous deposition, and is not obliged to use, in place of it, the judge's notes of the evidence on the first trial (*r*) A re-examination, with a view to the second trial, will be allowed on cause shewn, but not as a matter of course (*s*)

§ 1961 In order to the deposition being laid before the jury, it must be "established at the trial to the satisfaction of the Court by affidavit, or by oath in open court, that such witness is dead, or cannot attend owing to absence, age, or permanent infirmity" (*t*) Certificates will not be admitted for this purpose (*u*), except of consent The oath of one witness, however, is sufficient, if it is satisfactory to the Court (*x*) And the decision on the point by the judge who presided at the trial will not be disturbed on an exception, except in an extreme case (*y*) It has even been maintained that it is not subject to review (*z*)

§ 1962 The deposition will not be admitted on account of the witness being ill, unless the infirmity appears to be permanent, the proper course in cases of temporary illness being to postpone the trial (*a*) Where the witness is said to be abroad at the trial, that must be proved if he is a domiciled Scotsman, whose absence may be expected to be temporary (*b*) But proof of continued absence is not required in cases of those whose permanent residence is out of Scotland (*c*) [2] It is not necessary that the witness shall

(*p*) A S, *supra* (*r*) Willox v Farrell, 1848, 10 D 807—Muir v Muir, 1840, 2 D, 751 The judge's notes may also be used for this purpose, see *supra*, § 1934 (*s*) Muir v Muir *supra*—*Per curiam* in Willox v Farrell, *supra*—Paul v Commercial Ins Co 1832, 10 S 496 (*t*) A S, 16th Feb 1841, § 17

(*u*) Scott v Gray 1826, 4 Mur 63 (*x*) Willox v Farrell, 1848, 10 D, 807

(*y*) Willox v Ferrell *supra* (*z*) Ib (*a*) A S, *supra*—Gordon v Orrok 1849, 11 D, 1358—Setton v Setton's Tr, 1816, 1 Mur, 11

(*b*) A S, *supra*—Per L Ch St Leonards in Sutton v Ainslie, 1851 14 D 184, aftd, 1 Macq 299 (*c*) So held in Sutton v Ainslie *supra* See also Mackay v M'Leods, 1827 4 Mur, 278—Wight v Liddell 1820 ib 328, and 5 ib 47

[2] Boettcher v Carron Co, *supra* § 1953, note [6] 1861, 23 D, 322

have been requested to attend the trial (*d*) The Court may postpone the trial in order to enable a party to obtain the attendance of an important witness who is abroad, but is expected soon to come to this country (*e*) [3]

§ 1963 Evidence taken under the rules thus noticed is "subject to all legal objections to its admissibility" at the trial (*f*) And if the witness was examined *in initialibus* before the commissioner with a view to an objection to his admissibility the initial examination may be read to the jury, because, like that of a witness examined in court, it may contain matters important for the jury to consider in weighing the credibility of the evidence (*g*)

The depositions are usually sealed up by the commissioner in order to be used only in the event of their being held admissible The clerk of court may open them without the authority of the Court if both parties consent (*h*)

§ 1964 Former Acts of Sederunt directed that depositions which had been taken on commission should be cancelled or rendered illegible if the witnesses so examined were brought forward at the trial (*i*) But these acts have been repealed, and there is not any corresponding provision in the act which now regulates procedure in jury causes (*j*) The advantage of the alteration is seen in a case already noticed (*k*) At common law, however, a witness is entitled to have a deposition which he has previously emitted in the cause cancelled before deponing anew upon the same facts lest he should feel trammeled by the fear of contradicting his previous statement (*l*) [4]

(*d*) Armstrong's Tr *v* Leith Banking Co, 1834 12 S 440

(*e*) See Hyslop *v* Miller, 1816, 1 Mur, 43, note—Compared with Hyslop *v* Staig 1816, ib, 24, note (*f*) A S, 16th Feb 1841, § 17

(*g*) Geekie *v* Proctor, 1849, 12 D, 72 (*h*) Nicol *v* Sykes, 1850, 13 D, 182 (*i*) A S, 3d July 1823 § 4—A S, 29th Nov 1825, § 28

(*j*) A S, 16th Feb 1841 (*k*) Willox *v* Farrell, 1848, 10 D 807—*Supra*, §§ 1934 1962 (*l*) E Fife *v* E Fife's Tr, 1816, 1 Mur, 92—Kitchen *v* Fisher, 1821, 2 Mur, 590—Macf Pr 190—*Supra*, § 1750—See also 6 Geo IV, c 120 § 40

---

[3] A new trial was allowed where a material witness, who had been absent from the country at the time of the first trial, and whose evidence had been taken on commission, had returned But the case was very special, and the decision may be questioned, Stewart *v* Macfarlane, 1856 18 D, 787

[4] The system of examining witnesses on adjusted interrogatories is one which does not seem capable of being defended It is cumbrous, unwieldy, and wearisome,—impeding, instead of aiding, the discovery of the truth All the objections which can be stated against the tedious and unsatisfactory procedure in a proof on commission apply

CHAPTER VI.—OF TAKING THE DEPOSITIONS OF DYING WITNESSES IN CRIMINAL CASES

§ 1965 In criminal cases, where there is reason to fear that an important witness will die before the trial, his deposition may be taken by a magistrate in order to be read at the trial in the event of his death This is most commonly done on behalf of the Crown, in order to secure the evidence of those who are injured by crimes of violence (*a*) It is equally competent in principle, and is the practice, to examine other witnesses for the prosecutor whose lives are in jeopardy (*b*) And the prisoner may, by the same means, provide against loss of exculpatory evidence [1]

(*a*) 2 Hume 407—Bell's Notes, 291—2 Al, 511 (*b*) This seems not to have been doubted in Mackenzie, 1838, 2 Swin, 103, where the point was to some extent involved

with increased force to a proof taken on adjusted interrogatories The interrogatories are seldom exhaustive, yet they serve to fetter and embarrass the examination, they are intended to exclude irrelevant matter, and as a security for the protection and purification of evidence, but it is notorious that they fail to exclude irrelevant matter and that a deposition emitted in the usual way is considered of equal or superior trustworthiness There seems no reason why a deposition taken to lie *in retentis*, emitted in the ordinary form, and under the usual safeguards, should not be admitted in all cases at the trial, except where the party objecting is prepared to shew special cause why it should not be admitted A deposition taken *in initio litis* before the pleas are matured, may occasionally prove defective or irrelevant, but it is clearly unreasonable that it should be imperative to adopt one mode of examination *after*—while another, a simpler and more satisfactory, is competent *before*— the adjustment of issues

[1] It is competent, in a criminal case, to take the dying deposition of a party, "other than the party injured,' before a magistrate, who is not required to ascertain whether the party is aware that he is dying, and this deposition is competent and admissible evidence, which may be produced to a jury The point was argued at great length in the case of Stewart, but the Court were clearly of opinion that the evidence was admissible,—Lord Deas observing—'I have never understood that, by the law of Scotland, there was no way of preserving the evidence of a witness in criminal cases, however imminent the chances of his death before the trial and however important his evidence might be On the contrary, I think it may be done, and that it was rightly done here" But the Court will consider, on hearing the deposition read what parts of it could not have been competently emitted had the witness been examined at the trial and those parts will be deleted, H M Adv *v* Stewart 1855 2 Irv, 166 The English statute 11 and 12 Vict, c 42 § 17, provides, that where the deposition of a witness has been taken before a magistrate, the deposition shall be admissible at the trial "if it shall be proved by the oath or affirmation of any credible witness that any person whose deposition shall have been taken as aforesaid is dead or so ill as not to be able to travel' At common law in England the deposition of a witness who is kept away by the

§ 1966 The examination is obtained on application to a magistrate or the judge ordinary of the bounds, proceeding on a medical certificate It ought to be taken whenever there is reason for apprehending danger to the witness' life, and before his memory has become impaired, or his attention absorbed or distracted by fear of death (*c*) It is not necessary in this country that he should believe himself to be dying (*d*)

The deposition is taken on oath, upon questions asked by the magistrate or by the procurator-fiscal in his presence, and it is committed to writing and signed by the magistrate like a prisoner's declaration It is common in practice to examine the witness *in initialibus* At the trial the deposition must be proved by two witnesses (one of whom ought to be the examining magistrate), to have been emitted voluntarily when the witness was in his sound and sober senses (*e*)

§ 1967 Depositions of this kind being taken *ex parte*, are not so trustworthy as those which are emitted under the corresponding procedures in civil cases (*f*) No doubt, impartiality is secured to some extent by the presence of a magistrate, whose duty it is to put all questions which occur to him with the view of making the deposition fair and complete But this must often be a poor substitute for a cross-examination on behalf of the prisoner, by which the accuracy of the witness may be tested, and exculpatory circumstances be brought to light (*g*)

There is unfortunately, no procedure in criminal cases for examining witnesses who reside beyond the United Kingdom (*h*) and refuse to attend the trial

---

(*c*) Per L Just-Clerk (Hope) in Brodie, 1846, Arkley, 45 (*d*) Bell 1835, 13 S, 1179, Bell's Notes, 292, S C—Brodie, *supra* The opposite is held in England, Taylor, 473—1 Phill, 284, where, in general hearsay is inadmissible even where the witnesses have died (*e*) 2 Hume, 407 (*f*) *Supra*, § 1939

(*g*) See per L Just-Clerk (Hope) in Brodie *supra* (*h*) As to compelling witnesses in England and Ireland to attend the trial see *supra*, § 1894

---

practices of the prisoner is also admissible R *v* Gutteridge, 9 C and P 171 As to the conditions under which dying declarations are admissible in England, see R *v* Whitworth 1858, 1 F and F, 382 and R *v* Hind, 1860, 29 L J (Mag Cases), 147

CHAPTER VII.—OF THE RULE THAT WITNESSES MUST BE SWORN

§ 1968. One of the means by which the law endeavours to secure truthfulness in testimony is by requiring it to be emitted on oath. In this way each witness, before commencing to depone, is supposed to declare his belief in the moral government of a Supreme Being, in whose presence he emits his evidence, and whose vengeance he imprecates if he does not speak the truth (*a*). The practice is founded on the well known fact, that perjury is rare compared with false or coloured statements made without the sanction of an oath.[1]

An oath is required in all courts of law (*b*), and it is no less es-

(*a*) The view in the text is that commonly entertained of an oath. See Queen's case, 1820, 2 Brod. and Bing., 284—M'Gavin, 1816, Arkley, 69. It has, however, been considered that the idea of an oath does not necessarily involve imprecation—(in favour of this see Hebrews, vi, 13), and that its design is not to call the attention of God to man, but of man to God, not to call on God to punish the wrong-doer, but on man to remember that he will. Accordingly, an oath is said to be only an outward pledge given by the juror that his attestation or promise is made under an immediate sense of responsibility to the Deity, see 1 Starkie, 32—1 Greenl., § 328—Taylor, 918. But this is thought to be erroneous, for in taking an oath a person does not merely declare to man that he speaks under a sense of responsibility to God, he also makes God a witness to the transaction and declares himself amenable to the punishment which would be merited by impiously uttering falsehood in His august presence.

(*b*) Stair, 4, 43, 5—2 Hume, 376—Tait, Ev., 422.

[1] In M'Laughlin v. Douglas and Kidston, 1863, 4 Irv. 273, 35 Sc. Jur., 322, an oath in the following terms was administered to a Roman Catholic priest who objected to take the oath in the ordinary form:—"I swear by God I shall tell the truth and nothing but the truth, and whatever I shall say in this case shall be the truth." Lord Justice-General (M'Neill), in commenting upon this oath (from which the words "the whole truth" had been omitted), observed,—"The obligation to give evidence in the courts of law of the country is an obligation imposed by the law and the constitution on all the lieges. The obligation on a witness to tell the truth, the whole truth, and nothing but the truth, is an obligation imposed by the law irrespective of any oath. The administering of an oath is a means resorted to by the law to insure the fulfilment of the obligation to speak the truth, the whole truth, and nothing but the truth." The oath fell to be administered in the ordinary words, except in the cases excepted by statute. "But the law has also fixed the scope and sense of the words of the oath so as to be consistent with the legal rights or duties of the witness who takes the oath. The obligation to tell the whole truth is not extended by the words of the oath beyond the limits already prescribed by law. There are certain matters which the law itself excepts from the obligation to tell the whole truth, and these are as much excepted from the obligation after taking the oath as before. The obligation to tell 'the whole truth,' implied in the words of the oath, is neither more nor less extensive than the obligation to tell 'the whole truth,' imposed by the law. If there be anything which the party is in law entitled to refuse to disclose, the taking of the oath in the usual terms will not, in the slightest degree, deprive him of the right to refuse to disclose it."

sential in Small Debt and Police cases (*c*), than in important trials before the supreme courts Peers, when examined as witnesses, require to be sworn (*d*)

§ 1969 But the common law of this country allows Quakers and other sectaries, who have religious scruples against emitting oaths to give their evidence on solemn affirmation, declaring that what they are to say is "in the presence of God, who is their witness, and who will be their judge if they lie" (*e*) By statute Quakers and Moravians (*f*), and persons who have been of either of these persuasions (*g*), and those who are of the sect called Separatists (*h*), may both in civil and criminal cases be examined on affirmation in a prescribed form, wherever other persons would have to make oath A bill has passed through some stages for extending this privilege to all persons of whatever denomination, who have religious scruples against taking oaths[2] At present (May

(*c*) Home *v* Henderson, 1825 4 S, 30—Grant 1827, Syme, 144—Dykes 1829 ib, 262—Purvis, 1825, Sh Just Ca, 133—Bonnar *v* Simpson 1836, 1 Swin, 39—See *supra* § 1063

(*d*) Erskine *v* E Kincardine, 1712, 4 B Sup, 897—Cases noted *supra*, § 1504—Burnett, 451—Tait Ev, 423 In the trial of Mr Stewart for killing Sir A Boswell in a duel, Lord Rosslyn was sworn without objection, 10th June 1822, separate report, 44 See also the trial of the Earl of Macclesfield 1725, 16 St Tr, 1253, where a Bishop pleaded that he was privileged not to make oath, but waived his objection on an opposite opinion being indicated by Lord Lechmere It thus appears that in Ramsay *v* Nairne 1833, 11 S, 1033, the presiding judge erred when *proprio motu* he told the Duke of Gordon that he had the alternative of giving his evidence on oath or on his word of honour

(*e*) Stair, 4, 43, 7 (3)—Tait Ev 289 423

(*f*) 3 and 4 Will IV c 49, § 1 The statutory form is as follows —' I, A B being one of the people called Quakers (*or*, one of the persuasion of the people called Quakers, *or*, of the united brethren called Moravians, *as the case may be*), do solemnly, sincerely, and truly declare and affirm " This form is almost precisely the same as that prescribed by 8 Geo I, c 6, § 1, 9 Geo IV, c 29 § 13, and 9 Geo IV c 32 (which are subsisting) The act of Geo I abolished the old form required by 7 and 8 Will III, c 34

(*g*) 1 and 2 Vict, c 77 The form is, 'I, A B, having been one of the people called Quakers (*or*, one of the persuasion of the people called Quakers, *or*, of the united brethren called Moravians, *as the case may be*), and entertaining conscientious objections to the taking of an oath, do solemnly, sincerely and truly declare and affirm "

(*h*) 3 and 4 Will IV, c 82 The form is, "I, A B do, in the presence of Almighty God, solemnly sincerely, and truly affirm and declare that I am a member of the religious sect called Separatists, and that the taking of any oath is contrary to my religious belief, as well as essentially opposed to the tenets of that sect, and I do also, in the same solemn manner declare and affirm "

[2] The act 18 Vict, c 25, § 1, provides, that "if any person called as a witness in any court of civil judicature in Scotland, or requiring or desiring to make an affidavit or deposition, shall refuse or be unwilling, from alleged conscientious motives, to be sworn, it shall be lawful for the court or judge or other presiding officer or person qua-

1855) the law does not recognise the religious scruples of individuals on this point unless they are those of the denomination of which he is a member (*k*) And if a witness not being one of the privileged classes, refuses, either on account of religious scruples or from any other cause, to make oath, he may be imprisoned for contempt of court (*l*)

Where a witness makes affirmation under any of the statutes thus noticed, he must use the precise words of the statutory form, and not merely an equipollent for them (*m*) The rules as to examining children on declaration have been noticed already (*n*)

§ 1970 In this country the oath is administered in the following manner —The judge standing and holding up his right hand, delivers the oath to the witness, who stands in the same attitude, and repeats the words aloud, "I swear by Almighty God, and as I shall answer to God at the great day of judgment, that I will tell the truth, the whole truth, and nothing but the truth" This form must now be used in consistorial causes (*o*), in place of the more solemn oath which used to be administered in the Commissary Court, as representing the ancient ecclesiastical tribunals (*p*) As, however, the object of every oath is to bind the conscience of the witness, it will be administered in the form which he recognises as binding (*r*) A Jew, for example, is sworn with his head covered, and holding the Old Testament between his hands (*s*), and a Ma-

(*k*) 2 Al, 432 and cases there cited—Bonnar *v* Simpson, *supra* (*c*)—Tweedie, 1829, Sh Just Cr, 222 (*l*) Authorities in preceding note

(*m*) In M'Cubbin *v* Turnbull, 1850 12 D, 1123, the omission of the word 'truly" in the affirmation emitted by a Quaker, in place of an affidavit to a claim in a sequestration, was held to be fatal to his vote for the trustee on the estate

(*n*) See *supra*, § 1677 (*o*) 11 Geo IV, and 1 Will IV, c 69, § 37

(*p*) See this form in Boyd's Forms of Process (2d ed), 103 (*r*) 2 Al, 431 —Tait Ev, 423 (*s*) Rennie 1821 and Laidlaw and Spittal 1823, unreported, noted in 2 Al, 431Horn and Maclaren, 1831, Bell's Notes 265

lified to take affidavits or depositions, on being satisfied of the sincerity of such objection to permit such person, instead of being sworn, to make his or her solemn affirmation or declaration" in the words prescribed by the act The act 26 and 27 Vict, c 82, § 1 extends the provisions of the former act to "any person called as a witness in any court of criminal jurisdiction in Scotland, or requiring or desiring to make an affidavit or deposition in the course of any criminal proceeding" It was held, in Andrew Marshall, petitioner, 1862, 34 Sc Jur, 187, that the act 18 Vict, c 25, did not apply to the case of a notary-public, and that a notary-public still required to take the oath *de fideli* The following acts introduce changes in the form of oaths —Grand Jurors, 19 and 20 Vict c 54, § 2, Members of Parliament professing the Jewish religion, 19 and 20 Vict, c 49, Substitution of one oath for the oaths of Allegiance, Supremacy, and Abjuration, 21 and 22 Vict c 48

homedan is sworn on the Koran (*t*) It is said that a Roman Catholic should be sworn with his right hand on a cross drawn in pencil or chalk on the gospels, being the form which he considers most obligatory (*u*) But in a recent case the Justiciary Court refused to go through this ceremony, unless it were made to appear that the ordinary form was not binding on the conscience of the witness (*x*) So, in "the Queen's case," it was held to be irrelevant and incompetent to ask a witness whether he considers another form than that commonly used to be more binding (*y*)

Any objection to the form of oath should be stated before the witness is sworn, but this will not be insisted on, where the ordinary oath has been administered before the attention of counsel or of the Court was directed to it (*z*)

§ 1971. Whenever the oath is administered in the mode which the witness declares to be binding, he may be convicted of perjury, if he gives false evidence (*a*) And any one who makes statements on declaration under the statutes above noticed, incurs the same penalties as if he had been on oath (*b*)

CHAPTER VIII —OF THE MODE OF CONDUCTING THE EXAMINATION

I *Witnesses are examined separately*

§ 1972 As already seen, the exclusion of witnesses on the ground that they heard other witnesses emit their evidence has been almost entirely abolished (*c*) But it is still the practice in civil, as well as criminal cases, to examine the witnesses separately, in order that each may, as much as possible, speak purely from his own recollection

§ 1973 Witnesses on matters of opinion, however, used to be allowed to remain in Court during the evidence upon the facts on which their opinions were required, being removed whenever the evidence touched matters of opinion (*d*) This was more especially

---

(*t*) R *v* Morgan, 1764, 1 Leach C C 54

(*u*) Burnett, 457—2 Al 430

(*x*) M'Gavin, 1846 Arkley, 69

(*y*) Queen's case, 1820, 2 Brod and Bing, 281

(*z*) Queen's case, *supra*

(*a*) 1 and 2 Vict, c 105

(*b*) See statutes noted *supra*, § 1969

(*c*) See *supra* § 1758

(*d*) Authorities in following notes, compared with Newlands 1833, Bell's Notes 269—Jeffrey 1838, ib

the practice in regard to medical evidence both in civil (*c*) and in criminal (*d*) trials And it was common to all evidence of the same class, *e g*, that of sea-faring men as to the sailing of ships (*e*), and of chemists as to the nature of gases generated in certain manufactures (*f*) But about twenty years ago it became the practice in the Justiciary Court not to allow medical witnesses to be present during any part of the evidence (*g*), the reason being that, under the opposite practice such witnesses are apt not to form their opinions purely upon the facts relating to medical science, but to mix up moral presumptions and inferences from the general facts of the case, thereby substituting themselves for the jury the consequence of which may be that their opinions are in part based on views of the facts materially different from those which the jury entertain (*h*) It was observed that the late Dr John Hunter once allowed his opinion as a medical man to be influenced by the general evidence in the cause whereby he was led into errors which he afterwards acknowledged, and that the late Dr Abernethy declined to give evidence in similar circumstances (*i*)[1]

(*c*) Heddleston *v* Goldie, 1819 2 Mur 116—Stewart *v* Boyes 1838 Macf R, 27

(*d*) Newlands, 1833—Donaldson, 1836—Jeffrey 1838—Woods, 1839—Wilson, 1841—all noted in Bell's Notes, 269 Sir A Alison writing in 1833, says (vol ii p 544), "In all the late trials for murder in particular those of Mrs Smith Lovie at Aberdeen, and others, the medical gentlemen on both sides who were to give a professional opinion, were present during the whole of the trial" This practice was also followed in the celebrated trial of Burke and Macdowall in 1828 Syme, 345, *et seq*, and separate report (*e*) Harvey *v* Smith, 1818 1 Mur 307—Innes *v* Glass 1827 4 Mur, 161—Potts *v* Pollock, 1837 15 S 879—See also Cairns *v* Kippen, 1820 2 Mur, 251

(*f*) Hart *v* Taylor, 1827 4 Mur 311 (*g*) Gilmour, 1844 2 Broun, 23—Per L Just Clerk Hope in Gibson 1848, Arkley, 489—See also Howieson, 1831, Bell's Notes, 269 (*h*) Per L Just -Clerk (Hope) in Gilmour and Gibson, *supra*

(*i*) Per L Just -Clerk (Hope) in Gilmour, *supra* This alteration in the practice of the criminal courts has been challenged by an eminent medical jurist, Professor Christison, chiefly on the following grounds —That medico-legal inquiries often embrace facts, the precise character and bearing of which cannot be appreciated by persons unacquainted with medical science, that the expressions used by the witnesses to the facts will sometimes not be repeated accurately to the medical man, or they may be misunderstood in consequence of some words having different meanings in ordinary and in medical language It is also said that opinions formed upon hypothetical views of the facts will be more general and less adapted to the precise circumstances proved, than if they were founded upon these as heard by the medical witness, while he cannot fail to receive some impression, although an imperfect and probably incorrect one from the hypothetical views stated to him, and it were better (it is said) that he should know them correctly from being present throughout the trial See art on "The Present State of

---

[1] The present inclination of the judges is to allow medical witnesses to remain in

§ 1974. In a civil case, where the defenders in an action for the value of sugars, alleged to have been damaged by the leakage of their ship, moved that witnesses skilled in nautical matters should remain in court during the evidence as to the facts, Lord President Boyle refused the motion, chiefly, it would seem, on the ground that granting it would have occasioned constant watching over the evidence, lest there should have been matter of opinion stated, when the witnesses would have had to be removed His Lordship also considered that it would be incompetent to ask the witnesses their opinion on the whole complexion of the case, as that would be substituting them for the jury, and influencing the latter by the evidence of men of skill (*k*) This ruling by one judge, however, even when taken in connection with the later cases in the Justiciary Court, is hardly sufficient to alter the practice previously prevailing in civil trials

§ 1975 Even in criminal cases the rule will be relaxed, where that is advantageous for the ends of justice In a trial for culpable homicide, the prisoner's counsel succeeded in a motion that his medical witnesses should remain in court during the evidence adduced by the Crown relative to the *post mortem* appearances on the body of the deceased, but they were excluded while the Crown witnesses spoke to symptoms The Court, while they allowed this course on account of there being no written medical report on the *post mortem* appearances, treated the case as an exception, on ac-

---

Medical Evidence," Edinburgh Monthly Journal of Med Science, Nov 1851 The majority of these objections shew the necessity for care and accuracy in the examination of medical witnesses, rather than the propriety of a return to the former system The first is the most weighty of them But even it is more theoretical than practical, for there does not seem to be any instance in which error or real inconvenience arose from that source On the whole, therefore, it is thought that sufficient grounds have not been shown for returning to the former system, which involved at least as great risk of misdecision as that now followed, while it encroached upon the province of the jury as exclusively judges of the facts There are cases, however, where the disadvantages attending the present practice preponderate (*k*) Campbell *v.* Tyson, 1841, 4 D, 342

---

court while the evidence on the facts is being led At the trial of Alexander Murray the Lord Justice Clerk (Inglis) observed, that the great object ought to be to render medical evidence as valuable as possible, and that this was best attained by allowing the witnesses to remain in Court,—"So that the Court, the jury, and the medical witnesses might all proceed on the same evidence" But permission must be specially applied for in each case, H M Adv *v* Murray, 1858, 3 Irv, 262—See also H M Adv *v* Madeleine Smith 1857, 2 Irv, 641—H M Adv *v* M'Fadyen, 1860, 3 Irv, 650—H M Adv *v* Paterson, 1861, 4 Irv, 91—H M Adv *v* Milne, 1863, 35 Sc Jur, 170

count of peculiar circumstances, from the general rule, which they were satisfied was "most beneficial to the ends of justice" (*l*)

It has already been considered whether the rule, that witnesses should be examined separately, applies to the parties to the cause and their law-agents (*m*)

II *Of examining Witnesses* in initialibus

§ 1976. It used to be necessary, before putting any question to a witness on the merits of the case, to examine him *in initialibus* with the view of discovering whether any objection existed to his admissibility (*n*) But in the year 1840 it was enacted "that it shall not be necessary for any judge in Scotland, or for any person acting as commissioner in taking evidence in any action, cause, prosecution, or other judicial proceeding, civil or criminal, depending in Scotland to examine any witness *in initialibus*, provided always that it shall nevertheless be competent for any such judge or person acting as commissioner, or the party against whom the witness shall be called, to examine any witness *in initialibus* as heretofore" (*o*)

The initial examination, when required, is conducted before the jury, and although its proper object is to investigate objections to the admissibility of the witness, which is a question for the judge alone, it may bring out facts which the jury are entitled to consider in weighing the witness' credibility. Consequently where the evidence of a witness has been taken on adjusted interrogatories, the party against whom it is tendered may insist on the examination *in initialibus* being read to the jury (*p*)

III *Of Examination, Cross-examination, and Re-examination*

§ 1977. The witness after having been sworn, and examined *in initialibus* (if that is required), is examined in chief upon the merits of the cause In civil jury trials the form of procedure is, that "the counsel of the parties shall take the examination of the witnesses in such order as they shall arrange, but the counsel who begins the examination of a witness shall continue that examination throughout, without interruption from any quarter, (unless

(*l*) Gibson, 1848, Arkley, 489 (*m*) See *supra*, § 1760

(*n*) The rules as to this examination are noticed in considering the mode of proving objections to witnesses (*o*) 3 and 4 Vict, c 59, § 2

(*p*) Geikie *v* Proctor 1849 12 D 72

when an objection is taken to the legality of the question), until he exhaust the examination. After this, a counsel on the opposite side may cross-examine without interruption until he exhaust his cross-examination. Then the counsel who first examined in chief may re-examine, confining his re-examination strictly to such new matter as may have arisen in cross-examination, unless with permission of the Court (*q*). The counsel who cross-examined has not right to a second cross; but the Court allow him to put any questions which may be proper for clearing up matters which the re-examination may have left in doubt. Some judges, however, require such questions to be put from the bench. When the counsel on both sides have concluded, the Court put any questions which may suggest themselves, and this is sometimes done in the course of the examination from the bar. Jurymen are not allowed to interrupt the examining counsel by asking questions at the witness; but, when the counsel have concluded, the Court will put any competent questions which may be suggested from the jury-box.

These rules are also adopted in criminal trials, and, so far as applicable, in proofs on commission.

§ 1978. They will, however, be relaxed in order to suit the exigencies or convenience of individual cases. It is sometimes proper, for example, to adduce a witness upon one part of a case, and to delay his further examination till a later period of the trial, in consequence of the matter embraced by the first examination being preliminary, and requiring to be established by other evidence before the remaining facts are proved, or in consequence of his evidence being required upon independent branches of the case, which are proved at different stages of the trial. In England, the Court allow the counsel for the party against whom a witness is adduced to delay his cross-examination if he states that it would be inconvenient or prejudicial to his case to cross immediately after the examination in chief (*r*). In Scotland, the power to do so is embraced by an enactment to be noticed immediately (*s*).

§ 1979. At one time the cross-examination was limited to matters upon which the witness had been examined in chief (*t*). But this rule, after having been relaxed by acts of sederunt with reference to civil jury causes (*u*) and inferior courts (*x*), the rules of

---

(*q*) A. S., 16th Feb. 1841, § 28.

(*r*) Parlby *v.* Parlby, 1851, 16 Eng. Jur., 92, per Dr Lushington—Mitchelson *v.* Nicol, 1852, 18 Law Times, 198, per Martin, B.

(*s*) *Infra*, § 1981.

(*t*) Macf. Pr., 135—Tait Ev., 421—2 Al., 517.

(*u*) A. S., 16th Feb. 1841, § 30.

(*x*) A. S., 10th July 1839, § 78.

which were extended by analogy to proofs on commission (*y*), was abolished by statute, whereby it is "declared and enacted that in any action, cause, prosecution, or other judicial proceeding, civil or criminal, where proof shall be taken, whether by the judge or a person acting as commissioner, it shall be competent for the party against whom a witness is produced and sworn *in causa* to examine such witness, not in cross only, but *in causa* " (*z*). Yet where a pursuer has not led any proof of his own averments on a separate ground of action, and circumduction has passed against him, it would seem that he will not be allowed to cross-examine the defender's witnesses on that branch of the case, which he abandoned by not leading proof upon it (*a*)

§ 1980 The rules thus noticed apply where the party against whom the proof is led is allowed a conjunct probation, as well as where the interlocutor on which the proof proceeds is not in that form There is, indeed great difficulty in defining the term "conjunct probation", and it may be doubted whether it implies any investigation beyond what is competent at common law wherever a proof is granted (*b*) [2]

(*y*) Tait Ev, 425 (*z*) 3 and 4 Vict, c 59 § 4
(*a*) Observed *per curiam* in A B *v* C D, 1844, 6 D, 1148 (*b*) See *per curiam* in A B *v* C D, *supra*

[2] The following observations were made by the Lord Justice-Clerk (Inglis) in a recent case —' When an interlocutor has been pronounced allowing to a pursuer and a defender a proof of their averments on record, and to each a conjunct probation, the proper course is—(1) for the pursuer to lead his proof in chief, (2) for the defender to lead his proof in chief, and his conjunct proof in answer to the pursuer's proof, and (3) for the pursuer to lead his conjunct proof in answer to the defender's proof After this, the defender cannot be allowed a proof in replication unless he can show that matters of fact have been brought out in the pursuer's conjunct proof which he could not have anticipated It is never too late to allow a proof in replication when there is a necessity, and if the Lord Ordinary sees that there is ground for it in the present case, he may still grant it, specifying the particular matters of fact to which it is to be directed, but I entirely disapprove of allowing this proof in replication *per aversionem,* and reserving legal objections to the course of examination and to particular interrogatories to be determined afterwards" Strang *v* Stewart, 1862, 24 D, 955 In a still later case the Lord Justice-Clerk (Inglis) observed —' When a proof is allowed in cases in which no averments are made by the defender, the proper interlocutor is Allow the pursuer a proof of his averments, and to the defender a conjunct probation ', but when the defender makes averments, and both parties are allowed a proof a form of interlocutor, not unusual in such a case, viz, to allow both parties a proof and to either party a conjunct probation is erroneous and misleading In such cases the proper form of interlocutor is, 'Allow both parties a proof of their respective averments and to the pursuer a conjunct probation ', because the defender is bound to lead his conjunct probation when

§ 1981 At one time the general rule was against allowing a witness to be recalled after his examination had been concluded, and he had left the box, the reason being that, if witnesses could under all circumstances be called back, there would be risk of their being tampered with and tutored in the interim (c) But this rule was relaxed where it was expedient for the ends of justice to do so (d) The Law of Evidence Amendment Act of 1852, makes it "competent to the presiding judge or other person before whom any trial or proof shall proceed, on the motion of either party, to permit any witness who shall have been examined in the course of such trial or proof to be recalled" (e) This enactment evidently proceeds on the propriety of still farther relaxing the former rule, which does not accord with modern principles of evidence It may therefore be said that a party will now be allowed to recall a witness, whether adduced by himself or by his opponent, unless some good reason exists to the contrary, as for example, that the witness heard other evidence adduced on the matter on which it is proposed to re-examine him, or that he was tampered with in the interval [3]

§ 1982 If a witness, whether examined before a jury or before a commissioner, apprehends that he has made some mistake in emitting his deposition, he may, on application *de recenti*, get the mistake rectified (f) But it lies with the party, not with the witness, to obtain a re-examination for the purpose of bringing out new matters of fact, or of clearing up indistinct testimony (g)

(c) Macf Pr, 135—Tait Ev, 434 (d) Macf Pr, *supra*—Tait, *supra*—Compare Tait *v* Davie, 22d June 1815, F C—White *v* Clark, 1817, 1 Mur, 213—Baillie *v* Bryson, 1818 ib, 323—Smith *v* Jamesons, 1819, 2 Mur 101—Miller *v* Fraser, 1825, 4 Mur, 114—Clerk's Tr *v* Hill, 1827, 4 Mur, 206—in which cases the re-examination was granted, with Harvey *v* Smith, 1818, 1 Mur, 307, and Kilmahew *v* Cuningham, 1712, M, 16,723, where it was refused (e) 15 Vict, c 27 § 4 (f) Tait Ev, 434—Macf Pr, 137 (g) Tait, *supra*

he leads his proof in chief After the pursuer has led his proof in chief and the defender his conjunct probation and proof in chief, the pursuer is entitled to a probation conjunct to the defender's proof in chief, but, after that, the defender is entitled to no further proof, unless he can show that proof has been led in the pursuer's conjunct proof of such a nature as entitles him to a proof in replication, in which case he must apply to the Court for leave to lead such proof in replication, and must show special cause why it must be allowed", Magistrates of Edinburgh *v* Warrender, 1862, 1 Macph, 1[illegible] In the Justiciary Court, where it is doubtful whether the prosecutor is entitled to lead proof in replication, he has been allowed to anticipate a certain train of evidence in defence, *e g*, to put questions to his own witnesses tending to impeach by anticipation the credibility of a witness in the panel's list, H M Adv *v* Common, 1860 3 Irv, 632 See also Robertson *v* Baroness Keith, 1863, 35 Sc Jur 162

[3] Robertson *v* Mackenzie, 1856, 2 Irv 111

IV. *Witnesses when examined should not be led*

§ 1983 The examination of a witness must, in general be conducted without putting to him leading questions—that is, questions which suggest the answer which the party wishes the witness to give (*h*) This rule excludes not only such questions as "did not you see," or "did not the party say" so and so (*i*), but also those which in effect substitute a statement by the examining counsel, assented to by the witness, for a description or narrative by the witness in his own words (*k*) For example, in a question of boundaries a witness should not be asked "Was the march at Y one of the boundaries?" but "What was the march in that quarter?" (*l*) And it is improper to ask whether such and such persons were present on a certain occasion, the proper question being "Who were present?" (*m*), or to ask whether a person said so and so, instead of asking "What did he say?" (*n*) So a party may not ask a question which implies that a previous question has been answered in a particular way when that is not the fact (*o*), *e.g*, asking why a person did so and so, before proving that he acted in the manner supposed, or how much money was paid, when the witness has not stated that any payment was made

§ 1984 This rule, however, must be understood in a reasonable sense, for, if it were strictly adhered to, trials would be tediously and unnecessarily prolonged Where a witness is called to prove only certain facts in the case, he may be led up to them by recapitulating circumstances already proved, the strict rule, however, being applied to that part of the examination which is material (*p*) Circumstances may also be mentioned to a witness for the purpose of identifying the occasion or matter to which his attention has to be directed For this purpose the subject of the conversation, or a part of the contents of the document upon which his evidence is required, may be mentioned to him, the material passages being withheld (*q*) When the examination is upon dates, which are apt

(*h*) Burnett, 465—2 Al 545—Tait Ev, 427—Macf Pr 131—1 Greenl, § 434—Taylor, 931—Best's Pr of Ev § 611 (*i*) Burnett, *supra*—Al, *supra*—Tait, *supra* (*k*) 2 Al, 546 (*l*) Hunter *v* Dodds, 1832, 10 S 833

(*m*) Mackenzie *v* Murray 1819, 2 Mur, 511 (*n*) Walker *v* Robertson, 1821, 2 Mur, 510—Snadon *v* Stewart 1819, 2 ib, 70 (*o*) 1 Greenl, § 434

(*p*) Macf Pr 132—2 Al, 545—1 Greenl, § 434—Taylor 931

(*q*) Walker *v* Robertson, 1821, 2 Mur 509—Greenl, *supra*—Taylor, *supra*—Best Pr of Ev, *supra*—Compared with Aiton *v* M'Culloch, 1823 3 Mur 285—Macf Pr 132

to escape the memory, circumstances may be mentioned to the witness with the view of recalling them (*p*) So, in an English case, where a witness stated that he could not recollect the names of the members of a certain firm, but thought he might recognise them if they were suggested to him, that was permitted (*r*) And the same practice prevails in this country

§ 1985 In England the strict rule is not applied to cross-examination, because, as a witness is in general biassed in favour of the party for whom he is adduced, the suggestion is not likely to occasion a false answer (*s*) This is also the rule where a witness examined in chief exhibits unwillingness to give evidence, or hostility to the adducer (*t*) *E converso*, it would rather seem that if a witness shows a bias in favour of the party who cross-examines him, the right to lead will be restrained (*u*)

It is laid down by some text writers (*x*), and is said to have been decided in a criminal case (*y*) (the circumstances of which, however, are not mentioned), that there is not in Scotland any difference in this respect between examinations in chief and in cross. But the English rule was applied in a civil trial (*z*), and is recognised in the modern practice of our courts (*a*) [4]

When leading a witness in cross-examination is competent, the proper course is first to put the question in the ordinary form (*b*).

§ 1986 It is in the discretion of the Court, at the trial, to determine under what circumstances a leading question may be put, and a bill of exceptions on the point will not be entertained (*c*)

V *Witnesses must be examined on matter of Fact, not of Law Proving Foreign Law.*

§ 1987 Under the great rule, that the law of a case is for the

(*p*) Auchmutie *v* Ferguson, 1817, 1 Mur, 212—Macf Pr, 132—1 Greenl, § 435

(*r*) Accero *v* Petroni, 1815, 1 Stark R, 100, per Lord Ellenborough

(*s*) Taylor, 936—1 Greenl, 434, 447—Best Pr of Ev, § 611

(*t*) Taylor 931—1 Greenl, 135—Best, § 612

(*u*) Best Pr of Ev, § 612—Rosc Cr Ev, 168—2 Phil, 403

(*x*) Burnett, 466—2 Al, 547—Tait Ev, 427—*Contra*, Macf Pr, 132

(*y*) Stevenson and Others, 1808, Burnett, *supra* This case is of too old date to be of much authority on this branch of law

(*z*) Johnstone *v* Pennycook, 1818, 1 Mur, 289

(*a*) Macf Pr, *supra*

(*b*) 2 Phil, 401

(*c*) 1 Greenl, 135—Taylor, 933 So found in an American case, Moody *v* Rowell (Massachussets), 17 Pickering, 198, noted in Greenl and Taylor, ib

[4] H M Adv *v* Muir, 1858, 3 Irv, 280

Court and the facts for the jury, it is incompetent to ask a witness a question which involves an opinion on a point of law (*d*) The proper course is to get the facts from the witness and ask a direction on the point of law from the Court

This rule, however, only extends to the municipal law of the country in which the trial takes place. When the case involves a question of foreign law (which term, when used in Scotland, includes the laws of England and Ireland), it must be proved as matter of fact by persons skilled in the appropriate system of jurisprudence (*e*), the evidence of mere residenters or merchants accustomed to trade with the country not being admitted on the point (*f*) In questions as to the law of a colony which recognises the English system, the evidence of an English lawyer is usually taken (*g*) [5]

§ 1988. When the case is tried by jury, the foreign law is proved on oath like other parts of the case (*h*) But the Court may recall an order for issues to try the case by jury, and may direct the opinion of foreign counsel to be taken on questions of foreign law involved in it, if that course is deemed advisable (*i*) When the rest of the proof is on commission and in the numerous cases where no proof of the facts is required, points of foreign law are investigated by taking the opinion of one or more lawyers of the country on a case adjusted by the parties under the eye of the Court, or prepared by a neutral counsel whom the Court appoint (*k*) If the

(*d*) See, *e.g.*, Murray *v.* Tod, 1817 1 Mur, 227—E Fife *v.* E Fife's Tr, 1816, ib 106,7—Gibb *v.* Wathen, 1829, 5 ib, 65—Rawson *v* Johnston, 1833, 11 S, 1011

(*e*) Macf Pr, 207—Sanders *v* Reid, 1835, 14 S, 62—Mortimer *v* M'Nicol, 1835 14 S, 95 (*f*) Bell *v.* Bell, 1819, 2 Mur 132—Glegg *v* Levy 1812, 3 Camp, 166 (*g*) Robertson *v.* Gordon, 15th Nov 1814, F C—M'Alister *v* M'Alister, 1854, 16 S, 171—Trotter *v* Trotter 1826, 5 S, 78, affd on merits, 3 W S 407—Sinclair *v* Thomson, 1851, 14 D 217 (*h*) Maberly & Co, 1834, 12 S, 902 Here the Court refused to allow the evidence of English lawyers to be taken on commission, because there could not be any difficulty in procuring the attendance of such witnesses at the trial (*i*) Rutherfurd *v.* Carruthers, 1838, 1 D, 111

(*k*) Cases in following notes

[5] The statute 22 and 23 Vict, c 63, for ascertaining the law administered in different parts of her Majesty's dominions provides (§ 1), that a court in one part of Her Majesty's dominions may remit a case for the opinion in law of a court in any other part thereof The opinion, when returned, is to be applied (§ 3) by the Court making the remit It is competent (§ 4) for Her Majesty in Council, or the House of Lords on appeal, to adopt or reject the opinion The statute has been taken advantage of in Lord *v.* Colvin 1860, 23 D 111 and the Baroness de Blonay *v* Oswald's Representatives, 1863, 1 Macph, 1147 The statute 24 Vict c 11, contains similar provisions in reference to the laws of foreign states

foreign lawyers differ in opinion the Court will remit the case for the opinion of others (*l*) And if their opinions contain ambiguities or do not exhaust the case, it will be sent back to them for farther consideration (*m*) But if the opinion is clear, it will not be remitted to the counsel for re-consideration on one of the parties impugning it (*n*) And so, where a party concurred in a judicial remit to a New York barrister with regard to a point of the law of South Carolina, and an opinion adverse to him was returned, the Court refused to make a new remit to lawyers of the latter state, on an allegation that the practice there was different from that of New York (*o*) When foreign lawyers give opposite evidence in the witness-box, the point falls to be determined like any other question of fact, by balancing the conflicting evidence (*p*)

§ 1989 If the opinions returned on a remit are clear and concurring, the Court will apply them to the case, as conclusive of the points to which they refer, and will not take them to review or investigate authorities in the foreign law, to discover whether they are correct or not (*r*) But although the Court of Session will thus give conclusive effect to an opinion of English or Irish lawyers, the House of Lords, on the case being appealed will not hold themselves bound by it (*s*) If they did, the anomalous result would be, that while judgments pronounced by the supreme courts of these countries, after full argument, could be reviewed and corrected by the court of last resort, an erroneous opinion given by a counsel on

---

(*l*) Kerr *v* Fyffe, 1840, 2 D, 1001 (*m*) This is common in practice

(*n*) L Cranstoun *v* Cunningham, 1839, 1 D, 521 (*o*) Welsh *v* Milne, 1844, 7 D, 213 (*p*) *Per curiam* in Kerr *v* Fyffe, *supra*—Dalrymple *v* Dalrymple, 1811, 2 Hag Con Rep, 51

(*r*) Baird *v* Mitchell, 1854 16 D, 1088—Stein's Assig *v* Brown, *infra*—Duchess of Buckingham *v* Winterbottom, 1851, 13 D, 1129—L Cranstoun *v* Cunningham, *supra*—Aberdeen Banking Co *v* Maberly, 1837, 15 S, 1052—Trotter *v* Trotter, 1826, 5 S, 78, affd on merits, 3 W S, 407—Bennison, 1850, J Shaw, 453 It is not clear whether a Scotch court is bound by an opinion of English counsel as to whether an English deed is null on the stamp laws, for that is a question on the construction of a public British statute, see Taylor *v* Scott, 1847, 9 D, 1504 When the opinion of a foreign lawyer, taken as to the validity and construction of a will executed abroad, stated that it was valid, and that its construction did not involve any rule of local law, and the opinion concluded with giving what the foreign lawyer considered to be the right construction, the Court, while holding themselves bound by the opinion on the validity of the deed, construed it for themselves, and refused to adopt the opinion on the point, Sinclair *v* Alexander, 1851, 14 D, 217 The decision was pronounced on the opinions of a bare majority of the whole Court, and it would have been the other way if the opinion of one judge had been counted, who died after initialing the proof sheet of the print of it, an opposite opinion having been given by his successor

(*s*) Stein's Assignees 1831, 5 W S 47 (reversing 7 S 686)—Macpherson *v* Macpherson, 1852, 1 Macq, 24[illegible]—See also Trotter *v* Trotter, [illegible] W S, [illegible]

the same point, without hearing parties, would be final But it is doubtful whether this rule applies where the opinion on which a Scotch court proceed relates to a point of English ecclesiastical law, for the House of Lords have no jurisdiction in that class of cases (*t*).

§ 1990 A somewhat manifest improvement on this proceeding may be suggested—namely, to allow the parties to appear by counsel or solicitors before the foreign lawyer, as before a judicial referee By this means his attention would be fully directed to the merits of the question before him, and his opinion would be more deserving than at present of the finality with which it is regarded in this country This course seems to be the more necessary when the question is one on which the House of Lords cannot adjudicate in the manner above noticed.—According to the present practice, parties are not allowed to appear before the foreign lawyer (*u*), but

(*t*) See Geils *v* Geils, 1852, 1 Macq , 257, note

(*u*) Aberdeen Banking Co *v* Maberly, 1837 15 S , 1052 per L Cunningham Ordinary, acquiesced in The present mode of proving foreign law is objectionable, and admits of improvement whenever the point is one cognizable by the courts of England or Ireland —It may be a question *in apicibus juris*, on which different views would be entertained by the highest judicial authorities of the appropriate tribunal after full debate, and therefore to decide it on the opinions of counsel, not always the most eminent, given without hearing parties, and perhaps in the hurry of an extensive practice must frequently cause injustice Nor would the suggestion thrown out in the text remedy, although it might abate, the evil Still more objectionable is the practice of examining counsel as witnesses, for in them, as in all witnesses on matters of opinion there is a strong tendency to support the side of the party who adduces them, instead of giving a *quasi* judicial opinion on the question It frequently happens, too, that the best lawyers (for instance, Lord Ch Eldon) give their opinions with hesitation, while confidence and dogmatism often accompany superficial knowledge Accordingly, the jury are apt to be misled where they can only decide on the apparent preponderance of opinion on either side It is conceived that these evils would be remedied by allowing the Court of Session to send a case to the Supreme Court in England or Ireland, in which the question, if arising in either of these countries would be adjudicated, the decision of that court being obtained thereon, after hearing parties, as on a point of law reserved in a special verdict, and a reciprocal course might be adopted for determining questions of Scotch law when arising in an English or Irish court In this way the point would be decided deliberately by the appropriate tribunal, to which the parties probably looked when the transaction was entered into, and the judgment could be applied by the court in which the action had to be raised in consequence of a collateral question of domicile It may be added in support of these views, that under the former practice in this country questions of foreign law used to be submitted to the judges of the appropriate court for written opinion which was granted *ex comitate* on a recommendation from the court in which the suit arose, Paterson *v* Hall, 1620 M , 12,419—Cunninghame *v* Brown, 1676, M , 12,323—Ersk , 3 2, 42—Tait Ev , 127 [6]

[6] These suggestions have been given effect to in the acts 22 and 23 Vict , c 63, and 24 Vict , c 11, *supra*, § 1987, note [5]

the case frequently mentions the leading points maintained by the parties, with the authorities on which they respectively rely

VI *Witnesses should be examined on matters of fact, not of opinion —Evidence on questions of Science &c*

§ 1991 In general the examination of witnesses must be on facts which fell under their own observation, not on matters of opinion or inference, which are for the jury not for the witnesses Thus in an action for damages arising out of the overturn of a coach, a witness should be asked as to the circumstances which occurred at the time, and it is incompetent to ask whether in his opinion the driver was to blame (*x*) In an action of damages for adultery with the pursuer's wife, where a witness deponed to having seen the defender coming out of a bed in the wife's room, it was held incompetent to ask if the witness believed that she was then in the bed (*y*) A witness may not be asked whether he thinks that a certain prosecution was malicious (*z*), or whether the defender appeared to act maliciously (*a*) or whether the impression made on his mind by certain statements was that they were to the pursuer's prejudice (*b*) It has been held that a witness may not be asked whether a certain person acted with propriety (*c*), or whether one was taken to a certain place as a prisoner (*d*) or what was the pursuer's purpose in coming on board a vessel in which the defender was, the action being for damages for assault (*e*), or whether the witness believes that certain persons are partners (*f*), or whether it is his opinion that the pursuer believed a certain fact (*g*) It has also been held incompetent to ask a witness whether a party led him to understand so and so (*h*) In an issue of facility and circumvention a witness may not be asked whether, if he had been on a jury, he would have cognosced the party as *non compos mentis* (*i*) And in an action regarding the character of a servant it was held incompetent to ask a witness, who had

---

(*x*) Gunn v Gardner, 1820, 2 Mur, 197 (*y*) Baillie v Bryson, 1818, 1 Mur, 323 (*z*) Harper v Robinsons, 1820, 2 Mur 394

(*a*) Watt v Blair, 1828, 4 Mur, 573 (*b*) Harper v Robinsons, *supra*—Anton v M'Culloch, 1823, 3 Mur, 287, correcting Gibson v Stevenson, 1823 ib, 216

(*c*) Fowler v Paul, 1821, 2 Mur, 113 See also Burrell v Hodge, 1821, ib, 525

(*d*) Mannel v Fraser, 1818, 1 Mur, 392 (*e*) Lang v Lillie, 1826, 4 Mur, 81 (*f*) Chatto v Pyper, 1827, 4 Mur, 351 (*g*) Gibb v Watson, 1829, 5 Mur, 63—Brown v Cuthill, 1828, 4 ib, 476 (*h*) Hay v Boyd, 1822 3 Mur 12 (*i*) Mackenzie v Roy, 1830 5 Mur 260

given him a recommendation, whether he would have done so after a certain conversation with the defender, in whose service the party had been (*k*). In two different stages of a case (which occurred before the Jury Court was instituted), as to whether certain documents were written by a party, or under his directions, witnesses were allowed to be asked whether they knew or suspected by whom they were written or addressed (*l*). But this case has been justly questioned by Mr Tait (*m*).

§ 1992. There are however, some inferences which are deduced from a number of minor circumstances observed by the witness, not so much in their primary character as in the secondary fact which they concur in pointing to. This, as already explained (*n*), is the case in evidence of identity, whether of persons or things, and in proof of handwriting. It frequently happens indeed, that a person can confidently swear to identity and handwriting, without being able to describe the features of the individual, or the characteristics of the letters, far less to convey an adequate impression of them to the jury. Accordingly his belief on the point is every day received as evidence, the grounds of it being cross-examined upon, if that is thought advisable. So, where a witness is examined on a libel containing innuendos and blanks, he may be asked to whom he understands that they apply (*o*). In an action of divorce for adultery, a witness was allowed to be asked whether from what she observed on a particular occasion her impression was that criminal intercourse had then taken place (*p*). In the Justiciary Court, a witness is often examined upon the impression produced on his mind at the time by what he observed, as, for example, in order to bring out whether he thought that certain cries were those of a female in distress, or that the prisoner was skulking about certain premises, or that he was feigning insanity or distress. In like manner it has been held both in England and in America, that in an action of breach of promise of marriage, or damages for adultery with the plaintiff's wife, a witness accustomed to observe the mutual behaviour of the parties may give his opinion on the question

---

(*k*) Anderson *v* Wishart, 1818, 1 Mur., 433. (*l*) Chalmers *v* Douglas, 1784, M., 12,439. (*m*) Tait Ev., 427. See also Kingan *v* Watson, 1828, 4 Mur., 488. (*n*) See *supra*, § 245. (*o*) Edwards *v* M'Intosh, 1823, 3 Mur., 374.—See Daines *v* Hartley, 1848, 3 Wels. Hurl. and Gor., 200.

(*p*) King *v* King, 1842, 4 D., 590. It was observed that the question was put in too leading a form, as the witness should first have been asked what was her impression from what she saw.

whether they were attached to each other (r) Thus, also, in questions of facility and circumvention, it is the constant practice to ask instrumentary witnesses and other persons present at the execution of the deed, whether in their belief the party was of sound disposing mind And the witnesses to a prisoner's declaration are every day examined as to their opinion whether he emitted it when in his sound and sober senses

§ 1993 Again, where the issue involves the belief of a party in a certain fact, it would seem that other persons who were placed in similar circumstances may be asked whether they believed it (s), —as in a prosecution for uttering writings knowing that they were forged, where the witnesses had had the documents in their hands (t) Thus, also, in an action of damages for calling the pursuer a liar in making certain statements in a memorial on medical subjects knowing them to be false, where the defender took an issue of the *veritas convicii*, the Lord Chief-Commissioner (with whom sat Lords Cringletie and Mackenzie) allowed the pursuer to ask the President of the College of Surgeons whether he believed the statements to be true. His Lordship observed, "The nature of this evidence, I conceive, to be calling a person who, from his situation and profession is acquainted with the subject, and putting into his hands a memorial for the purpose of ascertaining whether he believes the statements true, and what follows is reasoning as to the probability of the pursuer knowing them to be false, when a person in the situation of the witness believes them to be true" (u)

§ 1994 Another exception to the general rule against examining witnesses on matters of opinion, occurs wherever the issue involves scientific knowledge, or acquaintance with the rules of any trade, manufacture, or business with which men of ordinary intelligence are not likely to be familiar (x) This exception is daily il-

(r) Trelawny v Colman, 1817, 2 Stark R 192, per Holroyd—M'Kee v Nelson, 1825 (New York), 4 Cowen, 355—1 Greenl § 440—Taylor, 911

(s) See Tait Ev, 433, 4

(t) In the trial of Humphreys for forging documents to prove his title to the Stirling peerage, the law agent who had produced the writings in the civil process was examined on behalf of the prisoner as to whether he believed that the documents were genuine 1839, separate report by Swinton, p 110

(u) Hamilton v Hope, 1827, 1 Mur 210 But this rule does not, in an action of damages for libel, admit evidence for the defender that other persons believed the libellous statements to be true, and still less that they suspected them to be so The reason is, that such suspicion or belief is not relevant in defence provided it was kept within the breast of the witness Yet the defender may prove that the slander was currently reported, as that will mitigate the damages, Kingan v Watson, 1828 4 Mur 488

(x) Tait Ev 433—2 Al 541—1 Greenl § 440—Taylor 941—Best Pr of Ev, § 495

lustrated in the examination of medical men in the criminal courts So the opinion of artists picture-dealers, and other persons familiar with the subject, is admitted in a question as to the value of a painting (*y*) In a question whether a purse won at a coursing match belonged to the owner of the winning dog at the time, or to a previous owner, the jury decided upon the opinion of sporting men as to the laws of coursing (*z*) And in an English case, where a libel consisted in imputing to the plaintiff that he had acted dishonourably in withdrawing a horse at a race, and he proved that the rules of the Jockey Club permitted such withdrawal, it was held that the witness might be asked, in cross-examination, whether such conduct, although in accordance with these rules, would not be regarded by him as dishonourable (*a*) It has already been seen that engravers, writing masters, bankers, and others accustomed to observe autographs, may be examined as to a *comparatio literarum*, although they have not previously been familiar with the handwriting in issue (*b*) Many other illustrations of the same rule might be given, in which engineers, persons in trade, mineralogists, and others skilled in particular branches of knowledge, have been examined on matters within their several departments

§ 1995 A foundation for such an examination must always be laid by ascertaining whether the witness is a person of skill, or an "expert" (the English term), under which is included those who have a theoretical acquaintance with the subject, as well as men who speak from practical knowledge (*c*) A peculiar fitness however, for the office in one of these respects is essential (*d*)

§ 1996 In conducting such examinations care must be taken not to encroach on the province of the jury, by laying before them an opinion founded partly on inferences which do not involve the peculiar skill or knowledge which the witness is supposed to possess[7] This is forcibly illustrated in the practice of excluding medical witnesses during the trial, in order that their scientific opinions may not be biassed by inferences from the general facts of the

(*y*) M'Lellan *v* Gibson, 1843, 5 D, 1032 (*z*) Gibson *v* Pollock, 1848, 11 D, 343 (*a*) Greville *v* Chapman, 5 Ad and Ell, New Ser, 731

(*b*) *Supra*, § 925 (*c*) See 1 Greenl, § 410, note

(*d*) See *supra*, § 1987, and M'Leod *v* M'Leod, 1821 3 Mur, 431

7 It was observed by the Lord Justice Clerk (Inglis) in Morrison *v* Maclean's Trus, that, in questions of insanity, the inferences to be derived from general peculiarities in the manner, speech, behaviour, and action of the alleged lunatic should be drawn by the jury for themselves, and that they should not be guided by the opinions formed by medical witnesses Morrison *v* Maclean's Trus, 1862, 24 D 626

case (*e*) On this account it is held incompetent in a question of facility to ask a witness "From all you have heard, do you think the deceased was capable of executing the deed in question?" (*f*) And a similar ruling was given as to examining nautical men in a question regarding the sailing of a ship (*g*) In England also a medical witness may not be asked whether in his opinion a particular act charged was one of insanity (*h*) And a skilled witness who has heard the evidence may not be asked his opinion on the case itself but on a similar case, stated hypothetically (*i*) This is also the mode of examination followed in criminal trials in this country, where the medical witnesses are kept out of Court during evidence upon the facts [8]

In a prosecution for rape it was held that a medical witness could not be asked whether, if the woman was a virgin, it was possible for the prisoner to have mastered her when one of his hands was behind her back and the other on her mouth, the question not involving a point of medical opinion (*k*).

§ 1997 But in a question, what was the port of delivery of goods under a written order, mercantile witnesses were allowed to give their opinions after perusing the document, like persons interpreting a deed in a foreign language (*l*)

§ 1998 In evidence of opinion it is essential to ascertain precisely the data on which the witnesses proceed For example, a physician often forms his opinion as to a supposed disease partly from the symptoms which he observed himself, and partly from statements by the patient as to his sufferings, and statements by another medical attendant or a sick nurse He may also have proceeded upon examination of evacuations or blood which he was informed came from the patient Nearly all his data will thus have come to him at second-hand, and may have been fabricated or erroneous He ought therefore to be examined with reference to different combinations of these supposed facts, corresponding to the different results at which the jury may arrive regarding their authenticity In like manner, a written medical report (*m*) ought to bear on its face the data on which the opinions contained in it

(*e*) *Supra*, § 1973, 4 See also *supra*, § 1756 (*f*) Stewart *v* Boyes, 1838, Macf, 27—See also Macleod, 1838, Bell's Notes, 267 (*g*) See per L Pres in Campbell *v* Tyson, 1811, 4 D, 312 (*h*) See R *v* Wright, 1821, Russ and Ry, 456—1 Greenl, § 440—Taylor, 915 (*i*) Sills *v* Brown, 1840, 9 Car and Pa, 601 (*k*) Henderson, 1836, 1 Swin, 316

(*l*) Schuurmans *v* Stephen, 1832, 10 S, 839 (*m*) See *infra*, § 2009

8 But see *supra* § 1973 note 1

proceed Its proper purpose is to set forth the inference deducible by a medical man from facts observed by himself (*n*) But if any information which he has derived from other sources would, if true, modify his opinion, he should state the results at which he would arrive on the hypothesis of the information being wholly or partially correct

These remarks may be applied *mutatis mutandis* to other evidence of opinion

§ 1999 There is perhaps, no kind of testimony more subject to bias in favour of the adducer than that of skilled witnesses, for many men, who would not knowingly misstate a simple fact, can accommodate their opinions to the wishes of their employers, and the connection between them tends to warp the judgment of the witnesses without their being conscious of it Hence it is that skilled witnesses in questions of handwriting can usually be got in equal numbers on either side (*o*),[9] and engineers are more frequently like counsel for their employers than like witnesses giving their real opinions upon oath Medical witnesses for the prosecution in criminal cases are an honourable exception, humanity and a sense of justice keeping them from bias Nor is medical evidence generally open to the censure which it deserved in the courts of this country some years ago, when medical polemics ran high in the metropolis, and when it was seldom difficult to get witnesses of one party to contradict the scientific opinions announced by their opponents (*p*)

§ 2000 In civil cases not tried by jury these evils are obviated by remitting the case to one or more competent persons, as assessors to the Court on the questions of science, or the like which it involves When both parties expressly consent to a remit of this kind, the report of the person remitted to is binding on them, like the award of a judicial referee for it would be absurd to allow a party, after agreeing to a particular mode of investigation, to repu-

(*n*) See Sheills, 1846, Arkley, 171

(*o*) See *supra* § 925

(*p*) See Prof Christison on Medical Evidence, Monthly Jour of Med Science, vol xiii 3d Series, p 404

[9] In a charge of forgery of a bill of exchange, the evidence of a bank officer, who had no knowledge of the signature except *comparatione literarum*, was disallowed, Lord Deas observing,—"Such evidence had been found of no use, for as many opinions could always be obtained on the one side as the other", H M Adv *v* Beveridge, 1860, 3 Irv 625

diate the decision on finding it to be against him (r) This is also the rule where the remit was made on the motion of the party who afterwards challenges the report (s), and where the consent of parties is inferrable from their conduct, as in their mode of dealing with the report, and in acquiescing in the remit (t) But it is doubtful whether one who merely does not object to a remit gives to it the element of consent, which is essential to the report under it being conclusive (u) Where the remit was made before answer, and without any understanding that the report should be final, the parties were held not to be bound by it (x).

§ 2001 In all cases the Court will make a new remit to the reporters to reconsider their report, if it is unsatisfactory or does not exhaust the case (y) If the reporters are equally divided in opinion, another person of skill will be joined with them, like an oversman (z) And if they have committed such irregularities that a second remit to them would be improper, the Court will rather make a new remit to other reporters than allow a jury trial or a proof *prout de jure* (a) Where a party applied to have certain works executed at the sight of persons to be named by the Court, and where, after the work had been executed at the sight of two persons so appointed, without objection from the party, one of them died before the work had been finally approved of, the Court made a remit to another competent person in his room, and refused the motion of the party who had obtained the remit, to allow the question to be investigated by a proof on commission, or by a jury trial (b) This decision, however, was not meant to encroach on

---

(r) Dixon v Monkland Canal Co, 1821, 1 S, 153, affd, 1 W S, 636—Rowat v Whitehead, 1826, 5 S 19—Meason v D Queensberry's Ex, 1827, 6 S, 326—Halkett v E Elgin, 1831, 9 S, 412—Brown v Love, 1852, 4 D, 386—See also Arnot v Brown, 1852, 1 Macq, 229 The report of persons remitted to of consent in the Sheriff Courts is final by 16 and 17 Vict, c 80, § 10 (s) Brown v Love, *supra*—See also L Blantyre v Glasgow, Paisley, &c Ry Co, 1851, 13 D, 570 (t) Dixon v Monkland Canal Co, *supra*—Wilson v Struthers, 1837, 15 S, 523—L Blantyre v Glasgow, Paisley, &c Ry Co, *supra*—Mackintosh v Ly Ashburton, 1834, 12 S, 518—See also Thomson v Moffat, 1831, 10 S, 124 (u) See per L Mackenzie and Fullerton in L Blantyre v Glasgow, Paisley, &c Ry Co, *supra*

(x) D Buccleuch v Pringle, 1827, 5 S, 677—Hunter v D Queensberry's Ex, 1827, ib, 678 (y) Compare Halkett v E Elgin, 1831, 9 S, 412—Dixon v Monkland Canal Co, 1821, 1 S, 153, affd, 1 W S, 636, where a new remit was allowed, with Rowat v Whitehead, 1826, 5 S, 19, where it was refused See also Brown v Love, 1842, 1 D, 386—Meason v D Queensberry's Ex, 1827, 6 S, 326

(z) Muir v Anderson, 1833, 12 S, 129 (a) Per L Pitmilly in Meason v D Queensberry's Ex, *supra* (b) L Blantyre v Glasgow, Paisley &c Ry Co, 1851, 13 D, 571

the principle that consent to a judicial remit to certain individuals, like consent to a judicial reference, involves a *delectus personæ*, and does not bind the party to agree to a remit to other persons on the failure of those originally named (*c*)

§ 2002 It is competent to allow the person to whom a remit is made to meet with the parties before making up his report (*d*), and this course is usually followed in practice without any special authority (*e*)

§ 2003 It would seem that the person to whom a remit has been made may be required to verify his report upon oath (*f*) But this practice has been disapproved of (*g*)

§ 2004 In questions of accounting remits are commonly made to accountants to prepare states and reports upon the documents and books founded upon The object is to put the case in shape for decision by the Court upon the disputed questions, and the accountant's report is not final, like that of persons remitted to on a matter of science (*h*) Yet a party may, by his conduct, bar himself from farther probation on the questions sent to an accountant (*i*)

VII *Witnesses must depone from their own recollection—Referring to memoranda to refresh memory.*

§ 2005 The evidence of a witness must in general be given from his own unaided recollection as at the time of examination. It is therefore incompetent for him to read a written statement upon the facts which he has prepared beforehand, otherwise one-sided evidence might easily be concocted so as to defeat the objects of examination before the jury (*k*) In like manner, if the examination is on interrogatories, the witness may not give in written answers which he has prepared, but must answer the questions orally (*l*) *A fortiori*, where a witness had noted certain cir-

(*c*) See per L Fullerton in L Blantyre *v* Glasgow, Paisley, &c Ry Co, *supra*

(*d*) Hunter *v* D Queensberry's Ex, 1827, 6 S, 89 (*e*) Brown *v* Love, 1842, 4 D, 386, per L Mackenzie (*f*) Per Lords Cringletie (Ordinary) and Pitmilly in Meason *v* D Queensberry's Ex, 1827 6 S, 326—Wilson *v* Struthers, 1837, 15 S, 523 See also D Buccleuch *v* Pringle 1827 5 S, 677

(*g*) Per L Pres Boyle in Brown *v* Love 1842, 4 D, 391 (*h*) Per L Just-Clerk Boyle in Cameron *v* Anderson, 1844 7 D, 100—Gibson *v* Ewan, 1852, 15 D, 211 (*i*) Gibson *v* Ewan *supra* (*k*) Kinloch, 1795, 2 Hume, 381—Elphinstoun *v* L Lothian, 1679, 2 B Sup 249—Burnett, 459—2 Al, 541

(*l*) Sayer *v* Wagstaff, 1842 5 Beav, 467

cumstances from time to time as they occurred to his memory, and at his request the solicitor of the party who adduced him had digested these into the form of a deposition, which he afterwards revised, corrected, and transcribed, his evidence emitted upon reference to that statement was held to be incompetent (*m*) It was also held in one case that a witness may not have a deposition which he had previously emitted read over to him before commencing to give his evidence the proper course being to cancel the previous deposition, if he is afraid he may make statements inconsistent with it (*n*) But opposite decisions have been pronounced, both in this country (*o*), and in England (*p*)

§ 2006 Notwithstanding this general rule, a witness called to prove that he wrote or attested a document, may depone that he recognises his handwriting and has no doubt of its authenticity, although he has not any recollection of the circumstances (*r*) If such evidence were not admissible, many genuine deeds might be imperilled in consequence of the writers or witnesses not recollecting the circumstances at a distance of time, an obliviousness very common among persons engaged in conveyancing business (*s*) It is also common in the criminal courts, in questions of identity, to ask a witness whether he identified the prisoner when he gave information at the police office, and in identifying productions, witnesses often depone from recognising their signatures to the labels attached to the articles, without being required to swear to the articles themselves at the trial

§ 2007 Another exception to the general rule allows witnesses, both in civil and criminal cases, to refer to memoranda in order to refresh their memories upon matters of detail, as, for example, dates and sums, measurements, and articles contained in bills of lading, inventories, and the like (*t*).[10] Such memoranda prepared

---

(*m*) A B, 1753, cited by L Kenyon in Doe *v* Perkins, 3 Durf and E, 752 With this case compare Hook *v* Hook 1852, 14 D, 545 (*n*) Cogan *v* Lyon, 1834 12 S, 569—See *supra*, § 1964 (*o*) M Lean *v* Sibbald 1819, 2 Mur, 121—Bell *v* Bell 1819, ib, 132—Mag of Brechin, 1835, 13 S, 556

(*p*) Vaughan *v* Martin, 1796, 1 Esp, 140—Smith *v* Morgan, 1839, 2 Moo and Rob, 259 In Laws *v* Reid 2 Lewin's Cr Ca, 152, a witness was allowed to refresh his memory from notes taken by counsel of his deposition on a former trial

(*r*) R *v* St Martins Leicester, 1834, 2 Ad and Ell, 210—Maughan *v* Hubbard, 1828, 8 Barn and Cress 16 (*s*) See *supra*, § 910

(*t*) Macf Pr, 135—Tait Ev, 432—Burnett 458—2 Al, 510, 540—Taylor 933—1 Greenl, § 436

---

[10] H M Adv *v* Wilson, 1861, 4 Irv 42

by the witness at the time are a great assistance to his memory and increase the value of his evidence both in precision and in confidence. Documents may be used for this purpose which are themselves inadmissible in evidence, *e g*, deeds null from want of stamps (*u*), improbative minutes of meetings (*x*), log books (*y*), notarial instruments where not required by law (*z*) and letters written by the witness (*a*). And it is not necessary for the document to be lodged as a production, or in criminal cases to be libelled on, for it is not used substantively as evidence, but merely as an aid to the witness' memory (*b*).

If the witness has become blind since writing the document, it may be read to him to refresh his memory (*c*).

§ 2008. It is essential to this kind of evidence, that the witness have some recollection upon the matter to which the memorandum refers; for if his memory is a total blank upon it, the document is not made part of his deposition but comes under the rules as to the admissibility and production of written evidence (*d*). It is also necessary that the memorandum should have been prepared shortly after the occurrence of the facts noted in it and while they were fresh in the memory of the witness, so that although an interval of a day or so will not prevent the document from being used (*e*), yet a witness may not refer to notes made from memory at considerable intervals (*f*), or prepared on the day of trial (*g*).

§ 2009. Evidence of this kind, when relating to inspections by medical men, engineers and similar witnesses, is often given in the form of a report, which is read over by the witness in the box, and sworn to as true. The reason is "that the medical or other scientific facts or appearances which are the subject of such a report, are generally so minute and detailed that they cannot with safety be intrusted to the memory of the witness, but much more reliance may be placed on a report made out by him at the time when the facts or appearances are fresh in his recollection" (*h*). A report

(*u*) See *supra*, § 1014. (*x*) Keirs *v* Penman 1830, 5 Mur 145—Gt Northern Ry *v* Inglis, 1851 13 D 1315 (affd on other points, 1 Macq, 112)—Wilson *v* Glasgow and S Western Ry Co, 1851 14 D 1. (*y*) Innes *v* Glass, 1827, 4 Mur, 164—Wight *v* Liddell, 1829, 5 Mur, 36. (*z*) Innes *v* Glass, *supra*.
(*a*) Graham's Tr *v* White, 1829 5 Mur, 95. (*b*) Macpherson, 1845, 2 Broun, 540—Graham's Tr *v* White, *supra*. (*c*) Catt *v* Howard, 1820, 3 Stark R, 3—2 Al, 510. See also Vaughan *v* Martin, 1796, 1 Esp, 440.
(*d*) Doe *v* Perkins, 1790, 3 Durf and E, 749—Oliver 1827, Syme, 224—See also Macpherson, 1845, 2 Broun, 430, *infra*, § 2010. (*e*) Wilson *v* Glasgow and S Western Ry Co, 1851, 14 D, 1. (*f*) Elder or Smith 1821, Syme, 114.
(*g*) Graham *v*. Loch, 1829, 5 Mur, 75. (*h*) 2 Al, 541.

prepared at the time is also likely to be much more precise in its language than the evidence emitted by the witness on referring to his original notes to refresh his memory The practice is daily seen in the criminal courts, and it has sometimes been followed in civil cases (*i*), in which, however, it is more common to examine the witness with reference to his report than to make him read it (*j*)

§ 2010 In criminal cases where reports are used in this way, it is necessary to libel on them, and lodge them with the clerk of court, like the other productions in the case (*k*) [11]

§ 2011 The question is often raised whether a witness may refer to a copy of the notes which he took at the time, without having the original with him to test the accuracy of the transcription On the one hand, the Court have allowed witnesses to refer to copies made by themselves from notes or memoranda, where there was no reason to fear mistake (*l*) And where a draft minute of a meeting had been prepared by the witness at his leisure, from short notes taken by him at the time the witness was allowed to use it to refresh his memory upon the *res gestæ*, although he had not the original notes (*m*) So in a trial for sedition, where a witness adduced to prove expressions used by one of the prisoners in a speech, had made short notes at the time, which he had extended a few days afterwards, and where he could not swear that the extended copy was *verbatim* the same as the original notes, although it was substantially so, the Court allowed him to give his evidence from his recollection of the words, aided

(*i*) Macf Pr, 133—Thomson v Bisset 1823, 3 Mur, 302—Callander v Eddington, 1826, 4 Mur 110 (*j*) Innes v Glass, 1827 1 Mur, 165—Mackenzie v Horne 1838, 16 S, 1286, M'L and Rob, 977

(*k*) Matheson, 1837, 1 Swin 593, Bell's Notes, 276—2 Al, 511 In Macpherson, 1845, 2 Broun, 450, where a witness called on to identify a bank note deponed that he could not do so without referring to a list which he made up at the time and that he had no recollection of the note more than of any other, the Court would not allow him to refer to the list, because it had not been libelled on and produced in process

(*l*) Thus a medical witness was allowed to refresh his memory from notes taken by himself of entries made in his day-book at the time of attendance, Forgie v Henderson, 1818, 1 Mur, 413 And it was held that a witness may, before coming into Court, use for the same purpose a memorandum book made up by him from other memoranda, Keith v Smart, 1832, 5 De and And, 236 A witness was also allowed to refer to a chartulary containing copies of deeds, in order to refresh his memory as to whether the original of one of them had been prepared by him as agent for a certain party, E Fife v E Fife's Tr, 1816, 1 Mur, 107 (*m*) Wilson v Glasgow and S Western Ry Co, 1851, 14 D, 1, per L Colonsay—See also *supra* § 1173

11 H. M Adv v Macnamara, 1861, 4 Irv, 131

by reference to the extended notes (*n*) In an English case, where transactions in trade had been entered by the plaintiff's clerk in a waste-book and the plaintiff day by day posted them into a ledger, each entry being at the time checked by the clerk, the Court allowed the clerk to use the ledger to refresh his memory, without accounting for the absence of the waste-book (*o*) An engineer was even allowed to give his evidence with reference to a printed copy of the report which he had prepared from his short notes of an inspection, the party against whom he was adduced not having cross-examined him to test the accuracy of his statement that the report was substantially the same as the original notes, and that the print was a copy (which the Court held to mean a correct copy) of the report (*p*)

§ 2012 On the other hand where a road surveyor deponed to the measurements set forth in a report prepared by him, and on cross-examination stated that he first took down notes in his pocket-book on the spot then wrote out a draft of his report on a slate at home, and that his son-in-law made the fair copy of the report from his dictation, but neither the original notes nor the draft of the report had been preserved, the presiding judge refused to admit the report, and directed the jury to disregard the evidence which the witness had emitted under reference to it, and this ruling was sustained on a bill of exceptions (*r*) The Court, however, carefully guarded themselves against laying down that, as a general rule, the original notes must be in the hands of the witness when speaking from an extended copy of them. They considered that every case of the kind depends on its own circumstances, especially on the nature of the notes and the object for which they were taken, as established by the evidence of the witness Lord Fullerton (with whom the other judges seem to have concurred) distinguished between notes taken by the witness as a description of the facts, which he afterwards digested into a formal report and mere notes of measurements, distances, &c , in figures or lines drawn on loose scraps of paper or even by notches on a stick, the report being framed from these notes immediately, with all the ad-

(*n*) Cumming and Grant, 1848 (J Shaw, 17), not reported on this point

(*o*) Barton *v* Plummer, 1834, 2 Ad and Ell , 341

(*p*) Mackenzie *v* Horne, 1838 16 S , 1286, and M'L and Rob , 977 The Court considered that as the party did not examine the witness upon the means used for securing the accuracy of the report and print respectively, he must be held to have been satisfied with the witness' general statement, and that in these circumstances he could not be allowed to infer that they varied materially from the original notes

(*r*) Campbell *v* Macfarlane 1840, 2 D , 663

vantages of recent recollection. His Lordship considered that in the former case the witness disburdens his memory into the original notes, and that the party against whom he is adduced is entitled to see whether the formal report corresponds with them. But in the latter case his Lordship held that the report itself is the original record of the witness' observations, and that the notes even if they could be got, would probably perplex rather than explain the witness' testimony. The learned judge also observed that when notes taken on the spot are called for as presumptively the best evidence, it lies on the party adducing the witness to show that they are not such as require to be produced.

In an English case, also, a witness was not allowed to refer to a copy made by himself six months after he had written the original, which although in existence, was not in Court (*t*).

§ 2013. These authorities show that while the rule which excludes secondary evidence does not apply strictly to documents used for this purpose, the Court will exercise a discretion in allowing a witness to refresh his memory from a copy of his original notes. Every case of this kind will therefore depend on its own circumstances, the object for which the document is required, the nature of the original notes, the circumstances under which the copy was made, and the means taken to test its accuracy, the question being whether the copy properly represents the memory of the witness as at the date of the matter deponed to.

§ 2014. In like manner, a witness may not, in general, refresh his memory from a document not prepared by himself, or refer to entries in cash-books which were not made in his own handwriting (*u*). Yet if they were written by his clerk under his eye (*x*), or if he perused them and satisfied himself of their accuracy while the facts were fresh in his recollection (*y*) they may be used for this purpose. So joint reports by medical men, written by one and signed by them both, are used in daily practice in the criminal courts.

§ 2015. Where documents are used by a witness to refresh his memory the counsel for the opposite party is entitled to see them in conducting his cross-examination (*z*).

(*t*) Jones v. Stroud, 1825, 2 Car. and Pa., 196.

(*u*) M'Neil v. M'Neill, 1822, 3 Mur., 149—Mackenzie v. Roy, 1830, 5 ib., 260.

(*x*) Gibson v. Stevenson, 1822, 3 Mur., 219.

(*y*) See Tait Ev., 433—2 Al., 510—Taylor, 935—Barton v. Plummer, *supra* § 2011, (*o*).

(*z*) Tait Ev., 433—2 Al. 510—Taylor, 938—R. v. Hardy, 1794, 21 State Tr., 821.

VIII *Witnesses may decline answering questions which infer a charge of criminality against them*

§ 2016 It has already been seen that a judicial examination and a reference to the oath of a party are incompetent on allegations which infer criminality in him (*a*). In like manner, *quod nemo tenetur jurare in suam turpitudenem*, a witness is entitled to decline answering any question which infers against him a charge of an indictable offence (*b*) This privilege has, for example, been recognised where the crime involved was murder (*c*), theft (*d*), perjury (*e*), carrying a challenge to fight a duel (*f*), and felonious abstraction of documents (*g*) It applies to questions inferring a charge of adultery (*h*), which is still a point of dittay, although prosecution for it is now unknown, and also to the examination of instrumentary witnesses as to whether they attested the deed without seeing the granter subscribe, or hearing him acknowledge his subscription because doing so infers the penalties of forgery (*i*) A witness was allowed to decline answering whether he took a bribe at a borough election (*k*) The privilege also applies to questions involving a charge of a serious assault (*l*) and sending a threatening letter (*m*), crimes which are punishable by imprisonment And it is thought that a witness is not bound to answer regarding any offence for which a criminal prosecution may lie against him (*n*)

§ 2017 The privilege, however, is limited to questions which may involve the witness in penal consequences (*o*) He must answer such as merely impugn his mercantile credit (*p*), or infer a ground of damages in a civil action (*r*) So a party to the cause

---

(*a*) See *supra* §§ 1396, 1548 (*b*) Tait Ev, 428—2 Al, 528

(*c*) Burke and Macdowall, 1828, Syme 364, *supra*, § 1796 (*d*) Miller, 1837 1 Swin 489 (*e*) Pender, 1836, 1 Swin, 25 Here a witness was allowed to decline answering whether on a previous occasion he emitted a false oath

(*f*) Hyslop *v* Millar, 1816, 1 Mur, 48 (*g*) Livingstone *v* Murray, 1830, 9 S, 161 (*h*) Stephens 1839, 2 Swin, 348—Don *v* Don, 1818, 10 D, 1046—See Brash *v* Steele 1845 7 D 539 (*i*) *Supra*, § 908

(*k*) Fortrose Election, noticed in Nicolson *v* Nicolson, 1770, M, 16,770

(*l*) Brown *v* Miller, 1828, 6 S, 561 (*m*) M'Callum *v* M'Call, 1825 3 S, 551 (*n*) Bell's Pr, § 2249—Macf Pr, 166—Stevenson *v* Scott, 1854, 1 Irvine, 603—*Supra*, § 1549—16 Vict, c 20, § 3—But see *contra*, Burnett, 463—Tait Ev, 428—2 Al, 528, and *infra*, § 2017 (*t*), where the privilege is stated only as to charges of crimes which infer infamy (*o*) Tait Ev, 428—2 Al, 529—Burnett, 463 (*p*) Pender, 1836, 1 Swin, 25 (*r*) Bell's Pr,

examined by his opponent under the Law of Evidence Amendment Acts (*s*), is bound to answer questions to his own prejudice, unless they infer criminality in him. In a case as to the fraudulent destruction of a deed of settlement, where a Sheriff-clerk was asked whether he knew how the deed had been taken out of the register under his official care, the Court overruled his objection that he was not bound to answer questions which might involve him in a charge of malversation of office, and it was "laid down as a rule that no objection made by a witness against his own deponing was to be sustained, except where the fact put to him might infer infamy, and accordingly, in exhibitions and other cases, witnesses are every day examined upon facts which infer against themselves fraud and damage" (*t*)[12]

In a late case however it was held that a witness may be asked whether she had frequently been found fault with by persons in whose service she had been, for listening at doors and windows and telling lying stories, it being explained to her that she was entitled

§ 2249—Tait Ev 428—2 Al 529—Burnett, 463—*Contra*, Chatto *v* Pyper, 1827, 4 Mur, 357, per L Ch Commissioner See also Inglis *v* Gardner 1843, 5 D, 1029

(*s*) 15 Vict, c 27, § 2—16 Vict, c 20, § 3 (*t*) Murray *v*. Murray, 1744, M, 16,752, Fch, "Witness," No 22 See also *supra*, § 1896

[12] In the examination of the wife of a bankrupt by the trustee, the Court held that it was competent to ask her whether she was aware that her husband had, at a certain date, drawn a large sum from a bank for which he was agent, although a criminal charge had been brought against him of embezzlement of the funds of the bank as at that date Lord Cowan observed, in reference to the criminating tendency of the inquiry —"This, it must be remembered, is a collateral inquiry, and not a case in which the husband is directly interested In such a case the law of England does not exclude such an investigation But further, suppose the bankrupt himself had been asked this question, I am prepared to say that the bankrupt could not have refused to answer Suppose there had been no charge of embezzlement against him, could he have said 'I will not answer this question, because it may criminate me in a matter which may ultimately become the matter of a criminal investigation' In my opinion he could not refuse an answer on any such ground He cannot shelter himself in an investigation as to his property under the Bankrupt Statute by pleading that he may criminate himself by bringing upon his head a charge of fraudulent bankruptcy". Sawers *v* Balgarnie, 1858, 21 D, 153 It has been held in England that a bankrupt is bound, when under examination, to answer all questions, although they may tend to criminate himself, and his answer may be given against him in a criminal charge Reg *v* Scott 1856 2 Jur, N S, 1096 It is no ground for refusing to answer that the answer may tend to expose the witness' customers to actions, Tetley *v* Easton, 1856, 25 L J, C P, 293 See also Adams *v* Floyd, 1858, 4 Jur, N S, 590—Mexican Co *v* South African Co, 1859, 5 Jur, N S 615—Reg *v* Baynes, 1861, 7 Jur, N S, 1158—Reg *v* Halliday, 1860, 29 L J, M C, 118—Scott *v* Millar, 1859, 5 Jur, N S, 868

to decline answering (*u*) But the objection was to the competency of the question, and the point of the witness' right to decline answering was not properly before the Court. In a case of rape the woman was allowed to decline answering whether she had had intercourse with other men besides the prisoner (*v*) The rule in England seems to be, that witnesses are not bound to answer questions put for the mere purpose of degrading them (*x*), although, if the question relates to the merits of the case, they must answer (*y*)

§ 2018 Where a *socius criminis* is examined in a criminal case, he is bound to answer all questions relating to the charge upon which he is adduced, for, although his doing so casts a stigma on his character, it cannot involve him in penal consequences (*z*) And for the same reason, it is thought that a witness who has been examined as a *socius criminis* may be compelled to answer as a witness in a civil action for reparation of the loss or damages caused by the act (*a*) So it is held in England and America that if the right to prosecute for the crime involved in an interrogatory has prescribed the witness is bound to answer (*b*) And in this country a witness must answer whether he has been convicted of a specified offence (*c*)

§ 2019 The right of declinature extends to examination on facts which indirectly infer guilt, or which may form links in a chain of circumstantial evidence against the witness, as well as to the direct question, whether he committed a specified crime (*d*) It lies with the Court to determine, from the circumstances of each case, whether the question comes within this rule (*e*) and they will generally be satisfied with the witness statement that it does, without requiring him to explain how the question bears upon the charge, for that would often in effect deprive him of his privilege (*f*)

(*u*) King *v* King, 1842, 4 D, 590 (*v*) Allan, 1842, 1 Broun 500 This may be questioned (*x*) Rose Ev at Nisi Pr 137—Taylor, 973—2 Phill 421—Best s Pr of Ev, § 126 (*y*) Phill, *supra*—Taylor, *supra*—Best *supra*

(*z*) Burnett, 463—Tait Ev, 428 (*a*) See Jantzen *v* Easton, 3d Feb 1814, F C—*Supra*, § 1396 (*b*) Roberts *v* Allat, 1828, 1 Moo and Malk, 192—Parkhurst *v* Lowten, 1816, 1 Meriv, 400, per L Eldon—Williams *v* Farrington, 1789, 2 Cox Eq Ca, 202—Taylor 972—1 Greenl § 451 (*c*) Johnston, 1845, 2 Broun, 403 (*d*) Hyslop *v* Staig, 1816 1 Mur 17, 18—Taylor, 972—1 Greenl, 451—Best Pr of Ev, 125—*Contra*, Hyslop *v* Miller, 1816, 1 Mur, 48, where the L Ch Commissioner ruled that although a witness may decline to answer whether he carried a challenge to fight a duel, he must say whether he delivered the same message as he received, the terms of which may be proved otherwise

(*e*) Taylor, *supra*—Greenl, *supra*—Best, *supra* (*f*) Taylor, *supra*—

The recent Law of Evidence Amendment Act (*e*) trenches somewhat on this principle, in making it competent to examine a witness as to whether, on any specified occasion, he made a different statement from that given by him when examined; for, although the question may involve a charge of perjury, it would seem that, in general, the witness may not decline answering. Yet if the previous statement was made on oath, he would be entitled to protection (*f*).

It may be added that little or no advantage can be gained from pressing a witness to answer a question where he states, although erroneously, that it may infer a criminal charge against him; for, in general, the declinature serves the party's purpose.

§ 2020. The right of the witness is limited to a declinature to answer. He cannot resist being put on oath and asked the questions to which his privilege applies (*g*). Nor has the party against whom he is adduced any right to interfere (*h*). It seems to be *pars judicis* to inform the witness of his privilege (*i*). If he waives it, as he is entitled to do, his evidence is competent (*k*). If he declines to answer, his doing so and his manner on the occasion are circumstances which the jury are entitled to consider in weighing the evidence (*l*), because an innocent man is far more likely to answer with an indignant denial than to avail himself of his privilege, and if he takes the latter course from indignation or sulkiness, the jury will probably discover that from his manner.

IX. *Examination by means of Interpreters.*

§ 2021. When a witness does not understand the English lan-

Greenl., *supra*—Fisher *v.* Ronalds, 1852, 17 Eng. Jur., 393, where Jervis, C.J., and Maule, J., considered that the answer of the witness would be conclusive. Williams, J., thought it unnecessary to decide the point. See § 1850.

(*e*) 15 Vict., c. 27, § 3.

(*f*) *Supra*, § 2016 (*e*).

(*g*) Don *v.* Don, 1818, 10 D., 1046. Here the alleged paramour in an action of divorce for adultery, pleaded that he should not be put on oath, because his examination could not be for any object except to prove criminal intercourse between him and the defender, no other allegations of adultery having been sent to proof. But the Court held that the pursuer was entitled to put him on oath and get his declinature.

(*h*) Nicolson *v.* Nicolson, 1770, M., 16,770—Marshall *v.* Anderson, 1798, M., 16,787—Thomas *v.* Newton, 1826, 1 Moo. and Malk., 48, note—R. *v.* Adey, 1831, 1 Moo. and Rob., 94.

(*i*) Dickson *v.* Taylor, 1816, 1 Mur., 141—Burke *v.* Macdowall, 1828, Syme, 364—Macf. Pr., 166—1 Greenl., § 451. But see *contra* Taylor, 976.

(*k*) Sutton *v.* Sutton's Tr., 1816, 1 Mur., 12.

(*l*) See Don *v.* Don, *supra*—Burke and Macdowall, *supra*. The English authorities are not agreed on this point. Compare 2 Phill., 129—Taylor, 976—1 Greenl., § 451, and cases there cited.

guage, he is examined through a sworn interpreter. In the celebrated trial of Humphreys, the prisoner's counsel moved that an interpreter whom he had in court should be sworn as well as the interpreter produced by the Crown, but this was refused, on the ground that the latter is not the interpreter for the Crown but for the Court. The prisoner's interpreter, however, was allowed to remain in Court, and he afterwards acted as sworn interpreter of the exculpatory evidence (*m*).

The rules as to examining deaf and dumb witnesses (*n*), and as to taking and proving declarations of foreigners (*o*), are stated in previous chapters.

X. *Remarks upon the Cross-examination of Witnesses.*

§ 2022. It has already been seen that the party against whom a witness is examined, is entitled to cross-examine him—that is, to ask him such questions as may test both his general credibility and the accuracy of his evidence when examined for his adducer. At one time nice distinctions were drawn as to what questions were, and what were not, cross to the examination in chief. But these do not require to be adverted to, for, as noticed above, a party against whom a witness is examined, has now right to examine him not only in cross, but also *in causa* (*p*).

§ 2023. The same general rules regarding the competency of the questions apply to cross-examinations as to examinations in chief. But they are not so strictly enforced in regard to the former class. Thus, while matters entirely irrelevant to the cause may not be entered into for the purpose of discrediting an opponent's witnesses (*q*), the Court allow a cross-examining counsel some license in this respect, because want of truthfulness in a witness can often be discovered by extending the examination to matters which bear but remotely on the issue, and on which he is, therefore, not likely to have prepared himself with answers (*r*). The

(*m*) Trial of Humphreys for forging titles to Stirling peerage, 1839, separate rep. by Swinton, 114, 185; Bell's Notes, 270, S. C. (*n*) *Supra*, § 1687.

(*o*) *Supra*, §§ 1419, 1422. (*p*) *Supra*, § 1979. (*q*) See *supra*, § 40.

(*r*) "The benefits of cross-examination are sometimes defeated by the interposition of the Court, to require an explanation of the motive and object of the questions proposed, or to pronounce a judgment upon them immediately; whereas experience frequently shows that it is only by an indirect, and apparently irrelevant inquiry that a witness can be brought to divulge the truth which he had prepared himself to conceal. The explanation of the motives and tendency of the question furnishes the witness with a caution that may wholly defeat the object of it, which might successfully be attained

rule against admitting parole of the contents of documents, is also relaxed in cross-examinations, where an answer given by the witness in chief represents partially or inadequately a document to which he has referred; for if this were not allowed, the jury might be misled by the answers given by the witness (*s*) [13] Again, where a witness has been examined upon certain statements made by the party against whom he is adduced, that party may cross-examine him upon other statements made on the occasion, in so far as that is required for laying before the jury a fair representation of the conversation, in place of selected passages in it (*t*) It would also seem that in this country, as in England, leading questions may to some extent be put in cross-examining an unwilling witness (*u*)

§ 2024 A cross-examination, if well conducted, is justly considered one of the most effectual means for detecting falsehood or error in testimony "By means of it, the situation of the witness with respect to the parties, and to the subject of litigation, his interest, his motives his inclination and prejudices, his means of obtaining a correct and certain knowledge of the facts to which he bears testimony, the manner in which he has used those means, his powers of decernment, memory, and description, are all fully investigated and ascertained, and submitted to the consideration of the jury before whom he has testified, and who have thus had an opportunity of observing his demeanour, and of determining the just weight and value of his testimony It is not easy for a witness who is subjected to this test to impose on a court or jury, for however artful the fabrication of falsehood may be, it cannot embrace all the circumstances to which a cross-examination may be extended" (*x*) On the other hand, cross-examination far more frequently increases than impairs the credibility of an honest and accurate witness; for by making his statements more circumstantiate, it gives them greater coherence and intrinsic probability, and if it should bring out a few errors in unimportant details, these, from the nature of the facts on which they occur, will often add to the appearance of candour and want of design exhibited by the

if the gradual progress from immateriality to materiality was withheld from his observation" Evans on Pothier, vol ii, App x, 269 (*s*) See cases noted *supra*, § 125 (*t*) See cases noted *supra*, § 1380 (*u*) See *supra*, § 1985

(*x*) 1 Greenl, § 116

[13] Where a pursuer denies that a contract was reduced to writing, the defender, before parole of its terms is admitted, may interfere, and prove that it was in writing. Cox v Couveless, 1860, 2 F and F, 139

narrative (y). Accordingly, the skilful tactics of an experienced counsel are often seen in his declining when he ought not to cross-examine; and there is perhaps no error more common or more injurious in the practice of young counsel especially when engaged on the prisoner's side, than an indiscriminate cross-examination of the witnesses adduced against their clients.

§ 2025. Cross-examination is an art which cannot be practised successfully without both natural talent and experience. It requires ingenuity and readiness, an intimate knowledge of human nature, a quick eye for truth or falsehood as indicated by expression, firmness and perseverance to force an answer from an unwilling witness, combined with a temper not easily ruffled by his falsehoods or attempts to evade the examination. The mode in which it ought to be conducted varies with the circumstances of each case, and the character and temper of the individual witness; while it also depends in a great measure upon the information which the interrogator possesses as to the witness' acquaintance with the facts. It is therefore impossible to lay down precise rules on the subject. The most that can be done is to offer a few suggestions, chiefly for the benefit of those who have not opportunities of observing how leading counsel deal with adverse witnesses.

The examination ought to be conducted differently according as its purpose is to prevent the *suppressio veri*, or to detect and expose the *expressio falsi*. In the former case, it is often injurious rather than beneficial to impair the credibility of the witness; and a conciliatory style of interrogation ought, in general, to be followed. The proper course is to begin with questions remotely connected with the essential parts of the case, and from these to proceed gradually to others of closer pertinency. In this way questions may sometimes be put in such sequence that the witness is unconsciously led to form round himself a net-work of circumstantial evidence, so that at last he cannot escape from answering the main questions when they are put to him. The result not unfrequently is, that the witness finding himself in the hands of a skilful interrogator, gives up the struggle and makes a full disclosure.

Pretended forgetfulness is the most common device of an unwill-

---

(y) It has been justly observed, that "Forgetfulness on the part of witnesses of immaterial circumstances not likely to attract attention, or even slight discrepancy in their testimony respecting them, so far from impeaching their credit often confirms it. Nothing can be more suspicious than a long story told by a number of witnesses agreeing down to the minutest details." Best's Pr. of Ev., § 631.—See also Evans on Pothier, vol. ii, App., p. 245. See also *infra*, § 2044.

ing witness It can often be cured by judiciously mentioning certain facts likely to recall the matter to his memory, and by firmly refusing to take a mere "*non mi ricordo*" when a more specific answer can be extracted It ought, however, to be kept in mind that partial recollection is to be expected in even impartial witnesses, whose attention has been purposely directed in precognition and afterwards by examination in chief to the facts which bear on one side of the case, and that many circumstances which may not have occurred to him at first or may have been withheld as unimportant, may be recalled to his memory in the course of cross-examination In general, a witness comes into court with the memory strongly bent upon those parts of a case which have occurred to him as material The revival of other circumstances is the result of a particular examination respecting them, and according to the usual operations of the mind, they will unfold themselves gradually, at first with indistinctness and afterwards with precision, unless this natural progress is prevented by an intimidating and acrimonious course of inquiry " (z)

Sometimes the witness becomes sulky, and doggedly answers, " I don't know," or ' I don't remember," without attending to the questions If so, he will generally be brought to his senses by asking him some question to which he had given a specific answer before, or on a matter relating to himself which he cannot but be able to answer if he chooses The likelihood is that he will blurt out his dogged answer, and bring down on himself a sharp rebuke from the Court

§ 2026 When the object of the cross-examination is to expose the falsehood of answers already given by the witness, it has been justly remarked that " the most effectual method is to examine rapidly and minutely as to a number of subordinate, and apparently trivial points in his evidence concerning which there is little likelihood of his being prepared with answers ready made, and where such a course of interrogation is skilfully laid, it is rarely that it fails in exposing perjury or contradiction in some parts of the testimony which it is desired to overturn " (a) Even if the witness does not contradict himself, the examination will have increased the chance of his being contradicted by other witnesses when taken over the same ground,—and that not only in unessential details, where inconsistency may be expected, but as to matters on which a truthful witness could not be mistaken

(z) Evans on Pothier, vol ii, App., p 248

(a) 2 Al., 516

A different mode of treatment usually succeeds with a loquacious witness, biassed in favour of his adducer. By encouraging his tendency to talk, the skilful advocate often draws him on from one exaggeration to another, till, in the keenness of his partisanship, he is betrayed into extravagance or absurdity which is repugnant to the common sense of the jury, and destroys the credibility of his whole evidence (*b*).

§ 2027. It is not necessary in Scotland, as in some other countries, to caution the young advocate against a browbeating or harsh style of cross-examination, for that is seldom resorted to, and is always discouraged, in our Courts. A truthful witness is entitled to be treated with courtesy, and with some allowance for being in a position, perhaps an anxious and painful one, which he rarely, if ever, occupied before. Nor should hesitation or even slight errors and inconsistencies on his part induce an opposite treatment, for they can usually be accounted for without supposing that he meant to deceive. Besides, imputing falsehood to a truthful witness, or treating him as dishonest, is impolitic as well as unfair, for it usually enlists the sympathies of the jury in his favour, and produces the very opposite effect upon the case from what the interrogator intended (*c*). Nay more, even "where a witness is evidently prevaricating or concealing the truth, it is seldom by intimidation or sternness of manner that he can be brought, at least in this country, to let out the truth. Such measures may sometimes terrify a timid witness into a true confession, but, in general, they only confirm a hardened one in his falsehood, and give him time to consider how seeming contradictions may be reconciled" (*d*).

(*b*) This paragraph is taken substantially from Best, Pr. of Ev., § 632, citing Hints to Witnesses in Courts of Justice, by a Barrister (Baron Field), London, 1815; Law Mag., vol. 25, p. 361.

(*c*) "Considering the subject merely as a matter of discretion, the adoption of an unfair conduct in cross-examination has often an effect repugnant to the interests which it professes to promote. In the case of Hunter *v.* Kehoe (King's Bench of Ireland in 1794, Ridgeway, &c., 350), Lord Clonmel observed that cross-examination had gone to an unreasonable length, but he had in general permitted gentlemen to go as far as they pleased, because, if there was an honest case on the other side, it would do them no good." Evans on Pothier, vol. ii., Appx., p. 269.

(*d*) 2 Al., 546. In the same strain are the following remarks of a shrewd and enlightened observer, Archbishop Whately (Rhetoric, 6th ed., p. 70):—"Generally speaking, I believe that a quiet, gentle, and straightforward, though full and careful examination, will be the most adapted to elicit truth; and that the manœuvres, and the browbeating which are the most adapted to confuse an honest witness, are just what the dishonest one is best prepared for. The more the storm blusters the more carefully he wraps round him the cloak, which a warm sunshine will often induce him to throw off."

It must be added that these suggestions are only offered with reference to the generality of cases, and as aids to the attainment of a difficult art. To tie down a counsel to a set of rules, however well devised, would hamper him in the free exercise of that discretion, without which cross-examination cannot be adapted, as it ought to be, to the circumstances and exigencies of each individual case.

CHAPTER IX.—OF WRITING OUT THE DEPOSITIONS

§ 2028. When a proof is taken on commission, the depositions must be reduced to writing in a regular form, and must be duly authenticated (*a*). The record, which is called the "report," of the commission, should state in a preamble the appointment of the commissioner, and his nomination of a clerk to the proof, to whom he administered the oath *de fideli administratione*. But the omission to mention this oath will be overlooked, on the presumption *omne rite et solenniter actum* (*b*). And where the clerk to a proof taken abroad was an official person, an objection on this score was overruled on the ground that he had taken the oath when appointed to office (*c*).

The report must set forth that each witness was sworn; and accordingly, where this was omitted, the Court ordered the proof to be taken of new, although it bore through that each witness "deponed" and the party offered to prove that in point of fact all of them were sworn (*d*). Each deposition should also conclude thus: "All which is truth, as the deponent shall answer to God." But the omission of these words will not be fatal, if the depositions are stated to have been emitted on oath (*e*).—Corresponding variations will be made in the report where the witnesses are examined on affirmation (*f*).

(*a*) See forms in Appendix. (*b*) Robertson *v.* Mason, 1841, 4 D., 159.

(*c*) Cuming *v.* Kennedy, 1707, M., 4433. (*d*) A. B., 1838, 16 S., 630. See also *supra*, § 1063. (*e*) Hook *v.* Hook, 1852, 1 Stuart's Rep., 518.—Falconer *v.* Kinnear, 1684, M., 1760, 12,531, 16,693, S. C.—Galloway *v.* Gilmer, 1830, 2 De. and And., 218.—Tait Ev., 436.—Shand's Pr., 356.—*Contra*, Craigie *v.* Moodie, 1685, M., 16,691. (*f*) See *supra*, § 1969.

§ 2029 The depositions, as emitted by the witnesses, are dictated by the commissioner to the clerk In general this is done in the form of a narrative But it is proper, in important parts of the proof, to record the question and answer *in ipsissimis verbis*, especially if there is a likelihood of the report being read to a jury (*g*) Any objections which may be stated to the examination with the answers thereto and the commissioner's deliverances, will be shortly noted If the competency of the examination is somewhat doubtful the question and answer should be taken on a paper apart and sealed up (*h*), provided they do not involve confidentiality, in which case the proper course is to make avizandum to the Court with the objection

§ 2030. In a series of regulations for conducting proofs on commission in the Court of Session (and which are applicable to all written proofs) it is recommended to the commissioners "to exercise their own judgment in the manner of conducting the proof, and particularly to allow no matter to be introduced which is not pertinent to the cause, nor any unnecessary pleading or altercation about the competency of questions or the admissibility of witnesses, and to check the parties if they attempt to load the proceedings with unnecessary evidence, or superfluous matter of any kind" It is likewise recommended to them to attend to the rules of evidence, and to give their own deliverances either *viva voce* or in writing as they see cause, upon any debate which may occur it being always understood that their whole proceedings shall be subject to the after consideration of the Court, upon application made by either party, in order to which the commissioner himself, or those acting for the parties, may take such notes, on a separate paper, as they think proper for the due information of the Court But nothing shall enter the report but what the commissioner himself may think material (*i*).

By another of these regulations, "if it shall appear to the commissioner that any witness is not disposed to tell the truth, or behaves in any unusual manner, it is recommended to him to take a note thereof at the time by way of assistance to his memory in case he should be appealed to on that subject by either of the parties when the proof comes to be advised, or, if he thinks proper, he may annex the same to his report of the proof" (*k*)

§ 2031 Each deposition must be signed by the witness and,

(*g*) See *supra*, § 1958 (*h*) Shand's Pr, 358 (*i*) A S, 11th March 1800, § 4 (*k*) Ib, § 7 if he cannot write, that fact and the cause of his inability should be stated. The want of subscription, without a reason assigned, has been held fatal to a written proof taken by a church court (*l*), although irregularities in mere form in records of ecclesiastical proceedings are overlooked (*m*). The decisions (which are of old date) are conflicting as to whether the want of subscription will be fatal in depositions taken in a foreign country which are authenticated according to the law of the place (*n*). Subscription by the commissioner who takes the proof is indispensable, not only in civil cases (*o*), but also in depositions taken in church courts (*p*). And where part of a deposition had been taken on a paper apart, and had been sealed up to lie *in retentis*, the Court held that the want of the commissioner's signature to it was fatal, although the docquet on the envelope was signed by him and although the signed docquet at the end of the report referred to the separate paper (*r*).

Each page of the report ought to be authenticated by the witness and commissioner. But it will be valid, if each separate sheet is so (*s*).

The report ought also to be signed by the clerk to the proof. This, however, is not essential (*t*).

§ 2032. The foregoing rules as to the mode of writing and

(*l*) Brown *v* Her. of Kilberry, 1825, 3 S. 480, aff'd, 3 W. S., 441—Dunbar *v* Presbytery of Auchterarder, 1849, 12 D., 284.

(*m*) See Ferguson *v* Skirving, 1850, 12 D., 1145, aff'd 1 Macq. 232.

(*n*) In Davidson *v* E. Middleton, 1673, M., 4432, where the oath on reference of a Scotsman residing abroad was reported under the hand and seal of the foreign judge (who acted as commissioner), according to the forms of his own law, the Court directed the party to be re-examined and to sign his second deposition. But in Burnet *v* Lutgrue, 1675, M. 4433, where the subscription of a foreigner, examined on commission abroad, was awanting, the Court sustained his deposition, which was adminiculated and adhered to by him in a letter under his hand. In Cumming *v* Kennedy, 1707, M., 4433, where, instead of the original report of the commission signed by the witnesses, an extract of it signed by the judge and clerk was produced, the Court admitted this, on account of the practice of the foreign country to retain the originals of such documents and only give out extracts. See Tait Ev., 436. If the witnesses have died, then unsigned depositions will probably be admitted, provided they are formal according to the law of the foreign country, see Falconer *v* Kinnear, 1684, M., 1760, 12,531, 16,693—*Supra*, § 1932.

(*o*) Robb *v* Campbell, 1824, 3 S., 301—Strachan *v* Tomlins, 1825, ib., 560—Baxter *v* Kilgour, 1825, ib., 595—M'Phun *v* Reid, 1836, 14 S., 339. The Court refused to overlook this irregularity where the parties agreed to waive all objections on account of it, case mentioned by Lord Mackenzie in A B, 1838, 16 S., 631.

(*p*) Lord Ivory's Note in Dunbar *v* Presbytery of Auchterarder, 1849, 12 D., 284.

(*r*) Cleland *v* M'Lellan, 1851, 13 D., 501.

(*s*) L. Ivory's Note in Dunbar *v* Presbytery of Auchterarder. See *supra*, § 659.

(*t*) Robertson *v* Mason, 1841, 4 D., 159—Sutherland *v* Presb. of Dornoch, 1850, 13 D., 190.

authenticating depositions used to apply to cases in the Sheriff-courts But a recent statute has enacted that in these the evidence shall be led before the Sheriff (or Sheriff-substitute), "who shall, with his own hand, take a note of the evidence, setting forth the witnesses examined and the testimony given by each, not by question and answer, but in the form of a narrative, and the documents adduced, and any evidence, whether oral or written, tendered and rejected, with the ground of such rejection, and a note of any objections taken to the admission of evidence, whether oral or written, allowed to be received, and the note of the evidence given by each witness shall be read over to him by the Sheriff, and signed by the witness (if he can write) on the last page, in open Court, before the witness is dismissed" (*u*) And if the Sheriff is unavoidably prevented from taking such notes with his own hand he shall dictate the same to any competent person he may select" (*x*)

§ 2033 In jury trials in civil cases the depositions are not formally reduced to writing, but the judge takes notes of them in order to guide himself in charging the jury These notes are also used in place of a formal record of the proof when the Court deal with bills of exception and motions for new trial on the ground of verdict against evidence The party applying for a new trial, however, is not entitled to obtain from the judge who presided a copy of his notes, unless the Inner House, on a motion to that effect, desire such copy to be furnished (*y*) [1]

The former practice in trials in the Justiciary Court and in criminal trials before the Sheriff with a jury, was to take down the evidence *ad longum* in writing (*z*) But it was enacted a number of years ago, that in the Justiciary Court the evidence should not be taken down except in the judge's notes, power being reserved to proceed in the old form in any case where the Court might see cause (*a*) A similar change was afterwards introduced in regard

(*u*) 16 and 17 Vict, c 80, § 10 (*x*) Ib (*y*) A S 16th Feb 1841, § 36—See Murray v Murray, 1839, 1 D, 363, where the Court refused an application to allow the notes to be printed because there was no motion for a new trial before the Court, but only a question as to the interpretation of the oath on reference of the party who had got the verdict (*z*) 2 Hume, 382—2 Al, 518

(*a*) 21 Geo II c 19, § 7—23 Geo III, c 45, §§ 3, 4

[1] When a case has been tried before a Lord Ordinary and a jury, the application for the judge's notes of evidence, with a view to a motion for a new trial, should be made to the Lord Ordinary and not to the Inner House, Campbell v M'Laren, 1853, 1 Macph, 216

to criminal trials by jury before Sheriffs, and it was provided "that the judge trying such causes or prosecutions shall preserve and duly authenticate the notes of the evidence taken by him in such trial and shall exhibit the same or a certified copy thereof in case the same should be called for by the Court of Justiciary" (*b*)

§ 2034 A formal record, however, is preserved of the evidence emitted by a witness who is suspected of perjury. In such cases the deposition is taken down by the clerk of court, and, after being read over to the witness is authenticated by his subscription and that of the judge, or by the judge alone if the witness cannot write (*c*)

§ 2035. In criminal trials before Sheriffs, Justices of the Peace, and other inferior courts without a jury (under the exceptions to be noticed immediately), the depositions are taken down by the clerk of court and signed by the witnesses (if they can write) and by the judge (*d*) This is not necessary when Sheriffs try cases under the police jurisdiction, conferred on them by 9 Geo IV c 29, but the Sheriff must take and preserve a note of the evidence and exhibit it or a certified copy when required by the Court of Justiciary (*e*) In trials before Magistrates, under the "Police and Improvement' Act of 1850, "no other record shall be kept of the proceedings except the complaint and the judgment pronounced thereon" (*f*), and a clause dispensing with any record or note of the evidence occurs in the Police Acts of most large towns

CHAPTER X —OF CIRCUMDUCTION

§ 2036 In civil cases, where a party has obtained an order for a proof on commission, or before a Sheriff without a jury, and the term for leading the proof with its prorogations (if any) has expired, the other party may obtain an interlocutor of circumduction (*a*), which is a formal declaration by the judge that the term

(*b*) 9 Geo IV, c 29 § 17 (*c*) 1 Hume, 375, 6—Burnett, 562—1 Al, 178 9 (*d*) 9 Geo IV, c 29, § 18—2 Al, 518 Sentences of police courts and of justices have been set aside on account of this not having been done Philips *v* Cross, 1818, 1 Shaw, 130—Christie *v* Adamson, 1853, 1 Irv, 293—Penman *v* Watt, 1815, 2 Broun 586 (*e*) 9 Geo IV, c 29, § 20 (*f*) 13 and 14 Vict c 33, § 318 (*a*) Stair, 4, 46, 6—Ersk, 4 2, 32 The interlocutor is in the [illegible]

is closed [1] It has been held that, in point of form, circumduction is necessary before the Court enter upon the merits of the case (*b*) But this is not strictly observed in practice in the Supreme Court Circumduction is premature so long as appeals against deliverances by the commissioner in the course of the proof are undisposed of (*c*)

§ 2037. After circumduction the chequer is closed against any evidence, or further evidence (as the case may be), on the points to which the previous order for proof applied (*d*) And if a pursuer has led no evidence upon a specific and independent ground of action, and circumduction has passed against him, it would seem that he is not entitled, under the act 3 and 4 Vict, c 59, § 4 (*e*), to examine the defender's witnesses on that branch of the case (*f*) But circumduction will be opened up wherever that is fair and reasonable in the circumstances (*g*), the Court, however, refusing to do so if the party, whether from negligence or with a view to delay, has obtained repeated prorogations of the term without availing himself of them (*h*) [2]

CHAPTER XI —OF THE NUMBER OF WITNESSES REQUIRED TO PROVE THE ISSUE OR LIBEL—AND OF CORROBORATIVE TESTIMONY

§ 2038 By the law of Scotland the testimony of one witness however credible, is not full proof of any ground of action or de-

---

terms,—"The Lord Ordinary (or Sheriff) circumduces the term for proving" Shand's Pr, 360 (note) (*b*) Renny *v* Cuthell, 1800, Hume D, 494

(*c*) Hook *v* Hook, 1851, 14 D, 39—See also Aitken *v* Weir, 1840, 2 D, 1029

(*d*) Stair 4, 46, 6—Ersk, 4 2 32—Shand's Pr 360 (*e*) See *supra*, § 1979 (*f*) See A B *v* C D, 1844, 6 D, 1148 (*g*) Lindsay *v* Thomson 1839 1 D, 434—Aitken *v* Weir, 1840 2 D, 1029—Shand's Pr, 360—See also M'Lean *v* Elder 1829, 8 S, 56—Duffus *v* Mag of Wick, 1831, 4 De and And, 383 (*h*) Finlayson *v* Mackenzie, 1829, 7 S, 717—Sharp *v* King's Tr, 1838 16 S, 659—Binnie *v* Binnie, 1848 11 D, 89—Montgomery *v* M'Clung 1848, ib, 131

---

[1] When the period for taking proof under a commission has expired, the proper course is to move the Court to renew the commission A motion to prorogate is incompetent, and any procedure following on such a motion (including the interlocutor of circumduction) has been held irregular, Aikman *v* Cockburn, 1857, 19 D, 279

[2] As to circumstances in which the Court has refused to recall interlocutor of circumduction, see Sutherland *v* Johnson, 1856, 18 D 626—See also Paterson *v* Mackenzie, 1856, 18 D, 663, where the Court refused to recall interlocutor of circumduction though *res noviter* was pleaded

fence, either in a civil or criminal cause (*a*) Accordingly, if the only evidence in support of a case is the uncorroborated testimony of one witness, it is the duty of the Court to direct the jury that the proof is not sufficient in point of law (*b*)[1]

§ 2039 But this rule does not require that two witnesses should swear to every fact in the case The direct evidence of one witness, supported by facts and circumstances is sufficient (*c*) In cases of theft proof by one witness of the essential fact that the articles belong to the person from whom they are alleged to have been stolen, combined with evidence from other sources of circumstances clearly pointing to the prisoner as the thief, is every day sustained as full proof (*d*), and in trials for rape there is seldom any direct proof of the fact of violence beyond the statement of the woman, the proof being completed by corroborative circumstances. An admission of guilt in the prisoner's declaration, with the evidence of one witness, will be complete proof in a criminal case (*e*) In an action of damages for uttering the same slander on two or more occasions the case may go to the jury on the evidence of one witness to each instance, for the witnesses mutually corroborate each other (*f*)[2] If, however, the slanders are different they must be proved independently (*g*) Again, a libel charging several acts

---

(*a*) Stair, 4, 43, 1, 2, 3—2 Hume, 382—Burnett, 509—2 Al, 551—Tait Ev, 437—M Lachlan *v* Campbell, 1822, 1 S, 302—Dougall *v* Dougall, 1833, 11 S 1020 Accordingly, in an action of reduction of a deed on the ground of forgery or informality in the execution, the evidence of one of the instrumentary witnesses in favour of the pursuer is not full proof, Cleland *v* Cleland, 1837 (first trial), 15 S, 1246, *supra* § 916, note (*u*) (*b*) See Cleland *v* Cleland *supra* (*c*) See this illustrated in Stair, 4, 43, 2—2 Hume, 384—Burnett, 511—2 Al, 551—Tait Ev, 438—Macf Pr, 227—Murray *v* Tod, 1817, 1 Mur, 230—Fraser *v* Maitland, 1818 2 Mur, 33—Smith *v* Jameson, 1819, ib, 102—Mackay *v* Waddel, 1820, ib, 205 (*d*) 1 Al 324

(*e*) Burnett, 519—2 Al 552 (*f*) Landles *v* Gray, 1816, 1 Mur, 79—Ramsay *v* Nairne, 1833, 11 S, 1033 1046—Dougall *v* Dougall, ib, 1020—Tait Ev, 438—Macf Pr, 227 (*g*) See Dougall *v* Dougall, *supra* In Cullen *v* Ewing, 1832, 10 S, 497, which was an action of damages for uttering against the pursuer slanders of the same tenor in a judicial pleading and in conversation, the Lord President (Hope) directed the jury that the judicial slanders were a corroboration of the evidence of one witness as to the conversations, sufficient to constitute full proof But, on the case being appealed, Lord Wynford stated that he entertained great doubts upon the point, 6 W S, 577, 581

---

[1] See as to the evidence required where *socii criminis* adduced H M Adv *v* Campbell, 2 Irv 232, *supra*, §§ 1691, 1697, *et seq*

[2] Where of three slanderous averments two are justified by proof of the *veritas*, the uttering of the third is not proved by the evidence of one witness, Wilson *v* Weir and Strang 1861, 24 D, 67

of adultery with the same person may be proved by the evidence of one witness to each act (*h*) It would even seem that one witness to each of several acts of adultery with different persons will be sufficient in point of law At least it has been held in England —where the evidence of one witness uncorroborated is not sufficient in this class of cases (*i*),—that a credible person swearing to criminality with one woman, corroborated by another witness to each of certain unsuccessful attempts upon the virtue of others, is full and convincing proof (*j*)

§ 2040 In criminal cases also, where several acts of the same crime are charged the proof of them will be sufficient in point of law, although there should only be one witness to each act, as, for example, in a charge of several acts of incest with the same person (*k*), or a charge of suborning several persons as witnesses in the same trial (*l*), or of several assaults upon the same individual about the same time In such cases the different acts are repetitions of the same offence, springing from the same impulses or motives, and unquestionably the proof of one of them strengthens the probability that another took place In like manner, in a charge of treason by two or more overt acts of the same description, proof by one witness to each act is sufficient (*m*)

§ 2041. The ordinary rule however, applies where the acts charged are only independent instances of the same kind of crime or offence, as for example, several charges of theft or robbery (*n*), uttering forged notes to several persons at different times and places (*o*) Yet even in this class of cases different offences may be so related that proof of one of them will supplement defective evidence in another, as, for example, where several acts of house-

---

(*h*) Mack Cr, 2 26, 14 (vol ii, p 259), and case of Maxwell there cited—2 Hume, 385—Burnett 511—2 Al, 552—Tait Ev, 438—Ly Milton *v* L Milton, 1667, M, 12,636—Murray *v* Murray, 1847 9 D 1556—Sim *v* Sim, 1834, 12 S 633 In the latter case the Court held the evidence to be sufficient in point of law but insufficient to satisfy their minds of the fact, as they did not believe the witnesses

(*i*) Evans *v* Evans, 1844, 1 Robertson s Ec Ca, 165—Simmons *v* Simmons, 1847, 11 Eng Jur 830 (*j*) Forster *v* Forster 1790 1 Hag Con R. 144—Soilleux *v* Soilleux, 1802 ib, 373 But criminal acts with other persons may not be proved unless they are libelled on otherwise the defender could not be prepared with counter evidence, if the allegations were untrue King *v* King 1842 4 D, 590

(*k*) Hume, *supra*—Barnett, *supra*—Al, *supra*—Tait Ev, *supra*

(*l*) Soutar and Others, 1738, Hume, *supra* (*m*) 7 Will III, c 3, §§ 2, 4 —Charge of Lord Pres Hope to Grand Jury in 1 Trea Tr 26,7—2 Russ, Cr 944—Taylor, 615 (*n*) 2 Hume, 385—Burnett, 512—2 Al 552

(*o*) Hume, *supra*

breaking are committed on the same night about the same place, by cutting a pain of glass with a diamond, going down a chimney, or in some other peculiar way The unity of character in such cases makes it highly probable that they were all parts of one thieving expedition, and it is thought that the Court would not require the prosecutor to withdraw one of the charges, because the direct evidence of one witness to it was not corroborated by circumstances connected with that charge individually.

§ 2042 Again, where the proof consists of circumstantial evidence alone, it is not necessary for each item of it to be established by two witnesses (*p*) The mutual interlacing and coincidence of the circumstances themselves form an ample corroboration of the witnesses who depone to them Indeed it is far more difficult to fabricate a consistent circumstantial proof, where the evidentiary facts come from independent sources, than to get two false witnesses to concur in a direct proof of the ground of action or defence (*r*)

§ 2043 The law of England recognises a different rule from that which has been thus noticed, the evidence of one witness, if believed by the jury, being sufficient in almost all cases (*s*) Yet, as has been well observed (*t*), this difference is more apparent than real, for the credibility of a single witness can seldom be ascertained without corroborating circumstances, the want of which often leads to an acquittal on the advice of the Court, while, in Scotland, the absence of a second witness may be supplied by circumstances, and, if there is such corroboration, it lies with the jury to say whether they believe the whole evidence

§ 2044 In concluding this subject, a word or two may be added upon corroboration and contradiction in testimony The natural and common characteristic of truthful testimony coming from different persons is consistency that of false evidence is discrepancy, and the more numerous the circumstances over which the examination extends, the more likely is it to bring out one or other of these qualities, as the case may be This is true in an especial manner where the examination has been extended to minute and unimportant circumstances, upon which the witnesses are not likely

(*p*) 2 Hume 385—2 Al, 551—Tait Ev, 438 (*r*) See this subject fully considered *supra*, §§ 280, *et seq* (*s*) Taylor, 615, *et seq*—Best Pr of Ev, § 559—2 Russ Cr, 914 The exceptions from this rule are treason, perjury, and cases in the ecclesiastical courts, Taylor and Best ib—*Supra*, § 2039 (*c*)

(*t*) 2 Al, 551

to have expected interrogation At the same time, complete uniformity is not to be expected in genuine evidence The human mind is so constituted that different persons who witness the same occurrence seldom or never receive precisely the same idea of it, circumstances which arrest the attention of one of them passing unobserved by another, and even the same circumstances presenting themselves in different aspects, according to the prepossessions or temperaments of the individuals who perceive them No less diverse are the memories of different men, for not only are there degrees of general retentiveness, but also some persons have peculiar aptitudes for recollecting facts which most men soon forget, while others have corresponding deficiencies in memory The consequence is, that two eye-witnesses to the same occurrence seldom or never tell precisely the same story, the extent of diversity increasing with the interval since the date of the transaction. Such discrepancies, therefore, as can be accounted for on this ground do not impair the credibility of witnesses whose general statements are in unison. Nay, if along with them there are coincidences on casual and minute circumstances on which preconcert is improbable, the narratives will have the ordinary characteristics of truth, whereas, if a set of witnesses repeat the same story in nearly the same words, there is considerable risk of the uniformity being artificial (*u*)

(*u*) This subject is very ably treated by Archdeacon Paley in his Horæ Paulinæ, and his Evidences of Christianity In the latter work he observes,—"I know not a more rash or unphilosophical conduct of the understanding than to reject the substance of a story by reason of some diversity in the circumstances with which it is related The usual character of human testimony is substantial truth under circumstantial variety This is what the daily experience of courts of justice teaches When accounts of a transaction come from the mouths of different witnesses, it is seldom that it is not possible to pick out apparent or real inconsistencies between them These inconsistencies are studiously displayed by an adverse pleader, but oftentimes with little impression upon the minds of the judges On the contrary, a close and minute agreement induces the suspicion of confederacy and fraud When written histories touch upon the same scenes of action the comparison almost always affords grounds for the like reflection Numerous and sometimes important variations present themselves not seldom also, absolute and final contradictions, yet neither one nor the other are deemed sufficient to shake the credibility of the main fact". Paley Evid of Christianity, part iii, ch 1 — See also *supra*, § 2024 (*y*)

BOOK FOURTH.

OF REAL EVIDENCE, OR EVIDENCE DERIVED FROM THINGS.

---

§ 2045. Real evidence, or evidence derived from things, is divided by Jeremy Bentham into—

1. The subject matter of the offence—*e.g.*, the person killed or hurt; the thing stolen or damaged; the document forged; the genuine money diminished; or the counterfeit money fabricated.

2. The fruits of the offence—*e.g.*, in cases of depredation, the goods taken; in cases of forgery, the profit obtained.

3. The instruments of the offence—*e.g.*, in the case of homicide or other bloody injury, the pistol, sword, knife, &c.; in the case of depredation by housebreaking, the picklock, keys, crow or chisel, or the ladder; in cases of incendiarism, the combustibles; in cases of forgery the engraving plates, and instruments for fabrication; in cases of monetary forgery, the coining tools.

4. Materials of the subject-matter of the offence, or of the instruments, when they happen to have anything appropriate in their nature, exclusively or peculiarly fitting them for being converted into instruments of the offence.—Examples, silver or gold in plates or other suspicious forms, where the offence is coining; laurel leaves for distillation, in cases of poisoning; drugs calculated for adulteration, found in the possession of dealers charged with adulterating articles.

5. Receptacles inclosing or having inclosed the subject-matter, fruits or instruments of the offence—for example, the clothes of the person injured; the ship, room, closet, case in which the goods stolen or destroyed, or the instruments of the offence, were contained.

6 Bodies circumjacent (though detached) with reference to any of the objects above enumerated Examples—the floor, chair, or bed where the person killed or injured was, the pathway spotted by his blood

" It is in virtue of some peculiarity in their condition that the things in question are qualified to become sources of real evidence, of evidentiary facts, with reference to the modification of delinquency in question—the fact indicated" (a)

The effect which these articles may have in proving the issue has been considered at some length in treating of circumstantial evidence (b) Here it is only necessary to notice shortly the rules as to producing them and making them available

§ 2046 In the criminal courts there are two different ways in which real evidence may be used It may either be a formal production that is, an article to be used substantively as part of the evidence in the case, being exhibited to the different witnesses, and produced in process, or it may be brought into Court by a witness as illustrative of his evidence, being taken away with him when he leaves the witness-box. In order to allow any article to be used for the Crown for the former purpose it must be libelled on and lodged with the clerk of court in due time before the trial, the period required being usually two days (c) [1] But neither of these proceedings is necessary in regard to articles which are merely used by witnesses to illustrate their evidence (d) Productions to be used properly as evidence in exculpation, and not merely by witnesses for the prisoner to illustrate their testimony, must in strict-

(a) Benth Rat of Jud Ev, book iv chap 3, § 1 (vol iii p 31 of ed 1827)

(b) *Supra*, § 248, *et seq*

(c) 2 Hume, 387, *et seq*—Bell's Notes, 278—2 Al, 588, *et seq* If the time is not sufficient to enable the prisoner's counsel to be instructed with reference to the productions on account of their number and importance, the Court will postpone the trial on a motion to that effect

(d) 2 Hume, 391—2 Al, 614—Bell's Notes, 278

[1] The inventory of productions in a criminal libel contained 'a pair of scissors' On these being shewn to a witness, it was objected that they had never been in the hands of the clerk, and it was argued, that if an article was not produced in the clerk's hands, the panel was entitled to conclude that it would not be used against him It appeared that the scissors had not been in the clerk's hands, but that no application to see them had been made to him by the panel's agents The Court repelled the objection Lord Ivory observing "If application had been made to the circuit-clerk and the productions had not been forthcoming, the case might have been very different", H M Adv v Davidson, 1855, 2 Irv 151 See also H M Adv v Kerr, 1857, 2 Irv, 608—H M Adv v Wilson, 1857 2 Irv, 626—H M Adv v Aimers, 1857, 2 Irv, 725—H M Adv v Watt, 1859 3 Irv, 389—H M Adv v Fairweather, 1861, 4 Irv, 119

ness be lodged with the clerk of court not later than the day before the trial (*e*)

In trials by jury in civil causes "all plans, maps, models, or other such productions proposed to be used at the trial of a cause, must be lodged eight days before the trial with the clerks (aforesaid) at the office in the Register House, if the trial is to be in Edinburgh, and either with the said clerks or with the sheriff-clerk of the county town where the trial is to be held, if the cause is to tried on the circuit, and notice of the lodging thereof shall be at the same time served on the opposite agent and no other productions shall be allowed to be used at the trial, unless by permission of the Court, on its being made out on oath, to the satisfaction of the Court, that such productions could not be lodged in time" (*f*) But it is competent in civil, as in criminal, cases for a witness to use an article to illustrate his evidence, without its being lodged in terms of this rule provided he takes it away with him, and it is not used as in itself real evidence for the party

The detailed rules on these subjects will be found in works upon practice (*g*)

§ 2047 The uniform practice in the criminal courts is to libel on, and (if they are portable) to produce all articles of real evidence, upon the identification or appearance of which, or any circumstances in their condition, the witnesses are to be examined Where they are too large to be produced, models, or plans and drawings of them, are often used in their stead The production of articles examined upon is a most useful practice, for it enables the witnesses to give their evidence with confidence and precision, while it affords to the jury an opportunity of judging for themselves on many matters on which there is no reason why they should form their opinions at second-hand Moreover, it follows from the rule which requires the best evidence, for the characteristics and appearances of the different articles, the marks upon them, and other similar matters, cannot be so satisfactorily proved by mere description as by exhibition of the things themselves At the same time, there does not seem to be any absolute rule that either the subjects or the instruments of a crime, or any other article of real evidence, must be produced in order to admit of witnesses being examined with reference to them The decisions on the point are somewhat contradictory

---

(*e*) See Harper, 1812, 1 Broun, 411 (*f*) A S, 16th Feb 1841, § 18 But the period may be shortened by consent of parties, Ib § 42 (*g*) 2 Hume, 389, *et seq* —2 Al, 588, *et seq* —Macf Pr, 81

§ 2048 Baron Hume, in noticing the question "how far, in cases of theft, housebreaking and the like, it is competent to interrogate the witnesses concerning such of the stolen articles as are not previously produced in the hands of the clerk of court more especially if the libel has not described these in so particular a way as to distinguish them from all other articles of the same kind," observes—' It is obvious that no such law could with any colour of reason be maintained with respect to certain species of stolen goods such as sheep horses or cattle which cannot be placed in the custody of the clerk But in the case even of such articles as might be produced, this pretention has justly been overruled in the only instance so far as I know, where it ever was advanced I allude to the trial of John Macdonald, 8th July 1782" (*g*) In that case the prisoner's counsel objected to the examination of witnesses upon certain stolen articles which had been lodged with the clerk of court, but were not mentioned specifically in the libel The counsel for the Crown answered (*inter alia*) that there is no rule of law that in a trial of theft the stolen goods must be produced Their production may be impossible, yet the evidence would not be the less complete or conclusive It was also pleaded that the witnesses might have produced the articles, and that lodging them with the clerk of court was an indulgence to the prisoner The Court "having considered the foregoing objection and answer they repel the objection" Here then, it appears that the production of the stolen articles as proper evidence for the Crown was held not to be indispensable, and Baron Hume gives the case the sanction of his high authority

A similar decision was pronounced on circuit in a trial of malicious mischief by throwing vitriol on the cushion of a carriage The cushion not being libelled on, could not be put in evidence, but a witness in whose hands it had been, was allowed to use it to illustrate his testimony on condition of taking it away when he concluded (*h*) It does not appear that the prosecutor stated any reason for failing to put the damaged article in evidence

Again, in a trial for housebreaking, where the production of the stolen articles was prevented in consequence of an objection from the prisoners as to the description of them in the libel, the prisoners were found guilty, although it was pleaded that the prosecutor had, in consequence of his own blunder, failed to lay before

(*g*) 2 Hume, 393

(*h*) Campbell, 1823 2 Al, 614

the jury the best evidence (*i*) Here however, the articles were in court, and the panels could not have been prejudiced by their not being used as evidence for the Crown

In a subsequent case, however, where certain bank notes which were libelled on as stolen and to be produced, had been all along in the possession of one of the witnesses, who was about to produce them in the course of his examination, Lord Moncreiff had doubts as to the competency of receiving the documents and censured the practice as loose, whereupon the notes were withdrawn (*k*) And the Court held it incompetent for a witness, when called on to identify a key libelled on as a stolen article, to do so by fitting it to the lock, which was in the hands of the witness, but was not libelled on (*l*)

§ 2049 Even where an article of real evidence, which had an important bearing on the case, was neither produced in process nor used by any of the witnesses to illustrate their evidence, the prosecutor has been allowed to lead proof regarding it Thus, in a trial for theft, where the prisoner objected to the Crown proving that a skeleton key found on the person of the panel but not produced or exhibited, had been applied to, and had opened the lock of a cabinet from which the articles were said to have been stolen, the objection was repelled, with the observation that it was open to the counsel for the panel to comment to the jury on the non-production (*m*) In like manner, in a trial for concealment of pregnancy, the Court repelled the objection that as the prosecutor had not produced a substance alleged to have come from the prisoner and to be an after-birth, he had not laid before the jury the best evidence, when it was in his power, on a fact on which the case mainly turned, and which was liable to much difference of opinion (*n*)

§ 2050 It is common in practice where a number of articles of the same general kind have been stolen, to prove them by means of samples libelled on and produced, the remaining articles being enumerated or referred to as by inventory This, for example, is done in extensive thefts of jewellery, or other articles stolen from shops, and in thefts of body clothes from persons in humble life

(*i*) Wilson, 1834, Bell's Notes, 278 (*k*) Pringle 1838 Bell's Notes, 275 The note of this case would indicate that the trial proceeded without the articles stolen being used at all (*l*) Goodwin, 1837, 1 Swin, 431, Bell's Notes, 279—See also Sutherland, 1837, Bell's Notes, ib (*m*) Smith, 1837, 1 Swin, 505, Bell's Notes, 278 There was considerable difference of opinion upon the Bench upon this case (*n*) Punton, 1841, 2 Swin, 572 Bell's Notes, 279

In such cases production of the whole articles would occasion great inconvenience to the parties from whom they had been stolen, and, in thefts from shopkeepers, might materially injure them in business.

§ 2051. In cases of forgery the prosecutor is bound to produce in evidence the writing in question if it is within his power (*o*), not only because parole of the terms of a document is inadmissible, but also because it is almost impossible to conduct successfully the investigation into the authenticity of the document, without its being in the hands of the witnesses. Yet, if the prisoner has destroyed the document, or if it has perished without fault on the part of the prosecutor, or persons for whom he is responsible, its non-production will not prevent him from making out his case by other evidence if he can (*p*).

It does not seem to be fixed whether, in charges of uttering base coin, the prosecutor is bound to produce the subject of the crime, unless prevented by a cause beyond his control. In one case, where the prosecution was brought under a statute by which the counterfeit character of "any coin produced in evidence" may be proved by any credible witness, although not an officer of the mint, it was held by Lord Moncreiff that the prosecutor adducing such proof, but omitting to produce the coin (although it was libelled on), had failed to prove his case by the best evidence in his power, and that the statute dispensed with skilled witnesses on the footing of the jury having the evidence of their own senses that the coin is base (*r*). Subsequently, however, a conviction was obtained under a direction by Lord Cockburn, although the coin, which was libelled on as a production, had been mislaid by the Crown authorities (*s*). Lord Moncreiff adhered to his own view in a later case, where, after a witness had sworn that the coin (a shilling) was bad, it became mixed up with two other shillings alleged to be base but not libelled on. The prisoner's counsel thereupon contended that, as the prosecutor could not identify and produce the coin in issue, the decision in the previous case of M'Ginnes applied, and Lord Moncreiff, with some difficulty, directed the jury to acquit (*t*). There

---

(*o*) 1 Hume 164—2 Ib., 388.

(*p*) Chatto, 1753, Cameron 1754, both noted in 1 Hume, 164—Hay, 1819, ib., note.

(*r*) M'Ginnes, 1839, 2 Swin. 435, and Bell's Notes, 279 per L. Moncreiff. His Lordship observed that there was a difference of opinion on the bench upon the point.

(*s*) Connoway 1840. 2 Swin., 503. Bell's Notes, 279. The previous case of M'Ginnes, *supra*, seems not to have been brought before his Lordship.

(*t*) Simpson, 1840, Bell's Notes, 136.

can be no doubt, however, that non-production of the coin would not be fatal if it arose from the act of the prisoner, or from some accident not imputable to the prosecutor. But the evidence of skilled witnesses would be required to prove that it was counterfeit, as such a case is not within the statute referred to. Whether a case of coining could go on if the fact of counterfeit were proved by skilled witnesses, but the coin was not produced from carelessness, or any cause for which the prosecutor is responsible, seems to be an open question.

§ 2052. But whatever may be said as to the cases thus noticed, there can be no doubt as to the propriety of following, wherever possible, the practice of libelling on and producing the articles of real evidence to which the different witnesses are to refer in their depositions.[1] Neglect to do so would inevitably produce unpleasant reflections from the Court, and might occasion an acquittal, where greater care would have prevented the guilty from escaping.

§ 2053. Every article which is produced in evidence must be identified at the trial. This is frequently done by two witnesses; especially in matters of importance; but the evidence of one witness is sufficient in point of law, because the fact being only one item of the case, comes under the principle already noticed, that the rule which requires two witnesses does not apply to the individual facts which jointly prove the issue (u).

§ 2054. In the criminal courts it has long been the practice, when the precognitions and declarations are taken, to attach to the articles to which they refer, labels which are signed by the declarants and the magistrate and are attached by means of seals. This practice enables witnesses when examined at the trial, perhaps at a considerable interval, to identify the articles with confidence from recognising their autographs on the labels. It has even been laid down that when a prisoner's declaration is proved by the magistrate before whom it was emitted, it is not necessary to identify in Court the articles referred to in it, provided they are correctly labelled and signed as relative thereto (y). The value of

(u) See *supra*, § 2039. (y) Smith, 1854, 1 Irv., 378.

[1] Among the list of productions attached to a criminal libel, were "a stone or other substance," and "part of a dress." It was held that the description was too vague, and did not sufficiently identify the articles, H. M. Adv. v. Wood, 1856, 2 Irv., 197. A book described in the indictment as a "day-book kept by the procurator fiscal," in which there was not a single entry, was rejected, H. M. Adv. v. Wilson, 1857, 2 Irv., 626.

this kind of evidence manifestly depends on the labels being attached to the articles at the time when they were signed by the persons who afterwards identify them, and on there not being any risk of their having been detached since Any carelessness in either of these respects, therefore, is both highly reprehensible and dangerous Similar precautions should be observed when substances have been taken from certain places for the purpose of chemical analysis or microscopical examination The practice is to have the boxes or bottles in which the substances are inclosed carefully sealed up, and if they are transmitted through a number of hands, the chain of identity is preserved by having the seals examined and proved to be entire before the articles are removed from the custody of the person who last had charge of them They are then delivered in his presence into the hands of a criminal officer, and taken to the person who has to perform any experiments on them by whom the seals are again inspected in the officer's presence,—being sealed up by him again when his purpose is served, and so on till the parcels are produced at the trial The necessity for care on this head was exhibited in a case of murder, where the paper parcel in which portions of the poison had been inclosed, was libelled on as a sealed packet, but was found at the trial to have been opened by cutting round the seals, which had been left entire. The parcel was laid before the jury under reservation of a question as to its admissibility and they returned a verdict of guilty but owing to a mistake in the terms in which the case was certified, the point did not come before the Court, and the prisoner ultimately escaped (z)

§ 2055 It may be added that when such preparations are lodged on behalf of the Crown the prisoner is not entitled at his own hand to open the parcels, in order that persons of skill may examine them on his behalf The proper course is to apply to the Court for authority to have the inclosures opened for the purpose; which will be granted under such safeguards against accidental or intentional alterations of the substances as may be deemed advisable In the trial of Humphreys for forgery some discussion took place as to the competency of permitting two chemists, adduced for the Crown, to retire with one of the documents for the purpose of making experiments upon it the prisoner's counsel having objected that this might produce alterations on the writing before it could be submitted to the exculpatory witnesses The Court were in-

(z) Fraser, 1852, 1 Irv, 1

clined to overrule the objection, but it turned out that a blank leaf was sufficient for the purpose, and on the prisoner's counsel consenting, a portion of that leaf was given to each of the chemists (after administration of an oath) to be subjected to whatever experiments they pleased, by each separately at home, and they were afterwards examined as to the results (*a*)

(*a*) Humphreys 1839, Bell's Notes, 257, separate rep by Swinton

ADDENDA ET CORRIGENDA.

P 4, note to § 4 It was held that the pursuers of a declarator of public road were bound to put in issue whether the road was used as a public road at some time within forty years prior to the date of the action, and the view taken by Lord Benholme, that it was enough for the pursuers to prove that the road was a public road at some period, though before the forty years and that it then fell on the defender to take an issue of loss of the right of public road by the negative prescription, was rejected—Davidson *v* Earl of Fife, 1863, 1 Macph , 874

P 5, note [6], add—See Bell *v* Gow, 1862 1 Macph , 183

P 11, note [17], add—A pursuer alleging breach of contract may sue for the penalty provided in the contract, with interest—without alleging damage—although the penalty be subject to modification, and the defender must take a counter-issue to prove that the damage actually caused was less than the stipulated penalty—Craig *v* M Beath and Stevenson 1863, 1 Macph , 1020 In an action as to a pauper's settlement, the onus lies on the parish of the pauper's birth to prove that the birth settlement has been lost by acquisition of an industrial settlement—Beattie *v* Leighton and Mitchell, 1863, 1 Macph , 434

P 31, note [8], and p 35, note [illegible] *For* § 34 in these notes, *read* § 37 Since this note went to press, the question was raised, whether the provisions of the 37th section of the statute, with regard to the forms of trial under the Coinage Offences Act applied to Scotland, and it was held that they did not The 30th section of the Act provides, that "all high crimes and offences, and crimes and offences against this act, which may be committed in Scotland, shall be proceeded against, and tried according to the rules and procedure of the criminal law of Scotland ," and the Court held that this section regulated the mode of procedure in trying offences under that act It would therefore appear that the view of the act stated in these notes is erroneous, and that trials for coinage offences under the new act will be conducted in the usual manner—H M Adv *v* Davidson and Francis, 1863, 35 Jur , 270

P 57, note to § 59 In H M Adv *v* Bryson, 1863, 35 Jur , 460, Lord Neaves, at circuit, refused to allow a previous conviction of theft to be stated as an aggravation of stouthrief, because stouthrief was an offence of the same kind as robbery

P 61, note to § 64 Since the acts of 9 Geo IV, c 15, and 3 and 4 Will IV, c 42, the power of amendment in civil cases in England has been largely increased by the Common Law Procedure Acts—See Best's Prin of Ev , 3d ed , p 381

P 76, note [2], *for* Clerk *read* Clark

P 89, note [12], line 11, add—H M Adv *v* John Stewart, 1855, 2 Irv , 166

P 99, note [12] The judgment in the House of Lords in M'Alister v Gemmil is reported in 35 Jur, 263

P 100, note [13], line 9, *for* these, *read* there

P 110, note to § 141 So held in Beattie v Paterson, 1836, 1 Macph, 279

P 111, note [4], add, in reference to the memoranda and articles of association of joint stock companies—The act 19 and 20 Vict, c 47, is repealed by the act 25 and 26 Vict, c 89 (§ 205, Third Schedule First Part) But (§ 206) the repeal does not affect anything duly done under that act The provisions of the act 19 and 20 Vict c 47, mentioned in the note as to subscription of the memorandum and articles of association of joint stock companies, registered under that act, are not repealed in the act 25 and 26 Vict, c 89 Under the latter act, the memorandum and articles of association are to be signed by each subscriber in the presence of, and to be attested by, one witness at least, which attestation is declared to be a sufficient attestation—§§ 11 and 16 Section 23 of the act defines the members of the company

P 111, note [4], second paragraph, line 7, *for* thus it has been, *read* thus it has been held

P 112, line 23, for *Scotæ* read *Scotiæ*

P 132, add to note—See Walker v Flint, 1863, 1 Macph., 417, and view of the judges there expressed as to the case of Wark v Bargaddie Coal Co

P 144, note to § 183 See Carson, Warren, & Co v Miller, 1863, 1 Macph, p 604

P 170, note [21], *for* 26 J, 50 *read* 26 Jur, 520

P 220, end of note [2], add—But this is only a rule of evidence, not a presumption of law—Ross v Fraser 1863, 1 Macph, 783

P 246, add to note [2]—Under Crown diligence the furniture of the Crown debtor was sold in his house, and the purchaser allowed it to remain in the house, where it was used by the debtor's wife and children, the debtor having absconded Nine weeks after the sale the landlord sequestrated the furniture for the current year's rent, and was about to sell it It was held that he had no right of hypothec, and that the purchaser of the furniture was entitled to interdict against the sale—Adam v Sutherland, 1863, 2 Macph, 6

P 254, note [4] In Dougal v Hamilton, 1863, 1 Macph, p 1112, in an action by the representatives of the drawer of two bills against the acceptor, proof *prout de jure* was allowed that they had been granted without value, and the Court, on considering the proof, held that the proof had not displaced the presumption in favour of the first bill, but they held that the second was merely a renewal of the first

P. 270, note. After *scripto vel juramento*, add—Robertson v Robertson, 1858, 20 D, 371.

P. 271, add to note—In the important case of Kennedy v. Rose, 1863, 1 Macph, 1042, the question as to the presumption against donation arose in the following circumstances —On the death of Kennedy, it appeared that in June 1858 he had deposited in bank £400, and had taken the receipt in favour of Rose, whose sister Kennedy had married, in June 1859 Rose indorsed the deposit-receipt, and Kennedy took it to the bank and got a new deposit-receipt, also in favour of Rose, for £408, being the £400 with £8 of interest In like manner, in 1860, Rose indorsed the new receipt, and Kennedy took it to the bank and got a third deposit-receipt in favour of Rose for £416 Kennedy died on 10th December 1860, and on

13th December Rose drew the £416. The sum was claimed by Kennedy's executor, and Rose maintained that it was a donation by Kennedy to him. The majority of the Court, Lords President M'Neill, Curriehill, and Ardmillan, held, on consideration of a proof which had been led in the Sheriff-Court, that the defence of donation was established. Lord Deas held that the presumption against donation had not been overcome. The Lord President, admitting the general presumption against donation, held that donation might be inferred from circumstances, and that the circumstances of the case were sufficient to support the inference of donation. His Lordship distinguished between the case in which the holder of a deposit-receipt indorses it to another, and the case in which one lodges money in bank and takes a deposit-receipt in name of another. In the former case, his Lordship observed, that the indorsation was a mandate which empowered the indorsee to draw the money, but that when it was drawn, the indorsee was debtor of the indorser for the sum, whereas in the latter case, the person in whose name the deposit-receipt was taken was thereby made the creditor of the bank. But Lord Deas rejected this distinction, holding that a deposit-receipt was not a negotiable instrument, nor equivalent to an assignation, nor an instrument habile to transfer the right to the fund. His Lordship's view was, the proof adduced of the design with which the deposit-receipt was taken in favour of Rose was competent, but that the presumption was against donation, and that the presumption was not rebutted by the proof. Lord Curriehill was of opinion that when a man took a deposit-receipt in favour of another, and retained it in his own hands, the presumption of law was, that he intended to make a donation *mortis causa*. The opinion of Lord Deas contains a review of the previous cases in which deposit-receipts have been founded on as constituting donations.

P. 277, note to § 377. The law appears to be, that it is always a question of circumstances whether a legacy is or is not additional to a previous provision or legacy of the same or similar amount, and that there is no fixed or strong presumption in favour of or against accumulation of legacies—Kippen *v.* Darley, 1856, 18 D., 1137, aff'd, 1858, 3 Macq., 203.

P. 332, note [6]. These cases have since been decided. It was held that prescription applied to the business accounts of London solicitors when sued for in this country, and that it applied to all outlays made by agents in the ordinary course of their business as such, but that it did not apply to outlays made by an agent in the capacity of a factor or cashier. Lord Deas held that the act might not apply to the case of a large exceptional fee, such as 1000 guineas, paid to a leading Scotch counsel to plead some particular cause in London. The majority of the Court (Lord Deas dissenting) held that the act applied to charges made by a Scotch solicitor for opposing railway bills in Parliament—Richardson, Loch, and Maclaurin and Lamond's Trustees, Pursuers *v.* James Merry and The Shotts Iron Co., Defenders, 1863, 1 Macph., 940.

P. 349, note [14], line 5, *for* on his oath, *read* in his oath.

P. 531, note. The decision in the case of Gollan *v.* Gollan, was reversed on appeal. It was observed in the House of Lords, that the rule of law in reference to an erasure in a deed of entail, is, that the words on the erasure are to be held *pro non scriptis*, and the Court is not entitled to presume, for the purpose of cutting down the entail, that different words, destructive of the entail, were written originally on the erased space—28th July 1863, 35 Sc. Jur., 641. In the case of Bontine *v.* Bontine, 19th March 1863, 1 Macph., 665, there was an erasure in the clause in a deed of entail prohibiting alteration of the order of succession, which the Court held not to vitiate the deed

P. 536, note [4], line 6, *for* in, *read* on Line 8, *for* 14 D., *read* 24 D. It has since been laid down in the House of Lords, in the case of Gollan *v.* Gollan, where the judgment of the Court of Session was reversed on appeal, that the Court ought not to assume that the words originally written on an erased space in a deed of entail were words destructive of the entail, Gollan *v.* Gollan, 1863, 35 Sc. Jur., 641.

P. 586, line 34, *for* granters, *read* grantees

P. 590, note [3]. Reported as Arnott *v.* Drysdale, 1863, 1 Macph., 797

P. 690, note [4] *for* Emslie *v.* Gabriel, *read* Emslie *v.* Alexander

P. 783 note to § 1328 In the Western Bank *v.* Baird, 1863, 2 Macph., 127, it was pleaded for the defenders that the pursuers were bound *ante omnia* to produce the books and documents founded on by them in the action As this would have involved the production of an immense number of books and documents, which could not be conveniently parted with, the pursuers declined to make the production but offered to give the defenders full access to the books and documents They contended, moreover, that the 3d section of the Judicature Act, requiring production with the summons or defences did not apply to jury causes The Court, holding that the books and documents were founded on in the sense of the statute, and that the statute applied to jury causes, required the pursuers to produce them, the Lord Justice-Clerk (Inglis) observing, that the act only required production and not necessarily permanent continuance in process and that it was in the power of the Court to make such regulations as were required for their delivery, after production to the pursuers.

APPENDIX.

APPENDIX.

No. I

ACT 3 & 4 VICT, CAP LIX

AN ACT FOR THE AMENDMENT OF THE LAW OF EVIDENCE IN SCOTLAND [7th August 1840]

Witnesses admissible notwithstanding relationship to party adducing them

WHEREAS the Law of Evidence in *Scotland* has in certain respects been found inconvenient, and inconsistent with the ends of justice, and therefore requires amendment Be it therefore enacted by the Queen's Most Excellent Majesty, by and with the advice and consent of the Lords Spiritual and Temporal, and Commons, in this present Parliament assembled, and by the authority of the same, That from and after the passing of this Act it shall, by the Law of *Scotland*, be no objection to the admissibility of any witness that he or she is the father or mother, or son or daughter, or brother or sister by consanguinity or affinity, or uncle or aunt, or nephew or niece, by consanguinity, of any party adducing such witness in any action, cause, prosecution, or other judicial proceeding, civil or criminal, nor shall it be competent to any witness to decline to be examined and give evidence on the ground of any such relationship

Examination in initialibus *may be dispensed with*

II And be it enacted, That it shall not be necessary for any judge in *Scotland*, or for any person acting as commissioner in taking evidence in any action, cause, prosecution, or other judicial proceeding, civil or criminal, depending in *Scotland*, to examine any witness *in initialibus* Provided always that it shall nevertheless be competent for any such judge or person acting as commissioner, or the party against whom the witness shall be called, to examine any witness *in initialibus* as heretofore

Presence in court not to disqualify witnesses in certain cases

III And be it enacted, That in any trial before any Judge of the Court of Session or Court of Justiciary, or before any Sheriff or Steward in *Scotland*, it shall not be imperative on the Court to reject any witness against whom it is objected that he or she has, without the permission of the Court, and without the consent of the party objecting, been present in court during all or any part of the proceedings, but it shall be competent for the Court in its discretion to admit the witness, where it shall appear to the Court that the presence of the witness was not the consequence of culpable negligence or criminal intent, and that the witness has not been unduly instructed or influenced by what took place during his or her presence, or that injustice will not be done by his or her examination

Examination of witnesses by the parties against whom they are produced

IV And be it declared and enacted, That in any action, cause, prosecution, or other judicial proceeding, civil or criminal, where proof shall be taken, whether by the judge or a person acting as commissioner, it shall be competent for the party against whom a witness is produced and sworn *in causâ* to examine such witness, not in cross only, but *in causâ*

Act may be amended this session.

V And be it enacted, That this Act may be amended or repealed by any Act to be passed in the present session of Parliament.

No. II

ACT 6 & 7 VICT, CAP LXXXII

AN ACT FOR EXTENDING TO SCOTLAND AND IRELAND THE POWER OF THE LORD HIGH CHANCELLOR TO GRANT COMMISSIONS TO ENABLE PERSONS TO TAKE AND RECEIVE AFFIDAVITS, AND FOR AMENDING THE LAW RELATING TO COMMISSIONS FOR THE EXAMINATION OF WITNESSES [22d August 1843]

Lord Chancellor to have the same powers for granting Commissions for taking Affidavits, &c in Scotland and Ireland as he now has in England

WHEREAS it would be convenient to extend to *Scotland* and *Ireland* the power of the Lord High Chancellor of *Great Britain* to grant commissions in order to enable persons to take affidavits, affirmations, and declarations Be it therefore enacted by the Queen s Most Excellent Majesty, by and with the advice and consent of the Lords Spiritual and Temporal, and Commons, in this present Parliament assembled, and by the authority of the same, That the Lord Chancellor, Lord Keeper or Lords Commissioners of the Great Seal, for the time being, shall have such and the same powers for granting commissions for the purpose of enabling fit and proper persons to take and receive affidavits affirmations, and declarations in *Scotland* and *Ireland*, and to perform the other duties of Masters Extraordinary of the High Court of Chancery in *England* as he and they now have in any part of the kingdom of *England*

Persons wilfully swearing falsely in any affidavit &c in Scotland deemed guilty of perjury, and liable to punishment in same manner as persons swearing falsely in open court

II And be it enacted, That all and every persons and person wilfully swearing or affirming or declaring falsely in any affidavit or affirmation or declaration to be made in that part of the United Kingdom called *Scotland*, before any person or persons who shall be empowered to take affidavits or affirmations or declarations in *Scotland* under the authority aforesaid, shall be deemed guilty of perjury, and shall be liable to prosecution and punishment for perjury, in the same manner, and to the same effect as if such persons or person had wilfully sworn falsely as a witness or witnesses in open court in any judicial proceedings in *Scotland*, or in any court of competent jurisdiction in that part of the United Kingdom in which such person shall be apprehended on such a charge, and it shall be competent to bring such prosecution, if brought in *Scotland*, either in the Court of Justiciary or in the Sheriff Court of the county within which the offence shall have been committed

Persons wilfully swearing falsely in any affidavit or affirmation in Ireland deemed guilty of perjury and liable to same pains and penalties as for swearing falsely in open court False declaration, a misdemeanor

III And be it enacted, That all and every persons and person wilfully swearing or affirming falsely in any affidavit or affirmation to be made before any person or persons who shall be empowered to take affidavits or affirmations in *Ireland* under the authority aforesaid, shall be deemed guilty of perjury, and shall incur and be liable to the same pains and penalties as if such person or persons had wilfully sworn or affirmed falsely in the open court in which such affidavit or affirmation shall be intituled, or in the court in which such person or persons shall be tried, and be liable to be prosecuted for such perjury, in any court of competent jurisdiction in *Ireland*, or in that part of the United Kingdom in which such person shall be apprehended on such a charge, and if any declaration which shall be made before any person who shall be empowered to take declarations in *Ireland* under the authority aforesaid shall be false and untrue in any material particular, the person wilfully making such false declaration shall be deemed guilty of a misdemeanor, and shall be punishable accordingly

What fees may be taken

IV And be it enacted, That every such person authorised to act under any such commission as aforesaid shall be entitled to receive and take such and the same fees, and none other, as Masters Extraordinary of the High Court of Chancery in *England* are now entitled to by virtue of the orders of that court, or of any Act or Acts of Parliament now in force

For compelling the attendance of witnesses

V And whereas there are at present no means of compelling the attendance of persons to be examined under any commission for the examination of witnesses issued by the Courts of Law or Equity in *England* or *Ireland*, or by the Courts of Law in *Scotland*, to be executed in a part of the realm subject to different laws from that in which such commissions are issued, and great inconvenience may arise by reason thereof, be it therefore enacted, That if any person, after being served with a written notice to attend any commissioner or commissioners appointed to execute any such commission for the examination of witnesses as aforesaid (such notice being signed by the commissioner or commissioners and specifying the time and place of attendance), shall refuse or fail to appear and be examined under such commission, such refusal or failure to appear shall be certified by such commissioner, or commissioners, and it shall thereupon be competent to or on behalf of any party suing out such commission, to apply to any of the superior courts of law in that part of the kingdom within which such commission is to be executed, or any one of the judges of such courts, for a rule or order to compel the person or persons so refusing or failing as aforesaid to appear before such commissioner or commissioners, and to be examined under such commission, and it shall be lawful for the court or judge to whom such application shall be made by rule or order to command the attendance and examination of any person to be named, or the production of any writings or documents to be mentioned in such rule or order

Punishment of persons disobeying rule or order to appear or to produce writings or documents required

V And be it enacted, That upon the service of such rule or order upon the person named therein, if he or she shall not appear before such commissioner or commissioners as aforesaid for examination, or to produce the writings or documents mentioned in such rule or order, the disobedience to such rule or order shall, if the same shall happen in *England* or in *Ireland*, render the person disobeying subject and liable to such pains and penalties as he or she would be subject and liable to by reason of disobedience to a writ of subpoena in *England* or in *Ireland*, and if such disobedience shall happen in *Scotland* it shall be competent to the Lord Ordinary on the Bills, upon an application made to him by or on behalf of any party suing out such commission, and upon proof of such disobedience made before him, to direct the issue of letters of second diligence, according to the forms of the Law of *Scotland*, to be used against the person disobeying such rule or order

For payment of witnesses, &c

VII Provided always, and be it enacted, That every person whose attendance shall be so required shall be entitled to the like conduct money and payment of expenses and for loss of time as for and upon attendance at any trial in a court of law, and that no person shall be compelled to produce under such rule or order any writing or other document that he or she would not be compellable to produce at a trial, nor to attend on more than two consecutive days, to be named in such rule or order

---

No III

ACT 15 & 16 VICT, CAP. XXVII.

AN ACT TO AMEND THE LAW OF EVIDENCE IN SCOTLAND

[17th June 1852]

WHEREAS it is expedient to alter and amend the Law of Evidence in *Scotland* Be it enacted by the Queen's Most Excellent Majesty, by and with the advice and consent of the Lords Spiritual and Temporal, and Commons, in this present Parliament assembled, and by the authority of the same, as follows, *viz* —

Witnesses not to be excluded by reason of crime, &c

I No person adduced as a witness in *Scotland* before any court or before any person having by law or by consent of parties authority to take evidence, shall be excluded from giving evidence, by reason of having been convicted of or having suffered punishment for crime, or by reason of interest, or by reason of agency or of partial counsel or by reason of having appeared without citation, or by reason of having been precognosced subsequently to the date of citation, but every person so adduced, who is not otherwise by law disqualified from giving evidence, shall be admissible as a witness, and shall be admitted to give evidence as aforesaid, notwithstanding of any objections offered on the above-mentioned grounds

Right to examine witnesses as to credibility not affected

Provided always, that nothing herein contained shall affect the right of any party in the action or proceeding in which such witness shall be adduced to examine him on any point tending to affect his credibility.

Not competent to adduce as a witness any person who shall be acting as an agent in the action

Provided also, that it shall not be competent to adduce as a witness in any action or proceeding any person who shall at the time when he is so adduced as a witness be acting as agent in the action or proceeding in which he is so adduced, excepting in so far as the same may be competent by the existing law and practice of *Scotland*, and

Where any person adduced has been an agent, no plea of confidentiality allowable

Where any person who is or has been an agent shall be adduced and examined as a witness for his client, touching any matter or thing, to prove which he could not competently have been adduced and examined according to the existing law and practice of *Scotland*, it shall not be competent to the party adducing such witness to object, on the ground of confidentiality, to any question proposed to be put to such witness on matter pertinent to the issue

Party to an action may be adduced as a witness, unless it be shewn that he has a substantial interest

II It shall be competent to adduce and to examine as a witness, as aforesaid, in any action or proceeding any party to such action or proceeding, even although individually named in the record or proceeding, unless it shall be shewn to the satisfaction of the Court, or of the person having authority to take evidence as aforesaid, that such party has a substantial interest in such action or proceeding, and is not merely nominally a party thereto

Witness may be examined as to having made a different statement

III It shall be competent to examine any witness who may be adduced in any action or proceeding as to whether he has on any specified occasion made a statement on any matter pertinent to the issue different from the evidence given by him in such action or proceeding, and it shall be competent in the course of such action or proceeding to adduce evidence to prove that such witness has made such different statement on the occasion specified

Witness may be recalled after examination

IV It shall be competent to the presiding judge or other person before whom any trial or proof shall proceed, on the motion of either party, to permit any witness who shall have been examined in the course of such trial or proof to be recalled

Laws and practice inconsistent with this Act repealed.

V All statutes, laws, and practice now in force respecting evidence in *Scotland* shall be and the same are hereby repealed, in so far as inconsistent or at variance with the provisions of this Act, but the same shall in all other respects remain in full force

---

No. IV.

ACT 16 & 17 VICT., CAP. XX.

AN ACT TO ALTER AND AMEND AN ACT OF THE FIFTEENTH YEAR OF HER PRESENT MAJESTY FOR AMENDING THE LAW OF EVIDENCE IN SCOTLAND [9th May 1853]

Be it enacted by the Queen's Most Excellent Majesty, by and with the advice and consent of the Lords Spiritual and Temporal, and Commons in this present Parliament assembled, and by the authority of the same, as follows

§ 2 of 15 & 16 Vict, c 27, repealed

I The second section of the Act of the fifteenth year of Her present Majesty, chapter twenty-seven, is hereby repealed

So much of § 1, of 15 & 16 Vict, c 27, as to incompetency of persons who are agents in actions being witnesses, repealed

II So much of the first section of the said Act as provides that "It shall not be competent to adduce as a witness in any action or proceeding any person who shall at the time when he is so adduced as a witness be acting as agent in the action or proceeding in which he is so adduced, excepting in so far as the same may be competent by the existing law and practice of *Scotland*," is hereby repealed

As to examination of witnesses, whether named in the record or not

III It shall be competent to adduce and examine as a witness in any action or proceeding in *Scotland* any party to such action or proceeding, or the husband or wife of any party, whether he or she shall be individually named in the record or proceeding or not, but nothing herein contained shall render any person or the husband or wife of any person, who in any criminal proceeding is charged with the commission of any indictable offence, or any offence punishable on summary conviction, competent or compellable to give evidence for or against himself or herself, his wife or her husband, except in so far as the same may be at present competent by the law and practice of *Scotland*, or shall render any person compellable to answer any question tending to criminate himself or herself, or shall in any proceeding render any husband competent or compellable to give against his wife evidence of any matter communicated by her to him during the marriage or any wife competent or compellable to give against her husband evidence of any matter communicated by him to her during the marriage

This Act not to apply to cases of adultery, &c

IV. Nothing herein contained shall apply to any action, suit, or proceeding instituted in *Scotland* in consequence of adultery, or for dissolving any marriage, or for breach of promise of marriage, or in any action of declarator of marriage, nullity of marriage, putting to silence, legitimacy, or bastardy, or in any action of adherence or separation

Adducing of party as a witness not to have effect of reference to his oath

V The adducing of any party as a witness in any cause or proceeding by the adverse party shall not have the effect of a reference to the oath of the party so adduced Provided always, that it shall not be competent to any party who has called and examined the opposite party as a witness thereafter to refer the cause or any part of it to his oath, and that in all other respects the right of reference to oath shall remain as at present established by the law and practice of *Scotland*

Not to affect authority of Court as to judicial examination

VI Nothing herein contained shall alter or affect the authority or practice of the Courts in *Scotland* as to judicial examination

---

No V

ACT 17 & 18 VICT, CAP XXXIV

AN ACT TO ENABLE THE COURTS OF LAW IN ENGLAND, IRELAND, AND SCOTLAND TO ISSUE PROCESS TO COMPEL THE ATTENDANCE OF WITNESSES OUT OF THEIR JURISDICTION, AND TO GIVE EFFECT TO THE SERVICE OF SUCH PROCESS IN ANY PART OF THE UNITED KINGDOM

[10th July 1854]

Whereas great inconvenience arises in the administration of justice from the want of a power in the superior courts of law to compel the attendance of witnesses resident in one part of the United Kingdom at a trial in another part, and the examination of such witnesses by commission is not in all cases a sufficient remedy for such inconvenience Be it therefore enacted by the Queen's Most Excellent Majesty, by and with the advice and consent of the Lords Spiritual and Temporal, and Commons in this present Parliament assembled, and by the authority of the same, as follows

Courts of Law in England, Ireland, and Scotland may issue process to compel the attendance of witnesses although not within their jurisdiction

I If, in any action or suit now or at any time hereafter depending in any of Her Majesty's Superior Courts of Common Law at *Westminster* or *Dublin*, or the Court of Session or Exchequer in *Scotland*, it shall appear to the court in which such action is pending or if such court is not sitting, to any judge of any of the said courts respectively, that it is proper to compel the personal attendance at any trial of any witness who may not be within the jurisdiction of the court in which such action is pending, it shall be lawful for such court or judge, if in his or their discretion it shall so seem fit, to order that a writ, called a writ of subpœna ad testificandum, or of subpœna duces tecum, or warrant of citation, shall issue in special form, commanding such witness to attend such trial, wherever he shall be within the United Kingdom, and the service of any such writ or process in any part of the United Kingdom shall be as valid and effectual to all intents and purposes as if same had been served within the jurisdiction of the court from which it issues

Statement to be made at foot of writ that it is issued by special order

II Every such writ shall have at foot thereof a statement or notice that the same is issued by the special order of the court or judge, as the case may be, and no such writ shall issue without such special order.

Witnesses making default to be punished by the courts of the country in which the process was served

III In case any person so served shall not appear according to the exigency of such writ or process, it shall be lawful for the court out of which the same issued, upon proof made of the service thereof, and of such default, to the satisfaction of the said court, to transmit a certificate of such default under the seal of the same court, or under the hand of one of the judges or justices of the same, to any of Her Majesty's Superior Courts of Common Law at *Westminster*, in case such service was had in *England*, or in case such service was had in *Scotland* to the Court of Session or Exchequer at *Edinburgh*, or in case such service was had in *Ireland* to any of Her Majesty's Superior Courts of Common Law at *Dublin*, and the court to which such certificate is so sent shall and may thereupon proceed against and punish the person so having made default, in like manner as they might have done if such person had neglected or refused to appear in obedience to a writ of subpœna or other process issued out of such last mentioned court

Persons not to be punished if it shall appear that sufficient money has not been tendered to pay expenses

IV None of the said courts shall in any case proceed against or punish any person for having made default by not appearing to give evidence in obedience to any writ of subpœna or other process issued under the powers given by this Act, unless it shall be made to appear to such court that a reasonable and sufficient sum of money to defray the expenses of coming and attending to give evidence, and of returning from giving such evidence, had been tendered to such person at the time when such writ of subpœna or process was served upon such person

Act not to prevent the issuing of a commission to examine witnesses

V Nothing herein contained shall alter or affect the power of any of such courts to issue a commission for the examination of witnesses out of their jurisdiction, in any case in which, notwithstanding this Act, they shall think fit to issue such commission

Not to affect the admissibility of evidence where now receivable

VI Nothing herein contained shall alter or affect the admissibility of any evidence at any trial where such evidence is now by law receivable, on the ground of any witness being beyond the jurisdiction of the court, but the admissibility of all such evidence shall be determined as if this Act had not passed

---

No VI

ACT 18 VICT, CAP XXV

AN ACT TO ALLOW AFFIRMATIONS OR DECLARATIONS TO BE MADE INSTEAD OF OATHS IN CERTAIN CASES IN SCOTLAND.

[25th May 1855]

Be it enacted by the Queen's Most Excellent Majesty, by and with the advice and consent of the Lords Spiritual and Temporal, and Commons, in this present Parliament assembled and by the authority of the same, as follows

Affirmation instead of oath to be allowed in certain cases

I If any person called as a witness in any court of civil judicature in *Scotland* or requiring or desiring to make an affidavit or deposition, shall refuse or be unwilling from alleged conscientious motives to be sworn, it shall be lawful for the court or judge or other presiding officer or person qualified to take affidavits or depositions, on being satisfied of the sincerity of such objection, to permit such person instead of being sworn to make his or her solemn affirmation or declaration in the words following, *videlicet* —

' I, A B, do solemnly sincerely, and truly affirm and declare that the taking of any oath is according to my religious belief, unlawful , and I do solemnly, sincerely and truly affirm and declare," &c

Which solemn affirmation and declaration shall be of the same force and effect as if such person had taken an oath in the usual form, and shall in like manner incur the pains of perjury in case of falsehood

Her Majesty may by Order in Council, direct provisions of this Act to be applied to all Courts in Scotland

II It shall be lawful for Her Majesty from time to time, by an Order in Council, to direct that all or any part of the provisions of this Act shall apply to all or any court or courts in *Scotland*, and such order shall be notified by the Secretary of State to the clerk or other officer of the court or courts therein named respectively, and shall be published in the Edinburgh Gazette , and within one month after such order shall have been so notified and published, such provisions shall extend and apply in manner directed by such order , and any such order may be in like manner from time to time altered and annulled

No. VII.

ACT 19 & 20 VICT, CAP LVI

AN ACT TO CONSTITUTE THE COURT OF SESSION THE COURT OF EXCHEQUER IN SCOTLAND, AND TO REGULATE PROCEDURE IN MATTERS CONNECTED WITH THE EXCHEQUER [21st July 1856]

Section 3 of 16 Vict, c 20, not to extend to revenue cases

XLIII The Third Section of the Act of the Sixteenth Year of Her present Majesty, Chapter Twenty, shall not be deemed to apply to any cause to be instituted under this Act relating to the Customs or Inland Revenue

---

No VIII.

ACT 26 & 27 VICT, CAP LXXXV

AN ACT TO GIVE RELIEF TO PERSONS WHO MAY REFUSE OR BE UNWILLING, FROM ALLEGED CONSCIENTIOUS MOTIVES, TO BE SWORN IN CRIMINAL PROCEEDINGS IN SCOTLAND [28th July 1863]

WHEREAS it is expedient to grant relief to persons who may refuse or be unwilling, from alleged conscientious motives, to be sworn in Criminal Proceedings in *Scotland* Be it therefore enacted by the Queen's Most Excellent Majesty by and with the Advice and Consent of the Lords Spiritual and Temporal, and Commons, in this present Parliament assembled, and by the authority of the same, as follows

Persons refusing from conscientious motives to be sworn in criminal proceedings in Scotland to be permitted to make a solemn affirmation or declaration

I If any person called as a witness in any Court of Criminal Jurisdiction in *Scotland*, or required or desiring to make an affidavit or deposition in the course of any criminal proceeding, shall refuse or be unwilling, from alleged conscientious motives, to be sworn, it shall be lawful for the court or judge, or other presiding officer or person qualified to take affidavits or depositions, upon being satisfied of the sincerity of such objection, to permit such person, instead of being sworn, to make his or her solemn affirmation or declaration in the words following, *videlicet*,

"I, A B, do solemnly, sincerely, and truly affirm and declare that the taking of any oath is, according to my religious belief, unlawful, and I do also solemnly, sincerely, and truly affirm and declare," &c

Which solemn affirmation and declaration shall be of the same force and effect as if such person had taken an oath in the usual form

Penalty for making false affirmation

II If any person making such solemn affirmation or declaration shall wilfully, falsely, and corruptly affirm or declare any matter or thing which, if the same had been sworn in the usual form, would have amounted to wilful and corrupt perjury every such person so offending shall incur the pains of wilful and corrupt perjury.

Short Title

III This Act may be cited for all purposes as "The Oaths Relief in Criminal Proceedings (*Scotland*) Act 1863

No IX

ACT 19 & 20 VICT, CAP CXIII

AN ACT TO PROVIDE FOR TAKING EVIDENCE IN HER MAJESTY'S DOMINIONS IN RELATION TO CIVIL AND COMMERCIAL MATTERS PENDING BEFORE FOREIGN TRIBUNALS [29th July 1856]

WHEREAS it is expedient that facilities be afforded for taking evidence in Her Majesty's dominions in relation to civil and commercial matters pending before foreign tribunals Be it enacted by the Queen's Most Excellent Majesty, by and with the advice and consent of the Lords Spiritual and Temporal, and Commons, in this present Parliament assembled, and by the authority of the same, as follows

Order for examination of witnesses in this country in relation to any civil or commercial matter pending before a foreign tribunal

I Where, upon an application for this purpose, it is made to appear to any court or judge having authority under this Act that any court or tribunal of competent jurisdiction in a foreign country, before which any civil or commercial matter is pending, is desirous of obtaining the testimony in relation to such matter of any witness or witnesses within the jurisdiction of such first-mentioned court, or of the court to which such judge belongs, or of such judge, it shall be lawful for such court or judge to order the examination upon oath, upon interrogatories or otherwise, before any person or persons named in such order, of such witness or witnesses accordingly, and it shall be lawful for the said court or judge, by the same order, or for such court or judge or any other judge having authority under this Act by any subsequent order, to command the attendance of any person to be named in such order, for the purpose of being examined, or the production of any writings or other documents to be mentioned in such order, and to give all such directions as to the time, place, and manner of such examination and all other matters connected therewith, as may appear reasonable and just, and any such order may be enforced in like manner as an order made by such court or judge in a cause depending in such court or before such judge

Certificate of ambassador, &c sufficient evidence in support of application

II A certificate under the hand of the ambassador, minister or other diplomatic agent of any foreign power, received as such by Her Majesty, or in case there be no such diplomatic agent, then of the consul general or consul of any such foreign power at London, received and admitted as such by Her Majesty, that any matter in relation to which an application is made under this Act is a civil or commercial matter pending before a court or tribunal in the country of which he is the diplomatic agent or consul having jurisdiction in the matter so pending, and that such court or tribunal is desirous of obtaining the testimony of the witness or witnesses to whom the application relates, shall be evidence of the matters so certified, but where no such certificate is produced other evidence to that effect shall be admissible.

Examination of witnesses to be taken upon oath Persons giving false evidence guilty of perjury

III It shall be lawful for every person authorised to take the examination of witnesses by any order made in pursuance of this act to take all such examinations upon the oath of the witnesses, or affirmation in cases where affirmation is allowed by law instead of oath, to be administered by the person so authorised, and if upon such oath or affirmation any person making the same wilfully and corruptly give any false evidence, every person so offending shall be deemed and taken to be guilty of perjury

Payment of expenses

IV Provided always, that every person whose attendance shall be so required shall be entitled to the like conduct money and payment for expenses and loss of time as upon attendance at a trial

Persons to have right of refusal to answer questions and to produce documents

V Provided also, that every person examined under any order made under this act shall have the like right to refuse to answer questions tending to criminate himself, and other questions, which a witness in any cause pending in the court by which or by a judge whereof or before the judge by whom the order for examination was made would be entitled to, and that no person shall be compelled to produce under any such order as aforesaid any writing or other document that he would not be compellable to produce at a trial of such a cause

Certain courts and judges to have authority under this act Lord Chancellor, &c to frame rules, &c.

VI Her Majesty's Superior Courts of Common Law at *Westminster* and in *Dublin* respectively, the Court of Session in *Scotland*, and any Supreme Court in any of Her Majesty's colonies or possessions abroad, and any judge of any such court, and every judge in any such colony or possession who by any order of Her Majesty in Council may be appointed for this purpose shall respectively be courts and judges having authority under this Act provided that the Lord Chancellor, with the assistance of two of the judges of the Courts of Common Law at *Westminster*, shall frame such rules and orders as shall be necessary or proper for giving effect to the provisions of this Act, and regulating the procedure under the same.

No X.

22 VICT, CAP. 20

AN ACT TO PROVIDE FOR TAKING EVIDENCE IN SUITS AND PROCEEDINGS PENDING BEFORE TRIBUNALS IN HER MAJESTY'S DOMINIONS IN PLACES OUT OF THE JURISDICTION OF SUCH TRIBUNALS

[19th April 1859]

WHEREAS it is expedient that facilities be afforded for taking evidence in or in relation to actions, suits, and proceedings pending before tribunals in Her Majesty's dominions in places in such dominions out of the jurisdiction of such tribunals Be it enacted by the Queen's Most Excellent Majesty by and with the advice and consent of the Lords Spiritual and Temporal, and Commons, in this present Parliament assembled, and by the authority of the same, as follows

Order for examination of witnesses out of the jurisdiction in relation to any suit pending before any tribunal in Her Majesty's possessions

I Where upon an application for this purpose it is made to appear to any court or judge having authority under this Act that any court or tribunal of competent jurisdiction in Her Majesty's dominions has duly authorised, by commission, order, or other process, the obtaining the testimony in or in relation to any action, suit, or proceeding pending in or before such court or tribunal of any witness or witnesses out of the jurisdiction of such court or tribunal and within the jurisdiction of such first-mentioned court, or of the court to which such judge belongs, or of such judge, it shall be lawful for such court or judge to order the examination before the person or persons appointed, and in manner and form directed by such commission order, or other process as aforesaid, of such witness or witnesses accordingly, and it shall be lawful for the said court or judge by the same order, or for such court or judge, or any other judge having authority under this Act, by any subsequent order, to command the attendance of any person to be named in such order for the purpose of being examined or the production of any writings or other documents to be mentioned in such order, and to give all such directions as to the time, place, and manner of such examination, and all other matters connected therewith, as may appear reasonable and just and any such order may be enforced, and any disobedience thereof punished, in like manner as in case of an order made by such court or judge in a cause depending in such court or before such judge

Penalty on persons giving false evidence

II Every person examined as a witness under any such commission, order, or other process as aforesaid, who shall, upon such examination wilfully and corruptly give any false evidence, shall be deemed and taken to be guilty of perjury

Payment of expenses

III Provided always That every person whose attendance shall be so ordered shall be entitled to the like conduct money, and payment for expenses and loss of time, as upon attendance at a trial

Power to persons to refuse to answer questions to criminate himself, or to produce documents

IV. Provided also, That every person examined under any such commission, order, or other process as aforesaid shall have the like right to refuse to answer questions tending to criminate himself, and other questions which a witness in any cause pending in the court by which, or by a judge whereof, or before the judge by whom the order for examination was made, would be entitled to, and that no person shall be compelled to produce under any such order as aforesaid any writing or other document that he would not be compellable to produce at a trial of such a cause

Certain courts and judges to have authority under this Act

V Her Majesty's Superior Courts of Common Law at *Westminster* and in *Dublin* respectively, the Court of Session in *Scotland*, and any Supreme Court in any of Her Majesty's Colonies or Possessions abroad, and any judge of any such court, and every judge in any such colony or possession who, by any order of Her Majesty in Council, may be appointed for this purpose, shall respectively be courts and judges having authority under this Act

Power to judges to frame rules &c, for giving effect to provisions of this Act

VI It shall be lawful for the Lord Chancellor of *Great Britain*, with the assistance of two of the judges of the Courts of Common Law at *Westminster*, so far as relates to *England*, and for the Lord Chancellor of *Ireland* with the assistance of two of the judges of the Courts of Common Law at *Dublin*, so far as relates to *Ire-*

land, and for two of the judges of the Court of Session so far as relates to *Scotland*, and for the chief or only judge of the Supreme Court in any of Her Majesty's Colonies or Possessions abroad, so far as relates to such colony or possession, to frame such rules and orders as shall be necessary or proper for giving effect to the provisions of this Act, and regulating the procedure under the same.

No. XI.

22 & 23 VICT., CAP. LXIII.

AN ACT TO AFFORD FACILITIES FOR THE MORE CERTAIN ASCERTAINMENT OF THE LAW ADMINISTERED IN ONE PART OF HER MAJESTY'S DOMINIONS WHEN PLEADED IN THE COURTS OF ANOTHER PART THEREOF. [13th August 1859.]

WHEREAS great improvement in the administration of the law would ensue if facilities were afforded for more certainly ascertaining the law administered in one part of Her Majesty's dominions when pleaded in the courts of another part thereof: Be it therefore enacted, by the Queen's Most Excellent Majesty, by and with the advice and consent of the Lords Spiritual and Temporal, and Commons, in this present Parliament assembled, and by the authority of the same, as follows:

Courts in one part of Her Majesty's dominions may remit a case for the opinion in law of a court in any other part thereof.

I. If in any action depending in any court within Her Majesty's dominions, it shall be the opinion of such court that it is necessary or expedient for the proper disposal of such action to ascertain the law applicable to the facts of the case as administered in any other part of Her Majesty's dominions on any point on which the law of such other part of Her Majesty's dominions is different from that in which the court is situate, it shall be competent to the court in which such action may depend to direct a case to be prepared setting forth the facts, as these may be ascertained by verdict of a jury, or other mode competent, or may be agreed upon by the parties, or settled by such person or persons as may have been appointed by the court for that purpose in the event of the parties not agreeing; and upon such case being approved of by such court or a judge thereof, they shall settle the questions of law arising out of the same on which they desire to have the opinion of another court, and shall pronounce an order remitting the same, together with the case, to the court in such other part of Her Majesty's dominions, being one of the superior courts thereof, whose opinion is desired upon the law administered by them as applicable to the facts set forth in such case, and desiring them to pronounce their opinion on the questions submitted to them in the terms of the Act; and it shall be competent to any of the parties to the action to present a petition to the court whose opinion is to be obtained, praying such last-mentioned court to hear parties or their counsel, and to pronounce their opinion thereon in terms of this Act, or to pronounce their opinion without hearing parties or counsel; and the court to which such petition shall be presented shall, if they think fit, appoint an early day for hearing parties or their counsel on such case, and shall thereafter pronounce their opinion upon the questions of law as administered by them which are submitted to them by the court; and in order to their pronouncing such opinion they shall be entitled to take such further procedure thereupon as to them shall seem proper.

Opinion to be authenticated, and certified copy given.

II. Upon such opinion being pronounced a copy thereof, certified by an officer of such court, shall be given to each of the parties to the action by whom the same shall be required, and shall be deemed and held to contain a correct record of such opinion

Opinion to be applied by the court making the remit

III It shall be competent to any of the parties to the action, after having obtained such certified copy of such opinion, to lodge the same with an officer of the court in which the action may be depending, who may have the official charge thereof, together with a notice of motion, setting forth that the party will, on a certain day named in such notice, move the court to apply the opinion contained in such certified copy thereof to the facts set forth in the case herein-before specified, and the said court shall thereupon apply such opinion to such facts, in the same manner as if the same had been pronounced by such court itself upon a case reserved for opinion of the court or upon special verdict of a jury, or the said last-mentioned court shall, if it think fit, when the said opinion has been obtained before trial, order such opinion to be submitted to the jury with the other facts of the case as evidence, or conclusive evidence as the court may think fit of the foreign law therein stated, and the said opinion shall be so submitted to the jury

Her Majesty in Council or House of Lords on appeal may adopt or reject opinion

IV In the event of an appeal to Her Majesty in Council or to the House of Lords in any such action, it shall be competent to bring under the review of Her Majesty in Council or of the House of Lords the opinion pronounced as aforesaid by any court whose judgments are reviewable by Her Majesty in Council or by the House of Lords, and Her Majesty in Council or that House may respectively adopt or reject such opinion of any court whose judgments are respectively reviewable by them, as the same shall appear to them to be well founded or not in law

Interpretation of terms

V In the construction of this Act, the word "action" shall include every judicial proceeding instituted in any court, civil, criminal, or ecclesiastical, and the words "Superior Courts" shall include, in *England*, the Superior Courts of Law at *Westminster*, the Lord Chancellor, the Lords Justices the Master of the Rolls or any Vice-Chancellor the Judge of the Court of Admiralty, the Judge Ordinary of the Court for Divorce and Matrimonial Causes, and the Judge of the Court of Probate, in *Scotland*, the High Court of Justiciary, and the Court of Session acting by either of its Divisions, in *Ireland* the Superior Courts of Law at *Dublin*, the Master of the Rolls and the Judge of the Admiralty Court, and in any other part of Her Majesty's dominions, the Superior Courts of Law or Equity therein

---

No. XII.

ACT 24 & 25 VICT, CAP XI

AN ACT TO AFFORD FACILITIES FOR THE BETTER ASCERTAINMENT OF THE LAW OF FOREIGN COUNTRIES WHEN PLEADED IN COURTS WITHIN HER MAJESTY'S DOMINIONS [17th May 1861]

WHEREAS an Act was passed in the twenty-second and twenty-third years of Her Majesty's Reign intituled *An Act to afford facilities for the more certain Ascertain-*

ment of the Law administered in one part of Her Majesty's dominions when pleaded in the courts of another part thereof And whereas it is expedient to afford the like facilities for the better ascertainment, in similar circumstances, of the law of any foreign country or state with the government of which Her Majesty may be pleased to enter into a convention for the purpose of mutually ascertaining the law of such foreign country or state when pleaded in actions depending in any courts within Her Majesty's dominions and the law as administered in any part of Her Majesty's dominions when pleaded in actions depending in the courts of such foreign country or state Be it therefore enacted by the Queen's Most Excellent Majesty, by and with the advice and consent of the Lords Spiritual and Temporal and Commons in this present Parliament assembled, and by the authority of the same, as follows, viz —

Superior Courts within Her Majesty's dominions may remit a case, with queries, to a Court of any foreign state with which Her Majesty may have made a convention for that purpose, for ascertainment of law of such state

I If in any action depending in any of the superior courts within Her Majesty's dominions it shall be the opinion of such court that it is necessary or expedient, for the disposal of such action, to ascertain the law applicable to the facts of the case as administered in any foreign state or country with the government of which Her Majesty shall have entered into such convention as aforesaid it shall be competent to the court in which such action may depend to direct a case to be prepared setting forth the facts as these may be ascertained by verdict of jury or other mode competent, or as may be agreed upon by the parties, or settled by such person or persons as may have been appointed by the court for that purpose in the event of the parties not agreeing, and upon such case being approved of by such court or a judge thereof such court or judge shall settle the questions of law arising out of the same on which they desire to have the opinion of another court, and shall pronounce an order remitting the same, together with the case, to such superior court in such foreign state or country as shall be agreed upon in said convention, whose opinion is desired upon the law administered by such foreign court as applicable to the facts set forth in such case, and requesting them to pronounce their opinion on the questions submitted to them and upon such opinion being pronounced, a copy thereof certified by an officer of such court, shall be deemed and held to contain a correct record of such opinion

Court in which action depends to apply such opinion to the facts set forth in cases, &c

II It shall be competent to any of the parties to the action, after having obtained such certified copy of such opinion, to lodge the same with the officer of the court within Her Majesty's dominions in which the action may be depending who may have the official charge thereof, together with a notice of motion setting forth that the party will on a certain day named in such notice, move the court to apply the opinion contained in such certified copy thereof to the facts set forth in the case herein-before specified, and the said court shall thereupon, if it shall see fit, apply such opinion to such facts, in the same manner as if the same had been pronounced by such court itself upon a case reserved for opinion of the court, or upon special verdict of a jury, or the said last-mentioned court shall, if it think fit, when the said opinion has been obtained before trial order such opinion to be submitted to the jury with the other facts of the case as conclusive evidence of the foreign law therein stated, and the said opinion shall be so submitted to the jury Provided always, that if after having obtained such certified copy the court shall not be satisfied that the facts had been properly understood by the foreign court to which the case was remitted, or shall on any ground whatsoever be doubtful whether the opinion so certified does correctly represent the foreign law as regards the facts to which it is to be applied, it shall be lawful for such court to remit the said case, either with or without alterations or amendments, to the same or to any other such superior court in such foreign state as aforesaid, and so from time to time as may be necessary or expedient

Courts in Her Majesty's dominions may pronounce opinion on case remitted by a Foreign Court

III If in any action depending in any court of a foreign country or state with whose government Her Majesty shall have entered into a convention as above set forth, such court shall deem it expedient to ascertain the law applicable to the facts of the case as administered in any part of Her Majesty's dominions, and if the foreign court in which such action may depend shall remit to the court in Her Majesty's dominions whose opinion is desired a case setting forth the facts and the questions of law arising out of the same on which they desire to have the opinion of a court within Her Majesty's dominions, it shall be competent to any of the parties to the action to present a petition to such last-mentioned court whose opinion is to be obtained, praying such court to hear parties or their counsel and to pronounce their opinion thereon in terms of this Act, or to pronounce their opinion without hearing parties or counsel, and the court to which such petition shall be presented shall consider the same, and, if they think fit, shall appoint an early day for hearing parties or their counsel on such case and shall pronounce their opinion upon the questions of law as administered by them which are submitted to them by the foreign court, and in order to their pronouncing such opinion they shall be entitled to take such further procedure thereupon as to them shall seem proper, and upon such opinion being pronounced a copy thereof, certified by an officer of such court, shall be given to each of the parties to the action by whom the same shall be required

Interpretation of terms

IV In the construction of this Act the word "action" shall include every judicial proceeding instituted in any court, civil, criminal, or ecclesiastical, and the words "Superior Courts" shall include, in *England* the Superior Courts of Law at *Westminster*, the Lord Chancellor the Lords Justices, the Master of the Rolls, or any Vice-Chancellor, the Judge of the Court of Admiralty, the Judge Ordinary of the Court for Divorce and Matrimonial Causes and the Judge of the Court of Probate, in *Scotland*, the High Court of Justiciary, and the Court of Session acting by either of its Divisions, in *Ireland*, the Superior Courts of Law at *Dublin*, the Master of the Rolls, and the Judge of the Admiralty Court, and in any other part of Her Majesty's dominions, the superior courts of law or equity therein and in a foreign country or state, any superior court or courts which shall be set forth in any such convention between Her Majesty and the government of such foreign country or state

No XIII.

FORMS FOR DEPOSITIONS.

I —FORM FOR COMMISSIONER'S REPORT OF DEPOSITIONS OF WITNESSES

At , the day of , in presence of A B, Esq , Advocate, Commissioner appointed to take the depositions of witnesses in the action depending before the Lords of Council and Session at the instance of C D against E F, conform to interlocutor pronounced by Lord , Ordinary, on the day of , of which interlocutor a certified copy was produced to the said commissioner, and the said A B having accepted of the said commission, Compeared G H, Writer to the Signet, agent for the pursuer, and I K, Solicitor before the Supreme Courts, agent for the defender—the said A B having chosen L M (*designation*) to be his clerk, and administered to him the oath *de fideli administratione*, there also

COMPEARED N O, farmer at , in the county of , married, aged forty years (*or otherwise as the case may be*), who being solemnly sworn and interrogated as A WITNESS FOR THE PURSUER, depones &c BEING CROSS-EXAMINED on behalf of the defender, depones &c BEING RE-EXAMINED on behalf of the pursuer depones, &c BEING INTERROGATED BY THE COMMISSIONER, depones, &c All which is truth, as the deponent shall answer to God Three words delete before signing, and one marginal addition on page

N O
A B, Commr
L M, Clerk

If the witness cannot write, the report will conclude—Depones that he cannot write, on account of injury to his hand (*or otherwise as the case may be*)

A B Commr
L M, Clerk

COMPEARED also P Q (*designation, &c , as above*), who being solemnly sworn as A WITNESS FOR THE PURSUER, and being examined *in initialibus* at the instance of the defender, depones, &c The defender objects that the witness is inadmissible on the ground of bribery (*or otherwise as the case may be*) the commissioner repels the objection, and the witness being examined *in causâ*, depones, &c —(*Or*) The defender objects that the witness is inadmissible on the ground of bribery, and although the said objection may not be proved by the initial examination of the witness yet the defender maintains that the same is well founded, as he will prove by other evidence, which he is not at present prepared to adduce, and accordingly he protests for reprobators against the witness, on the ground above stated The commissioner repels the objection, whereupon the witness depones, &c , as above —(*Or*) The commissioner appoints the deposition of the witness to be taken on a paper apart, and sealed up, to await the future orders of the Court

COMPEARED, also, as A WITNESS FOR THE PURSUER, R S (*designation, &c , as above*), who states that he is a Quaker (*or* Moravian, *or* Separatist *as the case may be*) and being examined upon his affirmation and declaration in the form prescribed by Act of Parliament to be emitted by persons of his persuasion in place of an oath, he does solemnly, sincerely, and truly, affirm and declare (*see the statutory forms, supra*, § 1969, *notes*) All which is truth

Signed as above

At the conclusion of the depositions a docquet is appended in this form —What is contained on this and the preceding pages, is the report of the commission set forth in the first page hereof, humbly reported by

A B, Commr
L M, Clerk

If the witness is examined on adjusted interrogatories (See *supra*, § 1951 *et seq*) *the report should bear*,—The first interrogatory being put to the witness, namely (*insert the interrogatory*), he depones, &c *and so on throughout all the interrogatories* *If any questions not embraced in the interrogatories are put by the commissioner, the report must state that they were so put* (see § 1959, *thus*—and the witness being interrogated by the commissioner depones)

II —FORM FOR COMMISSIONER'S REPORT OF OATH OF PARTY

When the commission is granted for taking the oath of a party the report may be in the form given above, with the exception that it should bear, Commissioner appointed to take the oath *in litem* (*or*, on reference, &c *as the case may be*) of the pursuer (*or* defender)

III.—FORM FOR COMMISSIONER'S REPORT OF DEPOSITIONS OF HAVERS

When the commission is for examining havers, the report should bear, Commissioner appointed for examining havers in the action, &c

COMPEARED, &c [*as above*], who being solemnly sworn and examined on behalf of the pursuer as a haver, and being required to produce the writings set forth in the specification No of process, or one or more of them, he depones that he has certain of the writings called for, being the writings following, viz [*describe them*], and he now produces the same, and they are marked by the deponent, commissioner, and clerk, as relative hereto All which, &c (*as above*)

When the writings are numerous, it is usual to produce them conform to inventory, which is mentioned in the report, in place of enumerating the documents, thus —He depones that he has fifty documents of the kind specified, and he now produces the same, as they are enumerated and described in an inventory thereof, which is marked by the deponent, commissioner, and clerk, as relative hereto, the writings produced being also marked with their initials

The writings are marked and signed by the haver, commissioner and clerk, thus —1st January 1856 —Referred to in deposition of Y Z, as a haver of this date

Y Z
A B, Commr
L M, Clerk

If referred to as in an inventory, they are simply initialed by the haver commissioner, and clerk, the inventory being signed by them

When the diet of proof is adjourned, the report should bear —
The commissioner adjourns the diet till the day of

A B, Commr
L M, Clerk

And at re-assembling, a minute should be prefixed to the depositions, thus —
At , the day of at an adjourned diet of the commission aforesaid, Present, the agents above mentioned for the respective parties, before the said commissioner —COMPEARED, &c.

NOTE —The report is usually in the form of a narrative, in which the witness appears to speak either in the first or third person, the question and answer being thrown together into a statement as if made by him But it is proper at important parts of the deposition, to take down the precise words of the question and answer, thus,—"Being interrogated," &c, 'depones, I," &c, in the first person This is peculiarly necessary where the deposition is likely to be used in a jury trial, as it enables the party against whom it is tendered to raise, in proper form, any objections he may have to parts of it. This form must, of course, be observed when any objection to a question is stated before the commissioner In mentioning such objections and any which may be stated to the admissibility of witnesses, the ground of the objection and of the answer thereto, with the reason on which the commissioner sustains or repels it, should be stated shortly The same course should be followed where the witness declines to answer, the question being stated at length, and the declinature mentioned thus —' The witness declines to answer the question, on the ground," &c.

When the depositions mention numbers, these ought always to be stated at length in words and not in figures Any additions which may have to be made to the depositions, should be written on the margin, and signed by the witness, commissioner, and clerk, writing their christian names on one side of each addition, and their surnames on the other Interlineations and erasures ought to be carefully avoided If any words require to be deleted, that should be done by drawing the pen through them, and their number should be mentioned at the conclusion of the deposition When the deposition extends over more than one page, each page should be subscribed by the person examined (if he can write), and by the commissioner and clerk When any deposition is taken on a separate paper to await the orders of court on an objection to the witness, or to any question put to him, the separate part must be signed as usual and sealed up, and the paper which incloses it should bear a docquet as in this form, "Deposition of Y Z, referred to in report of the commission in the action between C D and E F

"A B, Commr

"L M, Clerk

Depositions taken to lie *in retentis* should also be sealed up and docqueted in a similar manner

INDEX.

The Numbers refer to the Sections

FINIS

JOHN BAXTER, PRINTER JAMES COURT, HEAD OF MOUND
EDINBURGH

Lightning Source UK Ltd.
Milton Keynes UK
UKOW06f2155250714

235816UK00011B/279/P